CLASSICAL MEDITERRANEAN SPIRITUALITY
Egyptian, Greek, Roman

World Spirituality

An Encyclopedic History of the Religious Quest

1. Asian Archaic Spirituality
2. European Archaic Spirituality
3. African and Oceanic Spirituality
4. South and Meso-American Native Spirituality
5. North American Indian Spirituality
6. Early Hindu and Jain Spirituality
7. Post-Classical Hindu and Sikh Spirituality
8. Buddhist Spirituality: Indian, Siri Lankan, Southeast Asian
9. Buddhist Spirituality: Chinese, Tibetan, Japanese, Korean
10. Taoist Spirituality
11. Confucian Spirituality
12. Ancient Near Eastern Spirituality: Zoroastrian, Sumerian, Assyro-Babylonian, Hittite
13. Jewish Spirituality: From the Bible to the Middle Ages
14. Jewish Spirituality: From the Sixteenth-Century Revival to the Present
15. Classical Mediterranean Spirituality: Egyptian, Greek, Roman
16. Christian Spirituality: Origins to the Twelfth Century
17. Christian Spirituality: High Middle Ages and Reformation
18. Christian Spirituality: Post-Reformation and Modern
19. Islamic Spirituality: Foundations
20. Islamic Spirituality: Manifestations
21. Modern Esoteric Movements
22. Spirituality and the Secular Quest
23. Encounter of Spiritualities: Past to Present
24. Encounter of Spiritualities: Present to Future
25. Dictionary of World Spirituality

Board of Editors and Advisors

EWERT COUSINS, *General Editor*

Volume 15 of
World Spirituality:
An Encyclopedic History
of the Religious Quest

CLASSICAL MEDITERRANEAN SPIRITUALITY

EGYPTIAN, GREEK, ROMAN

Edited by
A. H. Armstrong

CROSSROAD • NEW YORK

1986
The Crossroad Publishing Company
370 Lexington Avenue, New York, NY 10017

World Spirituality, Volume 15
Diane Apostolos-Cappadona, Art Editor

Printed in the United States of America

Library of Congress Cataloging in Publication Data

Main entry under title:
Classical Mediterranean spirituality.

(World spirituality ; v. 15)
Includes bibliographies and index.
1. Spirituality—Mediterranean Region.
2. Mediterranean Region—Religion. I. Armstrong,
A. H. (Arthur Hilary) II. Series.
BL687.C55 1986   291.4′09182′2   86-8937
ISBN 0-8245-0764-9

Contents

Preface to the Series   xi

Introduction   xiii

General Bibliography and Abbreviations   xxii

Part One: Histories

1   The Faith of the Pharaonic Period
  J. Gwyn Griffiths   3

2   The Great Egyptian Cults
  of Oecumenical Spiritual Significance
  J. Gwyn Griffiths   39

3   The Ancient and Continuing Pieties
  of the Greek World
  A. H. Armstrong   66

4   The Spirituality of Socrates and Plato
  J. B. Skemp   102

5   Aristotle
  Patrick Atherton   121

6   Epicureans and Stoics
  A. A. Long   135

7   Roman Spirituality
    John Pinsent   154

8   The Piety and Prayers of Ordinary Men
    and Women in Late Antiquity
    H. D. Saffrey   195

9   Plutarch and Second Century Platonism
    J. M. Dillon   214

10 Neoplatonist Spirituality
    I. Plotinus and Porphyry
        Pierre Hadot   230
    II. From Iamblichus to Proclus and Damascius
        H. D. Saffrey   250

Part Two: Themes

11 Monotheistic and Polytheistic Elements
    in Classical Mediterranean Spirituality
    John Peter Kenney   269

12 The Love of Beauty and the Love of God
    Werner Beierwaltes   293

13 The City in Ancient Religious Experience
    Patrick Atherton   314

14 The Self in Ancient Religious Experience
    Frederick M. Schroeder   337

15 Body and Soul in Ancient Religious Experience
    K. Corrigan   360

16 The Religious Experience of Time and Eternity
    Peter Manchester   384

17 Cosmic Piety
    Jean Pépin   408

18   The Spiritual Guide
       I. Hadot   436

19   The Spiritual Importance of Not Knowing
       R. T. Wallis   460

20   In Praise of Nonsense
       Patricia Cox Miller   481

CONTRIBUTORS   506

PHOTOGRAPHIC CREDITS   508

INDEXES   509

Preface to the Series

T HE PRESENT VOLUME is part of a series entitled World Spirituality: An Encyclopedic History of the Religious Quest, which seeks to present the spiritual wisdom of the human race in its historical unfolding. Although each of the volumes can be read on its own terms, taken together they provide a comprehensive picture of the spiritual strivings of the human community as a whole—from prehistoric times, through the great religions, to the meeting of traditions at the present.

Drawing upon the highest level of scholarship around the world, the series gathers together and presents in a single collection the richness of the spiritual heritage of the human race. It is designed to reflect the autonomy of each tradition in its historical development, but at the same time to present the entire story of the human spiritual quest. The first five volumes deal with the spiritualities of archaic peoples in Asia, Europe, Africa, Oceania, and North and South America. Most of these have ceased to exist as living traditions, although some perdure among tribal peoples throughout the world. However, the archaic level of spirituality survives within the later traditions as a foundational stratum, preserved in ritual and myth. Individual volumes or combinations of volumes are devoted to the major traditions: Hindu, Buddhist, Taoist, Confucian, Jewish, Christian, and Islamic. Included within the series are the Jain, Sikh, and Zoroastrian traditions. In order to complete the story, the series includes traditions that have not survived but have exercised important influence on living traditions—such as Egyptian, Sumerian, classical Greek and Roman. A volume is devoted to modern esoteric movements and another to modern secular movements.

Having presented the history of the various traditions, the series devotes two volumes to the meeting of spiritualities. The first surveys the meeting of spiritualities from the past to the present, exploring common themes that

A longer version of this preface may be found in Christian Spirituality: Origins to the Twelfth Century, *the first published volume in the series.*

xi

can provide the basis for a positive encounter, for example, symbols, rituals, techniques. Finally, the series closes with a dictionary of world spirituality.

Each volume is edited by a specialist or a team of specialists who have gathered a number of contributors to write articles in their fields of specialization. As in this volume, the articles are not brief entries but substantial studies of an area of spirituality within a given tradition. An effort has been made to choose editors and contributors who have a cultural and religious grounding within the tradition studied and at the same time possess the scholarly objectivity to present the material to a larger forum of readers. For several years some five hundred scholars around the world have been working on the project.

In the planning of the project, no attempt was made to arrive at a common definition of spirituality that would be accepted by all in precisely the same way. The term "spirituality," or an equivalent, is not found in a number of the traditions. Yet from the outset, there was a consensus among the editors about what was in general intended by the term. It was left to each tradition to clarify its own understanding of this meaning and to the editors to express this in the introduction to their volumes. As a working hypothesis, the following description was used to launch the project:

> The series focuses on that inner dimension of the person called by certain traditions "the spirit." This spiritual core is the deepest center of the person. It is here that the person is open to the transcendent dimension; it is here that the person experiences ultimate reality. The series explores the discovery of this core, the dynamics of its development, and its journey to the ultimate goal. It deals with prayer, spiritual direction, the various maps of the spiritual journey, and the methods of advancement in the spiritual ascent.

By presenting the ancient spiritual wisdom in an academic perspective, the series can fulfill a number of needs. It can provide readers with a spiritual inventory of the richness of their own traditions, informing them at the same time of the richness of other traditions. It can give structure and order, meaning and direction to the vast amount of information with which we are often overwhelmed in the computer age. By drawing the material into the focus of world spirituality, it can provide a perspective for understanding one's place in the larger process. For it may well be that the meeting of spiritual paths—the assimilation not only of one's own spiritual heritage but of that of the human community as a whole—is the distinctive spiritual journey of our time.

EWERT COUSINS

Introduction

THE SPIRITUALITY with which we are dealing in this volume has very distinctive characteristics that give it a place of peculiar significance in the history of world spirituality. On one hand it is an example of archaic spirituality, and on the other it bears an extraordinarily intricate relationship to our own European Christian, anti-Christian, and post-Christian spiritualities. (The present editor is not competent to consider its relationship to the world of Islamic spirituality, though there is much to be learned here.) We must consider the second of these two connections because it is something alive in our own spiritualities, which consciously or unconsciously affects our feeling, thinking, and imagination about the old gods and the old pieties. And we shall gravely misunderstand these if we do not continually bear in mind the first. But we must only consider these questions of historical relationship in order to understand this old Mediterranean spirituality as it is in itself, insofar as we can ever understand a spirituality of another age and thought world, understand its beauty and value and such unity as it has. We shall fail to see the point and power of it if we suppose that it is just another "primitive" spirituality with a sort of European rationalist topdressing, or salute or reject it as a *praeparatio evangelica*.

The assumption on which this volume has been planned, which some may find highly disputable, is this: what gives classical Mediterranean spirituality such unity as it has, and the abiding beauty, interest, and power that it has, is that it is in a quite peculiar and distinctive way a reflective spirituality. It acquired this character under the influence of one particular Mediterranean people, the Greeks. It is therefore on the hellenized Mediterranean world that attention is concentrated in this volume. "Reflective" must not be understood too narrowly as equivalent to "philosophical." The people we classify as Greek philosophers were not the only Greeks who thought and talked about, and sometimes asked very awkward questions about, the gods and the myths and the rites. In particular, for centuries before philosophy appeared, and at least for a century or two after it appeared, the reflection of the poets played a decisive part in the development of Greek spirituality. It is in fact hardly possible to form any idea even of archaic Greek spirituality, as distinct from ritual practice, without continual reference to the poets. Nonetheless, it is true that in the post-classical period the direct and indirect influence of philosophical reflection on piety became more and more important, and the only "schools of spirituality" that can be discerned in the ancient Mediterranean world are what we please to call the "schools" of philosophy.

What this reflection on reflection means in practice will become clearer as we go on; but because so much is going to be made of it, it is necessary to insist very strongly on the archaic component in Hellenic or hellenized Mediterranean spirituality. A simple fact about the old Mediterranean world needs to be remembered here. The educated and articulate people, the only ones to whose thoughts and feelings we can possibly have any kind of direct access, were throughout the history of that world a tiny minority; and even in what is generally supposed to be the most "spiritual" period of that history, the first centuries of the Christian era and the last centuries of the Roman Empire, those who could in any way be called deeply spiritual were a small minority of that minority. A good deal of space in this volume is devoted to Neoplatonist spirituality. The great Neoplatonists, Plotinus and Proclus, figure largely not only in the articles devoted to Neoplatonism in part 1, "Histories," but also in the majority of the most important themes treated in part 2. This is right because of the value and continuing spiritual influence of their teaching. But the "school of Plotinus" in Rome was a small informal group of friends meeting in a private house, probably known only to that minority of the Roman upper class who had intellectual interests. The Athenian Neoplatonists, of whom Proclus is the best known, were an even smaller group in a small university town, compelled to avoid public notice as much as possible by their opposition to Christianity, then the official and increasingly intolerant religion of the Roman Empire—rather like some little group of Roman Catholic scholars and theologians in penal times in England. Our interests can lead here to a grave distortion of our understanding of that world as a whole. The great mass of the Mediterranean populations, then and on through the Christian and Islamic centuries till our own time, were peasants, whose deep-rootedness in and deep attachment to ways of life and thought and feeling, particularly but not only religious thought and feeling, go back in many ways to Neolithic times—or further, as those who have had the honor of some acquaintance with their last survivors will know. The cities of classical Greek times were spiritually and in every other way close to the country. This applies even to the greatest and most intellectually advanced of them, Athens. Most of the sovereign and independent cities of Greece were in size and character no more than country market towns. Even the relatively vast urban agglomerations of Hellenistic times—Rome, Antioch, and Alexandria—never developed the sort of distinctively urban, in the sense of nonrural and antirural, ways of thought and feeling to be found in our own megalopolitan culture. The curious and elaborate rituals of the state cult in Rome, carried out with meticulous accuracy till the suppression of pagan cults in the late fourth century A.D., though their meaning had often long been forgotten, were for the most part the rituals of a primitive agricultural community. There is therefore a deep rural archaism built into Mediterranean spirituality, and we also need to remember that the most reflective poets and philosophers and the most sophisticated and cynical literary figures were (as everyone is) ordinary people most of the time and felt and imagined and acted in religious matters as the ordinary people around them did. Socrates, Plato, and Euripides would have had phallic symbols at their doors, like everyone else in Athens. And, as it is highly probable that they had all been initiated into the Eleusinian Mysteries, each of them would have found himself, one fine autumn day, bathing in the sea in the company of a small live (and no doubt lively) pig as an indispensable preliminary to initiation. It is particularly important to remember this in thinking about ancient times, when there were no trained religious or philosophical professionals and no segregated academic culture. The primeval observances were there, immediately, for everybody.

It is of great importance always to bear in mind this continuity of archaic spirituality, carried by the holy places and the immemorial observances, always there and underlying all the changes right down to the establishment of Christianity in the Roman Empire and after. It is the combination of this archaic base with often intensely sophisticated and, to us, modern-seeming thinking and feeling that gives Hellenic and hellenized spirituality and culture its peculiar and enduring fascination. In the development of classical spirituality there were indeed changes, and great ones (though not as great as they have sometimes been represented to be in the interests of a particular ideology or philosophy of history). But they were, almost without exception, changes in the interpretation of the old tradition, not changes that aimed at its destruction or radical reformation. The philosophers were generally content to assume that the old rites and pieties would continue to provide spiritual sustenance for the mass of humanity and a customary environment for their own reflective piety, whether they regarded them with critical or respectful indifference or, as they came to at the end of antiquity, with passionate devotion. Plato was a severe critic of poetic theology and would have drastically censored the poetry used in public worship and taught in the schools, but in his ideal state he is content that the religious observances of the city should be ordained by Delphi on traditional lines (*Republic* 4.427). His last great work, the *Laws,* which set the tone for much later philosophical spirituality, is full of a deep, though not uncritical, piety toward the old gods and the old worships. Zeno of Citium, the founder of Stoicism, in his early, Cynic-inspired dream of a world state, the no-longer-extant *Politeia,* would have banished temples and images from it along with marriage and lawcourts. But later Stoics did not follow him in this; and in late antiquity, when the old religion and the culture of which it was the heart and life were increasingly felt to be in danger, the philosophers rallied even more strongly to its defense.

This archaic Greek piety had, from the earliest of times at which we can form any idea of it, some distinctive characteristics which contributed essentially to the development of classical spirituality. These are to some extent shared with other archaic spiritualities, but they acquired a peculiar importance in the piety of this extraordinary people, clear-sighted, down-to-earth, argumentative, and above all free. (By the fifth century B.C. the Greeks had come to think that what distinguished them most sharply from their Oriental neighbors was their freedom under the law: the imaginary conversation of Xerxes, great king of Persia, and Demaratus, exiled king of Sparta, in Herodotus 7.101–4 illustrates this well.) These characteristics will be more fully discussed in my article "The Ancient and Continuing Pieties," but since they affect the whole content of the volume, they should be briefly mentioned here.

It was a piety of worship, not of belief. Cult was primary; myth was secondary; and one could interpret cult and myth as one pleased. The worship was of many divine powers in one divine universe. The unity of the divine is, in the old piety, very much in the background, but it is always there. The universe is something given for gods as well as human beings, not the product of a divine creation. The oldest stories of its beginnings are stories of birth, not of making. The actions of the gods, the many powers in the one universe, are various and often unexpected. They can clash and conflict and do not appear to serve any great obvious overriding purpose. The gods do not seem necessarily friendly to humans, and the world in which they rule is a hard and dangerous world, apprehended unflinchingly by the Greeks in all its hardness and danger. But it is not a bad world, and the gods are beautiful and delightful to contemplate as well as terrible. People often felt that especially their local gods and the gods of their personal devotion were kindly disposed toward them and that one could love as well as fear the gods. It was from love and delight in the beauty of the gods rather than from fear that the various forms of reflective piety freely developed. (Excessive fear of the divine was, as it grew, increasingly felt to be superstitious and un-Greek.)

It is important for the understanding of classical Mediterranean spirituality to see clearly the reasons for the peculiar freedom of its development. When it was said above that the archaic piety was one of worship, not of belief, this did not, of course, mean that the worshipers had no beliefs. It means that it was common worship—with the implicit and unformulated faith that all genuine worship requires—which united them, not a common profession of a formulated faith in the sense in which we often use the word. Hellenic or hellenized piety from its archaic beginnings till nearly the end of antiquity was a piety without scripture or creed. A most important reason for this was that, as in other archaic pieties, there was no body of professional clergy who were authorized guardians and interpreters of the sacred stories and official teachers of doctrine and morality. A priest in the ancient world was a person who had inherited or had had conferred upon him or her by public authority (or, sometimes, had bought from the city) the right and duty of performing certain sacrifices and ceremonies. Doctrinal teaching and moral instruction were not a priest's business. Further, there was no special group or hereditary caste in society that was specially concerned with religious matters. There were no Brahmins or Druids in the ancient Mediterranean world, and in the ancient Greek world there was nothing like the vast temples of Egypt or the Near East with their numerous clergy. The priests of these temples were, of course, priests of their particular temple, concerned exclusively with its rites; they were not ministers of a teaching church. But their numbers and position in society gave their understanding of the cult a predominant weight in the development of local pieties. In the hellenized world of the Greek kings after Alexander the Great, whose domains extended over Egypt and the Near and Middle East, and in the Roman Empire these great temples were features of the religious landscape, and the ideas of their priesthoods sometimes had some influence. But the priests never became religious authorities for that world as a whole outside their own communities.

Consequently, it was easy and natural for reflective piety which was in no way sacerdotal or esoteric to develop, a piety of free ordinary people, certainly in no way "secular" but decidedly "lay." It was not secular because ancient Mediterranean culture, like other archaic cultures, was permeated by religion. There was no corner of it in which the gods and spirits were not continually brought to mind by the public ceremonies of cities and villages and the domestic rites of house and farm and family graves. The whole world was in some way apprehended as divine and full of divine presences. But it was lay because it was a piety of thoughtful people who were not members of a professionally religious group and had no special training in thinking and speaking about religion. The early poets sang, recited, and eventually wrote in and for a turbulent, independent-minded society of well-born warriors. The later poets and the philosophers who shaped Mediterranean spirituality into its classical forms were free citizens, that formidable kind of human being which the Greeks introduced into our world and which it has never proved possible since to banish from it permanently.

All this stress on freedom and philosophy may suggest that classical Mediterranean spirituality was of a shallow, rationalist sort, without spiritual depth or power to transform life, rather like the picture we usually have of upper-class eighteenth-century spirituality. But to suppose this would be to misunderstand the nature of ancient philosophy and philosophical piety. From very early times some of those who followed the philosophic vocation saw it as a way of life based on a comprehensive understanding of reality, which made considerable moral as well as intellectual demands on those who followed it. In the last centuries of the hellenized Mediterranean world before the establishment of Christianity, philosophers were expected to be (though of course they were not always) persons of austere goodness leading lives of reasonable and moderate asceticism, and philosophic wisdom was not supposed to be attainable without virtue and detachment from worldly concerns. The content of this wisdom became more and more explicitly religious in the first centuries of our era when the ancient Mediterranean spiritualities took their most powerful and enduringly influential forms. Philosophers were more and more thought of as spiritual guides, helping human beings to find the way to the divine. This meant that philosophic wisdom was not something that could be attained by observation and discursive reasoning (though these had their part to play as spiritual exercises). It became more and more a matter of direct insight, inner enlightenment, spiritual communion with the divine. This is why those small, informal, unprofessional groups of master and friends and disciples, which we see when we look closely at the evidence for "philosophical schools," can be regarded as schools of spirituality—and the only schools of spirituality in the hellenized Mediterranean world. Hellenic spirituality differs from much Christian spirituality in that it is not based on a particular revelation and does not recognize any *ex officio* spiritual authority; in that it is free, unorganized, and without special spiritual institutions; and in that it retains close links with the archaic piety of the divine in nature. It differs from some, especially later, Christian spirituality in that it recognizes no primacy of will or feelings over intellect and is, in its own way and its own sense, strongly intellectual. But it must be recognized as a real and deep spirituality which has continued to be powerful after the end of the old Mediterranean world and can still challenge many of our common assumptions about the nature of spirituality. My own observations on the encounter of Hellenic spirituality with Christianity and on how I think it can still work in our present in ways important for our future will be found in volumes 23 and 24; but many readers of volume 15 will, I think, find something in it that speaks to their condition without any assistance from me. They will feel, as so many have felt in the intervening centuries, that there is some present help in these old pieties and ways of imagining and thinking about the divine, if they are meditated on and developed in that spirit of freedom on which I have so much insisted in the first part of this introduction.

The Plan of the Volume

Even a much larger volume than this could not contain everything that might usefully be said about the spirituality of the Hellenic and hellenized Mediterranean world. It was, like other great spiritual worlds described in other volumes of World Spirituality, too vast, complex and long-lived ever to be exhaustively described. Further, the evidence is often scanty and difficult to interpret, especially, though not only, for the spirituality of ordinary people. Yet in spite of the difficulty a great deal can sometimes be done in particular places and periods to illuminate popular piety, as H. D. Saffrey's "The Piety and Prayers of Ordinary Men and Women in Late Antiquity" shows perhaps better than any other article in the volume. What we have tried to do is to show, in a considerable variety of different ways and from a number of different points of view, a selection of the things that each of us, and very often all of us, finds worth showing and thinking about in what we can know of these ancient ways of imagining and feeling and thinking about spiritual reality.

The volume is divided into "Histories" and "Themes." In both sections the choice of subjects to be treated was the responsibility of the editor, though the contributors have had full freedom to treat each as they thought best within the bounds of the general guidelines of World Spirituality. It is hoped that the selection offered will stimulate readers to think that there are other aspects of classical Mediterranean spirituality that may be worth thinking about and that the readers will use the suggestions for further reading to find the way to them. In part 1, the histories are of two kinds. There is a group of long articles that try to show what the ordinary piety or spirituality of the ancient world was like—not just the piety of the common people or the lower classes, but the common spiritual inheritance and environment of everybody. Of these the great articles on Egypt by J. Gwyn Griffiths stand somewhat apart, as Egypt stood somewhat apart in the ancient world. Geographically and eventually politically it was fully a part of that world and was spiritually in continual interaction with it, but it had its own distinctive spirituality, in many ways very different from the Hellenic and hellenized spirituality with which it interacted and which it influenced. The first article by Gwyn Griffiths, "The Faith of the Pharaonic Period," brings out very well its depth, originality, power, and beauty; and the second, "The Great Egyptian Cults of Oecumenical Spiritual Significance," not only shows the extent of its influence in the Hellenistic and Roman worlds but also gives, in its account of what Isis meant to her worshipers, an outstandingly helpful understanding of the spiritual power of a great ancient goddess. It should be read with Saffrey's account of what Artemis meant to the people of Ephesus and the remarks on goddesses in the editor's "The Ancient and Continuing Pieties of the Greek World." This last, with John Pinsent's account of Roman religious experience and Saffrey's "Piety and Prayers," gives a reasonably complete picture of the common spirituality of the Hellenic and hellenized Mediterranean world which endured as a strong and living piety down to the official ending of paganism in the fourth century A.D., and perhaps beyond.

The other histories are concerned with what, in the ancient sense of the word "philosophical," may be called philosophical piety. The reasons for this have, I hope, been sufficiently explained in the first part of this introduction. Ilsetraut Hadot's article "The Spiritual Guide" provides ample confirmation and documentation of what was said there. There has been no attempt to present anything like a complete history of philosophical religion. The object has been to bring out those aspects of reflective Hellenic piety that were of spiritual significance in their own time and may still have some meaning and value today. It was above all the Platonic tradition which manifested a growing, and finally in late antiquity a dominant, spiritual power and made the principal contribution to the inheritance that later spiritual traditions, Christian and Islamic, derived from the old Mediterranean world. For this reason no apology is made, or really needed, for devoting four histories to this tradition in its various stages of development or for the important place it occupies in part 2, "Themes." The themes treated in part 2 are subjects that were of importance throughout the history of Hellenic and hellenized spirituality. One of the chapters is devoted exclusively to the Platonic tradition, "The Love of Beauty and the Love of God" by Werner Beierwaltes. As he shows so well, this theme, which is so central in our whole spiritual tradition, became so because of the way in which it originated and developed in Platonism. R. T. Wallis's

"The Spiritual Importance of Not Knowing" is also mainly concerned with philosophy, and particularly with later Platonism. The other themes, though they have much to say about philosophical piety in general and Platonic piety in particular, range more widely and also treat aspects of the common nonphilosophical spiritual traditions of the Mediterranean world. This is simply because God and the gods, the human community, the self, body and soul, time and eternity, the physical universe, and spiritual guidance must come in one way or another into accounts of anyone's and everyone's spirituality. One theme, John Peter Kenney's "Monotheistic and Polytheistic Elements in Classical Mediterranean Spirituality," deserves special mention because it shows so clearly something of vital importance for the understanding of the relationship of Mediterranean spirituality to spiritualities of biblical derivation, that the reflective piety of the Hellenes produced in the end a highly developed monotheism very different from what Kenney, following general usage, calls "classical theism." The themes conclude with the article by Patricia Cox Miller on alphabetical piety, which bears the splendid title "In Praise of Nonsense." This owes its place to the conviction of editor and contributor that we can no longer neglect, deride, or denigrate wilder forms of spirituality. We may well find that we need in our own spiritual journeys help from people whose preferred name for God is something like AEEIOUO; of course, if our study of them is to be helpful we must not talk nonsense about their spiritual "nonsense," and Patricia Cox Miller in her praise of nonsense certainly does not.

I should like to express my particular gratitude to Dr. Peter Manchester for his invaluable help in preparing this volume for publication, without which, owing to a variety of circumstances, the work could hardly have been completed.

A. H. Armstrong

General Bibliography and Abbreviations

IN CASES WHERE AN ARTICLE is principally or extensively concerned with a particular author or group of authors, its bibliography includes texts and, if there are any available, English translations. Where this is not appropriate, a list of good modern works in English, many with full bibliographies, is given. In two cases, "The Spiritual Guide" by I. Hadot and "Cosmic Piety" by J. Pépin, little has been written on the subjects (especially in English) that is generally readable and accessible, and so it has seemed best to the authors and the editor not to supply particular bibliographies.

The short general bibliography appended here contains information on texts and translations of authors often quoted or referred to, a few general works of reference on ancient religion and philosophy, and a short list of modern books that may be relevant and helpful.

Texts and Translations

There are numerous good critical editions of the Homeric poems, Pindar, the Greek lyric poets, the tragedians, Plato, Aristotle, Vergil, and Cicero. For Plotinus the *editio minor* of the Henry-Schwyzer text should be used (*Plotini Opera* [Oxford: Clarendon Press, 1964–82]). The following English translations can be recommended.

Homer. *The Iliad*. Translated by R. Lattimore. Chicago: University of Chicago Press, 1951.
———. *The Odyssey*. Translated by W. Shewring. Oxford and New York: Oxford University Press, 1980.
Pindar. *The Odes*. Translated by R. Lattimore. Chicago: University of Chicago Press, 1947.
Greek Lyrics. Translated by R. Lattimore. Chicago: University of Chicago Press, 1960.

The Complete Greek Tragedies. Edited and translated by D. Grene and R. Lattimore. Chicago: University of Chicago Press, 1959.

Plato. *Collected Dialogues.* Edited by E. Hamilton and R. Cairns. Princeton: Princeton University Press, 1961.

Plotinus. *The Enneads.* Translated by S. MacKenna. 3rd ed. revised by D. S. Page. London: Faber & Faber, 1956.

———. *The Enneads.* Translated by A. H. Armstrong, with the Henry-Schwyzer text. *Plotinus.* Loeb Classical Library. Cambridge, MA: Harvard University Press, 1966–. Volumes 1–5 have appeared; volumes 6 and 7 containing the Sixth Ennead are ready for publication.

General Reference

Egypt

Frankfort, H. *Ancient Egyptian Religion.* New York: Columbia University Press, 1948. Reprint. New York: Harper, 1961.

Hornung, Erik. *Conceptions of God in Ancient Egypt.* Translated by John Baines. London: Routledge & Kegan Paul, 1983.

Morenz, S. *Egyptian Religion.* Translated by A. E. Keep. London: Methuen, 1973.

Religion

Guthrie, W. K. C. *The Greeks and Their Gods.* London: Methuen, 1950.

Nilsson, M. P. *Geschichte der Griechischen Religion.* 2 vols. Munich: Beck, 1941, 1950.

———. *A History of Greek Religion.* Westport, CT: Greenwood Press, 1980.

Rose, H.-J. *A Handbook of Greek Mythology.* 3rd rev. ed. London: Methuen, 1945.

Philosophy

Armstrong, A. H. *An Introduction to Ancient Philosophy.* Totowa, NJ: Rowman & Allenheld, 1983.

———, ed. *The Cambridge History of Later Greek and Early Medieval Philosophy.* Cambridge: University Press, 1970.

Guthrie, W. K. C. *A History of Greek Philosophy.* 6 vols. Cambridge: University Press, 1962–81.

General Works Relevant to
Classical Mediterranean Spirituality

Adam, J. *Religious Teachers of Greece.* Edinburgh: T. & T. Clark, 1908.

Brown, P. *The World of Late Antiquity.* London: Thames & Hudson, 1981.

Festugière, A.-J. *Personal Religion among the Greeks.* Sather Classical Lectures 26. Berkeley and Los Angeles: University of California Press, 1954. Reprint, 1960.

Nilsson, M. P. *Greek Piety.* Oxford: Clarendon Press, 1948.

Nock, A. D. *Conversion.* Oxford: Oxford University Press, 1933. Reprint, 1961.

Toynbee, A. J., ed. *The Crucible of Christianity.* London: Thames & Hudson, 1969.

Abbreviations

Diels-Kranz *Die Fragmente der Vorsokratiker.* Edited by H. Diels. Revised by W. Kranz. 12th ed. 3 vols. Dublin: Weidmann, 1966–1967.

EPRO Études préliminaires aux religions orientales dans l'empire romain.

OCD *Oxford Classical Dictionary.* 2nd ed. Oxford: Clarendon Press, 1970.

PG Patrologiae cursus completus. Series graeca. 161 vols. Edited by J. P. Migne. Paris: J. P. Migne, 1857–66.

PL Patrologiae cursus completus. Series latina. 221 vols. Edited by J. P. Migne. Paris: J. P. Migne, 1844–64.

Ross W. D. Ross, *Aristotelis Fragmenta Selecta.* Oxford: Clarendon Press, 1955.

SIRIS *Sylloge inscriptionum religionis Isiacae et Serapiacae.* Edited by L. Vidman. Religionsgeschichtliche Versuche und Vorarbeiten. 28. Berlin: de Gruyter, 1969.

SVF Stoicorum Veterum Fragmenta. Edited by J. von Arnim. Leipzig, 1903–24. Reprint, Stuttgart: Teubner, 1966; New York: Irvington, 1986.

Part One
HISTORIES

The Faith of the Pharaonic Period

J. Gwyn Griffiths

The Early Phases

It is in art and architecture that the early dynasties of Pharaonic Egypt achieved their widest acclaim. It was an era that began shortly after 3000 B.C., and artistically its finest achievement was undoubtedly the superb statuary of kings and queens and occasionally of private individuals. In architecture its most famous feat was the erection of the pyramids of Giza and of the Sphinx. Some have regarded the Giza pyramids as monuments simply to the excesses of compulsory sweated labor, while others view them as comparable with the nuclear extravagances of the late twentieth century A.D.[1] The purpose of the pyramids, however, was radically different: they were tombs built for eternity and they were specifically intended to ensure that the kings buried in them would enjoy this eternity in heaven with the sun-god Rê. Indeed, the shape of the pyramid itself suggested an ascent to heaven.

The Pharaoh as a Central Figure

Implicated in the aims and methods of these huge monuments of the Fourth Dynasty (ca. 2580–2466 B.C.) is a mass of information about ritual procedures and about the society that produced the beliefs behind them. It is clear that it was highly centralized society—itself a pyramid with the Pharaoh as its apex. He was the absolute ruler and wielded supreme power politically and religiously, being at once monarch, supreme judge, and high priest, even if various subordinates were entrusted with functions of these offices. If we seek to examine the religious faith that cemented this society together, we find that, although its broad outlines are apparent in the monuments of Giza (where the Sphinx significantly represents the Pharaoh Khefren fused with the god Horus), we must turn to a lesser group of royal pyramids, those of Saqqâra, for intimate details of the beliefs and rites. These pyramids belong to the Fifth and Sixth Dynasties (ca. 2340–2200 B.C.), and unlike the pyramids of Giza they bear long inscriptions on their inside walls. Primarily concerned with the burial of the Pharaoh entombed within (but not discovered in a single case), the Pyramid Texts reveal a great deal about the whole world of ideas, hopes, and frustrations that encompassed them. At the core of the religious message is the affirmation that occurs time and again that the Pharaoh has survived his death:

> O King, you have not departed dead, you have departed alive; sit upon the throne of Osiris, your sceptre in your hand.
>
> (Faulkner, *Pyramid Texts*, 40)

This might seem to be a simple and forthright statement. So it is; but behind it lies a whole plethora of theological doctrine and ritual practice. There is a hint of the ritual preparation in a slightly later text which begins with a reproduction of the statement:

> Hail, Osiris-King! You have departed living, you have not departed dead. Hail, Osiris-King! Go down and bathe with Rê within the Lotus Pools (?); don the clean garments upon the refuge with him who lives in his shroud.
>
> (Faulkner, *Coffin Texts*, 1:36)

Several points in the elaboration are noteworthy. To begin with, the king is now called Osiris, and this identification means that the renewal of life experienced by Osiris after death is now to be granted to the king. Then come the allusions to purification rites, in which the king is said to join the sun-god Rê in the lotus pools. The dead king's body was washed in the purification tent before being taken to the House of Embalming, and this process was believed to contribute essentially to the renewal of life after death. Never in its long history was the importance of ritual neglected in Egyptian religion. Moreover, it was often commingled with a belief in magic. Thus, the hieroglyphic texts on the walls of the pyramids of Saqqâra are an invaluable early source for our knowledge of the beliefs and rites indicated in them, and they were often repeated in later texts, notably in the Coffin Texts and the Book of the Dead; but the very act of engraving the texts on the tomb walls or of inscribing them on coffins or papyri was believed to produce a magical potency which guaranteed the efficacy of the radiant promises spelled out in writing.

Basic Cults Reconciled

The mention of the two gods Osiris and Rê in the passage we have quoted points to another facet of the early religion and indeed of the continuing religious tradition. Osiris was preeminently the god of the dead and of their domain; he was often called the Foremost of the Westerners, that is, of the dead who were buried in the west. His associations are therefore predominantly with the necropolis and with the rites there carried out. Rê, on the other hand, was the sun-god whose abode was in heaven, the supreme High God. There is certainly a contrast inherent in the conceptions of these two deities, and some have interpreted it as a struggle for the souls of the Egyptians and their priesthood. As time went on, however, the contrast was mollified and the different emphases reconciled. This applied especially to the doctrine that the sun-god Rê visits the Osirian underworld during the night and, by reemerging in the dawning day, confers new life on all the dead who have been in contact with him. In the New Kingdom a fusion of Rê and Osiris is explicitly attested.[2] It is only the sun, according to the Latin poet Catullus, that enjoys a return to life after setting; human beings face an eternal night. The ancient Egyptians sought to ally themselves with the forces of nature's renewal, so that every dawn was associated with the idea of life after death. Another aspect of natural renewal came to be linked with Osiris—that of the earth's vegetation.

Rê and Osiris were always the brightest luminaries of the Egyptian pantheon, and if there was any rivalry between them, it was Osiris who eventually won. He became far and away the most popular of the Egyptian deities, although he was eclipsed during the Greco-Roman period by his sister and wife Isis in a process that nevertheless preserved the Osirian doctrine intact. The Pyramid Texts, at the same time, present a host of other deities, and here we confront another paradox: in spite of the rigid centralization and absolute authoritarianism that mark the emergence of a united Egypt at the beginning of the third millennium B.C., the religious texts do not show an overpowering urge to secure uniformity of outlook and belief. It is true that the treatment of Horus, the falcon-god who was the royal and national god of the whole country, does show some signs of such an urge. There were many local falcon cults scattered throughout the land, and these gods bore a diversity of names. In the Pyramid Texts they are often called Horus, but with the addition, as an epithet, of the local name that was originally possessed, as in the case of Horus Sopd.[3] Again, the Pyramid Texts assign theological primacy to Heliopolis, the ancient city a little north of Memphis (the biblical On, which reproduces the Egyptian form). Although a polytheism of bewildering diversity is presented, the

Great Ennead of Heliopolis appears as the dominating group, with the sun-god Atum at its head and the genealogy of related deities arranged thus:

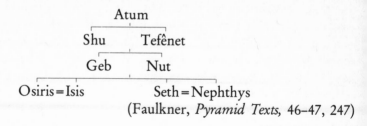

(Faulkner, *Pyramid Texts*, 46–47, 247)

Shu and Tefênet represent air and moisture respectively, Geb and Nut earth and sky. Unlike several other ancient cultures, Egyptian tradition makes earth male and sky female. Politically Heliopolis was not a predominant city in the early dynasties, but in the predynastic period it probably wielded great authority. It was the priesthood of Heliopolis—and the priests were also scribes—that secured for the city of the sun cult its prominence in the Pyramid Texts. Yet the same priestly scholars were ready to refer, in these texts, to a multitude of local cults throughout Upper as well as Lower Egypt.

A Lush Pluralism

If we pause to consider the lush pluralism of this attitude, we would do well to bear in mind the political antecedents. Before the unifying of Egypt politically under Menes, there was a long period of strife between different parts of the country. Eventually the competing areas, each equipped with its tutelary deities, crystallized into Lower and Upper Egypt, and in the final phase of conflict these areas, often called the "Two Lands," were under the religious aegis of Horus and Seth respectively. The triumph of Horus resulted, and the Pharaoh was identified with this god; indeed, the royal titulary constantly refers to the king as Horus. At the same time the result is often presented rather as a process of reconciliation, and in this religious picture it is the god Thoth who appears as the reconciler. His role may possibly represent a mediating political power, and he is said to achieve a settlement by means of arbitration. In the Coffin Texts (1:20b) he is described as "one who does not fight, who does away with fighting." In the Book of the Dead, Thoth states of his action:[4]

I am Thoth, who judged the Two Comrades. I did away with their fighting.
I wiped away their laments.

(Allen, *Book of the Dead*, 95)

It was a tradition that persisted.[5] The theology of the Egyptian united kingdom also persisted in showing Horus and Seth not as victor and vanquished but as deities who shared the tutelary power. There is clear indication of this in the beautiful reliefs from Lisht in Middle Egypt, which show the two gods in the ceremony of "uniting the Two Lands."

A doctrine of political reconciliation thus lies behind the priestly approach to dynastic Egypt, and it is reasonable to expect that this also colored the way in which the local traditions of the forty-two nomes were treated. Certainly the early texts show the greatest respect in providing details of them. A multitude of deities and a vast collection of mythological episodes—often mere scraps—enter into the funerary spells, and often they incorporate details of local origin, as, for instance, those relating to the towns of Buto and Saïs in the Delta. In religious experience generally the significance of what is near in place and time is very clear. Even a divine power that has a cosmic and universal dimension communicates more effectively when it has a local habitation and a name. This was particularly true in the Nile Valley of old, where the small village communities were often far from the capital cities and where a centralized system of gods and doctrines could not easily be imposed.

It may be argued, of course, as Henri Frankfort has done, that polytheistic systems are as inherently tolerant in their approach as they are pluralistic with respect to gods and cults. He contrasts the stage of mythopoeic thought with the quest of a single theory as pursued by the Greeks:

> The ancients did not attempt to solve the ultimate problems confronting man by a single coherent theory; that has been the method of approach since the time of the Greeks. Ancient thought—mythopoeic, "myth-making" thought—admitted side by side certain *limited* insights, which were held to be *simultaneously* valid, each in its own proper context, each corresponding to a definite avenue of approach. I have called this "multiplicity of approaches." . . . At the moment I want to point out that this habit of thought agrees with the basic experience of polytheism.[6]

A difficulty here is the distinction between the mythopoeic mind and the cultural receptacle in which its doings are eventually recorded and expressed. The works associated with both Homer and Hesiod, it may be agreed, give expression to many mythic details which are the fruit of the early myth-making stage. But a high degree of sophistication has entered into the presentation, and although some inner contradictions remain, on the whole their stories about the gods have a certain consistency. The priestly scribes of Heliopolis were certainly not without some ability in the task of ordering and selecting their material. Their main purpose in the Pyramid Texts was to secure the survival and well-being of the Pharaoh in

the afterworld which he had just entered; and we may infer from their practice that they saw a positive advantage in the wealth and variety of the
magical and mythical material available to them. Numerous contradictions
have resulted, and the less favorable interpretation of these is to posit a
process of recording, willy-nilly and unedited, a mass of local spells which
priests from other areas had provided. Even points of relationship between
the major gods remain unsettled. Was Seth the brother of Horus or his
uncle? Originally, it seems, he was his brother, but when the myths of
Osiris and Horus were conflated, a contradiction arose since Osiris is
described as the brother of Seth and yet as the father of Horus.

Doctrines of Creation

More important in our eyes are contradictions in doctrine. If we ask what
was the early Egyptian view of the origin of the world, the Heliopolitan
answer is that the prime mover and first creator was the sun-god Atum,
who is identified with Rê. He had no spouse and he was self-created. His
progeny—Shu, the god of air, and Tefênet, the goddess of moisture—are
said to be the result of masturbation, Atum being regarded for the nonce
as bisexual (He-She) and his hand being personified as his female consort. An
act of expectoration is alternatively indicated as the creative act. The rest
of the scheme is more logical. Shu, the god of air, is said to engender Geb
and Nut, deities of earth and heaven respectively, and Shu is credited with
the separation of these two elements. In more general terms the earth is said
to emerge as a hill from the primeval waters represented by the god Nun—
a parallel to the accounts in Genesis and Hesiod. Another early Egyptian
belief ascribed the origin of the sun to the sexual union of heaven and earth,
a pair regarded as female and male respectively by the Egyptians. The sky-
goddess Nut is thus the mother of the sun, but she is threatened by the
powers of darkness, which are led by the serpent Apopis. A victory won
against him ensured the ordering of the world under the goddess Mâat, the
daughter of the sun-god Rê. The rule of Rê was the blessed primal era for
humanity and the animal world. Again, according to the teaching of
Hermopolis in Middle Egypt, the primeval hill that emerged from the
waters of Nun produced a cosmic egg laid by Thoth in his ibis form, and
it was from this that the sun-god appeared. Yet a further variant saw the
sun-god coming forth as a child from a lotus flower.

The Hermopolite doctrine involves not nine but eight deities, who are
grouped in pairs of male and female representing cosmic entities. In each
case the female is a mere doublet with no conceptual difference. Thus, the
first pair consists of Nun, the primeval water, and his consort is called

Naunet. As opposed to the scheme of Heliopolis, this doctrine at least gives prominence to the female principle. In Heliopolis everything begins with the masturbating or expectorating male deity, who creates a male and female pair, but without female help. It would be fair, it is true, to compare the dominance of the male in the early Hebraic picture, where the God who created heaven and earth is himself male and where the first created pair, Adam and Eve, also gives priority to the male. The Hebraic account does not, however, assign to a self-begotten male an impossible process which contravenes the simple laws of nature. In the teaching of Hermopolis the role of Amûn and Amaunet seems to be connected with air or breath, whereas another pair, Kuk and Kauket, denotes darkness, so that Amûn and his spouse form the element that moves from a state of chaos. This has been compared with the *rûaḥ 'Elōhîm*, (the spirit of God), which is said to move upon the face of the water (Gen 1:2).[7] Yet another doctrine of creation emanated from the city of Memphis, which was the capital of Egypt in the Old Kingdom. The local links of the several doctrines are well pointed by S. G. F. Brandon in his chapter heading "Cosmogonies of Rival Sanctuaries."[8] At Memphis the leading god was Ptah, and in the *Memphite Theology* he is portrayed as a creator-god whose mouth *pronounced* the name of all things, thereby bringing them into being; and thus it is the divine utterance that has produced everything.[9] With the sovereignty of Thebes in the New Kingdom, creation is centered on Amûn, its dominant deity, who is now described as the god who was in the beginning and who had no father or mother.[10] He had already figured, of course, in the Ogdoad of Hermopolis, and to emphasize his self-begetting the strange phrase "bull of his mother" (*ka-mutef*) is used of him.

The immense diversity of these ideas, each linked to a particular cult center, may be explained on ontological lines. It may be that the intention is to reflect in this way the endless diversity of nature itself. Neither unity nor uniformity is found in nature, and the variegated viewpoints of the priests may simply mirror their belief about reality as they saw it. Hellmut Brunner, who has persuasively advocated this explanation, points out that "Egyptian hymns never tire of extolling manifoldness as a feat of Creation."[11] Here he is referring mainly to hymns of the New Kingdom in which the diversity of the human and animal world is praised, including the wealth of distinction between different races and nations with their variety of color, land, and language. It was only in the New Kingdom (after 1550 B.C.) that the Egyptians became acutely aware of the existence of many other nations, especially those of Syria, Phoenicia, Palestine, and the Aegean; and this consciousness affected them in many ways, resulting in the interplay of cultural and religious influences. This part of Brunner's argument will scarcely apply, therefore, to the literature of the Old Kingdom. At that time the Egyptian world view was limited, for the most part (with the exception of Nubia and the Sinai peninsula), to the confines of Egypt itself. Religion was firmly based on the nation-state, and the country's many divisions, which had previously been in a state of warlike rivalry with one another, were now purposively perpetuated in a bond of conscious cohesion. Before Memphis became the capital, it is likely that Buto and Heliopolis in Lower Egypt and Hieraconpolis and Abydos in Upper Egypt were places of both political and religious importance. Yet the advent of political unity centered elsewhere did not mean the obliteration of the associations that had so richly endowed these centers previously. What happened was quite the reverse. The sanctity of the ancient cult places was often invoked, as is clear in the Pyramid Texts, to fortify the continuing tradition. To some extent this was an unconscious process, and it was a feature of the conservatism that characterized the Egyptians in many spheres of life. Adolf Erman once stated this in an extreme way when he said that the Egyptians had a habit of carrying their eggshells about with them. In other words, they refused to discard traditional rites or customs that had really served their purpose.

It was a viewpoint that was, in its early stages, consistently inward-looking. To this nation the word "man" (*remetj*) could be applied only to Egyptians.[12] To them also, their king, the Pharaoh, was buttressed theologically to meet all the demands of defending Egypt and of carrying his sovereignty into the afterworld. In life he was Horus. In death he became Osiris. This was, of course, the official doctrine of the state religion, and it is presented as such in the elaborate texts which a literate minority have bequeathed to us on pyramid walls. It is true of ancient religions generally, as Professor Armstrong has well emphasized in his introduction, that detailed statements are available to us only from elite sources of this kind.

Primitive Echoes

Our earliest texts, as we have noted, come from the third millennium B.C. Although it was a period so distant from ours, Egypt was then already witnessing the stability of a settled agricultural community that was skilled in the arts of metallurgy. Silver, gold, and copper were expertly handled, and later bronze. Writing had already been developed and a calendar had been fashioned. A fairly regular rhythm of irrigation was made possible by the annual inundation of the land by the Nile. Behind all this, nevertheless, was a long vista of experience in the Neolithic and Paleolithic periods, when communities were far less settled. It is not therefore surprising that the religion of the Pyramid Texts and of other documents contains elements that hark back to primitive phases in Egyptian experience.

Early slate palettes bear representations that suggest tribal communities going to war under the standards of deities such as the falcon-god Horus. What is clear with regard to the Horus-king is that the leader of a community is identified with its sacred animal—a well-known feature of totemism as described by anthropologists.[13] Kinship with animals is an idea strongly imprinted on the Egyptian mind in other ways too, especially in the fact that animal worship was a conspicuous feature of their religion. Several of the major deities such as Horus, Thoth, Seth, Atum, Hathor, and Amûn were depicted in animal or partly animal form. Serpent, bull, jackal, baboon, and falcon were prominent in the cults, and they are cults that remind us that this religion was born in the African habitat with its teeming animal life. One element in animal worship was the ever-present sense of danger. I recall the experience of an Egyptian workman who was helping in an excavation of the Egypt Exploration Society in which I took part. During the heat of the previous summer his young daughter had arisen from her bed one morning and planted her bare feet on the sandy earth floor of the room. One foot trod on a scorpion, and she was dead within a short time. It is not surprising, then, that there have come from Egypt many spells to help one avert or overcome the attacks of snakes and scorpions. Yet we find a scorpion-goddess, Selket, and a cobra-goddess, Wadjet of Buto, who is the fierce defender of the Pharaoh in the shape of the uraeus on the front of his crown. The feelings of the worshiper are not hard to probe. There is the fear born of a sense of danger; there is the natural urge to make friends of the most dangerous enemy; and there is also the genuine admiration of power—even in a snake that carries deadly poison—and of grace and beauty in the wildest of animals.

Fear was undoubtedly an impelling force in this religion. According to the Psalmist (111:10) "the fear of the Lord is the beginning of wisdom" (or "the best part" of it). Statius, the Silver Latin poet, said more cynically that fear created the gods; and even in the analysis of the Holy which Rudolf Otto propounded, the element of fear, the *tremendum*, is present. The early phases of the Egyptian faith sometimes bear witness to this motivation in some of its crudest forms. It is the fear of danger, disease, and death that is often encountered, and death itself is naturally a central theme in funerary texts.[14] The atmosphere of sheer terror engendered by some of these texts is well exemplified by the Cannibal Hymn in the Pyramid Texts. It is a composition of considerable poetic power and begins with a description of disturbance in the heavens:

> The sky is overcast,
> The stars are darkened,
> The celestial expanses quiver,
> The bones of the earth-gods tremble,
> The planets (?) are stilled.
> Then comes the reason for the commotion:
> For they have seen the King appearing in power
> As a god who lives on his fathers
> And feeds on his mothers.

Here the expression "feeds on his mothers" might, by itself, simply imply the child's sucking of his mother's milk, but the previous expression "who lives on his fathers" shows that what is meant is the eating of their bodies. The King is presented as a god, the son of Atum, one who is yet more powerful than his father. At the same time he is depicted as a mighty hunter who kills and devours the gods as food. He is one who "himself prepares his meal" though he is aided by hunting attendants and butchers. He is "one who eats men and lives" on "the gods." It is said of these men and gods:

> It is the King who eats their magic
> And gulps down their spirits;
> Their big ones are for his morning meal,
> Their middle-sized ones are for his evening meal,
> Their little ones are for his night meal,
> Their old men and their old women are for his incense-burning.

The basic motive of the action is clear; it is to imbibe the magic and power of men and gods by eating their flesh and drinking their blood:

> He enjoys himself when their magic is in his belly;
> The King's dignities shall not be taken away from him,
> For he has swallowed the intelligence of every god.
> (Faulkner, *Pyramid Texts*, 80–83)[15]

That there is a background of cannibalism to this composition is hard to deny. It might be argued that the king's role as a hunter means that the picture of capturing with a lasso, then of cutting up and devouring, implies that wild animals and not human beings are being thus treated. But there are specifically human allusions, as to the "old men and old women" who are to serve only as material for incense burning. Animals, of course, may be incarnations of gods, and the eating of them, even after sacrifices, may denote the worshiper's unity with the gods by the absorption of their being. But animals are not the main victims of the king's triumphant feast.

If cannibalism rather is the background of the description, it can in no way be accepted as belonging to the period in which the pharaohs named in the pyramids actually lived. Even human sacrifices in any form are rarely

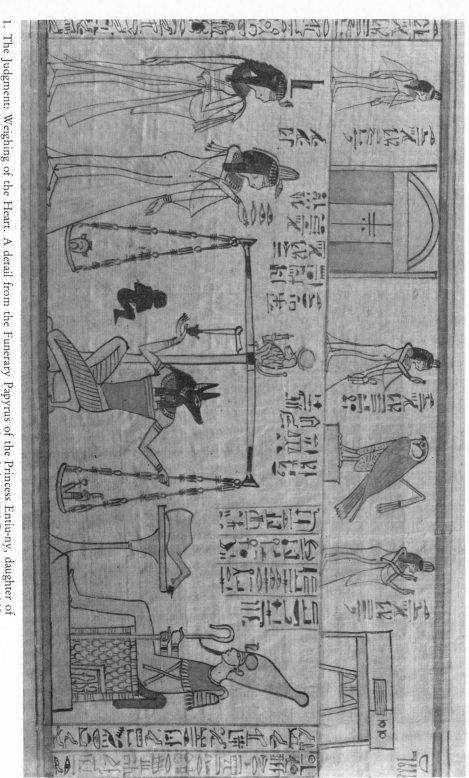

1. The Judgment: Weighing of the Heart. A detail from the Funerary Papyrus of the Princess Entiu-ny, daughter of King Pay-nudjem. From the tomb of the Queen Mother Meryet-Amun, at Bahri, Thebes. XXI Dynasty, ca. 1025 B.C.

attested in Egypt.[16] One is consequently obliged to transfer the horrific background of this poem to a period that long antecedes its composition. Faulkner has suggested that the statement "He has eaten the Red Crown and swallowed the Green One" must refer to the conquest of Lower Egypt, to which the red and green crowns belonged, by the white crown of Upper Egypt, which dates the whole piece to a past not so distant from the first united dynasties. This statement, however, can be explained as using the cannibalistic locutions in a merely metaphorical sense, and it is more likely that the cannibalism of the poem reflects a time far back in prehistory. Further, parts of the Pyramid Spells often reveal a disparity of origin in time and place. It is rather significant, as Faulkner points out, that the Cannibal Hymn is found only in the earliest two pyramids of the Saqqâra group. The later pyramids of the group omitted it, probably because the priestly editors recoiled from its crude reveling in primitive experience.

One has admittedly to be careful in one's attitude to such matters. The advance from the primitive to the civilized is not always in a straight ascending line; nor is it always necessarily an advance at all. According to Wilhelm Schmidt, cannibalism is not found in "pre-totemic peoples,"[17] so that the earlier phase here is also the less primitive in the condemnatory sense of the word. In a general way the distinction between what is primitive and what is civilized cannot be firmly drawn. The differences in material circumstances and technological usages are very plain, but modes of thinking show a continuity. "In my view," says a contemporary anthropologist, "there is no significant discontinuity in terms of either structure or form between 'modern' societies and 'primitive' societies."[18] It does not follow from this, unfortunately, that it is an easy task for modern observers to explain the thought processes and the religious emotions of primitive communities who are living today; and the task is doubly difficult with ancient primitives simply because they are no longer observable. In a discussion of Sir James Frazer's work *The Golden Bough,* where a multitude of data concerning contemporary primitive societies are assembled, Ludwig Wittgenstein finds that it is the explanations proffered that are unacceptable. He is drawn to this pessimistic assertion: "We can only *describe* and say, human life is like that."[19] He is particularly disturbed by Frazer's treatment of magic as a conglomeration of stupidities which characterized a primitive stage to be followed by the gradually more enlightened stages of religion and science. Wittgenstein avers that a book on anthropology might well be introduced in these terms: "When we watch the life and behaviour of men all over the earth we see that apart from what we might call animal activities, taking food etc. etc., men also carry out actions that bear a peculiar character and might be called ritualistic." He goes on thus:

But then it is nonsense if we go on to say that the characteristic feature of *these* actions is that they spring from wrong ideas about the physics of things. (This is what Frazer does when he says magic is really false physics, or as the case may be, false medicine, technology, etc.)[20]

Psychologically there is a clear kinship between modern technology and ancient magic. The majority of people today use the results of technology without understanding them; in their attitude of trust they are akin to those who relied on a magic that was seen to be working. Today, as of old, people have no aversion, for the most part, to killing their fellow-human beings in large numbers when they belong to other organized communities. High technology merely increases greatly the numbers involved.

Egyptian religion was certainly replete with both magic and ritual. At the same time, the Egyptians of the Pharaonic period showed a certain sensitivity about the taking of human life within the orbit of their own society — a reservation that clearly applied to the Hebraic commandment "Thou shalt not kill." A papyrus called the *Westcar Papyrus,* whose setting is placed in the Old Kingdom, tells of how King Cheops (Khufu) was entertained by his sons with tales of miraculous happenings. One of the sons, Prince Hardedef, seeks to vary the procedure by introducing a living magician who performs wonders before the king. Hardedef maintains that this magician, a man of 110 years called Djedi, is able to join to a body a head that has been severed. When Djedi appears before the King, he is questioned about his prowess:

> His majesty said: "Is it true, what they say, that you can join a severed head?" Said Djedi, "Yes, I can, O King, my lord." Said his majesty, "Have brought to me a prisoner from the prison, that he be executed." Said Djedi, "But not to a human being, O King, my lord! Surely, it is not permitted to do such a thing to the noble cattle!"
>
> (Lichtheim, *Lit.,* 1:219)

"The noble cattle" was a phrase strangely used of humanity. We are then told that the experiment was tried on a goose instead, and the severed head rejoined its body when Djedi had pronounced his magic. The same was then done, it is said, to a bird and an ox. It is an episode that touchingly illustrates a refinement of sensibility even if the king himself is not allowed to show it.

People and Priest

In theory the Pharaoh was the high priest of Egypt and he represented his people before the gods. It would be a mistake to construe the absolutism of his monarchy as implying that the people did not exist or count in any valid sense. Embedded in the Pyramid Texts, although they were written in the main to serve the royal prerogative, are several spells that were obviously in general currency, such as those against snakes. When we read a statement such as "I have not offended the King," it is clear that a commoner is defending his loyal record. On the other hand, when it is maintained that "this King rescues the people as a limb of himself," the cohesion of king and people is emphasized.[21] There are several words for "people" in Egyptian; some may refer to an original association with particular areas of the country; others, such as *hen-memet*, "sun-people," suggest a link with particular cult centers.

In the quest for a relationship with God, the Egyptians were served by many priests. The Pharaoh himself, as we have seen, fulfilled the supreme priestly role, but he delegated many functions to religious dignitaries. In the early phases of Egyptian religion there was no priestly caste. A complex system was evolved, but there was at first nothing to correspond to the priestly tribe of Levites among the Hebrews. The word for "priest" in a general sense was *wab*, which means "a pure one." This implies both ritual purity with its stress on personal ablutions and purity in the moral sense. Another frequent term for priest was *hem-netjer*, "servant of God," a term that sometimes attracts amplifying additions as in the phrase *hem-netjer wehem*, "servant of God who carries the message," applied to a priest who has the important task of managing the submission of questions and the delivery of responses in a context of oracular divine judgment.[22] The *hem-netjer* was normally a member of the higher hierarchy. At the same time, a large number of special priestly titles were used in particular centers. Thus, the high priest of Heliopolis was called "Greatest-of-Seers," that of Memphis "Leader of the Craftsmen." An inscription relating to a priest who is approaching a cult statue of a god represents him as saying, "It is the King who sends men to behold the god,"[23] a brief statement that sums up the status and duty of the priest in the temple: he has been delegated by the Pharaoh and his main task is to serve the god who is regarded as being present in his statue in the temple. This service included the cleaning and clothing of the statue, the presentation of food-offerings, and the expression of praise and adoration. Statues of the gods were kept in inner parts of the temple, and access was restricted to priests, who were considered to be employees of the temple. An elaborate division of duties was practiced, and the more learned of the priests were in charge of sacred texts and their use, including the ritual reading of them. Others of the scribal groups were concerned with temple administration, a task that covered the management of the considerable land owned by them. It follows that the priest was not usually a spiritual leader, nor did he have any caring contact with large numbers of believers. Normally he was not even a full-timer. The temple priesthood was divided into four groups, each being responsible for the temple for one month at a time, with the result that every group spent three months out of four pursuing their ordinary jobs in neighboring villages. During the periods of service, however, they adhered to strict rules. All priests had to be circumcised. They observed frequent washings and shaved themselves completely; they wore only dresses of fine linen and followed a food regimen that varied somewhat according to local traditions. Sexual intercourse was prohibited during periods of service.

The more specialized group of higher clergy spent their whole time in divine service. Attached to most temples was a House of Life (*Per Ankh*), which kept an assembly of books concerned with religious knowledge and indeed with a comprehensive field of knowledge, especially the art of healing. Questions of ritual and cult were settled by them, and they produced copies of sacred books such as the Book of the Dead, which was, in the New Kingdom and later, viewed as an essential vade mecum for the last journey. The House of Life became eventually a center of the Osirian ritual which gave believers a warrant of continued life in the afterworld. In general it is likely that the many priests who were engaged in funerary service were advised and guided from such centers, for the learned scribes there consulted could provide not only the religious texts of general import but also the personal details concerning the deceased persons. These details were naturally supplied by relatives and friends and often by the person himself during his lifetime, but the priestly scribes could alone produce the suitable compositions adorned with relevant depictions.

Several tombs of the Old Kingdom allow revealing glimpses of the lives of important citizens and in particular of the spiritual and moral standards by which those lives were assessed. They are tombs that provide a refreshing change from the social outlook which the Pharaoh dominates, although they almost always enumerate the posts held by the deceased under the Pharaoh. Artistically they are often of great appeal, and they are adorned with reliefs and paintings that show the deceased with his family and in scenes typical of his life on earth—scenes that look to the past and the future, for it was believed that a happy life after death would repeat the brightest episodes of this life. A fine example is the tomb of Mereruka at Saqqâra.²⁴ He was a vizier under King Teti of the Sixth Dynasty (ca. 2345 B.C. or later). Clearly the information supplied by such tombs in their depictions and texts does not illumine for us the faith of the ordinary Egyptian, even if we may assume that the details about ritual and about the gods invoked do not now point either to a royal prerogative or to religious benefits enjoyed exclusively by the higher echelons of society. Doubt is sometimes expressed as to whether the concept of the individual as a separate entity had emerged in Egypt at this early stage. The biographical material embodied in these tombs is sufficient, however, to give firm guidance on the point, for the career and achievements of these individuals are sometimes set out quite elaborately in the inscribed texts. Indeed, it has been rightly recognized that these writings constitute the first appearance in world literature of autobiography.[25]

An example occurs in the tomb of Nefer-seshem-re, also called Sheshi, at Saqqâra. It belongs to the Sixth Dynasty.

> (1) I have come from my town,
> I have descended from my nome,
> I have done justice for its lord,
> I have satisfied him with what he loves.
> I spoke truly, I did right,
> I spoke fairly, I repeated fairly,
> I seized the right moment,
> So as to stand well with people.
> (2) I judged between two so as to content them,
> I rescued the weak from one stronger than he
> As much as was in my power.
> I gave bread to the hungry, clothes to the naked,
> I brought the boatless to land.
> I buried him who had no son,
> I made a boat for him who lacked one.
> I respected my father, I pleased my mother,
> I raised their children.
> So says he (4) whose nickname is Sheshi.
> (Lichtheim, *Lit.*, 1:17)

Unlike several other tomb owners, Nefer-seshem-re does not tell us much about his career. The statements "I have done justice for its lord" and "I judged between two . . ." suggest that he held a judicial post of some kind, and there are several indications that it was in this context that he claims to have acted fairly and uprightly. A moral emphasis is seen in the *pietas* practiced, according to him, within his family, he has honored his father and mother and "raised their children"—presumably his younger brothers and sisters. He impresses us most, however, by the claim to actions that go beyond the norm of duty: he had rescued the weak from the strong, given bread to the hungry and clothes to the naked. A son was expected to show devotion and care in the burial of his father. Nefer-seshem-re has voluntarily taken on himself the duties of the son when need arose in other families, and a similar compassion for the needy is evident in the claim "I made a boat for him who lacked one." We have no means, admittedly, of checking these admirable assertions. What is clear is that a sensitive code of conduct here finds expression and that the collective representations (to use L. Lévy-Bruhl's phrase) that are reflected are of a high order.

Also from the Sixth Dynasty is the much longer autobiography of Weni, who gives a lavish account of his career in three reigns during which he was governor of Upper Egypt and a military commander. After recounting his achievements in these posts he is content with a very brief rehearsal of his more private virtues: "I was one beloved of his father, praised by his mother, gracious to his brothers" (Lichtheim, *Lit.*, 1:22). Much more revealing from the standpoint of ethical evaluation is the inscription of Harkhuf, who became likewise governor of Upper Egypt, as well as count, royal seal-bearer, sole companion, and lector-priest, the last-named position being clearly held in the quieter intervals of a busy public life. As a result of his expeditions to Nubia, Harkhuf was able to bring home a dancing pygmy to delight the boy-king Pepi II. The text includes the usual prayers for blessed burial and for the receipt of the food-offerings, which are regarded as a gift of the king and of the gods Anubis and Osiris. Traditional forms are used to describe Harkhuf's last journey: "May he journey in peace on the holy ways of the West, journeying on them as one honored. May he ascend to the god, lord of heaven, as one honored by / the god, lord of heaven /" (Lichtheim, *Lit.*, 1:23). When we come to the recital of virtues, we see at once that they are quite similar to those given by Nefer-seshem-re.

Georg Misch remarks that "the dead man's importance is measured by his success in gaining office and rank," but he concedes that an emphasis on "conduct" is found too,[26] as in these lines:

> I was one worthy —
> One beloved of his father,
> Praised by his mother,
> Whom all his brothers loved.
> (5) I gave bread to the hungry,
> Clothing to the naked,
> I brought the boatless to land.

Then comes a threat to possible maltreaters of the tomb and a resumption of the self-eulogy:

> I am an excellent equipped spirit (*akh*),
> A lector priest who knows his speech.
> As for any man who enters this tomb unclean,
> I shall seize him by the neck like a bird,
> He will be judged for it by the great god!
> I was one who spoke fairly, who repeated what was liked,
> I never spoke evilly against any man to his superior,

> For I wished to stand well with the great god.
> Never did I judge between two contenders
> In a manner which deprived a son of his father's legacy.
>   (Lichtheim, *Lit.*, 1:24)

This emphasis on compassionate and upright conduct recalls the statements made by Nefer-seshem-re; indeed, some of the assertions are closely similar, and the similarity indicates the development of a stereotyped form of *apologia pro vita sua,* which the priests were prepared to provide as requests came to them. One result is to rob the apologia of any intimately personal reference. On the other hand, the details about the person's career do have the stamp of individuality; it is the moral claims that lack specific application. There is a contrast here with the impressively subtle expression of personality revealed in the early statuary.[27] Yet the collective code of conduct is not without its high standard, and in later literature, including the funerary autobiographies, the presentation is more detailed, which allows one to understand much more fully the Egyptian's concept of the ideal man. What is further significant about Harkhuf's record is that it throws light on the spiritual motivation for the concern about upright living. A repudiation of evil speech is explained by a desire to avoid an adverse judgement by "the great god":

> I never spoke evilly against any man to his superior
> For I wished to stand well with the great god.

The threat to an abominator of the tomb is similarly buttressed:

> He will be judged for it by the great god!

The great god was probably Rê or Osiris.

Here we encounter a theme that became of the greatest importance in Egyptian belief: the conviction that every one faced a judgment after death. It is a theme to which we shall return, since it is best understood from the vantage point of its full development.

New Horizons

The political collapse of the Old Kingdom produced an unsettling effect on religious faith. Although it would be unwise to chart the changes in belief or disbelief too simply as a reflection of social and political upheaval, there are some very clear examples of such a process. Occasionally there are direct allusions to the chaotic conditions, as in *The Prophecies of Neferti:*

> I show you the land in turmoil,
> What should not be has come to pass.
> Men will seize weapons of warfare,
> The land will live in uproar.
> (Lichtheim, *Lit.*, 1:142)

If tenses here are future, the experience of a turbulent past is probably to be seen in the picture. The rejection of seemly tradition and the blatant pursuit of civil war are a part of the sad scene:

> Each man's heart is for himself.
> Mourning is not done today,
> Hearts have quite abandoned it.
> A man sits with his back turned,
> While one slays another.
> I show you the son as enemy, the brother as foe,
> A man slaying his father.

The inversion of the normal social grades is lamented:

> The beggar will gain riches,
> The great will rob to live.
> The poor will eat bread,
> The slaves will be exalted.

This is, of course, in sharp contrast to the Magnificat, where such an outcome is welcomed:

> He has brought down monarchs from their thrones,
> but the humble have been lifted high.
> (Luke 1:52)

A Confident Faith and Some Doubts

A severe jolt to the stability of the prevailing and accepted order of things can naturally bring an attitude of skepticism and of questioning. The classic example is the book of Job, although Job's troubles are more in his private sphere than in the world at large. In situations of this kind expressions of a new and challenging attitude tend to be intrinsically more interesting than the rather staid and loyalistic way in which a traditional faith is lauded. Even in a time of social and political chaos, the ordinary Egyptian probably continued to respect that faith in the practical sense of observing the rites laid down and the worship expected of him. As Professor Armstrong has said of the Greek attitude in his introduction, so it can be said of the popular religion of Egypt: "It was a piety of worship, not of belief."

When cult and faith do become articulate we can clearly discern in Egypt two basic beliefs firmly accepted, the one relevant to life in this world and the other to life after death. The first of these beliefs was centered on Mâat, who appears at once as a goddess and as an abstract principle. She is the goddess of truth and justice, the daughter of the sun-god Rê, and the principle embodied in her is that of harmony in human and divine life. It is only by upright living in obedience to Mâat that human beings preserve order and concord in their own sphere of life, and the same principle is honored in the ordered and harmonious life of the universe. That this is the spiritual foundation of the good life is made clear in the wisdom literature. Already in the Sixth Dynasty the *Instruction of Ptahhotep* throws light on this. Numerous words of advice are given there, many of them of a practical nature. Miriam Lichtheim thus sums them up (*Lit.*, 1:62):

> The cardinal virtues are self-control, moderation, kindness, generosity, justice, and truthfulness tempered by discretion. These virtues are to be practiced alike toward all people. No martial virtues are mentioned. The ideal man is a man of peace.

In this long document allusions to the gods are not frequent, but the importance of Mâat is brought out more than once, as in this section:

> If you are a man who leads,
> Who controls the affairs of the many,
> Seek out every beneficent deed,
> That your conduct may be blameless.
> Great is justice (*Mâat*), lasting in effect,
> Unchallenged since the time of Osiris.
> One punishes the transgressor of laws,
> Though the greedy overlooks this;
> Baseness may seize riches,
> Yet crime never lands its wares;
> In the end it is justice that lasts.
>   (Lichtheim, *Lit.*, 1:64)

Mâat is evidently envisaged here as operating in the sphere of justice in the legal sense, but also in the more general sense of a ruling principle that governs human affairs in the long term, however attractive ill-gotten gains may seem in the short term. Justice, we are told, is unchallenged since the time of Osiris—an allusion to the primal period of happiness when the gods ruled on earth, a concept paralleled in Hebraic and Greek thought. Ptahhotep goes on to preach the doctrine of a providence that ensures retaliation for evil:

> Do not scheme against people,
> God punishes accordingly . . .

> People's schemes do not prevail,
> God's command is what prevails.
> (Lichtheim, *Lit.*, 1:64–65)

This doctrine finds occasional expression in other contexts, but it is never elaborated with the thoroughness displayed in the Hebrew Bible. One reason may well be that the idea of judgment after death became increasingly dominant in the New Kingdom and afterward, tending to supplant the concept of divine punishment of evil in this life. The latter concept is admittedly conspicuous in the Demotic Chronicle, a document from the third century B.C. which firmly propounds the doctrine that prosperity on earth is linked to upright conduct. It is there said, for instance, of King Achoris, who died ca. 380 B.C., that he completed the time of his rule "because he was generous to the temples"; but then it is added that "he was overthrown because he forsook the Law and showed no care for his brethren."[28] Here the allusion to the law (*hep*)—and there are several others—is reminiscent of Hebraic usage and doctrine with its stress on the Torah.

A scene often depicted on the walls of Egyptian temples shows the Pharaoh presenting a figure of Mâat to a deity. She has a diminutive human form in a seated position and an ostrich feather emerging from her head. In a way the figure was representational in meaning: it was a summation of all offerings. Mâat is described as "the goodly word which comes from the mouth of Rê himself" and as the sustenance on which the gods live. When the king presents the figure of Mâat to a deity, he is also binding himself to follow and uphold upright conduct. "Speak the Truth, practice Truth, for it is great and powerful and endures" is an exhortation that illumines the approach.[29] Mâat is of vital importance too in the concept of judgment after death. At the same time there is often a conviction that the preservation of order and harmony, both in Egypt itself and generally in the universe, is dependent on the honoring of this deity. The idea is as early as the Pyramid Texts:

> Heaven is satisfied and the earth rejoices when they hear that King Pepi II has put Mâat in the place of falsehood (or disorder).[30]

The other basic belief of comprehensive importance was related to life after death. It was proclaimed unremittingly in the Pyramid Texts with reference to the dead Pharaoh, and it was present too in the texts inscribed in the tombs of private individuals. The elaborateness of their funerary preparations has sometimes led to an impression that the Egyptians were obsessed with the fact of death. Mummification and tomb construction are seen as among their principal concerns. We must bear in mind, however, that the archaeological record is inevitably one-sided, since the dwellings of the dead, located as they were in desert places away from the Nile Valley, have naturally escaped the ravages of time far better than the cities and temples of the living. In most cases the cities and temples have largely disappeared, the cities having become the sites of later settlements through many centuries. Yet it remains true that the tombs were the object of zealous tendance and forethought, and this followed logically from the firm belief that it was to be a house of eternity (*per djet*). It was to be the eternal abode of the body of the dead person, and this conviction gave rise to the idea that it was essential to preserve the body by embalming it. The main agent in this process was natron (hydrated sodium carbonate, found in a natural state), which was rubbed into the body after the intestines and brain had been removed. The heart was allowed to remain, and the whole procedure was assigned in myth to the action done for the dead Osiris by Anubis, the embalmer-god. By such means the life of Osiris was said to have been renewed or continued, and the urge to secure the same privilege for the dead Pharaoh led to his being identified with Osiris. In the later Saqqâra pyramids the Pharaoh is regularly called Osiris—in the form of a double name, Osiris-Pepi and so on. The procedure might seem a simple and superficial affair, but we should pause to recall that the name in ancient religion was fraught with profound significance. A god was thought to be present in his name in a special sense, and the Pharaoh who was identified with Osiris in death shared with the god his sovereignty over the realm of the dead. In life he had been the sovereign of the living, being equated with Horus. In death, like Osiris, his sovereignty applied now to another kingdom, that of Dat, the underworld, which was specifically the domain of Osiris. The king is assured that he will occupy the throne of Osiris, and other blessings are showered on him simultaneously. The gods of heaven, especially Rê, promise to ensure him a role of celestial bliss, but it is noteworthy that only in the case of Osiris is the dead king identified with a divine ruler.[31]

By the time of the Coffin Texts (ca. 2100 B.C. and after) the identification with Osiris is applied generally to all the dead. The term "democratization" has been used of the change, but it has no political character and it is doubtful whether it reflected social or political changes. It was an extension that implied an intellectual inconsistency. For the Pharaoh was linked to Osiris by his kingship, and this link was not present for any one else. The concept of kingship, however, had its collective and cohesive aspect, and it might have seemed natural that the Pharaoh's people should follow their sovereign—if not to a share in sovereignty, at least to a share in the blessings of the realm of Osiris. If we ask what it meant to them in the moral and

2. Coffin of Bekenmut (detail). Probably from Thebes. XXII Dynasty, ca. 900 B.C.

spiritual sense, the initial answer must be to some extent negative. It was an identification achieved by magical and ritual means, and the first emphasis was on being saved from death as he was saved. According to the myth, which was enacted dramatically in special rites, it was Horus who saved Osiris when he had been smitten by his enemies. Isis is also assigned the saving role, which includes the bestowal of new life. Osiris himself, therefore, is a savior-god only in the sense that he is the paradigm of a god who suffers and dies and is delivered from death. Those who believe in him and are identified with him are promised a similar deliverance. Nor is such a pattern of belief a notion to be scorned, for it has many parallels—not least in Christianity, since the savior is said to be "he who is risen from the dead and become the firstfruits of them that slept" (1 Cor 15:20).[32] The founder of Christianity was, of course, a historical person, and it is very unlikely that this was also true of Osiris.[33] This valid distinction should nonetheless be modified by a further remark: many of the Egyptians may have sometimes believed that Osiris had been an early king since he was placed with Rê and other gods among the first kings of Egypt.

It was not only from the Osiran faith that ideas about survival after death were drawn. If the body was secure in the tomb, it could also "come out by day" as the Book of the Dead maintained. Further, a person possessed two spiritual entities, the *ba* and the *ka*, the former envisaged as a human-headed bird and the latter as a continuing life-force. A third term, *akh*, denoted the transfigured spirit with which a person was glorified after death, provided the correct rites had been carried out. As manifested in the *ba*, the soul was deemed to enjoy freedom of movement away from the tomb and also freedom of existence in other forms of being. These forms were viewed as temporary and fleeting experiences since the *ba* was believed to return constantly to the body. In the fifth century B.C. the Greek historian Herodotus appears to have connected this doctrine with the Pythagorean idea of the transmigration of the soul to another form of life after death. The fact that the Egyptian doctrine included forms of animal or bird life was a persuasive element in the comparison; the important difference was the temporary nature of the new life thus envisaged. Relations between gods were also often indicated by assertions that one was the *ba* of another.[34] From the viewpoint of the individual's prospect in the afterlife it was the sense of freedom of movement and experience that was vital. It could be argued that it suggested at the same time the idea of the state of perpetual change which was inherent in life generally.[35] Did such an idea interfere with the belief in a continuing unified personality? This belief might indeed appear to be endangered likewise by a rather complex theory of what constituted one's personality. Apart from the body there were facets of spirit-existence manifested in the *ba* and the *ka,* and descriptions of the afterlife sometimes portray these beings as apparently enjoying activities independently of the body, which remained attached to the tomb. In addition, the dead person is regarded, as we have seen, as a glorified spirit (*akh*); it is clear, moreover, that the heart (*ieb*) was considered to have significant functions, especially as the seat of emotion, mind, and will and as the center of conscience—hence its importance in the ceremony of "weighing the heart." In spite of this complexity the Egyptian did not regard himself as a split personality. Aspects and functions might vary, but a unified being remained at the center.[36]

A guarantee of eternal life was one of the spiritual blessings conferred by the traditional religion. Its definition, however, is no easy matter, for it includes the idea of continuous creation. Two words are used—*djet* and *neheh*—and they denote different aspects: *djet* is associated with yesterday, with night, with Osiris, and with the end of existence; *neheh* is associated with day, with tomorrow, with the sun-god Rê, and with the beginning of life. Eternal static duration is expressed by *djet,* eternal cyclical movement by *neheh.*[37] A favorite symbol of eternity for the New Kingdom was the *ouroboros,* the serpent which forms a circle and bites its own tail; within the circle is envisaged the totality of existence.

Manifold experiences were regarded as possible after death, especially in the celestial orbit. Since the sun-god Rê is said to voyage through heaven on an encircling sea and to emerge in his barque in every dawning day after a nocturnal voyage through the realm of the dead, the desire to join Rê is a feeling often expressed. The achievement of this desire carries with it an assurance of immortality. There is located, at the same time, in the celestial paradise a blissful region of islands that contains the Fields of Food-offerings and the Fields of Reeds. Here the blessed dead live with the gods, and in the Fields of Reeds they are shown busily harvesting abundant crops of barley and wheat. Here we are clearly confronted with an idyll of the afterworld that only the early peasant farmers could have dreamed of. The Greek concept of Elysium and of the Isles of the Blessed is probably indebted to this source.[38] Egyptian tradition includes an Island of the Just, where Osiris is lord, and he is significantly the president of the court that awards the epithet Justified, Triumphant (*Mâa-kheru*) to those who have passed the test of the tribunal that examines the life record. Another island that figures much in funerary texts is Flame Island, where the sun-god is said to have been born at the time of the earth's creation. Every dawn is believed to imply not only the victory over the forces of night and darkness but also the glory of the First Time, when light emerged from gloom and chaos. In Flame Island the justified dead will know the joy of rebirth and the repelling of hostile and evil powers. Although often shown as joining the sun-god Rê in his barque, dead persons are sometimes presented as seeking the help of a ferryman and his boat. Unlike the Greek Charon, this ferryman is not prepared to take anyone with him. Only those qualify who can show that they are properly equipped morally and ritually; they must know the correct magic formulas.

The power of transformations enjoyed by the *ba* meant that a plethora of possibilities opened before the dead. The deceased could, for instance, become a bird or a star. From about 1400 B.C., the *Prayers of Paheri* (a royal scribe) portray the desired state:

> To become indeed a living *ba*,
> It shall thrive on bread, water, and air;
> To assume the form of phoenix, swallow,
> Of falcon or heron, as you wish.
> You cross in the ferry without being hindered,
> You fare on the water's flowing flood.
> You come to life a second time.
>   (Lichtheim, *Lit.*, 2:17)

There is confusion, of course, and even contradiction in the alternatives presented in such texts. The kindly explanation is to suggest that the very complexity of the possibilities was a means of strengthening the affirmation that a new life was to come. But it is also feasible to see in the complexity an underlying skepticism, a feeling that if one assurance proves ill-founded another will offer itself instead.[39]

A skeptical attitude is sometimes given quite clear expression. A papyrus of the Twelfth Dynasty, perhaps of the twentieth century B.C., which is now in Berlin, has been variously entitled "The Man Who Was Tired of Life" and "The Dispute between a Man and his Ba."[40] The author is a manic-depressive type who is thoroughly embittered and gives vent to a series of searing complaints about the trials and troubles that have afflicted him. He even expresses a longing for death, and the whole composition is in the form of a dialogue with his soul, who threatens to abandon him if he persists in being "in love with easeful death." The threat is a serious one, for it would mean losing the hope of a serene afterlife. In this debate the *ba* is the winner, since the man ends by extolling death and the promised eternity while being yet ready to face the present life. The writer's poetic power certainly has its enchantment:

> Death is before me today
> Like a sick man's recovery
> Like going outdoors after confinement.

> Death is before me today
> Like the fragrance of myrrh,
> Like sitting under sail on breeze day.
> Death is before me today
> Like the fragrance of lotus,
> Like sitting on the shore of drunkenness.
> (Lichtheim, *Lit.*, 1:168)

The images are simple, and the concluding stanza in the series conveys the universally appealing thought that death is a journey homeward, reinforced by the idea that it means freedom from captivity:

> Death is before me today
> Like a man's longing to see his home
> When he has spent many years in captivity.

The skeptical element in this work is rather similar to the attitude voiced in the "Songs of the Harpers," several of which have been found inscribed in tombs and were perhaps intended to be sung at family banquets held in the tombs—a lively custom that I have seen practiced in modern Muslim Egypt in the belief that departed members of the family now return to join in the party. It is unlikely, however, that the Muslim creed permits the outright challenge to established belief, which is apparent in some of the ancient songs. The song from the tomb of King Intef, for example, bewails the fact that splendid graves have crumbled, and it goes on to question the doctrine of life beyond the grave:

> None comes from there,
> To tell of their state,
> To tell of their needs,
> To calm our hearts,
> Until we go where they have gone.
> (Lichtheim, *Lit.*, 1:196)

Then comes an exhortation to pursue present pleasures. A reply to such daring hedonism is found in the song of the priest Neferhotep:

> I have heard those songs that are in the tombs of old,
> And what they relate in extolling life on earth,
> And in belittling the land of the dead.
> Why is this done to the land of eternity,
> The just and fair that holds no terror?
> (Lichtheim, *Lit.*, 1:195)

The Amarna Experience
and Its Aftermath

Although it is in some ways quite untypical of Egyptian religion, the vision of Akhenaten a little before the middle of the fourteenth century B.C. is one of the spiritual splendors of the tradition. It was to some extent a break with tradition, but remained in some degree indebted to it. After his death this remarkable Pharaoh was execrated as a heretic, and his influence seemed to be abruptly cut off. Excavations at the village of El-Amarna in Middle Egypt have revealed texts and representations that tell the story of a stormy but single-minded pilgrimage. It was on the site of El-Amarna that the Pharaoh had built his new capital, Akhetaten, "The Horizon of Aten," a doctrinal appellation that enshrined the name of his god, Aten, the god of the sun-disk. For a long time before this, Thebes had been the capital, and it was the king's opposition to the priesthood of Amûn at Thebes that was the major factor in his decision to abandon Thebes and build a new capital that would prove a more suitable center for a revolutionary religion. His opposition to the old religion is indicated also by his change of name— from Amenophis (Amenhotep), "Amûn is satisfied," to Akhenaten, "It is well with Aten." An element of fanaticism is manifest in Akhenaten's determination, eventually, to expunge the names of all gods from his monuments save for Aten. One is indeed tempted to wonder whether the driving force in his reforming seal was derived more from hatred of the established religious order than from a fervent conviction that his new vision deserved complete allegiance. In the history of religions there is often evidence of such a double approach. The prophets of the Hebrew Bible were unsparing in their condemnation of idolatry or of a degenerate monotheism. Zoroaster and the Buddha and Muhammad had a like facet to their teaching, and Jesus similarly condemned the Pharisees. Yet in each case the positive vision was far stronger than any negatively aggressive rebuke.

In the final phase of his pilgrimage Akhenaten established an uncompromising monotheism. His god, Aten, was regarded as embodied in the sun-disk and was naturally related, therefore, to the ancient worship of the sun-god Rê. The composite form Amen-Rê (combining Amûn and Rê) was a popular deity in the Eighteenth Dynasty before Akhenaten, but the element connected with Amûn now disappeared. Representations often show Aten extending his radiant rays to Akhenaten and his family, and the rays end in hands. They are helping hands, and there are few more attractive symbols in religious iconography. They indicate a creator-god who cares for all created beings. The hands are often shown holding and bestowing the *ankh* sign, which signifies life, so that Aten is depicted as the kindly bestower of life itself. Such representations are exquisitely confirmed by the Great Hymn to Aten. It is an original composition by Akhenaten himself and has long been recognized as a classic of religious literature. Parts of it are closely parallel to parts of Psalm 104.[41] The central theme is the praise of Aten as the divine power who creates and sustains life. He is "the living Aten, the beginning of life."[42] He is a deity who is both transcendent and immanent:

> Although you are far away, your ways are on earth.

When Aten appears in the sunrise, all created beings are awakened and rejoice; even the fish in the river dart before his face. The whole mystery of life is then extolled; Aten tends every form of life—the child in the womb, the chick in the egg—and his loving care is infinite: "you are the nurse even in the mother's womb." Nor is this solicitude confined to life in Egypt. It extends to foreign lands, and an eloquent passage lauds the amazing variety that marks the physical shape and color of different peoples as well as their languages:

> You have made the earth according to your desire, while you were alone, with men, cattle and all beasts, everything that is on earth going on its feet, everything that is on high flying with its wings, the foreign lands of Syria and Nubia and the land of Egypt. You set every man in his place and see to his needs; each one has his food and his time of life is reckoned. Their tongues are separate in speech, and their nature is likewise; the colour of their skin is different; you distinguish the peoples.
>
> (Brunner, "Egyptian Texts," 18)

Stress is laid on the existence of Aten as the only god: "O sole God, apart from whom there is no other!" Other Amarna hymns present the same vision, and the Short Hymn contains a memorable line:

> You are the mother and father of all that you made.
> (Lichtheim, Lit., 2:91)

"Mother," be it noted, comes before "father,"—and this in a society that was, at large, firmly patriarchal.

In some ways these works owe a spiritual debt to previous hymnology, especially that relating to the traditional sun worship. It is the enhanced sensibility and the unswerving monotheism that set Akhenaten's work apart. Other striking features are the rejection of mythology and the strong ethical color, which derives particularly from the emphasis on mâat (justice, order).[43]

The role of Akhenaten himself in the theology of Amarna is conspicuous but not without perplexities. At the beginning of the Great Hymn he is referred to as Aten's beloved son. At the end the same idea is repeated with the addition of the queen's name: Aten is said to have been creatively active "for your son who came forth from your body, the King of Upper and Lower Egypt, who lives from order, Akhenaten, and the great royal consort Nefertiti" (Brunner, "Egyptian Texts," 19). A little before that comes a remarkable assertion:

> There is no other who knows you, but your son Nefer-kheperu-Re Wa-en-Re [=Akhenaten], for you have made him to know your plans and your strength.

Brunner comments that "while every Pharaoh is mediator between the world of gods and the world of men and as such has a greater share in the world of the gods than do other men, there is no other period during which a king makes such a claim as does Akhenaten to exclusive knowledge of God's will and thus to worship."[44] The final phrase here probably refers to the representations and the prayers which indicate that the people venerated the king and queen together with Aten. To assume that they are worshiped on a par as a triad of deities would make nonsense of Akhenaten's conception of God. But a very special role is clearly assigned to the king, and his claims to exclusive knowledge of the divine betrays a kind of intensity of conviction that might, at the same time, invite the charge of arrogance. Yet religion that comes through revelation to an individual often bears the marks of a heightened assurance. Perhaps Hornung is near the truth when he gives an Islamic touch (however anachronistically) to the relationship in his summation:

> The new creed could, indeed, be summed up in the formula, "There is no god but Aten, and Akhenaten is his prophet."[45]

There is evidence that the ordinary people of Amarna were not ready to abandon all the old gods.[46] After the death of Akhenaten there was a restoration of the old order generally, although Amen-Rê did not regain his prominence nor was there a return to Thebes as capital. In language, political life, and religious art, the influence of the Amarna episode remained considerable; and if Aten disappeared from the pantheon honored by Akhenaten's successors, the sun-disk continued to be important in sacral symbolism.[47]

During the Ramesside era (1306–1070 B.C.) an attractive feature is provided by the hymns and prayers of humble folk. They often show penitence and devotion and a lively sense of the divine solicitude, as in the votive stela of Neb-Re:

You, Amun, are the lord of the humble man,
you come at the voice of the poor.
I call to you when I am oppressed,
and you come quickly, to save me in my wretchedness.
(Brunner, "Egyptian Texts," 33)[48]

The Judgment before Osiris

Although Osiris does not figure explicitly in the Amarna texts, his popularity greatly increased during subsequent eras, and in every funerary context he held supreme sway. The belief became widely prevalent that after death everyone faced a trial before him. In origin this belief was a part of the general tendency to ascribe to the afterlife all the activities of this life. Litigation was, of course, one of these, and early allusions to the idea often refer to possible litigation before the Great God, when an accusation may be brought against the dead concerning an action committed by him during life on earth.

There are some early allusions, as in the *Instruction of Merikare,* which show that the idea was extended to denote a compulsory court that everyone had to face:

> The Court that judges the wretch,
> You know they are not lenient,
> On the day of judging the miserable,
> In the hour of doing their task.
> It is painful when the accuser has knowledge,
> Do not trust in length of years,
> They view a lifetime in an hour!
> (Lichtheim, *Lit.,* 1:101)

A parallel development is that the idea of a general judgment is conveyed through the image of weighing in a balance. This occurs in *The Eloquent Peasant*[49] and in parts of the Coffin Texts, as in the following clear allusion:[50]

> Your evil is expelled, your iniquity is effaced by those who weigh with the balance on the day of the reckoning of qualities.
> (*Coffin Texts,* I, 181 a–e)

It was in the New Kingdom that an elaborate visual form was given to the concept. The heart of the dead was shown being weighed before Osiris, the president of the court, and forty-two assessors, a procedure to which detailed attention is given both textually and pictorially in Spell 125 of the Book of the Dead. We see the heart being weighed against a figure of the goddess Mâat. In charge of the balance is the god Anubis, and the recorder is the god Thoth. At hand is a composite monster, called the Devourer

(*Am*), who is ready to swallow the guilty. If a man's sins are numerous, this is regarded as depressing the scale in which his heart appears. What is therefore desired is an equilibrium.

Connected with the same process are the Protestations of Innocence or Negative Confessions, in which the deceased person is made to deny that he has committed specified sins, such as:

> I have not blasphemed God. I have not done violence to a poor man. I have not broken the taboo of a God. I have not defamed a servant to his superiors. I have not made (anyone) sick. I have not made (anyone) weep. I have not killed. I have not given orders to kill.
>
> (Brunner, "Egyptian Texts," 65)

From the catalogue of sins there indirectly emerges, of course, a code of conduct, and it is of interest that male homosexuality is condemned.[51]

A profound moral sensibility can be inferred from the basic idea of the Egyptian last judgment. For many, however, there was a magical way out of this crisis of the soul: if the tomb was equipped with a papyrus that contained the detailed denials, it was believed that a favorable result was assured. That a minority did not accept such a simple guarantee is demonstrated by the autobiography of Petosiris, a priest of Hermopolis in the fourth century B.C. He reveals a completely serious approach that views the day of moral reckoning as one which rich and poor, powerful and puny, alike must face:

> The west is the abode of him who is faultless,
> Praise god for the man who has reached it!
> No man will attain it,
> Unless his heart is exact in doing right.
> The poor is not distinguished there from the rich,
> Only he who is found free of fault
> By scale and weight before eternity's lord.
> There is none exempt from being reckoned.
>
> (Lichtheim, *Lit.*, 3:46)

An important part of this creed was the identification of the dead with Osiris, a belief that was developed more thoroughly in the Greco-Roman era, although it fell short of the ideal of mystic union with him.[52] It was a creed that endured in Egypt until the middle of the sixth century A.D., when Justinian closed the temple of Isis in Philae.

Notes

1. Kurt Mendelssohn, *The Riddle of the Pyramids* (New York: Praeger, 1974) 198–99.
2. Erik Hornung, *Conceptions of God*, 93–96 with pl. I.
3. Samuel A. B. Mercer, *Horus Royal God of Egypt* (Grafton, MA: Society of Oriental Research, 1942) 117–49, esp. 143; see also J. Gwyn Griffiths, *The Conflict*, 132–33.
4. See further Griffiths, *Conflict*, 82, where it is shown that other gods are occasionally assigned this role.
5. See Patrick Boylan, *Thoth the Hermes of Egypt* (London: H. Milford, 1922) 38.
6. Frankfort, *Ancient Egyptian Religion*, 4. Frankfort refers also to his discussion in *The Intellectual Adventure of Ancient Man* (Chicago: University of Chicago Press, 1946).
7. Kurt Sethe, *Amun und die Acht Urgötter von Hermopolis* (Berlin: Preussische Akademie der Wissenschaften, 1929) 77, cited by S. G. F. Brandon, *Creation Legends of the Ancient Near East* (London: Hodder and Stoughton, 1963) 47 n. 2.
8. *Creation Legends*, 14.
9. Compare the naming activity in Gen 1:5ff.
10. See S. Sauneron and J. Yoyotte in *La Naissance du monde* (Sources orientales 1; Paris: Editions du Seuil, 1959) 68–69; H. Kees, *Lesebuch: Aegypten*, 4.
11. In *Universitas* 17 (1975) 140.
12. See Siegfried Morenz, *Gott und Mensch im alten Ägypten* (Heidelberg: L. Schneider, 1965) 16.
13. See Griffiths, *Conflict*, 145–46. I am not suggesting that Egypt knew a full-fledged system of totemism. Claude Lévi-Strauss argued that totemism is an "illusion" produced by psychological factors (*Totemism*, trans. Rodney Needham [Boston: Beacon Press, 1963] 102. It appears that his case has not been generally accepted by anthropologists. See, for example, the essays by E. M. Mendelson and Peter Worsley in *The Structural Study of Myth and Totemism*, ed. Edmund Leach (London: Tavistock Publications, 1968) 119–59.
14. See the fine analysis by Jan Zandee, *Death as an Enemy according to Ancient Egyptian Conceptions* (Studies in the History of Religions, Supplements to *Numen* 5; Leiden: Brill, 1960).
15. See also Faulkner in *Journal of Egyptian Archaeology* 10 (1924) 97–103.
16. See my remarks ("Menschenopfer") in *Lex. Ägypt.* (1980) 64–65.
17. W. Schmidt, *The Origin and Growth of Religion*, trans. H. J. Rose (2nd ed.; New York: L. MacVeagh, 1935) 114.
18. Edmund Leach, *Social Anthropology* (London: Oxford University Press, 1982) 141.
19. L. Wittgenstein, "Remarks on The Golden Bough," in *The Human World* 3 (1971) 30.
20. Ibid., 33.
21. See Griffiths, *Osiris*, 231.
22. See Morenz, *Egyptian Religion*, 103.
23. Kees, *Lesebuch: Aegypten*, 36, no. 57.
24. See W. Stevenson Smith, *The Art and Architecture of Egypt*, 76 with pl. 51 B.
25. Georg Misch, *A History of Autobiography in Antiquity*, 1:20–33.
26. Ibid., 1:25.
27. Ibid., 1:24.

28. Alan Gardiner, *Egypt of the Pharaohs,* 373; see also Peter Kaplony in *Lex. Ägypt.* 1:1056–57.

29. For this and the previous quotation see Hans Bonnet, *Reallexikon der ägyptischen Religionsgeschichte,* 431.

30. Frankfort, *Ancient Egyptian Religion,* 55. Faulkner finds a future reference in the second part: "that the King will set right" (in the place of wrong . . .). (*Pyramid Texts,* 260 par. 1775).

31. Griffiths, *Osiris,* 232.

32. The Egyptians also frequently referred to death as sleep.

33. The view has occasionally been held; see Griffiths, *Osiris,* 4, 6, 23, 208.

34. Hornung, *Conceptions of God,* 93.

35. Rodney Needham sees this faculty of metamorphosis as a fundamental feature of mythology (*Primordial Characters,* 58–64).

36. Louis V. Žabkar, *A Study of the Ba Concept,* 97.

37. For these distinctions see Jan Assmann, *Zeit und Ewigkeit im alten Ägypten* (Heidelberg: C. Winter, 1975). Erik Hornung denies any meaning that goes beyond "time" (*Conceptions of God,* 183); see also his exposition in *Eranos Jahrbuch* 47 (1978) 269–307.

38. See my remarks in *Greece and Rome* 16 (1947) 122–26.

39. See A. H. Gardiner, *The Attitude of the Ancient Egyptians to Death and the Dead* (Frazer Lecture; Cambridge: University Press, 1935) 12.

40. The former title is given by R. O. Faulkner in *The Literature of Ancient Egypt,* ed. William Kelly Simpson (New Haven, CT: Yale University Press, 1973) 201–9; the latter title is given in Lichtheim, *Lit.,* 1:163–69.

41. See Lichtheim, *Lit.,* 2:100; Brunner, "Egyptian Texts," 16.

42. Brunner's translation has been used.

43. On the rejection of mythology, see Jan Assmann in *Lex. Ägypt,* 1:526–40; on the ethical aspect, see Louis V. Žabkar in *Journal of Near Eastern Studies* 13 (1954) 94–96.

44. Brunner, "Egyptian Texts," 19.

45. Hornung, *Conceptions of God,* 248.

46. See Kate Bosse-Griffiths in *Journal of Egyptian Archaeology* 63 (1977) 98–106.

47. Hornung, "Monotheismus im Pharaonischen Ägypten," in *Monotheismus im Alten Israel und seiner Umwelt,* ed. Othmar Keel (Biblische Beiträge 14; Fribourg: Verlag Schweizerisches Katholisches Bibelwerk, 1980) 84–97, esp. 95.

48. See also Brunner's instructive parallels on p. 32.

49. Lichtheim, *Lit.,* 1:181.

50. See Reinhard Grieshammer, *Das Jenseitsgericht in den Sargtexten* (Ägyptologische Abh. 20; Wiesbaden: Harrassowitz, 1970) 46.

51. "I have not had sexual relations with a boy" (Brunner, "Egyptian Texts," 66), though the translation is debated. Brunner states: "Homosexuality was strictly taboo."

52. L. Kákosy, *Selected Papers* (Studia Aegyptiaca 7; Budapest: ELTE, 1981) 227–37 with a review of studies by Morenz.

Bibliography

Editions

Buck, Adriaan de. *The Egyptian Coffin Texts.* 6 vols. University of Chicago Oriental Institute Publications, 34, 49, 64, 67, 73, 81. Chicago: University of Chicago Press, 1935–1956.

Budge, E. A. Wallis. *The Chapters of coming forth by day; or, The Theban recension of the Book of the Dead.* 3 vols. London: Kegan Paul, 1910.
Naville, Edouard. *Das aegyptische Todtenbuch.* 3 vols. Berlin: A. Asher, 1886. Reprint, Graz: Academic Press, 1971.
Sethe, Kurt. *Die altaegyptischen Pyramidentexte.* 4 vols. Leipzig: Hinrichs, 1908–1922.

Translations

Allen, Thomas George. *The Book of the Dead.* Studies in Ancient Oriental Civilization 37. Chicago: University of Chicago Press, 1974.
Brunner, Hellmut. "Egyptian Texts" (with Translations and Notes), trans. John Bowden. In *Near Eastern Religious Texts Relating to the Old Testament.* Edited by Walter Beyerlin. London: SCM, 1978.
Faulkner, Raymond O. *The Ancient Egyptian Coffin Texts.* 3 vols. Warminster: Aris & Phillips, 1973–1978.
———. *The Ancient Egyptian Pyramid Texts.* Oxford: Oxford University Press, 1969.
Lesko, Leonard H. *The Ancient Egyptian Book of Two Ways.* Translation with Notes. University of California Publications, Near Eastern Studies 17. Berkeley: University of California Press, 1972.
Lichtheim, Miriam. *Ancient Egyptian Literature.* 3 vols: 1, *The Old and Middle Kingdoms;* 2, *The New Kingdom;* 3, *The Late Period.* Berkeley: University of California Press, 1973, 1976, 1978.
Simpson, William Kelly., ed. *The Literature of Ancient Egypt.* New Haven, CT: Yale University Press, 1972.

Modern Works

Bonnet, Hans. *Reallexikon der ägyptischen Religionsgeschichte.* Berlin: de Gruyter, 1952. Reprint, 1971.
Clark, R. T. Rundle. *Myth and Symbol in Ancient Egypt.* London: Thames & Hudson, 1959.
Frankfort, Henri. *Ancient Egyptian Religion.* New York: Columbia University Press, 1948. Reprint, New York: Harper, 1961.
———. *Kingship and the Gods.* An Oriental Institute Essay. Chicago: University of Chicago Press, 1948, 1978.
Gardiner, Alan. *Egypt of the Pharaohs.* Oxford: Oxford University Press, 1961.
Griffiths, J. Gwyn. *The Conflict of Horus and Seth.* Liverpool Monographs in Archaeology and Oriental Studies. Liverpool: Liverpool University Press, 1960.
———. *The Origins of Osiris and His Cult.* Studies in the History of Religions, Supplements to *Numen* 40. Leiden: Brill, 1980.
Helck, Wolfgang, ed., with Eberhard Otto (later Wolfhart Westendorf). *Lexikon der Ägyptologie.* Wiesbaden: Harrassowitz, 1975.
Hornung, Erik. *Conceptions of God in Ancient Egypt.* Translated by John Baines. London: Routledge & Kegan Paul, 1983. A translation, with additional material, of *Der Eine und die Vielen.* Darmstadt: Wissenschaftliche Buchgesellschaft, 1971.
Kees, Hermann. *Religionsgeschichtliches Lesebuch.* 10, *Aegypten.* Edited by A. Bertholet. 2nd enlarged ed. Tübingen: Mohr, 1928.
Misch, Georg. *A History of Autobiography in Antiquity.* Translated by E. W. Dickes and Georg Misch. 2 vols. London: Routledge & Kegan Paul, 1949, 1950.

Morenz, Siegfried. *Egyptian Religion.* Translated by Ann E. Keep. London: Methuen, 1973.

Needham, Rodney. *Primordial Characters.* Charlottesville: Virginia University Press, 1978.

Posener, Georges, ed. *A Dictionary of Egyptian Civilization.* London: Methuen, 1962.

Smith, W. Stevenson. *The Art and Architecture of Egypt.* The Pelican History of Art. Harmondsworth: Penguin Books, 1958.

Žabkar, Louis. *A Study of the Ba Concept in Ancient Egyptian Texts.* Studies in Ancient Oriental Civilization 34. Chicago: University of Chicago Press, 1968.

2

The Great Egyptian Cults of Oecumenical Spiritual Significance

J. GWYN GRIFFITHS

WITH THE CONQUEST OF EGYPT by Alexander the Great in 332 B.C., the country's religion experienced several changes. The first of these was the result of placing Egypt wide open to foreign influences, especially Greek influences. It is true that this was not the first time in Egypt's history that the influx of foreign ideas was made possible. The country had previously been occupied, from the seventh century on, by Assyrians and Persians, but in neither case had the intellectual and religious influence of the invaders been extensive. Indeed, still earlier dominations by Hyksos, Libyans, and Ethiopians had made a greater impact. Contact with the Greeks, on the other hand, had also dated within Egypt to the seventh century, when the Greek colony of Naucratis had been established in the western Delta.[1] Moreover, there had been economic and political contacts with cities in Greek lands, especially with those of Ionia and with Athens; and intellectual interest had become evident in a two-way traffic, as the writings of Hecataeus and Herodotus had testified.

It was the foundation of the city of Alexandria by Alexander that signaled and elaborated the trends of a new situation. Naucratis still flourished too, and a third Greek city in Egypt emerged at Ptolemais in the Thebaid, founded by Ptolemy I Soter. If the Greek culture of the Macedonian regime was the dominating outside influence, there were several other strands in the variegated pattern of Alexandrian life, which included Jewish, Syrian, Anatolian, and of course Egyptian elements.[2] Among military settlers (that is, discharged soldiers) in various parts of Egypt, were Ethiopians, Arabs, Babylonians, Carthaginians, Lycians, Medes, Paphlagonians, and Indians. In religious matters an almost inevitable result was a readiness to identify deities of the differing traditions. Any polytheistic religion tends to be inherently friendly to other similar religions. But the process of syncretism, by which cults were combined, or of *theocrasia*, "mingling of deities," often meant that some attributes not originally present in a cult were absorbed from the cult with which it was identified.[3]

A National Religion Looks Outward

From the standpoint of Egyptian religion, a vital change now inaugurated was that the basically national character of the system was gradually transformed to a view of the world that was much broader. The most obvious feature of the nationally rooted nature of the Pharaonic system was its firm link with the gods Horus and Osiris. Every living Pharaoh was equated with Horus, every dead one with Osiris. The centrality of this belief was evident in all ritual that affected the state religion; naturally it did not enter so much into the local cults, and even in the Osirian cult — as far as this concerned the individual — the specifically royal connection had long since vanished. Yet the consciousness of Egypt's stamp on ritual and belief was deeply felt. Egypt was clearly regarded as the center of everything; only Egyptians were deemed to be fully human beings (*remetj*) — an arrogance shared, of course, by Jews and Greeks when they called other nations Gentiles and barbarians. National consciousness also entered into the role of the Pharaoh as high priest and representative of his people. In particular he was the upholder of *Mâat*, the principle of justice and concord that held Egypt together, and indeed the whole cosmic order; and with divine support the Pharaoh was believed to defend Egypt against her enemies. In some religious contexts, especially those concerned with temples or the attached House of Life, there was a taboo on the entry of "Asiatics."[4] There are parallels, admittedly, such as the restriction of the Eleusinian Mysteries to Greek speakers. In consonance with the national emphasis, the Egyptian deities who were venerated outside Egypt in the pre-Hellenistic era were viewed as representatives of the country and normally accompanied military and political expansion, as in Nubia and Syria.[5] Religion, like trade, often follows the flag. Further, the very distinctive character of Egyptian burial customs meant that when they were abroad, the people of Egypt had almost a terror of dying outside their country. The feeling is well expressed in the stories of Sinuhe and Wenamûn.[6] A wider consciousness embraced their fervent adherence to the whole native religion. John Barns has expressed it strongly but justly:

> Never, perhaps, was a people so profoundly influenced by environment as
> the Egyptians were by the land of the life-giving Nile, with its unique and

miraculously ordered seasonal phenomena. Philo accuses them of deifying their land; certainly it was for them the center of the universe of gods as well as humans. An illuminating document for the psychology of pagan Egypt, from its very deathbed in the late Roman period, the Hermetic *Asclepius* III, in a moving lament for the glorious past, calls Egypt "the temple of the whole earth."[7]

A problem therefore arose with the advent of an age when the Greek population of Egypt itself, under the rule of the Ptolemies, had to be guided to a religious situation in which both Egyptian and Greek aspirations seemed to demand recognition. The problem became more acute when Egyptian cults were exported to other countries. Were these cults now to be stripped entirely of their national character? Perhaps one might compare the problematic era of the early Christian church when it was beginning to spread outside Palestine. It had its origin in a phase of Judaism, and there was a powerful party which maintained that Jewish practices, including circumcision, should be followed by adherents of the new religion.

For the Greeks in Egypt the problem was partly answered by the prominence given to the cult of Sarapis. He was a god of Egyptian origin and derived from the worship of Osiris-Apis, called Osor-Hapy or Oserapis in the Memphite Serapeum. Behind this was the ancient cult of the bull-god Apis, but a human male form was assigned to Sarapis, and his appeal was mainly to the upper classes of the Greek population of Egypt. It has been urged that Ptolemy I Soter developed the deity specifically for them.[8] But "his Egyptian origin was never forgotten";[9] and if so it is hard to explain, as far as motive is concerned, his dual (Egyptian and Greek) nature, unless both Greek and Egyptian communities are taken into account. To some extent Sarapis was taking the place of Osiris as the consort of Isis. Greek dedications from Egypt often name Sarapis and Isis together. In a detailed survey of this material P. M. Fraser shows that Sarapis was worshiped "largely in Alexandria, and largely by Greeks"; he also points out that "the native Egyptians continued for their part to worship Osor-Hapi"—and, it may be added, Osiris.[10] It is to be expected, therefore, that the figure of Sarapis, hellenized as it was in form if not always in doctrine, appealed more to the Greeks in Egypt, however the precise purpose of the cult may be defined.

The persistence of a double stream of tradition in Ptolemaic Egypt is evident in other ways. We have referred to the traditional national religion as one based on the equation of Horus and the Pharaoh. During the Ptolemaic and Roman eras this tradition was stoutly maintained although the rulers of Egypt were now Macedonian and Roman intruders. It has been suggested that the Egyptians who carried out the elaborate Horus rites at the temple of Edfu were mentally identifying the Sethian enemy with the reigning Ptolemy and that under a show of loyalty they were messianically awaiting the "true Horus" who would liberate Egypt from the foreign yoke. It is an attractive theory, but no clear proof has emerged.[11]

"A very close connection between the cult and the Crown" is indicated for the third century B.C. in Egypt.[12] When the cult spread to Greek lands, together with associated Egyptian cults, a politically propagandist explanation was naturally forthcoming. Reference has been roundly made to the career of Sarapis in the Aegean as that of "an imperialistic religion."[13] Since the Ptolemies of Egypt ruled several areas at various times in the Aegean and Asia Minor, one might easily assume that the public cults established there might well derive from direct or indirect state instigation. Yet it has been shown, almost with the force of demonstration, that "the cult of Sarapis spread outside Egypt in the main through private action, by traders, mercenaries, priests and travellers who had acquired a personal interest in the cult, primarily in Egypt." In Cyprus and Cyrene the cult is said not to be strongly attested, although they were Ptolemaic possessions. Perhaps there was "a resistance to the cult . . . just because Sarapis symbolised Alexandria." Conversely, some independent communities, especially if they had close trade ties with Egypt, may have been ready to adopt the Alexandrian deity "to show friendship to the Ptolemies."[14] Trade and politics are often linked. Fraser's thorough analysis is confined to Sarapis, it should be noted. In the case of Cyprus, several other deities of Egyptian origin were venerated, as I had occasion to notice on a visit in 1983 to the museums of Limassol, Nicosia, and Larnaca, where the deities Bes and Isis were prominent in statuary[15] and other Egyptian deities, including Ptah, Sakhmet, Thoth, Shu, and Anubis are figured on faience pendants and amulets, often in pre-Hellenistic times.[16] The Hellenistic and Roman evidence for Cyprus embraces statuary of Isis and Osiris, with a notable Canopic Osiris.[17]

In the present study, however, our main concern is not with the economic and political implications of the dissemination of the Egyptian cults; it is rather with the nature of their appeal. What were the reasons — psychological, emotional, and doctrinal — which made them attractive to so many varied peoples? They had an "inner vitality" and a response to "urgent human needs"[18] which resulted in a widespread following. Ideally one should perhaps have to define those needs in the particular contexts of place and time in order to understand fully what was then going on in the souls of men and women. The Pauline example (1 Cor 1:22) confronts us with a challenging definition of what Jews and Greeks were anxious to experience in the first century of the Christian era: "Jews call for miracles (sēmeia). Greeks look for wisdom (sophia)." The call for miracles was certainly a feature of the popular mentality, and not only among Jews. The Egyptian cults offered a plentiful supply of both miracle and magic. Wisdom was an ideal of the minority, especially of those who knew something of the Greek philosophical schools. Two of these, the Epicurean and Stoic schools, had arisen in the early phases of the Hellenistic age. A reputation for *sophia* was ascribed to Isis by Plutarch and others, but in the Egyptian tradition it was magic, particularly healing magic, that was paramount in the Isiac ideology. It is generally accepted that in Greek lands after the conquests of Alexander the human needs of the individual were given a more pressing urgency by the dwindling importance of the autonomous city-states. Not that they were all directly placed under imperial domination. The term "Greek lands" embraces far-flung and scattered communities including those of the Greek mainland, islands of the Aegean and other parts of the Mediterranean, Asia Minor, as well as settlements in Italy, the Black Sea coast, and the North African littoral. A variety of political conditions prevailed. The case of Delos, roughly in the middle of the Aegean, is instructive. In 314 B.C. it passed from Athenian control and enjoyed political independence for some 150 years.[19] It belonged to a League of Islanders and had special relations from time to time with kings of Egypt, Macedon, Syria, and Pergamon. Commercially it was very flourishing, a fact that is doubtless the key to the amazing variety of its religious life. Greek cults were dominant, particularly of Apollo and Artemis, but numerous inscriptions and temple remains point to a vigorous flowering of the Egyptian cults, partly due, it seems, to the cosmopolitan character of the population. Clearly, Delos was exceptional in the vitality of its contacts in the Mediterranean world beyond. Yet many Greek cities were near the sea, and material commerce was conducive to commerce in religion. A large number after the death of Alexander became absorbed into the empires of his successors, Cassander of Macedon, Ptolemy of Egypt, and Seleucus of Syria.

Athens itself was uneasy under Macedonian domination,[20] and perhaps it was on the Greek mainland that "the decay of the city-state"[21] was most evident. Under the shadow of Macedonian imperialism the absence of the self-confidence that marked the independent city-states must have affected the outlook of the individual. The traditional Greek cults continued, and they were in practice largely communal, "the expression of the city-state's relationship to the gods"; but after the fourth century B.C. there was a "craving for a more personal relation to the deity and for a redemptive religion."[22] Although these two longings were answered—as Bell propounds in the passage from which we have cited—more in Oriental cults than in anything that the official Greek cults could offer, there were attached facilities in both categories that brought personal satisfaction in the social sense.

In Athens the lack of interest in political affairs led to the increased growth of private associations. "The alternative was to join a club,"[23] and the clubs were attached to cults of both Greek and non-Greek origin. Such clubs or associations of believers were a strong feature of Egyptian religious life both in Egypt itself and in areas to which the cults had spread.[24]

The principal deities of these cults were those grouped around Isis, Osiris, and Sarapis. Horus, the son of Isis and Osiris, appears in various forms. Nephthys appears as the sister of Isis and the wife of Seth-Typhon, but the latter is the archenemy of the family. Most prominent outside the family group are Anubis, the embalmer-god who has a canine head, and Thoth-Hermes, the learned scribe and recorder of the gods. It is Anubis that is sometimes linked with Hermes, especially as a guide of souls. A looser association was that with Bastet, the cat-goddess of Bubastis, and the popular Bes, an ugly monster-like figure who was the patron of sexual and other physical activities. Such was the predominance of Isis in Greco-Roman contexts that every other Egyptian cult was to some extent merged into hers. It was the attraction of her personal appeal, and especially the appeal of her very human story, that provided the initially impelling factor. In the early part of the second century A.D., the story was set down in detail by Plutarch; and he proceeded to add a series of elaborate interpretations. Whereas these are replete with Platonist and Stoic philosophical ideas, the main outline of the story is of authentic Egyptian origin, even if the native sources do not provide a comparably coherent account.

At the beginning of the story (Plutarch's chap. 12) mention is made of the birth of Osiris, "the great king and benefactor," at Thebes, and of other deities, among them Typhon and Nephthys. As a beneficent king, Osiris is said to have founded agriculture, a system of laws, and religion. Further, he is said to have traversed and civilized the whole world. (This is a transference to him of the tradition about Dionysus.) But after his return, Typhon, we are told, plotted against him and lured him into a chest, which was then thrown into the river and carried out to sea. This occurred in the twenty-eighth year of the reign of Osiris, and Isis then wandered in distress searching for the chest. In her sorrow she made the unhappy discovery that Osiris had mistakenly made love to her sister Nephthys, who gave birth, as a result, to the child Anubis. Yet Isis reared him, making him her guard and attendant.

In the meantime the chest was cast ashore in Syrian Byblos, where Isis followed it and became the nurse of the queen's child. Unfortunately Isis caused the child to be burned. (The whole episode in Byblos really belongs to a tradition about Demeter.) She recovered the chest, however, and brought it back to Egypt; and after opening it she embraced the body of

3. Coffin of Nakht. Egyptian. VII Dynasty.

Osiris. Then she journeyed to her son Horus who was in Buto in the western Delta. In so doing she had left the chest behind, with the untoward result that Typhon came upon it and cut the body into fourteen parts, which he proceeded to scatter to various regions of the country, thus causing the idea that Osiris had many tombs. Isis held a burial service over every part discovered by her. The only part that eluded her search was the phallus, which fish had eaten. However, she made an image of it and consecrated it.

Meanwhile Osiris came from the underworld to visit his son Horus, encouraging him to take up battle against Typhon, and Horus triumphed after a struggle that lasted many days. But Isis, when she saw Typhon tied up in bonds, did not kill him, preferring to release him. Thereafter Typhon brought a charge of illegitimacy against Horus, but with the help of Hermes, Horus was declared by the gods to be legitimate and won victories against Typhon in further battles. We are told, in conclusion, that Isis had sexual union with Osiris after his death, giving birth to Harpocrates, a form of Horus who was "prematurely delivered and weak in his lower limbs."

A Universal Goddess of Love Offers Salvation

Plutarch elevates Isis to the position of being "a pattern of piety" (*eusebeias . . . didagma,* 27.361E). In fact the phrase is a strange one when applied to a goddess, since *eusebeia* is a quality (like *pietas*) used of human beings in respect of devout and loyal behavior to both God and humans. Plutarch expounds his meaning fully: it was Isis who, as the sister, wife, and helper of Osiris, repelled the frenzy of Typhon, and after her struggles and wanderings and many deeds of wisdom (*sophia*) and bravery took care to enshrine the memory of them in the most sacred rites; thus it was that she "consecrated at once a pattern of piety and an encouragement to men and women overtaken by similar misfortunes." A similar note is struck in the prayer to Isis which Apuleius puts in the mouth of Lucius after his initiation:

> Thou in truth art the holy and eternal saviour of the human race, ever beneficent in helping mortal men, and thou bringest the sweet love of a mother to the trials of the unfortunate. (*Isis-Book* 25)

Like Plutarch, Apuleius was writing in the second century A.D. and his novel, the *Metamorphoses,* also called *The Golden Ass,* was probably composed about fifty years after Plutarch's work; its last chapter gives a memorable description of how Lucius, after his adventures as a man turned into a donkey, was restored by Isis to human form and then devoted himself to her worship.

To the human appeal of her story, therefore, Isis was able to add the inspiration of her courageous example and her miraculous blessings. In all religions the highest call is to the imitation of the divine (*imitatio Dei*); but it becomes a potent message only when the divine enters into the human condition. This was true of the way in which Isis was regarded, and in the process she came to be treated as a universal goddess who was equated with a host of other goddesses of varying functions. She was also herself envisaged as a divine power of cosmic and creative import. There are some suggestions within the Egyptian tradition of the importance of Isis as a mother-goddess and as a goddess of heaven.[25] But in the prayer ascribed by Apuleius to Lucius she is a cosmic deity whose power is all-pervasive.

> Thou dost revolve the sphere of heaven and illumine the sun, thou dost guide the earth and trample Hell under thy feet. For thee the constellations move, for thee the seasons return; the divine beings rejoice for thee, and the elements are thy slaves. By thy command breezes blow and rain-clouds nourish, seeds sprout and buds grow. Awe of thy majesty imbues the birds that move in the sky, the wild beasts that roam the mountains, the serpents that glide in the earth, and the monsters that swim in the sea. (*Isis-Book* 25)[26]

Here she is the creator-goddess who remains in close inspiring touch with her creation. Akhenaten's Great Hymn to the Aten is not dissimilar, it is true, although the universe that Isis guides is rather more expansively conceived of. Neither paean amounts to pantheism since God is not identified with the created cosmos, unlike the Hermetic text which avers that "God is totality" (*to pan;* Nock, *Corp. Herm.* 1.12.22). Still further away is the modern pantheism that both finds and loses God (as in Giordano Bruno's "world soul") in a depersonalized universe, recalling the vague recognition of the divine that led the philosopher Arthur Schopenhauer to describe pantheism as "polite atheism."

Some of the universalist emphasis achieved by Isis is due to her absorption of many other goddesses and their functions, a process expressed in the concept of Isis Panthea, which shows Stoic influence, and pithily summed up in the celebrated inscription from Capua: *una quae es omnia, dea Isis* ("thou who, being one, art all, goddess Isis").[27] It has been taken in the sense that she alone was worshiped all over the world since all other goddesses were subsumed by her. But the original Egyptian idea is an expression rather of a transcendent monotheism, the sense of one reality beyond the many manifestations of polytheism. The influence of Stoicism may be easily adduced if we compare the Hymn to Zeus by Cleanthes in the third century B.C. It begins:

> Most glorious of immortals, Zeus,
> The many-named, almighty evermore,
> Nature's Great Sovereign, ruling all by law . . .[28]

The epithet "many-named" might suggest an assimilation of other deities, but Max Pohlenz ascribes to a Stoic audience the view that *Logos* (Reason), *Physis* (Nature), *Pronoia* (Providence), and *Heimarmenē* (Fate) are the divine attributes intended by the implied names.[29] It is possible that both types of names are meant; for "gods" (*theoi*) are mentioned in the last line of the hymn. The previous line refers to "mortals" (*brotoi*); both groups are said to praise the general law of the universe which rules in justice. All existing things are embraced by this rule; the universe (*kosmos*) and the earth obey Zeus as the embodiment of it (lines 7–8).

The wide sweep of the Stoic viewpoint, while it involved a certain reductionism in the treatment of Zeus and other gods, reflected a cosmopolitan spirit that was characteristic of the Hellenistic and Roman ages. That there was, however, religious competition and rivalry in the disturbed world of the early Christian centuries is an inescapable fact. Indeed, T. R. Glover in 1909 entitled his study of the whole scene *The Conflict of Religions in the Early Roman Empire*,[30] giving primacy to this aspect. Yet the chief protagonists of the Isis-religion were singularly free of this approach. They favored a friendly syncretism, and their attitude is illumined by personal details of their religious life. Plutarch's friend Clea, to whom he dedicated his book on Isis and Osiris, had been initiated into the cult of these deities, but at the same time she was a priestess of Dionysus at Delphi. Plutarch himself held a priesthood of Apollo at Delphi; both he and his wife had been initiated into the mystic rites of Dionysus. It is probable, though not certain, that he had experienced an Isiac initiation, for his attitude to this religion is earnestly appreciative. His tolerant eclecticism in religious matters was shared by Apuleius, who in fact makes Lucius, the initiate-hero of the *Metamorphoses,* a kinsman of Plutarch.[31] In his *Apology* (55) Apuleius states that "he has taken part in a number of initiation ceremonies in Greece" and that he became acquainted with "holy procedures of many kinds, a great number of rites, and diverse ceremonies." It is likely that he had experienced both Isiac and Eleusinian initiations.[32] The Isiac cult therefore made no exclusive claim, and here perhaps lay its ultimate weakness vis-à-vis Judaism and Christianity.

In the longest of the "Praises" of the goddess, *Papyrus Oxyrhynchus* 1380, which was written down in the second century A.D. but probably composed in the previous century, we find a multitude of equivalencies with other goddesses.[33] Her universal sway is thus denoted, and the many epithets and abstractions assigned to her present a picture of divine benevolence. She is said to be "gentle" and "affectionate," a "giver," a "giver of favors," a "savior of men," a "supporter," a "bringer to harbor," "all-bounteous," "guardian and guide," "providing sweetness." By way of contrast, she is also "Lady of war and rule" and "in Rome warlike"; yet she is "enmity-hating" and the patroness of sexual union ("it is thy will too that women in health cast anchor with men"). If one word sums up her character it is "friendship" (*philia*). Nor is it surprising that in two places this papyrus uses the word *agapē* (love) of Isis, the word that is so prominently used in the New Testament of Christian love. In the first instance (line 28) the word is followed by a lacuna of nine letters, so that a longer word from the same root may have been present here in the original text. In lines 109–110 the phrase used is *a[ga]pēn theōn*, "the love of the gods" and it follows the words "in Italy." It is a phrase that agrees well with the main emphasis of the whole text, which is on the loving kindness of Isis, culminating in her saving grace. These qualities are offered, virtually, on behalf of a vast pantheon. In other words, Isis is the goddess who shows to humanity that god is love.[34] It is evident, however, that the idea of *agapē* here includes that of *erōs*, at least the sexual love that is socially acceptable within the divinely ordained context of the family. The Isiac and Christian uses of the term differ, then, in this respect. But why should Isis be *agapē* in Italy especially? This is a difficulty that has played a part in the emendation that some scholars have proposed:[35] in Italy she is *agathēn theon*, "the Good Goddess," that is, the well-known Bona Dea of Italian tradition. Yet this deity, as an independent goddess, was of Greek origin as Agathē. In the Italian and Roman tradition much store was laid by the idea that the *pax deorum*, "the peace of the gods," was attainable, and it is a felicitous extension of this idea to regard the divine, in the person of Isis, as actively loving and benevolent.[36]

In the same papyrus Isis is addressed as "Savior" (*Sōteira*) and a constant claim in relation to her is that she offers "salvation" (Greek *sōtēria*, Latin *salus*). Although the title Savior is used of many deities in the ancient religion of Greece, it is clear that in the Hellenistic age it took on a more urgent and more profound significance, particularly in the mystery religions. Salvation was one of the key concepts of the age for all who were seeking hope and assurance from religion. It is not surprising that an international conference held in Rome in September 1979, taking as its theme the oriental cults in the Roman Empire, was planned to concentrate on the concept of salvation. A bulky volume has resulted, in which many facets of the concept are treated.[37]

A development is discernible in the doctrine relating to Isis. In its ultimate form it became a doctrine of the double deliverance—from sin and from death. The early emphasis, however, is on the saving power of the goddess here and now. Men and women who are threatened by present dangers and the ravages of disease are said to be saved by the goddess. This idea is particularly evident in the "Praises," and a good example is seen in the text from Maroneia, from the first century B.C. It begins with a very personal expression of gratitude:

> With these eyes I have seen the sun, and I see the world which is thine.
> (*Aretalogy of Maroneia* 9)

The writer is thanking Isis for restoring his eyesight, and he then proceeds to praise her in more general terms.[38] In the same way, the Hymns of Isidorus praise Isis for saving human beings in their present troubles, although the hymns may also allude to her saving power in the after-world.[39] The salvation received by the Apuleian Lucius gives prominence to the latter thought, even if his immediate restoration to human form is the first saving act in his exalted experience. A cynical observer might be tempted to aver that he is being offered too much of a good thing—an extended span of life in this world and a blissful eternity in the next. If we examine the religious basis of the double deliverance offered by this religion, we find that an anomaly arises through the varying positions of Isis and Osiris. In the Hellenistic and Roman phases it is Isis who is mostly honored as the savior. Yet the pattern of belief throws the limelight unmistakably on Osiris. He is the prototype both of victory in the tribunal that awaits the souls after death and of triumph over death itself. In the fourth century of the Christian era Firmicus Maternus, who was a convert to Christianity, related to the initiates of a mystery religion the following oft-quoted lines:

> Be of good heart, initiates, because the god has been saved,
> For we shall have salvation from our troubles.
> (*De errore profanarum religionum* 22.1.)

The god referred to may be Attis, but is more probably Osiris.[40] His death and survival constitute the paradigm that is the basis of hope. Yet Isis in the myth is the divine agent who secures this, and to the initiate she is the unfailing helper who guides him to the "First and the Lord";[41] and a graffito of the second century A.D. from an Isiac sanctuary in Rome is a touching expression of this faith:

> Thou, Isis, thou art salvation to thy followers.
> (*Te Isis, te salus ad tuos.*)[42]

4. Isis Suckling Horus. Egyptian. 8th–6th century B.C.

The Initiand's Progress:
Confession, Judgment, Baptism, Forgiveness

For the emotional and psychological experience of full induction into the religion of Isis we have to rely very much on the account presented by Apuleius. It is one of the most impressive narratives of religious experiences that have come from the ancient world, and A. D. Nock justly hailed it as "the high-water mark of the piety which grew out of the mystery religions," remarking also that it contained "more than a touch of autobiography."[43] Whereas a few scholars have recently contested this view of the autobiographical element, it remains the accepted opinion.[44] In most of the first ten books of his long novel, Apuleius is following and adapting a Greek original. There is every reason to believe that the eleventh book, which differs so markedly from the burlesque conclusion of the Greek story, is an original work based on an authentic personal experience. This does not mean that the work is straight autobiography. Several of the details apply to Lucius as a native of Corinth or its environs, although Apuleius himself was a native of Madauros in North Africa. Punic was his first language, but he was a superb literary artist in Latin, and it may be argued, as indeed Fredouille has done, that the very perfection of the literary form displayed in the prayers and hymns to Isis prevents our regarding them as the expression of genuine conviction.[45] The relation between style and sincerity is, however, a difficult question. The Gospel of Mark is much less attractive as a Greek composition than is the Gospel of Luke, but it would be hazardous to infer, on stylistic grounds, that either shows greater sincerity of conviction than the other. Fredouille is prepared to concede that Apuleius was probably an accredited member, at least for a time, of the Isis cult.[46] If this is so, it follows that his account of the various phases of the initiations is likely to correspond, in outline, to the actual ritual sequence. Yet what is much more impressive is the authentic stamp of the inner experience. It has been rightly said that "his capacity of preserving the spirit of religious events is in any case quite extraordinary."[47]

It seems likely that in the prelude to initiation the candidate was expected to make an act of confession to the priest who was in charge of his personal induction. The priest's statement to Lucius in chap. 15 of *Metamorphoses* includes a sympathetic, albeit stern, analysis of his previous experiences, and it is natural to infer that the statement follows an intimate account by Lucius of the events that led to his sad asinine state, now terminated by the kindly intervention of the goddess. Apuleius himself does not refer to a confession. He states rather (in chap. 14) that "the priest had by divine communication, as ever, become acquainted with all my misfortunes from the start." Yet we are told in chap. 19 that Lucius tells the whole story to his relatives and former domestic servants, and the remarks made by the priest make it clear that he is concerned with much more than a mere narrative of the external events that have disturbed Lucius. He probes searchingly into questions of conduct, motivation, and responsibility. In effect, his analysis is the result of a spiritual examination that implies a long session of confessional responses to pointed inquiries. There is evidence elsewhere, too, for the role of confession in the Isis cult as well as in some of the other mystery religions.[48] Small crypt-like buildings which occur as adjuncts to the temples of Isis, as with the so-called megaron at Pompeii, would have been suitable for the converse of priest and novitiate, but their likely purpose has been variously interpreted.[49]

Doctrinally the priest's judgment in chap. 15 of *Metamorphoses* is the most important statement in the whole work, and it also has the function of binding its disparate parts together into a meaningful unity. Several of the apparently digressive tales have some relevance to the central motifs, as James Tatum has ably shown.[50] It is on a note of felicitation that the priest begins his comments.[51] Now that Lucius has experienced the transformation wrought by the goddess, he has at last reached after many troubles and storms, "the haven of Rest and the altar of Mercy." The cause of his misfortunes is then revealed in unflinchingly moral terms:

> Your high birth was of no avail to you nor even your position in society, nor yet the learning in which you are so rich, but on the slippery path of your hot-headed youth you fell into low pleasures and you have gained a grim reward for your ill-starred curiosity. (*Isis-Book* 15)[52]

The basic sins, then, for which Lucius is condemned are lust and curiosity, and both are clearly portrayed in earlier phases of the novel. When Lucius arrives in Thessaly on business, he stays with Pamphile, a woman skilled in magic, and becomes infatuated with her slave girl, Photis. Their erotic adventures formed part of the Greek original which Apuleius was here following, but Apuleius describes the episode with considerable relish and elaboration. Sexual immorality is also a conspicuous theme in the sequel, both in the main story of Lucius as an ass and in the subsidiary stories brought into the narrative. As for curiosity, the causal import of this interest is evident from the start. It was curiosity that made Lucius pry into the magical arts practiced by Pamphile, and when he wanted a temporary change into a bird, Photis gave him the wrong ointment and produced an all-but-permanent change into a donkey. Curiosity is also a basic motif in the story of Cupid and Psyche, a brilliantly told narrative introduced by

Apuleius. There it is Psyche who suffers through yielding to the impelling force of curiosity.

In at least three respects the priestly condemnation pierces through the mask of Lucius to the reality of the life of Apuleius. He was born of wealthy parents and gained renown as a philosopher and rhetorician of the "Second Sophistic." He certainly preened himself on his learning, including his mastery of both Greek and Latin, and he definitely showed much curiosity about magic, having been even accused of winning the love of a rich widow, Pudentilla, through the exercise of magic arts.[53] The religious significance, nonetheless, transcends considerations of autobiography, and we are fortunate in having the fine study by A.-J. Festugière as well as, more recently, the perceptive analysis by Friedrich Solmsen.[54] Not that these two scholars are always in agreement. Festugière points out that the charge of practicing magic which Apuleius faced was a very serious one—a matter of life and death—and that the memory of it may well have weighed heavily on him in later years when he wrote his novel. "He has there traced for us," Festugière suggests, "the story of a soul which fell, which suffered by reason of that fall, and which the merciful hand of Isis raised up and saved."[55] To this dictum Solmsen objects that "'the soul which fell and was rescued' introduces a Christian note into a story which includes no reference to 'soul' and where 'sin', as far as present, is not understood in Christian terms."[56] In fact, before this Festugière puts the matter of sin rather differently. He says that "the blunders of Lucius are presented as imprudent rather than sinful"[57]—a statement that belies the searing rebukes of the priest, especially "you fell into low pleasures" and "you have gained a grim reward," where the mere absence of words for "sin" and "soul" mean nothing and where a doctrine of retribution is clear. Downfall and degradation are certainly implied.[58]

The unhappy Photis unites the allurements of sensuality and of magic,[59] and in a way she is a counterfigure to Isis, the object of sublimated *erōs* and the vehicle of the highest wisdom. Yet Isis is traditionally also the mistress of magic, and the problem about curiosity as a sin is thus made more difficult. To the modern mind curiosity in the intellectual sense is the enlightened driving force behind much scientific endeavor. Two kinds were apparent to the ancients: the legitimate, truth-seeking, healthy kind, and the kind that is prying, illicit, and sinister. Apuleius uses the word *curiositas* only of the second kind. In his personal address to Lucius, the priest explains that the result of his moral failures has been his helpless exposure to the tortures inflicted by Fortune. This was an oppressive belief of the age, especially when Fortune or Fate or Destiny (*Fortuna, Tychē, Heimarmene*) was linked to the determinism of astrology. The priest assures

Lucius, at the same time, that Fortune is blind and has unwittingly led Lucius to his state of religious happiness in which Isis gives him victory over Fortune since she is herself a "Fortune that sees" (*Fortuna videns*)—an allusion to the worship of Isis Tychē. The priest concludes with a call to commitment, and here he uses a touch of paradox: accepting "the yoke of service" will give a sense of freedom. He also uses a metaphor which has parallels in Mithraism and Christianity: "enrol your name in this holy military service."

After this the confessional account is interrupted to describe the festive rites of the ship of Isis. Then, in chap. 19, Lucius is said to take a lodging within the temple area. He joins in the worship of the goddess and she visits him in nightly visions, telling him that he has been predestined for initiation and that the time has come. But now we are told of an unexpected episode. Lucius says that in spite of his ardent devotion he "was restrained by religious fear." He pondered on what would be demanded of him—"how arduous was the service of the faith, how extremely hard were the rules of chastity and abstinence"; and so he "kept delaying the matter." Here the psychology of hesitation and uncertainty has analogies in the cult of the god Asclepius as portrayed by Aelius Aristides, another writer of the second century A.D.[60]

When the hesitation is overcome, the desire for initiation burns the more ardently and urgently, and Lucius begs the high priest for admission into "the secret rites of the holy night." The priest administers suitable warnings, stressing that "the gates of hell and the guarantee of life were alike in the power of the goddess, and the very rite of dedication itself was performed in the manner of a voluntary death and of a life obtained by grace" (chap. 21). By this he means that the old life will end and that a new life will begin, for the goddess by her providence caused the initiate "in some way to be born again." He is not speaking here of Lucius but of Isiac initiates in general, so that the meaning cannot here refer to the physical transformation of the Ass-Man. Lucius receives further details from Isis herself. She specifies the expense of the preparations (a quite surprising detail) and names the priest who is to be in charge: it is the same high priest, called Mithras, that Lucius has previously encountered. He has been described as "a severe character and celebrated also for his strict interpretation of the faith."

The initial rites are of a preliminary nature. A "customary" ablution is followed by a baptism in which the priest "prayed for the forgiveness of the gods." There has been a hint of this before in the reference to "the altar of Mercy" (chap. 15). Since baptism is inherently a rite of purification, the idea of connecting it with the forgiveness of sins is not strange. In fact, that is precisely how the rite conducted by John the Baptist is explained by Mark: "he proclaimed a baptism in token of repentance, for the forgiveness of sins" (1:4). Long before that, in the Eleusinian Mysteries, ritual purity was an essential prerequisite.[61]

If we consider the possible Egyptian background of the sequence of confession, judgment, and forgiveness, we find that it is prominent in the concept of judgment after death, where the "Proclamations of Innocence" (in the Book of the Dead, 125) and the weighing of the heart suggest a similar process. A complete change of perspective, however, emerges in the later initiation rites. Here it is a process of spiritual regeneration that begins *in this life*. I have used the term "anticipated eschatology"[62] of this changed perspective, with a few allusions, at the same time, to signs of the change within Egypt itself, as attested, for example, by the Ptolemaic temple at Deir el-Medina, where a judgment scene apparently relates to the living.[63]

Encounter with the Divine, Apotheosis, Joyful Adoration

The rite of baptism is followed by an injunction that Lucius must spend ten days of strict regimen, "abstaining from all animal flesh and from wine." These rules he observes "with reverent restraint." Then comes the holy night when he is dressed in a new linen garment and led to the innermost part of the temple. The experience that is the heart of the initiation ceremony is related in deliberately brief and general terms:

> I approached the boundary of death and treading on Proserpine's threshold, I was carried through all the elements, after which I returned. At dead of night I saw the sun flashing with bright effulgence. I approached close to the gods above and the gods below and worshipped them face to face. (Apuleius *Isis-Book* 23)[64]

Although conventional classical terminology is used, this encounter with the divine has clearly to do with the nocturnal visit of the sun-god Rê to the Osirian realm of the dead. It is the central theme of the Book of Amduat, and it signifies triumph over death. The phrase referring to "the gods above and the gods below" is an apt allusion to the solar and Osirian deities, and the interpretation is confirmed by the divine garments assigned to Lucius, for they denote a solarized Osiris.[65]

The end of the initiation rites finds Lucius presented with twelve sacred robes. He is revealed to a crowd of admirers with "a crown of gleaming palm" on his head and with the leaves standing out like rays. He is described as being "adorned like the sun and set up in the manner of a divine statue"

5. Stela of Ofenmut: "Ofenmut Offering before Horus."
Egyptian. XXII Dynasty (?).

(chap. 24). The crown is that of triumphant justification while its form suggests the sun-god. An amalgamation of Rê and Osiris is a well-known development. What we see here, however, is the identification of the believer with his god, and Osiris is primarily meant. In a funerary context this identification is constantly present in Egypt, and it is accepted even more fervently in the Hellenistic and Roman eras.[66]

The phase of apotheosis has parallels, again, in other mystery religions where the savior-god is the pattern of salvation. In the case of Egypt, as we have already noted, there is a duality in the tradition in the sense that whereas Osiris is the god who died and lived again, yet Isis is the vehicle of saving power both for Osiris himself and for the believer. Here, then, is a phase of divine transfiguration, implying justification and immortality on the model of Osiris. Lucius expresses great pleasure, but it cannot be said that his response is exactly soulful. There follow "merry banquets" and a "sacred meal" which is regarded as consummating the initiation. But it is the goddess who still attracts the believer's devotion. Before returning to his Corinthian home, Lucius tells us that he "enjoyed the ineffable pleasure of the image of the goddess." He prostrates himself before her, wiping her feet with his tearful face, and then greets her with the exquisite prayer of chap. 25—too exquisite, as Festugière remarks, to be possible in such an emotional state.[67] It is rather an offering to Isis in which the rhetorical stylist presents his finest skills. After this Lucius says that he "embraced Mithras the priest, who was now as my father" (end of chap. 25). The priest has indeed acted as his spiritual father and confessor, and his name has some significance. If Isis seems at times to be making an exclusive claim, here is a reminder that the attitude to other religions was actively sympathetic.

Lucius eventually goes to Rome to undertake, in obedience to divine counsel, his Second and Third Initiations. These are concerned principally with Osiris, the supreme deity of the cult, although stress is laid on his close association with the faith of Isis. Lucius is favored with a vision of Osiris himself and is finally admitted to the Roman college of Osirian *pastophori*, a lower grade of priesthood. He faces his new tasks joyfully and in the meantime has become a successful barrister in Rome, having in the process mastered the Latin language. This success, he points out (chap. 30), has been made possible "by the generous providence of the gods." On both sides, indeed, the circumstances of the Second and Third Initiations are colored by rather mercenary considerations, since Lucius tends to resent the pressure of the priests in insisting on the additional rites and the further expenses involved.

Without question it is the dedication to Isis in the First Initiation that has produced the finest fruits of the spirit. This dedication is throughout infused, apart from the episode of hesitation and the bitterness of the priestly judgment, with a sense of radiant happiness. Joy (*gaudium*) is one of the key words. It stems initially from gratitude for the act of grace by which the goddess brings about his transformation, and it is a change that is both physical and spiritual. The grant of forgiveness is an experience that contributes much to this happiness as well as the knowledge, eventually, that Isis herself has called the new believer to the blessedness of initiation into her service. The sense of vocation is renewed and strengthened, while three times in the early narrative occur the words "sudden joy," a phrase that to a modern reader may recall Wordsworth's "surprised by joy," used afterward by C. S. Lewis to epitomize his own experience of conversion. Whether the term "conversion" can properly be applied to the experience portrayed by Apuleius is a moot point. It certainly includes spiritual regeneration, for the initiate is in some way born again. Isis, too, makes a special claim on the commitment of Lucius, but he is not asked to abandon all other religions.[68] Indeed the high priest who guides him is called Mithras, and the name, as we have noted, must have a deliberately syncretistic significance. Yet the quality of the adoration of Isis that Apuleius describes is rare in the annals of paganism.[69] It is a contemplative adoration that is absolutely disinterested, a devotion that seeks no recompense or return. It is a consciousness of divine love and protection, for in Isis is seen "the peculiar combination of majesty and love."[70] Doctrinally a rich and satisfying creed finds expression, particularly in the prayer of chap. 25, where Isis is at once the sovereign ruler of the cosmos and "the holy and eternal savior of the human race," one "who brings the sweet love of a mother to the trials of the unfortunate." She also provides the answer to the current fatalistic belief in the sway of Fortune over human affairs. At the same time the adoration offered by Lucius is intensely personal. Her "radiant commands in the dark night" (chap. 22) come through his dream-visions, and the "ineffable pleasure" of her image is much dwelt on, an emphasis that can only be appreciated when we recall the ancient belief that the deity was present in her statue. There is a strong sensuous element in such descriptions, and Henry Ebel expresses it well when he says that "Apuleius envisions a spirituality suffused with the tangibility of *Voluptas*."[71] Although Lucius is identified with the solar Osiris at the end of the First Initiation, his experience is basically one of mystic union with Isis. The sublimation of *erōs* is, of course, in the Platonic tradition, and it persists to some degree in the thought of Plotinus.[72]

Notes

1. For the Greeks in Egypt, see Alan B. Lloyd, *Commentary on Herodotus Book II*, 1:1–60.

2. P. M. Fraser, *Ptolemaic Alexandria,*1:189–301 ("Religious Life"). See also H. Idris Bell, *Cults and Creeds*, 3, 5.

3. Fraser, *Ptolemaic Alexandria*, 1:192.

4. *Papyrus Salt* 825.7.7 (ed. P. Derchain; Brussels: Palais des Academies, 1965); see his note on p. 168. This is a text of perhaps the Thirtieth Dynasty. Compare the similar interdiction in the temple of Esna: see Serge Sauneron, *Les Fêtes religieuses d'Esna* (Cairo: Publications de l'Institute français d'archeologie orientale, 1962) 345 with note on pp. 347–48.

5. See chap. 3 of S. Morenz, *Egyptian Religion*, trans. A. E. Keep (London: Methuen, 1973) 42–56. On the Horian focus of Egyptian statehood see Griffiths, *The Conflict of Horus and Seth* (Liverpool Monographs in Archaeology and Oriental Studies; Liverpool: Liverpool University Press, 1960) 22–27, 68, 147–48. The ideological function of Mâat in relation to the Egyptian state is ably presented by Jan Bergman in *The Myth of the State*, ed. Haralds Biezais (Stockholm: Alqvist & Wiksell, 1972) 80–102.

6. See John W. B. Barns, *Egyptians and Greeks*, 5–6.

7. Ibid., 8.

8. Fraser, *Ptolemaic Alexandria*, 1:250–52.

9. Ibid., 1:252. On p. 246 Fraser misleads when he says that "Isis, and with her Harpocrates (Horus) and Anubis are Egyptian deities of respectable, though not of great, antiquity...." In fact all three are as old as the Pyramid Texts of the third millennium.

10. Fraser, "Two Studies on the Cult of Sarapis in the Hellenistic World," *Opuscula Atheniensia* 3 (1960) 9, 19.

11. J. Gwyn Griffiths, "Egyptian Nationalism in the Edfu Temple Texts," in *Glimpses of Ancient Egypt*, ed. J. Ruffle et al. (Festschrift H. W. Fairman; Warminster: Aris & Phillips, 1979) 174–79.

12. Fraser, "Two Studies," 17.

13. T. A. Brady, *The Reception of the Egyptian Cults*, 7. Several previous writers took a similar view.

14. Fraser, "Two Studies," 49. Rhodes and Delos are noted as probable centers of diffusion.

15. See Vassos Karageorghis, *Cyprus from the Stone Age to the Romans* (London: Thames and Hudson, 1982) 173.

16. Ino Michaelidou-Nicolaou, "The Cult of Oriental Divinities in Cyprus," in *Hommages Vermaseren* (Leiden: Brill, 1978) 2:791–800, esp. 793; see the evidence for Sarapis in the third century B.C. at Salamis and Soli on p. 798.

17. Alfred Westholm, *The Temple of Soli* (Stockholm: The Swedish Cyprus Expedition, 1936) 200–201, 212, 215 with the relevant plates.

18. Ramsay MacMullen, *Paganism in the Roman Empire*, xi. Largely confining himself to the evidence of inscriptions, MacMullen scarcely succeeds in pointing himself to these spiritual resources.

19. W. A. Laidlaw, *A History of Delos* (Oxford: B. Blackwell, 1933) 94–168 ("Free Delos," 314–166 B.C.). The Egyptian cults there are presented in Pierre Roussel, *Les cultes égyptiens à Delos* (Paris: Nancy, Berger-Levrault, 1915–1916).

20. F. W. Walbank, *The Hellenistic World*, 92.

21. Bell, *Cults and Creeds*, 2.

22. Ibid.

23. W. S. Ferguson, *Hellenistic Athens*, 220.

24. Griffiths, *Apuleius: The Isis-Book*, 318–19; see also A. F. Shore in *British Museum Quarterly* 36 (1971) 16–19; on the abundant evidence outside Egypt see my remarks in *Journal of Egyptian Archaeology* 59 (1973) 233–36.

25. See Maria Munster, *Untersuchungen zur Göttin Isis* (Berlin: B. Hessling, 1968) 120, 191–92, 205; see also Griffiths, *The Origins of Osiris and his Cult* (Studies in the History of Religions, Supplements to *Numen* 40; Leiden: Brill, 1980), 50.

26. Griffiths, *Osiris*, 101–3.

27. The inscription is from the first or second century A.D.; see Malaise, *Inventaire*, 249, Capua, No. 1=Vidman, *SIRIS*, 502. Reitzenstein cites a similar attitude to Hermes Trismegistus (*Mysterienrel.*, 27–28). The antithesis between "The One" and "The many" (or "All") is deeply embedded in Egyptian ideology; see Horning, *Conceptions of God*, 184–85 and passim.

28. *SVF* 1:121, No. 537. Grant, *Hellenistic Religions*, 152 (tr.).

29. Pohlenz, *Die Stoa* (Göttingen: Vandenhoeck & Ruprecht, 1948), 1:108. One might add *Anankē* (Necessity), distinguished by Chrysippus from *Heimarmenē* (Fate) as an internal, as opposed to an external, factor; see A. A. Long in *Problems in Stoicism*, ed. A. A. Long (London: Athlone, 1971) 195 n. 15.

30. London: Methuen, 1909; 10th ed., 1923.

31. See D. A. Russell, *Plutarch* (New York: Scribner, 1973) 83. Philosophically Plutarch was not an eclectic. His dualistic approach shows the influence of Iranian thought, and he applied it to the opposition between Isis and Typhon. See John Dillon, *The Middle Platonists* (London: Duckworth, 1977) 202–6.

32. See Griffiths, *Apuleius: The Isis-Book*, 3–4, and p. 282 on a Roman who had received initiation into the Eleusinian, Dionysiac, and Mithraic mysteries.

33. See F. C. Grant, *Hellenistic Religions*, 128–30.

34. See my analysis in "Isis and 'The Love of the Gods.'"

35. G. Manteuffel, Erik Peterson, and Stephanie West; see the remarks by West in *Journal of Theological Studies* 18 (1967) 142–43, 20 (1969) 228–30.

36. See my discussion in "Isis"; see also R. E. Witt in *Journal of Theological Studies* 19 (1968) 209–11. Oda Wischmeyer writes on Agapē in extra-Christian antiquity and points out (p. 220 n. 41) that a corruption of *agathēn* into *agapēn* would be very unlikely (*Zeitschrift für die Neutestamentliche Wissenschaft* 69 [1978] 212–38).

37. See *Soteriologia*, ed. Bianchi. Much information on Roman Mithraism is given in a previous volume, *Mysteria Mithrae*, ed. Bianchi.

38. Yves Grandjean, *Une nouvelle Arétalogie d'Isis à Maronée* (Leiden: E. J. Brill, 1975) 17, with comments on pp. 24–29 concerning Isis as healer. He notes that she is sometimes believed to inflict blindness as a punishment. See also Witt, Reginald Eldred, *Isis in the Graeco-Roman World* (Ithaca, NY: Cornell University Press, 1971) 185–97.

39. V. F. Vanderlip, *The Four Greek Hymns of Isidorus*, 1:29–34; see also my remarks in *Journal of Egyptian Archaeology* 60 (1974) 284.

40. See A. J. Wedderburn in *New Testament Studies* 29 (1983) 345, but with a misleading reference to Cybele and Isis. See also Agostino Pastorino, *De errore profanorum religionum* (Florence: La Nuova Italia, 1956) ad loc. (p. 225) and M. J. Vermaseren, *Cybele and Attis* (London: Thames and Hudson, 1977) 116.

41. Plutarch *On Isis and Osiris* 2.352A. See C. J. Bleeker, "Isis as Saviour Goddess," 1–16. In the Roman era Osiris came into greater prominence. See Vilmos Wessetsky, *Ausgewählte Schriften* (Studia Aegyptiaca 6; Budapest: ELTE, 1981) 175–80; see also Robert A. Wild, *Water in the Cultic Worship*, 3 and chap. 3, esp. 101–2.

42. See Rita Volpe in *Soteriologia*, ed. Bianchi, 148.

43. Nock, *Conversion*, 138.

44. See Jean-Claude Fredouille, *Apulei Metamorphoseon*, 13–20, and my remarks in "The Concept of Divine Judgement in the Mystery Religions," 192–93.

45. Fredouille, *Apulei Metamorphoseon*, 14.

46. Ibid., 20.

47. Friedrich Solmsen, *Isis among the Greeks and Romans*, 149. He also thinks it "highly probable" that Apuleius was an initiate of the Mysteries of Isis.

48. See my *Apuleius: The Isis-Book*, 271; see also Nock, *Essays*, 119.

49. V. Tran tam Tinh, *Le Culte d'Isis à Pompéi* (Paris: E. de Broccard, 1964) 34–35 with pl. I, 4.

50. In *Transactions of the American Philological Association* 100 (1969) 487–527.

51. For the following remarks see my paper "The Concept of Divine Judgement in the Mystery Religions," esp. 192–205.

52. My version, p. 87.

53. In modern times a charge brought against the novelist Hermann Hesse is in some ways comparable. Both were acquitted.

54. Festugière, "Lucius and Isis," chap. 5 in *Personal Religion among the Greeks*, 68–84; Solmsen, *Isis among the Greeks and Romans* (1979).

55. Festugière, *Personal Religion*, 77.

56. Solmsen, *Isis among the Greeks and Romans*, 101.

57. Festugière, *Personal Religion*, 76.

58. Ibid., 75.

59. See the contributions by G. N. Sandy and C. C. Schlam to *Aspects of Apuleius' Golden Ass*, ed. B. L. Hijmans, Jr., and R. T. Van der Paardt (Groningen: Bouma's Boekhuis, 1978).

60. See Festugière, *Personal Religion*, 79–80.

61. A sacrificial pig was washed in the sea. See B. C. Dietrich, in *Soteriologia*, ed. Bianchi, 448. For the use of Nile water in the Isiac rite, see R. A. Wild, *Water in the Cultic Worship*, 2–5 and chap. 6.

62. "The Concept of Divine Judgement," 201–5, with a discussion then of its relevance to the other mystery religions.

63. The person facing the tribunal is not named, and L. Kákosy believes that the form figured in relief represents the deified Imhotep; see "Temples and Funerary Beliefs in the Graeco-Roman Epoch" in *L'Égyptologie en 1979* (Paris: Editions du Centre national de la recherche, 1982) 125–27.

64. My translation, p. 99.

65. For the view that the experience derives from the Greek tradition, see Solmsen in *Gnomon* 5 (1979) 555. The promise of new life in the Book of Amduat is well explained by Hornung (*Conceptions of God*, 155–56).

66. See L. Kákosy, *Selected Papers*, 227–37; see also my study in *Journal of Egyptian Archaeology* 68 (1982) 228–52, on paintings of the Roman era with judgment scenes.

67. Festugière, *Personal Religion*, 81.

68. Marcel Simon argues that in the pagan cults there was no conversion from one religion to another. "Conversion in our sense does not have a place in ancient paganism" (in *Mysteria Mithrae*, ed. Bianchi, 412).

69. See Festugière, *Personal Religion*, 80–84.

70. Solmsen, *Isis among the Greeks and Romans*, 112.

71. H. Ebel, *Arethusa* 3 (1970) 172.

72. A. H. Armstrong, "Plotinus," in *The Cambridge History of Later Greek and Early Medieval Philosophy* (also edited by him), 261–62.

Bibliography

Editions

Apuleius, *Metamorphoses*, XI.
Fredouille, Jean-Claude. *Apulei Metamorphoseon Liber XI.* Coll. Érasme. With Introduction and Commentary. Paris: Presses universitaires de France, 1975.
Griffiths, J. Gwyn. *Apuleius of Madauros: The Isis Book.* Edited with Introduction, Translation and Commentary. EPRO 39. Leiden: Brill, 1975.
Helm, Rudolph. *Metamorphoseon Libri XI.* Leipzig: Teubner, 1907, 1913, 1931. Reprint, 1955.
Robertson, D. S., with Paul Vallette. *Apulée, Les Métamorphoses.* Soll. Budé. Paris: Les Belles Lettres, 1956.

Plutarch, *De Iside et Osiride*.
Babbit, Frank Cole. *Plutarch, Moralia,* vol. 5. Edited with Translation and Notes. Loeb Classical Library. Cambridge, MA: Harvard University Press, 1936. Reprint, 1957.
Griffiths, J. Gwyn. *Plutarch's De Iside et Osiride.* Edited with Introduction, Translation, and Commentary. Cardiff: University of Wales, 1970.
Preisendanz, Karl. *Papyri Graecae magicae.* 2 vols. Leipzig: Teubner, 1928, 1931.
Vanderlip, Vera Frederika. *The Four Greek Hymns of Isidorus and the Cult of Isis.* American Studies in Papyrology 12. Toronto: Hakkert, 1972.
Vidman, Ladislaus. *Sylloge inscriptionum religionis Isiacae et Sarapiacae.* RVV 28. Berlin: de Gruyter, 1969.

Various Texts
Hopfner, Theodor. *Fontes Historiae Religionis Aegyptiacae.* Bonn: Mark & Weber, 1922–1925.
Malaise, Michel. *Inventaire préliminaire des documents égyptiens découverts en Italie.* EPRO 21. Leiden: Brill, 1972.
Nock, Arthur Darby. *Corpus hermeticum.* With French translation by A.-J. Festugière. Paris: Les Belles Lettres, 1945.
Peek, Werner. *Der Isishymnus von Andros und verwandte Texte.* Berlin: Weidmann, 1930.

Translations

Apuleius
Adlington, W. Revised by S. Gaselee. Loeb Classical Library. London and Cambridge, MA. Harvard University Press, 1915. Reprint, 1965.
Graves, Robert. Harmondsworth: Penguin Books, 1950. Reprint, 1976.
Griffiths, J. Gwyn. See under *Editions.*
Lindsay, Jack. Bloomington: Indiana University Press, 1932. Reprint, 1962.
Grant, Frederick C. *Hellenistic Religions: The Age of Syncretism.* With translations of various sources. The Library of Liberal Arts. Indianapolis: Bobbs-Merrill, 1953.

Plutarch
Babbit, Frank Cole. See under *Editions.*
Griffiths, J. Gwyn. See under *Editions.*

Modern Works

Armstrong, A. H., ed. *The Cambridge History of Later Greek and Early Medieval Philosophy.* Cambridge: Cambridge University Press, 1967.

Barns, John W. B. *Egyptians and Greeks.* Inaugural Lecture, 1966. Oxford: Privately published, 1973.

Bell, H. Idris. *Cults and Creeds in Graeco-Roman Egypt.* The Forwood Lectures, 1952. 2nd ed. Liverpool: Liverpool University Press, 1954.

Bergman, Jan. *Ich bin Isis.* Acta Univ. Upsal., Historia Religionum 3. Uppsala: Universitet, 1968.

Bianchi, Ugo. "Iside dea misterica. Quando." In *Perennitas: Studies for A. Brelich.* Edited by Giulia Piccaluga. Rome: Edizioni dell'Ateneo, 1981.

———, ed. *Mysteria Mithrae.* EPRO 80. Leiden: Brill, 1979.

———, ed., with Maarten J. Vermaseren. *La Soteriologia dei culti orientali nell' Impero Romano.* EPRO 92. Leiden: Brill, 1982.

Bleeker, C. J. "Isis as Saviour Goddess." In *The Saviour God: Studies for E. O. James,* 1–16. Edited by S. G. F. Brandon. Manchester: University Press, 1963.

Brady, T. A. *The Reception of the Egyptian Cults by the Greeks (330–30 B.C.).* University of Missouri Studies 10. Columbia, MO: University of Missouri Press, 1935.

Dunand, Françoise. *Le Culte d'Isis dans le bassin oriental de la Méditerranée.* Vol. 1, *Le Culte d'Isis et les Ptolémées.* Vol. 2, *Le Culte d'Isis en Grèce.* Vol. 3, *Le Culte d'Isis en Asie Mineure: Clergé et rituel des sanctuaries isiaques.* EPRO 26. Leiden: Brill, 1973.

Ferguson, W. S. *Hellenistic Athens.* London: MacMillan, 1911.

Festugière, André-Jean. *Personal Religion among the Greeks.* Sather Classical Lectures 26. Berkeley and Los Angeles: University of California Press, 1954. Reprint, 1960. [Esp. chap. 5, "Popular Piety: Lucius and Isis."]

Fraser, P. M. *Ptolemaic Alexandria.* 3 vols. Oxford: University Press, 1972.

———. "Two Studies on the Cult of Sarapis in the Hellenistic World," *Opuscula Atheniensia* 3 (1960) 1–54.

Grant, R. M. *Hellenistic Religions.* New York: Liberal Arts Press, 1953.

Griffiths, J. Gwyn. Commentaries on Apuleius and Plutarch. See under *Editions.*

———. "The Concept of Divine Judgement in the Mystery Religions." In *Soteriologia,* 192–222. Edited by U. Bianchi.

———. "Isis and 'The Love of the Gods.'" *Journal of Theological Studies* 29 (1978) 147–51.

———. "Isis in the Metamorphoses of Apuleius." In *Aspects of Apuleius' Golden Ass,* 141–66. Edited by B. L. Hijmans, Jr., and R. T. Van der Paardt. Groningen: Bouma's Boekhuis, 1978.

Hani, Jean. *La Religion égyptienne dan la pensée de Plutarque.* Paris: Les Belles Lettres, 1976.

Hornung, Erik. *Conceptions of God in Ancient Egypt.* Translated by John Baines. London: Routledge & Kegan Paul, 1983.

Kákosy, László. *Selected Papers.* Studia Aegyptiaca 7. Budapest: ELTE, 1981.

Leclant, Jean, with Gisèle Clerc. *Inventaire Bibliographique des Isiaca.* Leiden: Brill, 1972, 1974.

Lloyd, Alan B. *Herodotus Book II.* 2 vols. (continuing). EPRO 43. Leiden: Brill, 1975, 1976.

MacMullen, Ramsay. *Paganism in the Roman Empire.* New Haven, CT: Yale University Press, 1981.

Malaise, Michel. *Les Conditions de pénétration et de diffusion des cultes égyptiens en Italie.* EPRO 22. Leiden: Brill, 1972.

Muller, Dieter. *Ägypten und die griechischen Isis-Aretakigien*. Abh. Leipzig 53. Berlin: Academie-Verlag, 1961.

Nock, Arthur Darby. *Conversion*. Oxford: University Press, 1933.

———. *Essays on Religion in the Ancient World*. Edited by Zeph Stewart. 2 vols. Oxford: University Press, 1972.

Reitzenstein, R. *Die hellenistischen Mysterienreligionen*. 3rd ed. Leipzig: Teubner, 1927.

Solmsen, Friedrich. *Isis among the Greeks and Romans*. Martin Classical Lectures 25. Cambridge, MA: Harvard University Press, 1979.

Walbank, F. W. *The Hellenistic World*. Fontana History of the Ancient World. Glasgow: Collins, 1981.

Wild, Robert A. *Water in the Cultic Worship of Isis and Sarapis*. EPRO 87. Leiden: Brill, 1981.

3

The Ancient and Continuing Pieties of the Greek World

A. H. ARMSTRONG

A S A KIND OF BACKGROUND to the other studies in the volume, this article will deal with the thoughts and feelings about the powers of the divine world, the kind of piety or spirituality which we find established among the Greeks when we first begin to see them with any degree of clearness and which persisted as the spiritual environment of accepted practice and thought and feeling for all particular, more developed, and sophisticated pieties to the end of antiquity and even, in changed outward forms, beyond. The attempt will be only partly successful for many reasons: the fact that our evidence, though better than in many comparable areas, is not and could never be completely adequate; the extreme difficulty of entering into a spirituality that is so deeply different from and so strangely related to our own; and a reason that needs to be continually borne in mind when considering all ancient (and perhaps not only ancient) spiritualities but is not always as clearly stated and carefully remembered as it should be—that all pieties of the older kind, which are bound up with and live in worships and rituals, are intensely concrete, particular, and indefinitely various; but we have to speak of them, especially in a summary introduction like this, to a great extent in abstract generalizations. The point being made here has been excellently expressed by Günther Zuntz. Speaking of some of the very earliest religious images known to us, those at Catal Hüyük in Turkey, he states:

> Our interpretation cannot entirely divest itself of terms more or less abstract: in fact, though, the very power of these representations bespeaks the concreteness of this ancient experience. There is not really any thought of *vis vitalis*, but breasts and beak: no "concept of fertility" but the act and fact of birth; no "symbol of death" but horrid vultures feeding on bodies.[1]

In spite of the fact that it was the Greeks who inaugurated the habit of abstract generalization, the application of which to prehistoric religion Zuntz is deploring, his caution here is applicable to much in the far later ancient pieties of Greece. Zuntz speaks of the pernicious effects of a great book on ancient religion, A. Dieterich's *Mütter Erde*,

> . . . whose [Dieterich's] teachings have been generalized by a host of successors far beyond the intention of its author. The effect has been a dogmatism which frequently tends by a hackneyed symbolism ("fertility cult") to obscure the live variety and specific inspiration of the documents of ancient religion.[2]

This is a passage that all who write about ancient religion largely on the basis of other people's books about ancient religion need to bear continually in mind.

The Influence of Externals on Piety

The ancient and continuing piety or spirituality of the Greeks, within which grew those particular forms of spirituality which so deeply affected the whole hellenized Mediterranean world and gave it such spiritual unity as it had, not only was originally but continued to be a piety in essentials very like that of the neighbors of the Greeks, an archaic piety of rural communities that had been settled in their ways of thought and feeling long before the Greeks became clearly visible to us. It was a piety of the villages, which passed naturally to and continued in the cities as the cities developed. It was a spirituality that was carried and contained by the traditional rites of household and village and city. This was what gave it the strength and continuity that enabled it to last down to the end of the classical Mediterranean world. The rites of worship were not deliberately designed to express doctrines or even mythic imaginations. They were there, and the most varied ways of feeling, imagining, and thinking about the beings to whom they were directed grew out of them and were compatible with them. And they were there all the time for everybody. No religious reformer ever seriously attempted to embody a new way of thinking or feeling about the gods in an intrinsically different kind of ritual. This article is, in a sense, about the religion of the "ordinary person." But the term must not be understood in a pejorative sense. It is rather intended to indicate that all of us human beings, whether philosophers, saints, or emperors, are ordinary people most of the time and presumably need an ordinary spirituality when we are; and the ordinary spirituality of the ancient Greeks was that which went with and grew out of the rites.

If this is so, then it is clear that we should know something about the rites in order to understand the spirituality. It is certainly true that the more we know about them, in all their bewildering variety and at times extreme oddity, the better we shall understand the spirituality. But this is not a history of Greek religion, and there is no space for description of even a few rituals with sufficient detail and vividness to give any real feeling of what they were like. Generalizations in this field tend to be dull and unhelpful. All that will be attempted here is to say a few things about the rites which may help us to understand the spirituality. The first point that needs to be stressed is the pervasiveness of ancient shrines and ceremonies. There was a distinction between sacred and profane in the Greek world in the sense that there were places and times that were especially sacred and set apart exclusively for sacred uses, but there were no great secular spaces from which thought of the gods was excluded as inappropriate. The presence of the gods was everywhere and at all times evoked by shrines and rituals—in the home, on the farm, at the graves, and most impressively in the great sacred places and on the frequent religious occasions of the city. Most of the finest public buildings were temples, and all civic festivals were religious festivals, in which all the celebrations, including the great choral dances and dramatic performances—and a good deal of the eating and drinking—were part of the ritual. But it was probably the innumerable small shrines and rituals of house and farm and family life that made this ordinary spirituality so pervasive. Modern philosophers transported to Socrates' front door in ancient Athens would be confronted with what they might call two horrid little fetishes, an unshaped stone called Apollo of the Ways and another stone called a Herm with a head at the top and a phallus halfway down, which Socrates would tend at the proper times like every other Athenian householder. We do not need to find some shoddily "mystical" interpretation of his famous last words "Crito, we owe a cock to Aesculapius" (Plato *Phaedo* 118A.7–8) to see in them a moving religious significance. Socrates had vowed a customary offering to the god of healing in thanksgiving or prayer for the recovery of a friend, perhaps for Plato, who, in one of his very few mentions of himself in the dialogues, makes the narrator of the *Phaedo* say "Plato, I think, was sick" (*Phaedo* 59B.10). This was an obligation of ordinary piety that any good man, philosopher or not, would remember on his deathbed. Perhaps one of the most pleasantly vivid evidences of the way in which this common piety penetrated daily life is the poem that Xenophanes, the earliest and one of the severest critics of the poets' stories about the gods, wrote for (or about) a drinking party some years before or after 500 B.C.

Now the floor is clean, and the cups, and the hands of all, and someone puts wreaths woven of flowers on our heads, and another offers fragrant perfume in a flask, and the mixing-bowl stands there full of delight: and there is another wine ready in the jars, sweet and smelling of flowers, which says it will never betray us. In the midst incense sends up its holy scent, and there is water, cold and sweet and clear. Golden-brown leaves are ready, and a noble table loaded with cheese and sweet honey. There is an altar in the middle of the room, all decked with flowers, and there is singing and joy all around the house. Men of sense ought first to sing the gods' praises, with reverent stories and pure speech. When we have poured libations and prayed that we may be able to do right, for this is much the most suitable for us, there is no harm in drinking as much as one can get home with without a guide, if one isn't extremely old. (Fr. 1, Diels-Kranz 1:126–27; trans. A. H. Armstrong)

Holy Places and Temples

There were holy places, where the gods were thought of specially and tended, in every house, street, and farm; and the family graves were holy places where the cult of the ancestors continued from generation to generation. The sense of divine presence was universally diffused, as my introduction already indicated, in the ancient Mediterranean world (as it still is, under changed forms, in the modern, where anything of older tradition persists). But there were everywhere places that were particularly holy, where the gods were believed to be in some way specially present, and it was in these that the public worship of the communities, large and small, was centered. It is important for a proper understanding of this ancient spirituality that it was first and foremost the place, the sacred precinct, the area enclosed and set apart, that was sacred. One did not, as a general rule, make a place holy by putting up a temple, altar, or image there. One built a temple because the place was felt to be holy. The reasons for this sense of sacredness varied. Precincts in or near the central gathering ground of the people, the *agora,* were there because the gods, the most important members of the community, were felt to be there where the community met. The great sacred precincts of the citadels, the "high towns" or *acropoleis,* were sometimes, perhaps, there because the cult in them continued that celebrated by the ancient kings at the house shrines in their royal residences. But very often the reason may have been something about the place itself, a numinous beauty obscurely sensed though not fussed about with a self-conscious aestheticism. This seems to be particularly true of the little country places of worship and the great Pan-Hellenic shrines, where all Greeks would gather for the festivals of their gods. One is certainly vividly conscious of the powerful beauty of the place at the precinct of Apollo at

Delphi. Perhaps the best and strongest expression of this feeling for the sacred beauty of a place in all Greek literature is the last work of one of the three great Athenian tragedians of the fifth century B.C., Sophocles of Colonus. His *Oedipus at Colonus* is, among other things, a celebration of the local sanctities of his native village, culminating in the great central chorus. The tone is set from the beginning, when Antigone leads her old blind father to the shrine at Colonus where he is to meet his destined end and become himself one of the holy powers of the place. She tells Oedipus:

> This place is clearly holy, with its strong growth of laurel, olive and vine, and a crowd of nightingales fly and sing beautifully within it

And later in the first scene a local inhabitant tells him:

> All this place is holy: Poseidon's majesty possesses it, and in it is the fire-bearing god, the Titan Prometheus: the place where you stand is called the brazen threshold of this land, the bulwark of Athens: and the near-by glades boast the horseman Colonus as their lord, and bear his name, all together called after him: this is what the place is like, stranger, not honored in story, but more by living with it. (lines 16–18, 54–63; trans. A. H. Armstrong)

(More than six centuries later, the great Neoplatonist Plotinus applied this quotation to the whole material universe in his treatise *On Matter and Evil:* "All the place is holy," and there is nothing which is without a share of soul" [*Ennead* I 8 [51], 14, 37; trans. A. H. Armstrong].)

This sense of the sacredness of the place itself was expressed in and maintained by the fact that nearly all public worship took place in the open air. A Greek or Roman temple was not a house of assembly for the worshipers. It was the house of the god, who was represented in it by the image. The central sacrificial rites took place under the sky, at the great altar outside the main door of the temple, which was opened for the ceremony so that the god could take part symbolically. Peripheral rites might spread over a wide area and involve more than one shrine or sacred precinct. The poetic and athletic contests that were an important part of the greater festivals took place in open-air theaters and stadia in or near the precinct, and the great processions moved through the whole city or countryside. This open-air character of all sacred proceedings probably had an influence on spirituality. When the perceived environment of worship was the whole town or the whole countryside, it was hardly possible for the worshipers to feel that they were a special flock, a people set apart, separate from the whole world of nature and the common society of humanity. The difference of function between temple and church may have meant that the change from one to the other had a considerable influence on spirituality. Other features of ancient piety that worked against any sense of spiritual separation from the common natural world will be considered later, and the one very small authentically Hellenic group who did consider themselves a peculiar people set apart from common people, the Orphics, wil be described separately.

The Mysteries

There was one group of cults in which the worshipers did assemble inside buildings the functions of which were somewhat analogous to churches. These were the mystery cults. They need to be considered separately because they have sometimes been surrounded with a good deal of mystification. In less informed writing on ancient spirituality, mystery, mysticism, and mystification have tended to get mixed up, with unfortunate results. A mystery in the ancient world was simply a cult celebrated in strict privacy, admission to which was by initiation and from which noninitiates were rigorously excluded. This was why the rituals had to be performed in enclosed and private spaces and in church or chapel-like buildings, of which the best known is the Telesterion, the Hall of the Mysteries at Eleusis. But in other ways the mysteries conformed entirely to the pattern of the ancient spirituality of worship that we are describing. This is natural, because the gods of the mysteries were not different from the gods of public worship. Nearly all the divinities who had mysteries also had public cults, and the great festivals, which included initiation into and celebration of mysteries, often had impressive public celebrations. Our knowledge of the feelings that these divinities aroused in their worshipers comes mainly from accounts of these public celebrations. This is as true of the later mystery cults that entered the Hellenized Mediterranean world from Asia Minor, Syria, and Egypt as of the earlier Hellenic mysteries. Mithras is the only mystery god who did not also have a public cult, and he was generally identified in late antiquity with the Sun, who was often identified with Apollo.[3] This agreement with the general pattern of the piety of their world meant that no religious or spiritual teaching was given in the mysteries any more than in the public cults. Initiates did not learn secret creeds or esoteric wisdoms or spiritual techniques. Aristotle expressed this very well when he said that those being initiated into the mysteries did not have to learn (*mathein*) but to experience (*pathein*) and be changed by the experience (*On Philosophy* fr. 15, Ross 84).[4] They were changed by the deepening of their piety and the sense of have entered into a special relationship with the divinities to whom they were initiated, but their piety was not of a different kind and they did not acquire any new way of thinking about the gods. Any ideas that the initiates in later times had in their heads, any theological interpretation of their experience, for the most part derived from the only source of religious and spiritual teaching in the ancient world, philosophy. (More will be said about the undoctrinal character of ancient piety in the next section.)

The central figures in most mystery cults of any spiritual importance are female divinities who can be grouped under the general title of Goddess or Mother. The exceptions are Mithraic mysteries, which belong to a different spiritual world (see n. 3), and the Dionysiac mysteries; these, which were prominent only in Hellenistic and Roman times and were not of very great spiritual importance will be considered later in the context of other cults of Dionysus. What do we mean when we speak of the "Goddess"? It is, of course, a modern generalization covering a great multiplicity of cults and stories in the Mediterranean area. But they all have something in common that is very difficult to apprehend and perhaps impossible ever to understand fully: the feminine aspect of divinity in the world can mean so many things. The nearest approach to a successful statement of what it may be is perhaps what Zuntz says when speaking of an early form of the cult of the mother, that of the great Neolithic temples of Malta: "These men of an age from which not one word reaches us perceived and worshipped in their goddess the wonder of life unending, embracing death as a stage and step to its eternity."[5]

What is suggested here can still be felt in the mystery goddesses of greatest spiritual power in the Hellenic and hellenized Mediterranean world, the Egyptian Isis and the Two Goddesses of the greatest of all mysteries at Eleusis, Demeter and Persephone.[6] We know almost nothing and can safely conjecture very little about what went on in the mystery sanctuary at Eleusis.[7] But from what we know of the public cult and from the art and poetry it inspired, we can form some idea of how their worshipers thought and felt about these widely worshiped and deeply loved goddesses. Demeter, the mother, is the most loved, the kindliest, the closest to humanity of all forms of Mother Earth. She gives corn, the very stuff of ordered human life, symbol and reality of ordered fertility, and in giving it gives a life of order and concord attuned to the rhythms of its growth and harvesting. Her sorrow at the loss of her daughter brings barrenness and death to earth and humanity. With her joy at her recovery comes renewal of life. Persephone, the daughter, is at Eleusis the Korē, the Corn-Girl, who goes down every year into the darkness (she does not die; she is an immortal Greek goddess, not a mortal Near Eastern god) and comes back again bringing new life. But she is also Despoina, the mistress, the Queen of the Dead, always ready to receive her initiates in the underworld. In the western Greek lands, her own domain of Sicily, and the Greek settlements of southern Italy, she is a very great goddess indeed, reigning over lands and cities also here in the upper world. It is above all in the western Greek understanding of Persephone that we can see how in the goddess light and dark, death and life, are united—and so death, without being done away with or denied, is overcome.

The Spirituality of the Ancient Worships

We shall now try to understand something of what those who worshiped the gods in these ancient ways thought and felt about the gods, to get as near as we can to the ancient experience of divinity. This is not altogether easy. As has already been said, the gods and the cults and the experiences of divinity bound up with them were indefinitely many and various, and our evidence permits us to know about only a small part of them. Further, as has already been indicated in the Introduction to this volume (pp. xiii–xix) the development of the ancient pieties on this multifarious basis was free and informal. In the ancient world we are not dealing with a "religion" in any sense in which we normally understand the term nowadays. There is no scripture, no church, no body of authoritative interpreters of the tradition. The stories that the poets told about the gods and the way in which they expressed the common pieties certainly deeply colored people's imaginations and influenced their feelings about the gods. But they were not in any way authoritative. Poets could and frequently did disagree with each other about the gods, and anyone was free to disagree with the poets. The cults were the foundation of all piety, but there was much in them that never got into the poetry. The old-fashioned way of speaking of Homer as "the Bible of the Greeks" was decidedly misleading. And if there was no Bible, there was no church either. There was no organized religious community distinct from the general communities of families, villages, cities, and peoples and no clergy with the special function of safeguarding and interpreting a tradition arising from a scripture. Priests were representatives of families or officers of state whose business was to perform certain ritual functions, not to teach or to guide the development of spirituality. (Of course even in religious communities with a strong creedal and doctrinal base, there is often a good deal in the piety and spirituality of the members that does not fit in with and cannot be adequately explained by the creed and doctrine.) So ancient spirituality is bewilderingly free and various. Nonetheless, there are some general statements that can be made, tentatively and subject to correction and exceptions, about how the ancients thought and felt about the gods whom they worshiped and whose divinity they experienced in worship and prayer and the changes and chances of life.

What the Ancient Gods Meant to Their Worshipers

Perhaps the best starting point for understanding this ancient experience of divinity is power. The gods were apprehended and worshiped as far more powerful than human beings. They were not omnipotent and they did not stand free from the universe and act upon it from outside. They were powers in the world and were limited by the powers of other gods and the law of the whole. (Even when some spiritual leaders became aware that the divine far transcended the cosmos of our experience, a unity between the transcendent and the cosmos was preserved and the transcendence was apprehended as also deepest immanence.) A great god was a great force in the nature of things, powerful to help or harm. When the difference between gods and human beings is thought of as a difference in powers within the whole, it becomes easier to see how humans could sometimes come to be worshiped as gods. The gulf between gods and humans, the sense of distance and difference of the divine, is often very strongly stressed, especially in the early poetry, and we shall soon see that it was more than just a difference of power. But the gulf was never so great that the two species could not interbreed. The main themes of the ancient poetry were the doings and sufferings of heroic persons descended on one side from gods, and these "heroes" were worshiped all over Greece with rites that were not always easy to distinguish from those offered to gods. Two of them, Heracles and the god of healing Asclepius, were held to have passed beyond humanity altogether after their deaths and to have become gods without qualification; they were very much worshiped and loved. Even human beings of wholly human parentage could come to be worshiped with these heroic, divine, or semidivine honors after their death, as Brasidas, the Spartan general, was at Amphipolis, the city he had delivered from the Athenians (Thucydides 5.11). This was the Hellenic background of the worship of Hellenistic kings and Roman emperors in the hellenized Mediterranean world. It was often a thoroughly cynical and unspiritual business. It was not a blasphemous identification of the ruler with any First Cause or Creator, but simply a recognition of him as a great power in the world in his place and time. The point is well brought out in one of its earliest and most cynical expressions, the hymn that the Athenians sang to Demetrius I of Macedon near the end of the fourth century B.C.

> The other gods are far away, or have no ears, or do not exist, or do not pay the slightest attention to us, but we see you here present, not a god of wood or stone, but a true one.[8]

This great power of the gods in the nature of things was an everlasting power. They were immortal. This is one of the strongest and clearest differences between gods and human beings, which has a very important place in the ancient piety. They were not without beginning. All gods were born, and their birth stories were impressive and at times strange. The whole dynasty of gods now reigning, Zeus and his family, had been preceded by earlier generations. Everything in the most ancient divine universe had a beginning in some sort of natural generation. The ideas of the everlasting, without beginning as without end, and of the eternal which comprehends and transcends the whole of time are products of later philosophical reflection. But once the gods had been born they lived for ever. The Greeks were familiar with Near Eastern vegetation spirits like Adonis and Attis, who died and were reborn annually, and they were prepared to worship them in the appropriate ways when and where it seemed desirable, as they were always prepared to worship other people's gods. But there seemed to them something odd, exotic, un-Hellenic about dying gods. Their own gods lived forever, and it was from this early belief in divine immortality that the immensely powerful and enduring vision of divine eternity developed. Divine immortality is not merely everlasting life but life in perpetual youth, beauty, and strength. The Greeks were as vividly conscious as Jonathan Swift or Aldous Huxley of the horror of mere immortality. They expressed it in the story of Tithonus, the human lover of the dawn-goddess, Eös. She obtained the gift of immortality for him from Zeus, but unfortunately forgot to ask for perpetual youth. So, when old age came upon him, he gradually shrank into a little shriveled, paralyzed creature with a chirping voice going on and on forever, who had to be put away in an inner room behind locked doors (in a later version he turned into a cicada) (*Hymn to Aphrodite* [*Homeric Hymn* 5] 218–40).

The gods, then, lived forever in perpetual youth and beauty, exempt from old age and sickness, though not from occasional pain and grief. They could be physically hurt by humans in a fight and could feel deep grief for the death of mortals they loved. But hurt and grief soon passed away from them, and they returned untroubled to their life of joy and peace. It is in their apprehension of this that the old poets express most vividly their sense of the distance and difference of gods from human beings. The ancient imagination had two vivid and simple ways of showing this. One was to say that the gods had a different fluid in their veins from humans, *ichor*, not ordinary blood, and that this difference was maintained by their special food and drink, the food and drink of immortality, ambrosia and nectar. The other is in the description of their special home, where they spend their time when they are not visiting their shrines and festivals or intervening in human affairs. (It was philosophical reflection that showed the divine as omnipresent and omniscient: the gods of the old stories are neither, though they can perceive at great distances and move very fast.) This home is on Mount Olympus or in the sky, above the clouds and storms, in the light and peace of an everlasting spring day. The contrast between this happy life of the gods and the life of mortals is vividly and rather disconcertingly presented in the Homeric *Hymn to Apollo*. When Apollo arrives on Olympus the gods turn to singing and dancing, and to celebrate the joyful occasion the Muses sing beautifully:

> The immortal gifts of the gods and the miseries of men, how under the immortal gods they live witless and helpless and can find no cure for death and defense against old age. (*Hymn to Apollo* [*Homeric Hymn* 3] 189–93; trans. A. H. Armstrong)

It is important for a proper understanding of ancient spirituality to see that neither here nor elsewhere in the earliest poetry is there any sense of human jealousy or resentment of this rather unfeeling happiness of the gods. Their everlasting beauty and joy was something to delight in. Later on, as reflection on the old traditions continued, there was a good deal of questioning and criticism and an increasing demand for an account of the gods that showed them clearly as morally good and as ruling and caring for the human race and the world with a good moral purpose. More will be said about this in the next section. At this point it must be seen, if we are to enter as fully as we can into the spirit of this ancient piety, that their worshipers contemplated these powerful beings, living in perpetual youth and beauty in their world of light far above human miseries, with pleasure, admiration, and a kind of affection. The gods were from the beginning, long before questions about divine morality and divine care for humanity were raised, apprehended as good. One of the strengths of ancient spirituality is its instinctive recognition that there are other kinds of worshipful excellence in the universe than those that meet our moral concerns or our human self-interest. The old gods have the beauty and goodness of the sun, the sea, the wind, the mountains, great wild animals, splendid, powerful, and dangerous realities that do not come within the sphere of morality and are in no way concerned about the human race.

Gods and Human Beings

It is clear from what has been just said that the gods do not love the human race as such and cannot be relied upon to be kind to individuals. Indeed,

6. Sacred Relief: Mithras Slaying the Bull (Detail of Helios). Roman. 2nd century A.D.

they were often thought to resent any human success beyond the normal, and to bring to disaster any power or prosperity that might raise a person above the human level. As Herodotus makes the wise Solon say to the rich King Croesus: "All the divine is envious and liable to cause trouble" (Herodotus 1.32.1; trans. A. H. Armstrong).[9] The philosophers, from Plato on, were strongly opposed to this idea of divine envy, as quite incompatible with divine goodness as they saw it. But the goodness of the Platonic and Stoic gods was austere. (Aristotelians and Epicureans did not believe in any divine providential care.) It was directed to the whole, to the increase of goodness in the whole, and to the well-being of individuals only insofar as it contributed to the goodness of the whole. Ordinary piety was less rigid here. The gods could not be relied upon to be kind to and to care for individuals and particular communities, nor could they be relied upon not to. Both individual people and whole communities often felt that they had a special relationship with particular gods, with loving care on the divine side and affectionate gratitude on the human. This sense of being looked after, however difficult to justify rationally, seems to be an essential part of any normal human piety. The Athenians certainly felt like this about the great lady of their city, the goddess Athena (as the people of Constantinople later did about the Mother of God). And perhaps there was nothing in the ancient poetry that did more to stimulate this sense of being looked after than the story of the special friendship between Athena and Odysseus which runs all through the *Odyssey*. But a pious man in the old Hellenic world might also feel that he had a claim on a strange god, not one to whom he or his family or his city had a special devotion, on grounds, as we might say, of "common humanity." There is a passage in the *Odyssey* that illustrates this well and also shows the complexity which a person's relationships with the many divine powers might have. Toward the end of book 5 the shipwrecked Odysseus is swimming toward the savage, rock-bound coast of the fairy-tale land of Phaeacia, from which he is destined to get home to Ithaca. The great sea-god Poseidon has been doing his best to drown him. A minor sea-goddess, Leucothea, has been extremely helpful. The invisible presence of Athena is always with him, inspiring and helping. He comes to the mouth of a river, which is the only safe landing place on that coast, and this is how he prays to the river, whom he does not know and has never met before:

> "Hear me, although I do not know your royal name: for in you I find the answer to all the prayers I have made for deliverance from the sea and from Poseidon's malice. Even the immortal gods do not rebuff a poor wanderer who comes to them for help, as I now turn to you after much suffering and seek the sanctuary of your stream. Take pity on me, royal river. I claim a

suppliant's rights." In answer to his prayer the River checked its current, and holding back the waves made smooth the water in the swimmer's path, and so brought him safely to land at its mouth. (*Odyssey* 5.445–54; trans. E. V. Rieu)

This simple sense of experienced divine care and kindness and the affection for the gods that responded to it was an important part of ordinary ancient piety. But there was also, of course, a strong element in it of fear of the gods. As has already been indicated, they were powerful and dangerous and their actions were unpredictable. They might strike suddenly to destroy individuals, families, and cities. Sometimes this was for reasons that could be discerned as having something to do with the maintenance of the moral order of the universe (more will be said about this in the next section). But sometimes no reason at all appeared for divine anger and divine destroying: it was inexplicable, like storm or drought or those sudden deaths of the young which were said to be due to the arrows of Apollo or Artemis. Fear of the gods was always there in ancient piety, but its importance must not be exaggerated or misunderstood. The world of the ancient gods was a hard and dangerous world, apprehended unflinchingly by their worshipers in all its hardness and danger. But it was not an evil world, beset or dominated by powers apprehended as evil. (More will be said about this when we come to consider the piety of the great tragedians of the fifth century B.C.) There is no devil, no force of pure supernatural evil, in normal Hellenic or hellenized piety. The powers of darkness, of night and the underworld, were not evil powers, as we shall see. The fear of the gods was not the servile terror that produces neurotic religious depression. This was something the Greeks resisted when they encountered it in later centuries, strong in their conviction that the gods and the world were somehow good and beautiful.

Piety and Morality

It is a commonplace to remark that the old Hellenic gods were "immoral" or "amoral." This was said first, and very forcibly, by the Greek philosophers who inaugurated the tradition of reflective spirituality, above all by Plato. The first critic of the old stories about the gods was Xenophanes, whom we met earlier at a pious drinking party, and his criticisms of an all-too-human portrayal of the gods set the tone for later reflection:

Homer and Hesiod have attributed to the gods everything that is a shame and reproach among men, stealing and committing adultery and deceiving each other. (Fragment 11, Diels-Kranz; trans. G. S. Kirk)

The early Christians and most people since, till fairly recently, have repeated this kind of criticism, perhaps rather too uncritically. There are many serious questions to be asked about whether a very close association of morality and piety is good for either and in what fruitful or unfruitful ways they can be brought together. But even to raise them would go quite beyond the proper limits of this article or this volume. But what is essential for a proper understanding of this ancient Hellenic spirituality is to try to see why the spiritual leaders who so drastically criticized the morality of the poetic gods continued to observe the traditional cult practices and never attempted to introduce a new, irreproachably ethical divinity and corresponding new ways of worship. (In later times, when a nostalgic devotion to the whole of the great old classical Hellenic culture dominated the minds of educated persons, the war between poets and philosophers ended, and the philosophers turned from the former fierce criticisms of the poetic stories to allegorical interpretation—that all-too-easy way of dealing with embarrassing passages in ancient sacred texts. There is no very good reason to suppose that the ethical superiority claimed for the Judaeo-Christian God had very much to do with the triumph of Christianity.)

There may be more than one reason why the old worships and the piety that centered in them survived so easily the criticisms of the old poetic stories about the gods. The first is simple. Poetry, as has already been observed, was not scripture. If one did not approve of the old stories about the gods one did not have to believe them, and one's disbelief did not prevent one from taking part perfectly sincerely in the cults of one's family, village, or city—with which the best known and most scandalous poetic stories about the gods worshiped in them often had very little to do. But there may be reasons that go deeper. The gods in the stories were certainly no more morally respectable in their behavior than the human kings and nobles in whose image the poets imagined them. But they were always thought to be concerned with maintaining the world order, which was by no means altogether indifferent to morality, and with punishing human offenses that were thought to be major breaches of that order. Such offenses were treacheries involving the breaking of solemn oaths (of course a direct insult to the gods) and grave offenses against the family or against strangers and suppliants. The kind of consideration that Odysseus demands as wanderer and suppliant in his prayer to the river, quoted above, is stressed again and again in the old poetry as something morally essential and of great concern to the gods. This kind of moral concern, though restricted, could easily be deepened and broadened and was already sometimes being deepened and broadened by the old poets. Further, the strong Greek conviction that the gods were good in whatever sense of "good" seemed to them important at any time needs to be remembered here. It meant that, as soon as moral goodness came to be regarded as an essential part of human excellence, virtue and a concern for virtue would naturally and inevitably be attributed to the gods. This could be done without any serious difficulties except those arising from experience of the ways of the divine universe in which the gods were the ruling (though not omnipotent) powers. As has already been said, when the old stories conflicted with the new demand for divine moral goodness, they could easily be rejected or allegorically explained away without diminishing the piety of the old worships. There remained, of course, as we shall see when we come to consider Aphrodite and Dionysus, some forms of human behavior which the older piety could regard quite unselfconsciously as being divinely approved or inspired but which a thoroughly ethical religion simply had to exclude. At this point it is important to remember that the philosophical champions of a fully moralized spirituality never had more than the authority of philosophers, and their ethical piety never took over completely. The old cults went on and the old poetry was read, and this meant that the possibility of very strange forms of behavior being divinely countenanced could never be completely excluded or allegorized away.

Piety and Some Individual Gods

It will be helpful to our understanding of Hellenic and hellenized spirituality to give a few illustrations of how the worshipers thought and felt about a few individual gods. For reasons of space the number of these illustrations will have to be severly limited, and what is said about the thoughts and feelings of diverse men and women in very diverse communities through so many centuries may be in overgeneral terms or may be overinfluenced by particular examples. The gods chosen are, with one exception, gods who were worshiped all over the Hellenic and hellenized world from the beginning to the end of antiquity. The exception is the sun-god, Helios or Sol, who was only centrally important in the last century or so before the Roman Empire became officially Christian, but was so important then that he must be included.

Zeus

The great sky- and weather-god who was king of gods and humans was generally felt to be too high and mighty and too universal in his rule to be much concerned with individuals or particular communities, and he did not arouse much personal devotion. In the oldest poetry he is sometimes shown as being friends with and caring for individuals. The great Cretan king and lawgiver Minos is said in the *Odyssey* to have been the "familiar friend (*oaristēs*) of great Zeus" (19.178–79). When we come shortly to consider the relation of the will of Zeus to universal law, we shall see him deeply moved by the inevitable death of an individual hero. On the whole, however, ordinary people and even ordinary kings and emperors did not feel that Zeus was personally concerned about them and, as a rule, preferred more accessible gods as their divine patrons and companions. Nonetheless, Zeus cannot be left out of any account of ancient spirituality because it is in him that the sense of the divine unity and order of the whole cosmos finds its expression. When the gods are most vividly imagined in human form, as they are in the great epics, as the turbulent princes and nobles of a heroic kingdom, it remains a kingdom, not an anarchy, and it the king who holds it together. From then on it is thought and felt that Zeus is responsible, somehow, for the order and unity of the divine realm, for the fact that the world is a cosmos, not a chaos. There is a kingdom, not an anarchy, but the kingdom is not a despotism. Zeus is not outside the world any more than any of the other gods. The order and unity of the whole are not simply imposed by his will, nor are they exactly an impersonal destiny to which he is subject. Poetic and popular piety was not concerned with working out the relationship between the will of Zeus and universal law too precisely. There is a passage in the *Iliad* that images this undefined and rather mysterious relationship with superb vividness. Hector is in his last fight with Achilles and his destined day of death has come. Zeus, with the other gods, is watching the fight and, as he had done before when the death day came for his son Sarpedon, considers aloud whether he might save Hector, whom he loves, from his appointed death. Athena answers for the other gods, as Hera had done on the earlier occasion, that it would not be impossible for him to do so but that it would be improper and unethical, not the way the king and father of gods and humans should behave. So then:

> When for the fourth time they had come around to the well-springs then the Father balanced his golden scales, and in them he set two fateful portions of death, which lays men prostrate, one for Achilleus and one for Hektor, breaker of horses, and balanced it by the middle; and Hektor's death-day was heavier and dragged downward towards death, and Phoibos Apollo forsook him. (22.208–13, trans. R. Lattimore)[10]

Zeus balances the scales and sets the weights in them. But he does not choose the weights, or make the scales tip.

Athena

We now turn to the two children of Zeus who in general estimation stood closest to him and had most share in his authority. First, his daughter Athena, strangely born from his head. We know a good deal of how people thought and felt about Athena because of her legendary patronage of the very popular hero Odysseus and still more because she was the lady and protector of the great city that bore her name, Athens, about whose religious practice and feelings we know much more than we do about any other Greek city and whose great writers kept the whole Hellenic and hellenized world in mind of her. She must be given prominence in any account of ancient piety because she is the type for us of the city-goddess, whose loving care and defense of her people calls out a corresponding warmth of devotion. People of many cities, small and great, felt the same about the one of the many other gods, famous or obscure, whom they regarded as their special protector. She was not at all a soft or weakly and vaguely benevolent goddess. She was thought of as the calmest, most rational and self-possessed of the goddesses, full of practical wisdom, and patroness of craftsmen as much as of statesmen and leaders. She was not interested in sex and was, as befitted the protectress of her city, a warrior goddess, "champion and leader in war"[11] of her people, as the people of Constantinople later saluted the Mother of God. So she was often represented fully armed for battle. As warrior-goddess she could be really terrifying. Zeus showed her closeness to him by allowing her to use his aegis (*aigis*, goatskin), originally the skin cloak which he wore like his peasant worshipers in the mountains but soon, especially when Athena used it, represented as a shield with the Gorgon's head in the middle. When she raised the shield and shook it, it struck unspeakable terror into the enemy. This is how Pindar describes her birth:

> The great King of the Gods
> Soaked a city in golden snowflakes
> When, by the craft of Hephaestus
> And his bronze-beaten axe, from the top of her Father's head
> Athena jumped out, and cried with a monstrous shout,
> And the sky shuddered at her, and Mother Earth.
> (Olympian 7.34–37; trans. C. M. Bowra)

But powerful—at times austere and at times terrible—as she might be, she was felt to be of all the great divine powers the easiest to make friends with, for individuals as well as communities. And this was felt to the very end of pagan Hellenism. There is no more moving or enlightening story about late antique piety than that told of the great Neoplatonist Proclus. When in the fifth century Athena's great temple at Athens, the Parthenon, was converted to a church of the Mother of God and Athena's statue was turned out, she appeared in a dream to Proclus (who lived near by) and said to him "They have turned me out of my house, so I am coming to live in yours" (Marinus *Life of Proclus*, chap. 30)—a story that could have been told, with slight modification, about some pious Roman Catholic at the time of the destruction of the great shrines of Our Lady in sixteenth-century England.

Apollo

The greatest of the sons of Zeus is more distant, more obviously formidable, less easy to make friends with than the favorite daughter Athena. His beauty is always rather terrible. At the beginning of the great Delian hymn in his honor the poet says

> The gods tremble when he enters the palace of Zeus, and all rise hurriedly from their seats as he comes, when he bends his shining bow. (*Hymn to Apollo* [*Homeric Hymn* 3] 2-4; trans. A. H. Armstrong)

It is only when his mother Leto has disarmed and seated him and when his father Zeus has taken wine with him that the other gods sit down again and go on with the divine feast (at which, we hear later, he is the life and soul of the party) (lines 186–203). His special closeness to his father is not thought of so much in terms of a loving personal relationship as in terms of the fact that he is in a special way the spokesman of Zeus, the god of the great oracles at Delphi, Didyma, and Claros, and many lesser shrines. He is, not exclusively but predominantly, the god who declares the divine order in the world. Here we are close to his central significance in Hellenic and hellenized spirituality. From the beginning to the end of this ancient world he stands in people's aspirations toward and visions of the divine for light, truth, clarity, order, and moderation. He sets things in order (sometimes by very terrible means) and when the order is broken by grave human offenses he purifies human beings, primarily ritually. But ritual purity is not easy to separate sharply from moral purity, and the demand for one can easily pass into the demand for the other. He and his close associates, the Muses, are patrons and inspirers of *mousikē*, a word that in Greek can cover poetry, music (always primarily song in the ancient world), and dance—the whole numbered, rhythmical, and melodic ordering of speech, song, and movement—and can easily be extended in its meaning to cover philosophy and in the end the whole of humane culture. Poets and philosophers could feel themselves near to and inspired by Apollo. It is significant that in legend, and quite probably in historical fact,

Pythagoras was very closely associated with Apollo. He was the first Greek thinker to concentrate his mind on the divine ordered beauty that makes the world a cosmos, to see the essence of things not in the stuff of which they were made but in their mathematical and musical order and structure.

Aphrodite and Erōs

With the great goddess of love and her son in mythology we enter the realm of those powers who were seen as working predominantly within the human personality, and so were powerful, and often terrifying, in a very special way. The love of which the goddess and her son were the powers was the passionate sexual love for which the Greek word is the same as the name of the love-god *erōs*. This was very early felt to be a great universal force. In the earliest attempt that we have to connect up and set in order the stories about the gods, Hesiod's poem on divine origins (*Theogony*) it is said:

> Verily first of all did Chaos come into being, and then broad-bosomed Gaia [earth], a firm seat of all things for ever, and misty Tartaros in a recess of broad-wayed earth, and Erōs, who is fairest among immortal gods, looser of limbs, and subdues in their breasts the mind and thoughtful counsel of all gods and all men. (116–17, 119–22; trans. G. S. Kirk)

The world is born, not made, in ancient religious thought, and most things spring from the coupling of divine powers and sexual generation. This is why Erōs appears so early in the story and is such an important power. He is independent of his mother here, as he sometimes is in cult. In Boeotia, where Hesiod came from, he had a very ancient cult at Thespiae, in which his "image" was an unhewn stone. But in general it is difficult to assign them clearly separated and defined spheres of influence. They are the embodiment of sexual charm, and the excitement, sometimes amounting to madness, that it produces. Their power in animal and human life is universal, including regular mating and married love as well as wilder and more disorderly passions.[12] For a proper understanding of this ancient spirituality we need to see that their divinity was manifested most clearly when their power took its extreme form in a terrifying and destructive madness. What was thought and felt about them (and, as we shall see, Dionysus) shows that in ancient Mediterranean piety the wild as well as the tame, that which breaks all bounds and destroys all order as well as that which maintains order, had its place in the divine nature of things, as it does in the world of ordinary human experience.

Of course, the full power and terror of love-madness, though a splendid subject for poetry, was not often experienced in everyday life. But Aphrodite and Erōs were felt to be present, and at times kindly and helpful, in more ordinary manifestations of sexual passion, regular and irregular, serious and frivolous. The strongest expression of devotion to Aphrodite that we have from the ancient world is the great song in which Sappho of Lesbos calls her patron goddess to help her, yet again, in the latest of her transient lesbian love affairs, laughing at herself a little as she does so, and expecting Aphrodite to laugh at, and with, her:

> Aphrodite, undying in intricate splendour,
> Child of the Father, braider of snares, I beg you
> Do not, Our Lady, with torments and tribulations
> Crush me in spirit,
> But come! Come here, if ever in time beforehand
> Hearing my cries from afar you attended, and leaving
> The golden house of your Father you came to me, yoking
> Birds to your chariot.
> Then the quick beautiful sparrows brought you, circling,
> Wings beating thick and fast, over the dark earth,
> Down from the sky through the bright air, and suddenly
> There they were with me.
> Then did you, laughing with lips immortal,
> Blessed One, ask me what again was my trouble,
> Why I was calling again, and what most I wanted
> In my heart's madness.
> "Who is it this time you want beguiled to your loving?
> Who is mistreating you, Sappho? I tell you truly
> If she runs from you now she will soon run after you.
> If she, unloving,
> Takes no gifts, in unwilling love she will give them."
> Come now as then, and free me from cruel troubles,
> All my desires fulfil, and yourself stand by me
> In this love-battle.[13]

It was worth quoting at length even a clumsy and limping translation of these magnificently musical Sapphic stanzas because they illustrate something difficult but essential to understand about ordinary ancient piety and the spiritual consequences of its continuing survival as the normal background and environment of the mature reflective spiritualities of the philosophers. Philosophical spirituality was, like the great spiritualities that succeeded it in the Mediterranean world, austerely ethical. Plato and his successors gave Aphrodite and especially Erōs a very important place in their spirituality because they saw that the passionate power of sexual love was essentially the same passionate power that drove the philosopher on in spiritual ascent to the Absolute Beauty and to God. But it was only at this highest level that they could be admitted. From the viewpoint of an austerely ethical spirituality, the carnal frivolities of Sappho and her like could only be seen as sins or at best imperfections that had to be fully overcome at the beginning of the spiritual quest. God and the gods could not be held to approve and bless them. They were excluded from the domain of piety and not as in the old unmoralized spirituality included along with other disreputable passions and activities (which of course continue to survive and flourish in all religious cultures, whatever the official view of them, since we humans are the sort of creatures we are). In old Greek piety not only all sorts of sexual love but also thieving and cheating had their divine patron, the god Hermes. The great hymn in his honor tells most entertainingly how on his first day of life he hopped out of his cradle and stole Apollo's cattle. And the *Odyssey* tells us how he gave Odysseus's grandfather Autolycus the gift of surpassing excellence in cheating and thieving as a reward for his piety—a gift that his famous, pious, and god-beloved grandson inherited in full measure (*Hymn to Hermes* [*Homeric Hymn* 4]; *Odyssey* 19.394–98). Hermes, like Aphrodite, as the hymn abundantly shows, was not only (to put it politely) ethically broad-minded but also amused and amusing. His worshipers could not only turn to him with confidence in their shady activities but also laugh with him.

Dionysus

Dionysus was held to be master of the strangest and most terrible of all the wild powers that might work within human beings. But his power extended very widely and had other manifestations beside the Dionysiac madness. General accounts of his place in ancient religious experience have sometimes in the recent past been distortingly rigid and one-sided. In particular, the much-labored contrast between "Dionysiac" and "Apolline" in ancient Greek religion and culture belongs to German speculation rather than the cults and piety of the Hellenic or hellenized world. Apollo and Dionysus were in fact always regarded as in perfect harmony, and there was not felt to be anything incongruous in worshiping both. This was especially true at the great center of Apollo's worship at Delphi, which Dionysus from very early times shared, almost on equal terms: it may well be that the Delphic temple establishment, before recorded history began, had played an important part in domesticating the cult of Dionysus and bringing it to the important place it held in ordinary Greek piety.

The most common and commonplace aspect of Dionysus—as god of wine—is a good starting point for considering Dionysiac piety in all its forms. Wine is, of course, for the ancient Mediterranean culture and later cultures influenced by it both a central reality of daily life and a spiritual symbol of inexhaustible and varied significance. Dionysus as wine-god was first and foremost in the experience of his ordinary worshipers, the peasant farmers who formed the vast majority of the ancient Mediterranean population, a power in all the abounding vitality of fields and vineyards and the power who especially inspired its celebration in the country festivals, which have always in most cultures been cheerfully drunken affairs. In this aspect of Dionysus the phallus played an important part in his rites. (The male sexual symbol in the ancient Hellenic and hellenized world was sacred, but not exactly revered, except sometimes in later antiquity under Oriental influence. Ceremonies and celebrations in which the phallus was prominent were riotously cheerful occasions with plenty of bawdy humor. There was none of the deep solemnity which surrounds the *linga* of Siva in India, and the female sexual symbol, the *yoni* of India, was not important in Mediterranean piety.) From abounding vitality and its intoxicated celebration it is easy to pass to another aspect of this god: Dionysus was the god of masking and mumming, of illusion and hallucination, and so the god of drama, the patron of the great dramatic festivals at Athens, and in the later Hellenistic and Roman worlds of the traveling companies of professional actors, the "artists of Dionysus." And from intoxication and illusion we can pass to Dionysus as the calm, smiling source and center of a storm of furious life which sweeps out far beyond the bounds of farm and vineyard and village or city festival, beyond all the bounds of settled life and ordered society, to the mountain. The mountains which everywhere in Greece separate the cultivated valleys and plains were for the Greeks something like what the desert was for Syria and Egypt and the forest for India—the wild place, the place of nature untamed by humanity—and it was on the mountain that the spirit of Dionysus was believed to have raged in its fullest and most terrible manifestation.

It is difficult to be sure how much emphasis should be given to the full Dionysiac madness in an account of the spirituality of the Hellenic and hellenized Mediterranean world because the great stories about it are stories of the remote past, about the time long before the beginning of recorded history, when the cult of Dionysus was being introduced into Greece and was encountering opposition from local communities and their rulers. What happened in those remote times was vividly remembered in such sharp detail that much of what is said and pictured in poetry and art about the behavior of those possessed by the god can be recognized by those familiar with other forms of collective madness. In historical times this corporate possession by the god was ritually sought at festivals throughout the Greek world and sometimes, it seems, in some measure attained. The

7. Demeter, Triptolemos and Persephone. Roman copy of votive relief
from Eleusis. Ca. 440 B.C.

stories vary a good deal, but the general outline is something like this. The authorities of the community resist and try to persecute the new cult. The god then possesses the women of the community. They leave their homes and their children, whom they sometimes kill, and go to the mountain. There they run and dance in ecstatic communion with the wild nature of those wild places, with which they are one in the god who is in them and in it. They become the *Maenads*, the "mad ones." The most impressive of the ritual reenactments of this mountain dancing in historic times was at Delphi. Here at the winter solstice every two years bands of women from all over Greece, including Athens, called Thyiades (another word for Maenads) went up dancing to the very top of Parnassus, savage crags above the clouds, from the great precinct of Apollo (which Dionysus was believed to take over from Apollo in the winter). This could hardly have been done at all without some measure of the Dionysiac ecstasy, and there is some slight evidence that the women were in a trance-like state. But there is no clear evidence that the final climax of the Dionysiac mountain madness was ever authentically reproduced in the rites of historical times. This was when the running turned into hunting, when the wild spirit of Dionysus in the Maenads transformed them to beasts of prey and they hunted down and tore and ate the raw flesh of animals, and sometimes men. In the most powerful, beautiful, and disturbing poetic account of the old Dionysiac madness that has come down to us, the *Bacchae* of Euripides, Pentheus, king of Thebes, the god's cousin in mythology, persecutes Dionysus and his followers. But the god befools, bemuses, and hallucinates him and in the end mockingly leads the poor madman, dressed up as a Maenad, out to the mountain to be torn to pieces by his mother and sisters and the women of Thebes who have followed them there. A few lines from the concluding stanza of the entrance chorus may give some idea of how the Dionysiac mountain running was remembered in the fifth century B.C.:

> He is sweet upon the mountains. He drops to the earth
> from the running packs.
> He wears the holy fawn-skin. He hunts the wild goat and
> kills it.
> He delights in the raw flesh.
> He runs to the mountains of Phrygia, to the mountains of
> Lydia he runs.
> He is Bromius who leads us! Evohē!
>
> With milk the earth flows! It flows with wine!
> It runs with the nectar of bees!
>
> Like frankincense in its fragrance
> is the blaze of the torch he bears.

Flames float out from his trailing wand
   as he runs, as he dances,
   kindling the stragglers,
   spurring with cries,
and his long curls stream to the wind!
               (135–50; trans. W. Arrowsmith)[14]

This vivid remembering and continual reenactment of the mountain ecstasy of Dionysus shows most clearly how for the ancients the divine extended to and might be manifested in everything in the world and human experience, the wild nature of the mountain as well as the tamed nature of the lowlands, the horror of madness as well as the comfortable order of sanity. It is not the cult of Apollo alone, or of Dionysus alone, but the fellowship of the two at Delphi that best represents Greek spirituality.

But we should not look for this or anything else of deep spiritual significance in the mysteries of Dionysus which proliferated in Hellenistic and Roman times. The general spiritual atmosphere suggested by their monuments is a rather superficially pious one, that of a religious dining club or a well-to-do ladies' sodality. Martin P. Nilsson sums them up well:

> The mysteries of Dionysus appealed to well-to-do people who loved a pleasant and luxurious life. The banquet of the blessed dead appealed to the taste of a public that was fond of the pleasures of life and did not take religion too seriously. The mysteries of Dionysus appealed to people who from education and conservatism kept to the old culture and religion and yielded less easily to the lure of the more demanding foreign religions, but who still wanted a little thrill of religion as a spice to the daily routine. . . . These people were not in earnest about religion.[15]

The Earth Powers and the Dead

We must now turn to the dark powers of the lower world, the *Chthonioi*, "those of the earth." These were with the fullest right members of the divine society, not powers of evil or enemies of the gods. There are earth-born enemies of the gods in Greek mythology, the giants and monsters of mythical times, but they are not important in ancient spirituality. They were not the earth powers who were worshiped and were continually present to the religious consciousness. Hellenic and fully hellenized spirituality was not devil-ridden. The demon-haunted piety sometimes so apparent in late antiquity comes from other sources. It can cause grave misunderstandings if the line, whether in ritual or in piety, between the powers of the lower and the upper worlds, between Chthonians and Olympians, is drawn too sharply. In particular, it is impossible to see on which side of such a sharp line the Two Goddesses of Eleusis, Demeter and Persephone, are to be placed.

Persephone in particular belongs to and unites both dark and light, lower and upper worlds. The dark powers could certainly be unspeakably terrible. The groups of underworld fertility goddesses worshiped all over the Hellenic world as the *Semnai*, "The Venerable," or the *Eumenides*, "The Kindly Ones," were generally identified with the *Erinyes*, "The Furies," the old women who come up from the underworld and follow the trail of shed blood, especially kindred blood, till they hunt down the killer. But even in their most terrible aspect they remain part of the divine order and play an essential part in the maintenance of that order. They sometimes become in the reflective piety of the poets the embodiment of that divine order in its dark and terrible aspect. In the great conclusion of his three-play telling of the story of Agamemnon and Orestes, the *Oresteia*, Aeschylus at the end of the *Eumenides* shows how the wisdom of Athena reconciles dark and light, law and equity, justice and mercy, and how in that reconciliation lies the only hope for Athens and for humanity. The final procession song in which the Athenians escort the dark goddesses, now at peace with Athena and her city, to their cave-shrine may give an idea of how thoroughly the underworld powers were felt to be part of the divine order:

> Home, home, O high, O aspiring
> Daughters of Night, aged children, in blithe processional.
> Bless them, all here, with silence.
>
> In the primeval dark of earth-hollows
> held in high veneration with rites sacrificial
> Bless them, all people, with silence.
>
> Gracious be, wish what the land wishes,
> follow, grave goddesses, flushed in the flamesprung
> torchlight, gay on your journey.
> Singing all follow our footsteps.
>
> There shall be peace forever between these people
> of Pallas and their guests, Zeus the all-seeing
> met with Destiny to confirm it.
> Singing all follow our footsteps.
> (Aeschylus *Eumenides* 1032–47; trans. R. Lattimore)

In the oldest Hellenic piety the dead are felt to be down there with the underworld gods in the earth of the community of which they are still members, close and powerful to help or harm. The change, well before Greek recorded history began, from inhumation to cremation and burial of ashes does not seem to have affected this feeling. Any formulated ideas that ordinary ancient Greeks had about the state of the dead were probably decidedly confused. The picture in the Homeric poems of them as strengthless, witless, squeaking ghosts in the underground realm of Hades, which everybody knew, did not accord well with the feeling of their powerful presence in or near their graves which was implied in and maintained by the grave cult. And quite early, by the end of the fifth century B.C., more positive and cheerful ideas about life after death, generally somewhere up in the sky, were beginning to get about, as was also a good deal of skepticism about any kind of survival. In late antiquity the more positive ideas, under influences from the East and from popular Platonic philosophy, became very widespread and powerful, as the sepulchral art of the later Roman Empire shows. [16] It is not quite certain how deeply these developments affected the mass of ordinary people (those who have elaborate tombs tend to be fairly well-to-do and more or less educated), and it is unlikely that they altogether superseded the feeling of the presence and power of the dead in their native earth, which was required and evoked by the continuing grave cult. After all, very similar feelings may quite spontaneously and naturally spring up in ourselves at our family graves, even though we are sure that death is the end or hope that our loved ones are in heaven. The immemorial past is nowhere more powerful than in feelings about the dead.

Helios

From the dark of the underworld we return to the brilliantly illuminated pomp and circumstance of the imperial sun cult of late antiquity. Helios, the Sun, had always been regarded as a god in the Greek world. But, outside the great island city-state of Rhodes, of which he was patron and protector, he did not receive much public cult, nor, as far as we know, was there much private devotion to him (though Plato mentions that Socrates, after his twenty-four hours of concentrated thought at Potidaea, prayed to the sun at dawn [Plato *Symposium* 220D.4–5]). He was always thought of as a powerful and universally present god who saw everything that happened on earth and so might be specially called upon to disclose hidden crimes. From this came a persistent connection between the Sun and justice. From the later third century A.D., the Sun came to occupy a much more important place in at least the public religion of the Roman Empire under the influence of the sun cults of the Near East, where sun worship was really important, and of popular Platonic philosophy. The emperor Aurelian in A.D. 274 established at Rome with great splendor the cult of "the Sun, Lord of the Roman Empire." It is difficult to be sure of the extent to which the official cult ever became really popular with ordinary uneducated people, except among those in and from the East who were already devout sun worshipers. But the Sun certainly became for the ruling classes in late antiquity a powerful and enduring spiritual symbol. He was seen as the visible theophany, the manifestation in the material cosmos of the one transcendent God in whom all educated people by this time believed. He represented and effected the unity of the divine order and divine rule in the universe. And, in a world in which absolute monarchy was generally considered to be the best form of government, the analogy and close connection between the Sun ruling in heaven and the emperor ruling on earth was naturally attractive to emperors and those who served them. This whole complex of ideas and piety proved easily transferable to Christ, the "Sun of Righteousness." Devotion to the Sun seems to have been particularly strong in the Flavian house, the family of Constantine the Great (perhaps for reasons connected with their Balkan origin). It may have provided Constantine himself with a bridge to Christianity, and it certainly inspired in his nephew Julian a passionate devotion which gave him spiritual strength for his war against the new religion.

Piety in the Poets

This whole article is permeated with the influence of the poets. Without continual reference to them it would not have been possible to write an account of ordinary (in the sense of not explicitly philosophical) Hellenic and hellenized spirituality that would do justice to its real range and depth and the power in it that made it capable of influencing later European spiritualities. It therefore will be useful to end the article with some remarks on what is to be found of lasting spiritual significance in the writings of at least the two groups of ancient poets who provided the bulk of the Greek poetic classics, which were classics for the hellenized Mediterranean world as well as for Europe later, which were read and studied by all who were in any way educated down to the end of the ancient world, and whose survival or rediscovery has had at times a notable spiritual influence. These groups are the older epic and lyric poets from the eighth to the early fifth century B.C. and the great Athenian tragedians of the fifth century B.C.

Epic and Lyric

The great Homeric epics, the *Iliad* and the *Odyssey,* were composed for a society of warrior princes and nobles who were proud of their ancestry (which they liked their poets to trace back to a god or hero), and the portrayal of the gods in them is fitted to the character of the audience. When they are being considered as evidence for the spirituality of their own times, we should not suppose that what is left out or underemphasized in the poems (notably the piety toward the earth powers) was not important for other sections of their society than the ruling aristocracy. The most powerful continuing influence that they exercised on ancient Mediterranean spirituality was probably due to their uncompromising anthropomorphism. All peoples, including the Jews, have in some way returned God's compliment by remaking him in their own image, but it has seldom been done so straightforwardly, openly, and uninhibitedly as by the great Greek epic poets. Their poems are the most powerful literary expression, and perhaps for later generations to some extent the source, of the strong Hellenic conviction that the only proper way to represent divine beings was as glorified and idealized men and women. They were so represented not only in literature but in the cult images that stood in almost every temple (in a few of the oldest the symbol of the god's presence was aniconic). In spite of the artistic beauty of the best of them and the power of the literary descriptions that went with them, it does not seem that the images were of central importance in the Hellenic spiritual tradition. There were, of course, images that were supposed to work wonders and that inspired special devotion. But the Hellenic images never seem to have had the same degree of spiritual importance as the icons in later Christian tradition. They were, however, always there and no one ever thought seriously of abolishing them. It is likely that they have exercised a strong and long-continuing influence not only on Hellenic but also on later European feelings and thoughts about the divine. This poetic and artistic anthropomorphism may also have had an important negative effect on Greek reflective spirituality. The philosophers, from Xenophanes onward, were naturally hostile to the simple and unqualified anthropomorphism of the poets, and this led in the most powerful traditions of reflective spirituality to a frequent preference for impersonal ways of thinking and speaking about the divine, and finally in the late Platonism of Plotinus and his successors, to a subtle and continuingly valuable interplay of personal and impersonal ways of thinking and speaking about God.

The group of poems by or attributed to Hesiod, of which the most important for our purposes is the *Theogony,* seems to have been composed for an audience of peasant farmers rather than noblemen and are consequently rather different in tone and temper from the Homeric epics. But the account that they give of the gods is not in any essential way different from that in the epics. The *Theogony,* or account of the origin of the gods, was the first (or at any rate the first of which we know anything) attempt to bring the old stories together and order them systematically in the form of a history of the divine family traced back to its first ancestor Chaos (perhaps originally the "gape" or "gap" which appeared when the sky-god was lifted up off the earth-mother at the beginning of things). As such it provided a particularly convenient focus for the later critical reflections of the philosophers.

The earlier poems in the collection of hymns to be recited in honor of particular gods that is called the *Homeric Hymns*, do not depart in any essential way from the epic way of thinking and feeling about the gods. But because each is concerned with a particular god, they often provide valuable clues to the way in which worshipers thought and felt about that god (they must have been acceptable to large enough audiences at the festivals at which they were recited). This is particularly true of hymn 2, *To Demeter*, which seems to come from Eleusis, and the Delian hymn that forms the first part of hymn 3, *To Apollo*. Hymn 4, *To Hermes* (see p. 87), is excellent evidence for the humorous, unrespectable side of the older Greek piety.

We have only miserable remnants of the great mass of works of the lyric poets from the seventh to the fifth century B.C., some of whom the ancients reckoned among their greatest poets. We do have a considerable collection of complete choral songs by one who was considered among the very greatest, Pindar. But it represents only one of the many genres in which he worked, the songs in honor of victors in the sporting contests at the great Pan-Hellenic festivals. From what we have, and especially from the victory odes of Pindar, we can form some idea of the imaginative splendor with which the old gods were presented to their worshipers in the choral dances that were a most important part of the proceedings at all public festivals, though we must remember always as we read them that we have only the words of a sung and danced celebration in which music and movement contributed most powerfully to the general effect.

Athenian Tragedy

In the great serious plays produced at the Theater of Dionysus in Athens, which were called *tragōidiai*, the reflective spirituality of the poets appears at its deepest. One of the best ways of understanding what it felt like to be human in the old divine world and under the power of the old gods is to study the all-too-few plays that have come down to us from the three great Athenian tragedians, Aeschylus, Sophocles, and Euripides. The spirituality of the tragedians is not discontinuous with the spirituality of the epic. Aeschylus's account of the authority and the justice of Zeus, and so of the divine order in the world, does not differ in any essential way from that of Homer and Hesiod, as some interpreters have thought that it did.[17] (If the study of Greek tragedy is one of the best ways of understanding the old

Hellenic spirituality, the study of modern interpretations of Greek tragedy is one of the best ways of misunderstanding it.) In tragedy parts of ancient piety that are in the background in ancient epic are sometimes brought forward, notably the piety toward the earth powers and the great dead (one of the best helps in understanding this is the last play of Sophocles, *Oedipus at Colonus*). A new depth and a new intensity emerge in the presentation of the old spirituality, which enables us to see more clearly both its power and the difficulties it raises in its old, unsoftened, unmoralized form. The power is most apparent in the older two dramatists, Aeschylus and Sophocles, and the difficulties are seen in Euripides, who, though by no means an irreligious or antireligious rationalist, is sometimes uneasy and unhappy with the gods as portrayed in the old stories. This perhaps is why he can portray with such power the wildest and most terrifyingly incomprehensible operations of the divine, of Aphrodite in the *Hippolytus* and of Dionysus in the *Bacchae*. One of the reasons for the power of the tragic presentation is that these great serious plays are not about ordinary people (who, the ancient thought, were suitable subjects for comedy, not for tragedy), though they appealed strongly to ordinary people. They were about the kings and queens and princesses and heroes of legend, whose exalted position brought them perilously close to the gods and exposed them to the terrible interplay of the world-ruling powers. The ancients thought that power was always very dangerous for human beings. In history and daily life as well as in legend, it was in the powerful that human weakness and folly and the dark incomprehensibility of some of the gods' dealings with humans were most clearly manifested. It is as true of the tragedians as of ancient Greeks in general that the world is not experienced as a bad world and the gods are not felt to be powers of evil. But the dark side of the world experienced by all of us is prominent, though not exclusively predominant in tragedy. The heroic nobility of its characters is shown in their taking the terrible chances of their exalted position with courage and dignity, though not without lamentation, resentment, and at times open criticism of the gods. The tragedians, unlike the later Stoic spirituality, do not expect their heroes to be inhumanly impassive, and, unlike later religious traditions, they allow one to criticize the divine. They are not concerned with justifying the ways of the gods to humans. There is room for guilt, fear, grief, joy, and hope within limits in the tragic world but not for absolute hope—or absolute despair. Many of these great serious plays end sadly, but many also end happily, or more than happily. The *Oresteia* of Aeschylus ends in a blaze of glory with the liberation of Orestes and Athena's reconciliation of the powers of light and dark for the good of her city. Though one cannot insult the splendor of the mysterious conclusion of the last reflections of Sophocles on the story of Oedipus in his *Oedipus at Colonus* by calling it a "happy" ending, it is not in any ordinary sense a "tragic" ending either. It again brings a blessing to Athens, where the play was enacted. Underlying the tragedians' way of experiencing the world and the divine, as it underlies all Hellenic spiritual experience, is the perception of human life in terms of the rhythm of the natural world, the rhythm of day and night and the seasons and birth and death, the rhythm of an endless dance rather than a march to a goal. This is neither an "optimistic" nor a "pessimistic" way of looking at life. It does not issue in absolute hope or despair, because one can always look at it either way up: winter follows fall inevitably, but spring follows winter; birth is the first step to death, but people are always being born to replace the dead; a house or city falls, but a new one rises; war destroys everything, but peace comes and houses are built and trees planted again; and so it goes on forever. Here a close study of and long familiarity with the works of the great tragedians enable us to experience something that lies very deep in the spirituality of the Hellenic and hellenized Mediterranean world and perhaps mark it off most clearly from Jewish and Christian spiritualities.

Orphism

The small sectarian movement called Orphism, with its very distinctive spirituality, has been segregated in this way at the end of the article, both because it is quite unlike other forms of Hellenic nonphilosophical spirituality and any attempt to force it into a general pattern would be misleading and because its importance has sometimes been exaggerated. What we know about Orphism is that in the first half of the fifth century (the period to which our earliest evidence for Orphic groups and beliefs belongs) there were in the Greek world small (perhaps very small) groups of people who possessed a mass of books of poems which they claimed were divinely inspired compositions by Orpheus and other mythical singers of remote antiquity. They regarded these as a sort of inspired scripture and based on them a distinctive doctrine about the nature of humanity, peculiar rituals, and a special way of life. The movement seems to have been particularly strong in the western Greek lands and in southern Italy and Sicily. In spite of the claim that the movement went back to Orpheus, there is no real reason to suppose that Orphism was very much older than our first evidence for its existence. (Most of the Orphic literature of whose content we know anything seems to be later, sometimes very much later, than the fifth century B.C.) In particular there seems no ground for certainty that it was older than the great tradition of reflective spirituality inaugurated by

Pythagoras in the late sixth century B.C. This is important, because the Pythagoreans to some extent shared the distinctive world view of the Orphics, and it was from Pythagoreans that Plato took it over, with considerable modifications, and made it an integral part of the centrally important Platonic tradition of philosophical spirituality.

Though the Orphics had scriptures, they do not seem to have had a canon of scripture: the poems possessed by different groups may have varied considerably. Nor does there seem to have been an Orphic church. The little groups were independent, though there may have been some kind of mutual recognition. The central Orphic doctrine shared by all groups was that there is in the human person a divine and an earthly element. The divine in us is an actual being, a *daimōn* or spirit, which has fallen as a result of some primal sin and is entrapped in a series of earthly bodies, which may be animal and plant as well as human. It can escape from the "sorrowful weary wheel," the cycle of reincarnation, by following the Orphic way of life, which involved, besides rituals and incantations, an absolute prohibition of eating flesh and, it seems, of all use of animal products (one of the best attested facts about Orphics is that they would not be buried in woolen shrouds). This goes well with a belief in reincarnation, with its necessary corollary of the kinship of all life. One of the best ways of getting the feeling of this Orphic spirituality is by reading some of the surviving fragments of a poem by Empedocles of Acragas in Sicily, the great west Greek thinker, prophet, miracle worker, and political leader of the fifth century who wove Orphic-Pythagorean ideas about the nature and destiny of humanity into his extremely original philosophical system (though there is no reason to suppose that he was a member of an Orphic group). The poem was called *Purifications,* and a few lines from it will be an appropriate conclusion to this section.

On eating flesh:
Will ye not cease from ill-sounding bloodshed? See ye not that in careless folly ye are consuming one another? Alas that the pitiless day of death did not first destroy me before I contrived the wretched deed of eating flesh with my lips.

On his own incarnations:
For already have I once been a boy and a girl, a bush and a bird and a dumb sea fish.

On the end of the cycle of reincarnation and the return to the gods:
But at the end they come among men on earth as prophets, bards, doctors and princes; and thence they arise as gods, mighty in honor, sharing with the other immortals their hearth and their table, without part in human sorrows or weariness.

Friends who dwell throughout the great town of golden Acragas, ... I go about among you an immortal god, mortal no more, honored as is my due and crowned with garlands and verdant wreaths. (Fragments 136, 139, 117, 146-47, 112, Diels-Kranz; trans. J. E. Raven)

Notes

1. G. Zuntz, *Persephone* (Oxford: Clarendon Press, 1971) 14.

2. Ibid., 17 n. 5.

3. Mithras belongs to a different spirituality—namely, Iranian—and is fully discussed in his proper context in vol. 12 of World Spirituality.

4. W. D. Ross, *Aristotle: Select Fragments* (Oxford: Clarendon, 1952) 87.

5. *Persephone*, 53.

6. Isis is spoken of in the part of this volume that is devoted to Egypt; see chap. 2.

7. For a justifiably skeptical assessment of the dubious evidence, see G. Mylonas, *Eleusis* (Princeton, NJ: Princeton University Press, 1961) Appendix, 287-316.

8. J. U. Powell, ed., Collectanea Alexandria, p. 173, *Oxford Book of Greek Verse* (Oxford: Clarendon Press, 1951) No. 523, p. 524 (trans. A. H. Armstrong). If this is quoted as evidence for the irreligious and unspiritual character of the Hellenistic Age, some caution and qualification are needed. It was indeed, comparatively speaking, the most irreligious and unspiritual period in the history of the ancient Mediterranean world, but it was an age in which the ancient worships were everywhere kept up and splendid temples were built, like the temple of Apollo at Didyma near Miletus, and in which one of the most powerful forms of reflective Greek spirituality, the Stoic, developed.

9. This whole address of Solon to Croesus (1.30–33) is most helpful for understanding the Greek view of human life.

10. For Sarpedon, see 16.431–505. Here Zeus weeps tears of blood for his beloved mortal son whom he may not save (lines 458–59).

11. From the first line of the Kontakion of the office of the Akathistos Hymn, traditionally composed by the patriarch Sergius in the seventh century A.D.

12. The best short general account of what Greeks of the classical period felt and thought about sexual love, which corrects a number of widespread misconceptions, is K. J. Dover, *Greek Popular Morality in the Time of Plato and Aristotle* (Berkeley and Los Angeles: University of California Press, 1974) chap. 4E, 205–16.

13. *Poikilothron' athanat' Aphrodita* (Sappho Fragment 1 [in fact, the only certainly complete poem of hers that we have]; trans. A. H. Armstrong). Denys Page's commentary on the poem is most helpful (*Sappho and Alcaeus* [Oxford: Clarendon Press, 1955]).

14. The best guide to Dionysiac madness is that champion of Hellenic rationality who had such a deep and sensitive understanding of the irrational, E. R. Dodds, in his superb edition of the *Bacchae* (Oxford: Clarendon Press, 1944), and Appendix 1, *Maenadism*, in his *The Greeks and the Irrational*.

15. M. P. Nilsson, *The Dionysiac Mysteries of the Hellenistic and Roman Age* (Acta Instituti Atheniensis Regni Sueciae 8.5; Lund: Gleerup, 1957) 146–47.

16. A very vivid account of this sepulchral art and of the still rather confused beliefs it shows can be found in the account of the pagan tombs under St. Peter's in Jocelyn Toynbee and John Ward Perkins, *The Shrine of St. Peter* (London: Longmans, 1956) 109–17.

17. On this see Hugh Lloyd-Jones, *The Justice of Zeus* (Berkeley and Los Angeles: University of California Press, 1971).

Bibliography

Dodds, E. R. *The Greeks and the Irrational.* Berkeley and Los Angeles: University of California Press, 1951.
Festugière, A.-J. *Personal Religion among the Greeks.* Sather Classical Lectures 26. Berkeley and Los Angeles: University of California Press, 1954. Reprint, 1960.
Guthrie, W. D. C. *The Greeks and Their Gods.* London: Methuen, 1950.
———. *Orpheus and Greek Religion.* 2nd rev. ed. London: Methuen, 1950.
Nilsson, M. P. *Greek Popular Religion.* Oxford: Clarendon Press, 1948.
Otto, W. F. *The Homeric Gods: The Spiritual Significance of Greek Religion.* London: Thames & Hudson, 1954.
Rose, H. J. *A Handbook of Greek Mythology.* 3rd rev. ed. London: Methuen, 1945.

4

The Spirituality of
Socrates and Plato

J. B. SKEMP

Socrates

IN THE FAMOUS SCENE at the close of Plato's dialogue *Phaedo,* the friends of Socrates with tactful sorrow ask where he wishes to be buried. "Bury me if you can catch me," he replies. Any attempt to assess the spirituality of Socrates must face the same evasiveness. He cannot be encapsulated. There are special historical and critical problems: the quest of the historical Socrates is likely to continue.[1] My basic assumption is that Plato is our best witness if his evidence is rightly assessed. Aristophanes, who was almost a contemporary of Socrates, must be taken seriously. Xenophon is not to be neglected but is probably less able to understand the deeper levels of Socrates. Aristotle is neither historically nor psychologically fitted to give first hand evidence, and his words about "what one might justly attribute to Socrates" (*Metaphysics* 13.4.1078b27–30).[2] show that debate on this question had already begun. In Plato himself I attribute special value to the *Apology* and *Crito* as showing insight into some of Socrates' views that he himself did not share. Elsewhere in the dialogues I rely most on the personal touches in the dramatic presentation of Socrates, and I would not feel confident to accept without qualification as his any of the doctrines he puts forward in any dialogue.

There is one historical question that bears directly on the spiritual qualities of Socrates and on his influence in after times. This is his alleged conversion from interest in science and the universe to interest in ethics and in the individual. For the picture of Socrates in the *Clouds* of Aristophanes to be funny and have point, the theater audience in 423 B.C. must have been aware that he took some interest in scientific questions. It seems as certain as any evidence can be that when still young he heard Archelaus, a pupil of Anaxagoras, discuss scientific questions in Athens. He must also have had some contacts with visiting sophists, and the amusing sketch of the gathering at the house of Callias with which the *Protagoras* opens may well be something that Plato could imagine truthfully. In the *Cratylus,* however, Socrates deplores the fact that he is not well equipped to discuss the problems of language because he could not afford to attend Prodicus's fifty-drachma course and had to be content with a popular one-drachma lecture (384B). But we must not take without skepticism Plato's account in the *Phaedo* where Socrates is represented as saying that he abandoned a "scientific" approach because it failed to explain fundamental questions. The *Apology* also may not be free from special pleading on this question of Socrates' ignorance of the problems dealt with by Anaxagoras. On the other hand there is no need to posit a time in his life before he became concerned with ethical issues. This concern probably went back to the day when he left his father's workshop as an unsatisfactory apprentice and spent his days talking to all and sundry in the marketplace. Certainly the *Clouds* in 423 B.C. guys him as a guru to whom Strepsiades mistakenly entrusts his son. The *Birds* in 414 B.C. describes the young Athenians at that time wearing their hair long, siding with Sparta, and "gone on Socrates." In 405 B.C., when Athens is in real danger and about to be conquered by Sparta, Aristophanes explicitly points out the danger of young men gathering round Socrates in a corner chattering and scratching up ideas. In view of all this evidence it is safest to say that Socrates made no clear division in his life of asking and answering questions, even if in a worsening political situation he attached greater importance to purely personal ethical matters. He was always more interested in people than in trees, but he was always ready for serious question and answer with anyone about anything. It was natural that he drew around him especially the young men with leisure to talk and open minds. Personal attachments naturally followed.

This practice, however, was unwelcome to many of those he questioned, and we have to note two particular words of disparagement used against him, for they indirectly reveal his personal qualities. One was *eirōneia,* which we should not really translate "irony." We misunderstand it if we regard it as a positive, laudable quality. It is his opponents' word and does no justice to him. When he asked questions he honestly disclaimed knowledge himself; and yet he had a firm standard, a sense of objective truth and reality, by which he tested the answers to his questions. It was by this unexpressed standard that he proved the answers inadequate. Though his methods may well have foreshadowed logical methods later formulated, his own ruling purpose was to arrive at an enlightenment shared by questioner and answerer which had a bearing on life and behavior. All too often this

had the actual effect of enraging his partners in discussion. Thus Thrasymachus at the very outset of the *Republic* discussion on Justice complains
precisely of this "habitual irony" by which he asks questions to which he
knows the answers in order to nonplus his opponent. So he is unwilling
to enter another debate with Socrates on these terms. We speak of "Socratic
irony" as of "dramatic irony," but neither concept really reflects the Greek
word, which implies a curmudgeonly kind of understatement, often with
malicious intent.[3] Tragedy does indeed provide scenes where a character
speaks words innocently that are only too true, and Socrates can play on
paradoxes in the course of his desire to reach the truth. If we accept the
traditional use of the word "irony" for this, we must be clear that the
professed ignorance of Socrates was not a pose. He knew that he did not
know. When he exposed the conceit of wisdom in leading members of
Athenian society to the inordinate delight of young men listening in on the
argument, we must credit him with the serious intent of discovering any
clue that could lead to the solution of the problem discussed. It was of the
essence of Socrates that he met his fellow human beings on the basis of
readiness on both sides to "give and receive argument." For this reason he
insisted on short questions and direct answers, and he distrusted harangues
decked out with cosmetic phrases.

A second opprobrious epithet he attracted was that of *adoleschēs*, "chat-
terer," "idle talker." Such idle talk, as the Athenian politicians saw it, was
dangerous and distracting. If it was with their own sons, it was, in their
view, deadly. The son of Anytus, according to Xenophon, was among the
group around Socrates. No doubt his father believed that Socrates had so
shattered his sons's ideas that he had become a dissolute and disgraced
member of society (*Apology* 29–32). Anytus was the principal accuser of
Socrates in fact if not in name, and the charge of corrupting the young men
clearly weighed heavily against him at his trial (Plato *Symposium* 219D.1).[4]
Plato in the seventh book of the *Republic* makes Socrates recommend that
young men should not engage in dialectic until fully trained and matured
through mathematical discipline, for otherwise they will pull each other to
pieces like frisky puppies. This, however, is Plato and not the real Socrates,
who was made to drink the poison not least for what he had done to the
young men of Athens in the judgment of the leaders of the restored
democracy in 399 B.C.[5] Socrates paid dearly for his rationalism—or rather
for his faith in reasoning as a right and necessary human activity from the
practice of which the young would take no harm but rather would profit.

Consideration of this "corruption" of the young leads us to other elements
in Socrates. No doubt many Athenians, thinking that there is no smoke
without fire, suspected him of physical homosexual relationships. The

sophist Polycrates produced a kind of pamphlet against Socrates in 393 B.C. which may have hinted darkly at it. Both Plato and Xenophon sprang to his defense. Plato is particularly concerned with answering such smears in the *Symposium*, where he makes Alcibiades, drunk from a bottle party, enter a decorous group where Socrates, unusually well dressed for the special occasion, is a guest. Alcibiades with indecorous frankness tells in detail of his advances to Socrates and of the occasion when he slept by Socrates expecting and positively inviting response. But nothing occurred and Socrates slept peacefully through the night. We are told also that no one ever saw Socrates drunk. A story, told by Cicero but claimed by him to go back to Phaedo after whom the famous dialogue is named, says that Zopyrus, who read characters from faces, said when confronted by Socrates that he saw many signs of a vicious and lustful nature in him. The group round Socrates laughed Zopyrus to scorn for this, but Socrates defended him and said that the lusts were indeed there but were conquered by reason.

The maxim "No one does wrong deliberately" may or may not have been first uttered by Socrates, but it was later agreed on all sides that it represents his moral teaching and was a natural corollary of his teaching that human goodness is knowledge. This is not knowledge of facts but a more-than-instinctive moral perception and moral know-how. It belongs to humanity as such. It is more than alike in man and woman: it is identical. (This was indeed revolutionary teaching and elevated women, though it did not help Socrates to appreciate the femininity of Xanthippe.) Euripides did indeed question in Socrates' own lifetime the maxim that no one sins deliberately. He points out that we can know and recognize what is right but not put it into practice because passion is stronger than reasoned willing (*Medea* 1078; *Hippolytus* 377–81), and the same plea is made on behalf of humanity by witnesses as diverse as Ovid and Paul of Tarsus. But Socrates' view was only modified and not abandoned by Plato and Aristotle. Plato justifies the introduction of a penal system in the *Laws* (11, esp. 860D1–861D1),[6] and Aristotle carefully states and defines the condition of *akrasia*, failure of control, in the *Nicomachean Ethics* (7.1145b21–1152a36).[7] Yet in both great masters the optimism concerning reasoned morality remained firm. Behind this optimism about human moral potential lay the teaching and, more important, the life of Socrates. He was, says Plato at the close of the *Phaedo*, "of all men of that time of whom we had tested experience the best, the most moral and the most righteous." It was Socrates who made credible the doctrine that no one does wrong deliberately.

The basis of Socrates' readiness to follow the argument at all costs was his faith in the reality of right and wrong, just and unjust. He believed it possible to discern each, to follow the one and avoid the other. The human person has the duty, but also the capacity, to obey his or her conscience, and this conscience is an individual conscience. Invited by Crito to escape from prison, Socrates enters on his usual course of question and answer. What makes for bodily health? Avoidance of what hurts the body and use of what benefits it. Who knows what does so? The expert rather than the crowd. Who then knows how to maintain soundness in that which right conduct benefits and wrong conduct hinders? (This he says is "that of us, whatever it is, that has right and wrong behaviour as its proper concern" [Plato *Crito* 47E]. This is about as near as we get to a Socratic definition of the soul or *psychē*.) Who then knows what benefits this vital part of us? Who can judge whether it is right to stay in prison in Athens or escape to Thessaly? The one enlightened mind, which is the mind of Socrates himself, following faithfully in adversity the doctrines he has established for himself as true in the course of moral discussions throughout his life when his own security was not at risk.

This claim for individual conscience is of great importance in the history of ethics in Europe, but it is also important in the history of religion and of human spirituality. Much interest has been taken recently in the short dialogue *Crito*, which shows Socrates refusing escape from prison and death. His conscience will not let him disobey the laws of Athens, which are like parents to him and received a freely given pledge of allegiance from him when he consented to stay in Athens and did not decide to move to another community. It has been suggested that this hardly accords with his attitude in the *Apology* where he refuses in advance to abandon philosophizing if allowed to escape punishment on that condition. "Men of Athens, I greet you and I am fond of you, but I must obey God (or the god Apollo) rather than you, and so long as I have breath in my body and capacity to do it I will not cease from my task of exhortation. . . ." There is no real inconsistency. Decision to conform and obey, and decision to disobey and to accept the consequences of disobedience in hypothetical circumstances, are perfectly compatible decisions of conscience. Conscientious objectors to military duties constantly cite Socrates as their model. He had no objection to military duty and performed it stoutly when called to serve, but the principle that individual conscience is not to be overridden can fairly be regarded as Socratic. James Adam in his note on the passage in the *Apology* compares the answer of the Christian apostles before the Sanhedrin that they must obey God rather than men (Acts 5:29). There we have rather the corporate conscience of a committed group who disobey ecclesiastical authority conscientiously. But there is here also enough relevance to make Adam's note legitimate.

Here too we have to consider the motivation of the "mission" to his fellows from which Socrates was unwilling to cease. The paradoxical quality of his life is perhaps best seen here. He seeks to prove the Oracle wrong by finding a wiser man than himself, and yet he devotes himself, entirely neglecting normal duties and obligations, to persuading his fellow Athenians and anyone else ready for serious talk with him to take the health of their souls seriously. This "therapy of the soul" must come before all worldly ambition and crush degrading desires for wealth. He is in one respect a challenger of Apollo, but his challenge leads him in fact into humble service of the God in his moral crusade.

This stress laid on the "therapy of the soul" leads him to some teaching which he knows to be generally unacceptable but which he insists upon proclaiming. This is the doctrine that it is better (and safer for one's soul) to suffer wrong than to answer wrong with revenge. Revenge so injures the soul of the revenger that it must be renounced. To do wrong to another is worse than to suffer wrong from him. It is absolutely worse, but the emphasis is on the harm it does to the soul. This is not the motive for loving enemies put forward in the Christian gospel, nor are enemies required to be loved. Even so, the ethical and spiritual insight of Socrates stands out in contrast to normal Greek (and other) standards of conduct. There is no employment of nonviolence as a political tool as Gandhi used it. But there is honesty in Socrates' statement that he bore no ill feeling against those who had condemned him and that his only concern was for their false scale of values which no one would point out to them once he was gone.

It might be thought that any consideration of the spirituality of Socrates must concentrate on the *daimonion* or supernatural guide he claimed as his special possession, or perhaps as his special visitant. According to Plato its interventions were always negative or cautionary. Xenophon thought it did on occasion prompt a particular action or course of action. Later generations discussed this *daimonion*. We have writings on it from Plutarch and Apuleius, but the former is not too relevant and the latter is too rhetorical to be of much value.[8] It may well have injured Socrates at his trial, as both Plato and Xenophon believed it did. It lay behind the charge of inventing novel divinities and not believing in the gods the city believed in. We can really only say with any confidence that Socrates believed in a supernatural source of help in certain decisions in his daily life and was prepared to accept this guidance. We cannot say certainly how seriously he felt that the guidance always came from a quasi-personal being concerned with him exclusively (the word *daimonion* is neuter in gender but this is not decisive). We can, however, see the divine sign as part of the spiritual life of a man who was at once a mystic and a moralist.

Plato gives us in the *Symposium* the picture of Socrates standing still in
a trance for a day and a night (220C).[9] There is no reason to doubt the story.
It helps to explain the strong personal hold Socrates had over his contemporaries. It was not simply the external habits of an eccentric—the snub
nose, sidelong glances, rolling walk, shabby dress, and far-from-aesthetic
features. Nor was it simply what we now call charisma. It was the power
of a personality that combined intellectual challenge with strong moral
integrity and authority. Young Meno said it was a chill like that caused by
cold fluid from a cuttlefish and that it reduced one to a frozen inability to
think and speak. Others were not so chilled, but all were to some extent
awed or, in some cases, reduced to furious silence.

We have to ask what ground such a man could give for his accusers to
charge him not only with impiety but with virtual atheism. Laying aside
the political reasons behind the accusations, we must look for the grounds
for it in the minds of his contemporaries. The clue probably lies in the
phrase in the indictment "not believing in the gods in whom the city
believes."

This does not point to a direct onslaught on the Olympian pantheon,
though the discussion in the *Euthyphro*, which seems to have genuine
Socratic touches, rejects "dear to the gods" as an inadequate definition of the
Holy because what is dear to one god is not necessarily dear to another.
This would seem wicked freedom of utterance to Meletus as well as to
Euthyphro. What was the real position? The conversations of Socrates
recorded by Xenophon show a rather simple, even naïve faith in a general
divine providence. But they must be seen as in great measure designed to
defend or rehabilitate Socrates and to owe much to this motive in
Xenophon. The real truth is probably reflected in his words to the judges
just before they cast the decisive vote, as these are given by Plato (*Apology*
25E). If he appealed to them to acquit him because death was an evil he
feared to face, he would indeed be guilty of not believing in the existence
of the gods and of encouraging doubt in his fellows. "For I believe in the
gods in a way none of my accusers do, and I leave it to you the jurors and
to God to decide the matter in the way that is best both for me and for you."

I deliberately translated *tōi theōi* as "God" rather than "the god Apollo"
in the saying "I must obey God rather than you." The same applies to the
final words of the *Apology*, "Well now, the time has come to depart, I to
death and you to life. Which of the pair of us goes to the better way of
existence is hidden from everyone save God." But in so translating I do not
wish to bring in Judeo-Christian or Muslim connotations of the word
"God." Only a few sentences before that final one Socrates says that no real
evil affects the good man in life or after death and his welfare is never

neglected by *the gods*. Socrates was not alive to the issue of monotheism, but his way of believing in the gods rose above that of his fellow Athenians. He had achieved (or had by natural gift) a faith in a divine reality outside good persons but giving them support and underpinning their moral existence. To such a divine reality one can commit oneself and one's deeds.

Did Socrates, then, believe in immortality? It has frequently been held that he was an agnostic, on the strength of the words Plato gives him in the final section of the *Apology*, and it is hard to discredit this passage. He asks what death really is. He answers "Either annihilation or transmigration." He is quick to say that the former need not be feared: no dreams would come in such a sleep. But his real interest and hope is in the latter alternative, migration to another life. Greek uses the antithesis of *men* and *de* (on the one hand, on the other hand) frequently like this, stating after *men* what is possible or thinkable but after *de* what is likely or preferable. "If the stories they tell are true," he says of this brighter alternative. This means that he sits as loose to detailed mythical descriptions as a modern Christian does to harps and crowns. There is a playfulness which can be mistaken for disbelief but which expresses a deeper faith than "orthodoxy." The final quip that they will not then be able to bring him to trial and put him to death because he will be immortal exactly portrays this deep faith reflected in but not to be confused with "the stories they tell."

Inevitably much of our material in this assessment of Socrates has been taken from Plato, though past generations would have taken much more. One more argument that Plato reports must be mentioned, the so-called argument from the arts, which really is from the crafts. The craftsman in his own sphere has expert knowledge and therefore authority. The leap from such expertise to moral and political expertise is risky, but Socrates seems to have made that leap, and this has a bearing on his personal as well as his philosophical interest. He was on easy terms with all men and no aloof aristocrat, and he thought everyone worth talking to; but he had a respect for expertise that set him somewhat apart. Plato took this much further, but the seeds of the argument are in Socrates.

However that may be, Socrates is seen most clearly if all the doctrinal content attributed to him in Plato's dialogues is not taken into account. What is left is the powerful personal interest of a moral mystic who could capture the allegiance not only of Plato but of Simon the Cobbler, of Antisthenes and, through him and the Cynics, of the early Stoics. They all thought that Plato and his school were too intellectual and based their allegiance to Socrates on his pursuit of moral strength and discipline and on his frugal life-style. Plato is said to have called Diogenes the Dog in his cask in the marketplace "Socrates gone mad." It is a good story whether true or not; for it catches that element of individualism and that following out of principle that make Socrates an irreplaceable figure in the spiritual pilgrimage of the human race. It also shows the difficulty of his living out his life anywhere in our midst.

Plato

It is almost as difficult to isolate and assess Plato's spiritual qualities as we found it to be to assess those of Socrates. The difficulty now is abundance of evidence, not lack of it. One can readily do what has so often been done and treat Plato simply as a political theorist. One can virtually ignore his political involvement and treat him as a propounder of metaphysical doctrines which he afterwards modified. One can concentrate on his founding of the Academy, paying special attention to his connections with Syracuse, where politics, metaphysics, and the Academy combined in a practical challenge to action. Each of these approaches offers some insight into the man himself, but none of them uncovers his understanding of and commitment to that source of being and thought which he says is "on the further side of being" of which nevertheless every soul is dimly aware. The basic question is whether he thought of this ultimate being as in any sense personal and in any sense concerned about the life of the physical universe and its inhabitants. We shall see that we may have to accept a ragged answer, a belief in the ultimate eternal real and also in an ultimate first cause with personal characteristics.

There is again a prior question as to what evidence we may use. There has been a challenge recently to the use of Plato's dialogues as evidence for his inmost beliefs. The attempt has been made to extract and reconstruct evidence from his unwritten esoteric teaching and from a course of lectures on the Good of which we have only brief reports in order to discover more accurately what were his ultimate views. But such evidence as we have of this teaching and Aristotle's attribution to Plato (maybe meaning his school) of the ultimate principles of the One and the Indefinite Dyad or Great-and-Small (Aristotle *Physics* 4.209b3–210a2) give us reason to believe that what Plato in the *Republic* calls the Form of the Good represents at any rate the positive factor in his view of what ultimately exists. And so the concentration through the centuries on this account of what Plato believed to be real or more than real has not been seriously misguided, though it may not have said all that needs to be said.

When we permit ourselves to consider the dialogues, we find a vast amount put into the mouth of Socrates. We have seen good reason to treat its claim to be truly Socratic with the utmost caution. But if it is not

8. Three Goddesses Attending the Birth of Athena. Eastern pediment of the Parthenon. Ca. 435 B.C.

authentic Socrates, it must in some sense be authentic Plato.[10] There is important evidence of Plato's own position in the earlier so-called Socratic dialogues, but this is even more so in the great central dialogues *Phaedo, Symposium, Republic,* and *Phaedrus.* We must look to them to understand Plato's approach to divinity and the principles that guided his life.

A question of first importance arises here. We have to differentiate and evaluate the Socratic and the Pythagorean influence on Plato at the formative time of his life in his early thirties immediately after the death of Socrates. In the *Phaedo* he shows Socrates at his end surrounded by Athenian friends and devotees but also by two young Pythagoreans from Thebes. Phaedo is to take to the Pythagorean group in Phleious the story of Socrates' last hours. He does it at the request of the Phleiasian Echecrates. The implication of this would be that Socrates himself had close links with the Pythagorean refugees from southern Italy and Sicily now in exile in mainland Greece. But Plato also represents Socrates as countering the skeptical objections of the two young men to the doctrines of the soul's immortality. This at least suggests that Socrates, because he met the young men's objections with arguments, not with reference back to views of Pythagoras on these matters, had his own approach not dependent on Pythagorean doctrine. If so, we may conclude that Plato drew his own convictions about the immortality of the soul from personal contact with Socrates, although in his own great myths (in *Gorgias, Republic,* and *Phaedrus*) he takes over and uses elements of "Orphic" and Pythagorean teachings about judgment and rebirth. But he faces them with the elemental Socratic conviction about the inextinguishable value of the human psyche, which constitutes the human person as a responsible being aware of right and wrong and capable of that knowledge which is specifically human goodness, the *aretē* of human beings.

The other basically Socratic element in Plato is found in contrast to, but in productive tension with, this morality which is knowledge, this knowledge which is morality. This is Plato's account of *erōs,* which is far removed from what was later called "Platonic love." This is perhaps most explicit in the *Symposium* in Diotima's discourse, where Plato can make a wise woman tell Socrates what Socrates himself had made clear to Plato by his direct personal influence more than by arguments and doctrines. The ascent from passion for one beautiful body to vision of and union with "the whole ocean of the Beautiful" is the true account of Plato's ascent with Socrates to help him on. Socrates is the ugly Silenus figure with beautiful images to be discovered within him, images of temperance and sobriety. These inner graces of Socrates had helped Plato himself to scale the ladder of desire, and he makes Diotima and Alcibiades say what he clearly feels to be true in his own experience. The urge to "create offspring in the Beautiful" is the emotional force behind his philosophic striving for truth. The *Phaedrus* myth shows the same impetus but in subtler myth-making language. The human soul has fallen from the company of the gods as they ride around contemplating the Forms in the place above the heavens. The unruly steed of physical passion has caused its chariot to crash to earth. But it sees the light of pure Beauty before it sees any other form and forthwith its wings begin to grow again.

The meaning of all this is to be seen in the description of the true philosopher in the *Republic*. Now the ultimate object of vision is named as the Form of the Good, which is "the greatest object of learning" and the crown of a system of existents which it surpasses, for it is "on the further side of being, more excellent than being in its worshipfulness and its power." We note two developments here. Instead of the emphasis on levels of desire, we have emphasis on levels of vision. The Good is described by analogy with the sun, the source of all physical life and growth and the only true revealer of all natural phenomena. Second, the note of transcendence is sounded more strongly than before and with it the teleological emphasis, for *agathon* in Greek contains the notion of relevance, of being good *for* something.[11] The ultimate source of intelligibility also in some sense generates the existent objects that the intellect contemplates, though Plato does not explain the meaning of this sentence, which was taken as a basic text by the Neoplatonists. (The sun causes cabbages to grow, but does not create cabbages.)

On the other hand, neither desire nor beauty is absent from the account of the Good. It is introduced at 505E as "that which every soul pursues, the true object of all its acts of choice. It divines that it really is something but is at a loss and cannot grasp adequately what it can be, for it lacks the firm and settled awareness of this which it has in dealing with objects of its normal experience." When Glaucon at last understands what Socrates has said about the Good he exclaims: "This is a beauty we cannot cope with of which you speak, if it provides understanding within us and true reality outside us but is itself above both in its intrinsic beauty." *Agathon* does not supplant *Kalon:* it includes it.

The union of the intellectual and the passionate in the true philosopher is seen even more clearly in Plato's account of him at the beginning of the sixth book of the *Republic*. James Adam, in his note on 486A.3 remarks that "these and the following sentences admirably describe the genius of Plato himself." Pettiness, we are told, is a thing utterly distant from the soul whose desire will always be set on what is universal in things divine and things human. A mind that is really big and able to contemplate all time and all existence cannot really attach so much importance to human life as to regard death as anything that is to be feared. This high vantage point is, however, the climax of a struggle, and the climax is described in blatantly sexual imagery:

> [The true lover of learning] will have the natural endowment to fight his way through, not staying at each particular class of things men suppose to exist but going ahead with unblunted urgency. He will not cease from his passion till he seizes on each thing that really exists, using the faculty within him able to seize this prize, and that faculty is kin to its objects. When he has thus approached reality as a lover and has been mingled with the real in truly real intercourse, he will achieve knowledge, life that is true life, and true sustenance. Then he will cease from his travail,[12] but until that crowning moment never.

So for Plato intuitive apprehension of an unvarying supersensible reality and personal emotional fulfillment go together. But this is in no way at the expense of the reasoning faculty in the human person, for the highest function of the psyche, which Plato calls *noēsis* (pure intellection), acts dialectically. It is not a mystic absorption that spurns all reason and claims to be above it. So Plato wrestles with analysis and definition and comes to see that propositions about actual situations in life come under the same rules as statements about invariable forms. He also sees the need to restate the theory of Forms itself. But he restates the doctrine and does not abandon it, holding it to be a basic presumption of all process of thought. The seventh letter attributed to Plato is a puzzle to scholars, many of whom doubt its authenticity, but there is in it a passage describing arrival at truth, which Plato would certainly have endorsed.

> Hardly, after practising detailed comparisons of names and definitions and visual and other sense-perceptions, after scrutinising them in benevolent disputation by the use of question and answer without jealousy, at last in a flash understanding of each blazes up, and the mind, as it exerts all its powers to the limit of human capacity, is flooded with light. (*Epistle* 7.344B; trans. L. A. Post)

Here we must turn to the other guiding influence on Plato, that of the Pythagoreans. He was drawn close to them after the death of Socrates, when he was anxiously seeking answers to problems of life and thought in his early thirties. His visit to Archytas at Tarentum and Dion at Syracuse led him to decide to found a school for young men of influence in their various cities who had, or could be given, expertise in mathematics. Archytas had been chosen seven times as chief magistrate at Tarentum and was also a distinguished mathematician. But it was more than pragmatic consideration that led Plato to take the crucial step of founding his research center by the gymnasium dedicated to Academus. He was himself of distinguished descent and bound to be concerned about political life and doing the duty of a responsible citizen. He could not step aside from politics as Socrates had done, but he saw contemporary politics as degraded and unprincipled. The moral qualities of Socrates were desperately needed in political life, but how could they be introduced and then enabled to survive? His Pythagorean friends could help him, though they themselves had been driven out of political control. For them the principle of harmony applied in all spheres, in the Universe, in the human person, the "little Universe," and in human collectives. Harmony rested on mathematical relationships, or at least on relations mathematically expressible. To understand mathematical laws was both a discipline for the soul and a means of insight into the true working of ultimate forces. Number gave things meaning and relationship and effected the ordering of disorder, the limiting of the unlimited.

This was something other than the Socratic approach. We cannot be sure how much mathematical knowledge Socrates had. Xenophon's doubts about his knowledge of geometry and astronomy are quaintly put in *Memorabilia* 4.5.7 but may reflect fact; and, if so, his evoking an answer from Meno's valet about a geometrical diagram may be true of his method of evocation but the material on which he exercised it may not be typical. However, Plato could "marry" the Pythagorean mathematics with the argument of Socrates based on the craftsman's expertise. Plato was seeking "professionals" in the craft of politics, who must then have the authority of a craftsman within his own sphere and govern. Philosophers mathematically trained would be the enlightened ones and entitled to authority. But the training was vital. This was not a craft one might learn from one's father in his workshop. Vision of truth that at last gave full and competent authority in the state came after ten years' slog in mathematical studies and five years more in dialectic. This is the "prospectus" in *Republic* 7 and the ideal curriculum at any rate for the Academy.

The Pythagorean influence on Plato also explains the definition of Justice finally arrived at in the fourth book of the *Republic*. The attempt to reach an answer to the question "What is the Just?" on Socratic lines is not pursued after the first book, though the insistence on being just as distinct from seeming just continues the Socratic moral requirement. The new approach is through a threefold division of individual psyche and community with the requirement that each fulfill its peculiar function so as to produce a harmony in both state and individual which is the realization of Justice. Here Plato shows his faith in the ordering of the disorderly for the common good which arises from his belief in the real possibility of harmony. He struggles to keep this faith in the face of all the hard evidence of human nature in communities, which he analyzes with penetration in the eighth and ninth books of the *Republic*. When he seems driven to despair about its realization at the end of the ninth book, he takes up a new ground of hope. In a famous sentence he says that though the city they have just founded in words may not exist anywhere on earth now, a pattern of it is set out in the heaven for any who will to see and then to enfranchise themselves in it. The heaven intended is the one above us with its regular rounds of stars (in his astronomy) and planets. The *Timaeus* (47B) tells us that observation of the heaven is a gift of God enabling us to recognize the undeviating motions of world soul, stars, and planets too, and to seek to assimilate the perturbed motions of our souls to their unperturbed regularity. So Plato believed that the starry heavens without could foster and promote the moral law within. Macrocosm, microcosm, and human society all have potential of perfect orderliness and felicity, almost actualized in the heaven but to be painfully attained in humanity and society.

This high Pythagorean approach based on belief in order expressible mathematically in the world soul and also in the human soul built on the same mathematical basis created a difference of outlook in Plato, which led him away from Socrates. It has lost him much sympathy, particularly in recent years, and led to the view that he is nothing but a dangerous political reactionary and the enemy of democracy. The root of the problem is his equation of mathematics with ethics and of ethics with mathematics. This led him to explain decline from the ideal state in terms of failure to grasp the right numerical formula in arranging matings and births and to say that the philosopher is 729 times happier than the tyrant. We smile at this, but we have to recognize that Plato himself was serious, and his reverence for and devotion to mathematics is to be seen as part of his religious conviction and not only as part of his philosophy. It is dominant in his later view of the Universe.

We have tried to isolate the Socratic and the Pythagorean strands in Plato's spiritual makeup, but we must not think of them as antagonistic or that between them they exhaust the content of Plato's inner life. We must go on to consider how, especially in his later life, he brought in yet other ways of interpreting the highest reality. This is to be seen in the *Timaeus* in particular, where we find the Demiourgos, the fashioner and father of this Universe. He was himself good, so he fashioned it after the good and eternal model, molding in it all the species that model presented. Mathematical relations exist between fire, earth, air, and water that make its body, but above all they are present in the mathematical (and musical) ratios from which the stuff (not, of course, material stuff) of its soul was made. The

Demiurge is the Socratic craftsman at a higher level. Like the carpenter in *Republic* 10 and the auger and shuttle makers in the *Cratylus,* he "looks to" a permanent form or model and then works a copy of that form into the material proper to his skill. Guided by immaterial unchanging form, he imposes form on matter.

We see here an important development—the recognition of the function of mind as a creative organizer and of the psyche not only as capable of intelligence, but also as capable of creative action. This in turn arises from the new definition of the soul as the self-mover capable of initiating and sustaining movement in the lifeless in a purposeful way.[13] Soul can indeed be good or bad and its movements can promote order or disorder, but Plato believes that the soul sustaining and controlling the whole cosmos is a perfectly good soul. It can contain and override the wayward motions set up by contrary wills. Plato then takes over the belief in reincarnation from the Pythagoreans but explains it all in his own way as he seeks in *Laws* 10 to convince the young men in his proposed city of Magnesia in Crete that the gods exist and take notice of us. It is a doctrine of free will and individual responsibility in a preordained Cosmos with a divine Controller. This figure is called "our king" but also "the backgammon player" who makes the best cosmically of the "move" that the individual has made in his moral choices (*Laws* 10.903D.5 [backgammon player]; 909AB [king]). It is here, rather than in the careful plans for a religious cultus based on Delphi set out earlier in the *Laws,* that Plato comes nearest to stating his own faith and speaking in his own person.

Yet we need something more than the references to king and backgammon player to express Plato's belief in an ultimate cause of life and process in time and space. In the *Timaeus* the Demiurge actually makes the world soul as well as divine, human, and animal souls. Is this in fact another way of saying that the Form of the Good can act creatively? Ever since the *Timaeus* was written, there has been controversy over its interpretation. We are concerned here only with knowing whether Plato himself believed in a supreme being with personal attributes. Was he in any real sense a theist?[14]

It is clear from his attack in the *Republic* on legends about gods who deceive and misbehave that he was a radical critic of the gods of the "establishment" of his day. We need to realize how iconoclastic he was at this point. He is more cautious in the *Laws* and concerned in refuting atheism only to prove that gods in general exist, care for humans and note what they do, and cannot be appeased immorally by sacrifices that are bribes. Presumably he would still condemn stories of the gods that failed to uphold these moral standards. His attempt to base the cults in his Cretan colony on advice from Delphi is an attempt to make the state religion as enlightened and free from scandal as possible while keeping traditional forms. But his own religious faith is at a deeper level and serious enough for him to contemplate putting to death the heretic who after patient persuasion refuses to conform. It is equally logical on his part to exclude all private shrines from his Cretan city. This is for us a dark side of him, but it is there and must be acknowledged.

The traditional view has been that for Plato the Form of the Good is his equivalent of God. It is thought that he elevated an impersonal metaphysical first principle, an *ens realissimum*, to transcendent "worshipfulness and power." Faced with the language about the Demiurge in the *Timaeus* (which forged some links between Greek and Jewish thinkers in Alexandria), some have said that the *Timaeus* is mythical and not to be taken as teaching an actual creation of the Universe at the first moment of time but rather that it is an analysis of the ongoing levels of life in the cosmos, in which the Demiurge is a figure showing the constantly creative and so sustaining activity of the Form of the Good. This interpretation is often supported by citing a passage in the *Sophist* (248E–249D) where the Eleatic Stranger, speaking for Plato, says that "what is completely existent" includes not only static Forms but life, mind, and movement. It is then argued that this attributes life, mind, and in some sense movement to the forms and *a fortiori* to the Form of the Good, who is the Demiurge. But the *Sophist* passage seems rather to mean that the system of Forms does not constitute the sum of reality, and so it is here acknowledged that minds divine and human have the same degree of permanent reality as the permanent objects of their knowledge. Above all, *psychē* as an intelligent responsible center of existence is not to be submerged in an impersonal supreme principle.

There is a further consideration. In spite of what was said about intercourse with reality that brings the ultimate satisfaction of desire, it is not clear that the Form of the Good responds to those who contemplate it. In this respect it seems to be like Aristotle's Unmoved Mover, which never responds to the desire of the Universe centered upon it. At the risk of metaphysical untidiness Plato left room for religious faith in a discernible divine purpose which involves some measure of care and oversight. The god in the myth in the *Statesman* alternately controls the way of the Universe, its inhabitants, and their collectives and alternately leaves them to their own urges. But when these urges portend universal collapse, he intervenes, heals its sicknesses, reverses its direction, and takes over control once again. Here Plato is still myth making, but he goes beyond the needs of this particular myth to indicate more precisely what he hints at in the *Laws* in speaking of the king and of the backgammon player. Faith in a cosmic order and in a benevolent upholder of that order is clearly behind these hints and this kind of myth. Moreover there is no certainty that the creation story in the *Timaeus* is not to be taken literally, as Aristotle and Plutarch took it. If we do so take it, it becomes less likely than ever that Plato thought of the Demiurge simply as one aspect of the Form of the Good. Though the later Middle Platonic and Neoplatonic systems could look back to Plato for inspiration and cite his dialogues as best suited their own philosophy, we cannot find in Plato the firm doctrine of the One at the apex with mind and its objects in parallel at the next level downward and soul still farther down. If we look for Plato's spiritual insights, we must recognize at one and the same time firm belief in the eternal beyond seeming and change but also a firm sense, never codified, of a divine concerned control and an ultimate benevolent planning mind. This was no survival from his childhood or accommodation to prevailing ideas. It was something basic that cannot be ignored without reducing him as a man. As he saw it, human beings could and should grow like God as far as it lay within them to do so.

Notes

1. Among works that are very skeptical about reliable evidence on Socrates, the most important in recent times is Olof Gigon, *Sokrates, sein Bild in Dichtung und Geschichte* (Bern: A. Francke, 1947). Gigon also produced commentaries on Xenophon, *Memorabilia.*

2. Aristotle's judgment that Socrates took no interest in the philosophy of the universe as a whole is only an opinion, though of course he is right in saying that Socrates propounded no doctrines about it.

3. On the word's meaning in Greek, see W. K. C. Guthrie, *A History of Greek Philosophy,* 3:446.

4. The whole scene begins at 212D.

5. In 1954 John D. Montgomery edited a series of essays entitled *The State against Socrates* (Boston: Beacon Press, 1954). The essays are by a wide range of nineteenth- and twentieth-century authors, and many reflect on Socrates' personality and religious beliefs.

6. Trevor J. Saunders has important remarks on this passage in his translation of the *Laws* in the Penguin series (London and Harmondsworth: Penguin Books, 1970).

7. Socrates is expressly mentioned at the outset. On the ethical side Aristotle seems to have a clearer understanding of Socrates than on the metaphysical.

8. Plutarch *De genio Socratis* (*Moralia* 575–99); Apuleius *De deo Socratis.*

9. Alcibiades is made to state that Socrates was struggling with an ethical problem.

10. One must, of course, allow for the purely dramatic settings of the dialogues and speeches ascribed to speakers who clearly do not speak for Plato himself.

11. Note particularly 505A.2 where we are told that the Form of the Good is "that by which just things and the like, when they have summoned its aid to stabilize them, became truly useful and beneficial." This difficult phrase seems to mean that acts and attitudes normally called just need scrutiny in the light of the Form of the Good. Only

then can their validity be tested, and only then can they have the beneficial effect and value that are claimed for them. This emphasis on "good for . . ." does not equate good and beneficial, but it does point to the teleological strand in Plato's thought which becomes prominent in the *Timaeus*.

12. The word means "birth pangs" and at first seems strange applied to the philosopher, but *psychē* is a feminine word and can be thought to be "in labor." J. Lindsay translates "travail of his soul," which is fine if one does not try to equate the phrase with Isa 53:12, which belongs to another world of thought and experience.

13. The definition of soul as the self-mover (and the deduction from this of its inherent life and therefore of its immortality) meets us suddenly in Plato's dialogue *Phaedrus* at 245C. For a brief but penetrating discussion of this passage, see R. Hackforth's translation and commentary (*Plato's Phaedrus* [Cambrigde: University Press, 1952] 62–68). I have discussed the passage and the general account of motion in my *The Theory of Motion*.

14. I have written more fully on this and given some bibliography in the volume on Plato, published as a supplementary volume to *Greece and Rome* [New Surveys in the Classics 10; Oxford: Clarendon Press, 1976).

Bibliography

General Works on Socrates

Cornford, F. M. *Before and After Socrates*. Cambridge: University Press, 1932.
Gulley, Norman. *The Philosophy of Socrates*. London: Macmillan, 1968.
Guthrie, W. K. C. *A History of Greek Philosophy*. Vol. 3, Part 2. Cambridge: University Press, 1969.
Taylor, A. E. *Socrates*. London: Peter Davies, 1932.

General Works on Plato

Field, G. C. *Plato and His Contemporaries*. London: Methuen, 1930.
Robinson, T. M. *Plato's Psychology*. Toronto: University of Toronto Press, 1970.
Skemp, J. B. *The Theory of Motion in Plato's Later Dialogues*. 2nd enlarged ed. Amsterdam: Hakkert, 1967.
Solmsen, F. *Plato's Theology*. Ithaca, NY: Cornell University Press, 1942.

Articles

Burnet, J. "The Socratic Doctrine of the Soul." *Proceedings of the British Academy* 7 (1915–1916) 235–59.
Dodds, E. R. "Plato and the Irrational." *Journal of Hellenic Studies* 65 (1945) 16–25.
Düring, I. "Socrates' Valedictory Words." *Eranos* 44 (1946) 90–104.
Ehnmark, K. "Socrates and the Immortality of the Soul." *Eranos* 44 (1946) 105–22.
Morrison, J. S. "The Origins of Plato's Philosopher-Statesman." *Classical Quarterly* n.s. 8 (1958) 198–218.

5

Aristotle

PATRICK ATHERTON

T HE PRIMARY FORM OF KNOWLEDGE is, according to Aristotle, a
theology or a science of god, and this in two senses: god is both
the object of the first philosophy or highest science because he is
the cause or *archē* of all things, and he is the subject of this
knowledge because he alone possesses it or possesses it in the highest degree
(*Metaphysics* 1.983a5–9). The human desire to know the truth (*alētheia*) of
things is the very fulfillment of his entire being; and this contemplative or
philosophical knowledge is a sharing in god's knowledge of himself. It is
scarcely possible to estimate more highly than does Aristotle the scope,
power, and dignity of the human being's intellectual nature and its essentially religious character. This "god," in whom all knowing is grounded and
to whom all knowing aspires (for he is that which is in itself the most
knowable of all things), is *nous* or intellect—more properly, he is the self-
distinguishing, self-integrating activity of pure visionary knowing (*noēsis
noēseōs*) (*Metaphysics* 12.1074b34). This divine intellect "encloses the whole
of nature," and it was apprehended by the ancients in the form of myth
handed down by tradition (*Metaphysics* 12.1074b1–3). Besides what was
graspable of the divine *nous* through the consideration of nature, it was its
presence in humans—in their theoretical and practical activities—that
elevated them above the merely natural. Through *nous* the human being
was capable of science or universally valid knowledge and of moral life. The
state—the good life in community—was the realization of practical reason
in humans; in aesthetic experience, in art and poetry, through the productive force of *nous* humans got an image of those universal divine forces, in
their inner unity and distinction, which regulate their lives and on their
relation to which their happiness and misery depend. The spirituality, then,
of Aristotle is nothing less than a celebration of the power of *nous*, displayed in all nature, life, and intellectual activity—an exaltation of reason
as what is divine and, in particular, as what is divine in human beings.

Though all this is very largely a paraphrase of Aristotle's own text, the religious character of Aristotle's philosophy has received little emphasis in modern culture. Though for a thousand years Aristotle was considered a theologian as much as a logician or a natural philosopher—and a dangerous one for Christians and other believers in revealed religions—his banishment from the intellectual universe at the beginning of modern culture left him with a curiously ambiguous and distorted reputation. During the Enlightenment, a "mere shadow of a mighty name," he was of course not understood at all—as George Berkeley said, "Many an empty head is shaken at Plato and Aristotle." Yet his *Poetics* had a surprising vitality and authority. When the closer study of the Aristotelian texts revived in the nineteenth century, it was in circumstances unlikely to lead to any very just appreciation of the theological character of his works. Armed with what it took to be the superior authority of philological science and with a sharpened awareness of development in cultural phenomena (which by no means corresponded to any deeper historical sense) and with a profound distrust of speculative reason, the later nineteenth and earlier twentieth century saw the brief resurrection of a variety of Aristotle adapted to the requirements of the empirical and mathematical rationality of the times. When it was noted, as it could hardly be avoided, that the primary reality or Being of Aristotle was "god," it was hastily added that this "god" had nothing whatsoever to do with Greek religion.[1] Where, as in Neoscholasticism, a tradition more sympathetic to Aristotle might have been suspected, the interests of revelation were often thought to require a very low estimate of the range and character of his divine science. A better historical sense and a consequent detachment from extraneous presuppositions are required to permit that sympathetic exploration of the Aristotelian world which could disclose its proper foundation and native *archē*. For it is only by an internal critique, only within the perspectives brought to light by the Aristotelian criticism of the sensible, that a more just and more precise estimate of the divine *nous* and of its necessity to his position is possible.

A few external remarks about Aristotle and religion may serve as a preface. It is notoriously difficult to say what religion could be in the Greek language. Is it piety? So far as this meant respect for, and performance of, the traditional cults of the city-state, such evidence as we have (for example, from his will) suggests that Aristotle adopted the attitude of the conservatively cultivated Greek gentleman: the cults will have been performed with sincere propriety. The interpretation, however, of the gods and their actions found in the poets—the source of traditional wisdom about the divine—was another matter. Aristotle was indeed able to appreciate fully the value of the poets: they would not be banished from his state, for poetry was "more philosophical" (*Poetics* 1451b6) than a prose narrative of mere particulars. But as a philosopher he would certainly have refused to allow that the poets were the true measure of truth about the gods. Truth was grasped by philosophical reason, including the truth about the divine. Philosophical wisdom in its primary form was a kind of divine knowledge; religion, so far as it was enlightenment about the gods, coincided with philosophy. Because there was no church to defend the interests of religion, the Greek philosophers had no incentive either to antipathy or to partiality but could simply discuss the gods in accordance with the logic of their investigation. An Aristotle or a Plato could, with unparalleled freedom, directly consider the world and whatever gods it revealed, together with related phenomena, and allow the argument to go where reason led them.

From Nature to God

The Aristotelian conception of the gods and the divine life is distinguished from that of later times by one very conspicuous feature: the ascent to god is from nature to its divine source or *archē*—from a contemplative consideration of the moving and changing things of our immediate experience to a grasping of these objects in their universal forms or determinations, and then to a grounding of these forms in the primary unity of the Form of Forms. The revealed religions, however, can all proceed in the opposite direction: they can begin with the Beginning, with the *archē*, and descend from it to nature. Their interest is to understand nature in the light of a principle already attained and known as first. The Aristotelian wisdom, on the contrary, brings us within sight of the divine principle as that which is required to explain nature. It does not then proceed to the consideration of questions about the relation of the divine mind to nature, which inevitably arose once the *archē* had been sharply separated from it. This difference was to be of the greatest importance for theology and spirituality when, in the High Middle Ages, an integration of the two approaches was attempted. Meister Eckhardt is an instance of the explosive character Aristotelian wisdom can have on the religious tradition when its speculative content is grasped with any sense of its original force.

From the moving things of nature to their source in god: this is the motif of that immediate form of Aristotelian science—the philosophy of nature. How can this kaleidoscopic world of experience be known? For the great difficulty, which for Greek reflection at that point (as now as always) beset the entrance to the true path of philosophy, was the reduction of the sensible thing to its primary simplicity. The efforts of the earlier philosophers had reached an impasse in the powerful challenge of the Eleatic school: if this world of changing things was as "two-headed" mortals supposed it to be, then it could neither 'be' nor be known; it could not properly 'be' because change or becoming involved the impossible unity of being and not-being; and what could not 'be' could not be named or known, for only what in some sense 'is' can be known.

The Eleatic argument was, to the later Greek philosophical tradition, no mere play on words. No distinguishing between the 'existentialist' and 'predicative' sense of the copula could avoid its force, for predication was as impossible as change, if this meant that 'x' *is* 'y.' For how could whatever is self-identical (is 'x') *be* something other than itself (i.e., be 'y')? Predication as well as change involved the impossible unity of identity and difference. The Eleatic impasse had arisen because of a certain assumption the philosophers had made: they had assumed "that the sensible was the real or 'being.'" (*Metaphysics* 4.1010a2–3). Their argument had shown that this could not be so, but they did not themselves recognize that 'reality' and 'being' belonged to purely intelligible substances. It was Plato who first grasped that the proper object of knowledge was not the fluctuating thing of sensation but the Idea or Form, which the sensible particular merely imperfectly suggested or recalled. It was the Forms that were the true stable objects of scientific thinking (*noēsis*): Being belonged primarily to the purely intelligible and to Mind (*nous*). So came to light the great doctrine that the real is the intelligible and the intelligible the real—the common foundation of Plato's philosophy and Aristotle's.

For Plato the Form was divided from itself in the externality of the Receptacle, giving rise in this way to the multiplicity of sensible particulars encountered in experience. It was at this point that Aristotle parted from Plato. Aristotle considered that Plato had separated Forms from sensible things too sharply by giving an ambiguous substantiality or independent reality to the dyadic material principle. The quantitative, extended character of sensible things Aristotle reduced to a state or aspect, a derivative accident of their primary underlying reality or substantiality. This reality or *ousia* contained contrary quantitative or qualitative characteristics within itself but in all its changing states and aspects remained identical with itself—or, in Aristotle's language, it had itself no contrary (*Categories* 4a10–12). Matter—that by which things are multiple and divisible and not wholly one with their Forms—was mere potentiality or possibility. If we would give a true account or *logos* of any sensible thing we must recognize that it had two aspects: it had form so far as it had any determinate identity whatsoever, but it also had matter so far as it was *capable* of assuming new (and losing old) aspects or qualities, of moving in space, of disappearing altogether (with death or destruction). It was this very unity of matter and form that constituted the being or *ousia* of anything sensible,[2] and this unity of matter and form was not a tranquil or static being but was rather a transition. For Aristotle there was nothing real but what was passing into actuality. Distinguished alike from the flux of Heraclitus and the immobility of the Eleatics, the real for him was *development*—the fulfillment of what is potential. Aristotle's forms are not genera existing in their self-identity apart from the sensible world; they are active forces, universals that particularize themselves and are actual or real only in individuals. Substance is that activity by which a subject (a *hypokeimenon*) draws *itself* into unity with its Form—its inner identity. In a word, substance is subjectivity.

The vision of nature that Aristotle would disclose to us is of a world of the most intense dynamism and vitality: Being is movement and activity. His *physis* or nature has *within itself,* in its power of change, a likeness to the divine activity. Every item of the furniture of heaven and earth is, in its appropriate place in an ascending scale of Being, suggestive of the "activity of immobility" of the divine *nous* (*Ethics* 7.1054b27). Because the earlier thinkers had, according to Aristotle, reduced all entities outside the *archē* to compositions of contraries, they had been quite unable to explain either the unity of sensible particulars (how, in his language, matter and form were one) or how the totality of sensible—the universe—was related to the divine unity. His own doctrine of Being as activity or energy was proffered as a solution to these difficulties. Being was substance or *ousia;* an individual thing (this horse or this man) was a subject or substance that endured through movement, in which it unified and held together the various states of its existence. In this activity of realization the substance was related only to *itself* (it had properly speaking no contrary, though it contained contrariety within itself); in and through the unfolding of contrariety the substance preserved itself. It was this active power, which all natural things displayed, of remaining in relation to themselves through all their various changes which provided an analogue of the self-relation of the divine thinking in its knowledge of the Forms realized in the becoming of the sensible; in the divine intellection, god's knowledge of the Forms was only a knowledge of himself—a self-knowledge (*Metaphysics* 12.1074b33–34).

The approach to the divine principle was by an ordered ascent. For, though Aristotelian science could allow that natural objects were properly speaking substances and could therefore be known, the things of nature were not *wholly* real—they were incomplete actualities. And because nature was incompletely real, we can move from it to the completely actual or the supreme reality, to god as *actus purus* or pure act. Grasped as not completely actual, nature by its very defectiveness pointed to the divine *archē*, and, because all beings had the same logical structure (of form, and the relation of matter to form), a universal science of *being as being* was possible (*Metaphysics* 12, chap. 4). Thought, in understanding the incomplete reality of natural beings, was implicitly reaching to the wholly actual Being of god. Moreover, it was not "we" (i.e., the finite thinking human observers) who made this transition, it was nature herself in her ordered phases which ascended to the pure activity of the divine substance.

All natural substances were incomplete because they were penetrated with negativity or privation (*sterēsis*). This is the third essential element in the Aristotelian doctrine of nature. Besides matter and form, negation is a factor in the constitution of all natural being (*Physics* 1, chaps. 6–9). This negativity is shown most conspicuously in the fact that in the sublunary world any natural being can change in the most radical way: it can as well *not* be as be. *Within* natural substances negativity appears as the contrariety which all change requires in the various categories or primary divisions of Being: from black to white, for example, in quality; increase and decrease in quantity; up and down in place, etc. This negativity of nature is gradually overcome in the ascent up the scale of Being, from the non-living to organic being. Instead of the (comparatively) aimless movement in a straight line of the elementary particles to ends external to them, the end or *telos* is internalized in the changes a living being undergoes: it is an inward self-developing principle. Its function, therefore, is the actualization of this inward end. Non-living being had no activity except spatial movement, but substances have for their activity growth—not the mere mechanical addition of new matter, but assimilation, the taking into *themselves* of what was external to them, the making explicit, by appropriating their environment, of what was merely implicit.

The transition to life brings to light the motif of the Aristotelian doctrine of Being as movement and activity. Movement is essentially incomplete (*atelēs*) activity or activity in which the end remains for ever unactualized; whereas activity, as sharply distinguished from movement, is a process in which end and activity are one: a change that is a progressive realization of an end. It is this relation of end to activity which both connects and separates life from intelligence. In the noetic activity of god, the perfect unity of end and activity is exhibited; other beings are placed in the scale according to their proximity to this perfect identity.

Living beings overcome the utter externality (the infinite divisibility) of their bodily parts, dispersed in space and time, by knitting together their various states and aspects into a developing unity of self-preservation: the various movements of a living thing are so many forms of self-preservation in Being. First by nutrition the substance distinguishes itself from its

9. Athena Parthenos. Roman copy after Pheidias's original. Early 3rd century A.D.

environment and subordinates it to itself. Then by reproduction it produces another individual like itself. In this way (because it has but a weak hold on Being) in the cycle of birth, growth, reproduction, decay, and death it mirrors the eternal return upon itself of the divine thinking. The Form maintains itself eternally in the endless generation of mutable individuals (*De Anima* 2.415b2). In heavenly regions, removed from this terrestrial realm of generation and corruption, a more perfect approximation of the supreme reality is seen in the movement of the celestial bodies. Their bodies are made of a special element (*aithēr*) that is not subject to death or decay. In one sense only is it matter: it is capable of local motion in a continuous everlasting circular direction—the highest sensible analogue of the eternal divine activity.

The plant, though beginning the appropriation of externality to itself, could not *feel* itself; this comes with sensitive beings which have the power of movement in their quest for self-fulfillment and which feel pleasure and pain. Sensitive beings have bodies of more complex organization and are capable of an increased variety of functions (together with appropriate organs). In all the multiplicity of relations the animal sustains to the world, it comes to feel *itself*—a more perfect form of self-relation is manifested. Finally, in intellectual animals, in human being, a purer, freer self-relating activity is exhibited. The rational soul, which does not have parts but contains within itself the more elementary powers of *psychē*, is "potentially all things." The intellect is able to relate itself to all the genera of Being by appropriating their Forms to itself, and this assimilation of Form to itself is pure self-relation; for in noetic appropriation the knowing subject and known object are *one* actuality (*De Anima* 3.430a5).

As he surveyed the forms of nature in all their endless variety and restless productivity, Aristotle found one exception which could withstand the negativity all natural things displayed, and that was the rational soul. The intellectual soul in its completeness was self-conscious and in its self-conscious activity knew its relations to externality and its own body as involved in its own self-relation. It was capable of enduring the most complete contrariety and maintaining itself even in the face of the extinction of its own embodiment. It was immortal and its activity was a sharing in the divine life.

The sweep and range of the Aristotelian natural philosophy, from the movement of the elements to the self-developing activity of living intellectual beings, has for its purpose the disclosure of the true character of Form. All nature is nothing other than the manifestation of Form—conditioned manifestation, Form as related to Matter, but nevertheless Form. It is in this sense that one may speak justly of Aristotle's doctrine of nature as teleological. Aristotle's teleology was far from a pedestrian external teleology in which natural things are understood as existing for the accomplishment of limited, merely human ends—the moon is there to give light to weary mortals at night. The teleology of nature is, for Aristotle, simply a consequence of understanding the sensible as the actualization of Form. The substance, the Being of natural things, could only be realized through a *process* of development. In them the Form is not immediately self-identical but appears as the as-yet-unrealized completion, the end or goal, of the process. In nature *telos* or final cause and moving cause are not wholly one with the formal cause. But this dividedness of the causes is overcome in artistic production, and in the highest Being, in which there is no residue of potentiality, all the causes are reduced to the unity of pure form in its free activity. That Form appears as *telos* in natural movement testifies to the incompleteness, the negativity implicit in all sensible substance. Humans with their purposes (finite *nous* in its various modes) are aspects of, and are contained within, this absolute teleology. And though nature exists for *nous* as the means by which the end is realized, it is the divine *nous* that nature discloses. Only in the sense that the human being as finite *nous* can make itself one with the divine Mind can nature be said to serve human purposes.

God as Nous

The contemplative consideration of nature has brought to light that sensible things are derivative forms of reality: they are substances which can realize themselves only in matter and through a process of change. But this entire derivative dimension of changing Being—the heavens and the world of nature—depends upon an unchanging substance or *archē*. This substance is "eternal and unmovable and separate from sensible things" (*Metaphysics* 12.1073a4–5); it has no magnitude and is without parts and is indivisible. It is a pure Intellect which grasps its object as one with itself. In describing the divine *Nous* and our relation to it, Aristotle permits himself an unusual warmth in his normally austere scientific treatment:

> On such a principle, then, depend the heavens and the world of nature. And it is a life such as the best which we enjoy, and enjoy but for a short time (for it is ever in this state, which we cannot be) since its actuality is also pleasure. (And for this reason are waking, perception and thinking most pleasant, and hopes and memories are so on account of these.) And thinking itself deals with that which is best in itself, and that which is thinking in the fullest sense with that which is best in the fullest sense. And thought thinks on itself because it shares the nature of the object of thought in coming into contact with and thinking its objects, so that thought and the object of

thought are the same. For that which is *capable* of receiving the object of thought, i.e. the essence, is thought. But it is *active* when it *possesses* the object. Therefore the possession rather than the receptivity is the divine element which thought seems to contain, and the act of contemplation is what is most pleasant and best. If, then, God is always in that good state in which we sometimes are, this compels our wonder; and if in a better this compels it yet more. And God *is* in a better state. And life also belongs to God; for the actuality of thought is life, and God is that actuality; and God's self-dependent actuality is life most good and eternal. We say therefore that God is a living being, eternal, most good, so that life and duration continuous and eternal belong to God; for this *is* God. (*Metaphysics* 12.1072b12–29)

Aristotle takes great care to elucidate the nature of the self-relation involved in the divine thinking. It is not that there is for him on the one side a divine *Nous*, complete in itself out of relation to a world of objects, and on the other a complex of Forms, to which self-consciousness has to be yoked. It is rather that the Mind in pure intellection (*noēsis*) is only aware of itself *as it grasps objects*. Its relation to objects *is* its relation to itself:

> to *be* an act of thinking and to *be* an object of thought are not the same thing. . . . [But] in some cases knowledge *is* the object. . . . Since thought and the object of thought are not different in the case of things that have not matter, the divine thought and its object will be the same, i.e., the thinking will be one with the object of its thought.

It only remains to add that the object of the divine thought is not composite or 'put together': it knows all aspects as parts of one perfectly unified whole "so that through eternity it is the thought which has *itself* for its object" (*Metaphysics* 12.1074b33–1075a4).

These abbreviated and dense remarks have naturally given rise (particularly in modern times) to a variety of interpretations. Partly the difficulty lies in the extremely speculative character of Aristotle's comments: he is moving beyond the level of ordinary scientific thinking (*epistēmē*), which keeps to the distinctions of thought in their separation from each other. *Noēsis* is before the categorial distinctions which it knows as the unfolding of its own unity; it is therefore beyond the contrarieties of the finite and divided world of change, matter and form, good and evil. The problem of how god could know the Forms that involve matter is resolved by the doctrine that matter is potentiality. Without the reduction of Form and Matter to actuality and potentiality, Aristotle thought there could be no resolution of the difficulties the ancient philosophers had raised.

Here, in the divine thinking, is found that perfect identity of activity and end that is merely adumbrated in the lower forms of Being. Its activity is one of pure self-relation, so that in knowing all things in their Forms it is knowing only itself. This primary activity is also the perfect identity of knowing and willing, for "the primary objects of thought and desire are the same" (*Metaphysics* 12.1072a27). This pure self-determining act, the unity of Reason and Will, is what is most real, best, and most properly 'one' or a unity. The character of this unity is worth some attention because it is here that the later Neoplatonists found Aristotle most defective. Aristotle's principle is a *concrete* unity: it unites in the undivided energy of pure knowing the distinguishable but inseparable elements of subject and object. There can be no higher real unity than this. To seek a One prior to this primordial energy of subject and object was, in Aristotle's exact language, to grasp at an abstraction—something "torn from" the concrete unity to which it belonged as an attribute.

The divine energy is also the cause of all things. How exactly this causality is to be understood is a matter of great debate. Aristotle says: "Itself unmoved, it moves as loved" (*Metaphysics* 12.1072b4). Some have supposed this meant a final *as distinguished from* an efficient and formal causality. But Aristotle's answer on this point seems clear: "On our view, the medical art is in a sense health" (*Metaphysics* 12.1075b8–10). In the divine causality, final, formal, and efficient *aitia* (causes) are reduced to unity. *Nous* is, in the fullest sense, efficient cause only because it is the only true *telos* of all things. Aristotle's meaning is that all things aspire to that condition of Being that the principle enjoys directly. Their movement is an effort to attain the Form from which, as distinguished from the *archē*, they are divorced. But their matter is not an opposition, a contrary to Form; "for the primary has no contrary" (*Metaphysics* 12.1075b24)—there is no actual, "evil" principle. There is only the Good—in various modes of actualization.

The principle as Good exists both as separate from the finite (i.e., as transcendent) and as involved in it as the order of the parts (i.e., as immanent), just as the general in relation to the order of the army (*Metaphysics* 12.1075a13–14). For all things are ordered to one end. The End exists as a free, unconstrained energy—free not with the caprice of arbitrary choice but as not dependent on anything apart from itself. This free *archē* is present, more or less explicitly, in all the phases of Being, but preeminently in the intellectual life of the human being.

God and Human Beings

From the point of view of the later tradition, Aristotle's treatment of the relation between god and humans is most inadequate. It is often difficult to discern, in a discussion of *nous*, whether it is the divine or human Mind he is considering. Of the openness to human knowledge of the divine

Being, he expresses himself with a generous confidence. So divine is the wisdom attained by philosophy, that it might be thought beyond the range of human capacity. "The gods are jealous," claim the poets, and they resent those who excel in this science. But "the bards tell many a lie," says Aristotle, and the divine nature cannot be envious but must disclose itself freely (*Metaphysics* 1.983a1–10). The capacity of human beings for philosophical wisdom is both the completion of human nature and the highest approximation humans can enjoy to the divine Being.

Theoretical knowledge, that knowledge of the truth for its own sake (without attention to any utilitarian end), approaches the divine felicity: it is the activity in which human nature, though enslaved by need and want in so many ways, shows its dignity and freedom. The rational soul, in apprehending the Forms of things, does not discover an alien world, but comes into possession of *itself:* "the soul is potentially all things" and, through scientific knowledge (*epistēmē*) that culminates in intellectual intuition (*noēsis*), it possesses actually what lay implicit within it. In this condition it has achieved its proper perfection (*aretē*) and completion: the philosophically wise person is happy (*eudaimōn*) with that joy and happiness that god possesses eternally.

To attain this contemplative perfection, the human soul must first be brought to a certain condition. *Nous* is not only theoretical (in which it simply contemplates itself in the presentations of sense) but also practical (in which it actively molds what is external to it to bring it into conformity with itself). As Will, in its various relations to the world, the soul stabilizes itself in fixed habits—the virtues. It discerns a 'mean' in the satisfactions of sense and learns to maintain itself in the face of pain or terror. In the properly human community, the polis, the *nous praktikos* energizes more freely and shows its absolute power more universally. The distinctive feature of human association is that individuals, seemingly independent and separated from each other, share a common rational nature and discover a good in which they are not external to each other—a common end. Participation in the political life is the highest actuality of practical *nous*.

Besides its theoretical and practical manifestations, *nous* is also productive; through its power one can, in *technē*, subdue nature to one's purposes. In the creation of artifacts humans do consciously what Nature does without deliberation—they impose Form upon the matter provided for them by nature. But in production the object made remains external to the activity—the shoes are external to the shoemaker's activity. In moral and political life the end begins to be internalized in action—in *praxis* the end is a certain condition of the doer and the virtues perfect the agent. Finally, in *theoria,* a kind of pure looking or beholding, *nous* attains a perfect identity of end and activity.

For Aristotle the life of Reason in human beings *was* the divine life. Has any more momentous demand ever been made of intellect than Aristotle's charge to the human person "to live according to what is noblest in him"? The question is raised, Is such a life not too high for the human person? This is how Aristotle himself answers it:

> It is not in so far as he is a man that he will live so, but in so far as something divine is present in him; and by so much as this is superior to our composite nature is its activity superior to that which is the exercise of the other kind of virtue. If reason is divine, then, in comparison with man, the life according to it is divine in comparison with human life. But we must not follow those who advise us, being men, to think of human things, and, being mortal, of mortal things, but must, so far as we can, make ourselves immortal, and strain every nerve to live in accordance with the best thing in us; for even if it be small in bulk, much more does it in power and worth surpass everything. This would seem, too, to be each man himself, since it is the authoritative and better part of him. It would be strange, then, if he were to choose not the life of his self but that of something else.... For man, therefore, the life according to reason is best and pleasantest, since reason more than anything else *is* man. This life, therefore, is also the happiest. (*Nicomachean Ethics* 10.1177b26–1178a8)

Aristotle's utterly concrete view of the divine *archē* and of the relation of the world and human beings to god did not long maintain itself in Greek culture. It had been attained as the result of the religious and intellectual experience of the older Hellenic world; it was the distillation of the profoundest contemplative consideration of the life of the polis and the divine powers that animated its life. A vision of the divine Reason as distinguished from the world but partially realizing itself in all aspects of nature, life, and every facet of human intellectual experience, could not preserve itself *in precisely that form* in the conditions that began to prevail throughout the Greek world shortly after Aristotle's death. Even for the immediate successor to his school, Theophrastus, the cardinal point of the Aristotelian system had become problematical: Was there any connection or reciprocal communion between intelligible objects and the things of nature? The later Peripatetics abandoned altogether the teleological structure of the Aristotelian universe and contented themselves with a purely mechanistic physics. The reduction of all nature and finite reason to a universal divine purpose is not, however, simply discarded; it is present in a certain fashion in the opposed forms of Hellenistic philosophy—in the pantheism of the Stoics and the free individuality of the Epicureans. But that momentary glimpse of a concrete divine Principle, actual in the very movement by which it both distinguishes and relates itself to itself, could come alive again only in circumstances in which a much more complete unity of human and divine was desired.

Notes

1. For a Marxist critique of Aristotelian theology, see H. Marcuse, *Reason and Revolution* (New York: Humanities Press, 1963) 166.
2. See the discussion of 'sensible substances' in *Metaphysics* 12.1069b3–34.

Bibliography

The primary texts for studying Aristotle's thought on humanity and divinity are book 8 of the *Physics,* the *Metaphysics,* particularly the theological treatise of book 12, and book 10 of the *Nicomachean Ethics.* The Oxford translation is best and most conveniently collected in the edition of McKeon. On this aspect of Aristotle's work, the older Greek commentators and Aquinas are the most valuable; unfortunately these are not easily available in English. The two-volume work by Reale (1968) is the best guide to modern scholarship on the question and has excellent bibliographies. Some of his discussion is accessible in English in the recently translated related study, Reale (1980). Sir David Ross's *Aristotle* is the standard secondary work of reference to the whole system.

McKeon, Richard, ed. *The Basic Works of Aristotle.* New York: Random House, 1941.
Reale, Giovanne. *Aristotele: La Metafisica.* Naples: Loffredo, 1968.
———. *The Concept of First Philosophy and the Unity of the Metaphysics of Aristotle.* Translated by John R. Catan. Albany: State University of New York Press, 1980.
Ross, William David. *Aristotle.* 5th rev. ed. London: Methuen, 1971.

6

Epicureans and Stoics

A. A. Long

THE ENGLISH LANGUAGE of religious experience is indelibly colored by expressions we have inherited from ancient Greece and Rome. Theology, piety, mysticism, union, divinity, spirituality—all these, and many more, are terms originating from classical antiquity and suggesting thereby direct connections between ancient and modern patterns of thought. More specifically, Stoic references to God as the father of people or Epicurean mentions of salvation and savior remind us forcefully that these two pagan philosophies of Hellenistic Greece and Imperial Rome were firmly entrenched by the time that Christianity received its first written forms. The suggestions of a religious continuum are not, of course, fortuitous. Early Christianity developed out of a culture which, so far as most of the older theologians were concerned, was more Greek and Roman than it was Jewish. Christian apologists such as Tertullian, Origen, and Clement of Alexandria are important sources for Stoicism. This is not because they accepted its doctrines in the Stoics' own terms. They frequently opposed them. But their opposition itself is a back-handed compliment to the powerful influence of that philosophy, much of which was unavoidably drawn into the language and thought of the early church.

The critical and creative use of Hellenistic philosophy by Christian writers is a complex and fascinating subject. As historians, however, we need to start from the pre-Christian context if we are to grasp the specific contributions of Stoicism and Epicureanism, or any other Greek philosophy, to religious consciousness. Theology, though a Greek concept, was hardly a domain of study independent of cosmology in the broadest sense. Later Greek philosophers wrote books on the gods or on piety, but these included a much wider range of subjects (cosmological or ethical) than would be generally admitted under the aegis of theology today. Stoic and

Epicurean thinking on religion, like that of Socrates, Plato, and Aristotle, knew nothing of a system of truths revealed in a sacred book which was the basis of all worship or ritual observance. Their conception of the divine, even when expressed in highly personal language, never suggests that the supreme being is an individual to whom someone might be related in the manner of an Abraham or a Job. Sin and saintliness, heaven and hell, temptation and redemption are notions to which such Greek analogues as do exist mislead more than they inform.

Trickiest and most potentially misleading of all is the term *theos* or *deus*. If Greek philosophers speak of "god" in the masculine singular, this is generally to indicate everything encompassed by the divine or to distinguish a supreme god from lesser divinities; no formal commitment to monotheism is implied. Only rarely did any Greek philosopher question or deny the existence of gods. But in Hellenistic times (about 320–31 B.C.), this and every divine attribute had to be argued for. It was a matter of controversy whether, if gods existed, they were the world's creative and causal agents; whether they were providential or beneficent; and what their life and form were like. The connotations of *theos* and *deus* did not settle these questions. It was universally agreed by all but skeptics that gods were superior to human beings in power and longevity and that they enjoyed a happiness that humans rarely, if at all, could achieve. Yet exceptional men, especially rulers, could be called godlike and might even be elevated to divine status in life or after death. Such vagueness and fluidity in the general conception of the divine gave Hellenistic philosophers an almost open field for speculation.

At first glance, nothing could be more divergent than Stoic and Epicurean theologies. The Stoics made their supreme god, Zeus, responsible for providence and creative agency, immanence throughout all nature, and interest in human moral welfare. In Epicureanism, the gods have human form but are not in the world, and they take no part in its organization or in human affairs. Both philosophical schools could appeal to features of the cultural tradition in defense of their own theologies, and neither could lay claim to them all. For there was no consensus on what a god was or what a god did.

The inadequacies and incoherence of mythological representations of the gods had been repeatedly exposed during the fifth and fourth centuries B.C. Expurgation and refinement of the traditional stories had been an occupation of writers as different from one another as Heraclitus, Pindar, Euripides, and Plato. Once the Homeric and Hesiodic poems were critically scrutinized, the inconsistencies within these hallowed texts became conspicuous. They exhibited the gods as sometimes blissfully detached from human behavior, and at other times as interacting with people in characteristically human ways. The gods were there shown both as upholders of basic moral norms and as injuring one another or human beings from thoroughly reprehensible motives. The physical world and its processes were under the control of the principal gods with their particular prerogatives. But the Olympian gods had not created the world and were junior to the older divine domains—heaven, earth, sea—which they administered. Zeus, though sometimes spoken of as omnipotent, was subject to the mysterious power of fate and was capable of being deceived. It was fearful to risk a god's displeasure, but unclear how to avoid doing so. The gods demanded reverence, worship, and sacrifice from human beings; yet their own response to human needs, as judged by events, was capricious and unpredictable.

In developing their conceptions of god, the Stoics and the Epicureans, like earlier Greek philosophers, must be viewed as reformers of this impressive but alarming conglomerate of ideas. Discarding what was incoherent, crudely primitive, or morally unacceptable, they selected, interpreted, and added to those traditional notions which fitted their most basic intuitions. Thus, the Epicurean gods have the beauty and human form of the Homeric pantheon and are conceived to live a life of sublime detachment, free from all pain and disquiet; everything else that the tradition ascribed to them was removed. In Stoicism, by contrast, the selection of mythological motifs is quite different. The Stoics employed allegory and etymology to reconcile poetic accounts of the gods' anthropomorphic behavior with their own theories concerning natural processes. In their philosophy, what survived of the old tradition was not the gods' detachment and human form but their involvement in the world as causal agents and as moral arbiters.

As we proceed to describe the details of these two theologies, such roots as they have in popular tradition may seem to be concealed beyond recognition. But the continuity exists and is extremely important. Both philosophical schools made a point of insisting that their theologies were founded upon the common religious preconceptions of humanity, and both of them took account, however selectively, of popular Greek religion. In spite of, or perhaps because of, its complexity and inconsistencies, that tradition was still powerful enough in the early Hellenistic period to engage many people's fears and hopes. All features of daily life, from the salvation of one's city down to the mundane activities of eating, drinking, and sex were ostensibly the prerogative of some deity—how ostensive, moreover, was underlined by temples, icons, sacrifices, and official worship. Divine rewards for conduct pleasing to the gods and everlasting punishment for offenders were beliefs that many appear to have shared, even though popular religion offered little by way of formal doctrine or ritual to support them.

Epicureanism

Epicurus (born an Athenian citizen in 341 B.C.) made it his life's task to undermine all beliefs about the gods and human life that threatened mental security or derogated from the individual's entire responsibility and opportunity to achieve abiding happiness here and now. His teaching is both a philosophy and a religion, offering an account of the world and of values grounded in the self-evident data of sense perception and immediate feelings of pleasure and pain. The ultimate principles of everything are everlasting atoms and empty space. Though not directly observable, these principles are advanced as truths of reason, which are consistent with phenomena and necessary to explain them.

This scientific approach to the world was not advocated disinterestedly:

> Vain is the message of a philosopher through which no man's disease is cured; for just as no good results from a doctor's failure to eliminate bodily diseases, so too no good comes from a philosophy if it does not expel the soul's disease. (Porphyry *To Marcella* 31)[1]

Epicurus's motivation, as he makes plain here and repeatedly, was the saving of souls. He believed himself to have discovered the causes and cures of people's unhappiness. His entire system was designed to show how mental health and contentment could be achieved by a proper understanding of the nature of things.

The principal ailment that he diagnosed were false beliefs about the gods and natural processes, together with false beliefs, largely consequential on the former ones, about the sources of pleasure in life and the significance of death. For his "Herculean" achievement in removing these beliefs and attendant fears, Epicurus was venerated by his followers as a savior and even as a god himself.[2] His strikingly handsome and compelling appearance was widely distributed in statuary and other representations, to serve as a permanent reminder and emblem of the founder's good news.[3]

The school that he established in his garden just outside the city wall of Athens was exactly what we would call today an alternative community. Its members were not only pupils or teachers but also friends who may have been encouraged to live there with their families; and, what was thoroughly radical by conventional Greek standards, women were admitted on equal terms with men. This social organization realized and symbolized the Epicurean way of life—a community of people, freely associating together under a charismatic leader, in the conviction that his teaching had given them the attitudes and values necessary to live in a state of permanent confidence and personal fulfillment. It was an alternative community because conventional society, according to Epicurus's findings, represented utterly mistaken values and was organized in ways that outlawed true freedom, whether through superstition, money making, system of education, or politics.[4] In retreat from this "mad" world, the Epicurean was encouraged to learn that the basic requirements of human happiness are simple and easily acquired.

> We must reckon that some desires are natural and others vain, and of the natural some are necessary, others natural only; and of the necessary some are necessary for happiness, others for the body's freedom from stress, and others for life itself. For the steady observation of these things makes it possible to refer every choice and avoidance to the health of the body and the tranquillity of the soul, since this is the goal of the blissful life. For this is what we aim at in all our actions—to be free from pain and anxiety. Once we have secured this, all the soul's turbulence is released. (Epicurus *Letter to Menoeceus* 127–28)

It is difficult, in the latter part of the twentieth century, to perceive this prescription through the eyes of the original readers. Historically, however, its message was remarkable. In the category of "vain desires," Epicurus included objectives that had traditionally provided the tightly knit city-states of Greece with most of their purposes—family solidarity, economic and political success, athletic prowess, artistic display, and the individual's opportunities for litigation, self-assertion, aggrandizement, and entertainment. Epicurus was not the first to question the adequacy of such activities to satisfy the deepest human aspirations. But no one had previously suggested that society's ills stem chiefly from misplaced fears concerning death and the gods, which provoke insatiable ambitions to cheat the grave and placate the wrath of heaven.[5] Nor had anyone else heralded friendship as "by far the greatest thing that wisdom provides for blessedness of life as a whole" (Epicurus *Key Doctrines* 27)[6] or offered his own estate as the setting for a full-scale alternative community. Seen in this light, Epicureanism can claim to be an extraordinary experiment in discovering spirituality, an all-embracing context for establishing the foundations of internal well-being.

The theology that was basic to this spirituality has two sides, negative and positive. Epicurus totally rejected all accounts of the gods, whether popular or philosophical, that made them responsible for natural processes or human fortunes: the world is not designed by the gods, nor does anything that happens, including human behavior, please or displease them. This negative theology was defended on various grounds. Against the teleology of Plato, Aristotle, and the Stoics, the Epicureans argued that the world is too obviously imperfect to justify beliefs in divine providence or purposiveness and that it was the height of absurdity to credit the heavenly bodies with divine minds.[7] The regularities of natural processes, which their rivals regarded as the supreme evidence of divine rationality, were explained by Epicurus as due to the patterns of movement exhibited by the infinite and everlasting atoms—lifeless units of solid body.[8]

More relevant to our concerns in this chapter is the Epicurean conception of what suits the nature of the gods.

A The blessed and imperishable neither suffers trouble nor inflicts it on anything else; so it has nothing to do with passions or favors. For everything like this is found in what is weak. (Epicurus *Key Doctrines* 1)[9]

B First, regard god as an imperishable and blessed creature, as the common idea of god is in outline, and attach to him nothing alien to imperishability or inappropriate to blessedness, but believe about him everything that can preserve his combination of blessedness and imperishability. For there are gods—the knowledge of them is self-evident. But they are not such as the many believe them to be. For by their beliefs as to their nature the many do not preserve them. The impious man is not he who denies the gods of the many, but he who attaches to gods the beliefs of the many about them. . . . It is through these that the greatest harms, the ones affecting bad men, stem from the gods, and the greatest benefits too (i.e., affecting good men). For having a total affinity for their own virtues, people are receptive to those who are like them, and consider alien all that is not of their kind. (Epicurus *Letter to Menoeceus* 123–24)

C Unless you expel these ideas from your mind and drive far away beliefs unworthy of the gods and alien to their tranquillity, the holy divinity of the gods, damaged by you, will frequently do you harm: not because of the possibility of violating the gods' supreme power, and of their consequent angry thirst for bitter vengeance, but because you yourself will imagine that these tranquil and peaceful beings are rolling mighty billows of wrath against you. You will be unable to visit the shrines of the gods with a calm heart, and incapable of receiving with tranquillity and peace the images from the holy bodies which travel into men's minds to reveal the god's appearance. (Lucretius *De rerum natura* 6.68–78)

These three passages report the essence of Epicurus's positive theology. "There are gods—the knowledge of them is self-evident" (passage B). So pervasive is the belief in gods, Epicurus argued, that it must be natural to human beings and not simply a product of convention or social conditioning. As something universally acknowledged, the existence of the gods was in need of no proof. "Nature herself has imprinted the conception of the gods on all men's minds" (Cicero *De natura deorum* 1.43).[10] People have always, especially in dreams, seen figures of marvelous appearance and

prodigious size (Lucretius *De rerum natura* 5.1161-85). According to Epicurean theory, all our mental impressions, perceptual or imaginary, are
caused by atomic "images" which enter the sense organs or the mind from
outside; our impressions always faithfully report the images that cause
them. So the basic religious conceptions of humanity had a real foundation
in the nature of things—externally existing atoms that produce impressions
of gods.

"But they [the gods] are not such as the many believe them to be" (passage
B). Beliefs, unlike impressions, can be false as well as true. It is possible to
misinterpret our impressions and to attribute to their external causes characteristics that these do not have. Epicurus explained the "impious beliefs
of the many" as a misinterpretation of the superhuman figures perceived in
dreams. Primitive people, unable to explain the workings of nature, assigned
these to the gods of their dreams (Lucretius *De rerum natura* 5.1189-1240).
They endowed these figures not just with superhuman happiness and everlastingness, but also with active involvement in our world. Such a concern,
Epicurus insisted, was quite incompatible with divine happiness: "Unless
you expel these ideas from your mind . . . the holy divinity of the gods . . .
will frequently do you harm" (passage C).[11] Here we have Epicurus's most
fundamental theological thesis. The gods themselves do nothing that can
injure us (passage A), but we, through false beliefs, can endow their images
with powers that do cause us serious harm. Correspondingly, the gods do
not plan or deliberately send us blessings. Their images, however, will be
a blessing to us if we receive them with the state of mind that is proper to
a correct conception of the divine (passage C).

The correct conception—"everything compatible with blessedness and
imperishability"—persuaded Epicurus that the gods are of human form;
that is the most beautiful of all shapes and the only one capable of including
reason and virtue (Cicero *De natura deorum* 1.46-48). But his basic justification for anthropomorphic gods and for their bliss and imperishability was
consensus omnium—the common agreement of people. It is difficult not to
suppose that he was also strongly influenced by the idealized portrayal of
the calm and beauty of the gods in Greek art. His own support for the
official forms of worship shows that conventional religion was acceptable
to an Epicurean who could approach the manufactured images of the gods
in the right spirit.[12]

So far, we have been considering the relation of humanity to the gods.
What of their nature and life as such? On this question, the evidence is
extremely difficult to interpret, and scholars have advanced many different
theories. Here we shall have to be content with a brief account of what
seems to me to be the most convincing answer. The key passage is as follows:

D That appearance (of the gods) is not body but quasibody, and it does not
   have blood but quasiblood.... Epicurus ... teaches that the force and
   nature of the gods is of such a kind that it is, primarily, viewed not by
   sensation but by the mind, possessing neither the kind of solidity nor the
   numerical distinctness of those things ... he calls "solids"; but that we
   apprehend images by their similarity and by a process of transition, since
   an endless series of extremely similar images arises from the countless
   atoms and flows to the gods, and that our mind, by focusing intently on
   those images with the greatest feelings of pleasure, gains an understanding
   of what a blessed and everlasting nature is. (Cicero De natura deorum
   1.49–50)[13]

Ordinary objects in the world are "solids" and give off atomic images of
their surface qualities. Epicurus recognized that some of our impressions
are also caused by *mere* images, collections of atoms that have not issued
from any actual object. Here he is reported to have said that the gods
themselves are such images, lacking the solidity and numerical distinctness
of perceptible reality. To describe them thus is tantamount to saying that
the gods themselves, though not of course the atoms that form the images,
are objects of our imagination; and this is further suggested by the statement that we apprehend the images "by their similarity and by a process
of transition." These words refer to familiar Epicurean methods of concept
formation—ideas that we generate by putting similar images together or by
adjusting the images we receive to what we want to think about.[14] "An
endless series of extremely similar images ... flows to the gods" can be
plausibly read to mean that *we* project onto the images of superhuman form
characteristics that make them into our gods. The stock of such images is
endlessly similar; they are thus completely appropriate to provide us with
the conception of everlasting beings who are not subject to the mutability
and troubles of human life.

If this is correct, the Epicurean gods are not living beings with an objective existence independent of human minds. They are idealizations of
human life, constructed by the right-minded as projections from the appropriate images that they receive: with these images they associate their
natural understanding of the essence of sublime happiness. This interpretation, it should be noticed, also accounts for false conceptions of the gods
(see passages C and D) and varieties of religious experience, since people
picture the gods in terms of their own values and fears and desires: "they
are receptive to those [images] who are like them, and consider alien all that
is not of their own kind" (passage B). Some Epicurean texts, though nothing
that survives from Epicurus himself, suggest a different theory—gods that
really exist in a never-never land, the spaces between worlds (*intermundia*)—
eating, sleeping, and talking Greek to one another![15] Against so childish a

10. Cameo Glass Skyphos. Roman. Early 1st century A.D.

doctrine can be set not only Epicurus's silence but also the frequently made charge of atheism. Moreover, he was alleged to have reduced the gods to such imaginary creatures as centaurs—a travesty of the theory outlined here— but one intelligible from the treatment of the gods as our images (Cicero *De natura deorum* 1.105).

According to any interpretation, the only role of the gods in Epicurean philosophy was to serve as objects of thought and as models of beatitude. What interested Epicurus was our relation to the gods and not their own existence per se. The happiness that he taught was, he believed, a goal truly grounded in our own nature. The attainment of that goal rendered a person capable of "living like a god among men; for a man who enjoys immortal goods is unlike a mortal creature in his life" (Epicurus *Letter to Menoeceus* 135). As Epicurus wrote in a letter to his mother:

> Think that each day we advance towards a greater happiness, always acquiring something useful. For of no small importance to us are the things which make our disposition godlike, and which show that we are not, by reason of mortality, inferior to the imperishable and blessed nature. For when we are alive, we enjoy a happiness like that of the gods. (Diogenes of Oenoanda Fragment 52, Chilton)[16]

Epicurus, then, offered his followers a form of deification. This should be taken seriously and seen to be in harmony with his teaching about the images of the gods. Epicurus's own lifetime was short, but images of the man and his teaching survived to later generations. Rightly understood, the objectively existing images of the gods were worthy of worship and emulation. Like Epicurus himself, they provided people with the ideals their nature needed. Hegel stated the gist of the doctrine well:

> The Holy, the Universal, in concrete form . . . the gods are the altogether general images which we receive into ourselves. The general image, which is at the same time an anthropomorphic conception, is that to which we give the name of Ideal, only that there the source assigned to it is the reiterated occurrence of images.[17]

To some, Epicurus's theology will seem completely misnamed. By denying the gods control over the world and human destiny, he removed what many have supposed to be central to religious belief. His forceful rejection of life after death removed any prospect of a final judgment, setting right the injustices of this life, or punishing wrongdoers. His remote gods or conceptions of gods, heedless of people, afford none of the comfort or personal mediation promised by some other religions. It would be mistaken, however, to conclude that Epicureanism was not a spiritual ideal and that its theology is pretense or only a disguised humanism. Negative in its rejection of the superstition and fear of traditional religion, Epicurean theology is positive, and in harmony with the best of that tradition, in using the gods as ethical models of tranquillity, beauty, and friendship. In its focus on the way we ourselves should conceive of the divine, combining freedom from pain with injuring no one, his religious outlook ranks as among the most enlightened of antiquity.

Stoicism

If Epicurean theology strikes the modern reader as out of line with the main Western religious tradition, the integration of Stoicism within that tradition will show itself more clearly. We may recall the divergent positions the two schools took up concerning divine creativity, providence, and concern for human well-being. It is, of course, true that the religious tradition to which the Stoics contributed was far from uniform on many points. Unlike the Platonists and the Aristotelians, whose mark on the tradition is so conspicuous, the Stoics defended positions that they shared with the Epicureans—the perfectibility of humanity in its terrestrial existence, the corporeality and the eventual destruction of the soul. In their opposition to such doctrines the early Christian fathers can give the impression that Stoicism was no less anathema to them than Epicureanism. But, from a larger perspective, Stoics, Platonists, Aristotelians, and Christians could present a united front against the Epicurean dismissal of the gods from running the world. It was common ground to these other philosophies that what is divine is the ground of the world's being and of our own, that the world exhibits an order and system that give evidence of its divine principle, and that human beings are so designed that imitation of or likeness to god is essential to their well-being. We have seen how the Epicureans completely rejected the first two of these propositions, but we noted that their interpretation of the third is idiosyncratic in its denial of divine interest or design in human affairs.

Moreover, Stoicism incorporated un-Platonic and un-Aristotelian doctrines which could be interpreted in ways that made them attractive to the Christian fathers. As breath (*pneuma*), the human soul and the supreme deity Zeus are corporeal, but the bodily nature of *pneuma* is so unlike body as normally conceived that it is able to permeate "matter" completely.[18] Literally, and functionally in terms of modern usage, the individual soul and Zeus himself are "spirit," from the Latin equivalent of the Greek *pneuma,* which is the word in the New Testament that is translated "spirit" or "breath" of God. Further, the Stoics, unlike Aristotle (or Plato as he was generally interpreted), taught the literal creation of the world and its eventual destruction. They posited an ending to the world in a mighty conflagration, which then reconstitutes everything in a ceaseless cosmic cycle.[19] Christian teaching on the end of the world and the resurrection could observe affinities to its own beliefs in these Stoic antecedents.[20]

We should regard Stoicism, then, as an important constituent of the prevailing rationalist, teleological, and theological tradition of Greek philosophy. Its founders, Zeno of Citium, Cleanthes, and Chrysippus—all Greek speakers from communities tinged by Middle Eastern culture—laid the basis at Athens of a system of thought that dominated intellectual life in the Hellenistic world and the early Roman Empire. Their own books have survived in a far more fragmentary record than those of Epicurus. Nor should it be assumed that Stoic thinking on religion remained as uniform as appears to have been the case with his philosophy. But our main sources (which include Cicero and Seneca in Latin, Plutarch and many others in Greek, and the Roman Stoics Epictetus and Marcus Aurelius) indicate general agreement on the essentials of theological doctrine, though this is often interestingly colored by the writer's own emphases and modes of expression.

In what follows much will be said about divine and human rationality. Before we proceed, it is important to recognize that the Stoics' commitment to rationality as the essence of what is divine and good includes the *love* of wisdom, *philosophia* as most brilliantly described by Plato in the *Republic*, *Symposium*, or *Phaedrus*. The Stoics did not, as is frequently supposed, set up as their ideal one whose wisdom excludes all emotion or feeling. Rather, they extended the notion of rationality so that it included desires and "good feelings" (*eupatheiai*), in contrast to the passions and mental perturbations that characterize a soul whose reasoning faculty is disordered.[21] In Zeno's ideal state the god who promotes the city's security is Eros, turned from an irresponsible Cupid into "god of friendship and freedom" (Athenaeus *Deipnosophistae* 13.561C).

Zeno supposed that a society composed of the perfectly wise would not build temples (Plutarch *On Stoic Self-contradictions* 1034B). His reason for this proposal, however, was not irreligious but, on the contrary, the inadequacy of such buildings to indicate what is sacred. Speaking of that final part of physics which deals with theology, Chrysippus called it *teletai*, a word that combines the sense of mystic initiation with fulfillment (*telos*) (Plutarch *On Stoic Self-contradictions* 1035AB).

The Stoics, as these instances show, characteristically transmuted and built upon conventional religious ideas and discourse. No more than Plato were they disposed to discard all myth and traditional religion as misguided or superfluous. Their respect for popular beliefs is evident in their concern to incorporate them, wherever possible, within their own science and theology. Though they normally treat the divine as a unitary being, they named it Zeus and accommodated the lesser Greek divinities as references to particular features of the cosmos—calling the lower atmosphere Hera (her name being seen as a form of *aēr*, "air"), deriving Rhea as the name for the earth from "waters flow (*rhei*) out of her," and so forth. As the Stoic spokesman in Cicero's *De natura deorum* 2.71 says:

> Stories and beliefs (which represent the gods as in Homer) are full of non-sense and utter stupidity. But while we reject and scorn these myths, we shall be able to understand the identity and character of the deity which penetrates each element, Ceres the earth, Neptune the sea, and so forth; and we have a duty to honour and worship these gods by the name custom has given.

The Stoics prided themselves on the coherence of their whole system. As god is a pervasive presence in the world according to their view, so too in their philosophy. In order to focus this discussion, within the space available, I propose to consider three basic Stoic propositions: (1) god is the designer and agent of everything; (2) the human being is an offshoot and partner of god; and (3) the human being's function is to live in harmony with god. There is an intimate relationship between these three propositions. To observe this, we should turn first to Cleanthes' Hymn to Zeus, a poem written in the style and meter of a traditional paean, honoring a Greek deity.[22]

> Noblest of immortals, many-titled, ever omnipotent Zeus, director of nature, steering all with your law, hail to you. It is right for every mortal to address you: we are your offspring, and of all creatures that live and tread the earth we alone have been given a likeness to god. You, then, I shall hymn, and sing for ever of your power. All this world, as it whirls around the earth, obeys you wherever you lead, and willingly submits to your power. Such is the double-edged, fiery, ever-living thunderbolt which you hold at the ready in your unvanquished hands. For under its blow all the works of nature are accomplished. With it you administer the universal reason (*logos*) which passes through everything. . . . Nothing occurs on the earth apart from you, god, nor in the celestial realm nor on the sea, except what bad men do in their folly. But you know how to make things crooked straight and to harmonize what is dissonant. You love what is not loved. For you have so wrought together into one all that is good and bad that they have a single everlasting reason. The bad among mortals shun and ignore it, wretches, who ever seek the possession of goods yet neither see nor hear god's universal law, by obeying which they could enjoy a good life in company with intelligence. But of their own accord they senselessly rush after this evil or that, some in their contentious passion for fame, others all set on acquisition devoid of harmony, others for relaxation and the pleasurable acts of the body. . . . Bountiful Zeus . . . rescue mankind from its grievous misunderstanding. Scatter this from our soul, father, and give us the power of judgment, by

trusting in which you steer all things with justice, that by being honored we may repay you with honor, hymning your works for ever, as it befits a mortal. For neither men nor gods have any greater prerogative than to sing for ever in righteousness of the universal law.

These splendid verses show Cleanthes' skill in turning popular religion to philosophical account. Greeks of the archaic period had sensed a connection between the justice of Zeus and his acts in controlling the weather and other phenomena, but the connection was one that posed more questions for the religious minded than it solved. In Cleanthes' Hymn the traditional power of Zeus and his thunderbolt are symbols of god as everlasting designer and agent of everything. The thunderbolt loses its connotations of erratic destruction and becomes a name for the regulating instrument of divine agency. "Father of gods and humans" was a traditional appellation of Zeus. Here his paternity has acquired a profoundly spiritual resonance; the Stoic Zeus is a creator of beings who share his capacity for intelligence and moral understanding. He stands to humanity and the world as the embodiment and enactment of universal or natural law.

Cleanthes' poem enables us to see that this law, also described as universal reason, has objective and subjective aspects, or outer and inner manifestations. On the one hand, it refers to the inevitable order of events or natural processes—the sun's rising and setting, the particular structures of living beings, etc. All of these, we are asked to observe, display rationality and order; they fit together into a harmonious pattern. Second, universal law or reason refers to the moral order, common to god and human. In this sense, the community of law and reason is something that the individual persons have the capacity to discover within themselves—a mental disposition whereby their own good and self-fulfillment is perceived to belong to the good and self-fulfillment of all other rational beings.

The only way in which the inevitable order of events could coincide with the universal moral order is, it may seem, through their identification: everything that happens is deemed to be right, or what is right is deemed to be everything that happens. Without qualification, such a thesis would be as repugnant as it is implausible. But what Cleanthes says is that Zeus determines everything that happens "except what bad men do in their folly." Thus, Zeus is not responsible for evil, which is a purely human aberration.[23] Even evil, however, is ultimately harmonized with good, under divine direction: "you know how to make things crooked straight. . . ." The picture, then, is of a world in which everything *ultimately* fits together according to a divine pattern. To appreciate what this means for human beings and their spiritual or moral life, we should consider the second proposition stated above: "the human being is an offshoot and a part of god."

The Stoics' deepest religious intuitions are founded on their doctrine that the human mind, in all its functions—reflecting, sensing, desiring, and initiating action—is part and partner of god. Some further quotations from Stoic writers will serve to illustrate.

A Living in accordance with virtue is equivalent to living in accordance with experience of what happens by nature . . . for our own natures are parts of the nature of the whole. Therefore living in harmony with nature proves to be the goal of life, which is in accordance with the nature of oneself and that of the whole, engaging in no activity wont to be forbidden by the universal law, which is the right reason pervading everything and identical to Zeus, the director of the administration of existing things. And the virtue of the happy man and his good flow of life are just this—always doing everything on the basis of the harmony of each man's guardian spirit with the will of the administrator of the whole. (Chrysippus, cited by Diogenes Laertius 7.87–88)

B Can our souls be so bound and attached to god, as being his parts and offshoots, without it being the case that god perceives their every movement as related and belonging to his own nature? . . . When you close your door and make darkness within, remember never to say that you are alone, for you are not; god is within and your own guardian spirit. (Epictetus *Discourses* 1.14.6, 12–13)

C Provided I remember that I am a part of this kind of whole, I shall be content with all that happens. And so far as I am in a relationship of kinship with the parts like myself, I shall do nothing unsociable—rather, I shall make those parts my objective and direct my every impulse at the common interest, and remove it from the opposite. With the fulfillment of such principles, my life must flow well. (Marcus Aurelius *Meditations* 10.6)

The Stoics conceive of the world as a gigantic organism. God is its life or activating principle, present in every part. The activity of god, however, takes different forms. God structures every part of nature, but only human beings are endowed with reason (*logos*), which is the essence of god himself. Thus, as parts of the world, human beings are related to god in a special way, as his "offshoots" or kin (B and C above). This relationship between the human being and god is pictured as a partnership. Our function as human beings is to cultivate our own portion of divine rationality—that is, our own souls—in such a way that we achieve complete harmony between what we as individuals desire and seek after and what right reason in general, the universal law embodied in Zeus, prescribes (A above).

So far as humanity is concerned, the prescriptions of right reason have two aspects, internal and external. Internally, they constitute the principles of Stoic ethics, which locate all that is good in what conforms to right reason; what is natural for a rational being is to do everything in one's power to promote the common interest—rational harmony in general (C above). This is the goal for which we are equipped as rational beings, and it requires us to develop, as the moral virtues, modes of understanding how we should act so as always to promote the common good. Where the Epicurean retreats into his own community of like-minded friends, the Stoic seeks to transcend the limitations of political society by treating all rational beings, divine and human, as members of a *kosmopolis*, a world community.

Externally, right reason manifests itself in the actual course of events. As individuals, the Stoics reasoned, we find ourselves in a world where much that happens is outside our own control, and we note that fortune's favors (as popularly understood) are frequently dispensed without regard to a person's needs or deserts. This external dimension, however, is god's business, not our concern. To us it is morally indifferent. Yet, as Cleanthes' Hymn to Zeus declares, god sees to it in the end that everything works out for the best, even "what bad men do in their folly." Right reason, then, requires us to conform ourselves to god by doing all *we* can to partner him in promoting rational harmony. We do this both by initiating well-reasoned actions ourselves and by acquiescing in every situation that we are powerless to change for the better. Thus we will "flow smoothly through life."

Such is the essence of the third proposition stated above: "the human being's function is to live in harmony with god." Its converse, as Cleanthes' Hymn makes plain, is making purely private and irrational things one's objective—fame, wealth, relaxation, sexual pleasure. Such things, according to the Stoics' evaluation, are neither good nor bad in themselves. But the pursuit of them as supremely worthwhile is judged to be a gross failure of understanding, a denial of our specifically human nature, a misrepresentation of what our "guardian spirit" (see A and B above), that is, the internal voice of right reason, would have us regard as good.

Stoic theology is thus a bold attempt to reconcile a demanding moral code with an insistence that the world, as we find it, is the best that a benevolent deity can provide. That cosmic evil, or apparent evil, outside the human domain troubled the Stoics is clear, but we have no room here to explore their various solutions or the objections of their critics.[24] Such wholehearted commitment to divine providence seemed naïve or worse to ancient skeptics and Epicureans. What should be stressed here is that Stoicism shows no complacence toward the injuries that people do to each other. It is also pertinent to observe that, for better or worse, we moderns have found it possible to manipulate the external environment—nonhuman nature, that is—in ways the Stoics could never have imagined. The precariousness of life in antiquity will have lent cogency to a philosophy

which taught that pain and suffering, though not willed by god, are un-
avoidable parts of the good he promotes in nature as a whole. Whether we
call it emotional appeal or spiritual enlightenment, Stoicism reveals its
special blend of religion and humanity in the words of the ex-slave and
Stoic teacher Epictetus and the emperor Marcus Aurelius. First Epictetus:

> Having received everything and your own self, from another, are you vexed
> and do you blame the donor if he takes something away from you? Who are
> you and for what purpose did you come? Was it not god who brought you
> in? Did he not show you the light? Did he not give you fellow-workers, and
> senses, and reason? And as what did he bring you in? Was it not as someone
> mortal? Was it not as one to live with the endowment of a little flesh, and
> to share for a little in his procession and festival? Are you not willing, then,
> for as long as it is granted you, to observe the procession and the festival,
> and then, when he brings you out, to go with reverence and thanks for what
> you have heard and seen? (*Discourses* 4.1.104–5)

And now Marcus Aurelius:

> First thing in the morning, say to yourself: I shall encounter these sorts of
> people—meddlesome, ungrateful, violent, cunning, spiteful, unsociable.
> They have all got like this through ignorance of what is good and bad. But
> I, who have seen that beauty is the nature of the good and ugliness the nature
> of the bad, and that the wrongdoer's nature is akin to me . . . sharing with
> me intelligence and a divine portion, I cannot be harmed by any of them—
> for no one involves me in ugliness—nor can I be angry with my kinsman
> or hate him. We were born to work together, like teeth or hands or eyelids,
> or upper and lower rows of teeth. So it is contrary to nature to act against
> one another; and that is how we act when we are vexed or turn our back.
> (*Meditations* 2.1)

Notes

1. Quoting Epicurus (*Epicurea* 221, Usener).
2. See especially Lucretius *De rerum natura* 5.1–54.
3. The evidence on this and its significance have been very interestingly explored
by B. Frisher in *The Sculpted Word*.
4. See *Key Doctrines* (*Kyriai doxai*) 5, 7, 10, 13; Lucretius *De rerum natura* 2.1–60;
5.1105–57 etc.
5. This theme is a constant one in Lucretius and is well discussed by D. Konstan
in *Some Aspects of Epicurean Psychology*.
6. Cf. *Vatican Saying* 52: "Friendship dances round the world announcing to us all
that we should wake up and felicitate one another."
7. For a selection of the evidence, see Lucretius *De rerum natura* 2.1052–57,
1077–1104; 5.156–207, 218–34; Cicero *De natura deorum* 1.18–23.
8. See A. A. Long, "Chance and Natural Law in Epicureanism," *Phronesis* 22 (1977)
63–68.

9. Note its primary position in this collection of Epicurus's fundamental maxims; his followers would know these by heart.

10. Reporting Epicurean views.

11. Cf. Epicurus *Letter to Herodotus* 76–77.

12. The evidence on this is well discussed by A.-J. Festugière in *Epicurus and His Gods.*

13. I read "flows to the gods" (*ad deos adfluat*) with the majority of manuscripts and not "flows to us" (*ad nos adfluat*), the commonly accepted emendation by Lambinus. This interpretation of the gods' nature will be defended at length in A. A. Long and D. N. Sedley, *The Hellenistic Philosophers.* I gratefully acknowledge Dr. Sedley's work, and he deserves the chief credit for developing this interpretation.

14. Lucretius *De rerum natura* 4.722–822; Sextus Empiricus *Against the professors* 3.40.

15. Most of the evidence comes from fragmentary remains of the Epicurean Philodemus, first century B.C.

16. Quoting Epicurus.

17. G. Hegel, *Lectures on the History of Philosophy,* ed. and trans. E. S. Haldane and F. H. Simpson (New York: Humanities Press, 1955) 2:304–6. Even Plato has Socrates in the *Phaedrus* say: "What is immortal does not have its source in a single reasoned discourse, but we *fashion* god as an immortal creature, not having seen him nor conceived of him adequately" (246C).

18. See Long, "Soul and Body in Stoicism," *Phronesis* 27 (1982) 34–57.

19. See J. Mansfeld, "Providence and the Destruction of the Universe in Stoic Thought," in *Studies in Hellenistic Religions,* ed. M. J. Vermaseren, 129–88.

20. See Mansfeld, "Resurrection added: The Interpretatio Christiana of a Stoic Doctrine," *Vigiliae Christianae* 37 (1983) 218–33; and for a brief but judicious assessment of the suitability of Stoic thought for Christians, see F. H. Sandbach, *The Stoics,* 177–78.

21. For an interesting, though partly hostile, discussion, see Augustine *City of God* 14.8.

22. The text is quoted in Stobaeus, *Anthologium* 1:25–27.

23. The Homeric Zeus had complained that humans blame the gods for troubles their own wrongdoing brings upon them (*Odyssey* 1.32–34.

24. See Long, "The Stoic Concept of Evil," *Philosophical Quarterly* 18 (1968) 329–43.

Bibliography

Editions

Cicero. *De natura deorum.* Edited by Wilhelm Ax. Leipzig: Teubner, 1933.

Diogenes Laertius. *Vitae philosophorum.* Edited by H. S. Long. Oxford: University Press, 1964.

Diogenes of Oenoanda. Edited by C. W. Chilton. Leipzig: Teubner, 1967.

Epictetus. Edited by H. Schenkl. Leipzig: Teubner, 1916.

Epicurea. Edited by H. Usener. Reprint. Stuttgart: Teubner, 1966.

Epicurus. *Letters* etc. See Diogenes Laertius.

Lucretius. Edited by C. Bailey. Oxford: University Press, 1947.

Marcus Aurelius. *Meditations.* Edited by A. S. L. Farquharson. Oxford: University Press, 1944.

Plutarch. *Moralia* 13.2. Edited by H. Cherniss. Loeb Classical Library. Cambridge, MA: Harvard University Press, 1975.

Sextus Empiricus. *Against the professors.* Edited by R. G. Bury. Loeb Classical Library, vol. 4. Cambridge, MA: Harvard University Press, 1949.

Stobaeus. *Anthologium.* Edited by K. Wachsmuth, vol. 1. Reprint. Berlin: Weidmann, 1974.

SVF

Translations

Most of the translations in this article are by D. N. Sedley or myself and will be found with full discussion in our forthcoming work; the remainder are my own.

Long, A. A., and D. N. Sedley. *The Hellenistic Philosophers.* 2 vols. Cambridge: University Press.

Modern Works

Bailey, C. *The Greek Atomists and Epicurus.* Oxford: University Press, 1926.

Dragona-Monachou, Myrto. *The Stoic Arguments for the Existence and the Providence of the Gods.* Athens: National and Capodistrian University of Athens, 1976.

Festugière, A.-J. *Epicurus and His Gods.* Translated by C. W. Chilton. Oxford: University Press, 1955.

Frischer, Bernard. *The Sculpted Word: Epicureanism and Philosophical Recruitment in Ancient Greece.* Berkeley and Los Angeles, University of California Press, 1982.

Konstan, D. *Some Aspects of Epicurean Psychology.* Leiden: Brill, 1973.

Long, A. A. "Chance and Natural Law in Epicureanism." *Phronesis* 22 (1977) 63–68.

———. *Hellenistic Philosophy.* New York: Scribner, 1974.

———. "Soul and Body in Stoicism." *Phronesis* 27 (1982) 34–57.

———. "The Stoic Concept of Evil." *Philosophical Quarterly* 18 (1968) 329–43.

Mansfeld, J. "Providence and the Destruction of the Universe in Stoic Thought." In *Studies in Hellenistic Religions,* 129–88. Edited by M. J. Vermaseren. Leiden: Brill, 1979.

———. "Resurrection added: The Interpretatio Christiana of a Stoic Doctrine." *Vigiliae Christianae* 37 (1983) 218–33.

Merlan, Philip. *Studies in Epicurus and Aristotle.* Wiesbaden: Harrassowitz, 1960.

Rist, J. M. *Stoic Philosophy.* Cambridge: University Press, 1969.

———. *Epicurus: An Introduction.* Cambridge: University Press, 1972.

Sandbach, F. H. *The Stoics.* New York: Norton, 1975.

Schofield, M. "Preconception, Argument and God." In *Doubt and Dogmatism: Studies in Hellenistic Epistemology,* 283–308. Edited by M. Schofield, M. Burnyeat, and J. Barnes. Oxford: University Press, 1980.

7

Roman Spirituality

JOHN PINSENT

I N HIS *Marius the Epicurean,* Walter Pater, the Oxford don and essayist,
gives a somewhat idealized account entitled "The religion of Numa,"
the first chapter of the spiritual odyssey of his hero, which ends with
his death just before conversion to Christianity.[1] The book is set in the
reign of the emperor Marcus Aurelius (A.D. 161–180), whose own *Meditations* have been described by E. R. Dodds as "a breviary for contemplatives
throughout the centuries."[2] Pater set it at that time because, he told a friend,
"that age and our own have much in common—many difficulties and
hopes," and the book was intended "to show the necessity of religion."[3]

Early Roman Religion

Pater's chapter affords a good starting point for an examination of Roman
spirituality, because its attitude to the earliest known Roman religion, that
traditionally attributed to the second king of Rome, Numa Pompilius, is
very similar not only to that of the Antonine period, in which the book
is set, but also to that of the Augustan. Augustus, taking power at the end
of a period of a hundred years of civil war and strife (133–31 B.C.), instituted
a program of moral and social reform deliberately intended to restore the
earlier "pristine virtues" of a Rome still uncorrupted by foreign influences.

The Romans themselves were very conscious of the theme of degeneration, a process sometimes linked with the Etruscan theory of *saecula,* "centuries," periods of time the length of which was determined by the death
of the last person who had been alive at the celebration of the last *saeculum.*
The historian Sallust, writing under Caesar at the end of his own political
career in the 40s B.C., dates the beginning of the decline to the destruction
of Carthage, *aemula imperi Romani,* "rival of Roman rule," in 146 B.C.
Then, he says,

Fortune began to be cruel, and to mix up everything. Those who had easily borne labors, dangers, and events both uncertain and harsh, found peace and riches, things elsewhere to be desired, a burden and a misery. So the desire grew, first for money, then for empire: that was, as it were, the raw material of all evils. For greed subverted trust, honesty, and the other good arts; instead, it taught them pride, cruelty, to neglect the gods, and to consider that everything had its price. (*Catiline* 10.1–4)

The presence of the "neglect of the gods," "trust," and "honesty" in this list is significant. Patriotism and morality are elements in Roman spirituality as important as the performance of ritual.

The destruction of Carthage was continually urged by that prime example of pristine Roman virtue, the elder Cato (234–149 B.C.), called Censorius rather from holding the office of censor in 184 B.C. than from the severity with which he performed it. His words have become proverbial: *delenda est Carthago*, "Carthage must be destroyed." This was finally done in 146 B.C., after Cato's death and in the same year Greece was finally captured and Corinth destroyed. "Greece," as Horace puts it, "taken captive herself took captive her fierce conqueror, and brought the arts into rural Latium" (*Epistles* 2.156–57).

The Greek influence on Roman culture, both direct and earlier mediated through Etruria, was in fact earlier than the conquest of Greece and has been traced in the earliest religion of Rome. Even the literary and intellectual influence, of which Horace is primarily speaking, goes back to the period of the Punic Wars (262–201 B.C.). But Horace's words may be used to indicate the degree of Greek influence on especially the literary expression of Roman religious feeling. Almost all our sources are literary. It is therefore difficult to disentangle the specifically Roman elements of spirituality.

Horace himself, in the context quoted, which is that of the development of Roman drama, paints the same idyllic picture of "the religion of Numa" as Pater does.

The early farmers, brave men and blest with a little, after the grain was stored, refreshing in festival season their bodies and their very spirits, which endured hard things in hope of their end, together with their children and their wives, who used to share their labor, used to propitiate Tellus [Earth] with a pig and Silvanus [god of the woods] with milk, and, with flowers and wine, the Genius that is mindful of the brevity of life. (*Epistles* 2.139–44)

The truth that lies behind this idealized account of early Roman religion is less easy to discover. The Romans were obsessively tenacious of precedent and obsessively concerned that a ritual be performed correctly in every detail and in the exact words prescribed. In a number of bronze sheets from the Italian town of Iguvium in Umbria (the modern Gubbio), the precise words of prayers are recorded, together with the instruction that if a mistake is made, the prayer must be started again from the beginning. Similarly, the words of an ancient prayer have been preserved in an inscription that records the activities in A.D. 218 of the Arval Brethren, a Roman religious college. The language of the prayer is so obscure that it has been used to provide information about the early Latin language.

But the details of this case well illustrate the difficulties faced by the student of Roman religion, which have been brought out by Ronald Syme, who speaks of "the slender and fragile foundations on which adepts of Roman religion construct their edifices."[4] For the prayer, or hymn, is first recorded for 29 May A.D. 218, as has been noted. Activities of these Arval Brethren, *fratres arvales*, "field brothers," are attested earlier, notably under the emperor Domitian (A.D. 81–96), but the college had been revived and perhaps reorganized by Augustus, probably in 29 B.C. or, as Syme puts it, "revived, and all but invented."[5] Earlier still, they were known to the antiquarian Varro, active under Caesar in the 40s B.C. He describes them as those *qui sacra publica faciunt propterea ut fruges ferant arua*, "who perform public rites for this reason, that the fields may bear fruit," and gives them an etymology, *a ferendo et aruis*, "from bearing and fields," which suggests that he may have wanted to take *fratres* not as "brothers" but as connected with "bearing" and the whole phrase perhaps as "field bearers" (*On the Latin Language* 5.85).

But total skepticism such as that of Syme about the antiquity of this sacred college may be excessive. It may be accepted that it did go back to a period in Roman history when Rome was still primarily an agricultural community. The antiquity of the hymn is a different matter, though it may in origin be older than the written version. Some scholars have found Greek influence in its form, but this, either direct or through the Etruscans, would not have been impossible in the late sixth or early fifth century B.C., by which time writing was sufficiently attested in Rome.

The case of the hymn of the Arval Brethren has been considered in some detail because of the two points that it well illustrates. One is the obsessive importance which the Romans attached to ritual and the conservative tenacity with which they preserved it. The other is the role of antiquarianism in the preservation of old forms of ritual and language, in its interpretation, and, unfortunately, also in its distortion or even invention. The Greek poets and scholars of Alexandria also had antiquarian interests, and their influence was strong on Roman literature of all kinds, so that one potent form of distortion was the adaptation of Greek ritual and legend to the material of Roman religion. Antiquarianism, therefore, is another area in which Greek influence made itself felt in Rome.

These same factors affect also Roman historical writing. Indeed, the first written record of Rome, which can be recovered from its incorporation, more or less modified, imitated, or invented, into later and surviving written histories of Rome, was a record not of historical events themselves but of the ritual actions which those events generated or with which they were associated. There was no separation of church and state in Rome. The annual magistrates had important religious duties, and the priesthoods in the major and minor colleges, such as those of pontiffs and augurs, [6]were held by persons of political importance, and their activities were of direct importance to the Roman state. In particular, the regular performance of the religious duties of the state and immediate reaction to those events and prodigies that indicated divine displeasure, were necessary to ensure the preservation of the *pax deorum,* "peace with the gods," upon which depended the continued prosperity of the Roman state.

There is, therefore, a strong element of patriotism in Roman spirituality, which should neither be discounted nor disapproved of in the light of modern prejudice. Roman religiosity—in Greek *deisidaimonia,* "(excessive) fear of divine powers," "superstition"—was remarked in the ancient world. It contributed to the belief that the Romans were descended, through Aeneas, from the Trojans, whose punctiliousness in due sacrifice is noted once or twice in the *Iliad.* The rationalistic and even cynical Polybius, writing his history of Rome in the second half of the second century B.C. and commenting on this Roman trait, regards it by no means disapprovingly as "a deliberate imposture devised for political reasons by a cunning man" and employed to keep the common people in subjection by "uncertain fears and such dramatic measures" (6.56.6–15).[7]

But this is unfair to the Romans and underestimates the very real contribution made by their religion to the stability and the attractiveness of the Roman state. The extraordinary cohesion of Roman Italy in the face of the invasion of Hannibal in 217 B.C. and its ability to weather the Social War of 90 B.C. (itself in part the manifestation of a desire to become more rather than less Roman) testify to the Roman ability to command the loyalty of the conquered, an ability that later extended to the whole empire. The cult of Rome and of the emperor was the religious expression of this loyalty, which contributed to the remarkable duration of the empire and to the extraordinary hold that it has exercised on the minds of people since its fall. The Holy Roman Empire and the papacy are only two of the institutions that have been considered in some sense heirs and successors of the Roman

Empire. Almost all subsequent imperial powers (with the exception of those in the Far East and in the South American continent) have tended to see themselves in Roman terms.

Virgil and the Secular Games

There was never any doubt in official Roman ideology that Roman success depended on the favor of the gods. This is well exemplified in a prayer from the ritual of the Secular Games, as celebrated in A.D. 204. These games marked the end of an originally Etruscan *saeculum* (of which the definition was given above). The end of one *saeculum* and, perhaps even more important, the beginning of the next were ominous and significant in something of the same way as was the millennium in Christian thinking of the early Middle Ages and in that of some sects today. New emperors, and in particular the first emperor of a new dynasty, liked to celebrate Secular Games in order to mark the new order (the *novus ordo seclorum* to be found on the dollar bill), a new foundation of Rome by a new Romulus—even if to do so involved the type of creative manipulation of chronology at which Roman historians were so adept.

Augustus held such a celebration, perhaps originally intended for 23 B.C., and Virgil's "Messianic Eclogue" may well have been taken to refer to it, even though it originally expressed the longing for peace at the time of the apparent reconciliation of Octavian and Antony in 40 B.C. Its imagery is full of religious feeling, and Hebrew influence has even been suggested. Its Christian interpretation accounts for the presence of the Sibyls, the pagan prophets, along with the Hebrew prophets in the frescoes of the Sistine Chapel.

> The last age now comes of the Cumaean song.
> A great order of centuries is born afresh,
> Now the Virgin, too, returns, there return the kingdoms of Saturn,
> Now a new progeny is sent down from high heaven.
> Only do you, when the boy is born for whom first the iron
> Race shall cease, and that of gold arise for the whole world,
> Be favorable, chaste Lucina: already your Apollo reigns.
> (Virgil *Eclogues* 4.4–10)

These pregnant lines require some explanation before we return to the later celebration of the Secular Games and the prayer preserved from their ritual.

The Cumaean song is that of the Sibyl of Cumae, near Naples, the best known of the ten Sibyls from all over the Mediterranean world, listed by Varro.[8] She is the one who led Aeneas to the underworld with the golden bough in Virgil's *Aeneid* 6 and will be known to readers of T. S. Eliot's

Wasteland from the epigraph quoted from the *Satyricon* of Petronius, in which Trimalchio says:

> I myself saw with my own eyes the Sibyl at Cumae hanging in a little jar, and when the children used to say to her [in Greek], "Sibyl, what do you want?" she used to reply, "I want to die." (48.8)

The reference to the virgin is to Justice. In Hesiod's original version of the ages (Gold, Silver, Bronze, and Iron, with the Age of the Heroes of Troy and Thebes inserted between the Bronze and the Iron), Shame and Indignation (*Aidōs* and *Nemesis*) depart to Olympus, unable to bear the horrors of the Age of Iron (Hesiod *Works and Days* 109–201, esp. 197–201). Saturn was an old Italian agricultural deity identified with the Greek Kronos, under whom, for Hesiod, the people of the Age of Gold lived. In some versions, when Kronos was overthrown by Zeus, an event that may have marked the end of the Age of Gold, he went to the west, to the Islands of the Blest, and Italy was therefore sometimes known as Saturnia.[9] So the golden age, of which Virgil foresees the return, had once been located in Italy!

Here the Cumaean is the tenth Sibyl and presides over the last of the ten *saecula* which make up the "great order of centuries," at the end of which the Age of Gold returns, presided over by the newborn babe, whoever he was supposed to be. Later he was probably identified as Augustus, who would also have been seen in the Apollo of the last line of the quotation. Virgil later "prophesied" in the *Aeneid,* when Anchises is showing his descendants to Aeneas in the underworld:

> This man, this is Augustus Caesar, whom you often hear promised to you, the race of a god, who will found the golden centuries again for Latium, through the fields once ruled by Saturn. (6.791–94)

Lucina is the old Italian goddess of childbirth, who brings children into the light, *luc-*. She was originally identified with Juno, but later, and so probably here, with Diana, since her Greek equivalent, Eilithyia, was identified or associated with Artemis.

Virgil's lines thus, like a great deal of Roman religious poetry and thinking, combine the old Italian religion with Greek literary identifications and employ them in the patriotic celebration of the Roman state. It was some later lines that suggested the messianic prophecies of Isaiah:

> Of their own accord the she-goats will bring back home their udders distended with milk, nor will the herds fear great lions. Of its own accord your cradle will pour out alluring flowers. The serpent, too, shall die, and the deceitful plant of poison shall die also; instead Assyrian balsam shall grow everywhere. (Virgil *Eclogues* 4.21–25)

This, together with the references to a virgin and child and to a new order, helped to gain Virgil a reputation in the Middle Ages as a "soul naturally Christian" (Tertullian *Apology* 17.6)[10] and led to his appearance as Dante's guide in Purgatory. Milton's "Ode on the Morning of Christ's Nativity" is also influenced by Virgil, especially in the following lines:

> For, if such holy song,
> Enwrap our Fancy long,
> Time will run back and fetch the age of gold.

and

> Yea, truth and justice then
> Will down return to men,
> Orb'd in a rainbow. . . .
>
> (105–7, 113–15)

Enough has been said to illustrate the enduring potency of the Roman religious concept of the *saeculum*. L. Septimius Severus, emperor from A.D. 193 to 211, had, like Augustus, dynastic ambitions. He decided to hold a celebration of the Secular Games in A.D. 204 in furtherance of these ambitions to mark the new order that he too hoped to have founded. As Augustus had done, he had extensive records of the ceremony engraved on stone. Fragments of these have survived, the most recent of which was discovered in 1930. From these fragments one of the prayers can be restored. It was repeated on three nights to seven different divinities:

> As it has been written in these books for you, for these reasons, and that it may be better for the Roman people, the Quirites, so may the rite be performed for you [with specified victims and offerings]. I ask and pray you that, as you have increased the sovereignty and the majesty of the Roman people of Quirites, at war and at home, and as the Latin has always been submissive, you may grant to the Roman people, the Quirites, eternal safety, victory, and health, and that you may favor the Roman people of Quirites and the legions of the Roman people of Quirites, and may keep safe the common wealth of the Roman people of Quirites, and may willingly be propitious to the Roman people of Quirites, to the college of Fifteen, and to me, my house, and my family, and that you may be acceptors of this sacrifice.[11]

"Those books" are the Sibylline Books, books of oracles in Greek verse. They were consulted in emergency by a special college of fifteen priests. The story was that nine books were offered to L. Tarquinius Priscus, the fifth king of Rome, by a Sibyl, who, when he refused them, came back with first six, and then three, still at the same price, which finally convinced him of their value (Dionysius of Halicarnassus 4.62.1–6). "Quirites" was the earlier name of the *Roma-ni*, the people of the city of Rome. It survived in official and ritual contexts such as this. It may mean "the men banded together." "The Latins," the first speakers of the language known by their name, were the dwellers in the "broad land" (*lătus*), the coastal plain that runs southeast from Rome. The name at first applied only to those who lived between the Tiber and the Alban hills. The Latins were early allied to the Romans and were effectively dominated by them. At least from 338 B.C. they held a specially privileged position among Roman allies and in Roman law. Their appearance in this prayer reflects their importance to Rome even before 338 B.C., by which time they were increasingly resentful of Roman control. The phrase "as the Latin has always been submissive" is reflected in a version of a Sibylline oracle instructing the Romans to hold a celebration of the Secular Games, in order to bring back to their allegiance Latins who had revolted. The oracle is preserved by Phlegon of Tralles, a freedman of the emperor Hadrian (emperor A.D. 117–138), in an essay on the long-lived (as Sibyls were). It ends thus:

> And for you, all of Italy's land and all that of the Latins will have your yoke on its neck, always under your scepter.[12]

This suits a celebration of the Secular Games in 348 B.C., for which there is some evidence, since the Latins were then in revolt. The prayer is fully preserved for the games of A.D. 204 but may reasonably be restored in what survives of the record of the Augustan games of 17 B.C. But neither it nor the oracle can safely be considered a survival from 348 B.C. Both are probably the creation of Augustan antiquarians. Nonetheless, the ritual of the Secular Games does illustrate very well two of the strongest elements in Roman spirituality. The first of these is patriotism and the belief that the survival and success of the Roman state did depend upon right relations with the gods. The second is a strong sense of the living past, linked with the present by the continuation of age-old ceremonies, even if these had to be recovered and even at times "improved" by antiquarian studies.

Cicero, Lucretius, and Greek Philosophy

Cicero was a "new man," who made his way in Roman politics from the Italian town of Arpinum, at first by his skill in oratory and as a pleader in the lawcourts. He became consul in 63 B.C. and played a major role in politics for the next twenty years. This was the period of the civil wars between Pompey and Caesar, which ended in the dictatorship of the latter. Cicero then withdrew into private life and wrote a number of philosophical and religious works that express the attitude of the well-educated and cultivated Roman of the end of the republic. Cicero was well aware of the importance of the old religious practices in the life of the Roman state and made a clear distinction between superstition and religion.

In his book *On the Nature of the Gods* (*De natura deorum*), written in 45 B.C., he bases the distinction on some doubtful etymology.

> Those who used to pray for whole days, and used to sacrifice, so that their children might be survivors of them (*superstites*), were called superstitious, which name afterwards extended more widely. But those who carefully re-considered all things which belonged to the worship of the gods, and, as it were, re-read them, were said to be religious, from re-reading (*relegendo*). . . . So it was brought about that, of the words "superstitious" and "religious," that one was the name of a defect and one of a merit. (2.72)

The word *superstitio* is indeed connected with "survival," but not, perhaps, in the sense of an outmoded belief that survives among the ignorant or as a matter simply of practice, like not walking under a ladder. It may rather have meant that which survives, or which causes to survive, by reason of its superiority in magic or in divination. But the word was used pejoratively, as Cicero says, by the practitioners of *religio,* for which also there is an alternative etymology that connects it with the word for "binding," *religare.* If this is correct, religion is concerned with the links that bind humanity and the gods.[13]

How seriously Cicero himself took the distinction can be seen from his next book, *On Divination,* written in 44 B.C. In this dialogue he speaks in his own name and actually refers to the passage just quoted.

> So let this divination by dreams also be driven off, equally with the other kinds. For, that we may speak truly, superstition, spread through the nations, has oppressed the minds of nearly all, and taken possession of the weakness of men. That was also said in those books which are on the nature of the gods, and in this discussion we have argued it most of all. For we have thought that we will be of great service, both to ourselves and to our fellow citizens, if we have got rid of it completely. Nor really—for I want this to be carefully understood—if superstition must be done away with, is religion therefore done away with also. For it is the part of a wise man to preserve the institutions of our ancestors, by rites and ceremonies that must be retained. Also the beauty of the world, and the order of the heavenly bodies, compels the confession that there is some surpassing and eternal nature, and that it must be looked up to and admired by human kind. (2.148)

In this eloquent statement of his own beliefs, Cicero not only exhibits his own appreciation of the importance of the old religious practices but also demonstrates what he has added to his spirituality from the influence of Greek philosophy. His reasoning appears to be as follows: the natural order proves the existence of the divine; the historical gods of the Romans and others have been derived from a misunderstanding of what that order really

11. Dionysios, the Seasons, and Other Figures. Roman sarcophagus. Ca. 220-230 A.D.

is. In his book *On the Nature of the Gods,* just before the passage already quoted on superstition, Cicero says:

> Do you see, therefore, how from natural things, well and usefully discovered, the reason has been drawn to fabricated and invented gods? And this has begotten false opinions, confused errors, and superstitions that are almost old wives tales. (2.70)

These words are put into the mouth of Quintus Lucilius Balbus, who has been expounding the Stoic doctrine that the popular gods are "either names for benefits received from the Gods (1), or personified virtues and passions (2), or the spirits of departed benefactors (3), or personified forces of nature (4)."[14]

Nonetheless, he seems to argue, we may approve those religious ceremonies which have the sanction of age (and are also socially useful, though he does not make this explicit). We may do so even though those who do not know better direct those ceremonies toward inferior objects that only dimly reflect what is truly divine. His attitude is not unlike that of those modern Anglicans, Episcopalians, or Roman Catholics—and even of some whose religious views are less well defined—who continue to support the use of Cranmer's prayer book or of the Latin liturgy for the not-entirely-discreditable reason (however much it upsets theologians) that these familiar forms have acquired a charge of religious emotion that is not affected by the difficulty or unintelligibility of the text.

In his book *On Divination,* Cicero's vehemence against superstition continues with these words:

> And therefore, as religion also must be propagated, when it is joined with knowledge of nature, so must all the roots of superstition be cast out. For superstition presses on and attacks, and wherever you turn yourself, it pursues you, whether you sacrifice, or watch for a bird, if you see a Chaldean or an interpreter of entrails, if there is thunder or lightning, if something is struck from heaven, or if something like a portent is either born or happens. Since one or another of these things must necessarily happen most of the time, one is never allowed to rest with a quiet mind. (2.149)

This throws some light on the general religious climate of the late republic, from say 60 B.C. to 40 B.C. It also helps to explain why some Romans of the time were attracted to Epicureanism, which was in practice a non-religious philosophy though not an atheistic one. For Epicurus, the fact that human beings see gods in visions and in dreams proves that gods do exist—somewhere. It may account also for the religious tone of the poem of T. Lucretius Carus, *On the Nature of Things (De rerum natura),* which expounds the philosophy of Epicurus. Indeed, some of the words of Cicero, when he is himself expounding the Epicurean doctrine through the mouth of Gaius Velleius in *On the Nature of the Gods,* are very reminiscent of Lucretius. We know that Cicero partly approved of the work of Lucretius, for he says of the poem, when writing to his brother Quintus in 54 B.C., "Lucretius's poems are as you write of them: they have many flashes of genius, yet much also of art" (*Letters to His Brother Quintus* 2.9.3). The words in question are the following:

> Freed by Epicurus from these terrors [those of divination], and claimed for freedom, as if from slavery, we do not fear those who, we understand, neither make for themselves any difficulty, nor seek it for another, and in a pure and holy manner we worship nature, that excels and surpasses all. (Cicero *On the Nature of the Gods* 1.56)

With these words we may compare those in which, at the beginning of the poem after his invocation of Venus, Lucretius describes what Epicurus had done for men, though he does not name him but simply calls him "a Greek man."

> When human life lay foully before one's eyes, oppressed upon the earth under a heavy weight of religion, which showed its head from the regions of heaven, threatening mortals with horrible aspect from above, first a Greek man dared to lift mortal eyes against it, and first dared to oppose it. Neither the reputation of the gods, nor their lightnings, nor heaven itself with its threatening murmur curbed him, but the more thereby provoked the keen courage of his mind, to want to be the first to break open the closed bolts of nature's doors. Therefore the lively force of his mind won through, and proceeded far beyond the flaming walls of the world, and in mind and spirit traversed the whole immeasurable space. From there, as victor, he brings us back the knowledge of what can arise and what cannot, and, finally, by what principle the power of each thing is limited, and its boundary mark fixed deep. (Lucretius *On the Nature of Things* 1.62–77)

This is the language of religion and poetry rather than of philosophy. So are the terms in which he again addresses Epicurus at the beginning of subsequent books, but again he follows the convention of Latin didactic poetry and never addresses such a controversial historical figure by name. In book 3 he apostrophizes him in these words:

> You, who first were able to raise up in the darkness so clear a light, and to illuminate the advantages of life, it is you I follow, ornament of the Greek race, and in your prints I place the tracks made by my feet, not so much wanting to strive with you, as because, for love, I am eager to imitate you. . . . You are my father, the finder-out of things, you provide us with paternal precepts, and from your pages, famous one, as bees in flowery glades sip up what they can, so we in the same way feed on all your golden words,

for gold they are, and always most deserving of perpetual life. (Lucretius *On the Nature of Things* 3.1-6, 9-13)

Lucretius's language is even more extreme at the beginning of book 5. He starts by doubting whether any mortal is able to write poetry in a manner worthy of the majesty of the subject or to praise Epicurus as he deserves. He continues:

> For if, as the discovered majesty of things itself demands, one must speak out, he was a god, a god, renowned Memmius [*sic*] [Gaius Mummius, an opponent of Caesar in 58 B.C., and Lucretius's patron], who first found out that principle of life, which is now called wisdom, and who, by his art, saved life from such great waves and such darkness, and set it in such calm, clear light. (Lucretius *On the Nature of Things* 5.7-12)

He then, although an Epicurean, compares Epicurus with those gods who provided humans with benefits. It was a Stoic doctrine that gods were "the spirits of departed benefactors."[15] He compares him also with the great Stoic hero and exemplar Hercules, who purged the earth of monsters, as the mind is full of fears and worries, which must also be purged.

> He, therefore, who overcame all these things, and expelled them from our minds by his words, and not by arms, surely it will be fitting that this man be thought worthy to be in the number of the gods. (Lucretius *On the Nature of Things* 5.49-51)

Similar words are used at the beginning of book 6, in which the praise of Epicurus is linked with the traditional praise of Athens as source of the knowledge of agriculture. In a myth connected with the Eleusinian Mysteries, the goddess Demeter was said to have given this knowledge to Triptolemus, the son of the king of Athens.

> Athens, of famous name, first gave to wretched mortals fruitful produce, and refreshed their lives, and proposed laws, and Athens also first gave us the sweet consolations of life, when she bore a man found to have such a heart, that he once poured out everything from a truth-telling mouth. And although he is now dead, because of the divine things he discovered, his glory is spread abroad from of old, and carried to heaven. (Lucretius *On the Nature of Things* 6.1-8)

All these passages are a poetic and heightened version of what Cicero expressed more moderately and prosaically in his books *On the Nature of the Gods* and *On Divination*, in the passages already quoted. The only difference is that Cicero calls "superstition" what Lucretius calls "religion." As a public figure, and one more Erastian in temperament, Cicero found a value and even a pleasure in the ritual performance of actions that had been sanctified by immemorial usage. It is not always proper to deny to that feeling the name of spirituality.

But Cicero and Lucretius are alike in finding the satisfaction of the higher elements in their spiritual nature, not in the practice of the traditional religion of the Roman state but in philosophy. Lucretius at least gave to philosophy a spiritual tone that may properly be described as religious, as the passages quoted from his poem demonstrate. Much indeed of what we call religion and spirituality is to be found in the ancient world not in the practice of the state cults nor even, perhaps, at least among the educated, in what are generically known as mystery religions, but in philosophy. The phenomenon can be traced back to Greek culture, perhaps as far as to Xenophanes' criticisms of the moral qualities of the Homeric gods. Certainly, in the myths of Plato, and notably in that of the *Phaedrus*, the gods appear as little more than ideal men. They are capable, indeed, as men are not, of completing without mishap the procession beyond the rim of heaven, in contemplation of the true reality, but they are in no way essentially different from them. The qualities that in developed religions are ascribed to the deity are in Plato those of the Form of the Good, and in Stoicism and in Epicureanism they are ascribed to Nature.

This dissatisfaction with what had happened to the traditional religion of Rome in the last century of the republic may reflect more than its degeneration into superstitious practice of the kind that offended both Cicero and Lucretius. It may reflect also the political insecurity of the times, just as the similar insecurity of the Hellenistic kingdoms of the third century B.C. contributed to the rise of the philosophies of Stoicism and Epicureanism. These philosophies provided a more effective and rational defense against the vicissitudes of fortune than did the superstitious practices that were intended to give the same kind of consolation to those whose approach was less dauntingly intellectual. Augustus's revival of the traditional state religion is, as it were, the ideological side of a coin, the obverse of which is his provision of a political stability, so much longed for and so sincerely praised by both Horace and Virgil.

Catullus

Not every poet of the Roman republic had the same elevated sense of spirituality as had Lucretius. Gaius Valerius Catullus, a Roman from Verona in northern Italy, is best known for his poems to "Lesbia," which seem, to modern readers, to chronicle in passionately personal poetry the course of a stormy love affair. These twenty-five poems are not the first place one would think of looking for expressions of Roman spirituality. Yet Catullus was a Roman, and the "Lesbia" poems are only a quarter of his surviving output. He apparently died young, at about the age of thirty. He had not formally entered on the official career that might have been his. He had only accompanied his patron Mummius (who was also the patron of Lucretius) to Bithynia in Asia Minor in 57 B.C.

Yet in two of his love poems to Lesbia, Catullus gives expression to a distinctive characteristic of Roman spirituality—the quality which the Romans called *pietas*. Our word "piety" is derived from that Latin word, which has, however, a somewhat different meaning. It is well known as the adjective *pius,* regularly applied to Aeneas by Virgil. T. F. Higham quotes "a lecturer," who "once informed undergraduates: 'We translate it "good," but we understand by it "Aeneas, that trained liturgiologist."'"[16] It is indeed true that the proper and correct performance of due rituals was an important part of Roman piety, of Roman spirituality. But the word goes further than that and implies the recognition and performance of all due obligations—moral and emotional as well as ritual—to family, friends, country, and indeed to anybody with whom one comes in contact.

Catullus exhibits his recognition of this quality, though he calls it by a different name, in the second line of the poem that is often thought to mark the beginning of his relationship with "Lesbia." It is a translation of a famous poem by Sappho of Lesbos, which partly accounts for the name that Catullus gave the woman. In this poem Sappho describes the emotional and physical effect upon her of seeing a girl sitting opposite a man at a feast and talking to him. Sappho's poem begins:

> That man seems to me to be equal to the gods, who sits opposite you and, from near at hand, listens to you sweetly speaking and laughing desirably. (Sappho 199, Page)

Catullus renders it:

> That man seems to me to be equal to a god, even, if it is permitted, to exceed the gods, who, sitting over against you, again and again sees you, and hears you sweetly laughing. (Catullus 51.1–5)

He has exaggerated Sappho's "equal to the gods" by adding "to exceed the gods," but he qualifies the second phrase with the very Roman words *si fas est,* here translated "if it is permitted." These words bear, as Catullus knew very well and indeed intended that they should bear, the implication that it is not permitted.

The word *fas,* with its negative *nefas,* is a very important concept in the thinking of Roman spirituality, even if its use here by Catullus may, as the lexicons suggest, be what they call "a weakened sense." The ancients connected it with the verb *fari,* "to speak," from which *fatum,* "fate," "that which is (solemnly) said or pronounced," also is derived. But even if "to speak" implies a speaker, the identity, and even the personality, of the putative speaker is left unexpressed, as in so much early Roman religion. Indeed, it may be inexpressible. But *fas* is nonetheless securely located in the religious sphere.

This is the concept that Catullus is employing—and with some understanding of its overtones—in his adaptation of the poem of Sappho. At a later stage of his unfortunate love affair he attempts to console himself by recalling how well he has behaved toward Lesbia, so that he does not deserve the treatment she has given him. Again the language that he uses to describe his conduct is that of Roman piety and morality. Even if there was a convention of using this sort of language metaphorically in erotic poetry, yet his words in this poem do seem rather to be expressive of real spirituality, as he tries to rid himself of what he describes at the end of the poem as "a foul disease":

> I myself want to be fit, and to put off this foul disease.
> O gods, give me back this for my piety.
> (Catullus 76.25–26)

The first four lines of the poem are entirely expressed in the language of morality. The first reference to his "thankless love" comes in the sixth. The poem begins thus:

> If there is any pleasure for a man who recalls his previous good deeds, when he reflects that he is pious, and has not violated a sacred trust (*fides*), nor, in any contract, misused the godhead of the gods for the deceiving of men, many things remain prepared for you, in a long life, Catullus, joys from this thankless love. For whatever things men can say or do good to one another, these were said and done by you. (Catullus 76.1–8)

The oath originally played as large a part in Roman life as it did in Greek. There, indeed, the ability to deceive a person by an oath that was strictly true but from which one might make false inferences was much admired and was ascribed to the infant Hermes in the Homeric hymn to that god. But the oath was early formalized in the Roman legal system, in which some forms of procedure can be seen as developed from contrary asseverations by the two parties. "Lovers' oaths" were proverbial in Latin, and Catullus himself recognizes their unreliability when, in an epigram to Lesbia, he says:

> My woman says that there is nobody she would sooner make love to than me, even if Jupiter himself asked her. So she says. But what a woman says to an eager lover she ought to write in wind and swift water. (Catullus 70)

But the oaths to which Catullus refers in his description of good conduct do not appear to be oaths of this kind. In general, his catalogue of virtues seems as sincere as that of Psalm 15, which includes a similar commendation of him "swears to his own hurt and does not change" (15:4). Indeed, when Catullus refers to Lesbia's words in another poem, he also claims a special quality for his love:

> You used to say once that you knew only Catullus, Lesbia, and that you did not want to have even Jove in my place. Then I loved you, not only as a common man loves a mistress, but as a father loves his sons and sons-in-law. (Catullus 72.1–4)

It is for this reason that it is not entirely paradoxical to cite the love poems of Catullus for a certain constituent of Roman spirituality. There is in Catullus a stronger element of conventional Roman feeling than he is often given credit for. In the marriage song that he wrote for L. Manlius Torquatus (praetor in 49 B.C.) he expresses very traditional sentiments:

> Play as is your pleasure, and within a short time give us children. It is not fitting that such an old name be without children: rather it should always be bred from the same source. I want a little Torquatus, stretching out his soft hands from his mother's bosom, to laugh sweetly at his father with half-gaping lip. May he be like his father Manlius, and be easily recognized even by all who do not know him, and may he show by his features the chastity of his mother. May the praise he gets for having a good mother approve his descent, as the reputation of Penelope's Telemachus remains unparalleled for his, the best of mothers. (Catullus 61.207–22)

Such is the content of Roman *pietas* as it related to women and the family. Even less to some modern taste will be the sentiments Catullus expresses at the end of his second marriage song. That is an imaginative hexameter poem with no particular reference. It owes something to Sappho and to other Greek models:

> And do not you fight, girl, with such a spouse. It is not right to fight with the man to whom your father himself handed you over, your father himself together with your mother, both of whom it is necessary to obey. Your virginity is not wholly your own. It belongs partly to your parents: a third part is your father's, a third part is given to your mother, only a third is yours. Do not fight with those two, who have given their rights over you to their son-in-law, together with your dowry. (Catullus 62.59–65)

Unquestioning obedience to those to whom it is owed, to gods, state, and family, is one of the elements of Roman *pietas*, as it has been an element in the spirituality of other cultures and, indeed, is one part of the Christian inheritance of our time. It was his *pietas*, the loyalty he owed to the gods, to his son, and to the city he was to found, Alba Longa, and to its successor,

Rome, that led Aeneas, in Virgil's poem, to abandon Dido, even though by doing so he becomes a less sympathetic hero to some modern readers and even, perhaps, to Virgil himself.

The Influence of Foreign Cults

Catullus, in that most Roman of his poems, quoted above, came to see his infatuation with Lesbia as a "foul disease." Infatuation, madness (*furor*), and the self-destructive and irrevocable actions into which they can lead their victim are the subjects of another poem of Catullus, which may serve to introduce another element in Roman spirituality—the role in it of foreign cults. Roman religion was never exclusive, and the strong Etruscan and Greek influences on it have already been noted. The absorption of the gods of captured cities and countries was one of the ways in which the Romans linked those cities and countries to themselves. But the introduction, or the unofficial adoption, of foreign cults is sometimes an indication that the traditional state cults were failing to provide their worshipers with the strength and consolation that they needed in a time of stress.

During the Second Punic War, Hannibal invaded Italy in 217 B.C. and inflicted on the Romans a series of major defeats in two years. Though he failed to march on Rome, which he would probably have captured, he did control most of southeast Italy for fourteen years. Toward the end of that period, just before the Roman counterinvasion of Africa, the Sibylline Books were consulted, and an oracle was discovered which stated that "when a foreign-born enemy has brought war into the land of Italy, he could be driven from Italy and conquered if the Idaean mother were carried to Rome" (Livy 29.10.5). The Sibylline Books seem to have been responsible for the not inconsiderable number of imports of foreign gods into Rome from the fifth century B.C. on. Up to this time all such gods had been Greek; their temples had been situated outside the city; and they were worshiped in the Greek manner (*Graeco ritu*), with uncovered head and sometimes with new and less formal ceremonies, which provided the ordinary worshiper with a feeling of personal participation that may sometimes have been lacking in the state cult.

An example is provided by the *lectisternium*, the "strewing of couches," which was first introduced, again at the instance of the Sibylline Books, in 399 B.C., toward the end of the ten-year war with Veii. The ceremony is described by Livy, probably on the basis of an archival religious record:

> The Two Men charged with Performing Rites, when a *lectisternium* was first made in the Roman city, placated Apollo and Latona, Diana and Hercules,

Mercury and Neptune, with three couches strewn as richly as could then be provided, for the period of eight days. The rite was also celebrated privately. They say that in the whole city all comers, known and unknown, were offered hospitality, with open doors and the common provision of everything in the forecourts of the houses. Kind and friendly conversations were held with private enemies. Moderation was exercised in quarrels and lawsuits. In those days, the chains were taken off anybody fettered: religious scruples forbade that those, to whom the gods had already provided help, should be fettered. (Livy 5.13.6–8)

The latter part of this account is derived from the historian L. Calpurnius Piso Frugi, consul in 133 B.C. and censor in 120 B.C. It is therefore better evidence for the Roman spirituality of his own times than for the fourth century B.C. But the general point, that foreign cults provided satisfactions not otherwise available, is certainly valid.

Pessinus in Phrygia was the seat of the Great Mother (*Magna Mater*), Cybele, also identified as Rhea, the wife of Cronos and mother of the gods. It was then in the kingdom of Attalus of Pergamum, with whom the Romans had already had dealings during their war with Philip V of Macedon, which ended in 204 B.C. The introduction of the cult of the Great Mother to Rome was, therefore, also a way of cementing relations between Rome and Pergamum, always her firmest ally in Asia Minor. The whole story of the introduction of the cult has, in fact, strong political overtones and illustrates the manipulative element in the Roman state religion, which is one of its least spiritual traits.

The goddess was worshiped at Pessinus in the form of a black stone which had fallen from heaven. This stone or a second one was sent to Rome and set up in a temple on the Palatine hill. Cybele had a consort, Attis, who castrated himself in her service and perhaps originally died for her annually, like Adonis and other "dying gods." Her priests, the Galli, were similarly eunuchs, and no Roman citizen was permitted to serve as one. The Roman praetors celebrated in her honor the Great Games, the Megalesia (Greek *megalē*, "great"), on 4 April, but the procession in honor of the goddess was entirely a foreign matter.

It evidently fascinated the Romans, from whose spirituality the ecstatic element was notably lacking. Lucretius also describes the ceremony, though he prefaces his account with the words "old learned poets of the Greeks have sung of her," which may be an indication that he is following, or even translating, a Greek poem. He identifies the goddess with the earth and gives moralizing interpretations of the ritual (here omitted). His account, therefore, can only with caution be used as a description of what actually

12. Man and Woman with Winged Demon. Etruscan red-figured skyphos (side A). 4th century B.C.

happened at Rome. Nonetheless it does give some indication of elements of spiritual emotion notably lacking from the regular state cults.

> From her seat in a chariot she drives twin-yoked lions . . . and they have set a walled crown round the top of her head . . . and, endowed with these devices, the image of the divine mother is now carried in a frightening manner through great lands. Different peoples, by ancient custom of their rites, call her the Idaean mother, and give her Phrygian bands as companions. . . . They assign to her Galli. . . . Tight drums thunder to the palms of hands, and concave cymbals in a circle, and horns threaten with harsh-sounding song. Hollow pipes stir up the mind with Phrygian tunes, and they carry weapons before her in token of their violent madness, which can frighten ungrateful hearts and the impious breasts of the crowd, through fear of the godhead of the goddess. So, as soon as she is carried through great cities, she rewards mortals with her silent greeting, and they strew the whole path of the roads with bronze and silver, enriching her with lavish alms, and they snow her with roses, shading the mother and the bands of her companions. Here an armed band, whom the Greeks call by name the Phrygian Curetes, play amongst themselves with weapons and leap up in time to the music, blood-stained, and shaking their terrifying crests by the nodding of their heads. (Lucretius *On the Nature of Things* 2.600, 601–32)

The purpose of this ecstatic procession was evidently in part fund raising and perhaps also recruitment. Sir James Frazer has a vivid description of a similar festival at Hierapolis in Syria. Frazer's account is based on that of Lucian, a traveling lecturer and philosopher of the second century A.D., in *On the Syrian Goddess*. Frazer says:

> While the flutes played, the drums beat, the religious excitement gradually spread like a wave among the crowd of onlookers, and many a one did that which he little thought to do when he came as a holiday spectator to the festival. . . . When the tumult of emotion had subsided, and the man had come to himself again, the irrevocable sacrifice must often have been followed by passionate sorrow and lifelong regret. This revulsion of natural human feeling after the frenzies of a fanatical religion is powerfully depicted by Catullus in a celebrated poem.[17]

Catullus's poem is written in the characteristic meter associated with the Galli and named for them "Galliambics." The poem begins with the arrival of Attis in Phrygia, in search of the goddess, in whose groves he enters her service.

> Borne over the high seas in swift bark, Attis, as he touched the Phrygian grove with eagerly moved foot, and approached the shaded places of the goddess, surrounded by woods, there, goaded by raging madness and wandering in his spirit, he plucked out the weights of his groin with a sharp flint. (Catullus 63.1–5)

He then proceeds to lead the Galli, whom Catullus calls by the feminine form Gallae, in a rout until nightfall. When he awakes in the morning he laments his fate, only to be driven back to the grove of the goddess by an attack by one of her lions, which she loosed upon him. "There always, for the whole length of his life, he was a servant" (90). Catullus ends the poem with a prayer:

> Great goddess, goddess Cybele, goddess lady of Dindymus, may all your madness, mistress, be far from my house. Drive others whom you have aroused, drive others who are mad. (Catullus 91-93)

It has, of course, been suggested that Catullus, like Lucretius, was simply following or translating a Greek original. Others have thought that he came into contact with the worship of Cybele during his visit to Asia Minor in 57 B.C., and still others that, like Lucretius, his experience of the rites in Rome was sufficient. There may be some truth in each of these three explanations of the process of poetic inspiration, to which a fourth may be added. Psychologically it seems possible that Catullus was equating the infatuation of Attis and its damaging consequences with his own erotic infatuation with Lesbia. If so, the final prayer may be seen as equivalent to the final words of the poem in which he recalls how well he himself behaved toward her. There he asks the gods to deliver him from that foul disease, in return for the piety which was, for him, a very real and a spiritual emotion. (Catullus 76.25-26)

The Roman senate had itself introduced the worship of the Great Mother into Rome—perhaps for political reasons of its own. But the religious emotions that the cult was intended to satisfy were real enough. This is attested by the subsequent spontaneous introduction of Bacchic rites into Italy in the first quarter of the second century B.C. Almost all the cities of Greece had, with various degrees of success, endeavored to domesticate the Bacchic cult of Dionysus by incorporating it into the city religion. But it always retained an antisocial element that appealed particularly to women, whose position in the societies of the Greco-Roman world was not in all respects enviable.

Roman reaction to the cult is not unlike that of Pentheus in Euripides' play *The Bacchae* or that of the Roman state to Christianity. It is interesting that the more military cult of Mithraism did not arouse the same disapproval. Livy devotes ten chapters of his thirty-ninth book to an account of the discovery of what was regarded as "a clandestine conspiracy" (39.8.3). It is a romantic tale of a wicked stepfather and a noble courtesan who saves her lover, the stepson, from the dire effects of initiation into the Bacchanalia by denouncing the sect to the consul, whose action leads to a decree of the senate. By good fortune, a copy of this decree has been preserved in a southern Italian city.

Livy marks the importance of the occasion with a speech, the first lines of which point out the contrast between the traditional religion of the state and those unregulated foreign cults. He may well have intended his words to have a contemporary application:

> When the consul had gone through the solemn chant of prayer, which magistrates are wont to pronounce beforehand, when they address the people, he thus began. "Never at any meeting, Quirites, has this solemn invocation of the gods been not only so fitting, but also so necessary. For it advises you that these are the gods whom your ancestors set up for you to worship, to venerate, and to pray to, and not those gods who drive to every crime and lust minds that have been captured by wicked, foreign superstitions [*religionibus*, here used pejoratively]." (39.15.2–3)

What was believed about such cults is shown by Livy's introductory account, which may, indeed, have been influenced by Euripides' play:

> [The cult was established by] a low born Greek . . . , a sacrificing priest and prophet. He was not a man who infected the spirit with error through a disclosed cult, by openly declaring both his gainful occupation and his sect. He was the superior of hidden, nocturnal rites. There were initiations, at first given to a few, then made common among men and women. The pleasures of wine and feasts were added to religion, and the minds of many people were enticed by these. Wine inflamed them: the mixture of males and females, and of those of tender age with older persons, extinguished every distinction of shame: seductions of every kind began to take place, since indulgence was available to all of whatever was the nature of their preferred lust. The promiscuous debauching of free men and women was not the only kind of mischief. False witness, false seals and wills, false evidence, all proceeded from the same factory. So did poisonings and slaughters inside the sect: sometimes the bodies were not even available for burial. Many things were dared by guile, more by violence. But the violence was concealed, because in the presence of cries of ecstasy and the noise of drums and cymbals the voice of those crying for help could not be heard among the debauchery and slaughter. (39.8.3–8)

This is the language in which dissident practices have always been attacked by the establishment, though it may be justly conceded that such practices have always provided a fruitful field for the corruption of the innocent. The Roman reaction was to forbid the unauthorized holding of Bacchanalia, except, apparently, for small private gatherings of not more than five persons, two men and three women at most. Only the Roman senate could give such authorization, at a meeting at which at least one hundred senators were present, that is, one third of the senate of that date (186 B.C.).

Similar reactions to foreign cults are not uncommon under the empire.

Then Judaism and the cult of Isis are often the targets, together with unspecified "Chaldaeans" and even philosophers. The cult of Isis in particular excited the contempt of the satirist Juvenal, writing under the emperors Trajan and Hadrian in the first quarter of the second century A.D. He links it with that of the Great Mother among other cults of which the priests prey on rich women.

> Lo, the chorus of the raging Bellona enters, with that of the mother of the gods, and so does a huge half-man, whose appearance is to be venerated by his obscene inferiors. He has long ago cut off his soft genitals with a picked-up potsherd. The noisy battalion and the drums give place before him, and his fat plebeian cheeks are covered with a Phrygian cap. (Juvenal 6.512–16)

Bellona, an old Italian war-goddess, had by this time been identified with another Asian goddess, Ma of Cappadocia. The Gallus imposes extravagant (and profitable) penances on the rich woman, who is willing to do anything.

> If the white Io order it, she will go to the boundary of Egypt and bring water from burning Meroe to sprinkle on the temple of Isis. (Juvenal 6.526–29)

Io, in Greek mythology, was turned into a heifer by Hera, and Isis was also worshiped in the form of a cow, which is why Juvenal refers to her in this obscure way. There is archaeological evidence for Roman dedications at Meroe in Egypt, so that Juvenal is not, for once, exaggerating.

But it would be unfair to end this discussion of the role of foreign cults in the development of Roman spirituality on this negative note. One of the most powerful expressions of what, to modern eyes, is immediately recognizable as religious experience—something that is not common in Latin literature—is to be found in the *Metamorphoses* of Apuleius, a rich philosopher, rhetorician, and literary figure from Africa at the end of the second century A.D. This work, popularly known as *The Golden Ass,* recounts the often scandalous adventures of Lucius, who is turned into a donkey for meddling with a sorceress. He is turned back into a man at a festival of Isis, into whose mysteries he has been initiated. He then addresses her as follows.

> You indeed, holy one, the perpetual preserver of human kind, and always generous in fostering mortals, grant the sweet affection of a mother to the misfortunes of the wretched. Neither day nor any quiet time of night, nor indeed any moment passes by that is not occupied by your good deeds. You protect men by land and sea: when you have driven off the storms of life, you stretch out your saving right hand. With it you draw back the threads of the fates, however inextricably they are twisted together. You soften the storms of Fortune, and restrain the harmful passages of the stars. Those above worship you, those below respect you. You roll the globe, you light the sun, you rule the world, you tread down Tartarus. The stars answer to you, the seasons return, the godheads rejoice, the elements serve you. At

your nod, breezes blow, clouds nourish, seeds germinate, seedlings grow. The birds, passing in heaven, tremble at your majesty: so do the wild animals wandering in the mountains, serpents gliding on the earth, monsters swimming in the sea. But I am poorly provided with talent for reporting your praises. I have no property for providing sacrifices. My voice is not rich, for saying what I feel about your majesty. A thousand mouths, and as many tongues, are not enough, nor is an eternal succession of unwearied speech. Therefore I shall make it my care to bring about the only thing that I can do, who am indeed religious, but in other respects a poor man. I shall form an image of your divine countenance and of your most holy godhead, and I shall always keep it hidden within the secret places of my breast. (Apuleius *Metamorphoses* 11.25)

It would be necessary to go to the writings of the Christian mystics to find a similar expression of religious feeling. This passage does something to explain what were, by the time of Apuleius, clearly felt as the inadequacies of the other more traditional elements in Roman spirituality. It justifies the inclusion of foreign cults as another such element.

Roman Gods

There has so far in this discussion been little mention of specifically Roman gods. This is because the concept of an anthropomorphic deity with a distinctive personality seems to have been alien to the earliest form of Roman religion—the "religion of Numa," as it has been called. A list of gods has, however, been preserved in an ancient commentary on Virgil. It is attributed to Fabius Pictor, the first historian of Rome, who wrote in Greek just after the end of the Second Punic War (about 200 B.C.). But it may really come from a work on pontifical law written by a more eminent Fabius Pictor, the consul in 142 B.C.

Fabius Pictor enumerates these gods, whom the flamen calls upon when performing the Cereal rite to Tellus and Ceres: Fallow-plower, Renewer, Ridge-plower, Grafter, Plower-up, Harrower, Hoer, Weeder, Reaper, Gatherer, Storer, Bringer-forth. (Servius ad *Georgics* 1.21)

These cover, in fact, all the operations of the agricultural year, from the first plowing of the fallow to the issuing of the stored grain, either for consumption or for sowing. They were evidently invoked in order, most probably at the Festival of Sowing, a movable feast, at least in the second century B.C. How much earlier they were invoked is uncertain, since they may be the product of the Roman ritual delight in exhaustive lists. Many such functional names of gods are known, each referring to a single activity or event. They were later regarded as titles of a god. Augustine of Hippo follows

Varro in giving a list of titles of Jupiter—Victor, Unconquered, Help-[or Wealth-]bringer, Instigator, Stayer [of a military retreat], Hundred-footed [perhaps from the size of his temple, but Augustine explains it as "Holding steady" (on his hundred feet?)], Layer flat [perhaps in plowing], Beam, Fostering, Suckler—though his list is not entirely reliable (Augustine *City of God* 7.11). Other such names appear as qualities of a god, as in another list of invocations preserved by another antiquarian, Aulus Gellius, in the third quarter of the second century A.D.:

> Lua of Saturn, Salacia of Neptune, Hora of Quirinus, Virités of Quirinus, Maia of Vulcan, Heriés of Juno, Molés of Mars, and Neriés of Mars. (Aulus Gellius 13.23.2)

Not all these can be interpreted, but the "Destructive power of Saturn," the "Springing up of Neptune," and the "Manliness of Mars" (*Neriés*) are certain enough.

These lists and ritual invocations may seem to have little real spiritual content, but they attest the very real Roman feeling that every activity of life was under the influence of a divine power. This feeling lies behind their concern with auguries and omens. The obsessive, neurotic quality of Roman religion accounts for the survival of the hymn of the Arval Brethren (see the section "Early Roman Religion"). It is not fair to the Romans to deny that this feeling had a real religious and spiritual content.

Such named functions hardly deserve the Roman title of *numina,* the plural of *numen,* here conventionally translated as "godhead." The word seems to be associated with the nod of assent, and it was later applied to developed gods. But in the poetry of the Augustan period it is particularly associated with the feeling of religious awe induced by certain places and especially by groves, sacred or otherwise. Paradoxically again, the best expression of this feeling is to be found in the works of Ovid, who, like Catullus, is best known for his erotic poetry. But as in the case of Catullus, Ovid's fluency in this mode should not be allowed to obscure his value as a source for very Roman sentiments. One of his works is a metrical version of the Roman religious calendar, the Fasti, so-called because it listed the days on which it was *fas,* "permitted," to perform public business, and those on which it was not. The work was only half finished when Ovid was exiled, in A.D. 8, for having in some way offended the emperor Augustus, and it was not completed. It may have been intended to avert a catastrophe that Ovid saw coming, and he may have abandoned it half-way through at the end of the account of the month of June when it failed that purpose.

The first of March was the day on which the Leaping Priests of Mars, the Salii, moved the sacred shields, one of which was said to have fallen from heaven and to have been provided with eleven copies to preserve it from discovery and theft. Ovid links his account of the shield with the story of how Numa, the second king of Rome, learned from Jupiter the ceremonies to be performed when a spot was struck by lightning. He did so by bringing the god down from heaven to the place where there was later an altar of Jupiter Elicius, interpreted as "Jupiter Elicited (from heaven)." By his skill in interrupting the god, Numa was able to turn his request for the head and the life of a man into one for the head of an onion, the life of a fish, and the hair of a man, which were the traditional offerings.

But first Numa had to discover how to bring Jupiter down from heaven. He did so by capturing the gods Picus, a woodpecker, and Faunus, by making them drunk when they came to drink at a spring, which he had doctored with wine and honey. The story is told in its entirety by two other sources as well, one of which attributes it to the probably Caesarian historian Valerius Antias, who seems to have constructed it in part from Greek folktales. It is summarized here to give some idea of the sort of anti-quarian interest which the Romans took in their surviving rituals and of the way in which they tried to explain them. It also provides a context for Ovid's description of the spring, of which he says:

> A grove was under the Aventine, dark with the shade of holm-oak. If you had seen it, you could have said, "a godhead (*numen*) is in it." There was grass in the middle of it, and, hidden by flourishing moss, a perennial vein of water was flowing from a rock. (Ovid *Fasti* 3.295–98)

Ovid used a similar grove for the site of his imagined encounter with the Muses of Elegy and Tragedy in a poem from his first book of poetry, the *Amores*, originally published perhaps as early as 20 B.C., though the surviving second edition is some years later.

> There stands an old wood, uncut for many years. It is credible that there is a godhead in that place. A sacred spring is in the middle of it, and a cave overhung with rock. From every side birds sweetly sing. (3.1.1–4)

Earlier Virgil had used similar language to describe the Capitol and the Tarpeian rock, when the Arcadian king Evander, who had migrated there, is showing Aeneas the site of the future Rome.

> From there he leads him to the Tarpeian seat, and to the Capitol, now golden, then bristling with woodland thorn-bushes. Even then the awesome religious quality of the place terrified the fearful rustics, and they were frightened of the wood and the rock. "This grove," he said, "this hill with leafy summit, is inhabited by a god (which god is uncertain); the Arcadians believe that they have seen Jove himself, when, as he often does, he shakes the aegis, and with his right hand moves the clouds." (Virgil *Aeneid* 8.347–54)

The aegis, a fringed goatskin shield, and the clouds have come from Homer, where Zeus, the cloud-gatherer, shakes his aegis, though it is less directly associated with the production of thunder than it seems to be here.

Certain types of landscape were, then, even for sophisticated Augustan poets, firmly associated with religious awe and with the feeling of the presence of a divinity—what the German mystic, Baron von Hugel, has called "the sense of the numinous." But what is significant and important for our understanding of Roman spirituality is that the feeling was not originally associated with any particular deity. But even in the literary expression of these poets the reality of the religious experience can be felt.

This sentiment of the presence of an unspecified divinity in certain localities and as supervising diverse human activities helps to account for the fact that, despite or perhaps because of the multiplicity of divinities and ceremonies, Roman religion never has the same polytheistic feel that is characteristic of Greek religion. This is true even when the sentiment was later associated with particular minor gods or was seen as the manifestation of a particular major deity. It is because Roman religious practice was so strongly linked to ceremonies performed at particular times and at particular altars, shrines, or temples. The developed Homeric and Hesiodic pantheon was never, for the Romans, much more than a poetic device. Identification of Roman and Latin deities with members of that pantheon owed much to Etruscan influence, and the Roman gods remained closely tied to their ceremonial worship at Rome.

The Indo-European sky-god of thunder and lightning, whose name is formed on the root DI-, "shining"—the Greek Zeus (*Diweus*, accusative *Di[w]a)—is of course to be found in Rome as Jupiter (*Diw + pater* "father"). He is accompanied by a wife, Juno, who owes much, however, to an Etruscan deity, Uni, who has aspects of Aphrodite. He also had a daughter, Diana. But Janus (Dianus), the two-faced god of beginnings, is never considered to be the son of Jupiter. These family relationships are probably Etruscan in origin. The cult of Jupiter on the Capitol certainly is, and there he shares an Etruscan temple with Juno and Minerva, each of whom has an aisle. Minerva is identified with Athena and is probably also Etruscan. Jupiter Optimus Maximus, "best (originally "richest") and greatest," was increasingly identified with the greatness and majesty of expanding Rome. Some Greek poets (such as Aeschylus), philosophers, and religious thinkers could regard Zeus as in some sense the supreme deity. The Romans could regard Jupiter in the same way. Augustine says of the Christian god that:

> He is the God whom Varro, the most learned of the Romans, thought to be Jove, though he did not know what he said. But I think I must mention it,

because a man of such knowledge could not think that God was nobody, or cheap. He believed Him to be the one whom he thought was the supreme god. (Augustine *City of God* 19.22)

The church inherited the organization and the role of the defunct Roman Empire. It is not, therefore, surprising that the Roman abbreviation of Iupiter Optimus Maximus, IOM, is to be seen on churches transformed into DOM, read as *Deo optimo maximo*, "(Dedicated) to GOD, the best and greatest."

Mars is in modern usage, as it was also in the Latin of Livy and Virgil, a synonym for war. His warlike aspect was particularly important for Augustus, who ascribed to Mars Ultor, "Mars the Avenger," his defeat of those who had killed his adopted father Julius Caesar. But Mars has also an agricultural aspect. He is one of the few gods who deserve special mention here. He is invoked in the hymn of the Arval Brethren, which was noted above in the section "Early Roman Religion." So are the Lares, who were field gods before they became household gods, and the Semones, one of whom was later associated with the god of oaths as Semo Sancus Dius Fidius. The Semones may originally have been gods of sowing. The interpretation of the hymn is extremely uncertain, but it deserves to appear in a study of Roman spirituality. It is perhaps the oldest Roman religious text, and it illustrates the primitive roots from which that spirituality grew. The translation given is that approved by L. R. Palmer, the most recent historian of the Latin language. Each line is repeated three times.

> Hail, aid us ye Lares.
> Do not allow pestilence or catastrophe to afflict the people.
>   [Mars seems to be invoked in this line as Marmar.]
> Be thou sated, wild Mars, leap upon the boundary stone
>   and stand there.
> Call ye in turn all the Semones.
> Hail Mars aid us [Mars here is Marmar].
> Triumpe [the old Latin form of *triumphe*].[18]

But it is not entirely clear whether Mars's functions here are really agricultural or whether his protection is invoked as chief god or as war god. He opens the year with March, originally the begining of the Roman year: December then really was the tenth month (*decem*, "ten"), November the ninth (*novem*, "nine"), and October the eighth (*octo*, "eight"). July and August were originally called Quintilis (*quinque*, "five") and Sextilis (*sex*, "six"), until they were renamed in honor of Julius Caesar and Augustus. But the year that begins with Mars could as well be the military as the agricultural year. On the other hand, an originally agricultural god may have become militarized as warfare, at first an unpleasant annual necessity, became culturally more important to the Roman ruling class. But we are here in the realms of speculation.

Augustus gave a particular significance to Mars the Avenger. He was adopted by his great-uncle, Julius Caesar, whose sister was the maternal grandmother of Augustus. He thus became, in Roman eyes, a Julius instead of the Octavius he had been born, though for some time he retained the surname Octavian, which indicated his adoption from the Octavii. The Julii claimed a special connection with Venus. When the Romans first came into contact with the Greeks, as a power of which notice had to be taken, they were fitted into the Greek mythological pattern of the past by making them descendants of Aeneas, a conveniently surviving and anti-Greek Trojan hero, who seems to have been known in Latium in some capacity quite early. A number of Roman families, therefore, began claiming Trojan descent. Among them were the Julii, who did so by claiming that Aeneas's son, Ascanius, was also called Iulus: they either equated it with Ilus, the name of the eponymous founder of Ilium (Troy) or said that he adopted it when his beard (Greek *ioulos*) grew.

This descent became important when Julius Caesar gained power in Rome and when Augustus was able to take over that power. Caesar dedicated a temple of Venus Genetrix, "Venus the Mother, or Ancestress." The title probably identified her as mother of the Romans, rather than specifically of the Julii. But when Augustus came to be regarded as the second founder of Rome, the distinction was blurred. The connection of Augustus, as a Julius, with Venus accounts for the prominence of Venus in Virgil's *Aeneid*. Like all the other gods and goddesses in the poem she appears as an anthropomorphic deity modeled on the Aphrodite of the *Iliad*.

The Latin Venus was not identified with the Greek Aphrodite much before the third century B.C. Her first temple at Rome was dedicated in 295 B.C. In the Punic Wars a second was added in honor of the Venus of Eryx, in Sicily. The Romans had taken over Sicily in 241 B.C., after the First Punic War. The temple at Eryx was a Greek one, dedicated to Aphrodite, so the Roman dedication to the Venus of Eryx shows that the identification was by then secure. But the earlier Latin Venus seems to have been a *numen* responsible for the flourishing of vegetables, which thus possessed charm— which is what *venus* means. We can see in operation the process, not confined to Venus, by which originally impersonal Roman *numina* were anthropomorphized, at least for the purposes of cult (for an impersonal force hardly needs a house). The impulse for such change came, in the cases of Jupiter, Juno, and Minerva, from Etruria; in the case of Venus, from Greek Sicily.

Such anthropomorphized deities were susceptible, in the minds of thoughtful and educated Romans, to wider and almost allegorical interpretation. This was one of the devices by which such people reconciled their spiritual apprehension of deity with the sometimes offensive details of the mythology and cult of an anthropomorphic god or goddess. That religious atheist Lucretius, as an Epicurean, presumably believed that the gods inhabited the spaces between the worlds, from which the atoms that made up their images permeated to the dreams and visions of human beings. But the gods took no interest in the world of humans and exercised upon it no influence for good or ill. But by this type of allegorical interpretation Lucretius was able to invoke Venus at the beginning of his poem *On the Nature of Things* in a more than conventional or poetic manner:

> Mother of the sons of Aeneas, pleasure of men and gods, Venus, the nurturer, who, under the moving signs of heaven, fillest the ship-carrying sea and the fruit-bearing lands. Through you every kind of animate being is conceived, and, when born, looks on the light of the sun. The winds, goddess, flee from you and from your coming, and so do the clouds of heaven: for you the variegated earth sends up flowers: for you the waters of the sea smile, and the calm heaven shines with diffused light. For as soon as the vernal appearance of day is made manifest, and the creative breeze of Zephyr is unlocked and flourishes, then the winged creatures of the air mark you and your beginning, struck in their hearts by your force, goddess. Then the wild herds leap about the joyful pastures, and swim over swift streams. Taken by your grace all females eagerly follow you wherever you proceed to lead them. Finally, through seas, and mountains, and snatching rivers, through the leaf-bearing homes of birds and the flourishing plains, you strike seductive love into the breast of all things, and bring it about that they eagerly propagate their generations by their kinds. You alone govern the nature of things, and without you nothing rises into the shining shores of light, and nothing joyful or lovable is made. So I am eager that you should be my associate in writing these verses, which I am trying to compose about the nature of things. (1.1–25)

Lucretius starts from the cult title "Mother of the sons of Aeneas," which provides evidence for the original meaning of *Venus genetrix*. But he soon turns "Venus the Nurturer" into the highly abstract "pleasure" and then into the force that leads all things, and especially the females among them, to propagate their kind. At times in the invocation it almost seems as if Venus is identified with the spring. A similar identification is made in the much later anonymous poem known as the *Pervigilium Veneris*, "The Eve of St. Venus."[19] There were two Roman festivals of Venus in the spring, one on 1 April and the other on 23 April. It seems more likely that Lucretius has in mind the second. Then the new wine of the previous year was tasted, and it is the Roman version of the universal spring festival to which

13. Mosaic Floor with Orpheus and the Animals, with the four seasons in the corners. Gallo-Roman. 2nd–3rd century A.D.

Christianity has given a deeper and more spiritual meaning. The reader of Lucretius is strongly reminded of Botticelli's celebrated picture of *The Birth of Venus*.

But what is perhaps remarkable is that Lucretius totally excludes the human race from the realms inspired by Venus in the spring. It is not until his fourth book that he deals with human love, which he also calls Venus. But he has no very high opinion of it, calling it "frenzy" and "madness" (Lucretius *On the Nature of Things* 4.1117). Epicureans had a bad name for self-indulgence—Horace speaks of "a pig from the sty of Epicurus," perhaps referring rather to stupidity (*Epistles* 1.4.16)—but it was not deserved. Epicureanism was a highly intellectual way of life, based on the avoidance of disturbance. Sexual love was for Epicureans, as indeed for much of the ancient world, the most disturbing emotion possible and one that was potentially disruptive of the social order. In his invocation, therefore, Lucretius seems implicitly to be setting humanity over against the realm of nature, in which Venus is operative.

Lucretius continues by naming his patron, Mummius, for whom he is trying to compose these verses and whose family, like the Julii, claimed descent from Venus. "You, goddess," he says, "have at every time wished that he might excel, endowed with every quality. For this reason the more, goddess, give eternal grace to my words"—presumably in order that Lucretius may gain Mummius's favor (Lucretius *On the Nature of Things* 1.26–28) He then goes on to pray for peace:

> Meantime bring it about that the fierce duties of soldiering may be put to sleep, and be quiet through all lands and seas. For you alone can help mortals with tranquil peace. (1.29–33)

Venus is able to do this "since Mars, powerful in arms, rules the fierce duties of war," and he often reclines in Venus's bosom, overcome by love. This entirely anthropomorphic picture reminds the reader of another well-known picture by Botticelli. It is reminiscent of the love of Aphrodite and Ares in the *Odyssey*, though it lacks the adulterous overtones of that tale (Homer *Odyssey* 8.264–366). But though the scene is realized physically, Lucretius's prayer for peace is genuine:

> As he reclines, goddess, on your sacred body, embrace him, and pour sweet speech from your mouth, seeking placid peace, renowned one, for the Romans. For I cannot act with equanimity in this hard time for our country, and the famous child of Memmius [*sic*]cannot fail the common safety in such a crisis. (1.38–43)

Lucretius's invocation of Venus at the beginning of his poem thus exemplifies the many ways in which an educated and sensitive Roman thinker and poet could look upon the Roman gods. He recognized them as objects of cult and allegorized them as potent forces of nature. He employed the anthropomorphic iconography of mythology, but was still able to regard them as the fit recipients of sincerely meant prayers that reflect his personal insecurity in a time of political crisis.

Later Roman Spirituality

Almost all the examples of different aspects of Roman spirituality that have been discussed have been taken from the literature of the later Roman republic and of the Augustan period. Only Apuleius, from the end of the second century A.D., has provided an example of the spiritual content that a provincial Roman from Africa could find not in the traditional religion of Rome but in the exotic cult of Isis. His attitude contrasted with the horror with which Catullus prayed that he and his house might be free from the madness induced by the Great Mother.

This distribution is deliberate and not without significance. The period of the Roman Empire had many virtues. The historian Edward Gibbon was led to say that:

> If a man were called upon to fix the period in the history of the world during which the condition of the human race was most happy and prosperous, he would without hesitation, name that which elapsed from the death of Domitian to the accession of Commodus.[20]

That period—and, indeed, for most of the inhabitants of the empire the period from its foundation under Augustus—was indeed characterized by peace and prosperity. If happiness is to be judged by that alone, then it must be supposed to have been happy. But the impression is also created of a certain spiritual barrenness. The literature of the period is too often marred by artifice, triviality, and obsequious flattery, tempered only by the more or less sincere expression of philosophical commonplaces.

The early fathers spoke of the Roman Empire as a preparation for the gospel (Eusebius *Praeparatio evangelica* 1.4.1–5). The point has been taken up by modern apologists. It may be true in a sense that neither intended. The Augustan religious revival expressed the real feeling of relief, throughout the empire, that the period of the civil wars was over. But as a spiritual force, perceptible in the work of Virgil and, to a lesser degree, in that of Horace, it hardly outlived its founder and left, it seems, a spiritual desert. Just how much of a desert and how much or how little spiritual consolation was available to adherents to the traditional religion is demonstrated by the sad little poem that is said, probably correctly, to have been composed by the emperor Hadrian, though perhaps not, as the source tells us, on his deathbed. That is probably a mere inference from its content:

> Little soul, little wanderer, little charmer,
> Guest and comrade of the body,
> To what places will you now depart,
> Little pale one, little stiff one, little naked one,
> Nor, as you do now, will you make jokes?
> (*Scriptores Historiae Augustae Hadrian* 25.9)

This desert was filled by non-Roman universalist cults such as that of Isis, which was able, as was shown above in the section on foreign cults, to inspire real spiritual feeling in such a man as Apuleius. Another such was the cult of Mithras. This was an originally Persian cult, confined to men and favored especially by soldiers and merchants, who spread it throughout the empire. To the Romans, Christianity must at first have seemed a universalist mystery religion of the same type, but Christianity possessed certain qualities which distinguished it from the others and which contributed (on the human level) to its eventual success. One of these was its superior organization, which allowed participation of all its members. The official organization of the empire was more and more confined to the rich, who, in the fourth century A.D., sometimes clung to paganism as a kind of badge of social and educational superiority. It is symptomatic that a man of the caliber of Augustine of Hippo should prefer a Christian bishopric to a position in the official organization of his province of Africa. Christianity also enjoined, as the other cults did not, a superior morality, and it possessed also one characteristic that prevented it from ever accepting, or being accepted as having, simply the position of one cult among many, to be adopted at the whim, or in accordance with the spiritual needs, of the devotee. This was its exclusivity, which brought it into conflict with the authorities because Christians refused to engage in emperor worship.

Paradoxically, emperor worship may be regarded as the one spiritual innovation of the empire. From as early even as the fourth century B.C., the Greeks had been accustomed to paying semidivine, or even divine, honors to powerful mortals, especially when they came into contact with the despotic monarchies of the East after the conquests of Alexander. Greek polytheism easily permitted assimilation into a pantheon that already contained both divine and semidivine beings of different status. A superior mortal, especially one who offered or provided deliverance from social and political evils, could easily be hailed as a divine or semidivine savior. By the time of Augustus, the eastern empire was accustomed to paying such honors to their rulers. The custom was adopted by the emperors as a potent unifying force of loyalty to the empire. It was extended to the west, where it was made more acceptable by association with the cult of Rome.

The element of patriotism in Roman religion was noted at the very beginning of this essay. It finds expression in two works of literature, one from the very beginning of the Empire and one from the end. At the beginning of Virgil's *Aeneid,* Venus is concerned for the fate of Aeneas, cast up on the shores of Carthage. Jupiter reassures her by a prophecy of the future glory of Rome and makes two promises. The first is as follows:

> Romulus will succeed to the race, and will found the Martial walls, and will call the Romans by his own name. To them I have set no material boundaries nor fixed duration in time. I have given them empire without end. (*Aeneid* 1.276–79)

The second is as follows:

> There will be born, Trojan in his fair origin, Caesar. He shall bound his empire by Ocean, and his fame by the stars, Julius, a name derived from great Iulus. One day you will safely receive him in heaven, burdened with the spoils of the Orient. He too will be called upon with vows. Then the harsh centuries shall grow soft, as wars are put aside. Old Faith, and Vesta, Quirinus with his brother Remus, will give laws. The dread doors of War will be closed with firm iron bonds. Impious Madness, sitting within on fierce weapons, will rage with his hands bound behind his back with a hundred brazen knots, and his gory face will bristle. (*Aeneid* 1.286–96)

A number of themes already touched on are summed up in this passage. It sees Augustus as the founder of the golden age, when the temple of Janus is closed because the Romans are no longer at war. The civil war is over: it is symbolized by the earlier quarrel of Romulus and Remus. Romulus is deified as Quirinus, god of the Quirites, the earlier name for the Romans. Virgil at most hints at the story of how Romulus killed his brother for jumping over the walls of Rome as they were being built. The passage foreshadows the deification of Augustus, who is still known by the family name of his great-uncle and adoptive father, Julius Caesar. It was from Caesar that he gained the Trojan connection that meant he could be adumbrated as Aeneas in the *Aeneid.* The eminent pagans of the fourth century A.D. deliberately kept alive the traditions of classical Latin literature in which they had been educated. They were sometimes able to infuse what they wrote with genuine emotion and to use it to express their deepest spiritual yearnings, feelings, and experiences. One such was the author of the *Pervigilium Veneris,* "The Eve of St. Venus," a poem which resembles Lucretius's invocation in its identification of Venus with the spring. But it adds a frank celebration of passion that is far from the puritanism of Lucretius and has suggested the Middle Ages to many commentators. Yet it can also be seen as the expression of genuine spiritual feeling.[21]

Another eminent pagan of the fourth century A.D. was Rutilius Claudius Namatianus, who had been prefect of the city of Rome in A.D. 414, four years after the sack of Rome by Alaric the Visigoth. In A.D. 416, a year that he describes as the 1169th from the foundation of the city, Rutilius paid a two-month visit to Gaul, his native land. He wrote an elegaic poem describing his journey, and portions of it survive. He begins with an extended speech of farewell to Rome; it includes an encomium of the city as an apology for leaving it:

> Hear me, Rome, most beautiful queen of your world. You have been received among the starry poles of heaven. Hear me, mother of men and mother of gods. We are not far from heaven when we are among your temples. (Rutilius Namatianus *On His Return* 1.47–50)

He praises Rome especially:

> [. . . because] you have made one fatherland for diverse races. The unjust have gained when they are captured by you: for you become their mistress and you offer them partnership in your own laws. You have made a city of what was before then a globe. We acknowledge Venus, mother of the sons of Aeneas, and Mars, father of the sons of Romulus, as authors of the Roman race. The names of both these gods come together in your customs: for victorious clemency softens armed strength. From them you derive the good pleasure you take in both fighting and sparing. You overcome those whom you fear, and love those whom you have overcome. (1.63–72)

The deification of Rome is a consequence of her virtue, as that of Hercules was the result of his:

> You, like him, have embraced the world in law-bringing triumphs. You make all things live under a common treaty. Every part of the Roman world celebrates you, goddess. The necks that bear your pacifying yoke are free. The stars, which preserve all things in perpetual motion, have never seen a more beautiful empire. (1.77–82)

Rutilius was writing some four hundred years after Virgil, and some two hundred after the edict of the emperor Caracalla in A.D. 212 had made all free inhabitants of the Roman Empire into Roman citizens. There may be a certain element of cant in the Roman belief that their rule conveyed great benefits on their subjects. But there is equally an element of genuine idealism and of objective truth. Virgil expressed the same attitude in the much quoted lines spoken to Aeneas by his father Anchises in the underworld.

> Others, so I believe, will forge lifelike bronzes more delicately, and draw out living countenances from marble. Others will plead lawsuits better, and mark

out with a measure the stars as they rise, and name them. But you, Roman, be mindful to rule peoples in your Empire. These will be your arts. Instil in them the habit of peace. Spare those you have conquered, and make war upon the proud. (Virgil *Aeneid* 6.847–53)

The last line has been more cynically rendered by those who remember World War II. "Spare collaborators and crush resistance movements." The implied accusation is as old as Tacitus, who wrote under the emperors Nerva and Trajan in A.D. 97 and 98. He put an indictment of the Romans into the mouth of the Scottish chieftain Calgacus. "They make a desert and call it peace" (Tacitus *Agricola* 30.7). The testimony of Rutilius, who echoes the words of Virgil, shows that the indictment is not a true bill.

Virgil was deceived in his prophecy that the Roman Empire would never end. Thomas Hobbes of Malmesbury disguised his generally anticlerical sentiments under the cloak of a then acceptable attack on the Roman church, but he let his guard slip when he admitted that "it is not the Roman Clergy only, that pretends the Kingdom of God to be of this World, and thereby have a power therein, distinct from that of the Civil State." He saw the historical truth "that the *Papacy,* is no other, than the *Ghost* of the deceased *Romane Empire,* sitting crowned upon the grave thereof: For so did the Papacy start up on a Sudden out of the Ruines of that Heathen Power."[22] But he underestimated the power of the Spirit in calling it a Ghost. Subsequent events have vindicated Virgil. The concept of a universal civil order, founded upon justice and buttressed by religion, is perhaps the greatest single legacy bequeathed us by the spirituality of the Romans in all its manifestations, as they have been examined in this essay. It is, therefore, entirely fitting that this survey end with Virgil and with the ideals of the Roman state, founded as it was on the *pax deorum,* the "peace of the gods."

Historical Note

It is convenient to summarize here the different periods of Roman history referred to in this account of Roman spirituality.

The city of Rome developed as that river crossing of the Tiber that was closest to the sea. The Etruscans lay to the northwest, and the Latins to the southeast. The traditional date for the foundation of Rome is 753 B.C. It is indeed in the eighth century B.C. that the first traces of settlement at Rome have been found by archaeology. The earliest survivals of Roman religious cult may belong to this period. Toward the end of the seventh century B.C. the settlement was taken over by the Etruscans and becomes recognizable to archaeologists as a city.

Early in the fifth century (but traditionally in 509 B.C.) Etruscan political domination was overthrown, and Rome became a Latin republic. Etruscan religious influence remained, and anthropomorphic deities were worshiped in temples in the Etruscan manner. For over one hundred years the Romans were confined to the area around the Alban hills. Then, from the middle of the fourth century, they easily and rapidly conquered Italy. In 280 B.C. they were strong enough to resist invasion by Pyrrhus, the Greek king of Epirus. This is the period of the first Greek influence on Roman religion.

The Romans were then drawn southward into conflict with the Carthaginians in Sicily. In the course of a prolonged struggle, they were able to withstand the invasion of Italy by Hannibal. The defeat of Carthage in 202 B.C. marks the emergence of Rome as a power in the Hellenistic world. Greece and Carthage were both finally conquered in 146 B.C. In 133 B.C. King Attalus bequeathed his kingdom of Pergamum to the Romans. They made it into the province of Asia. There followed a century of expansion abroad and revolution at home, as the Romans struggled to adapt the customs and beliefs of a city-state to the possession of an empire. This is the second period of Greek influence on Roman religion. Many members of the Roman ruling class adopted Greek ways of life and Greek philosophical concepts.

In 31 B.C. Julius Caesar's great-nephew and adopted son, Gaius Julius Caesar Octavianus, became the first Roman emperor (the word is derived from *imperator*, "general"). He took the name Imperator Caesar Augustus and attempted to revive the old Roman religion and its practices. The next four Roman emperors, Tiberius, Gaius Caligula, Claudius, and Nero (as they are generally called) were all connected by birth or marriage with the family of Augustus, though none of them by direct descent.

A year of civil war in A.D. 68 led to the accession of a new dynasty, the Flavians. Its founder was Titus Flavius Vespasianus, an Italian general. The last of the line, Domitian, was assassinated for tyranny, and from Nerva (A.D. 96) through Trajan and Hadrian to Marcus Aurelius (d. A.D. 180) the position of emperor was filled by adoption, it was hoped, "of the best man." This is the period of which Edward Gibbon so approved. But it is of less importance in the history of Roman spirituality.

Marcus Aurelius's son Commodus seems to have been driven mad by power. He was assassinated in A.D. 192. Thereafter the empire was ruled by military leaders. The civilian and legal basis of what became an increasingly autocratic power was undermined. Few emperors were able to rule for long. In this period universalist Oriental cults became of greater importance than the traditional Roman religion. Aurelian (A.D. 270–275) introduced the cult of *Sol Invictus*, the Unconquered Sun, to try to give a spiritual authority to his rule. Diocletian (A.D. 294–305 as emperor, living on after abdication until A.D. 316), who reorganized the financial and administrative basis of the empire, saw himself, on the other hand, as Jovius, an incarnation of the Roman Jupiter.

Constantine (A.D. 334–337) accepted Christianity after his victory over his rival, Maxentius, at the Mulvian bridge in Rome. He is popularly supposed to have seen a vision of the Cross and to have heard the words *"in hoc signo vinces,"* "in this sign you will conquer." For a while he combined Christianity with personal devotion to *Sol Invictus,* as indeed the identification of Christ as the Sun of Righteousness survives in hymnody. He was not baptized until his deathbed, as was then not uncommon.

Constantine supported the Christian church and enlisted its support for the empire. This had, as has been noted, important consequences for both institutions. But paganism and the traditional Roman religion lingered on, especially among the aristocracy in Rome, well into the fifth century A.D., and loyalty to the concept of Rome almost to its end. The "last Roman emperor" was deposed by the German Odoacer, who became the first king of Italy under the overlordship of the eastern emperor. That emperor was called Romulus Augustulus. He had been given the first name for his grandfather, a count from the area of Steyrmark in Austria. That both should have been called Romulus attests even for that late period the emotional power of the "majesty of the Roman name."

Notes

1. Walter Pater, *Marius the Epicurean* (London: Macmillan, 1885) chap. 1.
2. E. R. Dodds, "Aurelius (1)," *OCD,* 153.
3. E. Adams Parker in Walter Pater, *Marius the Epicurean,* abridged and edited by E. Adams Parker (English Literature Series 130; London: Macmillan, 1931) vii.
4. Ronald Syme, *Some Arval Brethren* (Oxford: Clarendon Press, 1980) 110.
5. Ibid., 2.
6. H. J. Rose, "Augures" and "Pontifex, Pontifices," *OCD,* 147, 860.
7. F. W. Walbank, *A Historical Commentary on Polybius* (Oxford: Clarendon Press, 1957) ad loc., 1:741.
8. Varro *Res Divinae,* in Lactantius *Divine Institutes* 1.6.8–12.
9. Hesiod *Works and Days* 111; Pindar *Olympians* 2.77.
10. Tertullian used the phrase of the human soul in general, with no reference to any particular person.
11. *Corpus Inscriptionum Latinarum* 6.4.2, ed. C. Huelsen (Berlin: Reimer, 1902) nos. 32323–36, pp. 3237–55. The translation is of the restoration on p. 3241, lines 92–99. *Notizie degli Scavi di Antichià* 1931, p. 343. See A. Momigliano, review of A. N. Sherwin-White, *The Roman Citizenship, Journal of Roman Studies* 31 (1941) 165.
12. F. Jacoby, *Die Fragmente der griechischen Historiker,* vol. 2B (Berlin: Weidmann, 1929) no. 257, frag. 37, lines 37–38 of the oracle, p. 1191. Momigliano thinks the oracle an Augustan forgery (review of A. N. Sherwin-White, *The Roman Citizenship, Journal of Roman Studies* 31 [1941] 165).

13. A. Ernout and A. Meillet, *Dictionnaire etymologique de la Langue Latine* (3rd ed.; Paris: Klincksieck, 1951) s. vv. *"religio,"* pp. 1004–5, and *"sto (supersto),"* p. 1154. A. Walde and J. B. Hoffmann, *Lateinisches etymologisches Wörterbuch* (3rd ed.; Heidelberg: Winter, 1938–56) s. vv. *"dīligō (religiō),"* 1:352–53, and *"superstes,"* 2:632–33.

14. J. B. Mayor in *M. Tullii Ciceronis De Natura Deorum Libri Tres,* ed. J. B. Mayor (Cambridge: University Press, 1883) 2:xiii, *Bd.*

15. Ibid., ad loc., n. 28.

16. T. F. Higham, "Introduction: Part II," in *The Oxford Book of Greek Verse in Translation,* ed. T. F. Higham and C. M. Bowra (Oxford: Clarendon Press, 1938) xlii.

17. J. G. Frazer, *The Golden Bough* (abridged ed.; London: Macmillan, 1922) 350; see also Lucian *On the Syrian Goddess* 51.

18. L. R. Palmer, *The Latin Language* (London: Faber, 1954) 63.

19. Trans. J. W. Mackail, in *Catullus, Tibullus, and Pervigilium Veneris,* trans. F. W. Cornish, J. P. Postgate, and J. W. Mackail (Loeb Classical Library; Cambridge, MA: Harvard University Press, 1913; revised 1962) 341–67.

20. Edward Gibbon, *The History of the Decline and Fall of the Roman Empire* (London, 1776) vol. 1, chap. 3.

21. J. W. Mackail, "Introduction to *Pervigilium Veneris,"* in *Catullus, Tibullus,* 343–46. Walter Pater, who assigned the poem to the principate of Marcus Aurelius, describes the poem as "a kind of mystic hymn to the vernal principle of life in things" *Marius the Epicurean,* chap. 6.

22. Thomas Hobbes, *Leviathan* (London, 1651) part 4, chap. 47.

Bibliography

Bailey, C. *Phases in the Religion of Ancient Rome.* Sather Classical Lectures 10. Oxford: Clarendon Press, 1932.

Fowler, W. Warde. *The Roman Festivals of the Period of the Republic.* Handbooks of Archaeology and Antiquities. London: Macmillan, 1899.

——. *The Religious Experience of the Roman People from the Earliest Times to the Age of Augustus.* Gifford Lectures for 1909–10. London: Macmillan, 1911.

——. *Roman Ideas of Deity in the Last Century before the Christian Era.* London: Macmillan, 1914.

Halliday, W. R. *Lectures on the History of Roman Religion: From Numa to Augustus.* Liverpool: University Press; London: Hodder & Stoughton, 1922.

Liebeschutz, J. H. W. *Continuity and Change in Roman Religion.* Oxford: Clarendon Press, 1979.

MacMullen, Ramsay. *Paganism in the Roman Empire.* New Haven, CT: Yale University Press, 1981.

Ogilvie, R. M. *The Romans and Their Gods in the Age of Augustus.* Ancient Culture and Society. London: Chatto & Windus, 1969.

Rose, H. J. *Ancient Roman Religion.* Hutchinson's University Library 27. London: Hutchinson; New York: Hillary House, 1948).

Scullard, H. H. *Festivals and Ceremonies of the Roman Republic.* Aspects of Greek and Roman Life. London: Thames & Hudson, 1981.

8

The Piety and Prayers of Ordinary Men and Women in Late Antiquity

H. D. SAFFREY

ORDINARY MEN AND WOMEN, by definition, leave no personal mark on history. In urban centers, they are the people in the street; in the country, the peasants. At best, such people can only be grasped as a collective phenomenon or insofar as others who are more authoritative have granted them a voice to defend themselves where necessary and have expressed their inner thoughts out loud. It is the anonymous behavior on the most ordinary level of ancient society during the age of the empire that will be described here.

The City

Let us begin with the urban centers. Something of the collective sentiment of the person in the street is bound to be expressed by certain incidents or certain aspects of religious legislation. Let us take as an example the city Ephesus in Asia.[1] During the reign of the emperor Nero, in the middle of the first century, probably in A.D. 57, a huge demonstration took place in Ephesus in support of the national goddess, Artemis. The whole world knew Ephesus to be the city where this goddess, daughter of Zeus and Leto, was born and nurtured. Each year great numbers of her statues were exported and crowds of pilgrims came to her temple, one of the seven wonders of the world. But for a while, Paul of Tarsus, one of those who traveled around preaching about new divinities, had been publicly announcing, in season and out of season, that gods made by human beings were not true gods—a dangerous theory that everyone perceived as an attack on the

195

goddess Artemis. A group of citizens particularly concerned, the goldsmiths, who had for so many years been making the statuettes to sell to pilgrims near the temple and in the city's shops, headed a movement to put a stop to Paul's activities. On the day of the demonstration, they stirred up so much commotion among their fellow citizens that they formed a procession, shouting slogans. They even went into a theater close by, which was soon filled with an enormous crowd. For two hours everyone chanted the official liturgical acclamation "Great is Artemis of the Ephesians!" Their shouts spread throughout the whole area and gradually the entire city gathered together. The last ones to arrive did not even know why there was a demonstration, but they too shouted fervidly, with all their might, "Great is Artemis of the Ephesians!" By then it was no longer just a revolt among the goldsmiths; it was a state matter, which roused public opinion and reached the spiritual depths of the person in the street. The national goddess was not to be meddled with; Artemis reigned supreme in their hearts. In order to subdue this movement, the secretary of the municipal council had come in person and given his assurance that measures would be taken to avert the danger.[2]

The deep-seated love that each Ephesian felt for the goddess Artemis was to manifest itself again a century later under the emperor Antoninus. Each year the Ephesians celebrated the feast of Artemis, the national goddess who reigned over the city and the countryside. Her statue was taken out of the temple and carried solemnly, in a magnificent procession, to the theater, where it was placed in the center of the orchestra to receive the prayers and devotions of the whole city on the occasions of the sacrifices and of the competitions that were celebrated in her honor. The month in which the feast took place bore the name of the goddess herself: the month of Artemision. Then, in the second century, the people of Ephesus thought it insufficient to celebrate the goddess Artemis only on certain days of the month. They thought that the whole month should be consecrated to the goddess, so that Artemision would become the month of Artemis completely. The people's assembly and the council gathered and, having examined the project, passed a decree instituting "The month of Artemis." The text of this decree is in an inscription preserved in the British Museum. It records the agreement of the entire town on this point:

> It has pleased the Council and the People of the City of Ephesus, the foremost and greatest metropolis of Asia—whereas Artemis, the goddess who presides over our city, is not only honored in her homeland which through her divinity she has made into the most glorious of all cities, but also among Greeks and Barbarians so that there are sacred sites and enclosures to her everywhere; temples, altars and statues have been raised to her because of her

brilliant epiphanies, and besides, whereas the piety shown to her is very evident, for example, the month named after her, which we call Artemisiŏn and the Macedonians and the rest of the Greeks in their cities call Artemision, the month in which feasts and celebrations are held, in particular in our city, the foster-mother of her Ephesian goddess, the people of Ephesus though it would be appropriate for the entire month which has this holy name to be consecrated and dedicated to the goddess; by this decree, we have decided to establish the following cult in her honor: that the month of Artemisiŏn should be sacred throughout all its days and that on those days of that month, feasts and the celebration of *Artemisia* should take place, so that, in fact, the whole month should be consecrated to the goddess, the greater the honor rendered to the goddess, the surer our city is to remain ever more blessed with good fortune and glory.

This noble style is no doubt that of the municipal secretaries who drew up this fine text, but we can be in no doubt that it perfectly expresses popular feeling—that of an unconditional attachment to the goddess Artemis. Let us try to imagine the rejoicing of the people, taking hold of the town and of the whole Ephesian territory; it was to last a whole month. Canticles and hymns sung by the choirs of the town accompanied processions and sacrifices. On this occasion, at least among the populace, meat was eaten during the feast following the sacrifice and the actual ceremony, when the meat left over from the sacrifice could be bought. Then competitions were organized to test both body and mind, in which the athletes and poets vied with each other. Then there were dramatic performances, perhaps even some mystery plays, recounting the life of the goddess, and mimes, bringing relaxation after the winter months, or gatherings of orators who recounted the history of the city and celebrated its noble origins. When the prize-giving day came round, there were official speeches and the honors list, and everyone experienced great joy on hearing proclaimed the name of his favorite, or simply of a youth he knew. On the occasion, decrees were read out publicly, in which the city honored its friends or its sons who distinguished themselves in her name through other contests abroad. And the whole festivity ended with another long procession through the whole city, bringing the statue of the goddess back to her temple.

On another occasion, the statue of worship was carried to the port on the day of the official opening for navigation after the closure during the winter months. The priests reverently plunged the statue into the sea so that Artemis would protect navigators. For Ephesus, essentially a port, was the only outlet for the whole hinterland of Asia after the port of Miletus became totally silted up, and it was also the arrival point of all merchandise coming from the west. As a result, Artemis was not only the star of the sea but also the queen of commercial affairs, for peasants as well as for artisans and those engaged in industry. For all of them, her effigy, stamped on their coins, was the symbol of wealth and prosperity. This was another reason for the whole population to offer her many prayers. The liturgical acclamation "Great is Artemis of the Ephesians!" certainly expressed the solidarity of the whole population of Ephesus.

A century has passed. The first honorific title granted to the city of Ephesus was that of *neocorus* of Artemis, that is to say, guardian of her temple, which was at the same time one of the most famous sanctuaries in the world.[4] It was only later and incidentally that Ephesus was to qualify as *"neocorus* of the Emperors" and that temples would be built in honor of Domitian (and, after the *damnatio memoriae* of the latter, in honor of Vespasian) and in honor of Hadrian. But no other divinity would ever take the place of Artemis in the heart of the Ephesians. Such was their adoration of the goddess that often newborn babies were given the name Artemidorus, "gift of Artemis." In this way they received their children as gifts of Artemis, who grants safe deliveries. The most famous Artemidorus of all, the author of the *Key to Dreams,* said that to dream of the goddess was lucky because "Artemis is good to those who fear her and it is she who bestows good health." In praying to her, they recited litanies of a sort and addressed her as "Savior," "Sovereign," "Queen of the World," "Goddess of the Sky," "Most Great," "Most Holy," "Most Wonderful."[5]

Well into the third century, religious fervor was still intact at Ephesus. It was at that point that the municipal council of the city decided to have a sacred law inscribed, a sort of outline of the fundamental religious rites of the country, to recall men and women to their religious duties. The following is the text of the law:

> The Prytanis (that is to say, the first magistrate of the city) ignites the flame on all the altars and offers up incense and sacred herbs; he provides, at his own expense, victims to be sacrificed to the gods on the days laid down by the law, numbering three hundred and sixty-five (that is, one animal a day), namely, one hundred and ninety victims whose heart and thighs will be removed beforehand, and one hundred and seventy-five complete victims; the public hierophant will give him counsel and will teach him which victim is determined by law to be offered to the gods. He will have canticles sung during the sacrifices, processions, and nocturnal ceremonies where these are compulsory according to custom, and he will have prayers said for the Roman Senate, the people of Rome, and for the people of Ephesus. The Prytanis will give the appropriate honorarium to the hierophant, the sacred herald, the flute-player, the trumpeter, the second hierophant, and to the man who examines the flesh of the sacrificed victims and to the curete of the week.[6]

One can picture it: in the mid-third century, the mayor of Ephesus had the duty of lighting the altar fires each morning and of sacrificing each day in honor of the god celebrated on that particular day. He sets out through the town with the chosen victim and a small following of assistants to sacrifice and to interpret the omens, not to mention the artists in charge of musical accompaniment. After this, all who passed close to this altar at the cross-roads on the way to work or to business could cast in a few grains of incense, so as to offer their own prayers and to pray for all the people of Ephesus.

The cult of Artemis, the national goddess; the daily municipal worship of each god and each goddess, including, without a doubt, the Roman emperors—these form the framework of the spiritual life of the person in the street in a great populous city like Ephesus. Christianity had still brought no changes in the third century, and it seems as though the state of pagan worship remained unchanged until near the end of the fourth century. The emperor Julian's most important spiritual counselor from 360 to 363 in the emperor's attempt at an official return to the pagan religion was still the Neoplatonic philosopher Maximus of Ephesus.[7] What we have just demonstrated in the case of Ephesus could be generalized to cover all the cities of Greece; each of them celebrated the public cult of its own god or goddess, a cult that brought together all the citizens, not only the promi-nent ones who were responsible for it but also all the ordinary men and women, whose lives were governed by the religious calendar of feast days and who placed their hopes in divine protection.

The Country

Let us now turn our attention to the country. The peasants were indus-trious, dependent on the soil. Many were serfs, either on large imperial or private estates or on land that belonged to the priests of certain temples. Since they were serfs, they were subject to forced labor, which could go so far as conscripting people for work deemed urgent. Farmers were burdened by taxes, the bane of peasants at all times and in all places—Egypt, Syria, or Asia—taxes levied by the big landowners, by the emperor in cases of imperial estates, or by the priests of the big temples. The peasants had a hard life, working each day simply to feed their families, which were generally large, and no day was different from any other. Religious festivals were the only source of enjoyment in this hard life. What these festivities meant to this humble peasant population is made clear to us in a valuable text of the fourth century. It comes from Libanius, the orator from Antioch, famous in his day, who joined his voice to those of his compatriots living in the country in the face of the measures taken by the emperor Theodosius I against pagan temples and the practice of pagan worship, including country chapels. He found exactly the right tone to express the physical and moral injustices thus inflicted on the peasants.[8] (This was probably in 386.[9]) Libanius fiercely denounced to the emperor the fanatical activities of the monks, who were acting without orders or authority.[10]

> You yourself have neither commanded the closure of the temples, nor forbidden people to frequent them. You have not banned from the temples and the altars the sacrificial fire, nor the incense nor other perfumes for burning. It was those scoundrels in black robes [the monks], more voracious than elephants ... who hid these misdeeds behind their unnatural pallor. Yes, Sire, while the law still holds, they are storming the temples. ... Once the first one is overthrown, they rush to the second one and then to the third; it is an uninterrupted chain of trophies, all in contravention of the law. (Libanius *Pro templis* 30.8)

Theodosius's command was to forbid sacrificing to idols, but not to destroy the temples from top to bottom. And yet this is what these monks were viciously doing. Indeed, Libanius continues:

> They [that is to say, the monks] are spreading out like torrents across the countryside; and in ruining the temples, they are also ruining the countryside itself at one and the same time. For to snatch from a region the temple which protects it is like tearing out its eye, killing it, annihilating it. The temples are the very life of the countryside; around them are built houses and villages, in their shadow a succession of generations have been born up until the present day. It is in those temples that farmers have placed their hopes for themselves and their wives and children, for their oxen and for the ground they have sown or planted. A country region whose temple has been destroyed in this manner is lost, because the despairing villagers no longer have the will to work. It would be pointless to exert themselves, they think, because they have been deprived of the gods who made their labors prosper. (Libanius *Pro templis* 30.8)[10]

The monks naturally claimed that the peasants were sacrificing victims and violating the law. Libanius replied firmly, still addressing the emperor: "Can you believe that these wretches who turn pale at the very sight of the tax collector's cloak, would ever think of challenging the authority of the Emperor?" And he continues:

> So, someone will ask, haven't your countrymen ever slit the throats of animals? Certainly, for a banquet, for a luncheon, or for a festive meal. But then the oxen did not have their throats slit in the temples; their blood did

not fall on the altar, none of their limbs were burned on it; there was no barley sprinkled on their heads first and no libations afterwards. If a few individuals happened to assemble in a pleasant place, where they slit the throat of a heifer or a sheep, or both, and if then they happened to boil or roast some part of the animal and then to eat it, seated in the open air, I do not see what law they infringed. For none of your laws, O Emperor, forbids these festivities. You confined yourself to a single prohibition, and as to the rest, you left us free. So that even supposing they held a banquet with all sorts of smoke rising, they would not be guilty of contravening the law, any more than if, while drinking wine in an intimate gathering, they sang canticles and invocations in honor of the gods. . . . Formerly, it was the custom for the inhabitants of several villages to meet together on feast-days, in the chief centers. There they sacrificed, and after the sacrifice they made merry at a banquet. While they were permitted to offer sacrifices, they offered them; when this right was suppressed, they were still allowed to assemble and to follow the ancient customs, with the exception of sacrifice. So they celebrated the day and honored the divinity of the temple by means of authorized practices; but no one in these gatherings ever thought of asking for a sacrifice. (Libanius *Pro templis* 30.8)

It is clear that these were peasants' festivities, in the shadow of the temple — pauses in an exhausting life, moments of rest from unending labor. As long as they could celebrate the feast with a sacrifice offered to the gods, they did so; afterward, they confined themselves to an offering of incense and to a private family feast accompanied by songs and prayers. It has been possible to draw up a very long list of gods and local goddesses in Asia Minor, all types of Zeus or of Mèn, and mother goddesses of all kinds, who were respected and honored by the peasants as the protective divinities in their lives.[11]

In this speech in behalf of the temples, Libanius is obviously pleading for the peasants of Syria and the surrounding area. But he gives an interesting detail about Egypt. He points out that in Egypt, as in Rome, an exceptional authorization of sacrifices was maintained. This was because of the fertility of Egypt, attributed to the Nile.

This fertility is the work of the Nile and banquets are offered and victims sacrificed as an invitation to the Nile to overflow into the lands of Egypt. If this homage were no longer rendered in the appropriate form, by those authorized to do so, the Nile would refuse to irrigate those lands. I imagine that those who suppressed so many other sacrifices were well aware of this and did not dare to tamper with these particular areas, however much they might have liked to. They allowed the Nile to enjoy its centuries-old banquets in peace and to pay the accustomed price for them. But just because not every land has a river like the Nile, which is the benefactor of the human race, must its temples be destroyed and yielded up as prey to those pious destroyers? I should like to know if they would dare to suggest, to demand formally that the honors now paid to the Nile should be suppressed, thus demanding that the land of Egypt no longer be flooded, that it cease to be sown, cease to be harvested, cease to produce wheat and other foodstuffs; and lastly that its vessels cease to transport life and plenty throughout the world. They would not dare to make an utterance with such a far-reaching effect and thus what they are afraid to say gives the lie to what they actually do say. Do not venture to say: Deprive the Nile of its honors; that would be an admission that the honors rendered to the gods of the temples are important to the welfare of humanity. (Libanius *Pro templis* 30)

How exactly Libanius expresses the feelings and complaints of the peasants when he exclaims: "To snatch from a region the temple which protects it is like tearing out its eye, killing it, annihilating it." The gods of the peasants are the divinities of nature: Artemis is the queen of all living things in nature that have not yet been touched by human hands. It is there that the peasant has gathered a bouquet for the goddess, like Euripides' Hippolytus:

These flowers which I have woven into a wreath, O my queen, I gathered them for you in a virgin meadow. Where no shepherd would dare to graze his flocks, And no hand wield the scythe. Immaculate, only a swarm of bees visits it in springtime. (Euripedes *Hippolyta* 73–77)

Even today all along the roads of Greece, women place flowers at the icon of the virgin and light a lamp in front of it in the evening. The countryside is the place of eternal devotion.

Prayers and Offerings

To find out in greater detail in what way the ancients prayed to their gods, one must consult the collection consisting of book 6 of the *Palatine Anthology* under the title "Epigrams of Offerings to Divinities." Admittedly, these are short passages of erudite poetry, but they express the essence of actions of popular prayer and must have often served as models for the private prayer of men and women at all times in antiquity. A complete analysis has been done by A.-J. Festugière, who has managed to draw up a catalogue of offerings made to the gods in exchange for which a request was made of them. This is how his analysis ends: "A whole network of friendly relationships between the human being and his god embraced the Greek from his birth to extreme old age. This is clear from the gifts which the Greek offered to his gods. And evidence for such gifts is provided by the epigrams."[12]

A young mother who had perhaps risked her life bringing a child into the world would offer a girdle, a wreath, a veil, hair-bands, the *peplus* under which she had carried her twins in her womb, all gifts by which not only

14. Statuette of a Veiled Dancer. Greek.
Early 2nd century B.C.

15. Statuette of a Girl. Roman period.

16. Harpist. Cycladic. Ca. 2500 B.C.

17. Demeter of Cnidus by
Leochares (?). Ca. 330 B.C.

to express thanks but also to place the child under the protection of the goddess, usually Artemis. Somewhat later one could "dedicate" the child to a god or goddess by presenting a portrait of the child to the temple. On one occasion a mother apologized that "it was a bad portrait, because she was poor" (*Palatine Anthology* 6.355). On another, the mother asked Cybele to make her daughter Aristodice grow in beauty until her marriage, in memory of the ritual dances where, in front of the temple, the girl had let her hair fly free, according to the rite of the cult of Cybele (6.281).

When children reached adolescence they offered to the gods the toys of their childhood: balls, castanets, knuckle bones, or tops. They offered them to Hermes, the patron of the gymnasium, just before entering it for the first time. Most often it was a still more touching offering of a lock of hair symbolizing the persons themselves, an offering by which the children entrusted themselves to the god. There is a distinction to be made between boys and girls. For the boy, it was a consecration of manhood at the time of puberty; for the girl it was the offering of a lock of hair on the occasion of her marriage, with this prayer: "Take good care of your devoted servant" (6.280). Or again, the boy gave the toys and tools that he had used till the time when, leaving the *epheboi,* he joined the class of men. Hermes had protected him—he would leave with him his hat, his cloak-pin, his scraper, his bow, and his cloak.

Naturally, these offerings and prayers continued into adult life; women offered the work of their hands, men that of their industry or the products of their hunting. But the most touching gifts are the most humble ones: cakes, a cup of wine, olives, a bunch of grapes, a biscuit. Numerous offerings to nymphs have been recorded, goddesses of the springs that refreshed the traveler or the herd, making the shepherd grateful. So it continued through life. When persons could no longer work, they finally offered up their work tools and prayed: "In return for this, deign to nourish ever the one who was your servant!" (6.63).

In fact, these offerings and these prayers were those of ordinary people as well as the highborn. The goatherd Philoxenides carved a little statue of Pan from an oak tree, and, having sprinkled the altar with milk, he offered Pan a he-goat in exchange for which he requested that his she-goats should always give birth twice a year (6.99). The fisherman Menis offered Artemis Limnitis a small gift of fish, in exchange for which he hoped that his nets would always be laden with good catches (6.105). Sailors offered Phoebus a ship's biscuit, a goblet of wine, and a lamp, in exchange for which they sought protection and a favorable wind (6.251). It is clear that what counts is not the value of the gift itself but the gesture, and this gesture can be understood only if the giver is confident that the gesture is valuable in the eyes of god. This presupposes a feeling of friendship.

Pilgrimages

Friendship with a god was certainly also what led to pilgrimages. Lengthy journeys were organized, particularly in Egypt, where the gods were popular. But closer to home, many local shrines attracted pious visitors, for example, the oracular shrine of Apollo at Claros. In the second century A.D. the interest in oracles became particularly intense, and some texts of Pausanias, Aelius Aristides, and Lucian bear witness to the fame of Claros. This fame was confirmed by the excavations of the shrine, carried out twenty-five years ago by J. Robert and L. Robert.[13] A few oracles in verse have been discovered engraved in stone in Lydia, Thrace, Pergamum, and Iconium. Each year the towns used to send delegations to consult the oracle. The inscriptions discovered on the site date from the second and third centuries A.D. They are lists of the people who formed each delegation. At the head was the official consultant, and there were choirs of boys and girls under the leadership of a director, who were to sing a hymn to Apollo, sometimes indicating which poet had composed the hymn. The names are obviously those of boys and girls from ordinary families, who had been chosen for their voices. They came from all over Greece, but preferably from parts that were hellenized later or from Roman colonies. The old countries remained faithful to the older oracle of Didyma, near Miletus, but the more recently hellenized populations went to Claros. For example, in Caria, the Roberts found inscriptions of the delegations coming from Tabia, Heraclea of Salbaka, Sebastopolis, Laodicea of Lycus, Aphrodisias, and Amyzon. But they could also come a great distince, from Olbia on the southern coast of Russia or Odessus on the Bulgarian coast of the Black Sea or from Caesarea of Cappadocia. They consulted the night oracle by lamplight in an underground crypt where a spring flowed. Iamblichus, in the fourth century, speaks of this oracle at Colophon, the city closest to the temple of Claros, where the prophet delivers his oracles without being seen by those present (*De mysteriis* 3.11).

In the valley of Meander, another Apollo, honored in a cave in the spot called Aulai, near Magnesia on the Meander, used to fill his devotees with such enthusiasm that they were able to uproot a tree from his sacred wood and carry it, at a run, along mountain paths as far as the shrine of Dionysus at Magnesia. "Those possessed by Apollo, drawing their extraordinary strength from the statue of Apollo at Aulai, began their feat from there, uprooting trees and running over the surrounding mountains and ravines, to arrive in the city at Dionysus' shrine, where they placed the uprooted tree in front of the god."[14] This obstacle course brought together the sportsmen of this mountain each year, and we have proof that this pilgrimage to Apollo from Aulai was still undertaken by the most pious pagans in the fifth century.[15]

It was mostly in Egypt, however, which was always a sort of mirage for the ancients, that a real religious tourism occurred. Several inscriptions and graffiti, which are acts of adoration in honor of Egyptian divinities, have been found, first on the Colossus of Memnon, then on the temples of the Valley of the Kings, and then on the temples of the island of Philae. Mostly they are written in the following form: "I came, I adored . . ." or "I adored for . . ." or "I commemorated. . . ." In the case of these last, some person absent or dead is involved. These inscriptions bear witness to a multitude of tourist pilgrims, who used to come by the thousands to these holy places, making the pilgrimage they had dreamed of all their lives![16]

The Colossus of Memnon is, in fact, made up of two gigantic statues, one of which had lost its head. It was believed to represent the legendary king Memnon of Ethiopia, the son of Aurora, whose story is told in the *Odyssey* and Hesiod. In fact, the Eygptian holy places in general were referred to by the name "Memnoneia" in Hellenistic and Roman times. The statue of Colossus always made a sound when struck by the first rays of the rising sun, and one arrived at dawn in order to have the opportunity of witnessing it. This was regarded as an oracle of good omen. The great period for pilgrimages was the second and third centuries of our era, and the most famous pilgrim was the emperor Hadrian, who endorsed a fashion that would continue long after him.[17] Beyond the Colossus, the pilgrims went on to what were called the *Syringes*. A syrinx is a flute, and the two paths one had to follow to arrive at the tombs of the kings were like corridors so narrow in places as to give one the impression of trying to squeeze into a flute. The whistling of the wind could doubtless also be heard in them. Here again, thousands of inscriptions of adoration and graffiti may be counted. This pilgrimage was international, and all regions of the ancient world were represented: Greece, Asia Minor, Syria, Spain, the Gauls, and of course many local areas. Pilgrims came from all stations of life: emperors, prefects, officers, priests, magistrates, doctors, ordinary people, and slaves. There were poets who came to have their works inscribed there, philosophers who made their pilgrimage in honor of Plato and his alleged sojourn in Egypt, but most often the real moving force was simple curiosity reinforcing devotion, Often one can read the cry of admiration "I was astonished!" Finally, next to Colossus and the royal tombs was the shrine of the healing gods, who had established themselves in the funeral temple of Queen Hatshepsout, at Deir el-Bahari, on the left bank of the Nile opposite Karnak. Many miraculous cures took place there.[18] This whole collection of monuments around Thebes provided a religious pilgrimage tour. One started at Alexandria and traveled up the Nile as far as the Valley of the Kings, just as we do nowadays. These sacred sites have attracted tremendous crowds almost continuously from the first centuries A.D. on.[19]

The shrines of Asclepius were an attraction for pilgrims as well. Devotion at the famous temple of Pergamum is well documented, both in the sacred discourses of Aelius Aristides[20] and in the published inscriptions relative to the Asclepeion of Pergamum.[21] In Cilicia there was another famous temple at Aigeai. Using chapter 10 of Philostratus's *Life of Apollonius of Tyana*, L. Robert describes the atmosphere of worship.[22] He brings to mind the altar of the shrine during a large-scale sacrifice: the altar covered in blood, the victims, large cows and pigs, the actions of the people flaying and cutting up the victims, and also the consecration of precious stones. A rich man had come; he sacrificed lavishly and would make more sacrifices and offerings if Asclepius would take heed. In so doing, he has not conformed to custom, has not made supplication, and has not spent any time in the shrine, like the others. . . . Accordingly, Asclepius appeared to his priest in the night and ordered him to drive away this unworthy man.[23] This story is entirely characteristic of the life of the shrine. Pilgrims lived there, they slept there, they carried out the treatments prescribed. Sickness diminished all differences between rich and poor; these were ordinary men and women coming to the Savior God. They had to live in his temple, follow the course of the sacrifices and prayers, wait until the god revealed himself, and blindly carry out his orders.

Places and Practices

Most people did not have to go very far in order to render to the gods the worship due them. The places of worship were in town or even at home. One has only to read the description which Apuleius, in the mid-second century, sketches of his adversary Emilianus, the prototype of a man who neglects all his religious duties, in order to imagine by contrast how an ordinary man in Africa in these times lived.

> I know well that there are people, Emilianus at the head of them, who consider it very witty to laugh at divine matters. If the inhabitants of Oea who know him are to be believed, at his age he has never yet prayed to any god or frequented any temple and he would consider it a sin when he passes a religious building, to lift his hand to his lips as a sign of adoration. Even to the gods of the countryside, who give him food and clothing he never

offers the first fruits of his harvests, vines, or flocks; there is not a single shrine on his land, not a holy place nor a sacred wood. But why speak only of groves and chapels? Those who have been at his house have never seen even a stone anointed with oil or a branch adorned with a garland. (Apuleius *Apologia* 56.3-6)

It was clearly an ordinary habit to have some sort of oracle at home, with an image of the god of one's choice. In *Adversus haereses,* Irenaeus relates that the Gnostics "possess images, some of them painted, others made of various materials. They wreathe these images and display them with those of Pythagoras, Plato, Aristotle, and others. They render to these images all the other honors in use among the pagans" (1.25.6). Later on, in the fourth century, the historian Eusebius of Caesarea, speaking of images kept by Christians, Christ, Peter, and Paul, explained: "It was natural, because the ancients were in the habit of honoring these images in this way like saviors, without further thought, in accordance with pagan custom which existed before them" (*Historia ecclesiastica* 7.18.4). Household worship was an ordinary practice. Busts of Tiberius and Livia with a serpent have been found in a house in Ephesus. These imperial divinities were placed in a niche, accompanying the *genius loci* in the shape of a serpent, and they insured protection in everyday life.[24] Household worship was such an important factor in Greek and Roman religion up until the end of antiquity that an edict from the emperor Theodosius was needed in 392 to forbid sacred offerings of fire, wine, and incense by anyone.[25] By the end of this period, worship, both private and public, had become an everyday occurrence, as M. P. Nilsson has clearly demonstrated.[26] A large feast with sacrifices took place once a year, but incense was offered and hymns were sung every day in honor of the Egyptian gods, the emperors, Dionysus, and Asclepius. They had their altars in the city and their images in homes. A lamp was kept burning as a symbol of family prayer.

For some of the more scrupulous souls, prayers of praise or request alone were inadequate. We can state with certainty that there was at least a very localized practice in the center of Asia Minor during the second and third centuries of setting up confessional steles in temples. These were popular documents dedicated to local divinities. Someone offended a divinity; the divinity sent a punishment. The offender acknowledged it and repented by warning others about the god's power and by claiming to have become more pious through the consciousness of having sinned. These documents were mainly discovered in Lydia and Maeonia.[27] Let us offer a few recently published examples.[28] These came from a sanctuary in Maeonia called "of Zeus and the Twin Oaks." The inscription begins with an acclamation: "Great is Zeus of the Twin Oaks and his powers!" One Menophilus had bought some wood which came from the sanctuary. He was punished by the god and underwent many sufferings. The god then enjoined the son to free his father by redeeming his fault. By raising the stele the son warned all men not to be disrespectful of the god. The stele was erected in A.D. 191–192. Another example is the following: "Great is Zeus of the Twin Oaks! I Athenaios, punished by the god for a mistake made through ignorance, after receiving many punishments, was summoned in a dream to raise a stele and I wrote out the powers of the god. In acknowledgment, I had this stele engraved in the year 347 [A.D. 262–263]." Above the inscription a bas-relief has been carved, showing poor Athenaios raising his right hand in a gesture of prayer and confession and the priest next to him holding his sacerdotal wreath in his right hand, and in his left the scepter with which to tap the wrongdoer as a sign of reconciliation. A third example relates that in 252–253, a woman named Bassa had to undergo sufferings too terrible to mention, simply for not believing in the god. When she was released, she consecrated this stele as an acknowledgment and recounts her story here in covert terms.

Through these exceptional but very popular documents, we can perhaps achieve something rare for a historian—to penetrate the secret feeling of guilt in people's hearts. Public confession, with its remedy, is clearly expressed here.[29] I believe that it comes from an acute sense of the transcendence of the gods, because it is in this region as well that a series of acclamations has been found on an altar: "God alone is in the Heavens! Great is Celestial Mèn! Great is the power of the immortal god!" It is, of course, not a declared monotheism but the exaltation of a local god, Mèn, whose power penetrates the invisible and uncovers it.[30] In these steles of confession we can hear the cry of remorse and the call for deliverance even now from the men and women who had them engraved and displayed publicly in the temples.

It was deliverance without remorse of any kind that was avidly sought through astrological and magical means at the end of antiquity. Nothing was more widespread throughout all levels of society. The horoscopes of the great have been kept, from which they tried to interpret the signs of the times. All hoped to find the face of their destiny in the stars.[31] Philo of Alexandria expressed a common sentiment when he wrote, "The earthly realities are suspended from the celestial realities in virtue of a certain natural sympathy" (*De opificio mundi* 117). Franz Cumont has described the religious character of Greco-Roman astrology,[32] and magic was no less religious.[33] Through magic people tried to free themselves from the fate that hung heavily over their lives. "You who take care of powerful Necessity which governs my affairs and the thoughts of my soul and which no one can escape from—neither god nor angel nor devil—rouse yourself for me, spirit of this dead man. Do not force me to be violent with you, but accomplish what I have written here and placed in your mouth, at once, quickly, quickly" (*Papyri Graecae magicae* 19.1.13–16). This note was slipped into the mouth of a mummy so that the dead person could respond to this love charm from the beyond. Magic also made the gods appear or even made one deified and able to say: "You are me and I am you." The term "magic" meant the acquisition of temporal benefits or of happiness after death, and the magician tried to seize the divine power, which gave him the right to give commands. This mad ambition is in everyone's heart. For people in antiquity it is the case that the word "god" carried no such crushing connotation of respect and transcendence as it implies for us. This sense is expressed in the proverb according to which "man is a mortal god, and god an immortal man."[34] The sense of this familiarity between the human being and god is perhaps the secret of the very natural and varied forms of piety among ordinary people in antiquity.

Among all the gods and goddesses, the one most familiar to ordinary people, whether they came from the city or the fields, was the sun. In *Antigone*, Sophocles makes the chorus sing a salutation to this cherished and holy light:

> O ray of the most beautiful sun
> which ever yet shone
> for our Thebes of seven gates,
> you have it now at last,
> The eye of the golden day!
> (100–104)

This is the same salutation that Pope Leo castigated in the middle of the fifth century in reproaching the citizens of Rome for adoring the sun upon entering Saint Peter's Basilica: "Some people," he said, "are stupid enough to adore the rising sun at the birth of a new day, from elevated ground; and there are even some Christians who think they are performing a religious act when, before entering Saint Peter's basilica, on arriving at the top of the steps, they turn their whole body towards the rising sun and, bowing their heads, they bend in homage to the radiant disc!"[35] But this was the most ordinary gesture of prayer from a human to the god who was most noticeable because of his regular gift made every day.

Notes

1. On the city of Ephesus in antiquity, see the combined article by D. Knibbe and S. Karwiese in in Pauly-Wissowa, Suppl. Band 12 (1970) cols. 248–364 and that by W. Alzinger in cols. 1588–1704. For the Byzantine period, see C. Foss, *Ephesus after Antiquity: A Late Antique, Byzantine and Turkish City* (Cambridge: University Press, 1979).

2. The account of this manifestation is in Acts 19:23–40.

3. The text of this inscription may be read in *SIRIS*, no. 867.

4. See Acts 19:35; see also J. Keil, "Die dritte Neokorie von Ephesos," *Numismatische Zeitschrift* 48 (1915) 125–30; and L. Robert, "Sur les inscriptions d'Ephèse 6. Lettres imperiales à Ephèse," *Revue de Philologie* 41 (1967) 44–64.

5. See R. Oster, "The Ephesian Artemis as an Opponent of Early Christianity," *Jahrbuch für Antike und Christentum* 19 (1976) 24–44.

6. See D. Knibbe, "Der Staatsmarkt: Die Inschriften des Prytaneions," *Forschungen in Ephesos* 9.1.1. (Vienna: Verlag der Österreichischen Akademie der Wissenschaften, 1981) 57–59, no. D1.

7. On Maximus of Ephesus, see J. Bidez, *La Vie de l'empereur Julien* (Paris: Les Belles Lettres, 1930) 71–72; and A. H. M. Jones, J. R. Martindale, and J. Morris, *The Prosopography of the Later Roman Empire I* (Cambridge: University Press, 1971) s.v. Maximus 21, pp. 583–84.

8. On Libanius in general, see A.-J. Festugière, *Antioche;* and P. Petit, *Libanius et la vie municipale à Antioche au IVᵉ siècle après J. -C.* (Paris: Geuthner, 1955). On the discourse *Pro templis,* see Festugière, *Antioche,* 237–40.

9. For this date, see P. Petit, "Sur la date du 'Pro templis' de Libanius," *Byzantion* 21 (1951) 285–309.

10. Emile Monnier provides a fine French translation in *Discours choisis de Libanius* (Paris: C. Lahure, 1866) 343–44.

11. See, for example, J. Keil and P. Herrmann, *Tituli Asiae Minoris* 5.1: *Tituli Lydiae* (Vienna: Austrian Academy of Sciences, 1981) 283 in the "Index rerum sacrarum," s. vv. Zeus, Mèn, Mètèr. See also P. Herrmann, "Mèn: Herr von Axiotta," in *Studien zur Religion und Kultur Kleinasiens* (Festschrift F. K. Dörner; Leiden: Brill, 1978) 415–23.

12. See A.-J. Festugière, "*Anth' Hōn:* La formule 'en échange de quoi' dans la prière grecque hellenistique," *Revue des sciences philosophiques et théologiques* 60 (1976) 389–418, which I summarize.

13 L. Robert, *Les Fouilles de Claros* (Limoges: A. Bontemps, 1954); idem, "L'Oracle de Claros," in C. Delvoye and G. Roux, *La Civilisation grecque de l'Antiquité à nos jours* (Brussels: La Renaissance du livre, 1969) 305–12. The published inscriptions from Tabai, Heraclea of Salbaka, and Sebastopolis are in J. Robert and L. Robert, *La Carie* (Paris: Maisonneuve, 1954) vol. 2; those of Amizon are in *Fouilles d'Amyzon en Carie* (Paris: Broccard, 1983) vol. 1.

14. L. Robert, "Documents d'Asie Mineure III 2: Le dendrophore de Magnésie," *Bulletin de correspondance hellénique* 101 (1977) 77–88; 102 (1978) 538–43.

15. Compare the pilgrimage of Asclepiodotus of Alexandria in Damascius *Vita Isidori* fr. 117, Zintzen, p. 156.

16. See A. Bernand and E. Bernand, *Les inscriptions grecques de Philae* (Paris: Centre nationale de la recherche scientifique, 1969); and the review by A.-J. Festugière, "Les proscynèmes de Philae," *Revue des études grecques* 83 (1970) 175–97.

17. See A. Bernand and E. Bernand, *Les inscriptions grecques et latines du Colosse de Memnon* (Paris: Institut français d'archéologie orientale, 1960).

18. See A. Bataille, *Les inscriptions grecques du temple de Hatshepsout à Deir el-Bahari* (Le Caire: Institut français d'archéologie orientale, 1951).

19. See A. Bataille, *Les Memnonia: Recherches de Papyrologie et d'Epigraphie grecques sur la nécropole de la Thèbes d'Egypte aux époques hellenistique et romaine* (Paris: Institut français d'archéologie orientale, 1952).

20. The sacred discourses of Aelius Aristides were edited by B. Keil (*Aelii Aristidis Smyrnaei quae supersunt omnia* [Berlin: Weidmann, 1958]) and translated into English by C. A. Behr (*Aelius Aristides and the Sacred Tales* [Leiden: Brill, 1981]). On the piety of Aelius Aristides, see A.-J. Festugière, *Personal Religion,* chap. 6 ("Popular Piety, Aelius Aristides and Asclepius"), pp. 85–104.

21. See C. Habicht, "Die Inschriften des Asklepieions," in *Altertümer von Pergamon* 8.3 (Berlin: Georg Reimer, 1969). On the god Asclepius and his cult, see E. J. Edelstein and L. Edelstein, *Asclepius: A Collection and Interpretation of the Testimonies* (Baltimore, MD: Johns Hopkins University Press, 1945).

22. L. Robert, "De Cicile à Messine et à Plymouth, avec deux inscriptions grecques errantes," *Journal des savants* (1973) 161–211.

23. Ibid., 186–87.

24. See L. Robert, "Dans une maison d'Ephèse: Un serpent et un chiffre," *Comptes rendus de l'Académie des inscriptions et belles-lettres* (1982) 126–32.

25. See M. P. Nilsson, "Roman and Greek Domestic Cult," *Opuscula Romana* 1 (1954) 77–85 (reprinted in *Opuscula Selecta* [Lund: Gleerup, 1960] 3:271–85).

26. Nilsson, "Pagan Divine Service in Late Antiquity," *Harvard Theological Review* 38 (1954) 63–69.

27. The bibliography was collected by M. P. Nilsson in *Geschichte der Griechischen Religion* (2 vols.; Munich: Beck, 1961) 2:578–79 and n. 1. Extended each year, the bibliography can be followed through the "Bulletin épigraphique" of J. Robert and L. Robert in *Revue des études grecques.*

28. See L. Robert, "Documents d'Asie Mineure XXVII: Reliefs votifs 2. 'Zeus des Chènes Jumeaux,'" *Bulletin de correspondance hellénique* 107 (1983) 515–23, which I summarize or quote verbatim.

29. See E. Varinlioğlu, "Zeus Orkamaneites and the expiatory Inscriptions," *Epigraphica Anatolica* 1 (1983) 75–87, who published three steles of confession and analyzed the mentality behind them. He is researching the origin of this mentality up until the Hittites.

30. See E. Peterson, *Eis Theos: Epigraphische, formgeschichtliche und religionsgeschichtliche Untersuchungen* (Göttingen: Vandenhoeck & Ruprecht, 1926) 268–70; and L. Robert, "Documents d'Asie Mineure XXVII," 583.

31. See O. Neugebauer and H. B. Van Hoesen, *Greek Horoscopes* (Philadelphia: American Philosophical Society, 1959).

32. F. Cumont, *Astrology and Religion among the Greeks and Romans* (New York: Dover, 1960); idem, *L'Egypte des astrologues* (Brussels: G. P. Putnam's Sons, 1937).

33. The magic texts were edited by K. Preisendanz, *Papyri Graecae magicae* (2 vols.; Leipzig and Berlin: Teubner, 1928, 1931). The magic amulets were edited by Campbell Bonner, *Studies in magical Amulets* (Ann Arbor, MI: University of Michigan Press, 1950). Three other basic works are A. D. Nock, "Greek Magical Papyri," *The Journal of Egyptian Archaeology* 15 (1929) 219–35 (reprinted in *Essays,* 176–94); A.-J. Festugière, *L'idéal religieux des Grecs et l'Evangile* (Paris: Gabalda, 1932) Excursus E: "La valeur religieuse des Papyrus magiques," 281–337; M. P. Nilsson, *Die Religion in den Griechischen Zauberpapyri* (Lund: Araberättelse, 1948; reprinted in *Opuscula Selecta* [Lund: Gleerup, 1960] 3:129–66).

34. See E. R. Dodds, *Pagan and Christian in an Age of Anxiety* (Cambridge: University Press, 1965) 74 (translated into French by H. D. Saffrey [Grenoble: La Pensée Sauvage, 1979] 90).

35. *S. Leonis Magni Tracatus* (Corpus Christianorum, S. L. 138; Tournai: Brepols, 1973) 27.4, Chavasse, p. 135. On the subject of the adoration of the sun in paganism and ancient Christianity, see F. J. Dölger, *Sol Salutis* (Münster: Aschendorff, 1925).

Bibliography

Brown, P. *The World of Late Antiquity.* London: Thames & Hudson, 1971.

Festugière, A.-J. *Personal Religion among the Greeks.* Sather Classical Lectures 26. Berkeley and Los Angeles: University of California Press, 1954. Reprint, 1960.

———. *Antioche païenne et chrétienne.* Paris: E. de Broccard, 1959.

Foerster, Richard, ed. *Libanii Opera.* 12 vols. Leipzig: Teubner, 1903–27.

Nock, A. D. *Essays on Religion and the Ancient World.* Edited by Zeph Stewart. 2 vols. Oxford: University Press, 1972.

9

Plutarch and
Second Century Platonism

J. M. DILLON

IT IS SUITABLE, perhaps, to begin such an essay as this, as Plutarch himself would have wished, with a Plutarchan profession of faith and of humility in the face of the divine. By way of preface to his reply to certain objections to divine providence presented in his essay *On the Delays in the Divine Vengeance* 549E, Plutarch says the following:

> The fact is that we really have no part or parcel in Being, but everything of a mortal nature is at some stage between coming into existence and passing away, and presents only a dim and uncertain semblance and appearance of itself; and if you apply the whole force of your mind in your desire to apprehend it, it is like the violent grasping of water, which by squeezing and compression, loses the handful enclosed, as it spurts through the fingers. (Trans. Babbitt)

In a way, these are banalities (though the imagery of taking a handful of water is lively), but they appear also to be deeply felt. When one is approaching the question of the living faith of a man like Plutarch, who is both a Platonic philosopher in an age of scholasticism, and a scholar and an antiquarian in an age of profound conservatism and reverence for the past, it is no easy matter to disentangle the genuine beliefs from the formalities. This goes also for the other figures with whom we shall be dealing: Taurus, Atticus, Albinus, Apuleius, Maximus of Tyre, and Numenius, all second-century men enmeshed in traditional attitudes, but each with personal challenges to face. To adopt Plutarch's image, one must handle the evidence gently, lest the truth spurt out like water through our fingers.

Plutarch

What, then, were the guiding principles of Plutarch's spirituality? I would identify them as devotion to Apollo as god of Delphi and to Delphic

worship and ceremony; a cosmic dualism; and, in ethics, a civilized moderation—Peripatetic *metriopatheia* as opposed to Stoic *apatheia*. Let us discuss
each of these features in turn.

The Delphic Divinity

To begin with Apollo, it is plain that for Plutarch it is not the son of Zeus
and Leto who is to be worshiped nor yet the Sun (see his strictures in *De
Pythiae oraculis* 400D), but rather the supreme God of Platonism, the Good
of the *Republic*, the Demiurge of the *Timaeus*, who reveals himself preeminently as the god of Delphi. Apollo is to be etymologized, following
the Pythagoreans, as 'Not-Many', and, therefore, the Unitary and Simple
(*De E apud Delphos* 393BC):

> In fact the Deity is not Many, as is each of us who is compounded of
> hundreds of different factors which arise in the course of our experience, a
> heterogeneous collection combined in a haphazard way. But Being must have
> Unity, even as Unity must have Being. Now divergence from Unity, because
> of its differing from Being, deviates into the creation of that which has no
> Being. Whereafter the first of the god's names is excellently well adapted to
> him. . . . He is "Apollo," that is to say, denying the Many and abjuring
> multiplicity. (Trans. Babbitt)

Such a god may be symbolized in this world by the sun (as in the
Republic), but he is by no means to be identified with the sun (393DE). As
to his nature, Plutarch accepts, both here and elsewhere, the Platonic norms,
enunciated in *Republic* 2, concerning how God should be spoken of: he is
unitary, as we have seen, unchanging, beneficent, not subject to passions.
Any untoward supernatural manifestations must be attributed not to the
Supreme God but to an inferior deity, about whom we will have more to
say later, in connection with Plutarch's dualism and demonology. In chap.
39 of his *Life of Pericles*, he takes the opportunity to remark that Pericles
was called "Olympian" because "his pure and undefiled exercise of power
was an image of the immortal gods," and he criticizes the poets for attributing anything else than this to the gods.

In a passage like this, and in numerous others, Plutarch speaks of "the
gods" but it is not clear that in this he is paying much more than lip-service
to polytheism. If we are to talk of "gods," they can be seen at most as manifestations of the supreme deity in various roles; Plutarch is happier with the
more indefinite term *to theion*, "divinity."

Such divinity, of course, is not to be thought of as having human (or any
other) form, or human personality. In another passage from the *Lives*, the
Life of Numa, chap. 8, Plutarch, in discussing Numa's alleged Pythagoreanism,

notes that he followed Pythagoras (and, it is implied, right reason) in banning images of God in either human or bestial form:

> For that philosopher maintained that the first principle of Being was beyond sense or feeling, was invisible and free from mixture, and discernible only by the intellect.

But to a God so devoid of personal characteristics what personal devotion can there be? A good vantage point from which to discern Plutarch's attitude to the divinity is the prefatory portion of his essay *On Isis and Osiris,* addressed to his good friend, the Delphic priestess Clea. The whole passage (351C–352A) constitutes a useful statement of what one might term Plutarch's "philosophical *gnōsis.*"

He begins by stating that what one asks first and foremost of the gods is a knowledge of themselves—with the Platonic caveat "so far as such a thing is attainable by men" (see *Theaetetus* 176A). God, he explains, gives human beings the other things that they request, but of *nous* and *phronēsis* he gives them only a share (*metadidōsin*), since these are properties peculiar to himself. The excellence of God lies not in his power and strength but in his wisdom, both his acquaintance with Real Being and his providential care of our realm of Becoming.

So the striving after the truth, and especially the truth of the divine things, is a fulfillment of the injunction to become like unto God. It becomes plain, however, that 'knowledge of God' does not consist merely in fashioning true propositions about the godhead, but in the performance of approved rituals and religious observances. The end of these, he says (*On Isis and Osiris* 352A), is "the knowledge (*gnōsis*) of him who is the first, the Lord of All, the object of intellection." Isis constitutes a proper symbol and vehicle of this *gnōsis,* as her very name indicates (Plutarch etymologizes it as deriving from *eidenai to on,* "knowledge of Being").

One might feel here that he is saying much of this as a compliment to Clea, but in fact he did not have to embark on the enterprise of praising Isis at all, if all this did not reflect his deeper convictions; and there is no reason to suppose that it does not. To call Plutarch a "gnostic," then, is, I think, meaningful, if the term is carefully qualified (the usefulness of the term in its "traditional" sense, after all, is being seriously questioned by scholars these days). Plutarch plainly holds that knowledge of God is not simply a matter of philosophizing in the modern sense, but rather of training and disciplining the mind through ascetic practices and the observance of ritual. Of course, intellectual philosophizing—the practice of dialectic and other Platonic methods—is necessary also, but it will not achieve knowledge of God without the observance of a certain way of life. This position can, I think, be characterized as "gnostic."

This, however, addresses only the summit, so to speak, of Plutarch's system of belief. Like Philo in relation to the observances of Judaism, Plutarch held that possession of the higher gnosis did not exempt one from the observances of one's religion. He took great pride in being a priest of Apollo at Delphi and served actively as such for many years, even into old age, as he testifies in his essay *Whether an Old Man should Engage in Public Affairs* (792F):

> Now surely you know that I have been serving the Pythian Apollo for many Pythiads, but you would not say: "Plutarch, you have done enough sacrificing, marching in processions, and dancing in choruses, and now that you are older it is time to put off the garland and to desert the oracle on account of your age." (Trans. H. N. Fowler)

As the elderly Plutarch danced in his choruses, in whose honor did he consider that he was dancing? One does not dance, I think, in honor of the Good, or of the One. Possibly Plutarch felt, as did later Platonists such as Porphyry, Iamblichus, or Proclus (though not, I think, Plotinus), that the correct way to honor the deity was through the forms of ritual traditional to one's culture, but one may detect also in Plutarch, as later in Proclus, a delight in ritual for its own sake, which is only, after all, to put Plutarch in the mainstream of traditional Greek piety, as emphasized by A. H. Armstrong in the introduction to this volume.

Cosmic Dualism

Plutarch is notable, within the Platonic spectrum, for his dualist tendencies. It is the general consensus of modern scholars, as it was of ancient ones, that Plato was not a dualist, in the strong sense. He recognizes the disorderly influence of matter, certainly in the *Timaeus,* but even in *Laws* 10, despite appearances, there is no need to assume any such entity as an evil world soul. However, Plato does lay himself open to such an interpretation for those who want to find such an entity, and his description of the creation of the world in the *Timaeus* is ambiguous enough to persuade some distinguished modern scholars, such as Gregory Vlastos, that he envisages a precosmic state of disorderly motion, upon which order is then imposed. Plutarch was certainly of this opinion, which he presents in his treatise *On the Creation of the Soul in the Timaeus*—recognizing, however, that in this he is going against the views of his predecessors. It is his contention, carefully argued particularly in chaps. 6-7, that the cause of evil in the world cannot be matter, which has no qualities or propensities whatever, but an irrational, 'evil' soul and that this is Plato's doctrine in the *Timaeus*, *Philebus*, *Politicus*, and *Laws* (see particularly *On the Creation* 1014B).

I have suggested elsewhere that Plutarch may owe his dualism to his teacher Ammonius, whom he portrays in the *De E* (394A) as holding that the sublunar world is in the grip of a secondary god whose characteristics are antithetical to those of Apollo.[1] But wherever he derived it from, it seems to be part of his world view. It emerges strongly in the *Isis and Osiris*, where its Persian origin is also made evident (see 369A–E). It is worth quoting from this passage what is a definitive statement of Plutarch's dualism:

> There has, therefore, come down from the theologians and lawgivers to both poets and philosophers [he has quoted Heraclitus and Euripides] this ancient belief, which is of anonymous origin, but is given strong and tenacious evidence—that the universe is not kept on high of itself without mind and reason and guidance, nor is it only one principle that rules and directs it as it were by rudders and curbing reins, but that many powers do so who are a mixture of evil and good. Rather since Nature, to be plain, contains nothing that is unmixed, it is not one steward that dispenses our affairs for us, as though mixing drinks from two jars in an hotel. Life and the cosmos, on the contrary—if not the whole of the cosmos, at least the earthly one below the moon, which is heterogeneous, variegated and subject to all manner of changes—are compounded of two opposite principles (*archai*) and of two antithetic powers (*dynameis*), one of which leads by a straight path and to the right, while the other reverses and bends back. For if nothing comes into being without a cause, and if good could not provide the cause of evil, then Nature must contain in itself the creation and origin of evil as well as of good.

For Plutarch, the tensions within the cosmos center on the figure of the World Soul, symbolized in the myth of Isis and Osiris by Isis, who is not itself an evil entity but irrational and subject to the evil influence of the Indefinite Dyad, symbolized by Typhon, or Ahriman. This World Soul, however, strives blindly toward the light of order, represented by the One and its Logos, and accepts ordering from that source, which leads to the creation of the physical cosmos (see *Isis and Osiris* 372E; *On the Creation* 1026E–1027A). The same tension must be seen as present in the human soul, and thus Plutarch's spirituality may be seen as containing a more pronounced notion of 'original sin' than is usual for a Platonist.

On the other hand, Plutarch is no 'world-negater' in a gnostic sense, or even to the extent that this might be said of the Neopythagorean Numenius, whom we shall consider presently. He simply sees this world as a theater in which a cosmic drama is played out, resulting from the tension between opposing forces, but where the Good triumphs. His position in ethics bears this out.

Ethics

In the area of ethical theory, a Platonist of Plutarch's time had in effect a choice between adhering to the Peripatetic doctrines of moderation of the passions (*metriopatheia*) and of virtue as a mean, and the more austere Stoic doctrines of extirpation of the passions (*apatheia*) and of the almost unattainable level of virtue of the Stoic sage, the great majority even of philosophers being mere 'improvers' (*prokoptontes*), not yet possessing true virtue. Antiochus of Ascalon, in the previous century, despite his Stoic tendencies in physics, was Peripatetic in his ethics, as were Taurus and Albinus later, in the mid-second century, whereas Eudorus of Alexandria and Atticus (who was Plutarch's follower in other respects) favored the Stoic ethical system. This is not, of course, the way they would have seen it: Plato could be quoted in support of either position, and Aristotle's *Nicomachean Ethics,* in particular, seems to have been taken by Platonists to represent Academic teaching.

Plutarch himself, despite frequently striking Stoic attitudes in his popular essays, was firmly on the side of *metriopatheia* and the mean. The essay *On Moral Virtue* gives a definitive statement of his ethical theory. Here Aristotle's doctrine in *Nicomachean Ethics* 2.5–7 forms the basis of his position, though tinged with the Pythagorean conception of the mean as a quasi-musical harmonizing of the irrational soul by the rational (see *On Moral Virtue* 444EF). For Plutarch, the individual soul is a battlefield of opposing forces, even as is the cosmos. In the course of criticizing the Stoic conception of a unitary soul, he has the following to say (445B):

> In this last instance [the case of temperance], indeed, the irrational seems, with particular clearness, to allow us to observe the difference between itself and the rational, and to show that passion is essentially quite a different thing from reason. For self-control (*enkrateia*) would not differ from temperance (*sōphrosynē*), nor incontinence (*akrasia*) from intemperance (*akolasia*), as regards the pleasures or desires, if it were the same part of the soul that we naturally use for desiring as for forming judgments. But the fact is that temperance belongs to the sphere where reason guides and manages the passionate element like a gentle animal obedient to the reins, making it yielding in its desires and willingly receptive of moderation and propriety; but the self-controlled man, while he does indeed direct his desire by the strength and mastery of reason, yet does so not without pain, nor by persuasion, but as it plunges sideways and resists, as though with blow and curb, he forcibly subdues it and holds it in, being the while himself full of internal struggle and turmoil. (Trans. Helmbold)

He here invokes the Platonic image of the charioteer and horses, from the *Phaedrus* myth, as constituting a particularly striking image of the soul's true nature. Plutarch's moral stance is in fact no less stern than that of any Stoic; it is just that his vision of the world, and of the human soul, is different.

Daemons

I have not, so far, alluded to a popular topic in discussions of Plutarch, his views on daemons. This aspect of his belief structure should not be neglected, but it is wrong to single him out as unusual in this respect. Everyone in Plutarch's world, not least the Christians, believed in daemons, in the sense of intermediate beings between God and humans, beneficent or maleficent, to whom a great many phenomena affecting one's daily life could be attributed. It has been well remarked that daemons in the ancient world filled many of the roles taken on by germs today. They were responsible for diseases of both mind and body, as well as for many infelicities of the weather. But on a more philosophically significant level, they provided a bridge between a divinity who (or *which*) was not subject to change or passions nor even possessed a personality and suffering and hoping humanity.

Plutarch's views on daemons are not, I think, entirely consistent, but they are nonetheless interesting for that.[2] One can discern in his thought both a 'static' and a 'dynamic' doctrine of daemons. On the one hand, we have passages (e.g., *On the Obsolescence of Oracles* 416C–F) in which what seems to be envisaged is a permanent class of intermediate beings, relieving god of too intimate connection with the concerns of earthly existence; on the other, we have a remarkable doctrine of the apparently endless cycle of changes upward and downward on the scale of being, which souls may undergo as they pass from human to daemon to god and, it seems, back again (e.g., *On the Face in the Moon* 944 CD; *De defectu oraculorum* 415B).

It is not relevant to our present purpose to discuss Plutarch's theory of daemons as such. All that concerns us is to note that daemons serve, on the one hand, to exempt god from any imputation of malevolent behavior or of taking pleasure in bloody or cruel sacrifices, and on the other, to buttress Plutarch's belief in the immortality of the soul and reincarnation, which, though traditionally Platonic, has some distinctive aspects.

Soul and Intellect

Plutarch derives from somewhere a strong contrast between soul and intellect (*nous*) (e.g., *On the Daemon of Socrates* 591 DE) and, together with that, a belief in what he calls a "double" or two-stage death, set out in the myth of the dialogue *On the Face in the Moon* (945BC). Soul and intellect

18. Relief of Apollo and Nike. Roman. Neo-Attic school. late 1st century B.C.–early 1st century A.D.

depart from the body at what we call death and ascend to the region of the moon, but then intellect leaves soul behind and ascends to the region of the sun. The reverse process also takes place, the sun sowing intellects in the moon, and the moon sowing the new intelligized souls into bodies.

In another myth, that of the dialogue *On the Daemon of Socrates* (591DE), we learn more. Relations between intellects and the soul–body complexes they manage will differ widely; normally the intellect is separate, floating above the body "like a fisherman's buoy," and it is this that may be seen as our personal daemon, but sometimes, it seems, it is dragged down into body as well.

Such a belief in a separable intellect is reminiscent of a doctrine that turns up in the Hermetic Corpus (*Tractate* 10, esp. sections. 19–21), where we learn that not all individuals have a *nous* and that in some cases the relationship with the *nous* becomes so unsatisfactory that it constitutes an avenging daemon. Whether Plutarch derives any influence from that quarter is doubtful, but certainly this doctrine, like his basic dualism, is an accretion of his Platonism brought in from outside.

Basically, however, Plutarch's religion is that of a Platonist, and such is his resounding affirmation of the immortality of the soul, delivered in the course of an attack on the Epicureans, toward the end of his treatise *That Epicurus Actually Makes a Pleasant Life Impossible* (1105CD):

> Hence in abolishing belief in immortality, they also abolish the pleasantest and greatest hope of ordinary men.

> What, then, do we suppose they do to the pleasures of the good, whose lives have been just and holy, who look forward to nothing evil in that other world but instead to all that is most glorious and divine? For in the first place, just as athletes receive the crown not while they are engaged in the contest but when it is over and victory is won, so men who believe that life is done are inspired by their virtue to a most wonderful confidence when they fix their eyes on these hopes, which include that of seeing at last the condign punishment of those who in their wealth and power are injurious and insolent now and who in their folly laugh all higher powers to scorn. In the next place no one impassioned for the truth and the vision of reality has ever been fully satisfied in this world, since the light of reason, veiled by the body as by a mist or cloud, is wavering and indistinct; but like a bird that gazes upward, they are ready to take wing from the body to some luminous expanse, and thus they lighten and disburden the soul of the gear of mortality, taking philosophy as an exercise in death. (Trans. Einarson and De Lacy)

This, inspired as it is by Plato's *Phaedo*, gives no hint of the complexities arising out of one's relationship with one's *nous* or problems of identity resulting from reincarnation. What Plutarch really believed in that area is not clear, but certainly he held, with Socrates at the end of the *Apology*, that "nothing bad can happen to a good man."

We began with God, and let us end with God. The purpose of life, for Plutarch as a Platonist, is "becoming like to God," *homoiōsis theō*. We have seen this expressed in this passage from the dialogue *On the Divine Vengeance* (550DE):

> Consider that God, as Plato says (*Theaetus* 176E), offers himself to all as a pattern of every excellence, thus rendering human virtue, which is in some sort an assimilation to himself (*exhomoiōsin . . . pros hauton*), accessible to all who can "follow God." Indeed this was the origin of the change whereby universal nature, disordered before, became a "cosmos": it came to resemble after a fashion and participate in the form and excellence of God. The same philosopher says further that Nature kindled vision in us so that the soul, beholding the heavenly motions and wondering at the sight, should grow to accept and cherish all that moves in stateliness and order, and thus come to hate discordant and errant passions and to shun the aimless and haphazard as the source of all vice and jarring error; for man is fitted to derive from God no greater blessing than to become settled in virtue through copying and aspiring to the beauty and the goodness that are his. (Trans. Einarson and De Lacy)

Plutarch's spirituality, then, is basically optimistic and world-affirming. He recognizes a tension in the world between good and evil, but without falling into nihilistic, world-abhoring gloom. In that, at least, he is more akin to Plotinus after him than to many of his contemporaries, products of that "age of anxiety" which E. R. Dodds so acutely identified in his well-known book of that title.[3]

Other Platonists of the Second Century

It would be desirable, I think, to set Plutarch in the context of other second-century Platonists and Pythagoreans to see how representative or otherwise he is of Platonism in this era, but unfortunately the material for making such an assessment is very largely lacking. We know the names and something of the views of fully half a dozen figures of this period in Platonism, but we do not have much that tells us what religious beliefs they held.

What we know of L. Calvenus Taurus is derived primarily from the reminiscences of Aulus Gellius in his *Noctes Atticae*, and these reveal an urbane and donnish figure, not subject to mystical or ascetic excesses. However, we do learn, not from Gellius but from Iamblichus, in his *De Anima* (ap. Stobaeus *Anthologium* 1.378, Wachsmuth), that Taurus "and his followers" put forward two views as to why souls are sent by the gods into bodies—*either* "for the completion of the universe, that there may be as many living things in the cosmos as there are in the intelligible realm" (a doctrine derived from Plato's *Timaeus*) or (what is more interesting) "that the gods may reveal themselves through souls; for the gods come out into the open and manifest themselves through the pure and unsullied life of souls." This latter notion has, it seems to me, a distinctly religious content. We are placed on this earth as projections of the divinity, and it is up to us to live up to this high calling, necessarily by 'likening' ourselves to God, in the accepted Platonic manner. This is perhaps derivable in part from such Platonic passages as *Phaedo* 62B (we are here on guard duty, as it were, for the gods) and *Laws* 644DE (we are puppets of the gods), but the tone of it is rather different. However, on a doxographic notice such as this one should not build too much.

We are no better served with such figures as Atticus and Albinus. From the former we have a polemical tract directed against those who try to interpret Plato through Aristotle[4]—and thus against Aristotelianism. This includes a spirited defense of God's providence against Aristotle's effective abolition of it, which takes on distinctly theological overtones. Atticus was doubtless a man of exemplary Platonic piety, but one cannot, I think, derive a true idea of his personal spirituality from this rhetorical polemic. From Albinus, on the other hand, what we have is a dry scholastic handbook of Platonic doctrine, from which nothing that could be regarded as a personal spiritual stance can be extracted.[5]

The situation is not much different with the interesting figure of Apuleius, who also, in his self-styled capacity as a Platonic philosopher (he may more properly be regarded as a lawyer and rhetorician), writes a treatise on Platonic philosophy, as well as an essay *On the Daemon of Socrates*. These, however, are products of scholasticism and rhetoric respectively and reveal little about Apuleius's personal views, except that he was a Platonist. The personal devotion to Isis shown by Lucius in *Metamorphoses* 11 is possibly much nearer the views of the real Apuleius, but that is more relevant to the beliefs of "ordinary men" than of Platonists as such.

Another quasi-Platonist figure of whom we have evidence is the sophist Maximus of Tyre, a number of whose orations concern topics that could come under the head of "spirituality." Particularly interesting are Oration 2 (Hobein), *Who Is God according to Plato?*, which complements the descriptions of the divinity given by Albinus and Apuleius in the handbooks; Orations 8 and 9, *On the Daemon of Socrates*, which gives a comprehensive theory of daemons analogous to that of Apuleius; Oration 5, *Whether One Should Pray*; and Oration 13, *Whether, If Divination Exists, There Is Free Will*. It is in these last two orations, which concern the problem of providence and free will, that we may most possibly discover something of Maximus's own views, and indeed this topic may serve to unite our discussion of all the previous figures, since the conflict between the doctrines of God's providence and human free will is perhaps the most burning philosophical and spiritual issue in second-century Platonism.

For the Stoics, being materialists and determinists, there is no theological problem (though some logical ones remain), nor is there for the Epicureans, who allow a different sort of determinism to hold sway; but for Platonists (and Aristotelians) the contradiction between the all-foreseeing and all-directing providence of God and the urge to preserve initiative and free choice on the part of the individual was a very grave problem, over which much ink was spilled in this period and later. If all is foreordained, how can there be praise and blame for human actions, and what is the use of praying to the gods? If human beings are free agents, how can their actions be foreseen by God, and in what sense, therefore, is God omniscient?

Besides Maximus's rather superficial contributions, we have a whole essay *On Fate* falsely attributed to Plutarch,[6] another treatise of the same title by the Peripatetic Alexander of Aphrodisias,[7] and chapters in the handbooks of both Albinus (chap. 26) and Apuleius (chap. 12). There is no need in the present instance to go into the complexities of the scholastic solutions offered in particular by Pseudo-Plutarch. Suffice it to say that, although the problem can hardly be said to have been solved in this period, much progress was made toward defining its parameters. Somehow the concepts of providence, free will, fate, and chance have to be fitted harmoniously into an overall world view.

For a Platonist, it is axiomatic, first of all, that God cares for the world, has set the course of events in it in motion, and knows, at least in general, what will happen to it. But it is also axiomatic that the human will is autonomous (this guaranteed for later Platonists by the famous phrase in *Republic* 10.617: "The blame is with the chooser; God is blameless"). It was also generally accepted that, below the Moon at least, *heimarmenē* or Fate, in the sense of a chain of necessary causes, held sway in the physical world and had considerable effect on our lives. But it was held to be somehow subsumed into, or comprehended by, God's providence, and it still left room for *to eph' hēmin*, "what is in our power," or individual discretion. It is in trying to accommodate these two concepts to each other that most ingenuity is expended. Here is Albinus's attempt:

All things are within the sphere of [lit. "in"] Fate, but not all things are fated. (*Didaskalikos* 26)

Fate has the status of a law. It does not say, as it were, "Because so-and-so has done this, he will suffer this," for that would result in an infinity of possibilities, since the actions that take place are infinite, and the results of them are also infinite.

> [If all things are fated], then what is in our power (*to eph' hēmin*) will disappear, and therefore praise and blame and everything like this.

> [The chain of causality begins] because, if a soul chooses such and such in life, it will then also perform such and such actions, and such and such results will follow for it. The soul is thus autonomous, and it is in its power to act or not, and this is not forced upon it, but what follows upon its action will be brought about in accordance with Fate.

Whether we find this satisfactory or not is beside the point. The important thing is that the preservation of a role for individual free will is a basic condition of Platonic spirituality. Only on this basis do prayer, self-discipline, and the practice of the virtues have any meaning.

It remains to round out our survey by considering at least one important representative of the Pythagorean "wing" of Platonism in this era. I use this form of words, since I do not see Neopythagoreanism as an independent philosophical movement in this era, so much as an attitude that might be taken up within Platonism. Admittedly, there is a tension between devotion to Pythagoras and to Plato as founding fathers, since a Pythagorean will attribute all that is good in Platonism to Pythagoras and his immediate followers and regard Plato as one (admittedly brilliant) follower. One may even become quite belligerent, as does Moderatus of Gades,[8] against the alleged tendency of Platonists to appropriate all that is best in Pythagoreanism for themselves and leave Pythagoreans with the dross. But generally, Pythagoreanism simply means, besides a personal devotion to Pythagoras and particular enthusiasm for number mysticism and a mathematical model for the universe, a more austere stance in ethics and the observance of a certain *bios*, or way of life, involving abstention from meat and beans and the adoption of the other Pythagorean rules, or *symbola*.

Leaving aside the remarkable figure of Apollonius of Tyana, whom I do not see as a philosopher in the strict sense and who may in any case be largely a literary creation of Philostratus, the only Pythagorean of whose spirituality we can form much idea is Numenius of Apamea, and even with him the situation is not very satisfactory, since we have only fragments of his works (once again, as in the case of Atticus, in Eusebius's *Praeparatio evangelica*) and doxographic reports.[9]

One first aspect of Numenius's spirituality to note is his omnivorous hospitality to the great religions of the world. In fragment 1a, we learn from Eusebius of his great respect for the teachings of the Brahmins, the Jews, the Magi, and the Egyptians (only the Druids, it seems, escaped his benevolent attentions). Of course, respect for ancient wisdom is very much a part of Platonism from the time of Plato himself, but Numenius seems to have carried his interest rather further than others, especially in respect to Judaism. Origen tells us (fr. 1b and c) that he discoursed much about the God of the Jews in his dialogue *On the Good* and that he gave allegorical interpretations of the works of Moses and the prophets. There is the intriguing possibility that he was acquainted with the works of Philo, but this cannot be proved. At any rate, from our point of view, what is important is his sense of the unity of religious experience and its concordance with the teaching of Plato and Pythagoras.

Other features of his philosophy connect him in an intriguing way with an extraordinary production of the second century A.D., the so-called *Chaldaean Oracles*,[10] the composition (possibly through a series of mediumistic trances) of a certain Julian in the reign of Marcus Aurelius. Both Numenius and the *Oracles* make a strong distinction between a First God, whom both claim is generally unknown to mortals,[11] and a secondary, demiurgic god, who is immediately responsible for the creation and guidance of the world. This is not a distinction made by Plutarch, though some such distinction appears in chap. 10 of Albinus's *Didaskalikos*. The relations between these two in Numenius's philosophy are of great interest, but not immediately relevant to our purpose. More to our purpose is to observe the mode of approach that Numenius recommends to his supreme principle, since it anticipates to some extent that of Plotinus to the One and may well be in its turn influenced by the doctrine of the *Chaldaean Oracles* that the Father may only be known by the "flower of the intellect," the mystical element in each of us (fr. 1). Fragment 2 of Numenius's *On the Good* provides a striking image of the watcher on the shore catching glimpses of a tiny fishing boat between the waves:

> We can acquire the notion of any material object from the comparison of similar objects and by the distinguishing characteristics of objects available to our sense: the Good, on the other hand, it is quite impossible to grasp on the basis of anything present to us or similar to it, but like someone seated in a lookout post, who, straining his eyes, catches sight for one moment of one of those little fishing vessels, a one-man skiff all on its own, bobbing amid the waves, even so must one remove oneself far from the things of sense, and consort solitarily with the Good in its solitude, where there is neither man nor any other living thing, nor any body great or small, but some unspeakable and truly indescribable wondrous solitude, there where are the accustomed places, the haunts and pleasances of the Good, and it itself in peace, in benevolence, in its tranquillity, in its sovereignty, riding gently upon the surface of Being.

Numenius's view of the world is more starkly dualist than that of Plutarch. Not only does he believe in an evil principle at work in the world, which he identifies with the Indefinite Dyad of Pythagoreanism (fr. 52), but he feels a dualism within the individual soul, to the extent of postulating two souls within each individual (fr. 43), a rational and an irrational. The descent of the rational soul into body he sees as an unqualified misfortune (fr. 48), and no reconciliation, only constant struggle, can come about between these two souls. This "gnostic" view he shares with the *Chaldaean Oracles* (fr. 102–4, 107, 112), and it adds up to a distinctly world-negating attitude, in distinction to that of Plutarch.

The spirituality of the second-century Platonists is not, therefore, a uniform thing, but embraces a fairly broad spectrum of attitudes, particularly toward the physical world and our place in it. The full extent of the diversity of the views of these thinkers is obscured for us, however, by the nature of the surviving evidence. Especially in the case of Numenius, we may regret the loss of a full text of his dialogue *On the Good,* and a man like Atticus, when not incensed by Peripatetic pretensions, might have revealed spiritual depths. On the other hand, it was not the fashion among Platonists of this period, as far as one can see, to compose personal testaments; there is no Platonist equivalent of the *Meditations* of Marcus Aurelius. Plutarch comes nearest to such self-revelation, but his utterances are generally given the protective filter of dialogue. Nevertheless, in the case of Plutarch, at least, one can feel, in reading his works, that one is touching a man.

Notes

1. Dillon, *Middle Platonists,* 191.
2. See Guy Soury, *La démonologie de Plutarque* (Paris: Les Belles Lettres, 1942); F. E. Brenk, *In Mist Apparelled,* esp. chaps. 6, 7; and Dillon, *Middle Platonists,* 216–21.
3. Dodds, *Pagan and Christian in an Age of Anxiety.*
4. Fragments are preserved by Eusebius in his *Praeparatio evangelica,* but the material is most conveniently available in the Budé edition of É. des Places (Paris: Les Belles Lettres, 1977).
5. If indeed Albinus it is. The *Didaskalikos* is attributed in the manuscript to "Alkinoos." It has long been held that this was a scribal error for "Albinos," but John Whittaker (whose new Budé edition of the *Didaskalikos* may be expected shortly) has made a spirited effort to reestablish the name of "Alkinoos." The existing edition is that of P. Louis (Budé; Paris: Les Belles Lettres, 1945). *Didaskalikos* 19.10 contains interesting doctrine on the nature of God, but it cannot be claimed as personal to Albinus.
6. There is an edition by E. Valgiglio, *Ps.-Plutarco, De Fato* (Rome: A. Signorelli, 1964). See also vol. 6 of the Loeb edition of Plutarch, and Dillon, *Middle Platonists,* 320–26.

7. Now in a good edition by R. W. Sharples, *Alexander of Aphrodisias: On Fate* (London: Duckworth, 1983).

8. See Dillon, *Middle Platonists,* 346.

9. A collection of fragments and good introduction and notes are in the Budé edition of É. des Places, *Numénius* (Paris: Les Belles Lettres, 1973). See also Dillon, *Middle Platonists,* 361–79.

10. Fragments edited by É. des Places (Budé; Paris: Les Belles Lettres, 1971).

11. Numenius fr. 17; des Places; *Chaldaean Oracles,* fr. 7, des Places.

Bibliography

For the translations of Plutarch, I have used those by the various editors of his works in the Loeb Classical Library series, making such minor alterations as seemed desirable: *Plutarch's Moralia* (15 vols.; Cambridge, MA: Harvard University Press, 1949-). All other translations are my own. The relevant literature is not very extensive, but the following works may be helpful:

Babut, Daniel. *Plutarch et le Stoicisme.* Paris: Presses universitaires de France, 1969.

Barrow, Reginald Haynes. *Plutarch and His Times.* Bloomington: Indiana University Press, 1967.

Brenk, Frederick E. *In Mist Apparelled: Religious Themes in Plutarch's Moralia and Lives.* Leiden: Brill, 1977.

Dillon, John. *The Middle Platonists.* Ithaca, NY: Cornell University Press, 1977.

Dodds, E. R. *Pagan and Christian in an Age of Anxiety.* Cambridge: University Press, 1965.

Dörrie, Heinrich. *Platonica Minora.* Munich: W. Fink, 1976. (Collected essays on Middle Platonism).

Krämer, Hans Joachim. *Der Ursprung der Geistmetaphysik.* Amsterdam: B. R. Güner, 1967.

Merlan, Philip. *From Platonism to Neoplatonism.* 2nd rev. ed. The Hague: Nijhoff, 1960.

———. "The Later Academy and Platonism" and "The Pythagoreans." Chaps. 4 and 5 of *The Cambridge History of Later Greek and Early Medieval Philosophy.* Edited by A. H. Armstrong. Cambridge: University Press, 1970.

———. *Monopsychism, Mysticism, Metaconsciousness: Problems of the Soul in the Neo-aristotelian and Neoplatonic Tradition.* The Hague: Nijhoff, 1963.

Theiler, Willy. *Die Vorbereitung des Neuplatonismus.* Berlin: Weidmann, 1930.

10

Neoplatonist Spirituality

I. Plotinus and Porphyry

PIERRE HADOT

I N HIS *Life of Plotinus* (*Vita Plotini*), Porphyry admirably summarizes in
a few phrases the various aspects of his master's spiritual life.[1] In so
doing, he reveals his own conception of the spiritual life. By reading
and commenting on these lines of Porphyry, we are able, at one and
the same time, to reveal the spirituality of the disciple and to begin to be
admitted to that of the master:

Plotinus was present to himself and to others, and he never relaxed his self-
turned attention except in sleep; even sleep he reduced by taking very little
food, often not even a piece of bread, and by his continuous turning in contemplation to his intellect. . . . Yet, though he shielded so many from the
worries and cares of ordinary life, he never, while awake, relaxed his intent
concentration upon the intellect. He was gentle too, and at the disposal of
all who had any sort of acquaintance with him. . . . The oracle[2] says that he
was mild and kind, most gentle and attractive, and we knew ourselves that
he was like this. It says too that he sleeplessly kept his soul pure and ever
strove towards the divine, which he loved with all his soul, and did everything to be delivered and "escape from the bitter wave of blood-drinking life
here." So to this god-like man above all, who often raised himself in thought,
according to the ways Plato teaches in the *Banquet*, to the First and Transcendent God, that God appeared who has neither shape nor any intelligible
form, but is throned above intellect and all the intelligible. I, Porphyry, who
am now in my sixty-eighth year, declare that once I drew near and was united
to him. To Plotinus, "the goal ever near was shown": for his end and goal
was to be united to, to approach the God who is over all things. Four times
while I was with him he attained that goal, in an unspeakable actuality and
not in potency only. . . . Through inward and outward wakefulness, the god
says, "you saw many fair sights, hard to see" for men who study philosophy.

230

The contemplation of men may certainly become better than human, but as compared to divine knowledge it may be fair and fine, but not enough to be able to grasp the depths as the gods grasp them.

Obviously, in this description we recognize first of all one of the traditional elements of Platonic spirituality, the desire to escape from the world. "He did everything to be delivered and escape from the bitter wave of blood-drinking life here." This is an echo of Plato *Theaetetus* (176AB) and the *Phaedo* (65E, 66–67, 79C, 81B, 83BD, 84A). It is in this sense that, for Plato (*Phaedo* 67CE), philosophy is preparing for death, because it is the endeavor to separate the soul from the body. Plotinus and Porphyry also conceive of philosophy in this way (Plotinus I 2 [19], 5, 4; I 7 [54], 3, 22; I 8 [51], 7, 13; V 1 [10], 10, 25). Porphyry, for his part, has a veritable predilection for the expression "escaping from the body" (*Letter to Marcella* 10, des Places), which we find echoed in the young Augustine (*Soliloquia* 1.14.24).[4] To separate the soul from the body, a strict asceticism must be practiced, "to reduce the body and make it worse." (Plotinus I 4 [14], 14, 21–22).[5] The wise man takes care of his bodily health, but will not wish to be altogether without experience of illness, nor indeed also of pain (Plotinus I 4 [14], 14, 21–22).

Plotinus does not say how we ought to practice this asceticism, but Porphyry, describing his master's virtues, enters into detail: "very little food, sleeplessly"; and in the treatise *On Abstinence from the Flesh of Animals* he states the conditions of sleeplessness (*agrypnia*); he specifies not drinking wine, having a very light meal close to dawn, having a well-lit and well-ventilated house, open to the winds, and a simple, dry bed (1.27).[6]

Porphyry and Plotinus attach particular importance to abstaining from the flesh of animals (*Life* 2.4). It is a Pythagorean trait, adopted in the Platonic school, to which Porphyry too returns in his *Letter to Marcella:* "The gods have prescribed that we should keep pure by abstaining from flesh and sexual relations" (28, des Places). This asceticism, this escape from the body, this wish to detach oneself from the sensible world does not, however, mean that the philosopher is not interested in other people. Plotinus, Porphyry tells us, "was present at once to himself and others" (*Life* 8.19–24): he was concerned not only with his disciples but also with children whom high-ranking Romans entrusted to him, to look after both their education and the defense of their inheritance (*Life* 9.5–18).

On the subject of the philosopher's rapport with others, about this "presence to others" of which Porphyry speaks, we find no theoretical information in the treatises of Plotinus. But this does not mean that Plotinus was not aware of this aspect of spiritual life; we know from Porphyry that his treatises were not written to provide a complete exposition of his thought, but in reply to certain questions (*Life* 4.12; 5.6). In fact, philosophizing, in a general way, in all the ancient schools is philosophizing together (*symphilosophein*) (Diogenes Laertius *Lives* 5.52; 10.18). The philosopher's essential task is as director of conscience. In his *Letter to Marcella* (3) we see Porphyry presenting himself as the director of his wife's conscience and suggesting to her, in accordance with the usual method for the direction of souls, a whole series of maxims for meditations borrowed either from lessons he has given her, or from the tradition—primarily Pythagorean but also Epicurean. In the *Life of Plotinus,* Porphyry presents Plotinus as a director of conscience whose clairvoyance he had been able to experience (11.11–19). Porphyry tells us that Plotinus was present to himself and to others. For Porphyry and for Plotinus himself, at a certain level, these two presences are identical. In fact, all souls can communicate in the same spiritual presence, Porphyry writes to his wife Marcella:

> Of my shade, of this visible phantom, neither the presence, nor the sad absence will be of use to you if you apply yourself to escaping from the body. The surest method of reaching me purely, of having me present with you night and day by all that is most pure and beautiful in our union, without my ever being able to be separated from you, is to practice retreating into yourself. (*Letter to Marcella* 10, des Places; trans. P. Hadot)

The best method, then, of being present to others is to be present to yourself. Being present to yourself is in fact being present to the universal being, to the totality in which all beings commune. This is why Porphyry, in order to describe the intense presence to himself, which was one of the characteristic qualities of his master Plotinus, speaks of "his continuous turning in contemplation to his intellect" and adds that "he never relaxed his intent concentration upon the intellect" (*Life* 8.24; 9.18). Indeed, in his treatise *On Abstinence from the Flesh of Animals,* Porphyry proclaims the necessity of returning to the real self and that the real self is nothing other than the intellect, so that the goal of life is to "live according to the Intellect" (*zēn kata noun*) (*On Abstinence* 1.29.4). With regard to Plotinus, we shall see what meaning Plotinus himself was able to give this sort of formula, which is an echo of the famous Aristotelian formula which states that "what is proper to man is the life in the intellect" (*bios kata noun*) (Aristotle *Nicomachean Ethics* 118a6)

It will suffice for the moment to explain this identification of the self and the intellect, if we recall the doctrine of Plotinus according to which the summit of the soul is identical with the intellect, because this summit always remains in the intelligible (Plotinus IV 8 [6], 8, 1–6): this intellect is at the same time our intellect and the divine Intellect to which it is united.[7] To be present to the self, to be conscious of the real self, is thus to be present to God. In the little book that Porphyry entitled *Introductions to Intelligible Things*, which is composed, to a great extent, of extracts from Plotinus, Porphyry insists more than his master on the identity between presence to the self and presence to Being, that is to say, to God:

> To the extent to which you approach yourself (and yet you are present to yourself and inseparable from yourself) you approach Being as well, because it is certainly inseparable from you by essence as you are from yourself. . . . As to those who leave their own being and turn towards other things, they are absent from themselves and Being is absent from them too. (Porphyry *Intelligible Things* 40)[8]

Presence to self can thus be identical with presence to others on the condition that one has oneself reached a degree of inwardness sufficient for discovering that the self, the true self, is not situated in corporeal individuality but in the spiritual world, where all beings are within each other, where each is the whole and yet remains itself.

The Plotinian Experience of Union

Obviously, the allusion that attracts our attention the most in Porphyry's description of the spiritual life of Plotinus, which was quoted above, is that to the four experiences of union with God, which Plotinus went through in the course of the several years during which Porphyry stayed with him (*Life* 23.1–27). Here Porphyry lets us glimpse the ideas about the union with God that were accepted in the school of Plotinus. First of all, the goal of human life "is to be united to, to approach the God who is over all things." This goal can be reached during life, but only very rarely. It is a precise experience, which is transitory and cannot last. It is an experience of presence: God appears, we are close to him, we are united with him. This experience, which transcends intelligence, may, however, occur while we are engaged in an intellectual exercise: the first God appeared to Plotinus while he was uplifted in thought toward him, along the lines defined by Plato in the *Symposium*. Porphyry is obviously alluding here to the ascent to the Beautiful described by Diotima in this dialogue (Plato *Symposium* 210, 211).

It is precisely this experience of union that is connected with love. Porphyry tells us that Plotinus "loved the divine with all his soul." The God who appears in this experience is the First and Transcendent God, who . . . is throned above intellect and all the intelligible. It is the One, then, or the

Good, whose absolute simplicity, according to Plotinus, transcends the intellect and produces it.

The Journey of the Soul to God

The Plotinus texts confirm this description in part, but they reveal other aspects of the Plotinian experience. First, they describe the journey by which the soul can try to ascend toward the divine, so that the experience of union may be possible. In ascending through the hierarchical levels of reality, the soul passed through the stages of spiritual progress; that is to say, it brought about a radical transformation of its whole being. It, the real human, becomes conscious of itself; it discovers that it depends upon a superior divine Intellect which illuminates it and permits it to think; that it emanates from a transcendent Good that is superior to Intellect and subject to its attraction. It is not a theoretical journey undertaken by reason alone; rather, it is a movement in consciousness, which transforms its being,[9] and an exercise in inner unification.

In its first stage, this journey can take two different routes: one consists in reflecting on the existence of the sensible world; the other turns resolutely toward the interior of the soul. Both, however, are destined to attain the same goal: the spiritual separation of the soul and body, and life according to the Intellect. The first route consists, then, in contemplating the splendor of the sensible world in order to ascend to the soul of the world that begets it and to discover in this way the power, the superiority of the soul in comparison with the body (Plotinus V 1 [10], 2, 1-5). If the soul of the world has such a power and such an action, it is because it contemplates eternally the divine Intellect and the world of eternal Forms which is within the divine Intellect and which is the model of the sensible world (Plotinus II 3 [52], 17, 15 and 18, 10; II 9 [33], 2, 12-17; IV 3 [27], 6, 15). The human soul thus becomes conscious of being itself related, a "sister" of the soul of the world, which it must take for its model (Plotinus V 1 [10], 2, 40; II 9 [33], 18, 30; IV 3 [27], 6, 13). For the soul of the world remains immobile and impassive; it is not disturbed by the body of the world which it governs. It is thus the model for the wise person, who must not be disturbed by the body but must, like the soul of the world, unite the human intellect to the divine Intellect (Plotinus II 9 [33], 18, 20-35; IV 8 [6], 7, 26-32). This first route, then, leads the human soul to become conscious of itself as a force transcending the body and receiving its light from the divine Intellect.

The second route, which converges with the first, goes straight to the inner experience: first the ascetic experience, then the experience of thought.

On this route we begin by seeking to separate the soul from the body—that is to say, from the passions, desires, and cares caused by the body—so that the soul can find itself:

> The soul collects itself in a sort of place of its own away from the body and is wholly unaffected by it. (Plotinus I 2 [19], 5, 5)

But if we separate the soul from the body in this way from everything that is other than it, says Plotinus,

> [we] will see an intellect which sees nothing perceived by the senses, none of these mortal things, but apprehends the eternal by its eternity and all the things in the intelligible world, having become itself an intelligible universe full of light, illuminated by the truth from the Good, which radiates truth over all the intelligibles. (Plotinus IV 7 [2], 10, 32-37)

This sort of immediate jump, in which the soul leaps up, almost without passing from the body, which it believed itself to be, to the Intellect, which it truly is, is perhaps surprising. In this inner route, there is no stage where the soul stops to become conscious of its function as soul—that is to say, of its role in organizing and giving life to the body. Plotinus does not even stop at the properly rational activity of the soul; he describes this inner experience as the immediate passing to the purely intellectual and intuitive activity that is appropriate to the intellect. Here we meet a point of doctrine that is valuable to Plotinus and of prime importance for the whole of his spirituality. For Plotinus, the human soul is constantly united to the divine intellect through its summit. Although the human soul has fallen into a body, it is always present in the intelligible world through its own parts. In other words, it unceasingly participates, through one of its own parts, in the activity of the divine intellect:

> And, if one ought to dare to express one's own view more clearly, contradicting the opinion of others, even our soul does not altogether come down, but there is always something of it in the intelligible. (Plotinus IV 8 [6], 8, 1-3)

> Even before this coming to be we were there, men who were different, and some of us even gods, pure souls and intellect united with the whole of reality: we were parts of the intelligible, not marked off or cut off but belonging to the whole: and we are not cut off even now. (Plotinus VI 4 [22], 14, 17-22)

What is this intelligible world, then, in which the summit of the soul dwells continually without usually being conscious of it? It is, first of all, the world of Forms or the Platonic Ideas, but, according to an interpretation of Plato that had developed in Middle Platonism, it is the world of Ideas that has become internal to the divine intellect so that each Form, each Idea, is itself intellect, is itself alive and conscious. The intelligible world thus forms a system of essences mutually implying each other and at the same time a system of intellects that are mutually conscious of each other: everything is in the whole and each part is in the whole, in accordance with its proper mode as part (Plotinus V 8 [31], 4, 21–25; VI 7 [38], 2, 30–40).

The human soul, by that part of itself which does not leave the intelligible world, is thus intellect itself, in accordance with its proper mode: it apprehends it according to its proper mode and it is apprehended by it. Thus, in the intelligible world, there is a dynamic unity of essence. The divine Intellect, by the movement of its thought, engenders the various Forms, which are the subdivisions of the first Form, which is the first Being. All the Form-Intellects are at the same time themselves and the divine Intellect. Souls as well have the same type of existence. Despite their multiplicity, the soul of the world, the souls of the stars, and human souls are all one soul: they are joined in a single origin which is the essence of the soul. They form a system in which each part is identical with the whole. Each individual soul thus remains united, through the superior part of itself—in other words, its essence—with the single essence of soul which is a Form, constituting part of the intelligible world, and which is itself Form and Intellect (Plotinus IV 1 [21], 1–23; IV 9 [8], 5, 1–28).

This whole doctrine of the unity of the intellects and souls is designed to explain the concrete experience of the soul, which, by concentrating on itself and returning to its original source, abandons the body, surpasses its discursive activity, and experiences its union with the divine intellect. It discovers itself as an intellect which, through knowing itself, is a part, an element, of the total intellect. It also discovers that it is this union with the divine Intellect which permits it to reason, because this union assures the presence in the soul of the principles and norms that form the basis of rationality (Plotinus V 3 [49], 4, 14). In discussing this stage in the journey of the soul, in which, by surpassing rational and discursive activity, it experiences union with the divine Intellect, we can already speak of a mystical experience, as we shall see.

The Expression "Mystical Experience"

Can we use the term "mystical experience" about Plotinian spiritual experiences? The modern definition of mystical experience is first used explicitly at the end of the Middle Ages when, among others, Jean Gerson, referring to mystical theology, defined it as a "cognitio experimentalis habita de deo per amoris unitivi complexionem."[10] Thus, to use the term "mystical experience" with reference to Plotinus seems to be an anachronism. In fact, the

19. Grave Stele with Louthrophoros in Relief. Greek. Last quarter 4th century B.C.

word *mystikos* does appear once in Plotinus (III 6 [29], 19, 26), but it designates simply the "hidden meaning" that the ancients intended when choosing a form for the statues of the gods. Indeed, this is the usual sense of the word in antiquity as a whole (Aristotle *Nicomachean Ethics* 3.1.1111a). It is this usage that reveals the origin of the word "mystical" and the evolution that led to its modern meaning. If we reflect on this origin and this evolution, it seems we have the right, finally, to use the term to refer to the Plotinian experience.

In antiquity, the word *mystikos* refers above all to the mysteries of Eleusis. More precisely, the word designates the secrecy that initiates had to observe about what they had seen. The word is then used in a more general sense of a secret only accessible to the initiate: for example, the allegorical or hidden meaning of a myth. In Neoplatonism, at the end of antiquity, the word maintains its fundamental meaning, centering on the idea of a "secret," but its uses increase considerably. In particular, it now designates "secret" visions—in other words, visions of the initiate, perhaps of the philosopher, on the arrival at the summit of his interior ascent (Proclus *Platonic Theology* 3.18).[11] Plato in the *Symposium* and the *Phaedrus* had already presented philosophy on the model of the Eleusinian mysteries: he had assimilated the contemplation of the ideas and especially the vision of Beauty, to the *epopteia,* the secret vision obtained in the Eleusinian mysteries (*Symposium* 210A; *Phaedrus* 250B). The Neoplatonists, in calling philosophical contemplation "mystical" or secret, are simply being faithful to the Platonic tradition. We could say that, for them, "mystical" means "proper to the mysteries." This Eleusinian model has always remained implicit in the notion of mystical experience. In fact, when Pseudo-Dionysius, who decisively influenced the Christian usage of the word "mystical," wrote his *Mystical Theology,* largely under the inspiration of late Neoplatonism, the word "mystical" meant, for him, "belonging to the mysteries." The "mystical" darkness he speaks of is the secret darkness, darkness that is mystery. But mystery is not only what is hidden from the normal person and reserved for the initiate; it is also what forms the object of an experience. Dionysius tells us of Hierotheus that he had been initiated into the divine scriptures by divine inspiration "not simply through study (*mathōn*), but by an experience (*pathōn*)" (Pseudo-Dionysius *The Divine Names* 29 [*PG* 4, col. 648A]). In the opposition Dionysius establishes between purely intellectual study, which permits the acquisition of knowledge, and experience, which is received, we can recognize an allusion to the Eleusinian Mysteries. It was, in fact, Aristotle himself who had introduced this opposition between *mathein* and *pathein* precisely in relation to the Eleusinian Mysteries. According to Aristotle, the Eleusinian initiates do not learn anything intellectually (*mathein*), but they feel—they experience (*pathein*)—something (*On Philos-ophy* fr. 15, Ross),[12] and this experience is in fact a theopathy. Dionysius's text on Hierotheus was to influence all later Christian theories defining mystical theology as an experiential knowledge of God. Like the word "mystical" itself, this notion of the experience of God goes back finally to the philosophical interpretation of the Eleusinian Mysteries again. These mysteries, in the whole of the Platonic tradition, are the "model" of experiential knowledge of transcendent reality, and it is not surprising that Plotinus should formulate his "mystical experience" in terms of a vision and of light. As the *mystēs* receives his secret initiation into the vision (*epopteia*), the philosopher reaches the supreme goal in his search for the experience in which he will see, touch, and feel, in an obscure way, the Ideas, the Thought, the One, or the Good. The Eleusinian "model" leads to a conception of philosophy that promotes intuition and experience through contact with reason. P. Merlan has shown well how, in the Aristotelian tradition, the doctrine of the illumination of the human intellect by the Agent Intellect—as formulated, for example, by Alexander of Aphrodisias—led to the introduction of the mystical experience and illumination into the very center of philosophy, and how this Aristotelian mystique had influenced certain mystics of Islam.[13]

The Soul United with the Intellect

Plotinus stands directly in the Aristotelian tradition when he presents the union of the soul with the divine Intellect as an experience that transcends the normal activity of reason. Several texts of Plotinus that are usually interpreted as the description of a mystical union with the Good which transcends Intellect apply in actual fact to the soul's union with Intellect itself. For example, in chapter 10 of treatise V, 8, Plotinus describes, in a mythical form, using the vocabulary of the *Phaedrus* (246E; 252E), the soul contemplating the divine Intellect and the intelligible world it contains. He insists on the fact that this contemplation of the intelligible world is not the vision of a spectacle external to the soul (as the myth in the *Phaedrus* might lead us to expect), but that it is internal to the soul, which has become identical with the divine Intellect.

> But those who do not see the whole only acknowledge the external impression, but those who are altogether, we may say, drunk and filled with nectar, since the beauty has penetrated through the whole of their soul, are not simply spectators. For there is no longer one thing outside and another outside which is looking at it, but the keen sighted has what is seen within, although having it he for the most part does not know that he has it, and

looks at it as if it was something seen, and because he wants to look at it. But one looks from outside at everything one looks at as a spectacle. But one must transport what one sees into oneself and look at it as one and look at it as oneself, as if someone possessed by a god, taken over by Phoebus or one of the Muses, could bring about the vision of the god in himself, if he had the power to look at the god in himself. (Plotinus V 8 [31], 10, 32–43)

Whereas in the preceding lines, Plotinus made allusion in a mythical form to the contemplation of the Intellect by the soul, in the text we have just read, Plotinus presents this vision of the Intellect (or of intelligible Beauty) as a mystical experience (drunkenness is an indication of this), taking the form of an internal vision or even of an identification with the god who is none other than the divine Intellect. This state of union with the Intellect can be maintained only if we avoid trying to become too conscious of it:

This is a sort of intimate understanding and perception of a self which is careful not to depart from itself by wanting to perceive too much. (V 8 [31], 23–24)

The whole chapter 11 describes the coming and going that is established between the experience of union, in which consciousness of the self is all but lost, and the process of becoming conscious of the self, in which one loses union with the Intellect. In this passage it is certainly a union with the Intellect, as is clear from the context and especially this phrase:

In the higher world then, when our knowledge is most perfectly conformed to Intellect, we think we know nothing. (V 8 [31], 11, 33–34)

In fact, we only have the impression of knowing nothing because we are accustomed to the discursivity of reason and the reflexivity of our consciousness: the activity of pure thought which union with the Intellect produces gives the impression of a lack of knowledge.

The famous text at the beginning of treatise IV, 8, with its biographical interest, also makes reference to the union of the soul with the divine Intellect.

Often I have woken up out of the body to myself and have entered into myself, going out from all things; I have seen a beauty wonderfully great and felt assurance that then most of all I belonged to the better part; I have actually lived the best life and come to identity with the divine; and set firm in it I have come to that supreme actuality, setting myself above all else in the realm of Intellect. Then after that rest in the divine, when I have come down from Intellect to discursive reasoning, I am puzzled how I ever came down, and how my soul has come to be in the body when it is what it has shown itself to be by itself, even when it is in the body. (IV 8 [6], 1, 1–11)

Here again, by opposing the plane of the Intellect to the plane of reason, Plotinus clearly indicates that, in the experience he describes, the soul undergoes union with the divine Intellect.

There are several passages in the *Enneads* where this opposition between the state of the soul united with the Intellect and the state of the soul that has returned to its usual activity of reasoning can be seen (V 3 [49], 6, 12-15; IV 4 [28], 2, 3-8). Plotinus also describes an experience of the same type when he shows the soul trying to renounce its individuality, trying not to be "someone," in order to become the whole—or, for Plotinus, universal Being, the intelligible world contained in the Intellect of which it was and always is a part:

> Even before this you were all: but because something else came to you after the "all" you became less by the addition: for the addition did not come from being—you will add nothing to that—but from non-being. And when some-one has come to be also from non-being he is not all except when he rejects the non-being. You will increase yourself, then, by rejecting all else, and the all will be present to you in your rejection. (VI 5 [23], 12, 19-25)

To summarize, the experience of union with the divine Intellect has all the characteristics of a mystical experience as Plotinus usually describes it. It is compared with drunkenness produced by nectar; it is unusual; it appears suddenly and does not last. It transcends the inherent duality of consciousness of the self; it consists of a vision without discursivity of any kind, the vision of an internal light, of a pure presence beyond all deter-minate forms and all distinct objects. This experience is seen as an identifica-tion with a reality that is at the same time different from and the same as ourselves. We become different while remaining the same. To sum up this experience briefly in Plotinus's own terms:

> The man who knows himself is double, one knowing the nature of the reasoning which belongs to soul, and one up above this man, who knows himself according to Intellect because he has become that Intellect; and by that Intellect he thinks himself again, not any longer as man, but having become altogether the other and snatching himself up into the higher world, drawing up only the better part of the soul. (V 3 [49], 4, 7-12)

We might say then that the mystical experience begins when the soul enters into contact with the divine Intellect, when it rises into its own interior as far as the summit, that "fine point of the soul" (as the Christian mystics were to call it), which is constantly united to the divine Intellect.

The Two Kinds of Life
of the Divine Intellect

This union of the soul with the divine Intellect is not simply the start of the mystical experience; it is also its fulfillment: being united to the divine Intellect, the soul lives the same life as the divine Intellect does. Now the life of the Intellect, according to Plotinus, appears as double, corresponding to the phases in the formation of the Intellect, as described in several places in the work of Plotinus. In fact, Plotinus refuses to admit, as Aristotle had done, that the divine Intellect is the supreme reality. Thinking, even if it is thinking of itself, can only be a second-rank reality, because it implies a duality and postulates a prior unity that makes possible the identity with and the difference from itself, which are essential to the unity with itself. Thus, the Intellect undergoes a formation process. Thought emanates from the prior unity, or, the Good, which is absolute because it is entirely adequate to itself. Plotinus describes this formation in the following way (VI 7 [38], 15, 14; 16, 13; 17, 12; V 3 [49], 10, 42 and 11, 4; V 1 [10], 5, 5–17; V 2 [11], 1, 19; III 8 [30], 8, 30; II 4 [12], 4, 15–37). By its pure presence, the Good makes the existence of all things possible. This is to say that a pure indeterminate possibility emanates from it, which Plotinus calls formless movement, infinity, power, life, or *energeia*. The Good attracts this still-indeterminate possibility, and thus thought will be formed. It is the result of a double movement of procession—that is to say, of departure from the Good and conversion to the Good, which animates the reality that emanates from the Good but is still unformed. In the first phase, this reality, which is still unformed and indeterminate, desires the Good, looks at the Good without seeing anything distinct. It is, as Plotinus says, a vision that does not see, a life turned toward the Good. In that moment, the Intellect is not yet Intellect, but it looks at the Good in a manner that is not yet intellectual. The arising Intellect would like to turn back, to return to its source, but, being already existent, it can only retreat further and further; and, by the combined effect of the movements of emanation and conversion, it begins to circle round the Good as if round a center and thus takes on a structured and finished form. Indeterminate life will thus define itself, the arising Intellect will be able to grasp an object that is determinate and other than itself, and it will be able to engender, in a dialectical way, by an internal subdivision, the whole universe of Forms which, in its diverse and systematic character, reflects all the richness of the original Unity. The Intellect will be completely finished, completely Intellect when it thinks of the totality of the universe of Forms which it itself has given

rise to. It will think itself once it has become all things. The desire to see
the Good is realized, then, in an unforeseen manner (III 8 [30], 8, 33) by
seeing in itself the world of Forms which expresses the power of the Good.
The Intellect sees the Good, refracted in some way in this systematic
totality.

The two kinds of life of the Intellect which we spoke of correspond to
these two phases in the formation of the Intellect. The thinking Intellect
corresponds to the last phase, the Intellect "in its right mind" as Plotinus
says, which contemplates the Forms in itself. The Intellect that does not yet
think corresponds to the first phase, the Intellect that is "out of its mind,"
as Plotinus says, the Intellect that is coming into being and is still in immediate contact with the Good from which it emanates:

> Intellect has one power for thinking, by which it looks at the things in itself,
> and one by which it looks at what transcends it by a direct awareness and
> reception, by which also before it saw only, and by seeing acquired intellect
> and is one. And that first one is the contemplation of Intellect in its right
> mind, and the other is Intellect in love, when it goes out of its mind "drunk
> with the nectar": then it falls in love, simplified into happiness by having its
> fill: and it is better for it to be drunk with a drunkenness like this than to
> be more respectably sober.

The Intellect thus has a double rapport with the Good: a mediated
rapport when it contemplates the refraction of the power of the Good in
the system of Ideas; an unmediated rapport when it tries to remain in
contact with the Good from which it emanates, by trying not to be caught
up in the multiplicity of Ideas. As Plotinus says:

> The intellect must return, so to speak, backwards, and give itself up, in a way,
> to what lies behind it (for it faces in both directions): and there, if it wishes
> to see that first principle, it must not be altogether intellect. (III 8 [30],
> 9, 29–32)

On reading this text, we cannot fail to think of the formula that H. Bergson
used, more or less summing up his own philosophy:

> Intelligence, reabsorbing itself in its principle, will relive its own formation
> in reverse.[14]

In this way, thought is born from a sort of loving ecstasy in this type of
drunkenness, which is produced by nonintellectual contact with the Good
from which it emanates.

The human soul, through its own summit, which is continually united
with the divine Intellect, sees the life of the divine Intellect in a potential
and virtual way. The mystical experience, for it, consists in the exceptional
and temporary actuation of this potentiality; and it can take on two forms,

corresponding to the two powers, the two modes of life of the divine Intellect. In fact, by rising from the discursivity of reasoning to the immediacy of thought, the soul is already entering into "mystical" union, through an experience that transcends reason, to the movement of the divine Intellect which thinks itself. But then, in the last phase of the experience, by living the life of the divine Intellect, the soul participates as well in the state of the Intellect in which the Intellect, arising from the Good, experiences the Good through what Plotinus calls a non-thinking, which is drunkenness and loving joy (V 5 [32], 8, 24; VI 7 [38], 35, 30). It is to this love of the Intellect for the Good, to this non-thinking which gives rise to thought that the soul is united at the summit of the mystical experience. If the soul enters into contact with the Good, as Plotinus says, using a very fine comparison,

> [it is because] it is carried out of it by the surge of the wave of Intellect itself and lifted on high by a kind of swell. (VI 7 [38], 36, 17–18)

If, in order to attain the Good, the soul must discard everything, simplify itself completely and even renounce thought, it is because according to one of its kinds of life the Intellect is not yet formed, it is not yet Intellect, not yet anything but love of the Good, not yet anything but nonintellectual experience of the Good.

Furthermore, Plotinus stresses several times the necessity of the soul's becoming divine Intellect if it wishes to contemplate the Good.

> Therefore one must become Intellect and entrust one's soul to and set it firmly under Intellect, that it may be awake to receive what that sees, and may by this Intellect behold the One, without adding any sense-perception or receiving anything from sense-perception into that Intellect, but beholding the most pure with the pure Intellect, and the primary part of Intellect. (VI 9 [9], 3, 22–25)

Plotinus also says that it is because the soul has been "intellectified" (*nootheisa*) that it is able to attain the Good (VI 7 [38], 35, 4–5). Thus, we could say that the mystical experience of the soul consists in living the life of the divine Intellect and in associating itself with the immediate experience of the presence of the Good, as lived by the Intellect. In other words, the summit of the mystical experience of the soul is the mystical experience of the Intellect itself with which the soul has succeeded, for a moment, in identifying.

From this perspective, the Aristotelian definition of the goal of human life, as taken up by Porphyry—*live in accordance with the intellect*—takes on a stronger meaning, which includes the experiential union with the supreme Good.

The Mystical Experience of the Good

Although in the mystical experience of the Good the soul is with the Intellect, in the state in which it is in contact with the Good, in which it is the loving Intellect, "out of its mind," drunk on the divine nectar that the soul identifies with, the soul remains nonetheless the subject to which the mystical experiences in the Plotinian descriptions are referred. Plotinus is obviously concerned with guiding the human soul toward union with God. This is why the mystical experience is presented as an exceptional phenomenon and as transitory. Although the union of the Intellect with the Good is eternal (VI 7 [38], 35, 29–30), the unitive experiences of the soul are exceptional. They appear suddenly, and we cannot induce them ourselves. The exercise of internal unification that prepares for their reception is not enough to induce them; they also disappear abruptly (VI 7 [38], 34, 13; 36, 18; V 3 [49], 17, 29; V 5 [32], 7, 35; VI 9 [9], 9, 60–10, 2).

The experience of the Good, or of the One, is presented by Plotinus using the model of loving union:

> And if anyone does not know this experience, let him think of it in terms of our loves here below, and what it is like to attain what one is most in love with. (VI 9 [9], 9, 39; cf. VI 7 [38], 34, 3 and 14)

The soul participates in the infinite desire of the Intellect stricken with love for the Good from which it emanates. The relation to the Good can only be one of love: it is essential that the Good excite desire and that it be the object of love (VI 7 [38], 22, 1–36). But for Plotinus it is clear that this is not a reciprocal relationship. The Absolute cannot have a relationship with the relative. Only the relative is "relative" to the Absolute. Contact with the Good produces an unspeakable joy in the soul:

> But when the soul has good fortune with it, and it comes to it, or rather, being there already, appears . . . then, truly, it would not exchange this for anything in the world, not even if someone handed over the whole universe to it. . . . Then it has the ability to judge rightly and to know that this is what it desired, and to establish that there is nothing better than it. . . . What it speaks, then, is that, and it speaks it afterwards, and speaks it in silence, and in its happiness is not cheated in thinking that it is happy: . . . but if all the other things about it perished, it would even be pleased, that it might be alone with this: so great a degree of happiness has it reached. (VI 7 [38], 34, 8–38)

This love incites the soul to assimilate itself to the object it loves and to retreat from everything that could separate it from this object (VI 7 [38], 31, 11). Since the Good is without form and without thought, whoever loves it will wish to discard all form and all thought.

The discarding of all form is essential to the Plotinian mystical experience. It is a question of love. We cannot attach ourselves to the Good and remain at the same time attached to something else beside it. From this point of view, the discarding of all form corresponds first of all to asceticism: the soul must detach itself from the body, the passions, and all memories of external objects. The soul must detach itself as well from all ideas and all intelligible forms:

> The soul also, when it gets an intense love of it, puts away all the shape which it has, even whatever shape of the intelligible there may be in it. For it is not possible for one who has anything else and is actively occupied about it to see or to be fitted in. But one must not have evil, or any other good either, ready to hand, that the soul alone may receive it alone. (VI 7 [38], 34, 1–8)

Like all lovers, the soul wants to be alone with the one it loves, all the more since the one it loves is the only One (VI 9 [9], 11, 50). But the soul, following the Intellect, wants to abandon all form and remain with the Good primarily because the Good transcends all forms which might dominate it and determine it, because the Good is not a thing and is external to all things, in a word, because the Good is infinite. The soul refuses, then, to remain in any form, however elevated, and thus it experiences the infinite love of the Infinite:

> Truly, when you cannot grasp the form or shape of what is longed for, it would be most longed for and most lovable, and love for it would be immeasurable. For love is not limited here, because neither is the beloved, but the love of this would be unbounded. (VI 7 [38], 32, 24–28)

This is why Plotinus speaks of the Good as a light in which there is no distinct object, a light that we see in itself and not by means of some distinct organ (VI 7 [38], 36, 20; V 3 [49], 28 and 35). The image of light, for Plotinus, is the symbol of the infinity of the One without form and without thought. The other model to describe the mystical experience is that of "enthusiasm," of the possession of the soul by a god (V 4 [49], 14, 9; VI 9 [9], 11, 13)—a model that, incidentally, goes back to Plato's *Phaedrus* (244A–245C). The soul feels the presence of another with which it is identified, and it is no longer itself. It is transported outside itself and does not know any longer what it is, no longer having the opportunity to consider what it is when it considers the Good:

> So then the seer does not see, and does not distinguish and does not imagine two, but it is as if he had become someone else and he is not himself and does not count as his own there, but has come to belong to that and so is one, having joined, as it were, center to center. (VI 9 [9], 10, 14–17)

Mystical Union and Negative Theology

We have seen that, according to Plotinus, the soul has to discard all forms in order to enter into contact with the Good (VI 7 [38], 34, 29; VI 9 [9], 11, 7 and 7, 22). This concrete movement of discarding (and also of detaching itself from any affective attachments), which is essential to the mystical life, must not be confused with negative theology, which is, in fact, only a rational method of knowing, as Plotinus stresses (VI 7 [38], 36, 6). The negations tell us something about the Good, but the purifications actually lead us to it. In a more general way, we could make a certain number of distinctions in this area. First, with regard to the rational method of negation, we must distinguish two discrete procedures. The first, which could be called the method of abstraction, is mostly used in mathematics, where, for example, we define the point by saying that it is not extended, and the line, by saying that it has no surface. As applied to God in the Platonic tradition, it is not specifically a theological method; it is used in mathematics, but Aristotle, for example, also uses it to define matter (*Metaphysics* 7.3.1029a16). It is, properly speaking, a rational method. Another method that could be called negation is the one used in the first hypothesis of Plato's *Parmenides* (137C–142A): in the hypothesis where we posit the One as One, it is impossible to speak of it, because we would not be able to attribute any other attribute to it, since we cannot ever attribute being to it. No discourse about it and no knowledge of it are in any way possible. This type of negative method can be found in Plotinus (VI 7 [38], 38, 1; VI 9 [9], 5, 30; V 3 [49], 13, 4; V 5 [32], 10, 16; V 5 [32] 11, 5; VI 8 [39], 11, 5–13). It belongs to reflections on the notion of the One, but it is nonetheless an abstract method and a rational one, which puts us into contact with the One in concrete terms. We must not confuse these rational methods with the activity of discarding all forms, of renouncing everything, of detaching oneself from everything, which actually leads us to the One (VI 9 [9], 9, 51; VI 7 [38], 34, 3; VI 9 [9], 7, 15 and 20).

We must also distinguish the rational method of negative theology from the impossibility of being able to relate anything whatsoever about the mystical experience: while the contact lasts, it is absolutely impossible, nor has it time, to speak, but afterward one can reason about it (that is to say, practice negative theology) (V 3 [49], 17, 26). In other words, we must not confuse the fact that it is impossible to speak about the notion of the One if we posit it simply as One (as in the first hypostasis of the *Parmenides*) with the fact that it is impossible to speak of the experience we have of the One. Here, it is the experience itself that is inexpressible.

Plotinian descriptions of the unitive experience have profoundly affected Western thought and, in particular, Christian spirituality. This influence was exercised in history through the Dionysian and Augustinian traditions. On one side, the mystical Plotinian aspiration has continued to live in Greek Neoplatonism and has been received into Christianity through Gregory of Nyssa and particularly through Pseudo-Dionysius. On the other hand, in the Latin West, the Plotinian influence touched Ambrose and, through Porphyry, Augustine. In Augustine's *Confessions* we can discern a number of themes that belong to Plotinian spirituality, like the famous "ecstasy" of Ostia, or, more specifically, that belonging to Porphyrian spirituality, like the affirmation of the identity of the presence of God and to the self (*Confessions* 2.1.1)[15] In these two traditions, which meet in the Latin Middle Ages, we no longer find the Plotinian distinction between the two levels of divinity: the level of the divine Intellect and the level of the Good, which, as we saw, characterized the Plotinian description of the mystical experience. The Christian soul unites with this one God in three persons which are consubstantial. But the theoreticians of the mystical life will always admit that union with God can imply different levels of intensity and perfection. There is obviously an essential difference between the Plotinian and Christian descriptions of the mystical experience. For Christians, the mystical experience is a grace, given to the soul by a divine initiative. For Plotinus, there is no divine initiative in the proper sense. But we should not conclude that, for Plotinus, human beings can attain to mystical experience by their own means. They have to wait for this experience and never know if it will come about. The soul has to do all it can to prepare for it. But, says Plotinus, when the Good comes to it and suddenly appears before it, it is a "chance" for the soul (VI 7 [38], 34, 8). Thus, Plotinus expresses, in his way, the gratuitous and unexpected nature of all mystical experience.

Translated by Jane Curran

Notes

1. Porphyry, *Life* 8.19–24; 9.16–20; 23.1–28, trans. A. H. Armstrong, in *Plotinus* I, ed. A. H. Armstrong. Loeb Classical Library; London: Heinemann, 1966).
2. The oracle is quoted by Porphyry *Life* 22.13–63.
3. In Porphyry *Vie de Pythagore. Lettre à Marcella,* ed. É. des Places (Paris: Les Belles Lettres, 1982). Se also *De regressu animae* fr. 10, in J. Bidez, *Vie de Porphyre* (Gand: E. Van Goethem, 1913; reprint, Hildesheim: Olms, 1964) p. 38*.
4. See also *Retractationes* 1.3.

5. Trans. A. H. Armstrong. In this chapter, the texts from Plotinus come from the translation by A. H. Armstrong, *Plotinus* I–VI (Loeb Classical Library; London: Heinemann, 1966).

6. Porphyry *De l'abstinence,* book 1, ed. J. Bouffartigue (Paris: Les Belles Lettres, 1977).

7. See Plotinus I 1 [53], 13, 8–9: "For intellect too is a part of ourselves and to it we ascend."

8. Lamberz p. 50.10 in Porphyrius, *Sententiae,* ed. E. Lamberz (Leipzig: Teubner, 1975).

9. Porphyry too insists on the necessity of the internal transformation; see *On Abstinence* 1.29.6: "We have to change our present life for another one."

10. Gerson, *De theologia mystica lectiones sex, vicesima octava consideratio,* in Jean Gerson, *Oeuvres complètes,* ed. P. Glorieux (Paris: Desclée, 1973) 3:274.

11. Saffrey-Westerink p. 64.7 in Proclus, *Théologie Platonicienne,* livre III, ed. H. D. Saffrey and L. G. Westerink (Paris: Les Belles Lettres, 1978).

12. See J. Goeder-Croissant, *Aristote et les mystères* (Bibliothèque de la Faculté de Philosophie 51; Liège: E. Droz, 1932) 137–94.

13. Merlan, *Monopsychism, Mysticism, Metaconsciousness: Problems of the Soul in the Neoaristotelian and Neoplatonic Tradition* (The Hague: Nijhoff, 1963).

14. Bergson, *L'Evolution créatrice* (Paris: Presses universitaires de France, 1962) 193.

15. See also *De ordine* 1.2.5: "Sapiens prorsus cum Deo est, nam et seipsum intelligit sapiens"; *Confession* 9.10.23–25.

Bibliography

Editions

Plotini Opera. Edited by Paul Henry and Hans-Rudolf Schwyzer. Vol. 1, *Porphyrii Vita Plotini, Enneades I–III.* Vol. 2, *Enneades IV–V . . . Plotiniana Arabica* ad codicum fidem anglice vertit Geoffrey Lewis. Vol. 3, *Enneas VI.* Paris and Brussels: Desclée de Brouwer, 1951, 1959, 1973.

Plotini Opera. Edited by Paul Henry and Hans-Rudolf Schwyzer. 3 vols. Oxford: Clarendon Press, 1964–1983.

Plotinus. Translated by A. H. Armstrong. 7 vols. (*Enn.* I–VI) Loeb Classical Library 440–446. London: Heinemann, 1966–.

Translations

Plotinus. *The Enneads.* Translated by Stephen MacKenna. 4th edition revised by B. S. Page with a foreword by E. R. Dodds and an introduction by Paul Henry. London: Faber & Faber, 1969.

Modern Works

Armstrong, A. H. *The Architecture of the Intelligible Universe in the Philosophy of Plotinus.* Cambridge: University Press, 1967.

———. *Plotinian and Christian Studies.* London: Variorum Reprints, 1979.

———. "Plotinus" in *The Cambridge History of Greek and Early Mediaeval Philosophy,* 193–268. Edited by A. H. Armstrong. Cambridge: University Press, 1971.

Rist, John M. *Plotinus: The Road to Reality.* Cambridge: University Press, 1967.

II. From Iamblichus to Proclus and Damascius

H. D. SAFFREY

IAMBLICHUS WAS BORN IN SYRIA, probably between 245 and 250; Damascius was born in Damascus and died after 538; the dates of these two figures give a time span of roughly three centuries. Iamblichus lived and taught in Syria, and his pupils spread his doctrine to Pergamum and Ephesus in Asia, as well as to Athens. Syrianus, who was from Alexandria, and Proclus, whose origins were in Lycia, took up Iamblichus's heritage and nurtured it in Athens, where they headed a flourishing school of Platonic thought in the fifth century. The last head of this school was Damascius. So it was in the Oriental basin of the Mediterranean that, over the course of some three hundred years, Neoplatonic philosophy and spirituality grew and developed.

The works of all these Neoplatonic philosophers, from Iamblichus to Damascius, deal almost exclusively with the nature of the divine and the hierarchy of the gods. "Theology as a science" is, therefore, a notion that originated with and was developed by them. Moreover, as philosophy in Greece was always more a way of life than a mere intellectual activity, the spiritual life of these philosophers came to be a constant sort of prayer or liturgy—and this precisely at a time when Christian emperors were forbidding the worship of pagan gods, closing down temples, and removing statues of worship and transforming them into decorative garden pieces, that is, a time when prayer had become an inner or silent matter and liturgy a private or household one. In this context their philosophical activity itself was transformed into a cult of worship of the gods.

Theology as a Science

In the *Parmenides,* Plato has his hero, Parmenides of Elea, say that a philosopher should be completely trained in dialectic "if he really wants to perceive the truth" (136C5). Proclus comments here:

> What is the goal that Plato ascribes to this training? He says it is the vision of the truth. We understand this remark not to be about truth purely and simply, but about that same truth of which he told us in another dialogue

(*Phaedrus* 248B5–6) that it is the moving force of the immense effort to see where the region of the Truth lies. Our whole life is thus a training for that vision, and a roundabout journey via dialectic leads us to that haven; that is why he speaks of a wholly admirable method of elucidating it in depth: indeed, souls really obtain that vision through a series of multiple, intermediary steps. (*On Plato's Parmenides* 5.1015.33–1016.3, Cousin)

This is how Proclus explains the meaning of the spiritual life which he both leads and recommends to his disciples.

For Proclus, the expression "vision of the truth" has a very specific meaning, in that the truth that he is seeking is a theological one. Prior to Proclus, the Greek tradition had sought sources of theology in myths interpreted by allegorical methods, in acts of cult that were defined by the literature of the *Aitia*, and in the interpretation of the oracles; but no one had ever as yet attempted to draw these sources exclusively from the works of Plato, who, in Proclus's eyes, had become "the guide to true mysteries and the hierophant of integral and immobile apparitions" (Proclus *Platonic Theology* 1.1, Saffrey–Westerink). The immediate result of this development was the birth of a new type of theology. Indeed, if up to Proclus's time three types of theology were well known—that of myth, that of public cult, and that of the philosophy of nature—now, "theology as a science" was to be discovered and developed, inasmuch as the living sources of theology were to be drawn from the rational work of one philosopher. This gave rise to a "scientific theology," which was different from all the others because of the systematic and coherent nature of its discourse. Proclus supports this idea as follows: "Plato is the only one to have undertaken the establishment of proper distinctions and to have provided for the organized procession, in good marching order, of all the divine classes and their mutual differences, the characteristics common to all the categories and those which are specific to each one" (Proclus *Platonic Theology* 1.4).

As such, true spiritual life would henceforth consist of reading Plato—in particular the *Parmenides,* the theological dialogue *par excellence.* The Neoplatonists interpreted the negations of the first hypothesis as "a theological hymn in honor of the One" (Proclus *On Plato's Parmenides* 7.1191.34–35), a hymn that Proclus takes up in his own way in the *Platonic Theology,* when he says of the First God:

> Let us extol him by a sort of hymn without saying that it was he who brought the earth and the sky into existence, or that he created souls and the species of all living things (for, to be truthful, this was no doubt also his work, but only the very last one); let us extol him instead for having brought to light the whole intelligible class of gods and the whole intellectual class of gods, all the hypercosmic gods and all the encosmic gods; and let us say

that he is god among all the gods, henad among the henads, beyond the first *adyta*, more ineffable than all silence and more unknowable than all existence, a holy god, hidden in the holiness of the intelligible gods. (2.11)

Let us also add to this important text the prayer that opens Proclus's commentary on the *Parmenides:*

I beg all the gods and all the goddesses to guide my spirit towards the goal I am ascribing to myself and, having kindled in me the shining light of the truth, to deploy my intelligence so that it attains the true knowledge of Being, to open up the doors of my soul and allow it to receive the divinely inspired doctrine of Plato, and, having put into motion my cognitive faculty towards that which is most luminous within Being (*Republic* 7.518C9), to put an end to my claim to wisdom and to my wandering among non-beings, through the completely intellectual study of Being, on which the eye of the soul *feeds* and *drinks,* as Socrates says in the *Phaedrus* (247D2; 251B3); I pray to the intelligible gods for a perfect intellect; to the intellectual gods for elevating power; to the supracelestial masters of the universe for an infrangible energy, free of material knowledge; to the gods who have the world as their lot, for a life equipped with wings; to the angelic choirs for a true revelation of divine things; to the good demons for fulness of inspiration from the gods; to the heroes for a magnanimous, serious and sublime state of soul; in short, I beg all the divine classes to form in me a perfect disposition for participating in Plato's thoroughly epoptic and mystical doctrine, which he himself reveals to us in the *Parmenides,* as deeply as is appropriate to the realities he is handling, and which was developed after him, by one who, using his purest intuitions, truly imbued himself, along with Plato, with dionysiac inebriation, who was filled with divine truth and who has become for us the master of this doctrine and the true hierophant of these divine revelations. I would gladly say that this man [Syrianus] has come to represent among men philosophy for the sake of procuring the well-being of souls here below, to replace devotional statues, sacred ceremonies, and the whole of worship itself, and as a guide to salvation, at least for men of today and for those who will be born after them. (1.617.1–618.13)

If in "that which is most luminous within Being," one recognizes the first god, the Good/One, according to the exegesis of Proclus himself (*Platonic Theology* 2.7), one discovers in this fine text the complete classification of those gods that Proclus discovered in the first and second hypotheses of the *Parmenides.* To each of these divine classes, Proclus addresses his prayer, asking each one to bestow on him a specific virtue directed to the supreme knowledge of the first god.

Oracles and Theurgy

For Proclus, mystical knowledge and the masters of religious philosophy have taken the place not only of devotional statues but of all worship itself.

As already mentioned above, to read the *Parmenides* is to perform the true religious act, and the practice of philosophical virtues is real ritual purification. The ideal of the Neoplatonic philosophers thus becomes the celebration of divinity through the creation of scientific theology. In other words, the celebration of divinity has become an entirely intellectual process; it is the *religio mentis*.

At the origin of this movement and of utmost importance was the need to obtain the principles of philosophy from oracular-type revelations. This need goes back to the second century, when the Platonic orator Maximus of Tyre—asking himself the question: Who is god, according to Plato?— cried out: "Oh why have I no oracle to consult, be it Zeus's or Apollo's, so long as I obtain an answer which is neither obscure nor ambiguous?" It is worth noting here that it was during the second century that large collections of oracles were compiled, in which the gods not only answered questions about everyday life but revealed, above all, their nature and properties. The second century was indeed one of theological oracles, the most famous of which are the *Chaldaean Oracles*,[1] which probably appeared for the first time in Syria and which transmitted revelations through a medium who was understood to interrogate Plato's soul.[2] No wonder Plato recited his own philosophy in these oracles! They remained unheard of for one or two centuries, but then, thanks to Iamblichus, they became famous. Indeed, in his falsely titled *De mysteriis*, Iamblichus turned them into the ultimate theological authority, and he wrote an enormous commentary on them, which unfortunately is lost to us.

The entry of the *Chaldaean Oracles* into the domain of philosophy brought with it two important consequences. The first concerned spiritual life itself. Indeed, not only was theological speculation now nourished by an element infinitely rich in varied interpretations, but day-to-day life and personal piety were also transformed. The *Oracles*, by teaching that every living creature possessed a symbol or character trait that came directly from the gods, gave virtually everyone a means of recapturing this divine origin. Indeed, in order to conform to divinity, conscious beings could liberate the divine character within themselves or make use of material things that bore the mark of some specific divine symbol. Thereafter, all they had to do was to cultivate, manipulate, and adore these symbols so as to encounter the divine and possess it. This new esoteric practice, called "theurgy,"[3] was first developed by Iamblichus and his disciples, whose feats the historian Eunapius recounts. Iamblichus knew how to bring statues to life and bring about divine apparitions. His disciple Maximus of Ephesus, who became Julian the emperor's chief adviser on religious matters at a time when Julian was trying to restore pagan religion, used magic formulas to make the statue of the goddess Hecate smile and to light up the torches she held in her hands (Eunapius *Lives of the Sophists* 7.2.7–12, Giangrande). Indeed, the Neoplatonic philosophers were well versed in horoscopic methods, in arts of divination and the like. Proclus himself was favored with apparitions of Hecate; he could, at will, bring about rain and avert earthquakes; he practiced soothsaying by means of the tripod and called up oracles for himself! (Marinus *Life of Proclus* 28, Boissonade).

At the same time, the "theology of characters" sums up Proclus's entire mystique; indeed, he claims:

> There are three true characters which fill divine beings and extend across all the divine classes: goodness, knowledge, and beauty; there are also three true characters which bring together what has been filled; they are inferior to the first, but they extend across all the divine worlds: faith, truth, and love. Through them the world is preserved in existence and joined to the primordial causes by an intermediary, whether it be love's madness, divine philosophy, or theurgic power, which is better than all wisdom and all human knowledge, because it concentrates within itself the advantages of divination, the purifying forces of rites carried out, and, in short, all the operations performed when one is possessed by the divine. (Proclus *Platonic Theology* 1.25)

Theurgy is thus the surest means of attaining union with god.

The second consequence is perhaps even more important. The utilization of the *Chaldaean Oracles* as theological authority in fact gave the Neoplatonists a new way of reading and interpreting the Platonic texts. Since the *Oracles* were Platonic, Plato himself became a god capable of proffering oracles; his writings thus became the revelation of a sublime doctrine, a truly "holy scripture." Proclus is certain that

> the truth about the gods is spread throughout virtually all the Platonic dialogues and that in them are scattered, more obscurely in some, more clearly in others, the venerable, luminous, and supernatural concepts of the very primary philosophy, which awaken the consciousness to an understanding of the immaterial and transcendent existence of the gods, for those who are minimally capable of grasping them. (*Platonic Theology* 1.5)

After this, any reading of Plato becomes a *lectio divina*. One of the actual goals of Neoplatonic theology is thus to put Plato and the *Oracles* into full harmony one with the other: faith in one implies faith in the other! This attitude also explains the tremendous exegetical work on Platonic texts that was carried out, in particular, by the Neoplatonists of the school of Athens. Indeed, most of their philosophy consists of interpretations of Platonic texts, and these very interpretations resulted in their explication of "scientific theology."

Contemplation and Prayer

Thus shaped by a constant reading of the ancients, Proclus attained contemplative wisdom. Marinus tells us:

> He [Proclus] used to experience a dionysiac ecstasy for the first principles and to contemplate face to face the truly blessed visions of the Beyond. . . . [And then] not only did he grasp without any difficulty all theologies—Greek theology, Barbarian theology [that of the *Chaldaean Oracles*] and that theology which is hidden in fictional myths [the Orphic poems], but he brought them to light for those who wished to and were able to understand them, explaining all things under inspiration from the gods and making all theologies agree. (*Life of Proclus* 22)

He meditated and prayed, not only by day, but by night as well.

> Even when he allowed himself a little leisure after the labours of the day and finally gave his body over to sleep, perhaps even then his intellect did not stop thinking. In any case, as soon as he could, he always chased away this light sleep, considering it a kind of laziness of the soul, and since the hour of prayer had not come as yet, because only a small part of the night had elapsed, meditating on his bed, he composed hymns, or else, examining some point of doctrine, he found the solution and, rising at daybreak, he put it down in writing. (*Life of Proclus* 24)

Neoplatonic philosophers were contemplative people who meditated and prayed. Their practices in prayer are known to us not only from the hymns they composed that have come down to us but also from the theory of prayer that they formulated. This theory is well explained by Proclus at the beginning of book 2 of his commentary on the *Timaeus*. He reminds us here that Iamblichus used to explain that praying was principally the activity "of beings capable of being saved by Those who save the whole universe," that is, by the gods and their providence. Because prayers must accompany rites to explain thair meaning, "they perfect worship and bind us in an indissoluble way to holy communion with the gods" (Iamblichus *De mysteriis* 5.26). And Iamblichus continues:

> The first stage in prayer is to bring about contact: it puts us into contact with the divine and acquaints us with it; the second stage binds this agreement into a joint action, asking the gods to send us gifts from Above, before we have even spoken; and even before we have had a chance to think, the entire operation has taken place. In the last stage, the ineffable union is sealed; its entire efficacy relies on the gods and our souls are laid to perfect rest in them. (Iamblichus *De mysteriis* 5.26)

Proclus puts into practice his theory that the gods have stamped divine characters onto everything that exists when he shows us that praying itself consists of seeking these characters out and using them in order to ascend to their authors. He says:

> Thanks to the ineffable signs of the gods, which the Father of souls has sown into our souls, prayer attracts the benevolence of the gods: on the one hand, it unites those who are praying to the gods to which they are addressing their prayers; and, on the other hand, it unites the intellect of the gods to the reasoning of those who pray; it moves those who contain abundant good within themselves to a desire to distribute it generously; in general, it is through prayer that we persuade the gods and that we place in their hands all that pertains to us. (Proclus *On Plato's Timaeus* 1, Diehl)

These different stages of prayer are analyzed more completely by Proclus than by Iamblichus. First there exists the knowledge of the gods; then there exists the act of making oneself resemble the divine through personal purity, chastity, education, and good behavior; then comes the act of entering into contact with the divine essence through the summit of the soul; then one comes into close encounter with the gods; and, finally, one unites oneself with them. Proclus advises as follows:

> He who really wants to give himself over to prayer should do the following: render the gods propitious and, in general, activate within himself his notions of the gods; devote himself to the continuous cult of divinity; keep constant the order of divine works; strive for those virtues which free us from the earthly element and guide us up to god—not only that admirable triad, faith, truth, and love, but also the hope of true good unchanging receptivity to the divine light; lastly, the ecstasy which frees us from all other preoccupations so that we can unite ourselves to god alone. (*On Plato's Timaeus* 1)

The idea of uniting oneself to god alone is at the very heart of Proclus's mystique, and we can almost imagine Proclus composing his hymns in the middle of the night to celebrate the feasts of both Greek and barbarian gods. He held vigils of prayers for them, and John Lydus even refers to Proclus's "book of hymns" (*De mensibus*, Wuensch)

Hymns

From this book of hymns, only eight have come down to us. They are dedicated to the Sun, to Aphrodite (the mother of spiritual and physical love), to the Muses, to the gods of the *Chaldaean Oracles*, to Lycian Aphrodite (Proclus's origins were in Xanthos, in Lycia), to Hecate and Janus, to Athena of Good Counsel, and to Ares.[4] These hymns are all composed in the same manner. They are divided into two parts: the first is an invocation to the specific god or goddess, who is designated by name and by his or her traditional attributes, all of which are derived from the most learned

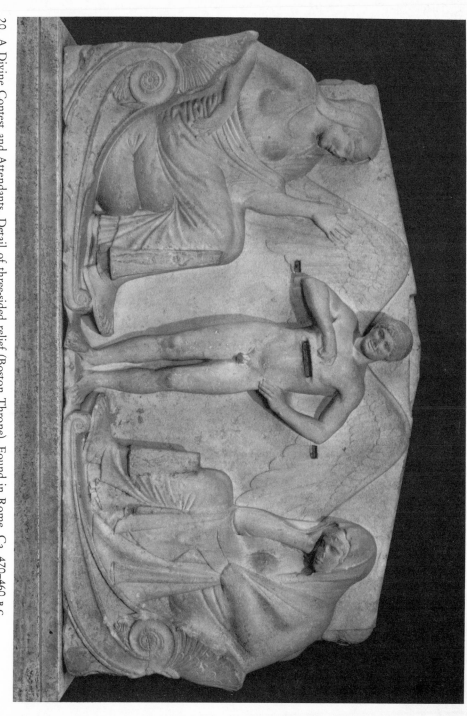

20. A Divine Contest and Attendants. Detail of three-sided relief (Boston Throne). Found in Rome. Ca. 470-460 B.C.

mythology; the second is a prayer of request, in which one is struck by the personal sincerity and tender devotion of its author. For example, Proclus's hymn to the Muses, the goddesses of intellectual life:

We sing of the light which leads mortals to the mountain-tops; we sing of the nine daughters of Great Zeus, goddesses with extremely sweet voices, who, through the immaculate rites conveyed by the books which give life to the spirit, deliver souls wandering in the depths of existence from worldly and mortal sufferings; by raising them up from above the deep tides of oblivion, they teach them to hasten to follow their footsteps and to ascend, completely pure, to the star which is related to them and from which they separated themselves the day they fell onto the shores of becoming, captured by a mad desire for material destiny.

Therefore, Goddesses, cause this urge in me towards worldly agitations to cease and inebriate me with the intellectual myths transmitted by the Sages; do not allow the race of men who do not know the fear of God to lead me to stray from the most divine, most bright, most fruitful path; and endlessly draw my wandering soul out of the pitiful confusion of becoming, towards pure light, loading it with the produce of your hives, food for the intellect, so that it ever preserves the glory of a beautiful song, filling the heart with enthusiasm. (Proclus *Hymn* 3, Vogt)

Proclus makes a special request to each of the divinities, in accordance with their specific natures. For example:

To the Sun:

Image of the Supreme Generative God, you who lead souls upwards, hear me, keep me pure at all times from all faults; receive my prayer which is full of tears; deliver me from wretched stain, preserve me from the avenging goddesses, by softening the sharp glance of Justice, which sees all. By your aid, which turns away evil, ever continue to grant my soul pure light in rich abundance and dissipate the poisonous clouds, destroyers of mortals, which obscure me. (*Hymn* 1)

To Aphrodite:

Hear me, and with your infallible arrows guide the sorrowful course of my life, O Sovereign, causing the icy urge of unholy desire to cease. (*Hymn* 2)

To Athena of Good Counsel:

Hear me, you whose face glows with pure light; grant to me, a wanderer on earth, a blessed port; grant my soul, in return for holy hymns composed by me in your honor, pure light, wisdom, love; breathe into my soul, through love, enough power and of a kind which will draw it out of the hollows of the earth and return it to Olympus, to the home of its Father. (*Hymn* 7)

The personal character of these hymns is striking; what also strikes one is Proclus's nostalgia for the region of pure light, for the kingdom of the divine.

Damascius gives us an idea of what constituted the "philosophical way of life," according to customs of the most rigorous piety, when he describes the life of Sarapion, an Egyptian friend of his master Isidorus:

> He lived alone in a very small house where he led a truly solitary life, and he only had dealings with certain of his neighbours for indispensable necessities. He lived, essentially, in prayer, and dressed as a common man, he made the rounds of sacred places, wherever traditional feast days led him. But most often, he spent his time at home, leading not a human life, but an absolutely divine one, while he continually proffered prayers, praises of divine marvels, either to himself, or directed to the gods; but on the whole, he pondered in silence. He was endlessly in pursuit of the truth and he was a natural contemplator. He refused to bother himself with the more technical points of philosophy, but concerned himself with broader questions leading to the state of divine possession. That was why he owned and read practically nothing but Orpheus. (Damascius *Life of Isidorus*)

Another collection of hymns that attests to this tradition of "prayer through hymn" in philosophical circles is the collection of so-called Orphic Hymns.[5] This collection appears to have been the "choir book" of a religious community in Asia Minor that in its religious devotion intermingled Orphic divinities and Dionysus. Each of these hymns is headed by the name of a god or goddess to which the hymn is addressed, and an indication is given of the kind of incense that should be offered up to the deity at the same time as the hymn is being sung. The idea that incense is offered at the same time as a hymn is sung is typical of pagan worship in late antiquity. This collection of Orphic Hymns begins with two hymns: one to Hecate (the goddess of the *Chaldaean Oracles*) and the other to Artemis (the patron goddess of Asia—in particular, of Ephesus); these two initial hymns are followed by a series of hymns addressed to the gods of Orphic theogony— the Sky, the Stars, the Moon, and Nature; these, in turn, are followed by a series of hymns addressed to the gods of Olympian mythology—Pan, Heracles, Cronos, Zeus, and, above all, Dionysus, in honor of whom seven individual hymns are addressed. One wonders how this "choir book" of hymns came down to us in the first place. There may be some indication, perhaps, in the fact that Proclus's hymns are contained in all the manuscripts of the Orphic Hymns. Moreover, we know from Marinus that Proclus was forced to go into exile in Asia for a whole year. As Marinus says:

> The gods provided him with the opportunity to make that journey so that he would not fail to be initiated into the more ancient rites as well, which are still kept up among the peoples there. In fact, he learned about their practices in detail and they, in turn, accepted his teaching because some of

their ceremonies had been neglected due to the passage of time; and the philosopher explained to them, in a more complete way, what divine worship consisted of. (*Life of Proclus* 14)

This important text shows the Neoplatonic philosopher as both one who collects ancient traditions and one who teaches those who are neglectful of their religious practices. The philosopher is thus not a mere armchair theoretician but also a sort of teacher or educator of the pious.

After Proclus and up until the end of paganism, there were other philosophers who composed hymns. Isidorus, a pupil of Proclus, for example, did a fair amount of composing; another of Proclus's pupils, Asclepiodotus, "increased the corpus of hymns," which is a further testimony to the fact that hymns were composed and collected in the school of Athens.[6] A generation later, Asclepiades, who was a pupil of Isidorus, composed a series of hymns in honor of the Egyptian gods, and it is possible that two acrostic hymns in honor of Dionysus and Apollo, which are preserved in the *Palatine Anthology* (book 9, nos. 524, 525), are related to this type of collection. Finally, attention has never been drawn to the fact that in Proclus's commentary on the *Cratylus,* one line is probably quoted from a hymn in honor of the goddess Hestia:

> Young men, hail Hestia, most ancient of the goddesses.
> (*In Cratylum* 138, Pasquali)

This fact is to be considered in connection with the official cult in the cities, where the goddess played the role of guardian of the prytaneum—in other words, of the town hall—for example, at Ephesus.[7] In Egypt, too, she appears on that extraordinary piece of tapestry, now kept in Washington, that actually represents "Hestia, full of blessings."[8] This portrayal is something like an "icon" of the goddess and of her gifts: light and fire, riches, joy, good reputation, the celebration of official banquets, virtue, and progress—in short, everything that a well-educated, good citizen could wish for. Hestia had always been the goddess of the family hearth, but with time she became also the goddess of the communal hearth of the whole city, on which the immortal or permanent fire was burning. Perhaps we are touching on a tiny but real trace of the influence of Neoplatonic spirituality on the urban citizens, which might even have played some sort of role in the resistance to the movement to christianize the empire.

Devotion

Devotion to traditional Greek divinities is thus a basic part of the spirituality of the Neoplatonic philosophers. Proclus is the one we know most about, in this respect, because of a funeral oration that Marinus composed in praise of him (a funeral oration falsely titled the *Life of Proclus*). We know from Marinus that Proclus considered his philosophical vocation to have come from the goddess Athena. Proclus was born in Constantinople, and the guardian goddess of Byzantium happened to be Athena. Of course, Proclus was born there purely by chance, because his father, a lawyer, happened to be there at the time of Proclus's birth—but, nevertheless, Marinus says: "I think that this fact led to his great affinity for the goddess [Athena], so much so, that he not only made a point of celebrating her feast-days, but he also performed her rites with utmost enthusiasm" (*Life of Proclus* 6). Years later, when Proclus returned to Constantinople with his professor of rhetoric, Athena appeared to him there and "urged him to study philosophy and visit the schools of Athens" (*Life of Proclus* 9). When Proclus finally arrived in Piraeus, he made his way to the acropolis and arrived there just as the doors were about to be closed. The custodian said to him: "I was actually going to close up, if you had not arrived" (*Life of Proclus* 10). Proclus, of course, interpreted this as meaning that before it was too late, he should take up the heritage of Athena's spirit, which still reigned in the Parthenon. Finally, several years later, when the cult statue of the goddess Athena was removed from her temple by the Christian emperors, Proclus heard the voice of the goddess telling him that she vowed to live with him evermore. Proclus's home thus became Athena's sanctuary (*Life of Proclus* 30). A closer or more intimate bond between a man and his god cannot be imagined. Indeed, Proclus considered himself a child of Athena.[9]

After Athena, the god probably most revered by Proclus was Asclepius. In general, this savior god was universally revered, and the cult of Asclepius, even more than that of the emperors, presented a challenge to Christianity. Marinus devotes two entire chapters to Proclus's relationship to Asclepius (*Life of Proclus* 30, 32), and he tells us how Proclus's prayers cured little Asclepigeneia:

> Asclepigeneia, the daughter of Archiadas and Ploutarche, the wife of our benefactor Theagenes, while still a little girl being brought up by her parents, was suffering one day from a serious illness which the doctors could not cure. Archiadas, whose hopes for posterity lay with her alone, was in great distress and, as one can imagine, in a pitiful state. While the doctors were despairing, he, as had been his custom in the most serious of circumstances, sought out the philosopher as his only hope, as his only savior, and with persistent supplications, he asked him to pray immediately for the recovery of his daughter. Proclus took along with him the great Pericles of Lydia, a man who was a great friend of wisdom, and together they went up to the Ascle-pieion, to pray to the god there, on behalf of the ailing girl. In fact, at the

time, the city still had the good fortune of benefitting from the presence of the god and the temple of the Savior had not as yet been pillaged. And while Proclus prayed, according to ancient rite, a sudden change took place in the little girl and she immediately felt easier: the Savior, inasmuch as he was a god, had truly cured her with ease. Having completed these ceremonies, Proclus visited Asclepigeneia and found her completely healthy, although she had just been relieved of the evils which were besieging her body. (*Life of Proclus* 29)

The philosopher cures diseases in hopeless cases; the theologian is truly a mediator between god and worshiper. This is the image that Marinus so admirably depicts in his *Life of Proclus*.

Another chapter in Marinus is devoted to Proclus's friendship with the god Pan and with the mother of the gods (*Life of Proclus* 33). In yet another chapter, Marinus tells us that "each month, Proclus observed the feast-days of the Mother of the gods, which were honored among the Romans,—even earlier, among the Phrygians; he observed the Egyptians' unlucky days better than the Egyptians themselves, and, in addition, he fasted on certain days for reasons peculiar to himself, namely, divine visitations." Marinus admirably depicts Proclus when he says: "Our most pious hero always had the following saying on the tip of his tongue: that the philosopher should not only be the priest of a single city or of certain particular peoples, but that he should be the universal hierophant of the whole world" (*Life of Proclus* 19). This was an admirable project indeed, and Proclus fulfilled it entirely, seeking throughout his life a constant harmony between the religious traditions of the entire universe.

Other Gods

To complete our description of Neoplatonic piety, we need to mention here that from the middle of the fifth century until the end of the school of Athens (529) the survival of pagan piety was clandestine because of the constant surveillance of the Christian authorities. An episode in Proclus's life that dates to the year 430–431 is highly symptomatic of this. The young Proclus had just arrived in Athens, and when he presented himself to Syrianus, the latter led him to the philosopher Plutarch, who was the head of the school of Athens at the time. Marinus tells us:

Also present at their meeting was Lachares, a man completely imbued with philosophical doctrines and who had been a pupil of philosophy under Syrianus himself. He was present, as I was saying, at their meeting. It was the twilight hour. They were still engaged in conversation when the sun set and the moon made its first appearance after its conjunction with the sun. They were trying to dismiss the young man, after having greeted him, inasmuch as he was a stranger, so that, once alone, they would be free to worship the goddess. But when Proclus started to move away from them, he too saw from the house that the moon was appearing and there, on the spot, he took off his shoes, and before their very eyes, he began greeting the goddess. Lachares, struck by the young man's daring, then said to the philosopher Syrianus exactly what Plato had said under divine inspiration on the subject of exceptional beings: "either this young man will be a great good or else he will be exactly the opposite" (*Republic* 6.491E1–6). (*Life of Proclus* 11)

This episode is most revealing of how cautious pagans had to be when practicing their religion. Indeed, they both wanted and had to be wary at all times of any actions or attitudes that could have been seen as provocation of Christians.[10]

In conclusion, we ask ourselves a very basic question, one that is bound to arise in the minds of modern thinkers: How were Neoplatonic philosophers capable of reconciling their worship of traditional Greek gods with their philosophy, which is somewhat monotheistic, in the sense that it leads everything back to the One. This "monotheistic" tendency needs, of course, to be correctly understood. For the Neoplatonists, the One is not actually the only god; rather, he is the first god, the one through whom all the others are gods as well. Furthermore, the multitude of different gods that exist within Platonic theology makes up a far larger and richer group than that which is represented in the Olympic Pantheon of the classical era. This is because it comprises all the henads of the classes of intelligible gods, intelligible-intellectual ones, and purely intellectual ones. And this rich hierarchy of gods is a sort of ladder which allows a soul seeking the divine to ascend its rungs and unite itself at the top with the first god, the One/Good. In general terms, the gods, placed as they are between the One and us, form classes, series, planes, orders; and we use them as a golden chain stretched out between the One/Good and ourselves, to lift us gradually toward the One/Good. Each of these steps is indispensable, and the philosopher, who knows both their nature and their hierarchical position, worships each of them in a fitting manner. But each god is not only a rung of the ladder leading up to the One/Good; to each one is also attributed a portion of the universe that is appropriate to him and that allows him to exercise his particular providence. A specific patron must be invoked, so that a specific effect can be obtained within a specific order of things. As such, even though the spirituality of the Neoplatonists is inspired by a certain "monotheism," this monotheism in no way excludes traditional polytheism; rather it assumes and confirms it.

In this article, we have quoted Proclus more than any other Neoplatonic philosopher. This is simply because, of all the Neoplatonists, he is the one we know best. Not only have a large number of his works come down to us, but, thanks to Marinus, we have a very lifelike portrait of Proclus and his work. Proclus, moreover, lived for over seventy years, over most of the fifth century, whereas Syrianus died at a young age. Yet it is through Proclus that we know Syrianus, who seems to have had a truly creative mind. After Proclus, Damascius is the most important of the Neoplatonists, and he presents himself as a critic of the works of Proclus. His works refute various positions in Proclus by returning to certain principles of Iamblichus. Whatever the case, Proclus seems to have been the strongest personality in the Neoplatonic school of Athens: it was he who organized the studious life as a kind of monastic life; it was he who organized the program of study as part of a true life of contemplation and prayer; it was he who viewed the philosophy of Plato as a "mystagogy," as an "initiation into the holy mysteries themselves, raised up in purity onto a sacred pedestal and installed, for eternity, in the home of the gods on High" (Proclus *Platonic Theology* 1.1). That is why, in our opinion, the spirituality of Proclus heralds the spirit of medieval philosophy.

Notes

1. See A. D. Nock, "Oracles théologiques," *Revue des études anciennes* 30 (1928) 280–90 (reprinted in *Essays on Religion and the Ancient World*, ed. Zeph Stewart [2 vols.; Oxford: University Press, 1972] 1:160–68).

2. See H. D. Saffrey, "Les néoplatoniciens et les Oracles Chaldaïques," *Revue des études augustiniennes* 27 (1981) 209–25.

3. See Anne Sheppard, "Proclus' Attitude to Theurgy," *Classical Quarterly* 32 (1982) 212–24.

4. See M. L. West, "The Eighth Homeric Hymn and Proclus," *Classical Quarterly* 20 (1970) 300–304.

5. The essential works on the Orphic Hymns are those of Otto Kern and Wilhelm Quandt, used by A. N. Athanassakis, *The Orphic Hymns* (Missoula, MT: Scholars Press, 1977).

6. Damascius *Life of Isidorus* 61 (for Isidorus), 209 (for Asclepiodotus), 164 (for Asclepiades).

7. See J. Keil, "Kulte im Prytaneion von Ephesos," in *Anatolian Studies*, ed. W. H. Buckler (Manchester: University Press, 1939) 119–28; and D. Knibbe, "Der Staatsmarkt, Die Inschriften des Prytaneions," in *Forschungen in Ephesos* 9.1.1 (Vienna: Österreichischen Akademie der Wissenschaften, 1981) 101–5.

8. See P. Friedländer, *Documents of Dying Paganism:* vol. 1, *The Hestia Tapestry* (Berkeley and Los Angeles: University of California Press, 1945) 1–26 (reprinted in *Studien zur antiken Literatur und Kunst* [Berlin: de Gruyter, 1969] 488–510). It will be noticed, however, that our interpretation of the document is not that of Friedländer.

9. On Proclus's devotion to Athena, see A.-J. Festugière, "Proclus et la religion traditionelle," in *Mélanges André Piganiol* (Paris: Centre de Recherches historiques, 1966) 1581–90 (reprinted in *Études de philosophie grecque* [Paris: J. Vrin, 1971] 575–84).

10. See H. D. Saffrey, "Allusions antichrétiennes chez Proclus, le diadoque platonicien," *Revue des sciences philosophiques et théologiques* 59 (1975) 553–63.

Bibliography

Editions

Damascius. *Vita Isidori*. Edited by E. Zintzen. Hildesheim: Olms, 1965.

Eunapius. *Vitae Sophistarum*. Edited by J. Giangrande. Rome: Typis Publicae Officinae Polygraphicae, 1956.

Iamblichus. *De Mysteriis*. Edited by E. des Places, with French translation. Budé; Paris: Les Belles Lettres, 1966.

Marinus. *Vita Procli*. Edited by J. F. Boissonade. Leipzig, 1814. Reprinted in *Procli opera inedita*, ed. V. Cousin. Amsterdam: Hakkert, 1966.

Oracles Chaldaiques. Edited by E. des Places. Budé; Paris: Les Belles Lettres, 1971.

Orphicorum fragmenta. Edited by Otto Kern. Berlin: Weidmann, 1972.

Proclus. *Commentarius in Parmenidem*. Edited by V. Cousin. 2nd ed. Paris: Bibliothèque nationale, 1864. Reprinted Hildesheim: Olms, 1961.

———. *Hymni*. Edited by E. Vogt. Wiesbaden: Harrassowitz, 1957.

———. *In Platonis Timaeum commentarii*. Edited by E. Diehl. 3 vols. Leipzig: Teubner, 1903–1906. Reprint Amsterdam: Hakkert, 1965.

———. *Théologie platonicienne*. Edited with French translation by H. D. Saffrey and L. G. Westerink. Budé; Paris: Les Belles Lettres, 1968.

Translations

Iamblichus. *Theurgia: or, The Egyptian Mysteries*. Translated by A. Wilder. New York: Metaphysical Publishing Co., 1911.

The Orphic Hymns. Translated by A. N. Athanassakis. Missoula, MT: Society of Biblical Literature, 1977.

Proclus. *The Commentaries of Proclus on the Timaeus of Plato*. Translated by Thomas Taylor. London: the author, 1820. Pacsimile reprint Ann Arbor, MI: University Microfilms, 1969.

———. *Platonic Theology*. Translated by Thomas Taylor. Kew Gardens, NY: Selene Books, 1985.

Modern Works

Lloyd, A. C. "The Later Neoplatonists." In *The Cambridge History of Later Greek and Early Medieval Philosophy*, 272–330. Edited by A. H. Armstrong. Corrected edition. Cambridge: University Press, 1970.

Nock, Arthur Darby. *Essays on Religion in the Ancient World*. Edited by Zeph Stewart. 2 vols. Oxford: University Press, 1972.

Wallis, R. T. *Neoplatonism*. London: Duckworth, and New York: Scribner, 1972.

Part Two
THEMES

11

Monotheistic and Polytheistic Elements in Classical Mediterranean Spirituality

JOHN PETER KENNEY

T HE TASK OF OUR PRESENT ENQUIRY is to analyze some concepts of divinity that were formative of, and embedded in, Greco-Roman spirituality. Discussion of the structure of the sacred cosmos might seem to suggest consideration only of formal theology or metaphysics, but this need not be so. In the study of any religious culture, one must adjust to the level of indigenous conceptualization found within that tradition. In the case of classical religion, there is a gradual development of religious thought toward exact and comprehensive reflection, so that our study must follow this tendency accordingly. Although our purpose is not historical, it nonetheless seems best to proceed with our analysis by tracing in a roughly chronological fashion the course of classical religious reflection, beginning with elements of archaic polytheism and ending with the special forms of Greco-Roman monotheism that manifested themselves in late antiquity.

Two further introductory points seem to be apposite before we begin. As they evolve, spiritual traditions may tend to refine and elaborate their accounts of sacred reality. In the process there can develop a measure of discrepancy between traditional cultic practices and religious metaphysics such that this sacred model may no longer fully endorse all aspects of received observance. Pressure for revision may be exerted from theological model to cult, or the reverse. While such reactions can sometimes be traced, our purpose requires only that we recognize the potential for such variance and incorporate this possibility into our terminology. When I speak, then, of polytheism and monotheism in an unqualified way, I will be using these terms to refer to positions in religious metaphysics. To signal discussion of the notions of divinity at the level of ritual behavior, I will preface these terms accordingly. For example, cultic polytheism—that is, the ritual observance of cults related to multiple gods. The significant point of concern, of course, is that, while the Greco-Roman religious tradition continued throughout its history to recognize many gods at the level of ritual, some versions of its reflective theology began through conscious revision to evince a type of monotheism. In such instances cultic polytheism was thus conjoined with monotheism in theology.

It is also necessary to be reflective about such theological concepts as polytheism and monotheism, notions often left freely floating in religious discourse. For our purposes, polytheism may be stipulated as the view that there are many final principles of order, power, and value. Monotheism would thus be the claim that there is one ultimate such principle. These might be treated then as the basic or root positions, which can obviously be developed in a number of different directions. We must be careful, however, not to allow any culturally familiar version of these concepts of deity to limit our considerations, especially in the case of monotheism. There is some tendency in Western religious thought to assume that monotheism denotes only the very sophisticated concept which emerged as the product of centuries of medieval Scholastic refinement. According to this approach, monotheism includes belief in a single, exclusive principle that is the ontological foundation of reality, the cosmological source of the structure of reality, the perfect foundation of all value, and so on. From this reading is derived the long list of divine attributes, for example, creator, omniscience, omnipotence, self-existence, infinity, eternity, immutability, etc. We must not think, by force of cultural habit, that this is the only conceptually possible version of monotheism, since doing so forecloses to our understanding other monotheistic options (e.g., deism or process theism) and prejudices anachronistically our recognition of forms of Western monotheism that emerged antecedent to this Scholastic construct. If we realize that monotheism as a core religious intuition can admit of a range of possible interpretations other than the one we naturally assume, then we will be free from a habit of mind that can blinker our assessment of classical religious thought and, indeed, that of other non-Western traditions.

It might be observed in anticipation that the monotheism which developed in the Greco-Roman world had many elements that differentiate it from our culturally dominant "Scholastic" model.[1] Besides the obvious differences that result from the gradual development of certain technical notions (e.g., existence, infinity), there was a distinct way of approaching the oneness of the divine.[2] Rather than rejecting polytheism by emphasizing the uniqueness of one divine being, as seems to be the case in the "exclusive" monotheism of the Jewish or Christian theological traditions, Hellenic monotheism tended to focus upon the ultimate unity of divinity behind its plural manifestations. This "inclusive" monotheism was thereby centered on a quite different way of understanding the divine nature, one that pressed beyond the many gods of polytheism to their final, divine ground. Although this theology was not opposed to cultic polytheism, it did seem to reject an intrinsically pluralized theological model for ultimate reality. Its intention seems to have been to understand the fundamental monotheistic intuition of the divine oneness in terms of final and inclusive divine unity rather than in terms of divine singularity, exclusivity, or uniqueness. Such is my provisional hypothesis regarding classical spiritual reflection; we must now consider some developments in the history of classical religious thought with this perspective on monotheism in mind.

Aspects of Ancient Polytheism

As one reflects upon ancient polytheism, the Homeric conception of the divine looms very large indeed, exercising a considerable power of imagination over our own understanding of traditional polytheism, as it did over later Greeks and Romans. We must recognize, however, that we have in these poems only a limited record of a much broader range of religious thought and behavior; even here there is ample evidence of a spiritual universe made complex by centuries of accretion and development. Besides this Olympian trajectory in ancient polytheism, there were other developments in early religious thought that are important to our enquiry, and these are to be found especially in Presocratic philosophy. I shall begin, then, by sketching out this archaic Olympian theology along with some of its later revisions; we can next consider a few interesting features of Presocratic thought.

The backdrop of the classical pantheon as we find it in Homer and Hesiod was provided by a generalized sense of the efficacy of divinity behind or within nature. This sense of the collective divine background with its immediate and particular forces (*daimones*) is pervasive in archaic Greek spirituality: the aweful, remote, and general power of divinity with its tremendous force of life manifests itself at a special time and place in the form of a present power or spirit. *Theoi*, "gods," may be treated, then, as manifestations of primordial divinity itself whose nature or character has been consistently revealed and whose differentiated identity has become the basis for a cult. As we shall see, this conception of the primordial divine fundament and its manifestations remains vivid throughout classical religious history and becomes the basis for important later modifications of the tradition.

The chief aspect of Olympian polytheism that served as a device both to associate and divide gods and humans was anthropomorphism. This conspicuous feature has sometimes been seen either as essentially the result of social projection or as primarily an element of rationalism, which helped humans to find some ground of likeness between themselves and the forces of divinity. Both of these perspectives are true to an extent. By characterizing manifestations of divinity in an anthropomorphic fashion, the religious imagination of the ancients was perhaps better able to draw out, as it were, the character of divinity itself and to make some elements of its obscure nature understandable. Divinity itself was doubtless easier to come to terms with in the form of gods who constituted the "highest anthropomorphic class," with motivations recognizable by their mortal adherents. It should be admitted as well that archaic social organization was clearly the basis for the Homeric projection of many aspects of Olympian behavior—in particular, the gods' pervasive concern for *timē*, "personal honor." Early Greek social organization rested upon a particular model of internal and reciprocal class relations in which honor and the physical manifestations of prestige were central to the aristocratic, warrior group. This model was certainly the speculative basis for the Homeric representation of the gods and of the relationship of this class to humans, and it remained an influential component of the Olympian tradition long after the original social structures that spawned it had decayed. Anthropomorphism was, therefore, an important feature of classical polytheism, which allowed this theology to find a means of representing the amorphous divine background in terms of a recognized group of specific and regular manifestations. As a result, classical polytheism was a religious cosmology in which the divine foreground of gods was sufficiently assimilated to humans that some means of communication were opened. The world was thus invested with religious meaning, and a covenant of order and significance was established within the universe.

We should also realize, however, that anthropomorphism was important in retaining the aweful distance of the divine, which is another common feature of traditional religious cosmologies. It might be said, contrary to common opinion, that this sort of projective representation of the divine tended also to disassociate the gods; for they were, one might say, sufficiently like humans for their real differences to become clear. This is particularly true of their immortality, as earlier citations indicated, and of their power. The power of the divine was viewed as tremendous and partly inscrutable, for it was never certain when and why divine intervention in human affairs might occur. In their Homeric portrayal, the Olympians, with the possible exception of Zeus, were prone to strong and varied emotions, and their involvement in the human world was in consequence spasmodic, willful, and elusive of final purpose. In such instances anthropomorphic characterization served not only to provide a limited access to divinity through an intelligible general depiction of their nature but also to underscore their awesome power and the uncertainty of its use. This is especially clear in the *Iliad*, as the fury of the gods leads them into combat. The overall portrayal of anger makes sense as an extension of human conflict, and yet the specific reasons for divine preference and action appear arbitrary. Throughout, the superiority and inscrutability of divine power are made plain by the anthropomorphic specification of the conditions of its use. Once again we can see in Homeric polytheism the stipulation of divinities that are very distinct from humans, in contrast to other archaic religious traditions, which would permit greater assimilation and even identification.

It is important to recognize as we proceed that, although archaic religious thought—such as that of Homer—is not systematic, there are nonetheless certain tendencies that can be identified and that provided the foundation for later religious reflection. One such tendency in particular should be noted: the Homeric gods, which became constitutive of classical polytheism, were frequently seen as regular, focal manifestations of the more obscure power which is divinity itself. They constituted the foreground of the divine over against its deeper primordial background. This is clear in many aspects of the Homeric account. The gods are not responsible for the origin of the universe; they are part of it and powers within it. Even in the cosmogony of Hesiod, sole responsibility is never placed in the hands of the gods; they are, in the person of Zeus, at best the fashioners who order primieval chaos. Neither were the gods in archaic thought in control of death, by which they were repelled, nor were they clearly in complete control of *moira*, "fate." There is instead a rather diffuse understanding of the divine, such that divine power was at times construed along the lines of purpose, and sometimes not, leaving a residue of potentiality below the level of anthropomorphic representation. The results of this complex understanding of the divine are obvious in Homer. For example, the death of Patroclus was attributed by Homer at times to Zeus, to the gods collectively, to Apollo, or to both Zeus and Apollo.[3] Similarly, the difficulties of Odysseus are attributed by him to Zeus, to a *daimōn*, or to the gods.[4] The cumulative effect of such references is to underscore the multiple ways in which divinity can be understood and to draw attention to the fact that the anthropomorphic foreground of divine representation alone would not suffice. There was more, then, to archaic polytheism than the gods.

At the same time, one can recognize in this archaic polytheism a growing tendency first to collect, as it were, the special powers of this anthropo-morphic foreground into a single principle, and then to connect this prin-ciple more closely with the underlying primordial power of divinity itself. This development within Homeric polytheism crystallized in the figure of Zeus, who is not only the central divinity of the Olympian hierarchy but also a god whose power exceeds all other Olympians combined. Most sig-nificant was the tendency to draw Zeus into a fundamental connection with the primordial force of divinity, so that he would thereby become the special god who most certainly and completely expressed the divine. This theme is effected by representing Zeus as clearly cognizant of fate and as a vital participant in determining its course. As just noted in the case of Patroclus's death or Odysseus's wanderings, it was acceptable to treat fate as being at least in part the result of Zeus's will. The prologue of the *Iliad* indicates the significance of the will or purpose of Zeus (*dios boulē*) in framing the story's course, for it was his intention that so many should have died. Besides exercising this admittedly vague control, he knows what will occur, such as is indicated when Zeus reveals the future course of the war to Hera (*Iliad* 8.470; 15.49ff.). It would be anachronistic to speak of omnipotence or omniscience in such contexts, but the germ of these concepts is present, and the result is a deepening of Homeric anthropo-morphism, allying the notion of the gods directly with the more general power behind them. Zeus's will, the *moira* of the gods, and *moira* as such, all seem interchangeable notions, which indicates this alliance between the relatively more knowable idea of the purposive will of the supreme god and the unknown power of divinity itself.

This tendency to emphasize the stature of Zeus and thereby to draw what I have called the unspecified primordial power of divinity into a closer rela-tionship with the anthropomorphic foreground of the gods is a significant element of traditional polytheism. As has been noted, this development can be seen within the Homeric poems, but it matured as Greek religious thought on the question of the justice of divine action continued.[5] It has sometimes been thought that the gods generally and Zeus in particular have no real interest in justice in any normative moral sense and that their interest in retribution is actually connected only to their concern to defend their *timē*. Particular social activities were the special concern of certain gods, and improper human actions that violated divinely mandated rules were an affront to the gods involved. Hence, the *Iliad* is said to revolve around the breaking of social customs governing guest relations and oaths, both of which intersect the realm of Zeus, whose provenance these areas are (as *Zeus Xeinios*, protector of strangers and guests, and *Zeus Horkios*, guarantor of oaths). This is indeed a possible, minimal analysis, but Zeus can also be seen as interested not only in the narrow scope of his concerns but also in providing his endorsement of the broad pattern of archaic social relations to which these two areas were vital. This reading would make Zeus into a figure whose concern is with social justice—or at least with something more than just a prerogative interest in his own sphere of influence. It must be admitted that Zeus does bring, or permit, evil in human lives, although this is mitigated in the *Iliad* by a slim recognition that Zeus may in fact punish humans for their transgressions through such evil (16.384ff.). The *Iliad* provides, then, the early elements of what would become a more consistent treatment of justice as central to the Olympians, and especially to Zeus. As a result, the gods began to be drawn more closely into an association with the underlying order of the universe.

The *Odyssey* intensified this theme whether by intent or as a result of the fact that its theme, the restoration of *dikē*, "social justice," in Ithaca, lends itself better to the issue. The speech of Zeus in the initial book emphasizes that it is humans who bring more evils on themselves than fate would have it.

> Oh for shame, how the mortals put the blame upon us gods, for they say evils come from us, but it is they, rather, who by their own recklessness win sorrow beyond what is given, . . . (*Odyssey* 1.31–34; trans. R. Lattimore)

In general, the *Odyssey* treats evil fortune as the just result of human action, with gods acting as arbiters, especially Zeus, for no god is deadlier. Subsequent writers continued this connection between the course of fate and the judgment of the gods. Given the conventions of archaic society, it need not have been a person's own offenses that were principally to blame, but those of one's ancestors, as in Herodotus's story of the doom of Croesus and his empire (*Histories*, book 1). Zeus is thought by Herodotus to be behind all this, although Herodotus continues, in the flexible world of Greek theology, to attribute such ancestral retribution to *daimōn*, or the divine in general. Nonetheless, this divine destructive activity is primarily marshaled against human beings who practice injustice.

One key, then, to understanding the ancient polytheistic model is the notion that, however complex the world may appear to be and however conflicting the divine forces seem which operate within it, there obtains a basic and fundamental pattern of order. In the truest sense, this is what divinity is, and it is to this root notion of the divine that the special activities and concerns of the Olympian pantheon were gradually made to be fully representative. Zeus was the major focus for this development, because he was the central figure of Olympian religion. It was Zeus who, although not especially concerned with mortals, was nonetheless responsible for bestowing and sanctioning social justice among them. It was Zeus who guaranteed the universal order and whose daughter Justice sat beside his throne looking after the affairs of humans along with myriad other immortals. The cosmogonic explanations of Hesiod were meant to underscore this, to set the present pattern and the current fate of humans into context; this is, therefore, a mythology meant to conjoin the basic pattern of universal order with the just intentions of Zeus, the primary anthropomorphic representation of divine power. It was this tendency, rather than any pantheism, which was behind the famous fragment of Aeschylus:

> Zeus is *aithēr,* Zeus is earth,
> Zeus is heaven, Zeus, surely, is all things,
> and whatever is higher than these.[6]

Zeus is the power of order within all things—within the universe and beyond it. He is therefore more than just the chief Olympian, preeminent among the dominant powers within the universe. He is something more, for he must be seen as grounded in the primordial order of the universe itself. Aeschylus has always been seen as a champion of this theme, if not an innovator, and the great choral hymn to Zeus from the *Agamemnon* exhibits this spirituality (160–84). As is made clear throughout the *Agamemnon,* Zeus does not punish the innocent, that is, those free from either personal or ancestral transgression. Although this conception assumes a continued corporate model of moral responsibility, the theology behind the sentiment is clear. The entire Oresteian trilogy illustrates that Zeus is relentless in his assertion of social justice—not as his personal perquisite but because he is identified as the principle of order within the universe. It is, therefore, Zeus who is best seen as the supreme divine power, giving humans the pattern of social order which is *dikē.* Although not specifically concerned with humanity, he is inexorable in his judgment. But it is through his retribution that humans achieve knowledge, a grace brought by violence.

In many ways these strands of religious thought forced attention upon the relation of a supreme deity within the Olympian pantheon and the primordial power of divinity that lay behind this level of religious representation. It would be foolish to suppose any certain consistency in this tendency or to assume linear development. My point is only that these elements are constitutive of a basic pattern of theology within Olympian polytheism, one that recognized in various ways the importance of a primordial divine unity behind the anthropomorphic foreground of the gods. Somewhat more exact reflection upon the nature of this divine fundament can be seen within that cluster of protophilosophical figures conventionally known as the Presocratics. Throughout this early philosophical theology there is evident a recurrent effort to specify the character of ultimate reality, something that was consistently described in theological terms.[7]

Xenophanes is a case in point.[8] Whatever his views may have been toward the anthropomorphism of Olympian polytheism, Xenophanes' speculation centered on a supreme divine power which is stable, intellective, and capable of action at a distance through thought:

> Always he remains in the same place, moving not at all; nor is it fitting for him to go to different places at different times, but without toil he shakes all things by the thought of his mind. (Kirk, Raven, and Schofield fr. 171)

> All of him sees, all thinks, and all hears. (fr. 172).

Although it is admittedly difficult to interpret with precision Xenophanes' views on this principle, I suggest that they be understood in the light of those aspects of the Olympian polytheist tradition that we have been considering. Xenophanes' principal god seems to have been a divine substance that permeates and gives life to the world. A force within and behind the world, it is, however, not simply to be identified with the world, given its intellective power and causal efficacy (Kirk, Raven, and Schofield pp. 172–73; fr. 174). Xenophanes seems, then, to have been rethinking the nature of the divine fundament, which he saw as having powers of intellection and causality exceeding those of the Olympian divinities.

This same effort of reflection upon the divine foundation of reality is to be discerned in the enigmatic pronouncements of Heraclitus. Behind the conflicting appearances of things, behind the qualitative opposites, there lies a common plan or measure, the divine *Logos*. The cognition of this hidden plan allows us to understand that, despite their discrete plurality and incongruence, all things have an inner unity and coherence: "Listening not to me but to the *Logos* it is wise to agree that all things are one" (Kirk, Raven, and Schofield fr. 196). This inner divine pattern is the basis for the manifest patterns of opposition and for the tacit balance and proportion in the world:

> God is day night, winter summer, war peace, satiety hunger, [all the opposites, this is the meaning]; he undergoes alteration in the way fire, when mixed with spices, is named according to the scent of them. (fr. 204)

Although the divine *Logos* is the inner connective feature of things for Heraclitus, it is difficult for us to know how he construed its relation to its constituent opposites. I think it is clear that it was neither just a term for the sum total of things nor some originative material still found within the fabric of things. It seems rather to have been the active divine fundament, also characterized by Heraclitus as fire. It is very important to notice that Heraclitus treated this principle as everlasting; as the divine constitution of reality, it cannot be assimilated to the common genetic model of natural production:

> This world-order (the same of all) did none of gods or men make, but it always was and is and shall be: an everlasting fire, kindling in measures and going out in measures. (fr. 217)

Heraclitus, by focusing upon an eternal world order, is revising the early Olympian idea of the fundamental divine rule (usually by Zeus) in accordance with a pattern of justice—although here the emphasis comes upon an eternal, compositional pattern or underlying arrangement for the cosmos. This *Logos* or Fire may be identified to some extent with Zeus ("One thing, the only truly wise, does not and does consent to be called by the name of Zeus" [fr. 228]), but it cannot be assimilated, as the divine fundament, into any cosmogony or theogony. To be the true foundation of the cosmos, it must be everlasting.

Such religious speculation upon an ultimate divine principle of the world was characteristic of Presocratic thought, and with it went continued efforts both to represent the way in which this power was related to the cosmos and to clarify its very nature. The notion of a divine intellect, pervasive but not merely a constituent of the cosmos, can be found, for example, in Empedocles: "He is mind alone, holy and beyond description, darting through the whole cosmos with swift thoughts" (Kirk, Raven, and Schofield fr. 397). This concept must have been attractive as a means of accounting for immanent cosmic unity, but it also brought with it some conceptual pressure to view this divine mind as transcending the cosmos to the extent that it served as a reflective principle of causation. Anaxagoras exhibits this tendency, although even in his philosophy mind remained a quasi-corporeal substance opposed to matter, so that the sense of divine transcendence through intellection is severely qualified:

> All other things have a portion of everything, but Mind is infinite and self-ruled, and is mixed with nothing but is all alone by itself.... For it is the finest of all things and the purest, it has all knowledge about everything and the greatest power; and Mind controls all things ... that have life. (fr. 476)

Despite such early philosophical accounts of divine intellection, there is no clearly resolved understanding of divine incorporeality and transcendence of the cosmos. Even the most sophisticated such principle, the primal One of Parmenides which exists fully, actually, and unchangeably, seems still to have the attendant concepts of sphericity and solidity attached (fr. 299). Archaic reflection upon the divine foundation of the world remained, therefore, intracosmic and quasi-corporealist.

21. Apotheosis of Homer. Greek. 2nd century B.C.

Ancient polytheism was thus a religious outlook that was entered on the sacrality of the cosmos, a world rich in powers often at conflict. There was as well within this older view a tendency to seek for a final understanding of the world order, for a pattern that was complete and purposive. As noted, religious reflection gradually became focused on the divine fundament, on the foundational order behind the plurality of gods and beneath the manifest opposing forces of the cosmos. It was this tendency in theology that initiated the later developments in Hellenic monotheism that we shall now examine.

Hellenic Monotheism

The monotheism of the classical tradition, "Hellenic monotheism," was an understanding of divinity that evolved from ancient spiritual reflection upon the obscure divine fundament behind the surface tale of polytheism.[9] We must be alert to the fact that this later monotheism was continuous with the elements of ancient polytheism already reviewed, so that it arrived at an account of divinity that was not in intention exclusive of divine plurality. It sought not to rend the august fabric of ancient polytheism but to revise it and to shift the focus of its emphasis. It was the ultimate ground of divine unity that mattered to Hellenic monotheists, a unity that could admit of multiple manifestations as proof of its efficacy and primordiality. It seems always to have been resonant with the sacrality of the cosmos, whose rhythmic, seasonal coherence bespoke a deeper presence of unity. To focus primarily on divine uniqueness or exclusivity would be to blind oneself to the genuine insight of this more inclusive sort of monotheism.

We must also not search for another prominent feature of traditional Scholastic monotheism: creation "out of nothingness." This cosmological concept was not important in classical spirituality, since separation of a single and unique god from the world was never the religious center of Hellenic monotheism. Although divine transcendence and ontological dependence became constitutive features of this type of monotheism, the whole cluster of ideas by which the divine nature was represented was a different one, and so we must attempt to understand it on its own terms.

It was Plato who devised many of the elements of what would become Hellenic monotheism. Paramount to his theology is a teleological religious outlook: that divinity is always good and that the cosmos has within it a pattern of excellence. This understanding required a reanalysis of archaic polytheism, and we find in Plato an effort not only to criticize those aspects of Olympian anthropomorphism that fell short of this standard but also to press out the implications of its obscure sense of divine unity behind the gods and the cosmos. Even so, Plato's theology remains in some respects a very traditional one, rooted in the sacrality of the visible world. This cosmic piety is evident in the *Laws* (10) with its deep reverence for the heavenly bodies and its recognition of the one or many good and divine souls which direct the universe,[10] as well as in the *Timaeus* (27C–53C), where the world soul is an immortal force of intelligent life which permeates the cosmos.

Nonetheless, it is this critical revision of ancient polytheism that is important for us. Impelled by the Socratic intuition of a moral universe, Plato pressed out the implications of the old notion of a foundational divine unity behind the cosmos and arrived at a two-world hypothesis. The Forms, the eternal constituents of Being, were to be seen as primordial archetypes of the physical world of change. As such, they were accorded a transcendent status: although they were in some sense present within their ontological clients in becoming, they were invested with a new and clear sense of separate existence. Forms had a higher level of 'being'; they held the eminent place in Plato's degree-of-reality hypothesis.[11] As perfect exemplars of value, the Forms exercised a telic force upon the elements of the lower world of becoming, which sought to imitate these paradigms. This understanding of reality thus provided a philosophic conception of the transcendence of divinity that continued to influence classical spirituality throughout antiquity. There was in this "Platonic inversion" of the Greek outlook on the visible world not only this sharp recognition of the divine transcendence but also a new understanding of divine causality in terms of ontological participation, and the consequent establishment of a firm divide in reality between the unchanging realm of the intelligible and the impermanent world of sense (*Phaedo* 99E–104A). The result of Plato's account of a moral, teleologically ordered universe was that a novel set of theological possibilities was opened for Hellenic religious thought.

While the Forms were multiple, there were several ways in which they evinced a higher unity. Although each Form had a distinct, definitional nature, Plato clearly considered them as making up an integrated realm, since definition of each Form called into play several others, so that there is a rich nexus of connectivity within being (*Sophist* 248–51A, 259E). For similar reasons, the Forms constitute a hierarchy of ever more universal principles, and as a result, being is not a loose collection of powers but an ordered and composite unity. Furthermore, Plato recognized, even if enigmatically, an ultimate principle for being, the Form of the Good, which is described in the *Republic* (508E–511E) as the ultimate source for the Forms, although itself somehow beyond this realm of being. Whatever Plato might have intended by this much-disputed remark, it certainly reinforces the theme of divine unity transcendent of the cosmos. Behind the visible world of flux there was not only some vague *Logos* but also a whole ordered world of perfections, constructed upon lines of logical inference and culminating in a hierarchical first principle, a perfect paradigm of value. Although there remains much obscurity in the relation between the constituents of being and becoming, there is no doubt that Plato helped thereby fix in the religious imagination of antiquity a new conception of divine transcendence and a new model for ontological dependence.

There is much in Plato's diffuse theology that must elude our consideration, but the cosmology of the *Timaeus* cannot be neglected. The *Timaeus* is a perplexing document, for it is difficult to decide how serious Plato was about his adoption of this cosmogony or some of its proposed entities, especially the Demiurge. But it can probably be agreed that some general theological themes do emerge with clarity. Plato seems, first of all, not to have considered Forms to be sufficient for the production of becoming; hence, his theology requires some other causal power to effect this generation. The *Timaeus* includes principally both a material cause—space or the receptacle—and the Demiurge.[12] The latter is an intelligent cosmogonic agent, responsible for actively fashioning the discordant motions or forces of the receptacle according to a paradigm, the absolute living creature. Although other principles are involved (e.g., subordinate gods), the theological point of the story seems to be that Forms require the active causality of a divine intellect. Plato also indicates through this cosmogonic model that the Demiurge's intellect, in exercising its necessary role of intelligent agency, does so to the best of its ability, and always in reference to exemplars separate and distinct from itself. There is no question of omnipotence here: the structure of being and of value is fixed as a brute, metaphysical fact, to which even active divine causality must refer.

Plato's theology in the dialogues was certainly not monotheistic, built as it was upon at least three principles: the realm of being, construed as a composite set of perfect paradigms; an active demiurgic intellect (or intelligent soul); and a material principle. His theology did, however, set the agenda for later Hellenic monotheists, providing the key notions of transcendence and causality for these systems. Aristotle's theology has a similar role to play, again as an important foundation for later Hellenic monotheism. Given his opposition to the theory of Forms and the two-world hypothesis of Plato, his theology did not stand as an endorsement of the Platonic model of transcendence. The great cosmological theology of *Metaphysics* (book 12) became, however, a formative analysis of divine intellect and an important assessment of purely immaterial divinity.

According to Aristotle's analysis, all motion and change are actualizations of potentiality and are dependent on something already actual to produce them (*Metaphysics* 12.6–9.1071b3–1075a11). Even the everlasting circular motion of the heavenly spheres requires something actual upon which it is dependent, and this prime mover would logically have to be something outside the chain of contingency in order to forestall regress. This line of thought evidently suggested to Aristotle the notion of a first cause which would be pure actuality and so without movement or change—that is, an unmoved mover. Such a purely actual substance would be purely immaterial as well, since matter is, for Aristotle, a type of potency. This was, of course, a model of ontological dependence different from Plato's thought, based as it is upon the concepts of actuality and potentiality, and in consequence Aristotle's divine first principle was distinguished from other elements of reality in a way somewhat different from the way Plato's Forms were. It was a supreme and pure sort of actuality and so it stood outside the chain of limited sorts of actuality, outside the class of changing, incomplete, and potential substances. There was not a higher stable degree of reality in which changing things participated ontologically, but rather a distinct type of reality, the fully actual and divine, which exercised a teleological attraction among potential things and generated cosmic motion. Its salient feature was intellection of a self-directed sort, in keeping with its self-sufficiency and complete actuality. It may be that Aristotle considered such full actuality as admitting of a class of instances, each an unmoved mover and a self-directed intelligence, perhaps all hierarchically arranged in relation to a principal mind.[13] However construed, it is divinity as a type of substance that receives attention, not the question of divine uniqueness. It is, one might say, the qualitative unity and essential character of divinity that mattered most to Aristotle, although the teleological force of his argument may well suggest a tendency toward one ultimate and supreme being. Once again it is the ultimate nature of things that is viewed as being divine, and it is the character of this final foundation of the cosmos that is more significant than its specific distribution.

Despite his striking account of divinity in terms of immateriality, self-intellection, and pure actuality, Aristotle's theology has a certain conservative aspect to it. The religious balance in his thought still seems to rest upon the cosmos as an organic unity—everlasting, revered, and sacred—of which divinity is a supreme substance. The divine is that inmensely significant power that draws all potentiality toward actuality and is in this way unique in type, but it remains in intention an element within the overall system, both its center and a part. This cosmos-centered perspective seems to have run very deeply in classical spirituality, and it remained, I think, a dominant theme in Aristotle's theology. This was certainly true of some other forms of theology subsequent to Aristotle, especially Stoicism.[14] Although it remained fundamental throughout later Hellenic monotheism, there was a gradual shift of emphasis toward locating conceptually the divine at a higher plane of reality separate from the cosmos. This development can be found, as might be expected, among later thinkers influenced strongly by Plato, and it is to this loose movement, known as Middle Platonism, that our analysis must now turn.

We know far too little about Plato's immediate successors in the Academy, Speusippus and Xenocrates, and our extant information on Middle Platonism and Neopythagoreanism is also limited, so that historical judgments in this area must remain qualified.[15] For our purposes a composite picture of this pre-Plotinian Platonism can be loosely constructed in order to understand better its contribution to the monotheistic dimension in classical religious thought. The distinctive theological concept for Middle Platonists was the supreme mind located at the level of true being. This intellect was identified with the Good of the *Republic* and was held to contain the whole world of being, the Forms, within the scope of its intellection as thoughts. This remarkable thesis of Forms as divine thoughts may have originated in the Old Academy with Xenocrates,[16] but its use by Middle Platonists helped to ensure that their supreme divinity would be seen as much as possible as an intellect which, like the Forms themselves, occupies an immaterial and transendent locus without the cosmos. The conception of the supreme mind which emerges is one of remoteness, of a self-thinking intellect wholly self-absorbed and free from outside activities interests, or diversions. This was, in consequence, a hierarchical theology, with many subordinate divine powers mediating between the supreme being and our lower world.

Its theological focus was thus two-fold: there was the exaltation of a supreme and transcendent object of contemplation and worship wholly disjoined from our concerns, and an attendant recognition of the intermediate divinities, whose religious importance derived from their greater accessibility. Exactly how this was worked out varied among the thinkers, but it was not uncommon for active governance of the world to be assigned to a secondary mind capable of outward-directed activity or to a tertiary world soul.[17] The range of lesser gods, astral divinities, and other powers of traditional piety could, of course, be accommodated within this theological model as well.

As a hierarchical system of theology, Middle Platonism treated divinity as a quality of which there could be degrees, and this position seems a natural one both because of the conventions of classical spiritual discourse and because of its Platonic ontological model. All of reality was charted on the scale of being, and, at that point where the divide into immateriality and immortality was crossed, it was appropriate to use the concept of divinity. There was here the common generic sense of the unity of the divine, which we have seen before, coupled with an increasing recognition of the special and even unique character of the supreme mind. The theologies of some Middle Platonists and Neopythagoreans began to accentuate the conceptual remoteness of this initial One, which is sometimes treated as ineffable and as a final unity beyond all other cosmogonic principles.[18] Nonetheless, the dominant systematic position among these pre-Plotinian thinkers was to view the initial divinity or supreme mind as itself locatable on the hierarchy of being—albeit in a preeminent position—and further to demur from considering it as immediately present at subsequent levels of being and divinity. We have not found, therefore, an absolute divine foundation of reality in this type of Platonism, only a supreme divinity within the hierarchy. Once again there is a pronounced tendency to assimilate the divine to the overall system of things, although in this later theology the transcendence by divinity of the physical and sensible cosmos is assured.[19]

It was in Plotinus that the monotheistic tendency in classical religious thought emerged with fully articulated clarity. His is a monotheism of divine simplicity, of the final divine unity which stands as the ultimate source for all reality while prescinding from any assimilation to that reality. Although it was a theology complex in its historical foundations and bordering often on paradox, it is, for our story, of unique importance, since it established in a rigorous theological way a model for Hellenic monotheism which would remain widely influential throughout late antiquity. According to this view, Plotinian theology does not stand strangely outside classical religious thought, but rather codified those elements that tended toward an inclusive sort of monotheism.

The One in the theology of Plotinus is the final divine unity; it is not so much numerically unique as distinctive for its position as the ultimate source of all reality. As against earlier Middle Platonic theologies, the One is not a supreme being that can be assimilated to the hierarchical system of being and divinity. It is intended to be separated from that hierarchy—an absolute principle, one might say, rather than a supreme first principle. Plotinus's theology is probably best understood against the backdrop of Middle Platonism, which he critically revised, and from that perspective the One appears as an attempt to represent final divine unity in a way that did not just set it at the apex of an ontological hierarchy. It seems not to have been sufficient for Plotinus to construe the ultimate foundation of reality behind the physical cosmos and the many divine levels as being simply the supreme being, since this obscured for him its true character. Nevertheless, his theology was continuous with the long tradition of classical religious reflection on divine unity, which we have reviewed, and pressed out many of its tacit assumptions.

The earlier Middle Platonic representation of the supreme principle as a transcendent mind was widely adopted in the religious thought of the first, second, and third centuries A.D., and it became common in theological culture and surfaced, for example, in the *Corpus Hermeticum* and the *Chaldaean Oracles*.[20] It was this model which Plotinus sought to reconstruct by focusing upon the supreme Intellect and examining this compendium of Platonic and Aristotelian theology. His criticism was based in part upon the deficiencies that he perceived in this account of divine unity and upon his heightened sense of this principle's role as the ontological source of all reality. The divine mind of Middle Platonism appeared to Plotinus as a complex entity, the locus of a multiplicity of divine ideas unified by the activity of divine intellection. His own spiritual experience seems to have suggested that such plurality was not authentic to the first principle;[21] no doubt this spirituality was in part given shape by some Neopythagorean treatments of an absolute unity beyond all number and their exegetical approach to the different notions of unity analyzed in Plato's *Parmenides*.[22] This absolute unity would be completely simple, and so it would be beyond the duality of standard predication. It would be transcendent even of the predicate "true being," so austere was its simplicity; and as a result it must be understood as existing beyond the Platonic realms of perfect Forms. This negative theology of Plotinus, grounded in the absolute simplicity of the primary divine principle, shattered the Middle Platonic hierarchical model, the consequences of which were considerable.

This new insistence upon absolute divine unity meant a radical departure for classical religious thought: its sources were traditional, but its implications were not. In Middle Platonic theology, there was a strong thesis of divine immateriality and separation from the physical world of change, and although the divine transcendence was thus secured, it was still possible to assimilate the supreme divine being to the other constituents of the hierarchy. Plotinus's thought might be said, however, to be a double-transcendence theology: the One not only stands without the lower world of sensible becoming; it exceeds as well the intelligible and immaterial realm of the divine. The resultant shift in spiritual focus is obvious in Plotinus: it is now the One that is the really significant center of the sacred. It should be clear that this theology of absolute divine unity was developed from elements within the classical tradition. Although it was not necessary or inevitable, it seems at least natural that religious speculation would press beyond the composite unity of the transcendent intelligibles and beyond the intellective unity of a supreme divine mind. Rooted first in the sacrality of the cosmos and then in the unity of an immaterial world bounded by intellection, this Platonic trajectory had now invested absolute unity and simplicity as the core of reality and divinity.

Closely connected with this abstractive aspect of the One is its role as ontological source of reality. The intensified Plotinian conception of the transcendence of the first principle helped make clearer its relation to the chain of lower realities; it was now possible to see the One as the separate source of all lower beings, and in this sense it was referred to by Plotinus as "father" (e.g., V 1 [10], 1, 8). The One was the first principle of all reality: in his ontology Plotinus was not a dualist.[23] In order to understand this point an important distinction should be made between ontology and cosmology, that is, between an account of the essential nature of things and an account of the production of the physical world. For Plotinus the physical cosmos was everlasting, but it was also ontologically dependent on an ultimate first principle. The cosmological idea of everlastingness is thereby conjoined to a theory of radical ontological contingency. All things are separate from and dependent on the One, and because it is thus construed as the transcendent source of all reality, it is also considered to be an infinite, fecund power.[24] The One is neither a supreme but finite being to be classed alongside others nor some nugatory void, an abyss stripped of all value and significance. Despite the negative theology, the One remains identified with the Good, infinite in ontological power and beyond all external limitation.

Rejection of finite conceptual circumscription and of assimilation to the hierarchy of being produced a significant change in religious outlook regarding the divine. Although all beings were now radically distinct from the One, Plotinus often tended to emphasize the immediacy of the presence of the One to its ontological derivatives (e.g., VI 9 [9], 7). Because it was not located on the hierarchical scale of being, as was the case in Middle Platonism, the One could be said to be omnipresent, which allowed for a new spiritual understanding of the divine relation to all aspects of reality. Divinity in its most primordial sense was therefore no longer remote from its derivatives but immediate to all levels.

Thus, Plotinus represents the coalescence of the monotheistic elements in classical religious thought; his theology is a *summa* of sorts for Hellenic monotheism. As we noted at the outset, if one is prepared to countenance a broader conception of monotheism than our culturally received model, then there seems no reason to deny that this Hellenic tradition in theology which culminates in Plotinus was monotheistic. To insist, on the contrary, that all the divine attributes associated with the Scholastic concept of deity are necessary for monotheism would be quite indefensibly anachronistic; indeed, many of the most significant Jewish or Christian figures from the late antique period, such as Philo or Origen. might also fail to qualify.[25] But if one considers the essence of monotheism to be belief in a final and transcendent ontological foundation for all reality, then it should be clear that Plotinus must be included. His was admittedly a different way of developing this basic position from the dominant model which emerged from the Middle Ages. There are major points of variance in cosmological imagery and in accounts of the nature of divine intellection or volition, both of which Plotinus was willing to consider in relation to the One only in a restricted sense.[26] Nonetheless, Plotinian theology was firm in its recognition of a final and transcendent unity that is the source of reality.

Plotinus's theology was not an anomaly in classical religious thought; drawing as it did upon that long reflective tradition which we have followed, it also influenced the great Neoplatonic theologians of late antiquity, who were the leading spiritual authorities in the waning days of classical Mediterranean religion.[27] It might seem surprising to suggest that figures so conspicuously associated with the last revival of cultic polytheism, such as Iamblichus or Proclus, were monotheists. I would suggest, however, that these later Neoplatonists continued the same inclusive approach to monotheism that we have seen already, and, as in Plotinus, their principal commitment in religious ontology was to the divine One. A few points should be noted on this question. The theological tradition associated with Iamblichus restored many of the hierarchical aspects of Middle Platonism. It avoided the Plotinian emphasis upon the immediacy of the One's presence and reconstructed a firm degree-of-divinity model, according a renewed remoteness to the One with the intention of promoting a shift of emphasis back to the multiple divine powers below the One, who were the subjects of petitionary prayer and theurgic ritual.[28] This school also developed the somewhat odd idea that on the level of the One there are multiple powers of unity, called henads, deputy 'ones' which exercise a role of ontological production over series of lower beings and mediate the infinite and now more remote power of the One. It might plausibly be thought that this reflects the reestablishment of theological polytheism, of multiple powers at the source of reality. It must be admitted that these developments were intended in conscious opposition to the contemplative theology of Plotinus and to his much looser attitude toward the divine hierarchy. They were, furthermore, part of an obvious apologetic strategy for cultic polytheism, one that both attenuated the degrees of divinity and improved the apparent status of divine multiplicity. But I do not think that the fundamental status of the One was ever in question: it remained that in which all things, even henads, participated and from which they derived their being. The necessary features of monotheism continued, therefore, to obtain. Indeed, it might even be said that the admittedly rather baroque religious ontology of these late classical theologians, with its proliferated ranks of divine beings and powers, was further witness to the character of the tradition that they concluded. For it was the manifest richness, fecundity, and power of the divine One to which this later Neoplatonic theology intended to call attention. In no sense were the henads meant to threaten the primal One: they were the constant witnesses, as is all reality, to the fact of its existence and the infinity of its power. That we tend by convention to approach monotheism differently may restrain our imaginations so that we neglect initially to recognize that multiplicity of manifestation can stand as important evidence for the divine One.

The Monotheistic Heritage

Hellenic monotheism was a theology of divine ultimacy. As a spiritual tradition rooted in ancient polytheism, its understanding of the divine began with the multiple divine powers and then focused on a primordial divine unity and a final principle of order and value for the sacred cosmos. Throughout this tradition the gods were not rejected, although they were superseded as theological interest was concentrated upon that absolute and transcendent principle into whose fecund unity all gods and divine powers could be resolved—for they were its manifestations at derivative levels of reality. Yet this theology was always an inclusive monotheism, for it seems to have been endemically modalistic—ever willing to consider whatever divine powers it could recognize as modes of this ultimate divine One. Hence, it was a religion of theophanies. Throughout its long history we find repeatedly the notion that primordial divinity may show itself in very many ways through its numerous powers, although a cohesive, if not always apparent, unity lies behind them all.

It is interesting to note that in the One of the late Hellenic theologies the idea of divine uniqueness has been arrived at by a search for an absolute divine unity. The One in Hellenic monotheism was in a sense single by virtue of its systematic position: the notion of complete simplicity as the ontological root of all reality is not an idea that suggests plurality. Because it is truly ultimate, the One is also unique. It is in this respect that the two major Western theistic traditions, the Hellenic and the biblical, find common cause in monotheism, though their cultural origins, cosmologies, and cultic practices are very different. It was also in this area that the historical influence upon the medieval Scholastic development of biblical thought by Hellenic monotheism was pronounced. The theological burden of exclusive monotheism has always been to justify divine singularity and to show why it is that the uniqueness and existence of this being is not just a contingent fact. That there just happens to be one God has never seemed quite enough. It is to Hellenic monotheism that medieval Scholastics turned to find theological accounts of divine simplicity and ultimacy, and these remained in their revised forms the enduring, reflective foundations of Western monotheism, invoked and honored whenever the idea of the ultimate ground of being is appealed to.

It might be said in closing that it seems often to be thought by students of religion that there is a vast hermeneutical space separating ourselves and classical religious thought, whose reflections can only be for us a theology of posthumous gods. I do not think this is so, and I hope that the elements of this tradition that I have traced indicate that a contrary case can be made. Classical theology should continue to be more than just a faint historical afterglow in modern religious thought. If we are really serious in our efforts to understand Western theology, we must come to terms with the whole of it, including this tradition, which can so strikingly combine divine ultimacy and immanence. Hellenic monotheism remains as an alternative understanding of divinity, deserving of renewed attention and respect as we weigh the resources of our Western theistic patrimony.[29]

Notes

1. Unfortunately, the term "classical theism" has become a common way to refer to the dominant Western monotheistic tradition. "Scholastic monotheism" might be a better term, referring to the systematic development of biblical thought by the Jewish, Christian, and Islamic schools of the Middle Ages. On the contemporary use of "classical theism," see H. P. Owen, Concepts of Deity, 1–48.

2. On existence, see John F. Wippel, "Essence and Existence," and on infinity, see John E. Murdoch, "Infinity and Continuity," both in The Cambridge History of Later Medieval Philosophy, ed. Norman Kretzmann, et al., 385–410, 564–93.

3. Iliad 16.252, 688 (Zeus); 693 (the gods generally); 791ff. (Apollo).

4. Odyssey 9.38, 67 (Zeus); 12.295 (a daimōn); 1.267 and 7.242 (the gods).

5. On this complex issue, see the discussion of Hugh Lloyd-Jones, The Justice of Zeus.

6. Aeschylus fr. 34, in Aeschylus, ed. H. W. Smyth; Appendix of Fragments, ed. Hugh Lloyd-Jones (Cambridge, MA: Harvard University Press, 1963) 2:403. The translation is my own.

7. On this subject, see G. S. Kirk, J. E. Raven, and M. Schofield, The Presocratic Philosophers; and Werner Jaeger, The Theology of the Early Greek Philosophers.

8. Kirk, Raven, and Schofield frs. 166–69. This and subsequent translations of Presocratics are drawn from their edition.

9. See n. 1 on the terminology.

10. Its expression in terms of Chaldaean astral theology, however, may have been somewhat novel.

11. W. K. C. Guthrie, *A History of Greek Philosophy*, vols. 4 and 5.

12. *Timaeus* 493B–53C (on space or the receptacle); 27D–30C (on the Demiurge).

13. See the discussion by Guthrie in *A History of Greek Philosophy*, 6:263–76. The chapter in question is *Metaphysics* 12.8.

14. Despite their historical importance, we must leave Stoicism and Epicureanism outside the scope of our enquiry. Suffice it to say that Stoicism represented an effort to construct a largely cosmos-centered theology, although (as in Heraclitus) the notion of an order immanent within the cosmos suggested a limited sense of transcendence. As for Epicureanism, its espousal of multiple and actually existent gods seems firm, although these gods take no part in the activities of the cosmos. Epicureanism seems to be, therefore, a deistic type of polytheism. On this period, see A. A. Long, *Hellenistic Philosophy*.

15. On the subject of Middle Platonism, which dates from about 100 B.C. to A.D. 200, see John Dillon, *The Middle Platonists*.

16. See Dillon, *Middle Platonists*, 22–38.

17. On Albinus and Numenius, see Dillon, *Middle Platonists*, 267–305, 361–79.

18. On Neopythagoreanism, see Dillon, *Middle Platonists*, 114–34, 341–52.

19. Because of its cosmological focus, I have left the so-called solar monotheism, which developed under imperial sponsorship in the third century A.D. aside; see A.-J. Festugière, *Personal Religion*, 121–23.

20. See the discussion of the influence of Middle Platonism in Dillon, *Middle Platonists*, 389–96.

21. Some of the major texts are the following: I 6 [1], 9; V 3 [49], 17; VI 7 [38], 34–36; VI 8 [39], 15; VI 9 [9], 11; V 5 [32], 12. See A. H. Armstrong, "Plotinus," in *The Cambridge History of Later Greek and Early Medieval Philosophy*, ed. A. H. Armstrong, 258–63; J. M. Rist, *Plotinus: The Road to Reality*, 213–30; R. T. Wallis, *Neoplatonism*, 82–90.

22. Dillon, *Middle Platonists*, 114–34, 341–52.

23. On this issue, see Armstrong, "Plotinus," 256–57.

24. See Rist, *Plotinus*, 21–37.

25. For example, the notion of temporal creation *ex nihilo* and its implications for an exclusive disjunction between the created and uncreated seem to have emerged from the Arian controversy of the fourth century A.D. Hence, there is ambiguity in earlier thinkers on this issue, for example, in Philo; see H. A. Wolfson, *Philo* (Cambridge, MA: Harvard University Press, 1968) 1:295–324. Origen's acceptance of a degree-of-divinity theology is another problem area; see Henry Chadwick, "Philo and the Beginnings of Christian Thought," in *The Cambridge History of Later Greek and Early Medieval Philosophy*, ed. A. H. Armstrong, 182–92.

26. See VI 8 [39] for Plotinus's full treatment; see also Rist, *Plotinus*, 66–83.

27. On Later Neoplatonism, see Wallis, *Neoplatonism*, 94–159.

28. On the question of theurgy and the hypostases, see Wallis, *Neoplatonism*, 120–34, 153–57.

29. I should like to offer memorial recognition of the benefit I derived from discussion of early Greek religion with my late colleague at Reed College, Professor William Lankford.

Bibliography

Armstrong, A. H., ed. *The Cambridge History of Later Greek and Early Medieval Philosophy*. Cambridge: University Press, 1970.

Berger, Peter. *The Sacred Canopy*. Garden City, NY: Doubleday, 1967.

Chadwick, Henry. "Philo and the Beginnings of Christian Thought." In *The Cambridge History of Later Greek and Early Medieval Philosophy*, 137–92. Edited by A. H. Armstrong. Cambridge: University Press, 1970.

Dillon, John. *The Middle Platonists*. Ithaca, NY: Cornell University Press, 1977.

Festugière, A.-J. *Personal Religion among the Greeks*. Sather Classical Lectures 26. Berkeley and Los Angeles: University of California Press, 1954. Reprint, 1960.

Geertz, C. "Religion as a Cultural System." In *Reader in Comparative Religion*. Edited by W. A. Lessa and E. Z. Vogt. New York: Harper & Row, 1972.

Guthrie, W. K. C. *The Greeks and Their Gods*. London: Methuen, 1950.

———. *A History of Greek Philosophy*, vols. 4, 5, 6. Cambridge: University Press, 1985, 1978, 1981.

Jaeger, Werner. *The Theology of the Early Greek Philosophers*. Oxford: University Press, 1947.

Kirk, G. S., J. E. Raven, and M. Schofield, *The Presocratic Philosophers*. 2d ed. Cambridge: University Press, 1983.

Kretzmann, Norman, Anthony Kenny, and Jan Pinborg. *The Cambridge History of Later Medieval Philosophy*. Cambridge: University Press, 1982.

Lloyd-Jones, Hugh. *The Justice of Zeus*. Berkeley and Los Angeles: University of California Press, 1971.

Long, A. A. *Hellenistic Philosophy*. London: Duckworth, 1974.

Nilsson, M. P. *Greek Popular Religion*. New York: Columbia University Press, 1940.

———. *Greek Piety*. Oxford: Clarendon Press, 1951.

Owen, H. P. *Concepts of Deity*. New York: Herder & Herder, 1971.

Rist, J. M. *Plotinus: The Road to Reality*. Cambridge: University Press, 1967.

Wallis, R. T. *Neoplatonism*. London: Duckworth, 1972.

12

The Love of Beauty and
the Love of God

W E R N E R   B E I E R W A L T E S

T
HE INTENTION OF THIS ARTICLE is to make clear the unity of the two aspects of the topic: love of beauty or the beautiful and love of God or the divine. What it means to bring them together can also be formulated in this way: Love of the beautiful is a manifestation of the Good and the divine itself; or again, love of God is the essence of beauty, is the absolute cause of the beautiful as idea or as individual beautiful object. Here a misunderstanding might easily arise. To exclude it from the outset, one should bear in mind that in Greek thought until late antiquity—in contrast to modern consciousness—the concept of beauty or the beautiful does not have primarily an aesthetic significance but, above all, an ethical one. The beautiful cannot be understood without the Good, but only through the Good. The beautiful is a manifestation or outward expression of the Good, an indication that a certain form of being or existence has attained its purpose or perfection or that it *is* perfection itself. For human beings, the beautiful is a successful inner way of life, or it is a fundamental ethical position that determines them—what Plato calls *aretē*, "virtue."

The loving turning of humans toward the beautiful as the divine or to God as the absolutely beautiful cannot be thought of in isolation (as though it were merely *alongside* other virtues), but is rather what fundamentally determines and directs their way of life and therewith all other virtues. It does not exclude a turning toward others, but, at least in the realm of genuinely Greek thought, it develops primarily as a relation of the individual to the divine principle. Because it fundamentally determines and directs a way of life, its realization at different times is also instructive for a history of spirituality.

If we attend to the connection or unity of the two aspects in the sense just outlined, a historical limitation follows. It is not our concern to analyze in a general way the loving relation or affection of human beings to God as it was originally conceived and practiced by the Greeks,[1] nor to analyze the loving turning toward the beautiful in the ethical-aesthetic way of life. Our intent is rather to characterize an event in the history of thought that makes it possible for the two spiritual movements to be considered as one. That event is the philosophy of Plato and the history of its influence in the spirituality of later antiquity. Plotinus and Proclus, above all, can serve as paradigms of this emanation of Platonic thought. Pseudo-Dionysius the Areopagite, on the other hand, shows that in spite of different historical conditions essential features of the Platonic and Neoplatonic conception of a way of life remained decisive for Christianity as well—a Greek inheritance that was in turn transmitted to the Middle Ages and the Renaissance, not least by Dionysius himself.

Characteristic of all these historical variations of the Platonic beginning is the close unity of metaphysical theory, or elements of theory, and a conduct of life that, on the basis of insight acquired by argument, allows itself to be guided by ideal principles, that is, principles determined by ideas, and that sees precisely in this the primary possibility of a development and perfection of the human self.

Plato

Plato was the first in the history of Western thought to think through systematically the interpenetration of love (erōs), beauty as idea, and divinity. Through him the connection of these three became a central moment in a conduct of life, guided by ontological principles, which remained decisive into the Renaissance. This fact is in certain respects identical with the history of the intensive influence of the Platonic Symposium and Phaedrus. In what follows, the relationship eros–beauty–divinity will be analyzed—above all from the interrogative structure of these two dialogues.

Of the garland of speeches on the essence and power of eros which constitute the Symposium, the last one is the most instructive for our investigation. In it Plato, through the prophetess Diotima, takes as his subject the question of the essence or idea of the beautiful and the closely associated question of eros as the essential force for the process of knowledge and for understanding the human situation. Personified and with echoes of the myth, eros is first presented as a daimōn (Symposium 202Dff.). However, according to its nature and activity, everything demonic—in the sense of the fundamental Platonic definition—is a "mean" between God and humanity. In contrast to the Christian notion of incarnation, for Greek thought the principle holds that "God mingles not with man" (203A1). Given this postulate—and *if* nevertheless a connection between the divine and the human is to *exist*—eros is not only a mean by virtue of status in being but an *active mediator* as well. Eros is the "interpreting" element that "conveys" the human to the gods and the divine to humans (202E2). Thus, "all the intercourse and converse of gods with men" occurs through its mediation.

The mythological genealogy of eros—his father is Poros (plenty), his mother Penia (poverty)—is most illuminating for the *de*mythologized or *non*-mythical nature of eros, insofar as it is considered the moving power of cognition, inherent in thought. Just as eros, according to the mythical notion, exists between plenty and poverty and therefore, though it strives for plenty or fulfillment, will always still remain limited by poverty and need (203D3), so too, as the movement of cognition, eros always seeks insight (*phronēsis*), the understanding that governs action and is its "mighty hunter" yet remains, nevertheless, somewhat limited by lack of knowledge or ignorance. It is the goal of eros to free itself from this ignorance by thinking and apprehending. The completion of this movement presupposes, to be sure, not a self-consciousness that is wrapped up in itself and self-sufficient, but one which—anticipating the 'what' of knowing—actually knows *that* there is something to be known and that what is visible and to be known is also what is *worth knowing*. Eros is accordingly what desires to know, in or by means of questioning. It is consequently that in human beings which strives beyond the present state of spiritual inadequacy, criticizing, changing, and fulfilling. By becoming conscious of what can be known and is worth knowing, through *conscious* dissatisfaction with and criticism of the hitherto existing situation, this movement at the same time initiates the search for what could fundamentally change these circumstances, that is, the movement of thought out of itself toward a goal that can be attained, even if not altogether obtained.

In the context of this ascending movement, Plato further understands eros as the striving—perhaps utopian—for an everlasting possession of the *Good*. This too in its highest form essentially approaches the realm of the divine or can even be thought of as the divine itself. The question of how this striving at least approximately realizes its goal takes us back to the original theme of the *Symposium*, to the inquiry into the *beautiful*. Plato understands its mode of realization metaphorically as a "begetting in beauty" (206B7f.)—corporeally and spiritually. In the spiritual begetting (*kata tēn psychēn*, "in the soul"), the relation to the Good is obvious. Reflection and justice—that is, essential forms of the basic ethical position, of *arete*, virtue—are to be generated or created in the *other* by means of *logos,* reason. In virtue, those things that belong together and mutually support each other according to their ontological status—the Good and the beautiful—become, sometimes, a practical unity guided by theory (*kalokagathia*).

The fundamental distinction between the corporeal and the spiritual, which Plato presupposes throughout, indicates the direction of the inquiring ascent of thought toward the pure, intelligible, true being of the idea. The basic aspects under which this transcending ascent is to be regarded are the graded manifestations or different degress of intensity of the One Beautiful itself *in* the many beautifuls. Through the *idea* of the Beautiful they are "akin" to one another (210B1f.; C5): that is, what appears in a number of different ways is based on one common or universal *eidos,* which exists in the most intense degree. The direction indicated leads away, therefore, from the corporeal to the beauty inherent in the soul—a quality that is ascribed to spiritual acts or to emotions determined by the spirit.

The forms of manifestation of the beautiful, through which thought passes and which it grasps in their essence, culminate in a "science" or cognition which has the being or essence of the One Beautiful itself as its object and which mediates this object to an insight. This insight occurs "suddenly," surprisingly, in a moment that is free of time. Only one who completes this methodical, rigorously conceived ascent as a continuity (210E3), in which understanding what is respectively higher depends on understanding what is respectively lower, will "suddenly perceive a nature of wondrous beauty for the sake of which all former toils were borne" (210E4f.). The methodically correct preparation, the return secured by argument from the sensible to an intelligible, from what is grounded to the ground, from the many to the One or universal, is the indispensable precondition for the evidential experience of the beautiful—beauty experienced sole and itself, in an authentic or true sense. In this context the beautiful is an outstanding paradigm of an idea. Its being is defined primarily in a negative or limiting way. The idea is thus to be understood through the beautiful in the following way:

> [as something] which in the first place is everlasting, not growing and decaying, or waxing and waning; secondly, not fair in one point of view and foul in another, or at one time or in one relation or in one place fair, at another time or in another relation or in another place foul, as if fair to some and foul to others, or in the likeness of a face or hands or any other part of the bodily frame, or in any form of speech or knowledge, or existing in any other being, as, for example, an animal, or in heaven, or in earth, or in any other place, but *beauty itself,* absolute, separate, simple and everlasting, which without diminution and without increase, or any change, is imparted to the

ever-growing and perishing beauties of all other things (211A–D16–27; trans.
B. Jowett [adapted]).

This means that the beautiful itself, as idea, is the ground of manifold
beauty and as such is free of time but acts in a temporal manifestation and,
furthermore, that it is not in the widest sense relative and thus is not confined to definite aspects of place and time but is rather absolutely itself. It
means, moreover, that it is nothing definite or individual ("a face or hands");
it is neither qualitatively further determinable outside of its own being nor
subject to the category of quantity; it is nothing *on* or *in* an other—thus
no attribute of an other, but rather pure being-in-itself. As such, however,
it is the basis of the participation in it of all other things which are called
and which are beautiful; as "simple" it is the one self-identical and invariable
ground of its own manifold appearance—in itself, for itself, with itself—
that is, beautiful in itself and through itself. The evidence of this beauty,
"which *exists*," "pure, clear, and unalloyed" (211C8; E1), or the knowledge
of the One-Itself, is at the same time the fulfillment of an erotic striving.
This kind of insight in the idea constitutes the only life worth living for
humans (211D2), their blessedness. That this is not equivalent to solipsistic
isolation in a "theoretical position" is already clear from the fact that, for
the one who is thinking in the idea of the beautiful, there is at the same
time an understanding of the normative principle of virtue. It is Plato's
conviction not only that "true virtue" is "touched" by the sight of the
beautiful but also that precisely this insight directs the actual "generation"
of the fundamental and perfect ethical position of humanity. To become
"inwardly beautiful" means to be good or to realize true virtue. This, however, is the core of Platonic spirituality.

If we wished, as indicated, to ask explicitly who the *Platonic God* is or
what simply the (absolute) divine in Plato's sense is, then the idea of the
Good or the Good itself as Plato develops it, particularly in the three
analogies of the *Republic,* might seem to be a fairly adequate response.
Plato, to be sure, never directly equates the 'idea of the Good' with 'God'.
This basic question of Platonic piety cannot be discussed in this connection.
Let it merely be said that essential predicates, which Plato also attributes
to the 'gods' or the 'divine', appertain to the idea of the Good as the universal principle (*Republic* 511B7), so that the Good—on the basis of its
priority to all things—must also be good in the highest or absolute degree
and consequently "most divine." Plato calls God truly good (*Rep.* 379B1),
which suggests that the expressions are interchangeable. Especially in the
analogy of the line, Plato favors the thought that the degree of being corresponds to the degree of divinity and that consequently what exists to the

highest and most intense degree would also be what is most divine, and vice versa. Because god is perfect being, he is self-sufficient (*Philebus* 20A4; 60C3f.). The Good, however, *is* the self-sufficient, because it is the foundation of all hypotheses yet requires no hypothesis or condition itself (=*anhypotheton; Republic* 510B7; 511B6). In this respect, the definitions of God and the Good converge in absolute unconditionality. They also converge in blessedness; the divine is the most blessed (*Theaetetus* 176E4; *Phaedrus* 247A5). Similarly, the *agathon* (good) is the "most blessed of beings" (*Republic* 526E3)—one of the many superlative designations of the idea of the Good that characterize its uniqueness and absoluteness. Furthermore, it must be remembered that the idea of the Good, as it is developed in the context of the Platonic concept of *paideia,* is considered just as much a measure of individual and public (political) activity as God is assumed to be in the *Laws* (716C4f.), which specify, in contrast to a subjective relativism in the manner of Protagoras: "Now God ought to be to us the measure of all things, and not man, as men commonly say."

The godlike character of the idea of the Good is decisive for the purpose of our consideration. It has already become clear that the *beautiful* stands in a special relation to the *Good.* Because the idea of the Good is the ground of the being, essence, and activity of every individual idea and is, so to speak, its structural principle, the beautiful can rightly be understood as an implication of the Good or as its manifestation. In the beautiful, then, the *divinity of the Good* imparts itself to the thinking and striving directed by eros.[2]

This notion, which is present in the *Republic* and in a different way also in the *Symposium,* is supported by a central passage of the *Phaedrus.* There, in the context of a myth of the soul that is concerned with the soul's ability to perceive the ideas, the beautiful is conceived of as the "most manifest and most lovable" (*ekphanestaton kai erasmiōtaton; Phaedus* 250D7) and thus also as a primary object of eros. This is already true for the beautiful that is accessible to sense perception (249D5; 250D3; 251A2). Through this fundamental characteristic it becomes the impetus for the anamnestic reversion of thought from the sensible to its intelligible ground. Eros introduces the anamnesis of thought into its own presupposition (249D6). It reactivates in thought what is, though as yet unconscious, entirely peculiar to it: "the soul has by nature seen true being" (249E5). In this anamnestic reversion of thought there becomes apparent, on the one hand, its own a priori structure and, on the other hand, the foundation of the sensible in the idea, its existence as image (250A6). The image is the motive for the erotic movement. In it the original appears, at least faintly or by analogy. The beautiful *in* the image leads back to the original because the latter, already present in the image as the cause of its beauty, also acts "attractively." The "plain of truth" in the *Phaedrus* is to be considered analogous to the dimension into which Diotima introduces Socrates. On this plain, which is to say in the realm of the purely intelligible and of the divine, beauty itself first appears to the percipient guided by eros—in "pure light" (250B5f.; C4). *What* appears in the light of absolute beauty, however, is the good and the true and the divine itself. Because Plato suggests that truth is what is in itself unconcealed as true being, we might well attempt the following formulation: Beauty or the beautiful is the truth of the Good, that is, the Good unconcealed and open; thus beauty is also the first manifestation of the divine.

Plotinus

Of the philosophers influenced by Plato, no one has thought through the connection between beauty, as a dimension of divine being, and the loving relationship to beauty and divinity more thoroughly and distinctly than Plotinus. These three forms of existence or of human conduct are essential elements of the way of life Plotinus outlines, which tends toward union with the One as the highest principle. For Plotinus too, then, the inquiry after the beautiful is determined by an ethical starting point and goal. Plotinus broadens the metaphysical foundation of this concept and the way of life it determines; he goes beyond the Platonic theory of ideas by asking and answering previously debated questions in a new way in his own doctrine of the three hypostases (the One, the intellect, the soul). The fundamental Platonic distinction between the sensible and the intelligible—and thus also between sensible and intelligible beauty—remains decisive for Plotinus as well.

Over against an identification of beauty with a purely formal concept of symmetry, Plotinus sets out a concept of beauty that is characterized primarily by intelligibility or "intellect, spirit" (Greek *nous*, German *Geist*). Beautiful is what participates in form or logos and is shaped by form and logos into a single ordered whole, whether by nature or by art. If form and logos mean not the external form of a thing but its inner structural principle—its intelligible foundation—then the identification of form and "idea" is justified. *Through itself*, that is, through its immanent activity, the "form" or logos that is added to unformed matter gives the formless material visible shape or form. The idea thus becomes the cause of the form that appears; it orders the parts into a unified whole which also appears outwardly as such (I 6 [1], 2, 19ff.). Plotinus's reflections on the concept of the beautiful, particularly as he develops them in *Enneads* I 6 and V 8, are, briefly stated, determined by the view that the *ground* of visible beauty is beautiful in the true sense. The joy, fear, delight, wonder, longing, and eros experienced already at the sight of sensible beauty become all the more intense in the face of the rediscovered or recollected intelligible, since this is the "true" itself (I 6, 4, 15). This experience is the result of an abstraction from what is purely corporeal and from the sensible *aisthēsis* (perception) possible to it alone. At the same time it is the result of a concentration of thought on itself, in order to reach as the real object of sight (5, 17) the intellect, which in the "history" of the return is a new form of the beautiful. This beauty now *exists* and *appears* in unity (18); as the unity of *being* and *appearance*, in the sense of a thinking self-manifestation, it is identical with what really exists. Thus, in Plotinus's view the extended answer to the question of what beauty is would have to be as follows: It is what really or actually exists, which is intellect or absolute thought (*nous*) and being itself; as such it gives rise to sensible beauty by means of logos or reflective thinking about the ideas. If the opposite of the beautiful, the ugly, is described as "dead," "outer," "below," or "dark" (5, 37ff.), then the beautiful is the living, the inner, the upper, and the light (5, 39; 3, 24; 9, 43).

The process of abstraction and purification, an anamnestic return of the soul into itself, leading to self-certainty, thus makes the soul itself the *eidos* and *logos*. The soul as a whole becomes intelligible and transforms itself into intellect. Because intellect gives rise to beauty through its act of reflection, the soul itself also becomes beautiful in this abstractive transformation and attains its own proper beauty (6, 18); only then does it become truly *itself* (6, 19; 7, 27). If in this return into itself, the soul rises to *nous* as its own ground or true self, then by becoming like such true *being*, which manifests itself as the unity of "good" and "beautiful," the soul itself becomes in a true sense *being*—good and beautiful. Although in I 6, 7, 30f. Plotinus considers the Good—identical with the One—as the first or most truly existing beauty, which at the same time beautifies, he later modifies this notion through a radical concept of the One. If the One, in itself the relationless not-many, cannot be a "form" because form always implies a differentiating statement and thus the mode of being of a limited or defined "something," then because on the other hand beauty and form and shape are indivisible, the One cannot be beauty. If therefore the One exists *prior* to the "something" and is thus utterly formless or more-than-being, then it is consequently also "beyond" beauty. Plotinus's designation of the One as "beauty beyond beauty" (*kallos hyper kallos*), as "superabundance" of beauty (*periousia tou kallous*) or "more than beautiful" (*hyperkalon*) shows not only the One's superiority to that realm which is beautiful in the actual sense but also the eminent beauty of the One—it is the "flower" or "summit" of the

22. Archaistic Relief, Procession of the Divinities: Artemis, Hermes, Demeter. Greek (Neo-Attic), 1st century A.D.

beautiful, *tou kalou anthos.*[3] The formlessness of the One and its associated inability to be beauty in the sense of a form or of a limited "something" elevate the beauty of the One to the constitutive *origin* and decisive *end* of beauty as noetic form or as psychical self-formation (*archē kallous kai peras kallous,* VI 7 [38], 32, 33). The beautiful, which is accessible as form or shape and which is to be called such in the "actual" sense, is accordingly the self-limiting manifestation of the origin: form as "trace of the formless" (VI 7, 33, 30). The latter, however, is identical with the timeless and consequently absolute nous, to which also the human intellect, conditioned by time, is drawn by eros (V 3 [31], 13, 12). The essence of nous is pure self-reflection. Through self-reflection everything in nous that is different is made into a unity, in or in spite of the difference.

> For all things there are transparent, and there is nothing dark or opaque; everything and all things are clear to the inmost part to everything: for light is transparent to light. Each there has everything in itself and sees all things in every other, so that all are everywhere and each and every one is all, and the glory is unbounded. (V 8, 4, 4f.; trans. A. H. Armstrong).

The different, that is, the particular different intelligible being or the respective individual idea, is considered "perspectivally," with a view to the whole, as an element of a dynamic unity. The whole, however, can only be understood from and through the individual. The moving force in the whole, which "stands" in itself, is thinking. Thinking is pure, inexhaustible life, a *sophia* (wisdom) that does not actualize itself discursively, in argumentative progression (V 8, 4, 34; 36f.), a contemplation that rather preserves the difference of the individual yet nevertheless concentrates this difference into a dynamic identity—"science itself" (*autoepistēmē*) or the foundation of all knowledge.

What is *in* nous is nous itself. Consequently, it thinks, within what it itself is, its own being. If the ideas are the intelligible differentiated in itself and if the ideas must nevertheless be considered identical with intelligible *being,* then nous thinks in the ideas its own being or itself. For this reason true, self-reflective *being* and *beauty* belong essentially together (V 8, 9, 34ff.) insofar as nous, as the totality of forms, is also considered the first beauty, primary in intensity and effect. As a result no mutual "causation" or "primacy" between "being" and "beautiful" can be conceived; rather, the degree of participation in being corresponds to the degree of participation in beauty (V 8, 9, 42ff.).

Plotinus's conception of nous as a reflective identity, dynamic in itself, which he considers "beautiful" on the very basis of its formedness, its unity, and its reflectively luminous liveliness, shows—modifying his earlier approach (in I 6)—that the beautiful may *also* be considered "symmetrical" in a higher sense, a sense determined by reflection and life (III 2 [47], 17, 64ff.). This assertion is supported by Plotinus himself, when he understands *truth* as that which effects the unity peculiar to absolute intellect or indeed *is* this unity. Truth of intellect does not accord with something external to it but only with itself, that is, with its own being (*ou symphōnia eis allo ekei all' autou hekastou houper alētheia;* III 7 [45], 4, 11f.; V 5 [32], 2, 18–20). This absolute self-agreement of the intellect, the dynamic identity of its ideas with itself, also constitutes its beauty. Thus the intellect's unifying, enlivening, and clarifying function in relation to the sensible becomes apparent.

The return of thought into itself through the medium of abstraction and purification (I 6, 8f.) leads not only to the vision of absolute beauty, but— now substantiated more precisely than in Plato—to the personal transformation of the human being into an inwardly beautiful *existence.* To provide a plausible motivation for this is one of the primary aims of Plotinian thought. The conclusion of *Ennead* I 6 formulates this in a penetrating way in the light of the Platonic concept of *homoiōsis* (coming to be alike):

> Go back into yourself and look; and if you do not yet see yourself beautiful, then, just as someone making a statue which has to be beautiful cuts away here and polishes there and makes one part smooth and clears another till he has given his statue a beautiful face, so you too must cut away excess and straighten the crooked and clear the dark and make it bright, and never stop "working on your statue" till the divine glory of virtue shines out on you, till you see "self-mastery enthroned upon its holy seat." . . . You become nothing but true light. (I 6, 9, 7ff.; 19; trans. A. H. Armstrong).

A person's intention to be or to become inwardly beautiful is brought to its perfecting end by the vision of the beautiful itself. This end can in turn only be attained by intensive preparation in the contemplative abstraction mentioned above. Movement and end mutually require each other. "No eye ever saw the sun without becoming sun-like, nor can a soul see beauty without becoming beautiful. You must become first all godlike and all beautiful if you intend to see God and beauty" (I 6, 9, 31–34; trans. A. H. Armstrong). It is clear for Plotinus that this transforming ascent of thought is motivated by *eros.* By virtue of being a mean, eros is the "eye of longing" (III 5 [50], 2, 40); it mediates between the desired and the desiring, tending *in* this desiring toward a "vision" of true being. In Plotinus's sense, to be sure, eros not only is a *pathos* (affect; III 5, 1, 10ff.) of the human but also has a universal form of being, from which the form of the individual is derived. Yet even in such a transcendent form (3, 23), eros is defined by vision: eros derives "its being from seeing," is "an eye filled" with the vision of being (3, 13). At the same time eros is that moment in the process of absolute reflection which mediates between vision and the object of vision. As daemon, eros is adapted to every form of the soul, not only to the individual soul but also to the transcendent soul, which proceeds from the intellect in the realm of the intelligible and whose own perfection of being consists in the vision of true being in nous (3, 19ff.). Yet eros belongs no less to the soul of the cosmos or to the world soul (3, 27ff.).

As the moving element in the ascent of the human soul, eros has essentially two points of reference: the intellect, which as reflective unity and formedness is identical with the beautiful, and the One, which as super-abundance or "flower" of the beautiful, and precisely because of its elevation above what is beautiful in the actual sense, is to be understood as its ground or origin. Both however are *divine:* the One as the God-himself, illustrated by the metaphor of the "king" (II 9 [33], 9, 35ff.), the intellect as the most intensive manifestation of this God-One: "second God" (V 5 [32], 3, 2ff.). Consequently the eros of the soul that assimilates itself to the intellect and tends toward the One is related in different ways to "God" or to manifestations of the divine itself. The goal of the abstraction, purification, self-clarification, concentration of vision, and associated increase in the soul's self-consciousness is the union with the One itself. In Plotinus's view this, or the Good which is to be understood as identical to it, is what is really "worth loving" and is the object of the most intense desire (e.g., VI 7 [38], 30, 29ff.; 32, 25f.; 32, 30; 33, 14). Again and again Plotinus compares the erotic movement toward the intellect and toward the One with the experience of *lovers:* they wish to *see* the beloved, to become *like* him, and to become *one* with him (VI 7 [38], 31, 10ff.; 33, 22ff.; 34, 14f.). The transformation of the soul into intellect and thus into truly intelligible beauty is the starting point for an eros that proceeds toward the One or the Good itself and has actually moved the soul from the beginning (VI 7, 31, 17f.). Because of its object this eros is "limitless," infinite. As already indicated, its origin—as overabundance of beauty or of what participates in form—is itself without shape or form (VI 7 [38], 32, 9; 24; 26–28; 33, 37), in order that it may take concrete form through an illuminating radiation in the beauty of the intellect. Conversely, this form or beauty becomes a "track" toward the limitless or formless Super-beautiful (33, 30)—from a dark reflection there arises an "eros for a great light" (33, 29). Plotinus distinguishes two basic faculties of the intellect—that of pure thought and the associated identification with its content, *and* that of intuitive abandon, a vision no longer defined by difference, which itself becomes the object of vision. This is the *loving intellect* (*nous erōn;* VI 7, 35, 24), in contrast to the intellect that is characterized by *phronēsis* (thinking insight). Although the intellect in the soul is first drawn to the realm of the intelligible as the

end of its identification, it nevertheless sees therein the luminous manifestation of Another, present in *all*—the Good or the One. For ultimately it
is the origin itself, which as a "higher" (more intense) light is fascinating in
its own appearance and which, through the splendor (*phengos*) or grace
(*charis*) of the beautiful, initiates an "intense" (*syntonos*) eros as the self-
mediation of the Good. Consequently, the Good or One, appearing *as*
beautiful, is both the origin and perfection of the soul's return into itself
and of its self-overcoming. Plotinus characterizes the ascent guided by eros
in the metaphorical language of the *Phaedrus:* the soul is "thrown into the
chaos of passion," "filled with barbs," "warmed," "awakened," "strengthened,"
"truly winged," and, in the movement of memory toward the origin, "made
light"; it "*becomes*" itself "*eros*" (VI 7, 21–22). Only this intellect of the soul,
radically shaped by eros—precisely the "*loving* intellect" as the most intense
and most unified form of intellect—is in a position to overcome and to
negate thought as its original and proper possibility and thus to join in an
ekstasis with the One or Good itself (VI 7, 35, 24ff.; VI 9 [9], 11, 23). The
union with the One as the "truly beloved," the *God* (VI 9, 9, 45f.; 56), is
also explicitly called an effect of eros: "The soul then in her natural state
is in love with God and wants to be united with him; it is like the noble
love of a girl for her noble father" (VI 9, 9, 33–35; trans. A. H. Armstrong).[4]
The One, or the truly existing Good that is above the beautiful—and only
in this way can the above-mentioned comparison appear meaningful—is no
abstract neuter but a substance that is itself capable of attracting and without envy shares its fullness and thus "strengthens" and "fulfills" (V 5 [32],
8, 11f.; VI 7, 31, 30ff.). It is *itself* eros, that is, as the purely transcendent
it remains in itself self-related: "love of itself" (*autou erōs:* VI 8 [39], 15, 1;
heauton agapēsas: VI 8, 16, 13). As such it is also the absolute goal of human
striving, which can even be experienced as "gentle and mild and delicate"
(V 5, 12, 33), which is in fact universally present but whose presence must
also be realized by the human person through reflection and practice. Such
a realization leads finally to an "abandonment of self" in the union (VI 9,
11, 23; V 5, 8, 11), which is not to be understood as "self-destruction" but
only as a "suspension" or "elevation" in what is highest—that is to say, an
identity with itself and with the origin. For the "lovers of the One" (VI 5
[23], 10, 7), such an elevation into the self-perfecting abandonment of self
appears to be the meaningful consequence of the previous relation of eros
and the purely "lovable."

It has become clear that Plotinus's reflection on the beautiful as a fundamental characteristic of the divine and on the eros of the beautiful forms
a peculiar dimension of his entire thinking. In his development of what
Plato had laid out, Plotinus gives the beautiful a systematically determined

place in the inquiry about the One and the intellect. He analyzes its origin and its manifestation, and understands it as a structure of being and absolute thinking, and yet also and equally as an ethically relevant essential feature of human existence. The movement of a thinking pervaded with emotion returns, step by step, from the most external trace of the beautiful, which appears in various degrees of intensity, to the intelligible form of the beautiful and finally to the formless origin of form. This is the quieting end of the erotic movement.

The connection, which Plotinus establishes, of absolute unity, intellect, and soul, first to divinity and beauty as their distinct essential features and then to human beings' relation (which takes the concrete form of eros) to their own divine cause, can be considered a convincing and historically influential paradigm of late antique spirituality. The concept "spirituality" is here intended to make apparent the indissoluble connection of philosophical reflection, piety or religiosity, and ethical activity resting on ascesis.

Proclus

In the Neoplatonism of later antiquity, Proclus in particular further developed the Plotinian concept of eros. In view of the principle that all that exists is moved toward the One by a never-diminishing *longing*—and that this longing is identical to the One in us, the prereflective awareness of the One itself[5]—*erōs* must be understood as the concrete realization of this fundamental striving. The theological and ontological significance of eros is revealed first of all in the triad *pistis–alētheia–erōs*, "faith–truth–love." While *pistis*, beyond rational knowledge and itself "without any otherness," grounds all existence in the One or Good, and while *alētheia* is the foundation of the visibility or illumination of all spheres of reality, *erōs* has the function, passing through from the intelligible to the worldly (cosmic), "to bring everything back to the divine beauty"[6]—this as cosmic moment *and* as inner motive power of thought. In accordance with Plato's *Phaedrus* (246D8–E1), the essence of the divine is defined as being beautiful, wise, and good. From this Proclus derived a triad in the following order: "goodness–wisdom–beauty." These three are closely interwoven characteristics of the realm of the divine. Beauty is understood on the one hand as a separately existing, intelligible structure and on the other as a "beautifying cause," origin of order and symmetry, of loving relation and unity, "form of forms" (*Platonic Theology* 3.8; 63.2, 25), as the most intense being of form *and* as the origin of all formedness. Proclus characterizes the effect of the beautiful, its power of manifestation and attraction—again with reference to Plato— by the following three aspects: (1) "delicate" or "mild" because in itself it mediates a participation in the Good; (2) "light," shining and illuminating other things, because it allows what is latent in goodness to appear as intelligible or divine light and thus also functions as a possibility of initiation into the cause of this light—"brighter and lovelier to behold than the morning star" (*Platonic Theology* 1.24; 108.25);[7] (3) "lovable to the highest degree," goal of longing and of eros, which—precisely on the basis of the Good, which manifests itself in the beautiful or as beautiful—brings about the reversal or return of that which developed from the One. In these three aspects, the beautiful recapitulates in its own way the all-moving and determining constitutionality of remaining, procession, and reversion—an intelligible circle completed by the distribution of the divine to the beautiful and by eros.[8]

The unifying and returning power of eros in the realm of the divine and cosmic is at the same time the reason why eros is also able to act in the sphere of *human* thought and activity (*In Alc.* 55.15f.; 32.9f.). In this realm eros is to be understood as the initiating, moving, and perfecting element of dialectical ascent and of assimilation to the origin. This "divine" eros— that is, an eros directed toward the divine—is to be thought of in general as "guiding, doing good, and perfecting, as cause of the intellect and of life according to intellect" (*In Alc.* 61.3–5). Eros thus becomes the basic attitude of the philosopher, guiding the search for truth and completing it in "faithful devotion." Eros unites dialectical and maieutic knowledge by converting an uncritical existence devoted to the sensible into a philosophical existence and, through delivery by Socratic questioning, making the respondent himself capable of recognizing what is true (*In Alc.* 28.7ff.). Whereas an unerotic and therefore unphilosophical existence rests upon the "oblivion and ignorance of original beauty" (*In Alc.* 48.9), a philosophy motivated by eros converts and returns from what seems beautiful to the divine *beauty* itself which is beyond being (*In Alc.* 30.15; 29.16; 33.6; 37.11; 52.12). Because eros effects "contact with a divine beauty" and "appropriation" of the "entire divine" (*In Alc.* 29.15; 52.11f.) and because the divine moreover is the unity of the beautiful, the wise (true), and the good, eros, itself moved by the origin, is revealed as the motive power of the return to the divine origin of beauty, truth, and goodness together. The beautiful itself contains an uplifting power and thereby becomes the moving force for the conversion and return through eros. Echoing Plato, Proclus derives the word *kalon* from *kalein* or *kelein*, "to call," and from the word draws conclusions about the object. Accordingly, the effect of the beautiful is to "*call* to itself what exists and thinks," to "*captivate*," and to "*enchant*" (*In Alc.* 328.12ff.).[9] At the same time, what "calls" and "enchants" distances thought from the beautiful appearance by becoming a "mean" that conveys or reduces the manifestation

of the beautiful to its being and essence. Although in the dimension of principles the beautiful, the good, and the just may indeed be related to each
other but must be regarded respectively as individual substances—for
Proclus just as for Plotinus, the Good as the source of the integral good is
beyond the beautiful in the actual sense (*In Alc.* 320.5f.)—they are nevertheless "unified with each other in the center of all being, which is the soul."
They can exist without each other just as little as can being, life, and
thought; they are equally *in each other.* If the beautiful is therefore identical
with what eros desires; if, furthermore, the lovable is the goal of desiring;
and if, however, all that is desirable is good, then eros strives *in* the beautiful toward the Good (*In Alc.* 329.23–25). The beautiful opens the way to
the *truth* of the Good as the ground of its own illumination. It "reveals the
hidden aspect of the Good, lets its loveliness shine forth and draws the
secret striving toward the Good into its own light" (*Platonic Theology* 3.18;
63.25ff.). The beautiful is thus itself light, in that it manifests the light of
its own ground or origin, the Good. Because truth is in beauty and beauty
must be understood as the luminous self-manifestation of the *Good,* beauty
can consequently also be thought of as the light of truth or as the luminous
self-manifestation of *truth.* When the soul "sees the unutterable as appearance, it rejoices and admires what appears" (*Platonic Theology* 3.18; 64.5f.).
Thus, eros leads the wondering soul away from the uncertain mere semblance into the bright sphere of the origin of beauty and thereby effects the
soul's transition into the intellect, its own *ellampsis,* "radiance." Proclus
explains this process by means of an analogy to the initiation into the
mysteries:

> As during the most sacred consecrations before the mystic spectacle a shud-
> dering (arouses) those being consecrated, so too, in the realm of the intelli-
> gible, the appearing beauty, prior to its union with the Good, makes the
> viewers shudder and converts the soul and, stationed in the antechamber,
> reveals how the hidden Good is within the sanctuary. (*Platonic Theology* 3.18;
> 64.6–12)[10]

During the search for truth which eros guides, the experience of divine
beauty through eros develops into an understanding of divine *wisdom,*
"filled with which the intellect recognizes what exists." Because, however,
wisdom (truth) and goodness are the same, it can be said that eros, as the
moving element in the search for truth, finds rest in the divine Good itself
as the luminous cause of truth and beauty. The Good is only revealed to
this kind of thought that has raised itself out of the movement of eros into
the "secure position," or which finally—negating and transcending thought
itself—surrenders to the One originative cause (*epididōsin heautēn; Platonic*

Theology 1.25; 111.18). The eros which mediates between sensible and intelligible, from the many toward the One, and which unites by concentrating, thus drives the soul which has become intellect in this movement beyond itself and unites the soul "with the primary and hidden beauty in a mode of life superior to intellectual thought" (*In Alc.* 64.14–17). The union with the beautiful and finally with the One itself is also for Proclus the goal of that thinking movement which seeks to arrive at its own, no longer thinking, origin. The essential intention of Proclean spirituality might thus be paraphrased by a single sentence of his commentary on the *Parmenides:*

> But it mounts toward the incomprehensible super-eminence of the One itself, borne in its direction by a longing for its nature, revolving round it, wanting to embrace it, seeking with supreme passion to be present to it, unifying itself as far as possible and purging all its own multiplicity so that somehow it may become perfectly one. (*In Parm.* 7.44.32–46.3; trans. G. E. M. Anscombe and L. Labowsky)

For the development of the idea that intimately unites the divine or God, beauty, and love with each other, it was of great consequence that Pseudo-Dionysius the Areopagite took over its main features from Proclus and adapted them to the Christian concept of a loving God. At the same time the Neoplatonic model of the ascent, loving and devoted to the beautiful, remains substantially preserved.[11]

For Dionysius beauty or "beauty beautiful beyond being" is an affirmative predicate of God. This predication implies identity with goodness. As such, the universal cause distributes itself and radiates like light without surrendering its substance (*Divine Names* 4.7 [*PG* 3, col. 701C]; 4.13 [*PG* 3, col. 712B]), thereby making the created beautiful and attracting it to itself, "calling it to itself" (*Divine Names* 4.7 [*PG* 3, col. 701C]).[12] Proclus, to be sure, introduces the concept of the *nous pronoētikos* ("preconceiving nous," the providential eros which acts "downward"), by means of which he makes philosophical the mythological notion that the gods love their own creature (a love that "saves," "perfects," and "unites" the beloved [*In Alc.* 55.10ff.];[13] this movement from the divine continues in the loving and caring turning of one person to another [*In Alc.* 32.16; 38.14f.; 41.11; 45.2ff]). Proclus does not, however, transfer the pronoetic loving attitude of the gods in the dimension *below* the One to the "essence" of the One itself because, in spite of its being a cause, its absolute transcendence might be disturbed by a commitment to its effect. To be "nothing of everything" also excludes an incarnation of the absolute. As *agathon* (good) the One does, it is true, share its abundance without envy but is not considered as actively loving. For Dionysius, on the contrary—based on the Christian conception that God himself is love (1 John 4:8, 16)—this fundamental characteristic of God is central. Although it can be asserted with a certain justification that Christian theology, starting with the New Testament, primarily used the term *agapē* for God's love, Dionysius defends the term *erōs* for the same content, prefers it in fact to *agapē*, and then uses both terms synonymously (*Divine Names* 4.11 [*PG* 3, cols. 708Cff.]; 4.12 [*PG* 3, col. 709B; 4.14 [*PG* 3, col. 712C]). "Divine love" (*agapē* or *erōs*) means exclusively God's own activity—as "cause of all he loves everything because of the excess of his goodness" (*Divine Names* 4.10 (*PG* 3, col. 708A]). His love is essentially "ecstatic" (*Divine Names* 4.13 [*PG* 3, col. 712A]);[14] in it or through it he proceeds out of himself, creating and "caring"; in it he loves what has been created and, equally, leads it back to himself qua attractive beauty. The *theios erōs* thus becomes the origin of an "eternal circle" of luminous procession (*Divine Names* 4.14 [*PG* 3, col. 712D]), which posits and sustains what is beautiful, *and of loving return*. The ecstatic divine eros is answered by the *ekstasis* of human love toward God, which leaves itself aside and devotes itself to him; it shows itself paradigmatically for Dionysius in Paul's statement: "I live, yet not I, but Christ lives in me" (Gal 2:20) (*Divine Names* 4.13 [*PG* 3, col. 712A]).

Notes

1. On this complex of questions, see A.-J. Festugière, *Personal Religion among the Greeks* (Sather Classical Lectures 26; Berkeley and Los Angeles: University of California Press, 1954; reprint, 1960).

2. The relation that Plato shows of eros to the realm of the ideas (see also *Republic* 490B2ff.) and finally to the idea of the Good has a metaphysically founded parallel in the cosmology of Aristotle. The latter considers the first principle of being—identical with the *theos*—as pure, self-thinking reality. This, while remaining unchangeably itself as first mover, is the origin of all cosmic movement and thereby lets "heaven and nature" be "dependent" on itself (*Metaphysics* 1072b13f.). In the moved or the changeable which is dependent on it, this reality also causes a kind of movement, which must be understood as an 'eros' toward it, the first divine principle: the first mover "moves like a beloved," *kinei de hōs erōmenon* (*Metaphysics* 1072b3). This notion is certainly close to Plato's cosmological thinking: in the *Timaeus* (32C2) he understands the mathematical analogy that constitutes the cosmos as *philia*.

3. *kallos hyper kallos*: VI 7, 32, 29. *periousia tou kallous*: 32, 33. *hyperkalon*: 33, 20. *tou kalou anthos*: 32, 31. Analogous to this notion is V 8, 13, 11: the "father" is "too great" to be named by "beauty," as is appropriate for the intellect.

4. From just this standpoint it is revealing to cast a glance at Philo of Alexandria, who on one side stands in the tradition of the original Platonism and from this position unites philosophical questions with the main features of biblical revelation to form a

hellenizing Jewish theology. At the same time, however, he also anticipates some aspects of later Platonism. The phenomenon of "love for God" he designates with the term "divine love" (*erōs theios*—not synonymous, to be sure, but a formulation already in Plato's *Laws* [711D6]), an intense spiritual and emotional movement of the human toward God, analogous to the Platonic and Plotinian eros. Compare *On Abraham* 32.17 (of Abraham ready for sacrifice); *Who Is the Heir?* 4.14; *On Flight and Finding* 11:58: *erōti kai philiai theou asarkōi kai asōmatōi kateschēsthai* (characteristic of eternal life); *On the Posterity and Exile of Cain* 12: we should be united with God in love (*adiastaton henōseōs*). In this context Philo develops the metaphor of the "soul as bride of God" (*On the Cherubim* 42ff.; 52: *en oikōi theou partheneuesthai*); *On Dreams* 2.34.232, in relation to the ecstasy of Moses: *ex erōtos theiou kataschetheis ho nous . . . theophoroumenos.*

5. *In Parm.* 7.58.12; 54.11, Klibansky–Labowsky.

6. *In Alc.* 51.15ff; 52.10ff., Westerink; *Platonic Theology* 1.25; 109.4ff., Saffrey–Westerink; in his commentary on the *Timaeus*, this triad in conjunction with "hope" is the precondition for *ekstasis* (1.212.21ff. esp. 23, Diehl). This goes back to Porphyry: in *Letter to Marcella* 24 Porphyry mentions as the four "elements" in the relation of humans to God "faith, truth, love, hope": "We must *believe* that the only salvation is the return to God, and believing this, strive as far as possible to *know* the *truth* about it and having come to know this, to *love* what is *known* and, loving this, to *nourish* the soul with good *hope* all our life."

7. Reminiscent of Aristotle *Nicomachean Ethics* 1129B28f., with reference to 'justice'.

8. On this, see 1.24; 106.5ff.

9. See also *Platonic Theology* 1.24; 108.7ff.; Plato *Cratylus* 416B6ff.

10. See also *In Alc.* 61.7ff.

11. Both from *The Divine Names* and from *The Mystical Theology* it may be demonstrated that it is difficult to agree with E. v. Ivánkas's contention that precisely through the concept of love, through the "substantial identity" [!] of the "depth of the soul" with God and through the ecstatic effect of love in the soul toward an immediate unification of the soul with God a "turning away from Neoplatonic thought in its essential point" occurs (*Plato Christianus* [Einsiedeln: Johannes Verlag, 1964] 283). First, "substantial identity" of the depth of the soul and God is not "given" in Dionysius but is at best *attainable* in *ekstasis;* and, second, Dionysius has also kept the notion of the way: the transition to *agnosia* presupposes a reflective ascent, whose breadth and intensity do admittedly appear limited in relation to Plotinus or Proclus. On the corresponding terms *diabainein, hyperbainein, kathodos* by affirmation and *anodos*—that is, *epanabasis*—by negation (the way down and up as encirclement by affirmation and negation) compare *Mystical Theology* (PG 3, col. 1000C; 1025B) and *Divine Names* 7.3. In addition, the philosophical and biblical predicates of God afford a differentiated possibility of reflection, which *mediates* toward *ekstasis*.

12. For the same etymology in Proclus, see *Platonic Theology* 3.8; 63.2, 25.

13. In view of the use of the concept *erōs pronoētikos* in Proclus, it is difficult to substantiate the attempt to contrast Dionysius with Proclus in this regard (C. de Vogel, "Amor quo caelum regitur," *Vivarium* 1 [1963] 16, 29ff.). The difference from Proclus in the transfer of this notion to God himself of course remains untouched by this.

14. Compare on this W. Beierwaltes, "Marginalien zu Eriugenas 'Platonismus,'" in *Platonismus und Christentum: Festschrift für H. Dörrie, Jahrbuch für Antike und Christentum,* Suppl. vol. 10 (Münster: Aschendorffsche Verlagsbuchhandlung, 1983) 71ff.

Bibliography

Editions

Dionysius the Areopagite, Pseudo-. *PG*, vols. 3, 4.

Philo of Alexandria. *Philo*. Greek texts with English translations by F. H. Colson and G. H. Whitaker. Loeb Classical Library. Cambridge, MA: Harvard University Press, 1966–71.

Porphyry. *Pros Markellan*. Edited with a German translation by Walter Potscher. Leiden: Brill, 1969.

Proclus. *Eis ton Platōnos Prōton Alkibiadēn*. Edited by L. G. Westerink. Amsterdam: North Holland, 1954.

———. *In Platonis Parmenidem commentaria, 7*. In *Plato Latinus*. Vol. 3, *Parmenides*. Edited with an English translation by R. Klibansky, C. Labowsky, and G. E. M. Anscombe. London: British Academy, 1953.

———. *In Platonis Timaeum commentaria*. Edited by Ernestus Diehl. Amsterdam: Hakkert, 1965.

———. *Théologie platonicienne*. Edited with French translation by H. D. Saffrey and L. G. Westerink. Paris: Les Belles Lettres, 1968.

Translations

For translations of Plato and Plotinus, consult the General Bibliography for this volume.

Dionysius the Areopagite, Pseudo-. *The Divine Names and the Mystical Theology*. Translated by John D. Jones. Milwaukee, WI: Marquette University Press, 1980.

Proclus. *Alcibiades I*. Translated by William O'Neill. The Hague: Martinus Nijhoff, 1965.

———. *The Commentaries of Proclus on the Timaeus of Plato*. Translated by Thomas Taylor. London: the author, 1820. Facsimile reprint Ann Arbor: University Microfilms, 1969.

Modern Works

Armstrong, A. H. "Platonic *Erōs* and Christian Agapē." *The Downside Review* 79 (1961) Reprinted in *Plotinian and Christian Studies*. London: Variorum Reprints, 1979.

———. "Platonic Love: A Reply to Professor Verdenius." *The Downside Review* 82 (1964). Reprinted in *Plotinian and Christian Studies*. London: Variorum Reprints, 1979.

———. "Beauty and the Discovery of Divinity in the Thought of Plotinus." In *Kephalaion: Studies in Greek Philosophy and Its Continuation Offered to Professor C. J. de Vogel*, 155–63. Assen: van Gorcum, 1975. Reprinted in *Plotinian and Christian Studies*. London: Variorum Reprints, 1979.

Arnou, René. *Le désir de Dieu dans la philosophie de Plotin*. 2nd ed. Rome: Presses de l'Université Gregorienne, 1967.

Burnaby, John. *Amor Dei: A Study of the Religion of St. Augustine*. 2nd ed. London: Hodder & Stoughton, 1947.

Keyser, Eugénie de. *La signification de l'art dans les Ennéades de Plotin*. Louvain: Bibliothèque de l'Université, 1955.

Kruger, Gerhard. *Einsicht und Leidenschaft*. 4th ed. Frankfurt am Main: Klostermann, 1973.

———. *Eros und Mythos bei Plato*. Frankfurt am Main: Klostermann, 1978. Excerpts from previous work.

Lasserre, François. *La figure d'Éros dans la poésie grecque*. Lausanne: Imprimeries reunies, 1946.

Markus, R. A. "The Dialectic of Eros in Plato's Symposium." *The Downside Review* 73 (1955) 219–30.

———. "Love and the Will." In *Christian Faith and Greek Philosophy*, 78–96. Edited by A. H. Armstrong and R. A. Markus. London: Darton, Longman, & Todd, 1960.

Nygren, Anders. *Eros and Agape: A Study of the Christian Idea of Love*. Translated by Philip S. Watson. New York: Harper & Row, 1969.

Rist, John M. *Eros and Psyche: Studies in Plato, Plotinus and Origen*. Toronto: University of Toronto Press, 1964.

Robin, Léon. *La theorie platonicienne de l'amour*. New ed. Paris: Alcan, 1933.

Scholz, Heinrich. *Eros und Caritas: Die platonische Liebe und die Liebe im Sinne des Christentums*. Halle: Max Niemeyer, 1929.

Theiler, Willy. "Diotima neuplatonisch." In *Untersuchungen zur antiken Literatur*, 502–18. Berlin: de Gruyter, 1970.

Trouillard, Jean. *La purification plotinienne*, 153–62. Paris: Presses universitaires de France, 1955.

Vlastos, Gregory. "The Individual as an Object of Love in Plato." In *Platonic Studies*, 3–34. Princeton: Princeton University Press, 1973.

13

The City in
Ancient Religious Experience

PATRICK ATHERTON

T HE POLIS OR CITY of the classical period was a religious as well as a
civic association: as much a "city-church" as a "city-state." The
civic attributes of the polis—the right of the *politai* or the citizens
to share in the government, to consider themselves equals, and
the demand of the polis that it should be free, that is, that it should *itself*
determine its life and laws—owe their character to the distinctive nature
of the gods that protected the communities. These gods were essentially intelligent, purposive beings; because humans shared with the gods a common
intellectual nature, they were capable of a form of community that was an
image of the life of the gods and raised them far above a merely animal
association founded on need and want. (The state was, according to the
Greeks, a distinctively human accomplishment, and contemporary views
that tend to reduce the state—and, indeed, the family—to an animal
bonding appreciably distort the nature of community [*koinonia*] among the
Greeks.) The philosophers of the classical period, who could look back
over the history of the city as it had matured through a long development,
found its source in practical reason. The city was the embodiment, the
realization of an active intelligence in human beings, and it was in intelligence, in *nous,* that the later Greek tradition would locate the divine.

The polis as a distinctive form of civic association had begun to appear
when there was recognition that the sovereignty of the community or its
archē was a common possession of the citizens; without the delineation of
a common sphere (including the most concrete geographical sense of a
"common" space or *agora,* where the citizens could meet and talk) there
could be no city. And the polis was an accomplished fact when it was established that it was the community (*to koinon*) that legislated—not kings or

314

priests or even the gods, directly. It was the *community* that selected magistrates, built the temples of the gods, appointed the priests, and commissioned the generals. Because they possessed a common nature, the citizens were obliged to recognize each other as "similars and equals";[1] in the early struggles to establish this equality it was expressly conceded that sovereignty belonged to the assembled peers (equals) or the *demos*.[2] Participation (in various degrees and forms) in the sovereignty of the state, a "share in ruling and being ruled," made the citizen. The share might be the very modest right to attend the sovereign assembly, but, as the polis matured, the participation became ever more complete until it included sitting on the council of the state or even, as magistrate, exercising the very *archē* itself. Relations between the equals had to be regulated and the distribution of power among the various classes fixed, not by the arbitrary authority of great individuals but by universal norms, applicable to all alike—by law. It was law that the early sages would glorify as the foundation of the polis: the people, said Heraclitus, should fight for the law as for their city walls (fr. 44, Diels-Kranz).[3]

The city as commonwealth, as the common possession of the citizens, regulating its life according to law within a cosmos or ordered world ruled by a universal or divine justice (*dikē*) was, the Greeks were well aware, not the only way in which human society had been organized. They were fully conscious of their originality in this respect and of how much they differed from their neighbors.[4] To measure the magnitude of the step the Greeks took when they discovered the polis, to chart its progress to maturity, and to recognize that both the initiation and the growth were entirely due to the conception they had come to form of the gods require first some brief acquaintance with the social forms and religious character that the Greeks in the properly Hellenic or polis stage of their culture had outgrown.

Setting the Stage

The ancestors of the Greeks first made their appearance on the shores of the Mediterranean as part of the general movement of Indo-European peoples in the early part of the second millennium before Christ. The same intrusion brought, for example, the Hittites to Asia Minor. At this period there was no cultural division between the two sides of the Aegean, and Crete, the most developed society of the region, was firmly oriented toward the kingdoms of the East. Some of the Indo-European tribes may have brought the horse with them: at least those who settled the Troad ("rich in horses" according to Homer) almost certainly made themselves formidable by the possession of the horse, and Poseidon was a horse-god before he became a god of the sea. By the last quarter of the second millennium these raw progenitors of the Hellenic achievement had acquired new social structures of astonishing complexity and had made themselves masters of the palace cultures of Crete. Mycenean Greece, now so much more known to us, was not at all like the polis-world of early Hellenic history but seemed to reproduce in a modified form the priestly cultures of the Near East. At the apex of the social order was a priest-king embodying in his person all aspects of power and authority; he was legislator, general, high priest, judge, and prime mover in an economic order of remarkable sophistication. All the aspects or facets of sovereignty, of the *archē*, that the city in its progress would separate out and allot to different magistracies were concentrated in the sacred person of the [*W*]*anax*. The [*W*]*anax* or "king," with his knowledge of the gods, was the very *raison d'être* of the community. The shrine where the community's gods were worshiped was the "private chapel" of the king. His commands were transmitted by a powerful priesthood, and the whole remarkable structure was made possible by the invention of writing. It is now recognized that the Myceneans spoke an early form of Greek but wrote it in a syllable script, adapted from Cretan sources. Nothing measures the division between Mycenae and the world of the polis more strikingly than the position of writing. In the city the ability to write in an alphabetic script could become a popular acquisition and an instrument of publicity; in Mycenae it was a scribal possession, truly an *arcanum imperii* and an instrument of social control because it was an aspect of the all-embracing authority of the priestly ruler or [*W*]*anax*. The accomplishments of Mycenean culture were undeniably impressive, but they were those of an alien heritage, the achievements of an order of life imposed over more primitive Indo-European ways that it was not able wholly to obliterate. Not until the apparatus of the Mycenean world—its palace bureaucracies, its scribal culture, and its sacred kingship—was swept away could Hellenic culture begin its authentic development.

The rise of the city cannot, therefore, be separated from the background of collapse and misery that occurred around the beginning of the first millennium, which the Greeks themselves knew as the Iron Age. A cataclysm of invasion and pillage swept over the entire world in the Bronze Age. In Greek lands, in the wake of what was later called the Trojan War, the Dorians, more primitive tribes living on the fringes of the Mycenean world, invaded and plundered and burned the great palace complexes. As they repeopled the Greek peninsula, they forced the older population to seek new homes across the Aegean. The [*W*]*anax* and the palace culture he sustained disappeared. In the general collapse of living standards, gold could no longer be used and building in stone was no longer possible; even the art of writing was lost, and the sea, now unsafe, instead of being a channel of culture became a barrier. The Greek world, never wholly integrated into the Bronze Age patterns of social order, now slipped out of their power altogether. Henceforth isolated in a provincial backwater, the Greeks were thrown back upon themselves. Because there was now no preponderant political power, no authoritative cultural model to inspire or imitate, the Greek world was free to develop from its own resources. When, later, the Greeks appeared in a clearer historical light, cultural life in all its aspects was beating to a new rhythm, and the focus of it all was that distinctively Hellenic achievement—the city.

The city had appeared when people had the strength to apportion by human decision shares in the *archē* or sovereignty: what had formerly been an aspect of a sacred king was now at the disposition of the community, the *koinon*, something to be settled after debate in a common or public space. How had people come to acquire the self-confidence to claim for themselves the *archē* which had earlier been the possession of the priest-king? The process has been called by some a "secularization" of the Greek mind. But it was quite unthinkable to the older Greek world that there could be an order of human life wholly independent of the gods. That the Greeks were capable of shaping freely a political order, of knowing themselves as free in the life of the city, was rather a result of the understanding they had reached of the nature of the Olympian gods and of human beings' relation to them. The polis was not a repudiation of the gods but a consequence of their nature, and the rationality inherent in the process was not something alien to the Olympians. The characteristic spirituality of the Greek world recognized in the intellectual life of humans, both theoretical and practical, their closest likeness to the gods. Though philosophy, that purely reflective grasp of the real, in its progress destroyed the older imaginative picture of the gods and proclaimed *nous* as the divine, it could only release the rationality inherent in the Olympian theology and strip it of its aesthetic embodiment; and the philosopher, no less than the poet, would celebrate the state as a religious society, a "communion of gods and humans."[5]

But what are these gods and how are they to be recognized? Humans, in contrast to the gods, are *thnētoi* or mortals. Things of a day, they come to be, flourish a little, and pass away. Only in the species, the *eidos* that renews itself endlessly in these transient individuals, do they attain any permanence. But the human species differs from the animals and the leaves of the forest in that it renews its life in the activity of ordered community. This life-in-community of the human species is set within a world, a cosmos of permanent substantial forces—the immortals, the *athanatoi,* "the deathless gods that are forever." The gods, then, are the enduring powers present in all nature and life and also (and most important for Greek spirituality) in all aspects of the intellectual life of humans. For the Olympian gods are new rulers of the world, who prevailed over the ancient gods through intelligence, and it is through the gifts of these intelligent gods that humans can turn against nature and subdue it to their purposes with their arts and sciences, and through their inspiration that, by sharing in the justice of the gods, they are capable of a properly human form of association. In the common life of the city, in the activity that drew the citizens, divided and separated by sectional and private interests, into one common purpose, the Greeks had an image and a share in the life of the gods. On the proper relation to these powers the success of the human enterprise depended. These many gods were not a mere chaotic multitude, devoid of relation or unity: they were interrelated and depended one on the other, forming a cosmos, a loose familial grouping under the power and authority of Zeus, "father of gods and humans." As humans were drawn out of separation and division into the common political life of the city, so the many gods were drawn into the unity of common purpose by Zeus. The transformation of Zeus from a nature-god of the bright sky into the preeminently political deity whose ruling authority was visibly present in the ordering of the human city is an abstract and brief summary of the essentially religious character of political association for the Greeks. Greek religion was a civic piety— not merely in the sense, important though it was, that it was the community that appointed the priests and performed the rituals, etc., but also in the sense that the very gods, toward whom this piety was directed, were recognized most adequately in the powers that presided over civic life.

How were these gods, the objects of this religion of civic piety, known and recognized by the Greeks? The most immediate (and in some ways the most enduring) form of piety was simply acknowledging the gods for what they were—the primary determining causes of all things. This required worship, recognition in word and deed that the gods were first—in short, cult and ritual. Since these were civic gods, they required worship by the community. The city's origin was normally the result of a divine initiative. Its survival and prosperity were the concern of some particular god. But there were many gods, and, simply *because* a city was particularly dear to one god, it might excite the anger of another. Dead heroes kept watch over it, manifesting themselves to encourage the citizens at moments of stress and crisis, as Theseus did at the battle of Marathon.[6] It was, therefore, as a citizen of Athens or Argos, not as a private person, that the individual

23. Athena Flying Her Owl.
Greek. 5th century. B.C.

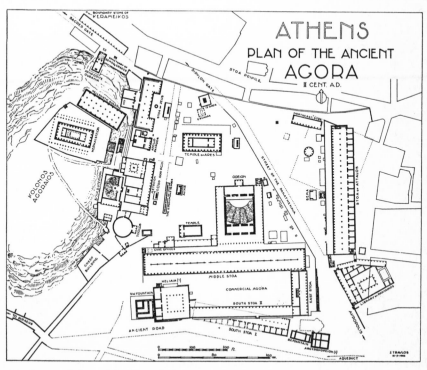

24. Agora, Athens. Plan in 2nd century A.D.

approached the shrines of the gods or joined the great procession that wound its way up the Acropolis to present a new robe to the goddess Athena. And it was a distinctive mark of the polis that, as it had appropriated all aspects of *archē* to itself, it made the priesthoods magistracies of the state and appointed officials for the cult of the community. The proper worship of the community's divine protectors was simply part of the public sphere that defined the city. The importance of cult and ritual in the civic awareness of the Greeks can hardly be overestimated; every aspect of life, domestic or public, was consecrated with its appropriate ritual. In later times, when the character of the city was profoundly changed and the concept of the divine radically altered, it would be the cultic practices, the old rituals, that would seem to many (the cultivated as well as the simple) to suggest most adequately the old Hellenic religion.

Besides recognition of the gods in the activities of civic life, acknowledgment in cult, and enjoyment of them in the games (see below), understanding of their nature and of the order they upheld was best attained by the older Greek culture through attention to the works of the poets. It has frequently been noted that the Greeks had neither official sacred texts nor a powerful priesthood; they had only the poets and their works and, in general, the plastic arts to interpret for them their beliefs and convictions and the presence of the gods in their lives. Hence the primacy among the Greeks of the work of the imagination and the aesthetic grasp of the divine, and the inevitability (as Plato claimed) of the conflict between the poets and the philosophers, when, as a result of its own internal development, Greek culture came to require a more rational conception of the gods. For the imaginative conception of the divine—which gave to everything a local habitation and a name—the gods became a plurality of sharply distinguished, perfectly formed human beings, caught forever at the moment of their acme and freed from the mutability and decay of mere mortals. The free imagination of the poets, inspired by the Muses, daughters of Memory, could rework the sages and folk memories to instruct the Greeks how these gods ordered all things: in particular, how they dealt with humans of superior ability (*aretē*). It was especially in stories of how great heroes of the past (transformed doubtless out of all merely historical verisimilitude) had conducted themselves in relation to the gods that the Greeks attained, through the poets, the surest insight of which they were then capable into the very nature of human excellence or *aretē* and its relation to those gods they already knew in the resolution of the conflicts within the life of the polis and recognized in the cult and ritual of civic piety.

The Homeric Foundation

The religion of the Olympian gods (and the order of the universe sustained by those powers) was the precondition of all the achievements of the polis, and the clearest guide to the content of this religion available to the early Greeks was the poetry of Homer. "It was Homer and Hesiod," said Herodotus, "who taught the Greeks the descent of the gods, and gave to all their several names, and honors, and arts, and declared their outward forms" (11.53). "Homer" predates the establishment of the polis (latter half of the eighth century?), but his poetry held a position of unrivaled authority among the Greeks until almost the maturity of the city in the fifth century. The evidence of Homer is, however, not easy for us to assess. Modern scholars with very different interests and preconceptions from those with which the early Greeks first listened to his inspired lays have often regarded the works as a rich storehouse of historical material, documents of sociology, a repository of myth (in the modern sense of a fanciful or arbitrary imaginative invention in no sense true), or antique legend. For the Greeks, Homer was primarily poet and religious teacher, and it was as such that he had authority over them. The bardic milieu to which Homer belonged preserved the sagas of the great heroes of the race: tales of warfare, of savage heroic deeds by which the people had been saved. Most of all it retained the memory of a great expedition to Troy under the control of the lord or great king ([*W*]*anax*) Agamemnon. The expedition had finally been successful and Troy had fallen. But the heroes had had no joy of it, for, on their return, they had all—with the exception of Odysseus—come to grief through the enmity of the gods. Homer's interest in this great event is not in our sense historical (though he undoubtedly believed the war had happened), just as our ancestors' interest in Adam and Eve—though our ancestors certainly believed Adam and Eve to have been a historical pair of individuals—was not historical (rather Adam and Eve were a means of considering the nature of human freedom and its relation to divine authority). Homer recollects the story of windy Troy through the inspiration of the Muses, and he shows the meaning of what happened in that great conflict and how the gods worked out their purposes in it. To understand something of the splendor and power of Greek religion, one must live for a time in Homer's world and make the effort of historical imagination to recognize in him the ancient "theologian."

From the mass of stories and legends surrounding the fall of Troy, the poet, with supreme art, selected one action through which he could illustrate the divine order upheld by the Olympian deities. The single action was the series of events caused and initiated by the wrath of Achilles. The progress and consequences of the hero's anger and its final resolution in the restoration of Achilles to the Greek host, with the consequent destruction of Troy's chief support, make up the *Iliad*. The poet tells us nothing about the fall of Troy and assumes we know much of the background to the expedition. His interest is limited to exhibiting the course and result of Achilles' anger as disclosing the purposes of the gods. Because the quarrel between Achilles and King Agamemnon is a dispute between the greatest hero that went to Troy, the hero *par excellence*, and the royal authority, the poem is a meditation on the nature of political power or sovereignty among humans and its dependence upon the gods: it is in this sense that the *Iliad* could instruct the Greeks on the nature of the power that regulates human communities and its origin in the authority of Zeus.

The story opens with a plague affecting the Greek army. The responsibility for discerning the origin of the plague and alleviating it falls to the king. The Greeks seek and expect to find a cause or explanation of events and catastrophes; here, of course, it has a divine origin, but it is assumed that the god who caused the plague can be known, that it is not merely a meaningless, opaque event. It is also assumed that social disorder is the result of bad government: when the king is bad, the people perish (here in the most literal sense). But on this occasion the king is blind to his responsibility; he ignores the people's plight and seeks no counsel to relieve the suffering. It is left to Achilles to suggest an assembly so that the army's predicament can be discussed. Achilles is the greatest of all heroes, and his worth or *aretē* is so outstanding that the Greeks could only think of it as almost more than human, nearly divine—and so Achilles was born of a human father and a divine mother. Yet this greatest of heroes (which, as the story will show, means the most kingly of men) is here in a subordinate position: he is not the king but is in an almost feudal relation to him—a situation pregnant with the possibility of conflict. Achilles is already showing his character in championing the cause of open discussion of the army's situation. In the ensuing debate it emerges that the source of the plague is the king's impiety: he has not shown proper respect for Apollo. When upbraided by Achilles for his selfish preference of his own interests, Agamemnon compounds his sin by threatening to dishonor him: he will take from him his external mark of respect, the concubine the army awarded him. Achilles, deprived of honor, is in this way driven to consider what worth and honor are—if he can be so easily stripped of them by the whim of a bad king. The quarrel has opened up a rift between Achilles and the Greeks that cannot easily be overcome. He withdraws from the battle and prays that Zeus vindicate his honor. Zeus is preeminently the royal or political god: it is by his authority that kings rule in the *Iliad,* as Agamemnon is quick to point out when he seeks to reprove Achilles for interference in his royal prerogative. How then can Zeus uphold Achilles against the anointed Agamemnon? At first, indeed, Zeus is reluctant to accept Achilles' prayer: Achilles has a claim, but then so have others. Finally Zeus accepts Achilles' request. He sees a way in which the vindication of Achilles is compatible with his purposes and the maintenance of the order he upholds. The working out of this vindication as the *boulē Dios* or as the will of Zeus is the story of the rest of the poem.[7]

If Zeus can grant Achilles' prayer as compatible with the order of things sustained by the Olympians, it is because he displays more of the *aretē* of a true king than he who has the formal authority. But to pray to have Zeus's favor is one thing; to merit it and to bear its demands are quite another. Zeus is the political god among the Olympians because it is he who brings the various particular gods with their rivalries into a common purpose, into a loose family unity, just as it is the king who establishes a common end amid the conflicting claims of persons and classes. To have the favor of Zeus, the highest god, is the highest honor a mortal can have. The favor of Zeus is not, as in later Jewish or Christian times, to know the one true divine end as raised above and separated from all finite goods (the gifts of the other gods, the Greeks would say). Zeus is neither merely one god among others nor the One above all others. He is the power that allows the various gods their free activity but can bring them all into relation to one another and to himself. To put this more clearly: the other heroes have particular gods as their divine protectors—Odysseus is watched over by Athena, Paris by Aphrodite—and this protection is not accorded capriciously. Odysseus is, to some extent, a human embodiment of Athena's power of practical reason, the man who can extricate himself from any difficulty or talk himself out of a threatening situation; Paris, the great lover, knows he is favored of Aphrodite. How then does one enjoy the favor of a god? Clearly, by being as like the god as possible. If Achilles is granted the favor of Zeus—and he alone among the great heroes (apart from royal personages) enjoys this privilege—and if he will be truly a son of Zeus, it must be that he realizes more adequately than others the gifts and powers of the supreme god. For Achilles is not satisfied with the favor of any one god; he appreciates them all, sympathizes with all human goods and ends. But he recognizes them all in their distinctive characters as interdependent and contained within Zeus's purpose. To know this is a hard and difficult truth. That no one of the ends of life has any stability except as involved in the accomplishment of the universal end of Zeus's will is a wisdom that is attained only with difficulty and must be dearly bought. The condition of its acquisition is to be stripped of attachment to finite ends or goods. Achilles would have liked to have the favor of Zeus—provided that it did not cost him his friendship with Patroclus. In the resolution of the poem, he is stripped even of this, so that, in the conclusion of the work—the scene between Achilles and Priam over the body of the dead Hector—these two great heroes, though no two men could be more divided, can, because each has been stripped of what most attached him to the ordinary ends of life, share a common insight and look unflinchingly into the divine order and accept what it has in store for them. The appeasement of Achilles' anger restores him first to unity with the Greek army and King Agamemnon, the quarrel forgotten now that the hero grasps what constitutes true *aretē*. At this point he is able to lead the Greeks to victory and kill Hector. He can then display himself as the son of Zeus that he is; he can play the king among men—not in the actual conditions of the expedition but in the ideal world of the games for the dead Patroclus. But his reconciliation to the full demands of Zeus's order is still incomplete; he distinguishes between a justice for Greeks and another order for Trojans. He cannot see that Zeus's justice is universal and embraces Greek and Trojan alike, so that his mutilation of Hector's body was an injustice, offensive to the gods. Finally he comes to this insight—only he and old Priam can move at this level—recognizes that there must be acknowledgment of Hector's virtue within Zeus's all-embracing *dikē*, and returns the body for decent burial.

To understand that the authority to rule humans depends upon *aretē* and to show what in principle this virtue involved is part of what Homer had to teach the Greeks. Even more important is to show how human societies regulated by these virtues are set within a cosmos structured and ordered by these intelligent and purposive Olympians. The divine order, as Homer understands it, can perhaps be best and most briefly illustrated by using an image he himself gives us. In the eighteenth book of the *Iliad*, Achilles is presented with new armor by the gods to replace what has been lost by Patroclus. Achilles is now ready to return to the battle and show himself as the hero he is. He lifts up his new shield, emblazoned with appropriate heraldic devices, in the way a crusader actually donned the cross—to exhibit externally his conviction and belief. But the divine order exhibited on this shield is very different from that presupposed in Christian belief. The circular shield is rimmed with ocean, the ever-rolling formless stuff of things. Then, farther in from the edge, come the earth and the heavenly bodies, the elements of nature. But within this natural setting, closer to the center of the shield, comes the human city, the social life of intelligent mortals. The community displayed embraces war and peace, the essential

activities of the city at peace—marriage and the administration of justice—
then the toil that the city's maintenance requires. But the center of the
shield has depicted on it the heart of its life, a display of leisure—the dance
and an acrobatic contest. The vision of the world is consummated in
leisure: it is in leisure and the activities of leisure (for example, the games)
that weary and fragile mortals catch a glimpse of the divine life and that
primal energy that sustains the world.

The Archaic and Classical City

According to the order of things displayed on the shield, the elements of
nature, the sensible world, have suffered a certain displacement with the
triumph of the Olympians. They (the elements) are now positioned at the
outer edge of things, removed from the center, which is reserved for the
life in community of intelligent beings. Nature in this view is no longer
primary but is reduced to being the appropriate condition for the display
of intellectual life. This appreciation of the natural and its subordination to
the purposes of intelligent gods are of incalculable importance for all the
ways of Greek culture and particularly for the life of the burgeoning city.
For the myth-making imagination, the old gods cast down by Zeus and the
Olympians, were raw, huge, misshapen monstrosities, whose brute force
availed little against the wit and intelligent power of the nimble younger
deities. Because these Olympian gods order in beauty this world of nature
(they order it; they do not create it) the Greeks were able with astonishing
rapidity to free themselves from the blank terror in the face of nature that
had weighed so heavily on older cultures. The early city was the setting for
a marvelous flourishing of curiosity and investigation into the events of
nature because the Greeks presaged an order and regularity in natural
occurrences which their minds could apprehend. Consequently, the miraculous has a relatively unimportant place in Greek religious life. To experience the divine as the power that overturns the natural order would have
seemed extremely odd to a Greek. The regularity of nature, as seen, for
example, in the unerring continuous circular motion of the heavenly bodies
was the surest evidence of the gods' presence—not the unexpected, the in-
explicably contingent event. The Greek gods are always known in relation
to nature: not "nature-gods" but gods who reveal themselves in the ordering
of the natural, they stimulated the aesthetic imagination to produce an ever
more adequate image of them. The Greeks were required by their religion
to produce an image of their god if the god was to be worshiped properly,
just as Jews were forbidden to attempt to picture a god who is above and
wholly removed from nature. Hence, when the Greeks became rich enough

again to build shrines of the gods in stone and to lavish their wealth in statue and frieze glorifying the rise and exploits of the Olympian order, the aesthetic achievement of the early city was not merely an external decoration but the very heart of the religious life of the community as it deepened its grasp of the nature of the gods.

But what of the social arrangements of the early polis that fostered so eagerly this primitive science and loved so ostentatiously the display of the *kouros* statue? When the city began to take shape, its differences from the dimly remembered Mycenean past (already for Homer a confused and distorted recollection) were striking. The [W]anax had completely disappeared, though the name was retained in prayers to the gods. But more than a name disappeared: the whole conception of a bureaucratic priestly royalty aided by scribes had evaporated. The *basileus*, the "king" that appeared in the early Greek city was a much humbler figure, probably the successor to the Mycenean *pa-si-re-u*, a sort of wealthy local squire or lord of a rural estate, who appears to have survived beneath the carapace of Mycenean institutions. The rediscovery of writing had an entirely new significance: an alphabetic script adapted from the Phoenician was easily learned and rapidly became a popular acquisition. No longer an instrument of control by a divine monarch, it became preeminently the means of publicity, and publicity belonged to the center of the city's life. Because the *archē* was no longer the private possession of a talismanic person but depended upon *aretē* or virtue, the nobles were easily able to dominate the government of the young city. At this stage it was readily assumed that virtue went with birth: the wellborn were the *aristoi*, who had the right to share in the *archē*. The aristocratic city prospered. In a new form of personal poetry, the lyric (Homer's poetry was conspicuously anonymous), the aristocrats exhibited their delight in the world they adorned with their virtue, their joy in their horses, in the competitive display of their *aretē* in the games, in their preeminence in the city. But the very prosperity of the aristocratic city required that the public nature of the *archē* be more fully comprehended. As external conditions for the Greek states improved and the seas became safe again, trading links with the Orient were resumed. New products and new aesthetic motifs flooded into the Greek world and, as the population increased rapidly, new homes had to be found. Under aristocratic leadership and the auspices of Apollo's priests at Delphi, new cities were dotted around the shore of the Mediterranean. With the new wealth came a period of great instability in the growing polis. The rich were no longer identical with the wellborn (to the disgust of the lyric poets), and even the prosperous farmer was wealthy enough to afford the new heavy armor of the

hoplitēs, "foot-soldier." The new form of military organization, the un-
broken line of shoulder-to-shoulder heavily armed foot-soldiers, meant the
decline of the horse-loving aristocrat. Not only did it require a new definition of the brave man (one form of aretē)—no longer the brave dash of the
individual hero (in the Iliad the battle was largely a "mosaic of duels") but
the steady courage to hold one's place in the line and not to break ranks—
but, as the city now depended for its survival on these military formations,
their claims to share in the archē could not be denied. For was virtue merely
a consequence of birth? The social turmoil of the time was settled by the
adoption of a constitution. A fundamental law, usually endorsed by the
Delphic god, fixed the proportion and share of the various classes in the
archē. The primacy of law in the life of the city became increasingly marked;
the early sages of Greek tradition were often connected with the introduction of codes of law or constitutional arrangements, and we have noted that
the early philosophers proclaimed the law as more essential to the city than
its walls.[8] Now laws are universals, norms applicable to countless instances.
In the administration of the city they meant the elimination of bias, the
regulation of relations between individuals and classes according to fixed
principles, known to all because they were now written down and open to
public inspection. As the circle of those claiming a share in virtue progressively expanded to embrace the entire citizen body and as citizens
demanded that law and even lottery should regulate the shares the equal
citizens enjoyed in the magistracies of the state, the Greek city had matured.

One achievement of the aristocratic city that deserves emphasis is the
institutionalization of the games as part of Greek civic culture; the Olym-
pics were traditionally thought to have been founded in 776 B.C. The games
were religious events in honor of the gods and departed heroes when the
Greek states were able for a short time to bury their ceaseless rivalries and
internecine wars, to join together in celebrating the Olympians, and to
enjoy—briefly—the peace of the gods. The game as religious worship was
already suggested on the shield, where it was depicted as the heart of the
community's life, but how did the games reveal to the Greeks the nature
of the divine? The game is essentially a leisure activity: that is, as opposed
to the normal life of toil or labor (ponos), where works are undertaken to
satisfy need or for ends that lie outside them, in leisure (scholē) the activity
is essentially its own end or has its purpose within itself and is not done
for anything outside itself—a free activity. Such is the divine life as the
Greeks glimpsed it in the games. No less important was the fiercely competitive side of the contests. As contrasted with the activities of ordinary life,
in which in pursuit of economic and political ends humans are divided from
each other and caught in destructive conflict, the competition of the games,

although it permitted the extremest self-assertion, did not destroy the unity of person with person, a common humanity, but rather discovered it in the simple rivalry to see that the best be done. The unity of humanity realized in an activity carried on by free and independent agents recalls the order of Zeus that prevails in and through the varied and opposed activities of the other gods. This peace of the gods, enjoyed in the games, is not possible in the divisive activities of ordinary existence. Human life, thought the Greeks, is at best a balance of toil and leisure, and they did not suppose that the restoration of a golden age before the necessity of toil had emerged was a possible object of historical striving; in this the Greek differs from the Roman (see below).

The polis had emerged and matured under the auspices of the Olympian deities. To the end of the archaic period, the growing city would find its ultimate sanction in its relation to the gods and their order. The law-giver Solon, in a period of great social stress, was confident that Athens would be secure because Athena, daughter of mighty Zeus, would hold her hands over the city.[9] But as the city developed and the common ends of life in community became more recognized and stressed, the tension between the political aspect of human existence and the satisfaction of domestic and private nature became more pronounced. Here the poetry of the heroic age was defective; it had originated in a period long ago, before the establishment of the polis and, though it pointed to a principle of order in social life, how that order would be embodied in the relations of a complex and developed society was not altogether clear. How was the Olympian religion to be understood in the conflicts between the claims of the magistrates, civic officials, and those of the family? These are the questions that the tragic dramatists of Athens, the most developed of the cities, would explore in the fifth century: could a king sacrifice a daughter to gain the favor of the gods? In this sense the work of the dramatists as "educators of the people" completed the work of Homer.[10] The dramatists exhibited the authority of the divine order and its all-embracing nature by showing a character of heroic virtue in conflict with it; the hero by a one-sided attachment to some one aspect of the divine (the favor of a particular god) comes into conflict with the claims of other, rival gods. He (or she) excites our sympathy (pity) as, at the same time, we are appalled at his destruction (fear), as the authority of the divine order *as a whole* reasserts itself. At the resolution of the conflict the sympathetic participant can acknowledge that in all that was done and suffered there was, as Sophocles said, "nothing here but Zeus."

But what was Zeus? With the strengthening of the city a new form of wisdom matured that would first challenge and then undermine the imaginative

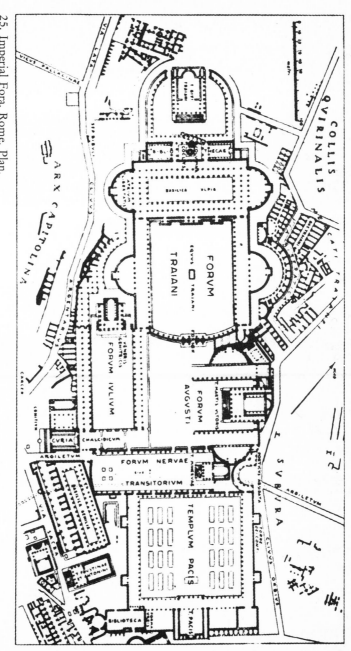

25. Imperial Fora, Rome. Plan.

grasp of the gods. This was that reflective knowledge of things the Greeks called philosophy. The Olympian gods had originally triumphed because of their wit and intelligence, and it was not foreign to their nature to exalt the power of mind. By the classical period the proponents of the new wisdom openly proclaimed that *nous* was the cause of all things; and, in general, philosophy in its maturity would teach that the divine is to be sought in *nous* and its life. The attempt to grasp the divine in the categories of the nonsensible could only have the profoundest repercussions, in time, on the life of the city and even its popular culture. The earlier philosophers had already transposed the vision of a cosmos sustained in being by a host of conflicting, individualized deities under the authority of Father Zeus into a divine substance which, by an inexorable law, adjusts and maintains itself in the ceaseless conflict of opposites, visible through nature. The divine as law or uniformity in cosmic change was retained, but the anthropomorphic, the vivid representational picture of the gods was increasingly repudiated, and the immoral and offensive features of the gods' activities, inseparable from their imaginative portrayal, were progressively challenged. The young had hitherto been encouraged to take as models of virtue the heroes in their conflicts as elucidated by the poets. When the primacy of *nous* was taken by the sophistic movement of the fifth century to reside in the power of human thinking over its images, the inspired pictures of the gods and heroes could be set aside as arbitrary products of merely human fancy. The effect of this could only be a seeming liberation of humans from groundless traditional restraint, and in this liberation the youth of the period joined eagerly—to the dismay of their elders, whose entire poetic culture from then on began to seem old-fashioned and antiquated.

The movement of sophistic enlightenment was challenged and arrested by the deeper rationality of Socrates. He found the wisdom of the Sophists as baseless as that of "the poets who uttered many fine things but did not understand what they had said." True to the Delphic god's command to "know himself," Socrates abandoned the guessing about the causes of natural phenomena and turned within himself to discover a foundation for knowledge. He quelled the chatter of the Sophists and their equivalent of the appeal to experience with the question "What is experience?" Reputed to have brought philosophy down from heaven to earth, Socrates was in truth the father of logic and metaphysics. He began with the apparently simplest of questions—"What do I know?"—and this was found to involve "How do I know it?" The knowing subject is discovered to be integral to the enquiry into the known object. His disciple Plato learned from this that a stable object of knowledge could not be found in the fluctuating images of the senses but only in the enduring forms or "ideas" of things, which were contained in or dependent on a supreme idea or *archē* in which being and knowing coincided. In the *Republic,* only a community that integrates the various classes in a just order, regulated by governors who understand the relation of all things in their forms to this primary principle or *archē,* can properly be regarded as a state. The rationality of the human soul can find its proper fulfillment only in the ordered political community. The state is the necessary condition for the individual's realized freedom—not a restriction of or something external to it. For Aristotle, who can say that "man is a political animal," the state is the embodiment of practical reason, of *nous praktikos.* In the state humans begin to participate in that activity of *nous* which, in its completed form of an undivided energy of subject and object in pure knowing, constitutes the divine life itself. The philosophers of the classical period restore to the city its divine foundation, but the clearer discrimination of the intellectual or rational from the imaginative or sensible presaged profound changes in the life and spirituality of the polis and the attitude of the citizens toward it.

The Hellenistic and Roman City

The epitaph of Aeschylus, the poet of the early classical city, recorded his services to the state at Marathon but not his distinction as a tragedian: poet and teacher were taken up in the pride of the citizen. In the Hellenistic period such an identification, even submersion, of the individual would have been unlikely. By the later part of the fifth century, the system of city-states had begun to betray a fatal instability. Athens and Sparta, the leading states of the time, clashed in a war that drew all Hellas into a desperate conflict. The result after thirty years—a peace of exhaustion with Sparta the nominal victor—was as ruinous for Hellas as the First World War was for the independence of the European states of the nineteenth century. Henceforth the Greek world, after enduring a series of short-lived hegemonies, could find a point of stability only in an outside power. This first appeared in Macedon: Philip humbled the city-states and Alexander completed their reduction at the very moment he posed as the champion of Hellenic interests against the barbarians and was to spread Greek culture throughout the East. Subsequently the old cities were swept up into the rivalries of the Hellenistic successor kingdoms and eventually into the province of Achaea as part of the empire of the senate and the Roman people. Never again would the Greek states be free self-governing communities. Though considerable independence might be left them to manage their own internal affairs, they were in truth pawns of remote political authorities, far surpassing them in power and military capacity.

To this altered political condition of the city there corresponded a new spirituality. The religion of the old city has been described as essentially a civic piety—an acknowledgment of and a reverence for the forces that ordered the ancestral community. Doubtless, much of this sentiment survived in the Hellenistic city, and the contrast should not be overemphasized. There were continuities as well as changes; priests were appointed, sacrifices offered to the gods as in the past. There is much evidence of a lively local patriotism and a devout attachment to the old ways and traditions. But the differences are striking. No one could confuse the quality of religious feeling that sustained the Panathenaic procession depicted by Pheidias with the sentiment that could vote such extravagant honors to Demetrius Poliorcetes, the Hellenistic conqueror of Athens—distasteful even to the goddess herself and allowed, interestingly enough, because "the old gods seemed far away . . . or heeded not at all."[11] The climate of religious sentiment was much influenced by the pronounced individualism characteristic of the period. From being a miniature church-state, all-embracing in the claims it made upon its members (so that Pericles could say that a person with no interest in public affairs was an oddity) and providing a focus for all their energies, the later polis had for many become primarily an administrative unit. It provided the necessary setting of order for the release of individuals to pursue a personal satisfaction which could no longer be confined within the culture of the ancestral community. Individuals in great numbers abandoned their cities and, as private persons, sought their fortunes as mercenaries, administrators, or scientific experts in the service of the Hellenistic monarchs. Individuals with religious interests could now roam the Mediterranean world in pursuit of their satisfaction. Many sought multiple initiation into various mystery cults with their exotic rituals. The mysteries had, in classical times, been absorbed into the state cult, as a subordinate element in the religious life of the city. Then, the citizen would have been initiated into the Eleusinian Mysteries as a citizen of Athens as part of his civic duty; now, a not uncommon sight was the religious devotee moving from city to city on a sort of pilgrimage, offering himself as a candidate for initiation. Fasting, ablutions, colorful novelties (there was a great interest in new cults, especially from the Orient)—all helped to create a condition of emotional excitement in which the initiate could experience religious exaltation and illumination.

The isolated individual could, if he belonged to the enlightened, take refuge in popular philosophy. The emergence of philosophical sects that offered a coherent body of doctrine and a recognizable way of life was an important ingredient in the spirituality of the period. The primary interest of the philosophies of the time was ethical; they sought to provide a rule of life to individuals conscious of their inner independence but inextricably involved in an inexorable external order. To gain a fairly widespread following these philosophies had to be readily comprehensible, and they were little concerned with the dialectical subtleties of the older, more speculative wisdom. In this way they easily became dogmatic and inevitably provoked a skeptical response. But whether Stoic, Epicurean, or Skeptic, all are concerned with the difficulty that arises for detached individuals who regard themselves as essentially separated from an order to which they nevertheless properly belong. Logically this meant a search for a criterion that would bridge the division between subjective conception and objective reality and would guarantee in this way the truth of the wall of private ideas which separated the thinking self from the reality of things. Morally there was a demand for a rule of life that would stabilize individuals in untroubled contentment within the fortresses of their own souls, in indifference to an external world from which they could not wholly free themselves.

These atomic individuals were in truth part of a teleological whole. The divine substance was an end-setting, purposive power, realizing itself in all aspects of nature and life, so that, in the social medium, the individualism of the time was balanced by an equally characteristic cosmopolitanism. The community to which a rational being owed allegiance embraced all rational nature, all humanity. There was truly only one city—the "cosmopolis" or city of the world. A point had been reached to cultural development in which there was recognized a demand for an absolutely universal community—in principle. In reality people actually lived in a multiplicity of powerless communities, populated by—so far as they shared in the contemporary philosophical enlightenment—deracinated individuals. The guides to the meaning of religion were now a distinct class, somewhat detached from popular religiosity. By no means necessarily hostile to those whose primary interest was in cult and experience, they were, at any rate, distinguished from them.

This Hellenistic world, with its aspiration to universal community, was gradually absorbed into the dominion of Rome as it spread its power over the eastern Mediterranean; the ancient city had entered its final phase. The Roman distinguished more sharply than the Greek the sphere of private interest from that of public concern, as the very name for the community, the *res publica* or "public thing" testifies. This private interest was recognized as legitimate—witness the formidable power of the Roman *pater-familias*—but then harshly subordinated to the common good. The hard Roman *virtus* was precisely the quality that could suppress private ends and feeling in the service of the state, and the myths of Roman origins—the consul ordering the execution of his traitorous sons, Aeneas abandoning

Dido—usually concerned sacrificial valor in the common interest. The original Roman religion lacked the imaginative transformation effected by the Greek mind. Any power (however prosaic) or anything that could affect the human enterprise for good or ill was a god, to be pressed into the Roman service in a relationship that was conceived of as essentially contractual, and the Romans duly considered themselves *religiossimi mortales,* "the most religious of mortals." What the Roman was sure of in the multiplicity of divine influences was the absorption of all forces into the realization of one divine end—the elevation and maintenance of the Roman state. Jupiter Best and Greatest was present historically in the expansion to universal dominion of the Roman people. The Romans actually made the whole world (*orbis*) one city (*urbs*), and the characteristic spirituality of the later Roman imperial order was the celebration as divine and eternal of a universal empire that had gathered all humanity into one city. The divine order was actually realized in history; the growth and extension of the city were the progressive realization in history of a golden age, a "kingdom of god";[12] and, finally, empire and ruler were appropriately worshiped as divine.

Immensa maiestas Imperii Romani: "The immense majesty of the Roman Empire." The civic experience of the ancients issued in an empire universal in aspiration (as embracing in principle all civilized humanity), eternal (as offering permanent fulfillment of human political needs), and divine (as embodying historically the divine purposes for human community). It was also, of course, the empire of the plundering general, of brutal conquest, of slavery, of unbelievable degradation. Both sides belong to the Roman experience—even religious experience—because once the essential submission or subordination of private ends to an external political will had been accepted as the basis of culture, Romans could pursue their private purposes with all possible vigor and with good conscience. Indeed, they could expect the help of the gods in these concerns. For, to the Romans, the divine was essentially the *useful,* that which assisted in the furthering of ends—their own and those of the state. Moreover, the ancient state could accept slavery easily (though with the emergence of Stoicism there was questioning of its justice), because it was only as a citizen—as an Athenian or as a Roman— that one was capable of freedom. Only as trained to virtue by the discipline of the state could one acquire free personality and hence own property. Birth could be overcome; one could become a Roman citizen. But acceptance of Roman law and culture was indispensable to full humanity. So the universality of the empire was not wide enough, and the emergence of a new religion that could embrace individuals in the primary divine community on a basis more fundamental even than that of citizenship was bound to come into insoluble conflict with the *Imperium Romanum*. The church might expand within the empire, but, equally well, it might go beyond the frontiers and evangelize the raw peoples hardly touched by *Romanitas*. Julian grasped the nature of the Christians very accurately from a Roman point of view when he said they were *philobarbari*, "lovers of barbarians." As the empire developed, civic piety began to lose its hold on its members. Pagan and Christian alike began to flee the city to reconstruct a new and purer life where private end and public good could be better integrated. It was not so much in the city as in the country regions, among the *pagani*, that the last traces of ancient *pietas* survived; in the simple rituals of country life something of the charm of ancient religion lingered. But to the end of the ancient world the human city remained a community only because of its relation to the gods. And it was not a mean or ignoble conception that could see in the growth and sweep of empire the habitation of Zeus among human beings: "All things are from thee, all in thee, all return to thee. There is one who says 'Dear City of Cecrops'; Wilt thou not rather say 'Dear City of Zeus'?" (Marcus Aurelius 4.23).

Notes

1. For a discussion of the importance of *isonomia*, of equality and reciprocity, in the early state, see J.-P. Vernant, *The Origins of Greek Thought*, 60ff.

2. See "The Great Rhetra," an ancient document that preserves the memory of the Spartan constitutional settlement; see also A. Andrewes, *The Greek Tyrants* (London: Hutchinson's University Library, 1956).

3. K. Freeman, *Ancilla to the Pre-Socratic Philosophers* (Oxford: Blackwell, 1948) 27.

4. See V. Ehrenberg, "When did the Polis rise?" *Journal of Hellenic Studies* 60 (1937) 147–59.

5. For Stoic texts on the *communis civitas* of gods and humans, see the collection in C. J. DeVogel, *Greek Philosophy: A Collection of Texts* (Leiden: Brill, 1964) 3:1069ff.

6. The story is told in Plutarch *Life of Theseus* 35.

7. See *Iliad* 1.1.5, where the poet says, "the will of Zeus was fulfilled" in the quarrel.

8. See n. 3 and Heraclitus fr. 44, Diels-Kranz.

9. Solon's verses are found most easily in the *Oxford Book of Greek Verse in Translation*, edited by T. F. Higham and C. M. Bowra (Oxford: Clarendon Press, 1938) 158.

10. Aeschylus regarded his plays as "slices from Homer's banquet"; see Athenaeus *Deipnosophistae* 8.347e.

11. Demetrius was "deified" by the Athenians: "son of the most mighty god Poseidon." The hymn saluting the new god—a most interesting document—is preserved in Athenaeus *Deipnosophistae* 6.253.

12. See Virgil *Eclogue* 4; *Aeneid* 6.790–800.

Bibliography

On the early city, see Ehrenberg; for its spiritual background, see the stimulating discussion in Vernant. For a sympathetic treatment of the Olympians and ancient spirituality, see generally Snell. For the relation of the ancient city and its institutions to religion, see Fustel de Coulanges. More factual is Fowler, *The City-State;* his *Religious Experience* is also helpful. On the relation of philosophy to religion and the city, see Caird, an older but well-written work.

Caird, Edward. *The Evolution of Theology in the Greek Philosophers.* 2 vols. Glasgow: J. Maclenose and Sons, 1904. Reprinted in 1 vol., New York: Kraus Reprint, 1968.

Ehrenberg, V. *The Greek State.* Oxford: University Press, 1961.

Fowler, W. Warde. *The City-State of the Greeks and the Romans.* London: Macmillan, 1952.

———. *The Religious Experience of the Roman People from the Earliest Times to the Age of Augustus.* Gifford Lectures for 1909–10. London: Macmillan, 1911.

Fustel de Coulanges, N. D. *The Ancient City.* Baltimore, MD: Johns Hopkins University Press, 1980.

Snell, Bruno. *The Discovery of the Mind.* Translated by T. G. Rosenmeyer. Cambridge, MA: Harvard University Press, 1953.

Vernant, Jean Pierre. *The Origins of Greek Thought.* Ithaca, NY: Cornell University Press, 1982.

14

The Self in Ancient Religious Experience

FREDERICK M. SCHROEDER

THE NOUN "SELF" IS *prima facie* embarrassing to the philosopher, since it seems to be little more than a hypostatized version of a reflexive and intensive pronoun. We may well ask, What is the difference between myself and my Self? How is either of these to be distinguished from me? The ancients were perhaps wiser in not rendering the equivalent Greek pronoun *autos,* or the Latin *ipse,* a substantive.

The present discussion is directed toward the place of the self in religious experience. Perhaps these perplexities may, for the moment, be suspended if we ask not after the definition but after the location of the substantive "self" in contemporary religious study. Three schools of thought presently address themselves to what purports to be the objective study of religion: structuralism, sociobiology, and depth psychology.[1] Of these, it is in the approach of depth psychology that the word "self" has its true currency.

The term "Self" (capitalized) is, for the purposes of that discipline, derived from its use by C. G. Jung and translates the German *das Selbst,*[2] a phrase that, on the face of it, does not yield much more sense than its English translation. In Jung the Self is the human being's objective (as opposed to the Ego as the subjective) identity.[3]

There are some solid reasons for not engaging the Jungian school on this subject. An encyclopedic survey would obviously be eclipsed by such debate, polemical or irenic. In addition, the depth psychologists are obsessed with the question of religious origins (as indeed are the other schools of secular religious study). It will not be the concern of the present article to seek by some reductive process the origins of Hellenic religious experience in primitive states of consciousness. We look to Greece not as a storehouse of primitive impulses but for a highly civilized approach to spiritual growth and understanding. The Jungians are, of course, also interested in such development, but from the horizon of their particular understanding of consciousness. We may, however, unpack their use of the noun "self" in a way that will be useful for our present purposes.

If I in my maturity write an autobiography, I, as a boy of sixteen, will become an object of my present reflection. I may be amused at what seemed or were to that boy pressing or embarrassing concerns. I may also see the seeds of the man I have become. I might say that I am interpreting the ego of that boy with reference to the self, the person, who I have become. His experience of life was but a part of an integrity.

We might also define "self" as a person's project in life. I might, for example, want to be one of several possible selves: a physician, a lawyer, a professor, a poet, a lover, or a holy man. I select one or another of these goals and progress toward it, perhaps throughout my whole life. Of course, I may progress, or even unfold, toward such a goal without at first being aware that I am doing so. If "self" is defined in terms of life project, of the final intentionality (conscious or unconscious) of sensitivity, thought, and action, then we shall have something both of the scope and the economy that this discussion requires. After all, to talk of self in religious experience in terms of, let us say, humanity and the gods, would be to transgress all reasonable boundaries. If we are then to speak of life project in relation to the divine, we shall have, perhaps, a reasonable point of departure.

Depth psychology, like the other secular approaches to the study of religion, also claims objectivity. This does not mean to say that it does not attempt to study religion from within. Obviously a psychoanalytic attempt will do so. Their claim to objectivity interprets itself to exclude *ab initio* the existence of the divine as a proper subject of investigation. We shall see that the ancients entertained the question of life project in its divine dimension very seriously. Ultimately, the kind of reflection that this undertaking demands may be seen to consist in asking whether the project of a human life must have a divine origin and goal.

The Life Story

In archaic Greek literature, the view of a human life, in the sense of life story (*bios*), falls easily within the compass of an understanding of "self" as we have defined it. A life may be interpreted only in its integrity. Thus, the motto "Count no man happy until he is dead" is not simply a counsel of despair. It is only at death that the picture is completed, and only the finished work will admit of evaluation.

This kind of biography is well represented in the story of Solon, the

Athenian lawgiver and one of the sages of Greece, and Croesus, king of Lydia, a man of fabulous wealth, recounted in Herodotus (1.30–33, 53–54, 86–91).[4] Croesus attempted in vain to impress his wise visitor with his wealth and solicited his flattery with the question "Who is the happiest man you have seen?" Solon produced two candidates for felicity whose lives seemed provokingly humble in fruits and attainment. Croesus was driven to ask directly after his own happiness. The sage replied that the gods are jealous and life a risky business. Of all the days that a man might be allotted in a span of seventy years, it takes but one day to undo happiness. Thus, a man may be accounted fortunate, but he may scarcely be esteemed happy until he is dead. Croesus later consulted the oracle at Delphi to enquire whether he should march against Cyrus, the great king of Persia. He received the ambiguous reply that if he marched against Persia a great empire would fall. In his defeat he was ruefully to recall the words of Solon.

This story may be fruitfully interpreted with reference to archaic notions of time. R. B. Onians observes, "In modern European thought there has prevailed the conception of time as a homogeneous medium analogous to empty space. . . . For the Homeric Greeks time was not homogeneous; it had quality."[5] In our story, Solon, after he has calculated the average life span at 26,250 days, remarks, "Not a single one of them is like the next in what it brings." In Homer, "the *ēmar* is not the day of the month nor is it shared by others, it is the time, the destiny experienced by an individual."[6] This may be seen in the epithets that accompany "day." Hector's death is described as *aisimon ēmar*, his "fateful day" (Homer *Iliad* 22.212). *Ēmar anankaion*, "the day of necessity" (*Iliad* 16.836) or *ēmar doulion*, "the day of slavery" (*Iliad* 6.463) describe the day when one is delivered into bondage. Odysseus reflects, "The father of gods and men makes one day unlike another day, and earthlings change their thought on life in accord with this" (Homer *Odyssey* 18.136).

Solon, in observing that life is subject to divine envy and fortune, remarks, "In the whole length of time, there are many things to see which one does not wish to see and many things to experience" (Herodotus 1.32.2). Time (*chronos*) in Homer never describes a point in time, but a duration, so that the word does not admit a use such as "at that time."[7] In the whole length of time, literally "in the whole, long time," there are many events that color the tapestry.

Notable in the story of Solon and Croesus is the passivity of humans before destiny. We are subject to what the day brings. Our chief virtue is to avoid sinful pride and to lead a humble life and leave a decent reputation behind us. It is sometimes said that Achilles entertains a choice between a peaceful and uneventful life into old age in his native Phthia and a brief and glorious life completed by death upon the field of battle. Plato indeed so describes the position of the hero, who prefers death and justice to life and injustice in his avenging of Hector's death (*Apology* 18D; trans. H. Treden-nick). Plato sounds in this context a genuinely Homeric note in Achilles' reflection that he would not want to become a laughing stock. This is appropriate for a Homeric hero to the extent that he lives within a culture of shame. Socrates, who scorns the opinion of the many, need only con-sider the issues of right and wrong.[8]

In Homer there is no notion of a choice on the part of Achilles, although, because of Socrates' interpretation, we are inclined to read this into the *Iliad*. In the *Iliad* Achilles says:

> For my mother Thetis the goddess of the silver feet tells me
> I carry two sorts of destiny towards the day of my death. Either
> if I stay here and fight beside the city of the Trojans
> my return home is gone, but my glory shall be everlasting;
> but if I return home to the beloved land of my fathers,
> the excellence of my glory is gone, but there will be a long life
> left for me, and my end in death will not come to be quickly.
>
>   (9.410)

After the death of Patroclus, Thetis tells Achilles: "It is decreed that your death must come soon after Hektor's" (18.96). Achilles replies "I must die soon, then; since I was not to stand by my companion when he was killed" (18.98). This is not so much a choice as it is a natural consequence of the death of Patroclus under the condition of Achilles' withdrawal. It is not invited, but demanded, by the heroic code.

Both Plato and Herodotus entertain a qualitative sense of time, in which destiny unfolds like a sort of tapestry. Both Plato and Herodotus differ from Homer in their sense of moral exegesis in beholding the end of a man's life. Yet Herodotus retains the sense of human passivity before destiny. Is it simply that Plato, in representing Achilles' destiny as a matter of choice, rejects the passivity of the ancient view? In the myth of Er, Plato represents the soul as choosing its destiny and its life (e.g., tyrannical or philosophical) before birth (*Republic* 617DE; trans. P. Shorey). For Plato, the notion that a life unfolds unto a unity and completion is true as it is for Herodotus. Yet he combines this view with one of free choice in an ante-natal act of decision.

In geometric art, diachronically sequential events are portrayed in hori-zontal succession. Thus, in a funeral scene, the corpse is, in successive depic-tions, anointed, dressed, laid on the bier, lamented, and buried.[9] In view of this qualitative conception of time, it may be reasonable to think that it was seen as a plastic medium. For this reason, Herodotus believes that the happiness of a person's life may not be judged until the picture is completed in death.

The tradition of considering a choice among several possible lives is preserved in their classification in Aristotle, where we may select the life of enjoyment, the life of politics, or the life of contemplation (*Nicomachean Ethics* 1095b14–1096a11). It might be thought that this view of life would undermine individuality, because we are speaking here not of my life but of a desirable life. In the archaic period, however, Croesus may be seen as a type of the hybristic and wealthy man who confuses happiness and good fortune rather than as an individual. Similarly, Oedipus would be a type in the sense that he is the complete monster of unhappiness. The consistency of thematic material and the tendency to view a character in terms of his salient characteristic in Homer may also point in this direction (although we may allow the poet to transcend the limitations of the craft of oral poetry).

Gods

For the Greeks, a god (*theos*) is fundamentally a power to be propitiated or won over. Any unexpected or awesome manifestation of power can be divine. The chorus in the *Bacchae* of Euripides addresses Earthquake with an apotropaic formula (585; trans. W. Arrowsmith). Here is a divinity with no cult, addressed only when its terrible power is revealed.[10] An unexpected or chance meeting with a friend can be a *theos*.[11]

The word "god" appears in Greek as a predicate.[12] Thus, Eros (love) is a god (Plato *Symposium* 194E–195A; trans. M. Joyce). We may contrast this with the biblical statement that "God is love" (1 John 4:8) in which the attribute appears in the predicate and God is the subject of the sentence. Eros is seen as a power, often destructive (Sophocles *Antigone* 781–809; trans. J. Moore). Thus, a power, Eros, is a god. The equation of power with divinity leads very naturally to the predicative use of the word "god."

This manner of predication is not restricted to the divine sphere. In the *Iliad*, the muse is invoked to sing the wrath of Achilles (1.1). The hero is possessed by this emotion. Heracles is commonly described with the formula "Heraclean might" (*Iliad* 2.650; 5.638; 18.117; *Odyssey* 11.601). In this example we can observe that the name Heracles bears to his most prominent characteristic an adjectival relationship. The use of stock epithets (swift-footed Achilles, Ajax good at the war cry, Hector of the glancing helm) points in the same direction. The person is seen almost as a function of his most prominent or powerful aspect.

In Earthquake we see an example of an external power that is, by virtue of that power, divine. In Eros we have what we would call a psychological force that is within. Perhaps it would be better to say that what we would call an inward force, if it is revealed in power and surprise, may, by those qualities, be regarded as divine.

All of this presents us with a fascinating logical problem. The same manner of predication applies to both divine and human spheres. A human emotion may be manifested with such power and surprise that it may admit of a divine predicate. We say that a man is possessed by a god, for example, Eros. It is as if he were invaded by some external power. Yet, according to another way of looking at it, the human emotion has taken on divine dimensions by the nature and extent of its power. This suggests that the boundary between human and divine is tenuous.[13]

In the *Iliad* Agamemnon explains his petulant behavior toward Achilles:

> I am not responsible
> but Zeus is, and Destiny, and Erinys the mist-walking
> who in assembly caught my heart in savage delusion (*atē*)
> on that day I myself stripped from him the prize of Achilleus.
> Yet what could I do? It is the gods who accomplish all things.
> Delusion (*Atē*) is the elder daughter of Zeus.
>
> (19.86–91)

It is not to be thought that Delusion here is only a personified face-saving device. This is a divine power. There is, of course, personification in the sense that Delusion is the elder daughter of Zeus. Delusion is a particularly interesting example of what we are looking for. It is both subjective, the psychological state of delusion, and objective, the ruin which that state brings about. The boundaries between inward and outward, human emotion and divine possession, are blurred.[14]

Homeric personification does not conceal that a god is fundamentally a quality or an aspect endowed with power. This may be seen particularly in the case of lesser divinities: Deimos (terror), Phobos (fear), and Eris (hate) are the companions of Ares, the god of war. These are no allegories, but, as anyone experienced in war would know, real and operative powers on the field of battle. Homer tells us:

> Ares drove these [the Trojans] on, and the Achaians grey-eyed Athene
> and Terror (Deimos) drove them, and Fear (Phobos) and
> Hate (Eris) whose wrath is relentless,
> and the sister and companion of murderous Ares.
>
> (*Iliad* 4.439–41)

Here Eris is personified as the sister of Ares and walks amid the hosts (*Iliad* 4.445). Ares orders Phobos and Deimos to harness his horses (*Iliad* 15.119), yet these forces remain shadowy and without personality. Ares himself is not the god of war, but the god War. As a spear is fixed in the heart of Alcathous, "Then and there Ares the huge took his life from him" (*Iliad* 13.444; cf. 16.613; 17.529). As an Olympian, Ares is person enough to have a love affair with Aphrodite (*Odyssey* 8.266–69), yet the tendency to divinize power and aspect is clearly evident.[15]

Even where personification is much to the fore, we can see the same principles at work. Achilles is in great anger and in the act of drawing his sword when Athena suddenly appears from heaven to persuade him to stay his hand (*Iliad* 1.8.188–222). In view of the great power of his wrath, it is cause for amazement that Achilles should not slay Agamemnon. The allaying of the wrath must be a manifestation of divine power.

The boundary between human and divine may thus be regarded as theoretically tenuous. A manifestation of unexpected or miraculous power may be seen as a mark of divinity, whether it is (as we would put it) external or internal to the human person. If a man displays miraculous power, is there the possibility that he might become divine?

The hero is, for the Greeks, upon his death an object of veneration and a source of protective power and blessing. He is not, indeed, divine, but is nevertheless a supernatural, chthonic force. In the *Oedipus at Colonus*, Sophocles portrays the very process of Oedipus's heroization.[16] He had fallen from kingship, the position of a sage, and happy family life when his own relentless enquiry revealed his incest and parricide, crimes unknown to himself. Oedipus was a monster of unhappiness. Yet it is in this very character that he may exhibit spectacular power upon his death and bring protection to his kind Athenian hosts.[17]

Pindar declares that the race of humans and gods is one but that they are separated by power (*dynamis*) (*Nemean* 6.1–11). Humans may resemble the gods in mind or strength, but their fate is uncertain. Heracles is, in the words of Pindar, *hēros theos*, both hero and god (*Nemean* 3.39). Both aspects of his nature constitute his integrity and to stress one at the expense of the other is always to err.[18] Yet he is the only hero to succeed in becoming a god among the Olympians. His divinity is reflected in the fact that, whereas a normal hero has one cult site, the place of his burial, Heracles' popularity enjoys many.[19] We may think that the power of Heracles is so great that it exceeds heroic dimensions.[20]

Empedocles proclaims, "I go to and fro among you as an immortal god, no longer mortal" (Diels-Kranz fr. 112.4–5; trans. K. Freeman). He lays this claim on his ability to practice the art of divination and to cure diseases (Diels–Kranz fr. 112.10–12). Obviously the claim to divinity proceeds from an assertion of power. The difference from the divinity of Heracles consists partially in the fact that divine status is achieved before death. What is more significant, Empedocles does not, like Heracles, become god, as his power burgeons of itself beyond mortal limits. He arrogates the position of god unto himself.[22] In all of this we may wish to see not only the confidence of a philosopher but also an "Orphic" and magical character. The guardians of the other world address the Orphic initiate in the words "Happy and blessed one, thou shalt be god instead of mortal."[23]

We have already seen from the story of Solon and Croesus how the god of Delphi is a humbling force. This aspect is, of course, also evident in the tragic story of Oedipus, in which self-knowledge brings destruction. Over the temple of Delphi stood the words "Know Thyself" (Plato *Phaedrus* 229E, trans. R. Hackforth; Xenophon *Memorabilia* 4.2.14, trans. H. Tredennick). Both Plato (*Charmides* 164E; trans. B. Jowett) and Heraclitus (Diels–Kranz fr. 116; trans. K. Freeman) understand that these words are the counsel of temperance and humility.[24]

The story is told in Diogenes Laertius that a Milesian fisherman discovered in the sea a sacred tripod. The tripod was sent to one after another of the Seven Sages of Greece until finally it was presented to Solon. Solon dedicated it to Apollo on the grounds that the god alone is wise (*Lives* 1.28; trans. R. D. Hicks). This folk story is reflected in the Platonic *Apology of Socrates*, in which Chaerephon consults the oracle of Delphi and asks who is the wisest of men (20E–21A; trans. H. Tredennick). The oracle replies that it is Socrates. Socrates shows appropriate humility in interpreting the oracle as a command to scour Athens in search of a man wiser than himself. When he fails to find such a person, he concludes that his wisdom must consist in his knowledge that he has no wisdom (23B). Here again the implication is clear: only the god is wise. That the consultation of Delphi is a project in self-knowledge is suggested by Heraclitus: "I consulted myself" (Diels–Kranz fr. 101; trans. F. M. Schroeder).[25] In this fragment the word for "consult" (*dizēmai*) is a verb that is used of oracular enquiry (Herodotus 7.142.1).

The Platonic *Apology* is also Delphic in that it is riddled with ambiguity and partings of the way. Socrates regards philosophical abandonment of Athens as an unholy desertion of the post to which the god has assigned him (28D–29A; 37CE). It is as an Athenian that he urges the care of the soul upon his fellow citizens (29D). Yet he asks the court for the same indulgence toward his manner of speaking as they would accord to a foreigner (17D). While Socrates is the autochthonous Athenian who will not, except on military service, leave his native city, he ironically casts himself in the role of both foreigner and wanderer. In this exercise of

26. Symmachi Diptych. Roman. Late 4th century A.D.

ambiguity Socrates resorts to Heraclean language. His enquiry and pere-grination within the city are a wandering (*planē*) (22A6)[26] and his actions are labors (*ponoi*) (22A7).[27] His work for the god is service (*latreia*) (23C1),[28] and he is a benefactor (*euergetēs*) (36C).[29] In Heracles, we behold a man who has become both hero and god. How strangely this contrasts with the humbling strains of Apollonian piety.

The Apollonian and the Heraclean are opposed ideals. Mortal humility and temperance belong to Delphic self-knowledge. Heracles is the man who became not only hero but also god. Perhaps Plato is suggesting that Delphic ambiguity may, in the figure of Socrates, transcend itself. From the path of Apollo there is also a parting of the ways toward the high road of Heracles. The Socratic choice of Achilles which we discussed above is an example of a departure from the passivity that we observed in the Homeric Achilles and, indeed, in the Apollonian fate of Croesus. It is perhaps in his Heraclean humanism that Socrates succeeds where so many failed in searching out the oracles of Delphi.

Care of the Self

In the *Theaetetus* Socrates argues that flight from the miseries of human existence consists in imitation of God (176AB), but he qualifies this state-ment by saying that this imitation is to be accomplished as far as possible. Here we may see that aspiration to divinity which belongs to the Heraclean Socrates. Yet it is pulled short by the considerations of Apollonian piety. The world of late antiquity was not to be so bashful. Plotinus declares that our concern should be not to be free of sin but to become a god (I 2 [19], 6, 3–4; cf. I 2 [19], 1, 1–4). We shall discuss later the Plotinian celebration of Heracles.

Socrates' response to the Delphic oracle, like that of Oedipus, consists in enquiry. It is also a project in self-knowledge. Yet Socrates is not, like Oedipus or Croesus, passive before circumstances beyond his control. In obedience to the god, he engages in the task of Socratic care (*epimeleia*) (*Apology* 29DE). This response is again Heraclean. In the story of Heracles at the crossroads, which Xenophon ascribes to Prodicus, Virtue tells Her-acles that the gods give nothing good or fair to humans without toil and care (*epimeleia*) (Xenophon *Memorabilia* 2.1.28.2). Heracles is not passive, as he chooses a life (*bios;* 2.1.21.9) of virtue over a life of vice. The Heraclean parting of the ways is clear, as the hero rejects the advances of the comely young woman, Vice, and follows the path of that more forbidding lady, Virtue. We can see here the difference between the passivity of a life accord-ing to the archaic view and active choice manifest in Heraclean care.

Socrates urges the Athenians to care (*epimeleisthai*) for the soul before their bodies or their wealth (*Apology* 29DE). He urges every Athenian to care for himself (*heautou*) before he cares for his affairs and to place care for the city itself above care for the affairs of the city (36C). It is obvious that care for the soul and care for oneself are equated. It is to be noticed that the Greek does not express care for the Self but care for oneself, using the reflexive pronoun.

Socrates is here playing with the traditional proverb that the man who best takes care of his affairs will best take care of the affairs of the city (Herodotus 5.29; Thucydides 2.40.2; 6.9.2; Plato *Protagoras* 318E). Clearly Socratic care is communal. The care for the soul is not a species of romantic withdrawal. It is also familial. Socrates urges the care for the soul upon his fellow Athenians as a father or an elder brother (*Apology* 31B). This provides us with a valuable key to interpretation. Parents would indeed wish children to prosper in their affairs. This is a major end of sophistic education (*Protagoras* 318E). Yet love will distinguish between this practical concern and the development of the child as a complete person. Socratic care is humanistic in its purpose to free the individual from entanglements in the world of business and politics. Yet this is a political humanism in that it wishes to base community upon the foundation of Socratic care. Care for the "city itself" may be understood in the light of Pericles' statement in Thucydides that the Athenians should become passionate lovers of their city, adorning it with great works of public art (2.43.1).[30] For the Socrates of Xenophon, care begins with the individual and extends in concentric circles to one's household, to friends, and to the city at large (*Memorabilia* 3.7.9; 4.5.1).

Care (*epimeleia, therapeia*) is a medical term.[31] It is used in Plato in a psychotherapeutic dimension, observing an analogy to medicine. In the *Charmides* Socrates recounts how, when he received a wound in Thrace, a shaman gave him an herb (156C–157C). Yet the therapy would not work unless at the same time that he received the herb upon his tongue he received an incantation into his soul. The whole person must be addressed by medical practice.[32] It is to be observed that, in the *Apology*, the physical aspect of care is not neglected. The Athenian is urged to care for the soul before the body (30A7–B1). It is a question of priority. The body should also be cared for, but true care begins with the soul or self. We may see in this a parallel to modern concern with holistic medicine.

It is a cliché of textbooks that compare Christian and pagan thought to remark that, whereas Plato entertains a dualism of body and soul, the church proclaims the wholeness and integrity of the human being.[33] The demonstrative context of the arguments in the *Phaedo* of Plato may be explained by the Pythagoreanism of Socrates' interlocutors, Simmias and Cebes.[34] This will account for the appearance of a rather crude dualism of body and soul in that dialogue. The serious student of Plato, however, will recognize that the soul is not, for that philosopher, a pale spirit temporarily entrapped in a tenement of clay. We are used to the notion that, for Plato, the soul (*psychē*) is equated with self (*autos*), that it is the locus of ethical decision and philosophical reasoning (*Apology* 29DE, 36C).[35] When Plato speaks of the body (*sōma*), he does not always refer only to a physical object. He also describes the body as subject. In the *Phaedo* the body as object is indeed mentioned, when Socrates ridicules the explanation of his presence in prison from the disposition of his bones and nerves (98CD). The body also, however, is the place of fears and desires (66BE) and, as such, the origin of greed, civil strife, and war. It is obvious that the body is also, besides the soul, self which makes (on the basis of delusion) ethical decisions. It is the task of the philosopher to separate the soul from the body (66Ea; 67A1; 67D). This is not merely the separation of the soul as subject from the body as object, but the separation of the philosophical from the bodily self ridden with fear and desire. The unpurified soul, which shares too much the desires of the body, becomes body-like (*sōmatoeides;* 81B5; 81C4; 81E1) and is drawn back to haunt the earth as a ghost (81BE).[36] We may see in the Socratic practice of death (*meletē tou thanatou;* 81A) not merely a rehearsal for physical death but the transformation of self, a dying to the identity that experience, circumstance, and inclination may have presented to us. Thus, the *Phaedo* is very much about life, a life in which archaic passivity before fate is replaced with contemplative will and control. It is another dimension of Socratic care.

The Unity of Virtue

In the archaic period self is seen as the sum of events as displayed over the tapestry of time. For Oedipus, to know himself is to know that he killed his father and married his mother. Knowledge of self is expressed externally, and freedom of will is not relevant in an essentially passive experience of life. For Socratic wisdom, as in the choice of Achilles as it is portrayed in the Platonic *Apology of Socrates,* care is expressed in freedom of will. For the Socratic Achilles, of course, freedom of will may result directly in acts. More profoundly, however, it is a way of contemplative inwardness which transforms the person. The acts of such a developed human being will flow naturally from the transformation itself.

In the *Republic* Plato speaks of the "inner man" who controls the multifarious beast of passion (589A7).[37] Virtuous acts or works flow from the cultivation of inwardness. In the same dialogue, he draws a distinction between "the external practice of one's affairs" and "the internal practice which is truly concerned with oneself and one's affairs" (443D; my translation). This reflects the language of Plato in the *Apology* where Socrates counsels the Athenians not to care for their affairs before they care for themselves, or to care for the affairs of the city before they care for the city itself (36C).

The inwardness of virtue has much to do with the notion that virtue is a unity. In the *Phaedo* Plato describes civic virtue as a mere exchange of counterfeit coins (69AB). We exercise courage in one matter or temperance in another only to avoid this pain or attain that pleasure. The good person will exchange all of this currency against the one true coin of the realm. In the *Protagoras* Socrates argues for the unity of virtue and attempts to show that Protagoras's inability to argue the question demonstrates its unteachability (329B). Later in the same dialogue, Socrates, arguing that virtue is knowledge, concludes that it must be teachable.

The question may well be asked whether such knowledge is merely the sum of correct moral definitions? Are we dealing with information or with transformation? In the *Republic* the philosopher's vision of light upon the completion of his education is described as a turning about, as if upon a revolving stage (518C21). After his ascent upon the ladder of love, the true lover is, in the *Symposium,* turned toward the whole sea of beauty (211D4). In each case, the object of vision is one. We are not speaking here of yet one more item of information, but of the turning about, the conversion of the person.

Bruno Snell argues that, since the word *sōma* (body) never refers in Homer to the living body but only to the corpse, Homer, who describes the physical entity of the human person as a disparate collection of limbs and parts, does not see the human person as a corporeal unity.[38] R. Renehan replies correctly that this argument from silence is insufficient, and he adduces passages from early texts in which indeed the word *sōma* does appear to be used of the living body.[39]

In the invocation to the Muse that begins the *Iliad,* the poet sings of the wrath of Achilles, which "hurled in their multitudes to the house of Hades strong souls / of heroes, but gave their bodies to delicate feasting of dogs, of all birds" (1.1–3). Lattimore, in this translation, happily paraphrases the Greek pronoun *autous,* "themselves," as "their bodies."[40] Certainly the *psychē* is scarcely to be identified with the seat of human identity and has a joyless existence in the Book of the Dead in the *Odyssey.* Achilles tells Odysseus that he would far rather be a poor man's slave in the land of the living than king in the realm of the dead (11.489–591). We may see a gulf between the care for the *psychē* as the seat of personality and ethical decision and intelligence in the Socratic tradition and the place of the *psychē* in Homer.[41] The funeral of Patroclus and the ransom of Hector's body in the *Iliad* demonstrate the enormous importance accorded to the corpse of the hero in Homer. A fine contrast of the difference in attitude may be seen in Plato's *Republic,* where it is urged that we should not rob the bodies of enemies, which are merely tools with which they fought and not themselves (469CE).

Snell argues, as we have seen, from the absence of a word for "living body" to the lack of a concept of corporeal unity in Homer. He further contends that the use of a variety of words other than *psychē* to describe psychic attributes shows a lack of any sense in Homer that the human being is a unity.[42] This view admits of the same refutation that is addressed to the supposed lack of corporeal unity in Homer. As Renehan observes, "For 'Homer', as for later Greeks, man was both a unified whole and an aggregate of discrete parts. His point of view was determined in each case by the needs and emphasis of the particular context."[43]

Happiness

Certainly Plato and his successors, with their philosophical focus upon inwardness, locate human identity in the soul,[44] soul in its rational aspect, or mind.[45] We have seen that, in the archaic period human identity consisted in the pattern of events that made up one's life. It was suggested that the philosopher introduced a measure of free will in offering us a choice of lives. Philosophical eudaemonism seeks the happy life for the human being (Theophrastus *apud* Cicero *De finibus* 5.29.86). If, however, human identity is located in the soul or mind, are things external to myself *qua* soul or mind crucial to my identity? If self consists in the attainment of a happy life, are things external to self as soul or mind necessary to that happiness and completion of identity?

This is a question that was much debated in antiquity. The answers range from the assertion that external goods are necessary to the happy life, to the view that the best life will include them, although happiness may consist in inwardness alone, to the notion that they are irrelevant to happiness.

In the *Philebus,* in examining the Delphic injunction "Know Thyself," Plato canvasses three kinds of ignorance: To think yourself to have more property than you have, to think your body superior to what it is, and (most common) to think yourself better than you really are in soul and in virtue (48CE). This passage demonstrates that human identity may be associated with the body and with wealth as well as with the soul.

27. Young Hunter with Dog. Red-figured Lekythos by the Pan Painter. Attic. Ca. 470–460 B.C.

28. Black-figured Terracotta Amphora. Athenian. Ca. 530–520 B.C.

Socratic care for the soul does not exclude the body and external goods. In the *Apology* Socrates reproaches the Athenians for caring more for money and honor than for wisdom, truth, and the soul (29DE). He goes on to say, "Wealth does not bring goodness, but goodness brings wealth" (30B). Burnet is scandalized by the notion that wealth might proceed from virtue.[46] He need not be. It is a question of priority. Similarly, Socrates urges the Athenians not to care for their bodies or wealth as much as for the soul (30A7–B1). This need not exclude concern or care for the good of the body.

For Aristotle, happiness consists in activity that is in accordance with virtue. Contemplation belongs to our noblest part and is therefore the activity in accordance with the highest virtue to which we may attain. Therefore, contemplation is the most complete happiness (*Nicomachean Ethics* 1177a12–19). He also argues that the wise one requires the necessities of life as much as others (1177a28–35). If these, however, are supplied, one has autarchy as compared with the just, brave, or temperate person who requires others for the practice of appropriate virtue. So, for Aristotle, although the life of contemplation is the happiest life, the wise one still requires external goods.

For the Stoics, happiness consists in virtue and virtue does not admit of degrees. Therefore, for Zeno, the wise one may be happy even on the rack (Cicero *De finibus* 5.29.85). The Stoics identify the ego with the governing principle, the chief part of the soul (Galen *De placitis Hippocratis et Platonis* 2.2, Müller). The Epicureans are, of course, at another extreme because of their equation of the good with pleasure. For them, in consequence, the ego is not the soul but the composite of soul and body (Plutarch *Adversus Colotem* 20.118D = *Testim.* 314 Usener; cf. 21:119A). Antiochus of Ascalon presents a compromise. He distinguishes between the happy life and the happiest life (*Academica priora* 1.6.22).[47] The former may consist in virtue alone; the latter requires external goods.

Humanity and the Gods

There are in antiquity two fundamental traditions concerning the relation between humanity and the gods. According to one, there is one race of humans and another of gods (Pindar *Nemean* 6.1–2). Another is that humans are of the same race as the gods (Orphic fr., Diels–Kranz 18; trans. K. Freeman). In Greek philosophy, the intellect is regarded as a divine element in our makeup.[48]

Empedocles teaches that we know like by like (Diels–Kranz fr. 109). We cannot perceive unless there is something in our composition that is of the same nature as that which is perceived. We know earth by earth and water by water. In the *Phaedo* Plato brings affinity and the Empedoclean epistemological principle together in a proof of the soul's immortality (79C–90D). We know the Forms not by the body but by the soul. The soul must be like the Forms, if it can know them. This likeness arises from affinity. The Forms are eternal. The soul has affinity with the Forms. Therefore the soul is immortal.

The imitation of God in the *Theaetetus* seems to be by way of knowing, for it consists in becoming "righteous with the help of wisdom" (176A). This would be knowledge that results in transformation of self, a becoming like the divine in knowing the divine. In the pseudo-Platonic *Alcibiades Major,* it is argued that if the soul wishes to know itself, it should look to its most divine part, the intellect (133BC). In this it will see, as in a mirror, both itself and God. Chrysippus interprets the Delphic commandment "Know Thyself" in accordance with the Stoic doctrine that we should live in agreement with nature (*apud* Cicero *De finibus* 3.73). Human beings, like all other animals, have a natural tendency to know themselves. But if they are to live in agreement with nature, they must first know the system of the universe and how it is administered. As the Stoics equate nature, reason, and God (Seneca *De beneficiis* 4.7–8 = *SVF* 2:1024), self-knowledge may in this context also be knowledge of God.

For Plotinus the beauty of the intelligible world is reflected in the world of sense. Thus the beauty of a temple exalts the mind toward the Soul (IV 3 [27], 11, 1–8). The discursive mind, when it enters quiet and ceases from its busy labors, may in contemplation reflect the hypostasis of Nous as in a mirror (I 4 [46], 10). Consciousness, for Plotinus, may exhibit a triadic structure. The intelligible world may at once be reflected both in the mirror of art and in the mirror of the mind. The discursive mind addresses itself in the first instance toward the sensible object. In the moment of reflection, both the mind and its objects are exalted and transformed. We may see in this the influence of the *Alcibiades Major* (133BC).

Plotinus also offers an itinerary to God which consists in introspection. If our waking consciousness is, upon analysis, seen to be insufficient to explain itself or the world, we must look elsewhere for an explanation. Thus, when the mind finds that all its explanation of beauty in terms of color, symmetry, and shape fails to explain such examples as a lone star in the night sky, it looks inward to Form and that in itself which is able to apprehend Form (I 6 [1], 1–3).

The hypostasis of Nous discovers the One in analysis of its own cognitive tools:

If it were only one, it would be sufficient unto itself and would not need to take consciousness of itself. Since indeed "Know Thyself" is addressed to those who, because of their multiplicity have the task of numbering their parts and learning their quantities and qualities and do not know all things, or know nothing, neither what is the ruling Principle, nor what is the Principle in accordance with which they are themselves. If the Principle is anything, it is greater than to be grasped by knowledge, thought, or consciousness itself. (VI 7 [38], 41, 22-27; trans. F. M. Schroeder)

The One is, in any case, always present in the consciousness of Nous, for the One is the light by which Nous sees itself and the Forms (VI 7, 16, 19-22). The quest for self and fulfillment in classical antiquity is, then, one that leads the human being into a relationship with God, who is the ground of identity.

The philosophical examination of self, in its direction of inwardness, displays a difference from the archaic view. It is more optimistic. The sense of biography, so important for the archaic mentality, is lacking. This may be seen in a striking interpretation of a text in Homer that is offered by Plotinus. In the *Odyssey*, Odysseus in the underworld recounts his vision of the shade of Heracles:

> Next I saw the strength of Heracles,
> An image (*eidōlon*); but he himself (*autos*) with the immortal gods
> Rejoices in abundance and has slender-footed Hebe,
> The child of great Zeus and Hera of the golden sandals.
> (11.601–4; trans. F. M. Schroeder)

This passage is doubtless an intrusion into the Homeric text and may proceed from post-Platonic Pythagoreanism.[50] There is a rich tradition in antiquity of philosophical and literary interpretation of this passage which reflects the questions that we have been discussing.[51]

Plotinus interprets this passage in such a way that the lower soul is Heracles the historical figure, and the higher, rational soul is Heracles himself.[52] It is asked whether, for the higher soul, there is memory of friends, children, wife, and country (IV 3 [27], 27). The lower human remembers these with passion, but the higher human retains these memories passively. Heracles in heaven will consider them slight. At this point a further Heracles is introduced. The Heracles who has been translated to the Plotinian Nous, where the divine mind is rapt in eternal contemplation of the Platonic Forms, will have no such memories (IV, 3, 32, 24; IV 4, [28], 1, 1–11).

In this consideration of Heracles, we may see that biography, which was crucial to the archaic sense of self, although still of contributory importance, is actually discounted in favor of the inner life. In communion with

Nous, it is not even remembered that here we have philosophized (IV 4, 1, 4–5). The passivity of the archaic view is overcome in the sense that philosophical care for the soul is a way that may be chosen and can lead to final happiness. On the other hand, the overcoming of that passivity does not emerge directly in action. It is resolved rather in the development of the interior life, the fruits of which may indeed be evident in a person's works. These are themselves, however, not a matter of final importance.

Notes

1. On structuralism as it pertains to Greek religion, see G. S. Kirk, *Myth: Its Meaning and Function in Ancient and Other Cultures* (Cambridge and Berkeley: University of California Press, 1970); idem, *The Nature of Greek Myths* (Harmondsworth: Penguin Books, 1974). On sociobiology, see W. Burkert, *Structure and History in Greek Mythology and Ritual* (Berkeley, Los Angeles, and London: University of California Press, 1979); idem, *Homo Necans: The Anthropology of Ancient Greek Sacrificial Ritual and Myth*, trans. P. Bing (Berkeley, Los Angeles, and London: University of California Press, 1983). On depth psychology, see E. Neumann, *The Origins and History of Consciousness*.

2. C. G. Jung, *Die Beziehungen zwischen dem Ich und dem Unbewussten* (Olten and Freiburg im Breisgau: Walter-Verlag, 1971) 65.

3. E. F. Edinger, *Ego and Archetype: Individuation and the Religious Function of the Psyche* (Harmondsworth: Pelican, 1973).

4. Herodotus, *The Histories*, trans. A. de Sélincourt (Harmondsworth: Penguin Books, 1954).

5. Onians, *The Origins of European Thought*, 411.

6. Ibid., 413.

7. H. Fränkel, "Die Zeitauffassung in der frühgriechischen Literatur," in *Wege und Formen frühgriechischen Denkens* (Munich: Beck, 1960) 1–2.

8. B. Snell, *Scenes from Greek Drama* (Berkeley and Los Angeles: University of California Press, 1964) 1, 17–22.

9. T. B. L. Webster, *From Mycenae to Homer* (New York: Norton, 1968) 205.

10. U. von Wilamowitz-Moellendorf, *Der Glaube der Hellenen* (Berlin: Akademie-Verlag, 1931) 1:12.

11. G. M. A. Grube, *Plato's Thought*, 150; Euripides *Helen* 560, trans. R. Lattimore.

12. Wilamowitz, *Glaube*, 17.

13. B. Snell puts forth the controversial view that Homeric man, failing of psychological unity and will, is the subject of divine manipulation ("The Homeric View of Man," in *Discovery*, 1–42). Snell argues elsewhere that in Homer the gods do not stand outside of nature ("The Olympic Gods," in *Discovery*, 23–42). If this is the case, then divine intervention is not supernatural. We may view it as an expression of an unexpected, internal event or a manifestation of power—hence divine.

14. E. R. Dodds, *The Greeks and the Irrational*.

15. H. Fränkel, *Dichtung und Philosophie des frühen Griechentums* (New York: American Philological Association, 1951) 86–88.

16. Trans. D. Grene, in *The Complete Greek Tragedies*, ed. Grene and Lattimore, 2:11–76.

17. C. M. Bowra, *Sophoclean Tragedy* (Oxford: Clarendon Press, 1944) 308–9.

18. U. von Wilamowitz-Moellendorf, *Euripides Herakles* (Berlin: Weidmann, 1895) 1:38.

19. H. A. Shapiro, "*Heros Theos:* The Death and Apotheosis of Herakles," *Classical World* 77 (1983) 9.

20. The Homeric *Hymn to Heracles* links the surpassing power of Heracles' feats in mortal life with his present divine status on Olympus (lines 6–8; trans. A. Athanasakis in *The Homeric Hymns*).

21. Cf. fr. B 146, where prophets and physicians are among those who attain to the last reincarnation and become gods.

22. Empedocles may be "thinking of his imminent release and apotheosis as already achieved"; see W. K. C. Guthrie, *A History of Greek Philosophy* (6 vols.; Cambridge: University Press, 1965) 2:246.

23. See Otto Kern, *Orphicorum Fragmenta* (fr. 32C, p. 107); and Guthrie, *History*, 246 (who offers this translation), 262; on Orphism and the fate of the soul, see K. Corrigan, "Body and Soul in Ancient Religious Experience" in this volume.

24. Wilamowitz, *Glaube*, 2:123.

25. For the usual translation of Heraclitus "I have searched myself," see K. Freeman, *Ancilla to the Pre-Socratic Philosophers.*

26. See also *Tragicorum Graecorum Fragmenta*, ed. B. Snell (2nd ed.; Hildesheim: Olms, 1983) Adespota 284=Diogenes Sinop. 88F4.

27. See also the story of Heracles at the crossroads in Prodicus *apud* Xenophon *Memorabilia* 2.1.28.

28. See also Sophocles *Trachiniae* 70; 830; trans. M. Jameson.

29. See also Euripides *Heracles* 1252, trans. W. Arrowsmith.

30. Cf. Pindar fr. 64, Bowra; Euripides *Medea* 824–865, trans. R. Warner.

31. For a medical use of *epimeleisthai*, see the Hippocratic treatise *Peri Technēs* 7.8–9; cf. the Hippocratic treatise *Peri Iētrou* 1.4; Plato *Laws* 720CE, trans. A. E. Taylor.

32. Pedro Lain-Entralgo, *Therapy of the Word*, 108–38.

33. R. Niebuhr, *The Nature and Destiny of Man* (New York: Scribner, 1941) 1:6–7.

33. See the reference to Philolaus in *Phaedo* 61D, trans. H. Tredennick. For the soul in Pythagoreanism, see K. Corrigan, "Body and Soul in Ancient Religious Experience" in this volume.

35. See also John Burnet, "The Socratic Doctrine of the Soul," in *Essays and Addresses*, 126–62.

36. See also W. K. C. Guthrie, "Plato's View on the Immortality of the Soul," in *Entretiens Hardt*, 3:4–22.

37. "Inner man" is my own translation. See the translation H. Tredennick in *Collected Dialogues*, 40–98.

38. Snell, "The Homeric View of Man," in *Discovery.*

39. Renehan, "The Meaning of *Sōma* in Homer," *California Studies in Classical Antiquity* 12 (1980) 279.

40. Ibid., 280.

41. Burnet, "The Socratic Doctrine of the Soul."

42. Snell, "The Homeric View of Man."

43. Renehan, "The Meaning of *Sōma* in Homer," 280. The nature of the debate will emerge well from the following: R. Renehan. "On the Greek Origins of the Concepts of Incorporeality and Immortality," *Greek, Roman and Byzantine Studies* 21 (1980) 105–38; D. B. Claus, *Toward the Soul*; J. Bremmer, *The Early Greek Concept of Soul*; L. Woodbury, review of the two foregoing books in *Ancient Philosophy* 8 (1983) 200–210. See also K. Corrigan, "Body and Soul in Ancient Religious Experience" in this volume.

44. Plato *Laws* 726A; 959B3–4; *Phaedo* 115CD ("I am this Socrates who is talking to you now," that is, the soul as distinct from the corpse which is to ensue upon his execution); the pseudo-Platonic *Alcibiades Major* 130C, the pseudo-Platonic *Axiochus* 65E.

45. Euripides fr. 1018, Nauck; Aristotle *Protrepticus* fr. 6, Ross (trans. *The Works of Aristotle*, ed. D. Ross, vol. 12, *Select Fragments* [Oxford: Clarendon Press 1952] 34–56); *Nicomachean Ethics* 1166a16–19; 1168b32–34; *Metaphysics* 1043b2; cf. 1032a8 and Ross's comments on both passages (trans. R. Hope, *Aristotle's Metaphysics*); Cicero *Republic* 6.24=*Somnium Scipionis* 8.26, trans. C. W. Keyes; Marcus Aurelius 1.22.52, trans. M. Staniforth.

46. *Plato's Euthyphro, Apology of Socrates and Crito*, ed. John Burnet (Oxford: University Press, 1924) ad loc.

47. See also J. Pépin, *Idées grecques sur l'homme et sur Dieu* (Paris: Les Belles Lettres, 1971) 64.

48. Plato *Timaeus* 73A; 88B; 90C; *Republic* 589E; Aristotle *Eudemian Ethics* 1248a27; *Nicomachean Ethics* 1248a27 and b28; pseudo-Platonic *Alcibiades* 1.133C; Cicero *Republic* 6.24=*Somnium Scipionis* 8.26; see also Pépin, *Idées*, 3–10.

49. See my "Representation and Reflection in Plotinus," *Dionysius* 4 (1980) 54–56.

50. J. Pépin, "Héraklès et son Reflet' in *Le Néoplatonisme, Colloques Internationaux du Centre National de la Recherche Scientifique, Sciences humaines, Royaumont 9–13 June 1969* (Paris: Éditions du Centre National de la Recherche Scientifique, 1971) 167–70, 187–92.

51. Ibid. (the entire article).

52. Ibid., 174–76; Plotinus VI 4 [22], 16; I 1 [53], 12.

Bibliography

Translations

Aristotle. *Aristotle's Metaphysics*. Translated by R. Hope. New York: Columbia University Press, 1952.

———. *Nicomachean Ethics*. Translated by M. Ostwald. Indianapolis, IN, and New York: Bobbs-Merrill, 1962.

Marcus Aurelius. *Meditations*. Translated by M. Staniforth. Harmondsworth: Penguin Books, 1964.

Cicero. *De Finibus*. Translated by H. Rackham. Loeb Classical Library. Cambridge, MA: Harvard University Press; London: Heinemann, 1971.

———. *Republic, De Legibus*. Translated by C. W. Keyes. Loeb Classical Library. London: Heinemann; Cambridge, MA: Harvard University Press, 1966.

The Complete Greek Tragedies. Edited by D. Grene and R. Lattimore. 4 vols. Chicago: University of Chicago Press, 1953–58.

Diogenes Laertius. *Lives of Eminent Philosophers*. Translated by R. D. Hicks. Loeb Classical Library. New York: Putnam; London: Heinemann, 1925.

Freeman, K. *Ancilla to the Pre-Socratic Philosophers*. Oxford: Blackwell, 1948.

Herodotus. *The Histories*. Translated by A. de Sélincourt. Harmondsworth: Penguin Books, 1954.

Hippocrates. *Collected Works*. Translated by W. H. S. Jones. Loeb Classical Library. New York: Putnam; London: Heinemann, 1923–31.

Homer. *The Homeric Hymns*. Baltimore, MD: Johns Hopkins University Press, 1976.

——. *The Iliad.* Translated by R. Lattimore. Chicago and London: University of Chicago Press, 1951.

——. *The Odyssey.* Translated by W. Shewring. Oxford and New York: Oxford University Press, 1980.

Pindar. *The Odes.* Translated by R. A. Lattimore. Chicago: University of Chicago Press, 1947.

Plato. *The Collected Dialogues.* Edited by E. Hamilton and H. Cairns. Princeton, NJ: Princeton University Press, 1961.

Plotinus. *The Enneads.* Translated by S. MacKenna. 3rd edition revised by D. S. Page. London: Faber & Faber, 1962.

Plutarch. *Adversus Colotem.* Translated by B. Einarson and P. H. De Lacy. *Moralia* 14. Loeb Classical Library. Cambridge, MA: Harvard University Press; London: Heinemann, 1967.

Thucydides. *A History of the Peloponnesian War.* Translated by R. Warner. Harmondsworth: Penguin Books, 1954.

Xenophon. *Memoirs of Socrates and the Symposium.* Translated by H. Tredennick. Harmondsworth: Penguin Books, 1970.

Modern Works

Armstrong, A. H. *An Introduction to Ancient Philosophy.* London: Methuen, 1965.

Bremmer, J. *The Early Greek Concept of Soul.* Princeton, NJ: Princeton University Press, 1983.

Burnet, J. "The Socratic Doctrine of the Soul." In *Essays and Addresses,* 126–62. London: Chatto & Windus, 1929.

Claus, D. B. *Toward the Soul: An Inquiry into the Meaning of psyche before Plato.* New Haven, CT, and London: Yale University Press, 1981.

Dihle, A. *The Theory of Will in Classical Antiquity.* Berkeley and Los Angeles: University of California Press, 1981.

Dodds, E. R. *The Ancient Concept of Progress.* Oxford: Clarendon Press, 1973.

——. *The Greeks and the Irrational.* Berkeley and Los Angeles: University of California Press, 1951.

Festugière, A.-J. *Personal Religion among the Greeks.* Sather Classical Lectures 26. Berkeley and Los Angeles: University of California Press, 1960.

Galinsky, G. K. *The Herakles Theme.* Oxford: Blackwell, 1972.

Grube, G. M. A. *Plato's Thought.* London: Methuen, 1931.

Guthrie, W. K. C. "Plato's View on the Immortality of the Soul." In *Entretiens Hardt,* 3:4–22. Vandoeuvres and Geneva: Fondation Hardt, 1955.

Lain-Entralgo, P. *The Therapy of the Word in Classical Antiquity.* Edited and translated by L. J. Rather and John M. Sharp. New Haven, CT, and London: Yale, 1970.

Neumann, E. *The Origins and History of Consciousness.* Translated by R. F. C. Hull. New York: Pantheon Books, 1954.

North, Helen. *Sophrosyne: Self-Knowledge and Self-Restraint in Greek Literature.* Ithaca, NY: Cornell University Press, 1966.

Nilsson, M. P. *Greek Piety.* Oxford: Clarendon Press, 1948.

Onians, R. B. *The Origins of European Thought about the Body, the Soul, the World, Time, and Fate.* Cambridge: University Press, 1951.

Renehan, R. "On the Greek Origins of the Concepts of Incorporeality and Immortality." In *Greek, Roman and Byzantine Studies* 21 (1980) 105–38.

————. "The Meaning of *Sōma* in Homer." *California Studies in Classical Antiquity* 21 (1980) 269–82.

Schroeder, F. M. "Representation and Reflection in Plotinus." *Dionysius* 4 (1980) 37–59.

Shapiro, H. A. "*Heros Theos:* The Death and Apotheosis of Herakles." *Classical World* 77 (1983) 7–18.

Snell, B. *The Discovery of the Mind.* Translated by T. G. Rosenmeyer. New York: Harper Torchbooks, 1960.

Woodbury, L. Review of D. B. Claus, *Toward the Soul,* and J. Bremmer, *The Early Greek Concept of Soul, Ancient Philosophy* 3 (1983) 200–210.

15

Body and Soul in
Ancient Religious Experience

K. Corrigan

MONG THE EARLIEST NOTIONS of soul perhaps the simplest is the idea that something survives the death of the body. Sometimes the sacred snake is possessed of the soul of the dead. Frequently the soul-ghost and the corpse are hardly distinguishable. The soul (especially that of the hero) continues to live in (and/or near) the tomb; it depends upon offerings of blood, food, or the trappings of earthly power for its well-being and can exert beneficent or maleficent influence. In both Greece and Rome the dead continue to play a part in the life of the living. On certain festivals they enter the upper world and must be appeased. In Hesiod the men of the golden age become spirits (*daimones*) after death and the guardians of their descendants. The classical latin *genius*, though originally the life force of the family or clan incarnated in the father of the family, is connected with the notion of ancestor guardianship and a strong sense of family continuity. Not only does the earth receive the dead; it also gives life and wealth.

The Greek *psychē* and *thymos*—and even more so the Latin *anima*, *animus, spiritus*—are connected with wind, breath, and air. In one version of the flood myth, humanity is formed anew when Athena and Prometheus breathe the winds into the clay figures they have molded. In Homer, female animals are thought to be impregnated by the wind, and in the art of later periods the various ideas of the soul as shade, bird, and air are frequently combined in the representation of the soul as a winged ghost-image hovering over the hero's head. In earliest times, then, the body is felt to be earthen, but the life principle something different, no matter how earthbound. And, of course, the idea that everything is endowed with soul and body, that everything is alive, either in its own right or by virtue of some divine agency, is very old.

Finally, the folk notion that a person's life depends upon something that can be distinguished from the person is seen in the legends of Meleager and Nisus, where life depends upon the preservation of some external object in which the "external soul" resides. The case of the shaman, whose soul leaves his body often for long periods of time, is also early.

Homer

The anthropomorphic gods of the Greeks and Romans shine with light, power, and intelligence. Supremely alive, they manifest the fullest meaning of body and its central importance in religious experience. In Homer the gods are arranged on the model of a human clan, and Zeus is the father of gods and humans. In Pindar we are said to resemble the gods in intelligence and bodily nature (*noos, physis*), but, although both races are born from one mother, the two classes in this feudal clan are separated by a great gulf (*Nemean* 6.1). Perhaps the most important difference between the two is that mortals possess a *psychē*, a life principle that can be lost in death. With very few exceptions, the *psychē* is never ascribed to a god.

Homer has no organic view of the body (for him the body is an aggregate; *sōma*, the later word for living body, most often means "corpse"), but the body and its life are the center of his attention. Three principal words cover the area of the soul: *psychē, thymos,* and *noos*. The *thymos* is the conscious, feeling soul, and the *noos* is the action and seat of intelligent seeing. They belong to the body and they perish with it. The *psychē* alone survives: in the living person it is simply the life that can be lost; in death it is the pallid, strengthless shade. It is connected with the breath that escapes from the hero's mouth at the moment of death. The Homeric souls disappear like smoke or chirp like bats or birds (*Odyssey* 11.206; 24.6; *Iliad* 23.10). It is also connected with the blood of the fatal wound through which the soul escapes. In the opening lines of the *Iliad* a sharp distinction is made between the heroes *themselves,* that is, their dead bodies, and their soul-shades sent down to Hades. The soul-shade, therefore, is less real than the dead body. For Homer, to live means to live the life of the body, and this remains true of those special instances in the *Odyssey* (4.561–69) and also in Hesiod (*Works and Days* 167–73) where certain heroes escape death and are conveyed *body and soul* to the Elysian Plain or the Isles of the Blessed, situated at the ends of the earth. But if the only function ascribed to the *psychē* in the living person is that it leaves the person, what importance does the Homeric *psychē* have for later development and what bearing, if any, upon religious experience?

Psyche

Although the Homeric *psychē* is a limited notion, its dramatic significance is much greater. The hero is not a closed unit with the well-defined boundaries of later thought. All his thoughts and emotions are displayed on a common stage as he addresses himself or the god who so often initiates his thinking.

The *Iliad* concerns the wrath of Achilles, the *Odyssey* the homecoming of Odysseus. Prominent in both poems in different ways is the fundamental struggle *for life*. In the fifth century, Empedocles will proclaim that he is a fugitive, an exile from the gods. Achilles is not a fugitive, but his mortality is in strong contrast to his immortal connections. Agenor says of Achilles: "There is psyche in him, and men say that he is mortal" (*Iliad* 21.569). With bitterness Achilles makes it clear that material possessions and all the trappings of external rank are not worth the life (*psychē*) one has to lose: "You cannot steal or buy back a man's life, when once the breath has left his lips" (9.401-9). The *psychē* is not an abstract conception so much as an objective entity that expresses value even more effectively for its negative "shade" connotation and for its very concreteness. Since death always lurks in the background whenever it is mentioned, a dramatic tension and an intensity are produced. The *psychē*, then, acts as a dramatic pivot.

In the opening lines of the *Odyssey*, Odysseus is said to have suffered many pains in his *thymos* in striving for his *psychē* and the return of his companions. This striving for life/*psychē* is here represented for the first time in the form of a journey to a mortal home. In book 5, so different from the figure we have expected, Odysseus weeps inconsolably on Calypso's island, a mortal unable to abide the promise of eternity. Odysseus is literally a fugitive from immortality.

This journey to a mortal home, however, is intimately linked to religious experience. Athena is everywhere in the *Odyssey*. Sacrifice, libation, prayers, dreams, visitations are major parts of the communion between gods and humans in both poems, but humans must also live their own lives. For on that stage there is an intensity that expresses something divine about humans—their courage, endurance, intelligence, etc.—qualities that are heightened by proximity to and personal contact with the gods, but also qualities that in the literal sense cannot be ascribed to divinity itself.

Body

Related to this is the case of body. In classical Greek sculpture the ultimate objective was to fashion the body in such a way that the spirit shone through the perfection of the physical form. Much earlier, in the *Odyssey* and the *Homeric Hymns,* the special quality of divinity and divine favor was the enhanced and luminously beautiful body. Demeter, in the *Hymn to Demeter,* casts off her disguise of old age, and immortal radiance fills the house with brillance (*Hymn to Demeter* 275–80). Divine light also guides human beings and transfigures their environment (*Odyssey* 19.30). Athena's transformations of Odysseus in Ithaca are a means of indicating the true stature of his soul. But here the picture is complex. There is, first, the contrast between the beggarly outward appearance and the persisting inner identity of Odysseus, and it is noteworthy that the principal recognition (by Penelope) is not physical but intellectual. This indicates the very strength of the man's whole being over his external appearance. Whether by accident or by design on the part of the poet(s), Athena merely magnifies Odysseus's limbs. Second, it is not so much that the inner is to be chosen for its own sake, but that the wretched outer appearance (the disguise) can be a more fundamental, more honest level of being. Odysseus, the beggar, discovers the true dispositions of everyone connected with his household. His position of maximum vulnerability is also one of maximum potentiality. Dramatically, he has "nothing" to lose and everything to gain. Here we encounter the power in the other pole of transfiguration: in the most wretched being divinity can reside. The suitors themselves are aware of this; Antinous throws a stool at Odysseus but is rebuked by another suitor on the grounds that the beggar, Odysseus, might turn out to be a god from heaven (*Odyssey* 17.484–87). Here, then, are several ways of apprehending divinity: in the light and beauty that augment the human form and give it deeper meaning, and, in contrast, in the recognition of value in the unlikeliest shape and size, the impoverished, unattractive stranger, protected by Zeus himself.

Poetic, Prophetic, Telestic, and Erotic Inspiration

In the seventh to fourth centuries there was no master idea to account for the rise of new conceptions of soul. The gulf between gods and humans was bridged by (1) translation (in which the whole person, body and soul, achieved immortality), (2) the hero cult, and perhaps also (3) the idea of the helping and suffering god (i.e., Prometheus and Cheiron and Asclepius). But even here, as in cases of the attempted immortalization of human beings, the outcome tended to intensify the plight of mortal creatures.

In poetic inspiration, however, and in the personal voice of the god at Delphi, speaking through the Pythia and granting divine knowledge, purification, and healing, there was a living relationship with divinity. At the same time, the development of a concept of law brought a new sense of the importance of the individual within the clan. Furthermore, the presence of dynamic, religious individuals and movements and the inner needs they answered were most important to a new and heightened conception of the soul.

The ecstatic worship of Dionysus from Lydia or Thrace offered a new form of union with the divine and an enhanced sense of one's being. The bacchants fled from normal sensibility into the wilds and at the height of their ecstasy tore to pieces a beast, which they believed to be the god himself, and ate its flesh raw, thereby enhancing their own vital powers. We cannot say how far this rending (*sparagmos*) and eating (*ōmophagos*) are connected with the concepts of death and resurrection which appear in the cult of Dionysus in later times. This temporary union, however, was seen as a purification of the soul and an inner commitment, shared by all the bacchants, to Dionysus, which must have offered some hope for the quality of survival the soul-shade might expect after death with Dionysus, the lord of souls. Here the normal barriers or limits of the personality were destroyed, and the soul entered into the community of fellow initiates (Euripides *Bacchae* 72–77), experiencing a kinship with the whole of nature, which was transformed together with it (*Bacchae* 726–27).

The notion of an inner, hidden self is suggested also by the deepest experience of love. Archilochus proclaims that he is unsouled (*apsychos*) by love (fr. 84, Edmonds), which suggests that the experience is a kind of death. Sappho describes how, when she unexpectedly sees her beloved, all the visible world becomes distant and her "psyche flew away with her wits" (fr. 118A, Edmonds). Here the flight of the Homeric *psychē* suggests that the experience is more intense than the life of normal consciousness and points to the emergence of a new consciousness, however unidentifiable.

Orphics and Pythagoreans

The first mention of the soul's divine origin occurs in a fragment of Pindar (fifth century) where the Homeric values of body-life and soul-shade are inverted (fr. 131, Sandys). Although the body must die, what survives is an image of life (*eidōlon aiōnos*), which sleeps during normal bodily consciousness but wakes up while the body sleeps and foresees future events in prophetic dreams. This "image" survives because it alone is from the gods.

The waking–sleeping antithesis and the idea that the divine reality of the soul is perceived only in isolation from the body and its functions are related to Orphic and Pythagorean views, according to which the human soul is immortal, subject to punishments or rewards in the underworld after death, and capable of being incarnated in beasts. If the soul survives death, it must also have existed before birth. Thus arise the theories of metempsychosis and cycles and a more vibrant conception of the soul-shade in Hades. This also leads to a radically pessimistic view of the relation between body and soul: the body is thought of as a tomb, in which the soul is buried (Plato *Cratylus* 400C), or as a prison, in which the gods keep the soul locked until it purges its guilt (Plato *Phaedo* 62A–E), or (by Empedocles in the fifth century) as "the strange garment of alien flesh" (Diels-Kranz fr. 126). According to an Orphic myth, the human race is born from the soot of the Titans who are destroyed by Zeus for the rending and devouring of the child Dionysus. Humanity, therefore, has two elements in its composition: a Titanic nature, the evil inheritance, and a Dionysiac nature, a spark of divine life, the soul.

This soul is conceived in a concrete fashion. It is, for the Orphics, borne upon the winds and it enters the body from the universe by respiration (Aristotle *On the Soul* 410b27). For the Pythagoreans it is identified with the dust motes in the air (or with that which moves them) (*On the Soul* 404a17). In Empedocles we are made to feel the torment of a personal experience, as the soul, which for him is a divine spirit (*daimōn*)—"in me you see a deathless god and no longer mortal" (fr. 112)—is compelled by its sin to enter the cosmic cycle and pass through many forms before it returns to god (fr. 115). In several places in Pindar we find the idea that this life is parallel to the waking life of the soul after death. The soul lives in both lives alternately and can sin or do good in both, but the ultimate aim is freedom from the wheel of rebirth (frs. 129–31, 133–34, 137, Sandys; *Olympian* 2.65). One of the principal demands, therefore, prompted by such beliefs is moral purity and purification from bodily pollution. This takes the form of an *askēsis*, in which the avoidance of animate foods is a major requisite. Like any regimen, especially one that disdains the body as evil, this can devolve into superstitious practices. But the major impetus of both movements is decidedly positive. The line between soul and body, although clear in death, is enormously flexible in life, since the soul too is conceived of in such a material way that the whole of nature is charged with its significance. Because of the kinship between all life—divine, human, and animal— a new respect for life and a sense of its greater dimensions are established.

In the *Cratylus* (400C), in his report of the Orphic body-tomb (*sōma-sēma*) doctrine, Plato mentions two other etymologies of the term *sōma*: (1) that it is kept safe (*sōzetai*) and (2) that it is the sign (*sēma*) of the soul, in that the soul gives signs to body. These two explanations are perhaps not unconnected with the idea (from Pindar above) that the soul sleeps in the body during normal consciousness. This thought is developed in Xenophon (*Cyropaedia* 8.7.21), Plato (*Republic* 571D), and Aristotle (fr. 10; cf. Aeschylus *Eumenides* 104): when the soul is alone (in sleep) it possesses true prophetic insight. This became the foundation for the Stoic philosophy of divination and also a regulating force in normal temple procedure. When in need of healing or initiation at one of the great shrines, the pilgrim waited for the confirmation of a god-inspired dream. Earlier, in the Hippocratic writings, it was developed into a theory of the soul's primacy and charge over all psycho-physical well-being (*On Regimen* 4.86). Even the nonrational intuition of the soul, therefore, was thought to have a decided effect upon the ordinary running of *this* life.

Finally, the Pythagorean spiritual ideal "to follow god" also included a rational discipline: the contemplation of the order of the universe and of the rhythmical relations, expressible in mathematical proportions, of music, song, and dance (Diogenes Laertius *Lives* 8.8). This led the Pythagoreans to the value of practical pursuits—medicine to purify the body, music to purify the soul (Diels-Kranz 1:468, 20). The physician, Alcmaeon of Croton, theorized that physical health is the harmonious mixing (*isonomia*) of opposites. This notion later became linked (perhaps in the Pythagorean Philolaus) to the soul; thus, the soul is seen as the harmony or attunement of the body. In the orators and in Democritus (where the soul is first contrasted to the body) the discovery of a proper balance between excess and defect depends upon the moral perfection of soul (Lysias 24.3; Democritus frs. 31, 187, 191; cf. Antiphon the Sophist fr. 2). Here, as earlier, the soul is conceived of as material and vulnerable. If in Homer the *psychē* serves as a dramatic pivot between life and death, and if for the Orphics and the Pythagoreans it is a traveler between life and death, perhaps it is not accidental that in the opposition between health and sickness, where human vulnerability is most deeply revealed in conscious life, the soul should assume another pivotal role as the balance or balancing agent between physical or moral opposites.

Soul, Body, and Sky

Let us return to the apprehension of divinity in the light that augments the human or divine form. Zeus, above all, is associated with fire and lightning. In Homer, "to see the rays of the sun" means "to be alive" (*Iliad* 16.188; *Odyssey* 11.498). In a passage of Pindar, in contrast, the dual nature of the human being appears sharply silhouetted: the human being is nothing but a dream of a shadow. "But, when a gleam of sunshine comes as a gift from heaven, a radiant light rests on men and a gentle life" (*Pythian* 8.95; cf.

Sophocles *Ajax* 125–26). However metaphorical, this suggests that the illumination in human nature is something granted to humans over and above their mortal nature and yet that it is also in some sense natural to them. Heraclitus transfers this luminosity to the soul itself, and for the first time the soul is associated with wisdom: "A gleam of light is the dry soul, wisest and best" (fr. 118; trans. C. H. Kahn; cf. test. 15). The temperate soul shines out like a beacon, just as a man "strikes a light for himself in the darkness, when his sight is quenched" (fr. 26).

The Greek *psychē* also means breath, as does the Latin *anima*. One of the early Milesian philosophers, Anaximenes, believed that the air is god, and he drew an analogy between the air, which sustains the universe, and the human soul: "As our soul, being air, holds us together, so do breath and air (*pneuma, aēr*) surround the whole universe" (fr. 2).

This theory is developed by Diogenes of Apollonia in the fifth century. Human beings and the other animals live on air, by breathing, and this is soul and mind to them (*psychē, noēsis*) (fr. 4). There is a hierarchy of air: air outside the organism, air inside, and air in the upper sky. "The soul of all animals is the same, namely air which is warmer than the air outside, in which we live, though much colder than that near the sun" (fr. 5, 14–17). Ultimately, air is an intelligent force that directs everything in the universe (fr. 5; cf. Aristophanes *Clouds* 224–30).

The Greeks also distinguished two layers in the atmosphere: *aēr*, a lower layer, comprising haze, mist, and fog;, and *aithēr*, the pure, luminous upper sky. Sometimes *aithēr* means air, sometimes fire; it is the home of Zeus and is sometimes identified with him (Euripides fr. 877). In the fifth century it became part of popular belief that the souls of the dead, their breath, fly off to the *aithēr*, while their bodies revert to the earth.[1] A line of Aristophanes indicates that the stars were popularly supposed to be the souls of dead men, and an old Pythagorean *acousma* shifted the Elysian Fields and the Isles of the Blessed from a mythical point in the west to the sun and moon (Aristophanes *Peace* 832ff.; Pythagoreans, Diels-Kranz 1:464, 6).

The Term Psychē
from the Sixth to the Fourth Century B.C.

Alongside this opening up of the cosmic dimensions of humanity, *psychē* itself in the sixth to fourth centuries bears a wide variety of meaning. It remains vulnerable and material. It assimilates the functions of the Homeric *thymos* (the conscious, emotional self) and becomes the seat of passion, courage, and love. But this intensifies its value; the *psychē*, therefore, is the moral self, because true or inner values are what make life (or the life after death) worth living (Pindar *Olympian* 2.70; *Nemean* 9.39; Hesiod *Works and Days* 686; Theognis 530; Sophocles *Antigone* 322 [cf. 1063]; Euripides *Andromache* 418). In this usage it is seen as the mental correlate of body (*sōma*), but it can also stand for the living or dead (shade) person, as can *sōma* (Sophocles *Oedipus Tyrannus* 64, 643; Pindar *Olympian* 9.33ff). It has a nonrational intuition and can establish contact with the supernatural in dreams. It also comes to possess an intellectual element (Sophocles *Philoctetes* 55, 1013; fr. 101; *Electra* 903; *Antigone* 227; Euripides *Orestes* 1180; Antiphon 4.1.17; 5.93). The idea of *psychē* as an intellectual agent seems to stem from earlier usages in which an intense, intellectual decision must be made in the context of *psychē*/life: Odysseus performs every mental trick to save his life/*psychē*; Theognis is "bitten in his *psychē*" concerning which course of life he will choose (*Odyssey* 9.422–23; Theognis 910; cf. Pindar *Pythian* 3.40–42).

The Internal/External Distinction and Heraclitus

The lyric poets develop the epic's distinction between outer appearance and inner reality. In the priamels of Sappho, against the background of every conceivable external good, "the fairest thing is the one I love." For Archilochus an outward show of splendor detracts from the inner good. As B. Snell has argued, this points to a new conception of soul, at once more individual and more interior.[2]

This antithesis is also important in the ordinary ritual of Greek religious life. The story is told of a man who made costly sacrifices at Delphi and asked the oracle who did the gods the greatest honor. To his astonishment the Pythia gave the name of an obscure man who regularly performed all the little offices of the domestic worship of Hermes and Hecate. Proper ritual piety, therefore, is expressed in fulfilling the god's prescriptions exactly and in avoiding unnecessary external panoply.[3] In serious situations of need, purification or continuing purity comes principally from normal and exact religious observances, which are not simply an external therapeutic but a natural transformation of the person, an organic spiritualization of the ordinary person who observes the sacred throughout life.

In the difficult but powerful fragments of Heraclitus we find a new moral, religious, and intellectual outlook on soul and body. Heraclitus's whole attitude to popular religious practice is characterized by a new inner perceptiveness. Fr. 119, "character is destiny" (*ēthos anthrōpōi daimōn*) focuses attention upon the human being rather than on superstitious fear of the unknown.

Heraclitus's view of soul is physiological, and yet it also breaks new psychological ground. First, the soul is a nature like air, *aithēr* or fire (fr. 118), related to the cosmic fire. Drunkenness is, for example, harmful to soul's dry nature (fr. 117). Second, the soul is, in one testimony (67), likened to a spider that has its seat in the center of a web (the body), but can move to any point of the web to effect repairs. In this analogy the soul is self-moving and creative; it is a central faculty that interprets sense data by its power for connected reasoning. Third, the notion of soul opens upon a larger spiritual dimension. As Snell has shown, the soul exhibits spiritual depth: "You could not find the ends of the soul though you traveled every way, so deep is its logos" (fr. 45).[4] It exhibits a capacity for augmentation from within, in contrast perhaps to the traditional divine "magnification" from without: "The soul has a divine *logos* which increases itself" (fr. 115). Finally, it exhibits comprehensiveness: "The divine logos is common" (*koinon;* fr. 2); it pervades everything and everything shares in it.

As opposed to the esoteric and nonrational knowing of the soul in the "Orphic" fragment of Pindar, the *psychē* in Heraclitus is a principle of rational cognition. But its new cognitive and spiritual nature cannot be separated from its physiological functions nor from the elementary tension between meanings which constitutes its being. At every point Heraclitus exploits *psychē*'s ambiguity, life or shade, and its pivotal balance between life and death. But most important, he transforms the dynamic intensity of soul, central to the epic drama, into a persisting balanced tension between opposites in an ever-changing world. This dynamic grasp in eternal flux is wisdom. Because of the constant change of all things, everything is vividly and dramatically new[5]—taut with discovery, since all necessary intellectual ingredients are present, and balanced between life and death. Soul is the principle of this intensely vital balance.

The Cosmic God and Presocratic Philosophy

In the Presocratics generally the soul is linked to a new conception of god, no longer anthropomorphic but cosmic, a god who in Anaximander is conceived of as boundless, eternal, unaging, and, therefore, divine. For Xenophanes this one god is similar to mortals neither in body nor in thought (fr. 23–26; cf. Empedocles fr. 133). All divine actions are whole and complete in themselves. In Heraclitus the divine logos is the basis of human cognition. Human beings' inner purity and indeed also their happiness depend rather on it than on external rituals or bodily pleasures (frs. 69, 4).

Together with this spiritualization, the human being is seen as the world in microcosm. For Diogenes of Apollonia the human soul is related to its

body as god to the universe. Air, the cosmic principle, is literally comprehensive. It reaches everywhere, arranges everything, and is in everything
(Diogenes fr. 5, Diels-Kranz 2:61, 6–8). In the early Milesian philosophers
this first principle is a stuff eternally self-moving, and everything is sorted
out by differentiation. Gradually the idea of a moving force (already implicit
in Hesiod's Love), separate from what is moved, emerges. Ultimately the
traditional belief in the divinity of the heavenly bodies is challenged, and
the sun, to the shock of Athens, is described as "a lump of incandescent
rock." Anaxagoras terms his new principle *nous,* and perhaps his major
reasons for doing this were because the term *psychē* still bore material and
vulnerable connotations and because his *nous* was both a physical and an
intellectual principle, which knows and anticipates all things but which is
not part of the mixture (fr. 12).

If all nature is alive with the divine, how can one draw a distinction
between the living and the nonliving? This was felt to be a question of
degree. The cosmos exhibits a hierarchy of vitality or mobility, from the
perpetual (and, therefore, divine) mobility of the heavenly bodies, likened
to soul mobility by Alcmaeon (test. 12), to the comparative lack of mobility
in "inanimate" solids. In Atomism the body is composed of large, rough
atoms and the soul of smooth, round fire-atoms (like quicksilver), which by
their greater mobility move the body (Democritus, tests. 104, 103). Democritus drew a sharp distinction between body and soul (frs. 37, 187); but he
also thought that all things, even dead bodies, share in soul of a kind
because they still retain a portion of heat and of the sensitive faculty when
the greater part has been dispersed by air (test. 117). Soul, therefore, forms
a hierarchy of finer matter; body, of denser matter.

Two further notions are important: the "independent" living body and
the "extended" soul. In Empedocles and Anaxagoras we find theories of
natural composition based upon the mixing of basic ingredients. In the
former, the evolution of natural forms takes place without divine purpose
(Aristotle *Physics* 198b–199a). However, in Anaxagoras and Diogenes the
structure of body would not have been possible without a teleological principle of creative order, Mind. For a Pythagorean like Philolaus, the human
being is a microcosm of the whole chain of life: the brain is "human," the
heart "animal." The navel (i.e., the root) is held in common with plant life,
and the reproductive organs are common to all things, since all is from seed
(Philolaus fr. 13). Here, then, the living body begins to assume an independence and to exhibit a natural hierarchy of functions and organic
composition. It progresses toward higher consciousness—soul or mind.

In contrast, the idea of soul or mind is implicitly extended to include the
divine, spiritual, and intellectual motive force as well as the mortal

29. Grave Stele of Apollonia. Hellenistic. Ca. 100 B.C.

consciousness. The life–death, immortal–mortal, opposition remains fundamental, but soul's vulnerability stands in antinomy to its new comprehensiveness. One of the major problems resulting from this antinomy is how
the two are related, a problem that in Eleatic philosophy is cast in the
antithesis of the One and the Many, the way of Being and the way of
Seeming.

On the other hand, in many of the Sophists (notably Critias fr. 25) not
only are human beings themselves spontaneously generated from earth and
water by the action of heat, but so are their religion and ideals too. Once
the human being becomes the measure of all things and soul is identified
with perception (in Protagoras), although the soul is still conceived of as
a critical balance, that balance is no longer dramatic as in Homer. There
is no other spectator of the soul nor extra dimension in which the solitary
perceiver can realize deeper (and also perhaps tragic) expressions of the
world.

Suffering and Illumination

There is a further type of purification that has a profound influence upon
the idea of the soul: the discovery of illumination in either the most
ordinary object or the extremity of darkness and need. In the Eleusinian
Mysteries the death and rebirth of the annual deity, so central a part of
archaic and pre-archaic religious ritual, find a deeply human expression in
the story of Demeter's anguish, her disguise and transformation, the discovery of Persephone (the life-principle or soul of the blossoming earth)
and her return to the light. The climax of the mysteries was something
seen, perhaps a dramatic reenactment of the myth, culminating in a brilliant
light, and the display of a sacred ear of corn—the germ of life, the ordinary
transformed by brilliant meaning. Doubtless a different quality of life after
death was promised by initiation. But the major emphasis was upon understanding and illumination in this life (Pindar fr. 137, Edmonds; Euripides
Bacchae 72–75; cf. Hymn to Demeter 480). Cicero states that by virtue of the
mysteries "we have been brought out of our barbarous mode of life to
humanitas and learned the real principles of life" and that "we have received
the means of living with happiness and of dying with a better hope" (De
legibus 2.14.36).

Plutarch compares the passage of soul into the other world with the
inspiration of initiation into the great mysteries. Like the soul, the initiand
is wholly changed and transformed. At the moment of greatest weakness
illumination comes; out of the feebleness of the soul a new soul is disclosed
(Stobaeus Anthologium 4.107–8).

Nowhere is this insight more poignantly illustrated than in Sophocles' presentation of Oedipus the king. In successive scenes Sophocles "strips" Oedipus of his benevolent priesthood and kingship, then of his "tyranny" (lines 300–462, 513–648), then even of his family and domestic relationships. Oedipus cannot even remain in the temporary comfort of being a "child of fortune," nor is he allowed to rest with the acceptance of the lowliest birth. He must be made equal to the terrible truth in which, as the chorus immediately proclaims in apostrophe, you generations of men are "equal to the nonliving" (lines 1186–87). Out of this zero point, a way is found back into life, and Oedipus becomes at Colonus a source of life for Attica in his death. The old hero cult is here given new spiritual significance since the tragic flaw and subsequent struggles of Oedipus contrast strongly with the exploits of the typical Greek hero. In the *Oedipus Coloneus* Oedipus asks his daughters to make reparation to the Eumenides on whose holy ground he has trespassed: "for I think that one soul suffices to pay this debt for ten thousand, if it comes with good will to the shrine" (lines 498–99). This thought reflects upon Oedipus himself and suggests a complex view of the relation between soul and body. Soul is the moral and spiritual achievement of the whole person (Sophocles fr. 98). It has won the right of interceding for many, but strikingly it is from the wretched body, or corpse, that Attica will be blessed: "I came to give you the gift of my miserable body (*demas*), not much to look at; but the benefits from it are greater than fair shape" (*Oedipus Coloneus* 576–79).

Socrates

Socrates is just a little like Oedipus—an ugly old man, but one of enormous inner vitality, with great courage, integrity, and marvelous powers of intellectual concentration—in short, a man to transform the meaning of *psychē*. The Delphic oracle changed his life by pronouncing him the wisest man in Greece. His subsequent search for knowledge led him to the conviction that his only wisdom consisted in the knowledge of his own ignorance and that knowledge of the good could not be inculcated by an external Sophistic technique, but must spring organically from the soul's full and immediate realization of the good. Under Socrates' questioning, or "midwifery," the soul of his interlocutor undergoes a painful process of giving birth: out of hopeless perplexity it is brought to see the truth for and in itself. Here the soul is the intellectual and moral personality for the first time, no longer simply a part of medical regimen but the most precious part of the human being, the source upon which all health depends (Plato *Charmides* 155D)— no longer the life of the body alone, but true insight into the good and just life (Plato *Crito* 48AB; *Republic* 353–54; *Gorgias* 504B–C). For the first time, both animals and *gods* possess life (*psychē*), which suggests a hierarchy of soul functions with the divine soul at the summit (Plato *Euthydemus* 302DE). It is also part of Socrates' deep and personal reverence for the gods that the world is ordered to the best by good, intelligent divine powers. Each thing, therefore, possesses its own good and since the natural good of humans is the health of their souls, it is a religious duty to care for the soul above all else (Plato *Apology* 30B; *Laches* 185E) and to make it good by realizing objective goodness in themselves.

Plato

This is part of the inheritance of Plato. We may add the following: (1) the Pythagorean theory that there is an eternal order underlying sensible reality which is expressible in number, harmony, and geometrical pattern; and (2) the Orphic-Pythagorean idea that the soul is a fallen god, imprisoned in the body, which existed before birth and which can after death realize its divinity. In the eschatological myths of Plato the soul retains in the underworld the personal and intellectual consciousness of its historical existence and bears full responsibility for its choice of a new life, animal or human. Plato believed that the only true way to save ethical norms and even physical objects, ourselves included, from either the relativism of naming by convention or the eternal flux of sensual existence was to posit an inherent value in those objects themselves, to recognize their objective, eternal reality, or Idea, independent of the mind which knows them. The human faculty that knows these Ideas, "themselves in themselves," is the soul. Since the body is no longer "like" god, the human being's likeness to god lies in this soul, which contemplated these Ideas before birth and can be reminded of them during life.

This way of thinking naturally produces an antithesis between body and soul, between the sense world of Heraclitean flux and the unchanging, intelligible world of Forms. Nowhere is this antithesis more pronounced than in the *Phaedo*. Here soul is a unity of intellect as opposed to the body, which is the seat of sense perception, passions, etc. The soul must be withdrawn from the body and purified, for it is immortal and kin to the eternal Forms. The philosopher must "practice death," that is, the separation of soul from body.

Perhaps paradoxically, however, the real focus of the *Phaedo* is this life. The dialogue reexamines the original Homeric context of *psychē*, the dramatic tension between life, loss of life, and death. Socrates takes the place of the epic hero, but he faces a slightly different set of alternatives: death will bring either oblivion or a new life. An intense dramatic value resides in the fact that whereas Socrates, in confronting death, embodies the very substance sought in the discussion, we, like his companions, are only too aware of imminent loss and of the gap between the reality of soul and the arguments employed to make us see its reality. The prospect of Socrates' death, therefore, brings us to confront the dramatic and religious value of soul here and now. Soul is an objective (and vulnerable [*Phaedo* 81BE]) reality; it is *ousia*, all that makes life worth having.

In contrast to the primary emphasis of the *Phaedo*, some of the middle and later dialogues explore the idea of soul as a multiplicity, a locus of internal conflict in the human being. First, the soul is more comprehensive, comprising not only the reason (*logistikon*), located in the head, but also the higher emotions (*thymos*), located in the breast, and the lower passionate part (*epithymetikon*), in the belly.[6] In the *Phaedrus* the rational faculty is likened to a charioteer, and the other faculties to two horses, one good and one bad. Here the tripartite soul is in fine tension, since its focus, bad or good, depends on the proper control of the lower elements by the charioteer. When controlled, each faculty fulfills its own task properly (*Republic* 586E–587A). The lower soul is mortal; the higher has been given to us by god as a *daimōn*. Second, in the *Phaedrus*, the souls of the gods are composite, like ours, but the essential differences seem to be that they are unmixed with evil and free from the degenerate effects of having bodies and in this way are perceived as pure unities (*Phaedrus* 246A; *Republic* 611A–612A). Third, in the *Symposium*, in the speech of Socrates on *erōs*, Plato combines the celestial and terrestrial poles of love in the theory of soul. Love is both immortal and mortal, since it is born from the union of Plenty and Poverty in the garden of Zeus. Need and beggary, therefore, for the first time are seen to play an essential role in the natural growth of soul; for out of need, in conjunction with the fullness of the intellectual object, soul rises to its most perfect expression. In the *Phaedrus*, at the sight of earthly beauty the soul remembers absolute beauty, and this *causes* its agony as its wings begin to grow (250C). Hence, *erōs* can unite all the faculties of soul and direct a stream of passionate desire upward or downward. At the same time, as the soul grows its wings, it procreates upon the beautiful and leaves intellectual progeny behind it. Soul's ascent, therefore, is conceived of as having powerful and practical effects: the Socrates of Alcibiades' eulogy is the embodiment of this converse with the Beautiful. And although he proclaims his own infertility, he acts as a craftsman upon the souls of others. Ultimately, in the *Timaeus*, God, the supreme Craftsman, makes the soul and fashions the physical world to the degree it will permit. For Plato, then, the soul becomes more than a traveler between this life and Hades; it is the creative intermediary between the worlds of Being and Becoming.

Soul is also the originator of all movement, self-movement in animate things, movement *ab extra* in inanimate things. It is implied that the higher the soul ascends, the more completely it can control or cause movement (*Phaedrus* 246C). In contrast, the closer that soul becomes involved with body, the more it is fashioned in body's likeness. This has two major consequences. First, the highest spiritual object is the truest source of self-realization. The more one turns "the eye of the soul" to the Good or Beautiful, the more fully does one become oneself. In this sense the Platonic ascent through Forms and Genera is not diminishment but augmentation. On the other hand, this spiritual realization is, like the Demiurge of the *Timaeus*, "difficult to find and impossible to tell." For Plato the truth cannot be communicated except by the sudden illumination that floods the diligent enquirer (*Letter 7* 341D–344D). The second consequence is a new cosmic religion. The perfect relationship between soul and body is exemplified physically, intellectually, and spiritually in the circular movements of the heavenly bodies, whose regularity had been demonstrated by fourth-century astronomers. Rational order reveals that the physical world is good, encompassed and directed by an intelligent cosmic soul. In the *Timaeus* this comprehensiveness of soul is such that each physical particle is charged with its presence, so that the dividing line between living and nonliving becomes blurred. Since the human soul is composed of the same ingredients as the cosmic soul, its movements can be brought into harmony with those of the heavens, for its origin and destiny are with the stars, where it may be attached to a pure heavenly body. Plato's search for the Ideal City and the Ideal World, therefore, brings him back to the problem of body and to a concrete understanding of how the soul, immersed in this world, can achieve perfect immaterial freedom.

Aristotle

Plato's vision is intrinsically religious. Aristotle has to find his independence, and his vision is very different. The development of the concepts of form and matter, act and potency, enable him to explore the inward nature of the physical object in an analytic and synthetic way without recourse to a separate world of Forms and to express the continuity of life at the different levels of the natural hierarchy: nutrition, sensation, thought. Each level manifests a fuller development of soul, a greater capacity for life; the higher is more comprehensive than, but depends upon, the lower.

There is a radical discontinuity, however, between the higher and lower powers of the human being. For Aristotle, soul and body form one substantial unity. Soul is "the first actuality of a natural, organic body potentially having life" (*On the Soul* 412a27). For the first time the nature and capacity of the recipient are specified. It stands in a potential relationship toward its principle, *kinēsis;* and the soul, as its actuality or form, is a truly immaterial cause making the body actually live. Soul and body are two aspects of one thing, only separable in thought, not in reality. Therefore, the soul cannot be immortal, but it is a fully immaterial principle.

What alone is immortal is the separable intellect (*nous*), which Aristotle says "comes from outside." And yet this is also conceived of as the highest power in the human soul. Here there is not simply a discontinuity between the soul as animator and the intellect as thinker, but one between the rational life of the corruptible human being and the meaning of rationality itself, just as one might distinguish between the rational action of a hand and the principle that produces that rationality.

There is no resolution of this discontinuity, except for the very fact that it exists and that Aristotle is perhaps aware of it. For Aristotle, the dividing line between living and nonliving is flexible. As a biologist he seeks the purposes of nature in the least prepossessing of animals and finds there a profound rationality (e.g., *On the Parts of Animals* 645a4–25). Each sublunary creature in its own way imitates the perfect rationality of the heavenly bodies. All of nature exhibits that movement which is completed by pure actuality, and the highest form of life is the life of God, which is the actuality of Mind. Although Aristotle characteristically refrains from overemphasizing the point, it is love of mind that causes all movement and is ultimately worth the relinquishing of one's sublunary composite existence (*Nicomachean Ethics* 1177b26–29). It is clear that this pure activity, however mysterious and unfathomable in his thought, is not simply the *siccum lumen* of God's solitary thought, but something that we too share in and is valuable in and for itself (*Metaphysics* 12.7). When we live according to this "theoretic" life, we seem to be living "not like men, but by virtue of a divinity" in us. Yet, in fact, this is what we really are "and it would be absurd to choose not one's own life, but that of another" (*Nicomachean Ethics* 1177b27–1178a8). Like the *psychē* of Homer and that of Plato's *Phaedo*, Aristotle's *psychē-nous* marks the parting of two paths: the loss of body–soul related experience, but the fullness of pure *nous*.

In Aristotle and Plato, then, there are two different approaches to spirituality: in Plato we find a cosmic and a hypercosmic spirituality, both of which liberate the soul from the narrower confines of body and permit it to explore either the regions of the heavenly spheres or an intelligible world of pure significances illuminated by the Good. In Aristotle we remain firmly rooted in the sublunary world, but from the lowest to the highest there grows an impetus to the contemplative life which brings one to the threshold of a new understanding of immaterial substance.

Stoicism

In Aristotle's psychology *pneuma* (described as "hot air") is the vehicle through which the soul operates on, and communicates with, body. It is the seat of the irrational soul (i.e., nutritive and sensitive) and of the imagination, and it contains something analogous to the aether (Aristotle's fifth element, of which the stars are made).

The Stoics took the further step of identifying *pneuma* with soul. God, the divine Fire or highest form of *pneuma,* is present in every form of matter, but the degree of tension (*tonos*)[7] in the *pneuma* differs in different cases. *Pneuma* has the tension of cohesion (*hexis*) in inanimate objects, of *physis* in plants, *psychē* in the lower animals, and rational *psychē* or *nous* in humans. Body grows into the greater fullness of higher soul, which is literally a portion or spark of the World Soul (the Divine Fire).

This opening up of the spirit to the cosmic dimensions of God (consubstantial in different ways with body and soul) and to the dynamic continuum of vital forces held in fine balance by pneumatic tension gives rise to new religious views of the nature of soul and body. On the one hand, God is the world and the world is a great city, united by the sympathy of all its parts, of which man is an organic part, a citizen; he is also a son of God and finally a brother to all men (Epictetus *Discourses* 2.10.1–30). One must act nobly toward others, therefore, and give a (Stoic) consent to the workings of immanent providence, since freedom is obedience to the divine logos ("animum debes mutare, non coelum" [Seneca *Epistulae morales* 55.8]). On the other hand, strong emphasis is placed upon the inner person. The early Stoics do not believe in the immortality of the soul, but in the late Roman Republic and Empire the mind is thought to be the true self: "Know that you are a god," the celestial spirit of Scipio Africanus proclaims to Cicero (*De republica* 6.24). And even under the stern injunction always to look to the good of the All, never to oneself, the idea grows of living continually in happiness and inner calm with the gods by retreating into their sacred presence within our minds. Marcus Aurelius hopes to enjoy the indwelling presence of God after death, which he has come to know in life (*Meditations* 5.29.1; cf. 5.27; 2.13). Here, then, is the source of a personal relationship to God to balance the more common notion of impersonal reabsorption into the Cosmic Fire.

Celestial Immortality

A second development was the emergence of a new geography of soul. The Homeric Hades had been transformed by the Orphics and Pythagoreans, by the vivid representations of the afterlife in Plato and later in Virgil, and had been challenged by the Epicureans' disbelief in any survival of the soul, by the mockery of the comic poets, and by the perennial skepticism of the ordinary person. With the discovery that the earth hangs free in space, Hades was no longer situated under the earth, but in the lower hemisphere. When it became known that the earth revolves upon its axis, the *Inferi* were transferred to the sublunary atmosphere, also inhabited (in both philo-sophical[8] and popular thought) by good and bad daemons. After death the soul ascends through the earth's atmosphere, where it is progressively purified, to the moon; here it lives until its second death, when intelligence is separated from it to pass into the sun. Alternatively, the soul ascends through the seven planetary spheres to the sphere of the fixed stars, where it arrives fully purified of all the qualities associated with each planet. These qualities form an ethereal or pneumatic envelope ("astral body"), of finer matter in ascent or grosser matter in descent, which acts as an intermediary between the intelligent soul, the irrational soul (to which the shade—*eidōlon, umbra,* or *simulacrum*—is assimilated) and the densely compacted body on earth. Here is a cosmological basis, therefore, for the solar or astral religions of late antiquity. But the religious feeling, giving life to these conceptions, is based on the conviction that the human soul or intellect is the friend of God and the rightful traveler of these heavenly regions.

The Hypercosmic Dimension: Plotinus

Related to this is the continuing development of a hypercosmic dimension. From the physical universe, which manifests the order of an intelligent world soul, one passes to a conception of an intelligible universe in which the world soul's intelligence contemplates the Eternal Forms of all natural objects and thereby knows itself. However, God is not simply Intellect. In the Platonic hierarchy of Ideas there is an Absolute One or Good which is nothing but itself and which transcends substance. The highest God, then, is ineffable and only knowable either by analogy or insofar as the soul, or intellect, can ascend to mystical union and negate all its own deter-minations to enter upon the boundlessness of God (Albinus *Didask.,* p. 165 [H]). This conception of three great principles—Soul, Mind, and Unity—

we find in an undeveloped form in Albinus, Plutarch, Numenius, and especially the Neopythagorean Moderatus (second century A.D.): but it assumes a new and revolutionary importance in the thought of Plotinus (third century A.D.), for whom these principles are both external and internal realities (*hypostases*) to be realized by our becoming aware of their presence within ourselves.

Plotinus was a philosopher and a mystic, and both of these capacities are united in his thought. For him, philosophy is the religious quest of the soul to find itself and its source, to recognize that in its substance the human soul always remains undescended in the intelligible universe and that in and through mind it can meet the One God who stands beyond all knowing and being and yet from whom mind and soul have come. In such a vision the position of body has to be lowly. Human beings must live as though they were out of the body; body is only a pale reflection of the intelligible world. The physical world is not evil in itself, but it *is* the *locus* of evil. On the other hand, the relation of soul and body is more complex. Soul extends from the Divine Mind down to the last shadow of reality in bodies, where it is found as Nature. This spiritual presence of soul is always dynamic and creative; for, although the physical universe is not created in time, it *is* eternally created by soul and the Divine Mind. Body also exhibits a hierarchy, from the inanimate stone to the plant, the animal, the human, and on up to the moon and the planetary spheres, to the fixed stars. When the soul descends from the intelligible world, it will, logically speaking, descend first to the highest and most noble part of the heavens and there assume an ethereal envelope. But, for Plotinus, the notion of the celestial hierarchy of soul and body is subordinated to that of immaterial power and its manifestation. The more a body manifests power, the "closer" it is to soul, and in this sense greater "distance" between body and soul signifies greater imperfection, even pain. Closeness signifies pleasure. Again we meet the paradox we noted in Plato above: to live the life of the body means, for Plotinus, to isolate and diminish oneself. Therefore, the spiritual soul must free itself from bodily involvement and seek the greater dimensions of the spirit. On the other hand, the more that body approaches soul, that is, realizes its capacity or potential for life, the more perfect is the relationship between the two.

Three further points should be made. First, a major problem of the post-Aristotelian period was to define humanity in a way that would embrace all human experience. Cicero, for instance, gives two characteristic definitions, the compound (soul and body) or the mind, body being merely a receptacle (contrast *De finibus* 4.10.25–26 [cf. *Lucullus* 45.139] with *Tusculanarum* 1.22.51–52). For the first time Plotinus combines human spiritual and material potential in a practical way when he suggests that the human being is a compound, "soul in a *logos* of a certain kind" (VI 7, 5, 1–5). Since the body is a *logos,* a *logos* of matter, the material element is part of the definition without obscuring the spiritual reality that gives it meaning.

Second, the question of the origin of evil was an urgent problem in late antiquity. Plutarch and Atticus posit an evil world soul; the Demiurge of Valentinian Gnosticism is ignorant; Numenius makes the rational and the irrational soul into *two* different souls. Plotinus's attitude has a characteristic subtlety: in his view it is never evil to give light to something else. If there is evil, the fault must be traced to the illuminated object (I 1, 12, 24–26; I 8, 14). Now, if we speak of the soul as evil, what we must *mean* is not the illuminating or creative soul, but the soul that is bound to the *locus* of the physical object. We can see that this object is only evil to the degree that it is unformed, and our physical and moral experience shows that there is something that causes unformedness. It would seem logical, therefore, to trace this lack of form to the foundations of the physical object and to say that matter is evil to the degree that it resists form, but good and positive because of the greater creative power of Form (see generally II 4; I 8). This positive-negative conception of matter is of the utmost importance for all future religious thinking. In later pagan thought, however, this confidence in soul is lost, and the human soul, no longer a *de facto* member of the intelligible, descends into the physical universe.

Third, soul encompasses the whole range of possible experience for Plotinus: (1) it is the great intermediary between the intelligible and the physical Worlds; (2) it can sink to its own "death" in material existence, but (3) it can also pass through Mind and enter into union with the One (VI 7, 35). There is a tension here between soul's being and soul's experience. Although an eternal reality in its own right, Soul-Mind must "cut away everything" and wait in nakedness for the sudden light of the Good. This is the "flight of the Alone to the Alone," but it can also be an experience even during our earthly lifetimes of the greatest, if unspeakable, fullness of Spirit.

From Homer to the Neoplatonists the soul's range of intensity expanded but remained balanced between its capacity for life, health, and purity on the one hand and its mortality or vulnerability on the other. Consequently, the soul in antiquity was capable of expressing both physical and spiritual motion, one intensity of which is thought and the vision of the Good. Body played an important role in this development. At different levels of reference, body and soul may appear as opposites, correlates, or even parallel universes, but ultimately the higher meanings of body—animate or inanimate—have to be interpreted in the light of soul. For even a truly immaterial conception of the immortal soul and of the spiritual life naturally strives to express the value of body therein.

Notes

1. See the Potidaea epitaph: "*Aithēr* received their souls; their bodies, earth"; see also Euripides fr. 971; *Helena* 1014–16; *Supplices* 533f.; fr. 839.8.
2. See Snell, *Discovery*, 43–70.
3. See M. P. Nilsson, *Greek Piety* (Oxford: Clarendon Press, 1948) 49.
4. Snell, *Discovery*, 17.
5. Compare Heraclitus fr. 6 ("the sun is new each day") with the Pythagoreans, for whom "nothing was absolutely new," in Porphyry *Life of Pythagoras* 18, 19.
6. In the *Republic* and the *Timaeus.*
7. See *SVF* 11:442, 446, 836, 879, 911.
8. See Xenocrates frs. 25, 23, 15; sublunary daemons are very common in the Middle Platonists (first and second centuries A.D.).

Bibliography

Editions and Translations

Works of most ancient writers referred to in the notes have been cited from the readily available editions of the Greek and Latin texts, with English translations, in the Loeb Classical Library from Harvard University Press. The fragments of Antiphon the Sophist are in *Minor Attic Orators*, vol. 1; Archilochus is in *Greek Elegy and Iambus*, vol. 2; Sappho in *Lyra Graeca*, vol. 1.

In addition to the Loeb edition of the hymns of Callimachus, there is a useful new edition and translation of the *Hymn to Demeter* by N. Hopkinson (New York: Cambridge University Press, 1985).

Fragments of the early Greek philosophers are cited according to the numbering made standard by H. Diels (*Die Fragmente der Vorsokratiker*, revised by W. Kranz [3 vols.; 12th ed.; Dublin: Weidmann, 1966–67]). They are most easily consulted in English in K. Freeman, *Ancilla to the Pre-Socratic Philosophers* (Oxford: Blackwell, 1948), which translates Diels's German translations and follows his numbering system.

Modern Works

Adam, J. *The Vitality of Platonism and Other Essays.* Cambridge: University Press, 1911.

Burnet, J. "The Socratic Doctrine of the Soul." *Proceedings of the British Academy* 7 (1915–16) 235–59.

Claus, D. B. *Toward the Soul: An Inquiry into the Meaning of Psychē before Plato.* New Haven, CT, and London: Yale University Press, 1981.

Cumont, F. V. M. *Afterlife in Roman Paganism.* New Haven, CT: Yale University Press, 1922.

Dillon, J. *The Middle Platonists.* Ithaca, NY: Cornell University Press, 1977.

Dodds, E. R. *The Greeks and the Irrational.* Berkeley and Los Angeles: University of California Press, 1951.

Farnell, L. R. *Greek Hero Cults and Ideas of Immortality.* Oxford: Clarendon Press, 1921.

Guthrie, W. K. C. *The Greeks and Their Gods.* Boston: Beacon Press, 1950.

Jaeger, W. *The Theology of the Early Greek Philosophers.* Oxford: Clarendon Press, 1947.

Nilsson, M. P. *A History of Greek Religion.* Oxford: Clarendon Press, 1925.

Onians, R. B. *The Origins of European Thought about the Body, the Soul, the World, Time, and Fate.* 2d ed. Cambridge: University Press, 1954.

Rohde, E. *Psyche: The Cult of Souls and Belief in Immortality among the Greeks.* Translated by W. B. Hillis. 8th ed. New York: Harper, 1966.

Snell, B. *The Discovery of the Mind.* Translated by T. G. Rosenmeyer. New York: Harper, 1953.

16

The Religious Experience of Time and Eternity

Peter Manchester

S OMETHING SIMPLE IS WORTH SAYING right away about our topic, the religious experience of time and eternity in the late classical Mediterranean world. Famous complications that have taxed the greatest philosophers cannot in the end be avoided, but a good quick insight is available from reflection on a very simple proposition: time and eternity make one topic, not two.

This was the position of the Platonic tradition both early and late, as I will show in some detail before we are done. But how they are bound together can be sketched in more general terms, and in a way that will help us bring into play from the start our own very different experience of temporal matters. Whenever it is made, I argue, the distinction between time and eternity is resolved out of a complex but tightly integrated experience. The two aspects of that experience must be considered together, each in relation to the other. As a name for this single embracing topic I use the term "temporality."

To be temporal is to have a future, a past, and a present. If we understand the "having" of such a thing as a future very broadly, then everything is temporal, but the concept of temporality belongs primarily to what exists historically. Within any living historical experience, the past and the present and the future are woven together in mutual interaction; yet one or the other of the three can be dominant. One of the great contributions of religious reflection is to make the temporal structure of historical experience explicit.

Where the past is dominant, temporality is experienced as fate or destiny, as that larger pattern in life that one does not see as it unfolds but which appears under an aspect of inevitability as the course of events finally brings it into view. If the present begins to disengage itself from the past, temporality becomes "the present age," "this world" in a series of worlds, where "worlds" are ages or epochs—whole world orders including human political accomplishments, which come to an end and are succeeded by new ones in a great recurrent cycle of totality. When the past and the present come to be overshadowed by the future, temporality can be experienced directly as history, that larger human story in which many acts of freedom, both of individuals and of peoples, work together to transform the scope of human action. Fate, the present age, history: each of these is *temporal* because for each there is a characteristic way of encountering the past, entertaining the present, and taking orientation from the future.

Time and eternity are horizons that come into play in a characteristic way within each of these possibilities for temporal experience. By 'horizons' I mean backgrounds for different directions in which the experience can be projected for interpretation. From the point of view of the history of religions, time and eternity are distinguished in the same way that the lives of mortals and the lives of gods are distinguished. Vast as this difference may be, it may fairly be claimed that all religious experience depends on the premise that mortal life and divine life are not altogether incompatible, that they impinge on each other and figure in the same stories together. Religious philosophy, grounded in the living immediacy of the mortal–divine encounter, appeals to the conceptual distinction of time and eternity in order to account for the union, not the separation, of humans and gods.

Because so little remains of a seminal religious experience in contemporary philosophical accounts of eternity and time, these are regularly understood to be not merely distinct but contrary notions. Eternity has dwindled to a construction of logic, mere abstract timelessness; time has been emptied into a dimension of the physical world, the measure of a kind of scattering of things. There is no road to recovery of the rich original intuitions through rehearsal of recent theories. For the more roundabout route that I will traverse, some orienting introduction will therefore be helpful.

The Road to Recovery

Perhaps the most familiar narrative track in mythology is the one that begins "on high" among primordial divine doings, but soon slips into a history of mortals that is more and more recognizable and continuous with our own. In such a way, perhaps, one could portray time and eternity making connection with each other, but this would be at an obvious cost to their distinction. It does not seem that the primordial "when," the "time of the beginning" in the myths, is eternity at all, since within the narrative it stands in a sequential and therefore timelike relationship with mundane times. The theoretical problem here was much discussed in ancient and medieval philosophy in the form of the question how the act of an eternal creator could be the first moment of a history in time. In this form, the question is probably unanswerable, because it confuses different forms of temporal experience. The oldest, mythical way of distinguishing a time of divine actions from a time of human actions is in a way an eternity–time distinction, but the philosophers' question about the eternal creator draws from another temporal experience altogether. In the latter experience, though the conceptual separation is much more sharply drawn, the interplay of the horizons and therefore of the divine and the human is very much more intimate.

For the philosophical religions that flourished around the Mediterranean in the Hellenistic and early Roman periods, divine life was taken to be imaged, or even directly experienced, in a certain kind of presence of mind, of intellectual alertness and intuitive grasp, with which a person could become immediately familiar in reflection. Here humans and gods come together not just in story or dramatic representation but in intersecting consciousness. And here it becomes possible to describe a living experience of eternity, to explore and delineate directly its contrasts with ordinary experience of time.

The philosophers made the experienced timelessness of pure intellectual self-possession into a theme of its own, considering it apart from the contemplation, prayer, or related religious practice in which it first arose. Eventually, especially in late Platonic thought and its Christian adaptation by Aurelius Augustine, this interior reflection on the life of the mind came to approximate the modern, post-Cartesian fascination with individual personal consciousness or the "ego," But even in Augustine, where Christian premises allow for a highly personalized experience of encounter with the divine, contemplative ecstasy is never reduced entirely to the psychological state of an individual. It remains the mark of a more-than-individual, indeed more-than-human, Presence.

It is presence, suggested by metaphors from vision—light, radiance, glory—which shaped the emerging philosophical account of eternity. And it is presence again, the same dimension of experience, which yields the interpretation of time we still use in natural science today.

But presence of what?

The Greek answer was Nature in its *kosmos.* "Cosmos" is the Greek name for the beauty of order. A literal translation is "world order," meaning world system, the arrangement of things and lives in intelligible and harmonious patterns. But cosmos means order in such a way as to mean beauty too, which explains how the adjective *kosmetikos,* "cosmetic," could wind up in English meaning pleasant, designed to please. If one removes the artifice and superficiality, merges "cosmetic" with "cosmic," something of the grandeur in the old sense of cosmos still can be heard. The orderliness of nature is not just lawlike but beautiful, not just beautiful but powerful, not just powerful but living. The great cosmetic array of things is not a fact but a Presence.

In appreciating nature as cosmos, Greek experience was strongly shaped by astronomy; it stands in direct line with that most challenging dimension of modern astronomy which is speculative cosmology. For this reason the movements of the sky were given special importance in understanding how this world of arising and perishing interacted with the divine ordering power present within it. The *ouranos* or sky is also the heaven; its dramatically final, universal, and all-encompassing presence represents at once the farthest and highest reach of human vision and at the same time the mode of presence of divine life itself. At first, among the Ionian naturalists of the sixth century B.C., study of the sky was "meteorology," where *ta meteōra,* "aerial things," included phenomena of the weather, planets, and stars all on one level. Later, especially in Pythagorean studies, the phenomena of the high sky, the stars and planets, became a domain of their own, on account of the regularity of their movements. The perfect completedness of the sphere came therefore to be the figure of eternity; and its movements, themselves seen as circular, became the definitive signs of the nature of time, an "image of eternity moving according to number," as Plato had his old Pythagorean Timaeus put it (*Timaeus* 37D).

If our goal is the religious experience of eternity and time in the late classical Mediterranean world, we will have to recover some feeling for this strange complicity of Heaven with Mind, of macrocosm with microcosm, of the cosmological sky with the human self. Against the grain of an older portrayal of the emergence of a science of nature in Greek philosophy, this new experience was not in its inception a rejection of the older world of myth and ritual, but a radical appropriation of the old experience of temporal transcendence. It belongs to the unity of temporality that the present never dawns except where there is also a past. Since, according to our leading premise, this is true not just of time but of eternity as well, the proper first step in our exploration should be an account of the "eternal Past" as it survived into even postclassical times.

The Preparation of the Eternal

How should a narrative of the whole of time begin? "In the beginning" is the obvious answer. But when was that? In the past, for sure. But here there is a problem; how does one imagine the past? What knowledge of it or contact with it makes it real to us?

The answer, even for educated modern people, is never "information about past events." However ready we may be to trust our sources and to submit our imagination to the perspective on the course of time that they embody, the times in question are not our own experience. Pastness itself, on the other hand, *is* part of immediate experience. It is with us in the present in the way that memory is always with us. I refer not to memories in their latency, experiences "stored up" somehow outside of attention, but to living, active memory, which is constantly a factor within the patterns of ongoing experience. It may well be the character of this constant factor to be inconstant, to come and go, dilate and foreshorten, now to seize our attention and now to slide away unobtrusively, but in every experience it brings up close to us, places behind us as we say, a kind of space in which things *appear*, though with the particular quality of having been, of pastness.

In what way does this immediate pastness have a beginning? One answer is that Now is the beginning of the past; it is always "just now" that things begin to have been, and it makes perfectly good sense to say that experiences are "first" present "and then" past, so that the past follows upon the present. But this is plainly not the beginning one has in mind in asking about the beginning of past time itself. We want the other beginning, the other side of the past, so to speak.

Still confining the question to the past as it is immediately a part of living experience, this is to ask for the beginning of memory. But here there is something remarkable to observe. Sigmund Freud called it "infantile amnesia," stressing the absence in adult memory of any of the events of very early childhood. This is indeed an interesting psychological problem, since two-and three-year olds do have memories at the time, but it is only an external observation of the specific kind of vacancy that one experiences oneself in the effort to remember the beginnings of memory. Searching within memory, one confronts a curiously vague sort of horizon, a darkness or abyss whose depth cannot directly be discerned. From the threshold of that abyss, individual childhood memories may survive that are vivid and distinct, but they come back to us all self-contained, suffused with an inner light that does not seem continuous with the chronology made available by our later memories. The evasiveness in the time we experience as farthest past is not a matter of declining intensity but of broken continuity, disconnection, loss of context. The beginning of memory is nothing like a first moment of time, even a forgotten one. It is instead like an ocean, a surface with unseen depth on which initially only islands are seen to float.

The historical past out along which we arrange the events about which we are informed by chronicles is no simple extension of the personal past that memory holds open. The alignment of the personal past with the historical past is a complex achievement of imagination, no less remarkable for the fact that in modern consciousness it has become habitual. In his famous discourse on memory in the *Confessions,* Augustine recognized that it is in many ways more natural to align the past of our own beginning with the absolute past of Genesis, the divine past of the creation of the world (book 10).[1] Fully convinced that a long history extended from one to the other, his sense of this strange coincidence between lifetime and the transcendent time of the divine was nevertheless so strong that it was only with difficulty that he finally abandoned the theory of a literal preexistence of the soul that seemed to bridge the gap.

In the oldest cultures, for whom the time of chronicles has not yet been discovered, the past in which divine action takes place is not projected outside the lifetime at all. To the contrary, it is necessary and possible through the possession of myths and their attendant rituals and festivals, repeatedly to bring lifetime back into contact with primordial time. As the historian of religion Mircea Eliade has shown, where myth is still a living religious presence, the sacred time of the narrative, *illud tempus* as expressed in the "in the beginning" or "when on high," is not a far past, farthest of all and getting farther, but a primordial Past that is in many ways nearer than the remembered past and in preliterate cultures may even displace it.[2] Before there were cities and writing and dynasties of kings, all of which come together in the origin of chronicles, events as near as the grandparents' generation were sometimes given little mind, so that the remembered past trailed off very quickly. The past to which the shaman or the priest gave mind was instead the mythical Past, cherished not as lore about the distant but as the most relevant and illuminating horizon of immediate experience.

What commands attention and seems meaningful to the imagination that builds up chronicled time is the novel, what happens once and is unique: this king, that battle. What commands the attention of the mythical imagination is what happens cyclically, again and again, typically and in recurrent patterns: the seasons of the year, the movements in the heavens, the phases of life (childhood, youth, majority, age). For each of these transitions there is a myth that explains how it emerged "in the beginning," and to each myth there belongs a rite or festival in which this life is made contemporary with that beginning or, better, in which the Time of Beginnings is brought back again, reconveying the creative power displayed by the gods in the story. In the temporal experience that Eliade describes as Eternal Return, the cyclic time of aboriginal religious experience, what *is* is what *has been*—either repeatedly, as marked in the yearly passage of rituals and festivals, or singly and paradigmatically, in the great Past of the deeds of the gods.

To the degree that festival calendars and the living tradition of ritual observances remain important, this sense of having-been-ness or pastness as the eternal aspect of human affairs outlives the emergence of high urban culture, with its chronicles and its emerging sense of history as the drama of the present. To the new consciousness the old eternity seems more and more like living in the past, in the sense of nostalgia or old-fashioned ways, but that is a mistaken view, because the meaning of the past itself is transformed in historical consciousness. A bridge to the archaic can be attempted, through the creation of a hybrid mythical history of the kind we see among the Greeks in Hesiod and among the Jews in Genesis, where a succession of Ages of the World or patriarchal generations interposes between the time of the beginning and nowadays, but this is finally literary artifice and unsatisfactory, as the Greeks were the first to see.

Beginning with the Homeric critique of the mythical world view, Greek enlightenment distanced itself from the Eternal past not by abandoning myth but by recovering it as poetry, which relativized its political force.[3] The gods and goddesses of the old myths were never, as a now-outdated scholarship used to argue, personified forces of nature; they and their deeds provided the paradigms for familial, civic, and political life. This was the basis of the great inertia of the old piety in the face of citified enlightenment. It was really the new civics of the Greeks—the notion that became constitutional in Athens of *nomos* or law as an accomplishment of human art and reason—that turned the stories of the gods into entertainment or poetic figure. In town and country, in piety and practice unimpressed by the new cultivation, mythic experience and ritual time had a long afterlife, certainly all the way into Greco-Roman times and perhaps, transposed into Christian liturgy, into the modern world.

It was a peculiarity of this survival among the Greeks that the rituals quite regularly outlasted their original mythical contexts. Perhaps because of the dislocations that set in with the Doric invasions of the late second millennium B.C., it was common for rituals and festivals to be preserved whose original meaning had been forgotten. New myths would be supplied, but they were derived, somewhat speculatively, from the rituals; and it was the latter, the rituals themselves, that carried increasingly the weight of an experienced interaction with the divine. Together with the great fascination of the Greeks with things oriental (Egyptian, Chaldaean, Persian), this laid the groundwork for a particular development within ritual religion in which the experience of transcendence preserved from the archaic spirit made a kind of last stand—still authentic, yet ready for a transformation. I refer to the increasing popularity of what we call the mysteries, especially in Hellenistic times among cosmopolitan seekers who had detached themselves from traditional civic pieties.

Through these initiatory rites, the archaic religious concern for maintaining solidarity between the living and the dead gave rise to a new search for security concerning one's own personal immortality. Taken up as a central theme by the most widespread and long-lasting of the mystery religions, Christianity, personal immortality has remained so important to popular religion in the West that in many minds it is the defining concern of religion itself. It can therefore be disorienting to discover that in archaic religion the notion of human immortality is either absent or, when present, involves either a kind of collective absorption into the life of the gods, in which individuality does not continue, or at best a kind of shadowy, semiphysical persistence which the living must take into account (the cult of ancestors) but which is nothing like a continuation of life past death for the personal self.

From about the eighth century B.C. on, in the Greek world as in India, the persistence after death of this shade or ghostly extract of the life-force came to be more graphically and personally imagined. In one tendency, the world beyond death was seen as offering different sorts of afterlife depending on the virtue or defect of one's earthly life. In another, associated with the legendary Pythagoras, representations of an Indic kind began to creep in: reincarnation into this world after death, within a great cycle of lives through which one might pass, now rising to the divine life of the stars, now sinking to that of a beast or a slug.

At first, these more personalized views of the afterlife made no assault on the gulf that lies between the human and the divine in archaic religion, uncrossable except by mythical heroes whose exceptional stature only emphasizes the lot of ordinary mortals. The kingdom of Hades, though an underworld, is again a world, like this world, however shadowy. The immortality that passes through cycles of reincarnation is expressly this-worldly. But already in the oldest and most indigenous of the Greek mysteries, those of Demeter at Eleusis, and even more clearly in the new Orphic cult of Dionysus Zagreus, the emerging urgency about one's status in afterlife, one's weal or woe in Hades or one's rank in reincarnation, began to take on a different dimension. The question shifted from that of one's status among the dead, in an afterlife that was real in the same way as successive cycles of Eternal Return, to that of whether one had awakened, in *this* life, to a transcending spiritual and interior life that knows its own eternity *already* and in death is released from the cycle of birth and death and from worldly existence altogether.

The rites called mysteries made something of this experience available to large numbers of people all the way into Roman times. The term "mysteries" seems to have attached first to an ancient celebration at Eleusis, near Athens, and was associated with the goddess Demeter. Like all mysteries, the Eleusinian Mysteries were reserved to initiates (the word *mystērion*, "mystery," derives from *mystēs*, "one who is initiated"), but at Eleusis all who knew Greek and were willing to be purified were welcomed. The cult of Demeter at Eleusis is attested already in Homer, so that one of the compelling features of her mysteries was their authenticity, expressed in the legend that they had been taught by the goddess herself in immemorial antiquity. In this sense they were a survival of the archaic experience of ritual time. More characteristic and compelling still was the sense of security they induced concerning one's personal good fortune in the world to come. For many, this would be merely a magical security, as external a transaction as the gaining of indulgences in early modern Europe. But, for others, conviction seems to have come through an immediate experience and insight concerning the reality of their own interior life or soul, an enlightenment not unlike that of Buddhism.[4] Later, other mysteries from the East joined the Eleusinian in providing this experience. Those of Egyptian Isis or Persian Mithras or the Syrian Great Mother were popular in Roman times. The mysteries of Jesus Christ, baptism and eucharist, were not untouched by this sensibility as they spread through the Greco-Roman world.

In a drastic statement to which some of the philosophers would subscribe, the mysteries accomplished an awakening and showing of *the divine within the self*. These were the terms of the Orphic mysteries, rooted in the myth of the god Zagreus (assimilated to Dionysus), who was torn apart and consumed alive by Titans from whose ashes human beings have been made. In this image, human life is composed of Titanic ashes and is therefore earthly and bodily, but within it a life that is divine has been instilled. The soul, according to the "ancient discourse" of the Orphics, is a god. Hence, the work of the purifications and initiations must be to release this god not just from its imprisonment in the body but from the entire cycle of birth and death to which embodiment subjects it.

The Orphic cult was far more private and restrictive than the popular mysteries, but it was also geographically more diffused. The problem of its origin and that of its half-mythical, half-legendary poet-singer Orpheus is probably unsolvable. But its outcome is clear and profound. It was with Orphic instigation that Pythagoreans and Platonists would pursue the experience of a divine and interior presence that we have been describing. Rooted in ritual time and the eternity of beginnings, it broke out of time in a new direction entirely: no longer recovering a transcendent Past but aspiring to a transcending Presence. It was to name this new phenomenon that the word "eternity" itself, in Greek *aiōn,* came into use.

The Eternal and Its Image

Eternity is to time, I have said, as the lives of gods are to those of mortals. Religious experience is possible because these overlap, because they can be con-temporal. In the temporality of the divine–human encounter, something is manifested about each.

For the temporality oriented by the past, we have seen, the lives of the gods took place in an elevated and primordial "time of beginnings," a time which was none of the times of profane experience but which held all of them within its power and so was a kind of species or prototype of eternity. Mortal times were cyclic, called back in Eternal Return to past paradigms. The characteristic religious problem in this temporal experience was to find the human place in the unifying thread of life that ran through birth and death, manifestation and occultation, the Land of the Living and the Land of the Dead.

Though this archaic experience survived, the religious experience of eternity and time that is distinctive of Mediterranean spirituality in our period is an orientation to temporal presence. With this we arrive at the notion of eternity proper, the Greek *aiōn.*[5] As I said above, it is an experience of a divine Presence in the human present, a presence reflected both in the cosmos of nature and in the life of the mind. Here the characteristic religious problem is the competence of speculative mysticism to encounter divine creative power. This formulation is deliberately general, because it spans ambitions as disparate as the mathematician's desire to touch in his own reasonings the ordering power displayed in natural law, the theurgist's search for the hidden names and maneuvers that put divine actions within the scope of his will, and the contemplative's discipline of emptying the soul of all sensible activity in order to awaken the perfect intellectual composure in which the goodness, truth, and beauty of things shine forth.

Each of these pathways to the experience of the Eternal Present comes to a crossroads in the thought of the philosopher Plotinus in the third century A.D. Not himself a mathematician or astronomer, he nevertheless drew out with new clarity the implications of the Pythagorean and Stoic traditions in these fields. He was even less a participant in ritual religion or theurgical practice than he was a scientist, but his principled reverence for the divine presence in nature still had much to teach the later sacramental sensibility, both non-Christian and Christian, in religion and art. What gave him such creative influence outside the domain of his own activity was his power as a learned and contemplative master of Platonic philosophy. The concept of eternity is usually traced back to Plato, yet it was Plotinus who first enforced the understanding of the concept that we now find there—not just in Plato but in his predecessors. The most natural way to prepare for an account of the classical experience is therefore to imbibe its distillation by Plotinus. This receives a sustained exposition in the treatise *On Eternity and Time* (III 7 [45]).

In that treatise Plotinus asks us first to contemplate eternity and then to "come down" in our reflections, from eternity into time, in a fashion that replicates the origin of time itself. This procedure is doubly remarkable.

First of all, it presupposes that eternity and time stand in a relation of such intimacy to each other that a passage between them of any kind is plausible. Thus far, at least formally, he has the highest of authorities on his side. The most famous of all statements about eternity and time is the one to which reference was made above, the metaphor introduced by the Pythagorean cosmologist Timaeus in the great monologue that makes up the bulk of Plato's *Timaeus*. The context is an elaborate myth that Timaeus relates about the making of the cosmos. Fairly late in his story, after both the body and the soul of the world have been constructed by a father or maker who seeks to realize intelligibility and beauty in his handiwork, Timaeus says:

> When the father and creator saw the creature which he had made moving and living, the created image of the eternal gods, he rejoiced, and in his joy determined to make the copy still more like the original, and as this was an eternal living being, he sought to make the universe eternal, so far as might be. Now the nature of the ideal being was everlasting, but to bestow this attribute in its fullness upon a creature was impossible. Wherefore he resolved to have a moving image of eternity, and when he set in order the heaven, he made this image eternal but moving according to number, while eternity itself rests in unity, and this image we call time. (*Timaeus* 37D; trans. B. Jowett)

This famous proposition, that time is an image of eternity moving according to number, is the source of my own initial assertion that eternity and time are together one topic. In saying this I was merely repeating what

30. Heroic Banquet Relief. Presumably from Attica. Ca. 340 B.C.

Plotinus finds in the doctrine: eternity and time are two manifestations of one life, bound to each other like a presence and its image in a mirror. He claims therefore an unassailable precedent not just for conjoining eternity and time within one treatise but for moving from one to the other on the basis of interior relatedness between them.

Less easily explained, however, is the *directionality* of his procedure, the movement *from* eternity *to* time. This is a move from the unfamiliar to the familiar, from the divine to the natural, and would seem quite backward as a logic of discovery, excluding anyone who has not already advanced to the deepest insights. Plotinus himself facilitates this objection. At the end of the first chapter of his treatise, he allows:

> If someone, before contemplating eternity, should form a picture in his mind
> of what time is, it would be possible for him, too, to go from this world to
> the other by recollection and contemplate that of which time is a likeness,
> if time really has a likeness to eternity. (III 7, 1)

It is Plotinus's constant refrain that the study of eternity and time is a reflection on living experience, not the acquisition of venerable lore. Since a genuine seeing of time would make possible an insight into eternity, why not begin where we find ourselves, which is, after all, in time? Why instead does he confront us at first with eternity, in a portrait as terse and peculiar in its logic as it is familiar in its rhetoric?

This is no easy question to answer. The problem is conditioned by the deepest ways in which the Plotinian experience of eternity and time is religious as well as philosophical. There is in fact no answer at all ahead of the exercise itself. Let us therefore let Plotinus confront us with eternity:

> One sees eternity in seeing a life that abides in the same, and always has the
> all present to it, not now this, and then again that, but all things at once, and
> not now some things, and then again others, but a partless completion, as if
> they were all together in a point, and had not yet begun to go out and flow
> into lines; it is something which abides in the same in itself and does not
> change at all but is always in the present, because nothing of it has passed
> away, nor again is there anything to come into being, but that which it is,
> it *is*. (III 7, 3)

This tells us that eternity is not just presence but life. Yet the illustrations are geometrical and somewhat austerely conceptual. A few chapters later, writing of the experience of eternity, the same conceptual elements are evoked in a different voice:

> Eternity could well be described as a god proclaiming and manifesting him-
> self as he is, that is, as being which is unshakeable and self-identical and
> [always] as it is, and firmly grounded in life. But if we say that it is made up

of many parts, there is no need to be surprised, for each of the beings There is many through its unending power, since endlessness, too, is not having any possibility of failing, and eternity is endless in the strict and proper sense, because it never expends anything of itself. And if someone were in this way to speak of eternity as a life which is here and now endless because it is total and expends nothing of itself, since it has no past or future—for if it had, it would not now be a total life—he would be near to defining it. (III 7, 5)

This is the discourse that caught the attention of later theologians, and its concluding definition of eternity was transmitted to the Latin Christian tradition nearly verbatim by Boethius.[6] The underlying note of the passage, that eternity is not simply the condition of divine life but its "proclamation and manifestation," provided in later mystical speculation the line of connection between the biblical God of revelation and the God of Platonic cosmology.

Now because the divine eternity has been so long celebrated in theology, these two descriptions have taken on a veneer of familiarity. This familiarity does not, however, survive closer inspection. That eternity is changeless is expected; but how then is it radiant life and power? Self-identical, very well; but how then unshakable composure, limitless sufficiency? Simple and total in partless completion; how also made up of many parts, each enjoying the same endlessness of power? Very quickly, an attentive reading discovers unexpected themes, and it is these that lead to the deeper insights.

Most familiar of all in the rhetoric of eternity is the exclusion of pastness and futurity, the consolidation of everything into presence. From this it becomes plausible to speak of eternity as a "now," a moment differing from those that make up life in time by being stationary, but like them in that its structure has the point-like simplicity of instantaneousness, all-at-onceness. Eternity then becomes a *nunc stans*, a "standing now," in the Latin tag that derives from Augustine and Boethius. The former of the two texts cited might seem to support this image, since it describes the components of eternity in a "partless completion, as if they were all together in a point. . . ." Yet upon reflection, the figure becomes surprising: the point that is like eternity is not the point-now, which divides a familiar time-line into past and future segments, but the point that is the center for a radial outflow, a spherical radiation. If anything about time that comes to attention when we say "Now!" is instructive about eternity, it will not be the compression, elusiveness, and instantaneity of the now-point. This is because, to begin our interpretive exposition, eternity or *aiōn* does not differ from time by being simply devoid of duration!

The word *aiōn* is still in use in English, having arrived through the Latin spelling *aeon*. This has been the source of much puzzlement, however, since if *aiōn* is 'aeon', it is not at all clear how it could have come to denominate eternity. We speak quite properly of aeons of time, whereas eternity, we are assured by those seeking to impart its secret, is altogether timeless.

This is not quite correct. Aeons are epochs, eras, great stretches across time. In one respect they are standard intervals, measured usually in some large number of years, but the defining property is not that they are lengths of time but that they are forms of completion for what goes on in time. Within them the arrangement of events has a kind of logical finish; there is a beginning and a middle and an end.

The archaic cosmologies that survive into our period construct the totality of the cosmic process out of a plurality of aeons. Within each aeon the pattern of events achieves its own self-contained finish and perfection, and the perfection of the whole is a pattern of such patterns. In a Zoroastrian system, for example, there are four ages of the world: a first age of chaos; a second age of protean creativity, where the Wise Lord has the upper hand; a third age of struggle, where the Adversary tends to come out on top; and a fourth age of resolution, where the Wise Lord prevails again. Egyptian and Chaldaean systems had more complicated astronomical patterns, but the same basic structure, subcycles integrated into a grand cycle of the whole, can be seen in them. The whole is not an aeon but, in the old phrase, an aeon of aeons.

The mark of the present aeon is therefore some present configuration in events, not some distance elapsed since a past time of beginning or transition. Aeon is a present power, a reigning Presence. *Aiōn* could therefore be treated as the name of a god; it could and did translate the Persian name Zurvan, the divinity from whom the Wise Lord and the Adversary are engendered. Zurvan is Primordial Time, primordial not as the archaic but as supervening present power. Zurvanism arose in fourth- or third-century B.C. Persia, perhaps under Greek influence, as a corrective to the unmediated back-and-forth quality of Zoroastrian conflict dualism. Some historians have attributed the elevated notion of eternity that becomes thematic in Plotinus to Persian influence, but such a relationship is inside out. *Aiōn* already meant presence and power and primordial time as the form of such regnancy, long before it lent itself to syncretic theologies.

Confusion is inevitable as soon as one looks for the sudden intrusion of a *durationless aiōn* into the history of a term that originally meant "lifetime," "time span," "aeon." But eternity is never, even full-blown as we find it in Plotinus, timeless in the sense of without all activity, motion, or duration. Eternity is something *intensive* about time rather than *extensive,* and it intensifies *something about time:* time as the bearer of ordering power, time as the figure of a living presence.

We are already on the road to Plotinus, therefore, in a *gnōmē* of the fifth-century B.C. philosopher Heraclitus, in which we find the earliest surviving use of the term *aiōn* in Greek philosophy.

> *Aiōn* is a child, moving counters in a game;
> the royal power is a child's.
> > (fr. 52, Diels-Kranz)[7]

Here, correctly enough if the underlying insight be sound, some translators supply "time" for *aiōn*. Certainly it would be overtranslation to write "eternity" for a text this early, but one needs to save "time" to represent *chronos*, which makes its first appearance in the sole surviving fragment of the sixth-century Milesian Anaximander, one of the "founding fathers" of Greek nature philosophy. Yet *chronos*, time, in Anaximander could perfectly well be translated "aeon," the ruling presence. What we really find at the earliest moments of discussion of eternity and time in Greek philosophy is a synthesis of both concepts, in an intuitive experience of natural beauty and truth.

What is certain is that even if final clarification of the concepts took place a millennium later in Plotinus, the time that is the image of eternity is a discovery of archaic Greek nature philosophy. To appreciate that discovery, we need to ask a primitive question ourselves: What should we understand by time? To what does the word time draw attention?

To the phenomenon of time, of course. But this answer is no help, given our recognition that there can be differing temporal experiences, in which different aspects of the world get noticed and regarded as time-like or time-showing. The characteristic Greek philosophical experience begins to show itself as soon as the word time is used to draw our attention to nature and to natural motions and changes. Time is then experienced as something about nature. Previously it could just as well have been something about rituals and the cycles of festivals, or about the fates that are acted out in the interactions of mortals and gods, or about dynasties of kings and chronicles of empires. But the new philosophical writing of the sixth and fifth centuries finds its creative center in reflections "On Nature," in Greek *Peri Physeōs*. Such books would later be called *ta physika*, and from them evolves our "physics." At first with hesitation, but soon with commanding originality, archaic Greek physics identifies and then begins to expound the timelikeness of nature.

I emphasize that it is nature that supplies the phenomena in which time is identified, because, strictly speaking, time itself is not a phenomenon. That is to say, like space or pure matter or pure consciousness, time is invisible by itself, transparent and empty. A phenomenon is something that appears and can be subjected to scrutiny. By nature Greek philosophy means the phenomenal in general, the domain of what we would call sensible reality.

Nature, then, is physical existence as it appears in perceptual experience. What is physical is not just material, however. Whereas modern physics excludes living nature and restricts itself to material being, it was the biological aspect of sensible presence that most shaped Greek physical imagination.

Living things arise and subside; they show themselves openly or withdraw into latency; they are generated and they perish. When life is the clue, when physics is physiology, physical appearing is like an emerging or an unfolding, not simply the blank overtness of matter. The Greek word itself says this: *physis*, "nature," is from *phyein*, "to emerge or appear," which is the verb for what a *phyton* does, a "plant." Plants do not just emerge in the sense of growing, adding stature by accretion. They unfold their form from out of themselves, budding forth as though from some invisible interior reservoir of form. Whether or not such a botanical image was at work in the original choice of the term *physis*, a late writer like Plotinus certainly hears it there. He quite regularly lets the image of a plant stand for sensible being as a whole.

The arisings and subsidings of things are part of a coherent process that shows patterns. This is the most primitive observation of any possible empirical science. It directs the most primitive of possible analyses, an account of the structure of pattern itself. To these topics archaic Greek physics devoted itself, and so it was primitive. But here primitive means fundamental.

Time in the old physics was associated with the patterns in natural motions and changes, not just with the seriality of one thing after another. And so the question of the identity of time was quickly directed to the structure and power of pattern and order. The oldest surviving original text from Greek physics is a sentence from Anaximander the Milesian, and in it the word time itself, *chronos* in Greek, plays a pivotal role. In order to cite it, a bit of context is necessary. Because this requires reconstruction of lost argumentation some uncertainty is involved, but the general outline is clear.

Anaximander put a name on what was later called the *archē*, the first principle of things. He called it the Limitless, which could also be translated the Infinite. Itself not manifest, it was the source or substrate of all that is manifest. If the source is called Limitless, what arises from it will exhibit Limit, limitation. It appears that Anaximander distinguished two stages in the constellation of the patterns of limitation displayed in nature. At a higher stage, directly engendered from the Limitless, he placed the simplest form of limitation possible, that in which polar contraries stand apart from one another: day/night, hot/cold, up/down and the like. At a lower stage, deriving from these fundamental oppositions, he placed the much more complicated limitations that emerge among individuals which become and perish.

Sketchy as this may be, it is enough of his position for us to recover the train of thought that leads to our surviving fragment. Begin on the level of the cosmological opposites. Hot stands apart from cold. Let loose the limit here, the difference between these opposites, and they cancel each other, lapsing back into the undisturbed Limitless. Hold the limit, however, and a tension is created from which motion and change might take rise. Drawing from a whole inventory of such simple and intelligible contrasts, the world of sensible becoming is a life modulated by necessity and balance. But what holds the limits open, what calls them into play among the individuals that are born and die? Anaximander says time does.

> Into the same things from which generation comes to existing things, perishing too takes place, in accordance with what is needful; for they give satisfaction to one another and make reparation for their injustice, in accordance with the order of time. (fr. 1, Diels-Kranz; trans. P. Manchester)

This is a very rich text, the vocabulary full of allusion: justice ("satisfaction") given and injustice repaired suggest jurisprudence, for example, and have much to tell us about the earliest sense of natural "law" and the emerging importance of the tribunal in Greek civics. It is also an ambiguous text: which are the "they" in the give-and-take, the cosmological opposites or the becoming things that derive from them? Many such questions are still disputed among scholars. Happily, what is needed for our account is relatively clear: it is the "order of time" that articulates the necessity and orchestrates the justice that prevails in natural processes. Time for Anaximander is an ordering power, not just a succession in events. As the force on whose behalf the Limitless allows itself to be broken open into limitation, time is the name of creative power itself. Its order is not simple sequence but meaningful structure, pattern; not just "this after that" but "this for the sake of that," "this in order for that."

At this earliest moment of its career in philosophy, time is in fact the name for something more than time, since the concept includes the intelligibility and power that will later be reserved for eternity. Even when the concept of eternity makes its entrance in the Platonic tradition, time never entirely loses its association with an order stronger than mere sequentiality.

In a similar way, eternity itself enters Greek philosophy as the name for something not yet altogether separate from time. In Anaximander's successor Heraclitus, in fact, *aiōn* plays very much the same role as *chronos* in Anaximander.

Whereas Anaximander had seen a necessity at work in nature and specified it through metaphors from jurisprudence, Heraclitus was the first to characterize the lawlike or intelligible quality of natural process as *logos*, "reason," the source of our term logic. He too was concerned with the relationship between truth on the level of fundamental reasons for things and the flux of transformations that is the face of nature to sensation. To his mind, this was a relation of great intimacy and immediacy. To discern the Logos at play in nature required no appeal to some other world of gods, but simply a transformation of attention and intuition, from self-involved and limited human concerns to the universal common cosmos. I speak of the Heraclitan Logos "at play" in the world to bring out the spontaneity and, as we would say, naturalness of the patterned beauty of truth, which he was at pains to defend against the artifice of divinity as the poets portrayed it. It was to make this point that he compared *aiōn* itself with child's play in the aphorism previously cited:

> *Aiōn* is a child, moving counters in a game;
> The royal power is a child's.

Aiōn here could never mean eternity in the sense of a higher order of truth, separate from what transpires in time, because the whole point of the statement is to celebrate the effortless rationality of the flux of natural changes. Yet it could also never mean time, except in the enriched concept at work in Anaximander, where its flux is a purposive and creative ordering power. As the two terms *aiōn* and *chronos* evolve into their more specialized denotations, which have begun to stabilize in the vocabulary of Plato, they retain this reciprocal implication, this reference to one another within that interplay of rationality with sensibility which is nature.

Eternity then is the pure presence of intelligibility, time the image of that presence in the natural cosmos. But what of the mind, the whole interior dimension of the experience of eternity and time, which is so distinctive of the Plotinian development of the theme? As mentioned above, mind, like time itself, is not directly a phenomenon on its own, but meets itself in reflection on that in which its presence is made manifest. Once individual consciousness or self-awareness is identified with mind, as it has been in European philosophy since the seventeenth century, this reflex closes in on itself all too quickly, to create that strange and solitary node we call the Ego. Mind comes to itself in the Greek experience of eternity and time, however, in an apprehension not of the Ego but of the Sphere of the All, the *ouranos* or sky.

It is no accident that the famous description of the origin of time as an image of eternity in Plato's *Timaeus* has astronomy as its context. Mediated to Greek philosophy above all by the Pythagoreans, the Egyptian and Chaldaean vision of the heaven as the paradigm for the beauty and intelligibility of order produced a tradition in which the Sphere is the epiphany of eternity and the figure of time. Plato has *Timaeus* tell us that all living things learn the obedience to number which is the principle of order from the primordial twofold of the day/night cycle (*Timaeus* 39C).[8] Even Aristotle, who thinks that only the regularity and observational convenience of the movements of the sky give the sky any priority in regard to time, still cites the tradition in which the Sphere shows something deep about the nature of time (*Physics* 4.10.218b1–2; 14.223b19–223a1). That contemplation of the sky as the Sphere of the All can be a religious experience is, of course, evident from the connotations of the alternate translation of *ouranos* as "heaven," the disclosure space of divine presence. In a place where he calls attention to this very distinction, Plotinus says:

> The gods in that higher heaven, all those who dwell upon it and in it, contemplate through their abiding in the whole of that heaven. For all things and earth and sea and plants and animals and men are heaven, everything which belongs to that higher heaven is heavenly. (V 8 [31], 3, 34–36; trans. A. H. Amstrong)

Under this aspect the sky is the epiphany of eternity. There is, of course, a silly version of this notion in popular imagination, ancient and modern, in which God or the gods dwell in the sky in such a way that their nonappearance to a cosmonaut can be promulgated as evidence for atheism. This is an obvious fallacy. A more sophisticated version would station God beyond the sky, somehow on the other side. But this too is excluded by modern cosmological geometry.

As we learn from Plotinus, I believe, all such interpretations of the exaltation that is experienced when microcosm meets macrocosm under the sky are inside out; they mistake up for down. Plotinus is often said to be a mystic, and the mystic is regularly portrayed as someone elevated, always seeking to ascend, in caricature to float off the ground. The gift of Plotinus was instead his capacity to descend, to come down in his thoughts and be perfectly present and attentive to persons and affairs, yet without interruption of his contemplative presence-of-mind, his contact with the above (Porphyry *Life of Plotinus* 8.11–21). He describes this descending as the originary motion of time itself, in which the soul opens up eternal intelligible being into temporal forms which can be participated in by sensible motions. At the pivotal point in his treatise "On Eternity and Time," where he makes the transition from eternity to time, he writes:

> What it means to be in time and what it means to be in eternity may become known to us when we have discovered time. So, then, we must go down from eternity to the enquiry into time, and to time, for there our way led us upwards, but now we must come down in our discourse, not altogether, but in the way in which time came down. III 7, 7, 6–11)

What is the experience of coming down from eternity with time? Since astronomy has provided so many key ideas in this connection, we try again a meditation on the sky. It is like the ecstatic apprehension in which, prostrate beneath the hemisphere of heaven to which our vision is at any time restricted, as much by the one-sidedness of our gaze as by the earth that interposes between ascendant and descendant hemispheres, we suddenly complete the Sphere in imagination, surround ourselves with wholeness, intuit not just the Two of time but the One of eternity, and find ourselves concentric with its all-inclusiveness and finality. The heaven opens around us as an abyss into which we are falling; it is the dizzying abandon to this All-At-Once-Now that is the true exaltation of the religious experience of eternity and time.

It is not just the doctrine but the experience of Plotinus that Presence There *reaches* presence here. Duration, once touched by this insight, is never again merely time, nor is it only eternity.

Epilogue: The Eternity of the Future

There remains a third form of temporal experience from which follows a characteristic religious experience of eternity and time, that which places the future in the first place. Its foundational events and literature were contemporary with the rise of the spirituality of presence which has been described, but it did not really come into its own until the post-Reformation period in Christian Europe and the dawning of modern historical consciousness. It is therefore only an epilogue to our story here. I refer to the temporal orientation of that extremely intense but short-lived religious experience which produced the visionary Jewish literature called apocalyptic, out of which in turn earliest Christianity emerged.

For the apocalyptic sensibility, eternity is the "world to come," time the dimension of "this world," which is already coming to an end. Its visions use an elaborate allegorical imagery to reveal (Greek *apokalyptein*) how events in time—in one's own time, which is the last time—have come into a constellation that proves that the New Age is at hand. The characteristic religious problem confronted in this experience is divine judgment, which is to say, the meaning of human life and history in the perspective of the end of the world.

If we say that this experience involves a kind of looking to the future, we will be misled if we supply a modern notion of future as the away-from-now into which expectation, progress, planning, and prediction reach. Apocalyptic speaks out of an experience of the immediate moment, the time of call and decision—in Greek, the *kairos*. This is the Now not of Presence but of Advent, and it is very much a group experience: "It's us! We're the ones who will see! Lo, the Judgment is already being revealed!" The future of the Day of the Lord is present, not absent. It approaches us, we do not march toward it, and certainly we do not bring it about.

This approach, indeed preliminary arrival, is the eternal aspect of the divine. The ecstatic embrace of the end of this world is very much a consolation for the historically beleaguered communities and traditions that produce apocalyptic religions, far removed from the morbid satisfaction of nihilism or the wicked defeatism that cries out, "We are doomed, let it all come down!" Apocalyptic movements, notably the early discipleships of John the Baptizer and Jesus of Nazareth, regularly experience the return of prophecy, as though water had returned to a well long dry. Like prophecy itself, which along with Zoroastrian conflict dualism is one of the principal sources of apocalyptic, the revelations are diagnostic more than they are prognostic. They face the future in the sense that they inculcate a certain state of readiness *now*, an acceptance, not a plan.

The old hasidic predecessors of the Pharisees, whose scholarship went back to Persian times, experienced an outbreak of apocalyptic in late Hellenistic times, in the Maccabean period, when it seemed that the syncretism and idolatry of Empire was all-contaminating and all-destroying. Two centuries later, the disciples of John and of Jesus saw the whole rich world of intertestamental Judaism shattered by the iron fist of Rome. The most important and fully formed apocalyptic visions that survive to us are from this period, the most elaborate from the circle of John (which we know in a Christian redaction as the book of Revelation), the most perfect from the circle of Jesus (chapter 13 of the Gospel of Mark).

In the end apocalyptic always has the problem of outliving itself. It is not true that the world has not ended. Worlds do end, again and again. But tradition outlives the end. In Christianity, apocalyptic experience was mastered institutionally by the two principal Christian mysteries, the baptism by water and the blessing of bread and wine. Spiritually, it quickly ceased being the center of experience of eternity and time within Christian tradition itself and gave way, like the mysteries themselves and the archaic temporal experience in which they were rooted, to the contemplative orientation to Presence.

Perhaps today the moment of that eternal Presence has passed, but that hardly means that it is gone. Eternity has drawn the burden of the past and the anxiety of the future into its divine composure before, and it can do so again. The spirituality of the Greek Mediterranean world is not everlasting in time, but it is certainly still eternal.

Notes

1. Augustine, *Confessions*, trans. R. S. Pine-Coffin (New York: Penguin Books, 1961).

2. Mircea Eliade, *The Myth of the Eternal Return*.

3. The familiar argument that the *Iliad* and the *Odyssey* begin the transposition of epic imagination from the divine to the human and are in that sense already the humanistic critique of mythology that becomes classic in Plato is expounded in relation to the developing concept of eternity by John S. Dunne, *The City of the Gods*, chaps. 3 and 4.

4. An instructive juxtaposition of the *deiknymenon* at Eleusis, the showing of the ripened ear of grain, with the Flower Sermon of the Buddha, concludes C. Kerényi's discussion of "Kore" in *Essays on a Science of Mythology*, 151–55.

5. There is a complicated philological problem in the existence of a second Greek term *aïdios*, meaning "everlasting" but sometimes translated "eternal." In early writers— and even in Plato and Aristotle, in the opinion of some—it is not clear whether a sharp distinction is understood between *aïdios* and the adjectival form of *aiōn*, *aiōnios*. Those who worry about this problem do so in the supposition that the mature conception of *aiōn* is an 'eternity' that is utterly durationless, whereas what is everlasting plainly has duration. Since, as argued in what follows, eternity transcends time not by excluding duration altogether but by intensifying certain of its aspects, the ambiguity of terminology in early writers does not pose any problem for this analysis, and *aïdios* will not enter the discussion.

6. "Eternity is the whole, perfect, and simultaneous possession of endless life," in Boethius, *The Consolation of Philosophy*, Book V, Prose 6, trans. Richard Green (Indianapolis, IN, and New York: Bobbs-Merrill, 1962) 115.

7. Translation adapted from that of Philip Wheelwright, *The Presocratics*, 71.

8. He calls it "the revolution of the Selfsame."

Bibliography

Editions

Plotinus. Translated by A. H. Armstrong. 7 vols. Loeb Classical Library, 440–446. Cambridge, MA: Harvard University Press; London: Heinemann, 1967 (vols. 1–3, 1984 (vols. 4–5).

Translations

Aristotle. *The Basic Works of Aristotle.* Edited by Richard McKeon. New York: Random House, 1941.

Augustine. *The Confessions.* Translated by R. S. Pine-Coffin. New York: Penguin Books, 1961.

Boethius. *The Consolation of Philosophy.* Translated by Richard Green. Indianapolis, IN, and New York: Bobbs-Merrill, 1962.

Plato. *The Collected Dialogues.* Edited by Edith Hamilton and Huntington Cairns. Bollingen Series 71. New York: Bollingen Foundation, 1981. Distributed by Pantheon Books.

The Presocratics. Translated by Philip Wheelwright. Indianapolis, IN: Bobbs-Merrill, 1960.

Modern Works

Dunne, John S. *The City of the Gods: A Study in Myth and Mortality.* Notre Dame, IN: University of Notre Dame Press, 1978.

Eliade, Mircea. *The Myth of the Eternal Return: Cosmos and History.* Translated by Willard R. Trask. Princeton, NJ: Princeton University Press, 1954.

Jung, C. G., and C. Kerényi. *Essays on a Science of Mythology: The Myth of the Divine Child and the Mysteries of Eleusis.* Translated by R. F. C. Hull. Bollingen Series 22. Princeton, NJ: Princeton University Press, 1969.

17

Cosmic Piety

JEAN PÉPIN

NOTHING SEEMS MORE FOREIGN to today's mentality than to make the *cosmos*, the organized universe, the object of a religious attitude. The Christian tradition, with which we are to some extent imbued, has imposed on us the idea of a sort of rivalry between the universe and humanity in which the latter is by definition the victor:

> Even if the universe were to crush him, man would still be nobler than that which destroys him, because he knows that he is dying and what advantage the universe has over him; the universe is unaware of it. (Pascal *Pensées* no. 347; Brunschvig, *ed. minor*, p. 488)

This famous saying of Pascal brings to mind, in certain respects, another saying, no less famous, of the Jesus of the Gospels:

> For what does it profit a man if he gains the whole world (*ton kosmon holon*) and loses or forfeits himself? (Luke 9:25)[1]

Accordingly, we are not surprised to note in the New Testament, particularly in the Pauline writings, various condemnations of cosmic religion. The Letter to the Romans recalls that the worst moral disorders struck the ungodly, who were guilty of having "worshiped and served the creature rather than the Creator" (1:25, *esebasthēsan kai elatreusan*—two technical terms of Greek worship). The religion of the world is sometimes discredited as being the religion of the "rudiments of the world," an obscure and disputed phrase, but one whose cosmic reference at least is undeniable. Thus, in the warning addressed to the Christians at Colossae, the hostile evocation of philosophy (the sole use of the word in the New Testament) reminds us that cosmic religion was, in fact, as we shall see, the concern of the greatest philosophers of the Greek tradition:

408

> See to it that no one makes a prey of you by philosophy and empty deceit, according to human tradition, according to the elemental spirits of the world (*stoicheia tou kosmou*). (Col 2:28)

It is probably also the cult of the world, of the astral world in particular, that is denounced in the Letter to the Galatians as an old practice, outmoded but still attractive:

> Formerly, when you did not know God, you were in bondage to beings that by nature are not gods; but now that you have come to know God, or rather to be known by God, how can you turn back again to the weak and beggarly elemental spirits, whose slaves you want to be once more? You observe days, and months, and seasons, and years! I am afraid I have labored over you in vain. (4:8–11)

Moreover, the Pauline letters on this point are rooted, though with different wording, in the Jewish and Greek Bibles. If Yahweh on Horeb was heard without being seen, it is as Moses said to the people of Israel:

> Beware lest you lift up your eyes to heaven, and when you see the sun and the moon and the stars, all the host of heaven, you be drawn away and worship them and serve them, things which the Lord your God has allotted to all the peoples under the whole heaven. (Deut 4:19)[2]

Later, the hellenized Jewish author of the Wisdom of Solomon was to rage similarly against those who, ignorant of God,

> supposed that either fire or wind or swift air, or the circle of the stars, or the turbulent water or the luminaries of heaven were the gods that rule the world. If through delight in the beauty of these things men assumed them to be gods, let them know how much better than these is their Lord. (13:2–3)

It will be apparent from these two extracts that, as in the Pauline texts, the express condemnation of the divinization of the world concerns the astral world above all. We shall soon see that this emphasis conforms to the reality of cosmic religion.

There was some point in quoting fundamental texts of Judaism and Christianity to explain how the religion of the world, so enduring and vigorous in classical antiquity, may seem strange to modern eyes. It is because these pages of the Bible echoed through the centuries and shaped mental attitudes. We cannot deal with the history of this topic here. It must suffice to take two examples from the patristic age. In his account of the orthodox faith, which concludes his *Refutation of All Heresies*, Hippolytus of Rome (third century) remarks that the world is not God because it comes from nothingness, as opposed to the Logos which, coming from God, is God (10.33). It was not long before his death (430) that Augustine expressed the same idea, but from different premises, in the context of a theory according to which the world had a soul that made it a living being. As usual, the African bishop appears perplexed and rather skeptical about this theory, dear to so many philosophers, but which did not convince him, either by reason or by the authority of the scriptures.[3] One point, on the other hand, is, in his view, beyond question: that this world, whether it has a soul or not, is not a god for us (*deum nobis non esse istum mundum; Retractions* 1.10.4). Numerous positions of this kind could be found in the writings of the fathers and the medievals, particularly in their commentaries on the passages of scripture quoted above.

The Tradition of Cosmic Piety

Plato and the Old Academy

A convenient way of approaching the history of cosmic religion in Greek thought is to read the sketch of it from the pen of Cicero, in the first book of his dialogue *On the Nature of the Gods* 1.8.18–1.15.41; its polemical style comes from the fact that the author makes the Epicurean Velleius deliver it.[4] As in a portrait gallery, we see a procession of philosophers: first of all, certain Pre-Socratics, from Thales to Diogenes of Apollonia (25–29), then Plato and his school, in which Aristotle takes his place, followed soon afterward by his own school (30–35); and finally the Stoics from Zeno to Diogenes of Babylon (36–41). The vast majority of these thinkers are seen as authorities on the divine universe; they recognize "a spherical fiery god, caught up in a circular movement" (*rotundum, ardentem, volubilem deum*); (18). The doctrinal accounts devoted to each one of them and their assessment by Epicureanism are equally stereotyped, which prevents us from having blind confidence in them. Mostly these philosophers are credited with attributing divinity simultaneously to the whole world and to several of its parts, whether souls or cosmic intellects, aether, sky, stars, etc., and this pluralism is denounced by the Epicurean spokesmen as a contradiction (*inconstantia*). There is the same monotony in the other critique, in which it is continuously argued that the cosmic god, in perpetual movement, is a challenge to the absolute quietude of the gods of Epicurus.[5] Nevertheless, Cicero's list has the merit of throwing into relief the three principal centers of the religion of the world—that is to say, Plato and the Academy, Aristotle while still a Platonist, and Stoicism, in comparison with which the influence of the Pre-Socratics is minimal and disputed.

In any case, what Cicero says about Plato faithfully reflects his teaching:

> In the *Timaeus,* as in the *Laws,* he says that the world is god, as are also the sky, the stars, the earth, and their souls. (*On the Nature of the Gods* 1.12.30)

On the subject of the divinity of the world, in the *Timaeus* 34A, the distinction between the Demiurge and the world is rendered as that between "the god who is always" and "the god who will be." The world is referred to here as "the blessed god" (34B), "the sensible god" (92C). These terms would indicate a god on a lower level. *Laws* 7.821A does not support this hypothesis: "the totality of the world" seems there to be called "tbe greatest of gods." Still more frequent is the attribution of divinity to the stars, "visible gods" (*Timaeus* 40D), "gods whose revolving is manifest" (41A), "gods of the skies" (*Laws* 7.821C, cf. 822B), "gods and divine things" (*Laws* 10.886D, where, exactly as in Cicero, this term is applied to the earth). All the stars together are called "the celestial species of gods," "the divine species" (*Timaeus* 39E–40A). In this system, the sun and the moon are separated (*Laws* 12.950D) and are both "great gods" (*Laws* 7.821B). A negative formulation of the same view is that those who believed the starry heavens to be filled solely with inanimate bodies have been many times accused of "atheism" (*Laws* 12.967C). The divinity of the cosmic soul is expressed, above all, in *Laws* 10: when the universal soul is joined to the divine intellect, it is itself a god (897B; text uncertain); the soul that moves the sun is a god, as are other souls that are causes of all celestial movements (899AB).

All these texts of Plato set forth and support the theses of cosmic theology, but there are others, mostly in *Laws*, where we detect corresponding feelings of devotion and even actual religious practices. In the refusal to see impiety in the compulsion to examine the causes of the divine universe (*Laws* 7.821A), we can infer, on the contrary, the idea of a certain cosmic piety. This, moreover, shows through in all sorts of gestures, regarded by Plato with a favorable eye or even recommended by him. Just as Socrates offered up a prayer to the rising sun (*Symposium* 220D), the Greeks and barbarians prostrated themselves and worshiped at the rising and the setting of the sun and the moon (*Laws* 10.887E). Those who knew nothing of astronomy could not sing, in honor of the gods of the stars, the hymns that were truthful and appropriate (*Laws* 7.822C). It is proper to decide the following:

> that our citizens and young men should be informed about the gods of the sky; that they should know enough about them all so as not to blaspheme about them and so as to speak of them reverently each time they sacrifice or, in their prayers, call upon them with piety. (*Laws* 7.821CD)

This tends to confirm the Platonic authenticity of the little dialogue *Epinomis*, which agrees with and reinforces what we have just seen. The god of the sky is said here (977A) to have the advantage over all the other daemons and gods. In the "divine species of the stars," each one is "absolutely divine" (981E–982A; cf. *Timaeus* 39E, quoted above). Whether divine or a god—and the affirmation occurs several times (983E, 984C, 987A and D, 988A)—planets or fixed stars, all are gods of equal dignity (980B); in short:

> The visible gods, the greatest ones, those most worthy of honors, those whose glance is the most penetrating on all sides must be numbered among the first rank; they are, by their very nature, the stars. (984D)

In this glorification of the stars, the *Epinomis* barely exceeds the *Laws*, but it shows more invention when deriving applications from them relevant to religion or even culture. To begin with pious feelings, there is admiration for the celestial order (986C), veneration of it (*semnynein*), and the honors (*timan*) due to it (977A, 984D, 987A). There is one allusion to hymns (*hymnēteon*) in honor of the stars (983E). Without wishing in any way to abandon the traditional religion, the author deplores the fact that these visible gods should be ignored through slackness:

> deprived of ceremonies (*anorgiastous*) though they also are gods in another way, and not receiving the honors due to them.

> How, then, seeing the sun and moon excluded from all honor, could we not for our part, long to bring them, brilliant in the eyes of all, to a place of honor to establish feasts (*heortas*) for them and sacrifices (*thysias*) or to distribute the time which each of them has for its revolution into longer, or often shorter, annual periods? (985DE)

There is in this the idea of a sacred veneration of the stars, and even of a sort of liturgical time-scale determined in conjunction with the duration of their course. This notion recurs shortly afterward (986C), when the necessity becomes clear of giving all the stars their share and the time-scale of their own circuit, instead of being limited to the solar year or the lunar month. Even if the stars proved not to be actual gods, they were at least images of gods, statues of a sort (*hōs agalmata*) wrought by the gods themselves, which, more than any others, call for honors and veneration (984A). But we should observe how the final word in this little dialogue about the worship of the stars takes the form of a profession of faith in the ability of the Greeks to absorb foreign elements. Undoubtedly Egypt and Syria were the first, on .account of their clear skies, to become conscious of the star gods (987A and D).[7] It is incumbent on us Greeks to outdo the barbarians in this belief and this cult (*phēmēs te hama kai therapeias*), by drawing upon our culture, our oracle at Delphi, and all our established worship.[8]

Whether *Epinomis* is the work of Plato or one of his disciples (Philip of Opus), no other text of that school was to exalt to a greater extent the religion of the world. But a trace of it is found among Plato's successors as the head of the Academy. One of them, Xenocrates, thought "that the sky is also a god and that the fiery stars are the Olympic gods" (fr. 15, Heinze

p. 165, 3–4). Expressing another view, very close to that of the *Epinomis* (987B), he counted eight gods—five planets, all the fixed stars combined to form a single god, the sun as number seven and the moon as number eight. (fr. 17, Heinze p. 165, 19–23). A doxographic reference to his disciple Polemon reports very classically that "he professed that the world is god" (Aetius *Placita* 1.7.29; Diels, p. 303b30–31).

Aristotle

In his best-known works, which arise from his teaching as head of a school, Aristotle leaves no room even for the possibility of a religion of the world. But probably it was not always so. Various later authors attribute to Aristotle by name a belief in the divinity of the world, especially the celestial world, and even say that he allowed true religious emotion to appear in this context. The authors who inform us of this could not have had the scholarly Aristotelian treatises in mind, as we have seen. They must, then, be transmitting the contents of other works of Aristotle, which we know there were, lost as complete works and known only from what was said or preserved by their ancient readers. For reasons that it would be inappropriate to develop here, it is thought that belief in the divinity of the cosmos was expressed in a dialogue *De philosophia,* in which Aristotle had not yet repudiated all the Platonism by which he had been formed.[9]

A few references to this dialogue, taken from Cicero and Philo of Alexandria, include the following:

> (1) I wonder whether Aristotle was not acting in a pious and holy fashion (*eusebōs kai hosiōs*) in opposing [preceding opinions] when he said that the world was not generated and incorruptible and when he accused of a terrifying atheism those who defended the opposite thesis and refused to recognise any difference between the works from the hand of man and this immense visible god (*horaton theon*) who encompasses sun, moon and in fact the whole "pantheon" (*pantheion*) of the other stars, planets and fixed stars. (Aristotle *De philosophia* fr. 18, Ross p. 85 = Philo *On the Indestructibility of the World* 3.10)

If we restore this extract to the context of the Philonian treatise from which it comes, we can see that the ideas attributed to Aristotle are opposed, in a dialectical procedure, not taking chronology into account, to those of the Atomists Democritus and Epicurus as well as those of the Stoics.

Nevertheless, the view violently rejected by the Aristotle we see here objectively corresponds more than any other view to that of the Platonic theory of the origin of the world with its artificialist implications. His passionate opposition to the comparison with manual works will nourish the Epicurean objections to the *Timaeus* with its world "seemingly made by hand" (*manu paene factus*).[10] The anger thus leveled at a theory that is one of Plato's is surprising when coming from Aristotle, fresh from the Academy. It is certainly from the *Timaeus*, as we remember, that this expression "visible god" comes (40D), supporting divinization of the heavens in the direct line of Platonism. Philo, on the other hand, emphasizes Aristotle's cosmic piety, as in the following text.

(2) "respect (*aidous*) for the visible [god]" (fr. 19a, Ross p. 86 = Philo *On the Indestructibility of the World* 5.20)

(3) Therefore, since it is in the ether that the stars are born, it is universally admitted that they possess sense and intelligence. For this reason, the stars are to be numbered among the gods (*in deorum astra esse dicenda*) (fr. 21a, Ross p. 90 = Cicero *On the Nature of the Gods* 2.15.42)[11]

(4) Finally, the movement of the stars is voluntary. Anyone who, on seeing this, denied that they were gods would be acting not only in ignorance but with utter impiety. (fr. 21b, Ross p. 91 = Cicero *On the Nature of the Gods* 2.16.44)[12]

Stoicism

The observations made about the Stoics by Cicero, through the mouth of the Epicurean Velleius, in the first book of *On the Nature of the Gods,* were referred to above. But the second book of the same dialogue brings into the foreground a Stoic, Lucilius Balbus, whose long exposition Cicero has constructed from reliable Stoic sources.[13] In it, there are, somewhat haphazardly several attestations to the belief in the divinity of the world and particularly of the stars (8.21–28, 73). The transition from one theory to the other can be read in paragraph 39:

After having examined the divinity of the world as a whole, it remains to recognise the same divinity in the stars.

These affirmations are for argued according to a plan that is often as follows: the world (or the sky) possesses the type of character that requires it to be proclaimed a god. For example, the world is wise from its beginnings (par. 36). The perfection of its nature—that is to say, virtue—is within it (par. 39). It is a living being, endowed with senses, intellect, and reason (par. 47); *ergo,* it is god. Furthermore (par. 54), when we see in the stars the presence of intellect, reason, and resolution, "we cannot fail to number them among the gods" (*non possumus ea ipsa non in deorum numero reponere*). The last two fragments of Aristotle, which are constructed on the same model, are also extracts from this discourse of Balbus.

We find a related argument, proceeding to the same conclusion, framed in a Stoic context in Sextus Empiricus (*Against the Schoolmasters* 9.95–98).[14] The starting point is a page of Xenophon on the teleological argument (*Memorabilia* 1.4.2–8), which Sextus uses as an inductive proof with the following result in brief. If there exists in you a fragment of earth, water, air, and fire, this means that those elements exist in great quantity in the world. Equally:

> If there were no intellect in the world, there would be no intellect in you; but there is intellect in you, thus there is one in the world also. It follows that the world is intelligent. But, being intelligent, it is at the same time god.

We cannot overstress the importance of the intellect of the world in the cosmic theology of the Stoics. It is not one god among many; it is the god to whom the other realities of the world owe their divinity. To return to Cicero, the Stoic will not recognize that it is daylight now with more conviction than he would affirm the following:

> that the world which we see is wise, that it has an intellect produced by itself, it has produced the world and guarantees the orderliness of all things, their movement and their direction; he will also be convinced that the sun, the moon, all the stars, the earth and the sea are gods because a living intelligence spreads through all these beings and circulates among them. (*Lucullus* 37.119)[15]

And here is a Greek testimony that in fewer words awards the honors to the universal intellect:

> [The Stoics recognize] as gods the world, the stars, the earth and, superior to them all, the intellect in the ether. (Aetius *Placita* 1.7.33)[16]

It is no doubt this same distance, between the primordial divinity of the cosmic intellect and the consequent (but no less real) divinity of the universe which is indicated by Zeno, Chrysippus, and Posidonius: "The entirety of the world and the sky is the substance of God" (Diogenes Laertius *Lives* 7.148)[17]

The history of Stoicism, needless to say, was far from finished with Chrysippus, and the religion of the world was one of the alternatives adhered to for some time to come. Thus, in the first century B.C. the Stoic Varro, a friend of Cicero, was responsible for a theory very similar to the one we have just seen among the founders of the school, but more radical: the primacy of the god as universal soul had so developed that, without suppressing the divinity of the sensible universe, it almost made it arise from a metonymy *a parte ad totum*. This is how Augustine attests to this point of doctrine:

> Varro says that, in his opinion, the soul of the world which the Greeks call
> *kosmos* is god and that the world which we see is itself god; but [he continues]
> just as rational man, although composed of body and soul, is nevertheless
> called rational because of his soul, in the same way the world is called god
> because of its soul, although it is composed of soul and body. (Varro *Antiqui-
> tatum* 16, fr. 226, Cardanus p. 96 = Augustine *City of God* 7.6)

The formulation is overrefined, but the idea is clear: it is the soul of the
world which is originally god. The world is only god through it and not
through its body; this explains the reaction of Augustine, who continues
immediately: "Varro appears here, in some degree, to profess One God."
Finally, to complete the Stoic line, we should draw attention to the poet
Manlius, a contemporary of the emperor Augustus and the author of a great
fresco in verse entitled *Astronomica*. The first book of this work attests on
several occasions to a belief in the divinity of the world and, above all, of
the sky (known as *mundus*). Manlius appears captivated by the eternity of
the latter, *a parte ante* as *a parte post* and its unchanging permanence: "it will
always be the same because it has always been the same" (line 521). This is
the reason put forward for its divinization: the firmament "is a god, which
does not change in time" (523); and again in lines 483–85:

> I cannot see an argument as powerful to demonstrate that the world, in its
> movement, obeys a divine power and is itself a god.

Imperial Platonism

Celsus was a Platonist at the end of the second century A.D., who was an
anti-Jewish and anti-Christian polemicist on a large scale. His *True Discourse* has been lost, but luckily many quotations from it survive in
Origen's refutation, entitled *Against Celsus*. Celsus addressed this reproach
to the Jews:

> They venerate the sky and the angels in it, but they ignore its most venerable
> and powerful parts, the sun, the moon and the other stars, the fixed stars and
> the planets; as though it were admissible for the whole to be god and for its
> parts not to be divine!" (Origen *Against Celsus* 5.6)

It is immaterial whether the accusation was well founded or not; but
Celsus's argument, which concludes *a toto ad partes*, from the worship of
the sky to the necessity for a cult of the stars, has a long history.[18] It shows
that the authors who applied this reasoning to this subject were, for easily
comprehensible reasons, devotees of the religion of a world considered
divine in its totality at the same time as in each of its constituent parts. It
is safe to include among these believers the Platonist Celsus, faithful in this
regard to Plato his master from centuries before.

After quoting these lines from Celsus, Origen discusses them and challenges the argument. It is an opportunity for him to deliver some information of extreme interest about the different modulations of cosmic theology, and he implies, in a rather astonishing way, that all Greeks are supporters of it:

> Greeks, it is clear, say that the world in its totality is god, Stoics say that it is the first god, Platonists that it is the second and certain others that it is the third. (*Against Celsus* 5.7)

Faced with evidence of this kind, historians will not rest until they can make general formulas precise by the use of appropriate names and until they can reshape the points of doctrine by using other texts. This is rather difficult: nevertheless, the meager results which can be obtained allow the diachrony of cosmic theology and even its conceptual field to be appreciably extended.

There does not seem to be any Stoic document available to support the idea of the universe as first god, but we can read a doxography according to which, in the eyes of Chrysippus and other Stoics,

> the world in its totality being alive, animate and rational, has as its guiding principle (*hēgemonikon*) [. . .] the purest part of the ether: they even call it first god. (Diogenes Laertius *Lives* 7.139)[19]

It is conceivable that, given a certain shifting, this sort of formula might be the source of Origen's testimony. The fact that the Platonists named the world as "second god" harmonizes completely with the sketch in the *Timaeus* (28C, 41A, etc.), which represents the Demiurge as the "father" of the universe. If we make him the "first god" (which does not seem to contradict the way of thinking in the *Timaeus*), we get very close to Origen's formula. And this step is not without precedent; it is to be found, indeed, coming from the pen of the doxographer Aetius (*Placita* 1.7.31; ed. Diels p. 304b31–305b8),[20] including the reference to *Timaeus* 28C:

> The other divine beings are descendants of this father and creator. . . . The sensible descendants of the first god are the sun, the moon, the stars, the earth and the world which embraces all things.

Finally, Origen attributes to "certain Platonists" the conception of the world as a third god. This is clearly a reference to an author whom he knows well, the Platonist and Neopythagorean Numenius, probably a contemporary of Celsus:

> Numenius, in fact, claims three gods and calls the first "Father," the second "Creator" and the third "Creation"; because the world, for him, is the third god. (Numenius fr. 21, 1–3 des Places)

It is very probably Numenius again who is referred to in a passage from Porphyry, in which, exactly as with Origen, he takes note only of "certain Platonists." The system attributed to them comprises "the first god," then the soul of the world, then "the other gods," namely, the world, the fixed stars and the planets, visible gods, to whom sacrifices must be offered in thanksgiving (*On Abstinence* 2.37.1–3). The hierarchy of the divine principles is less accentuated here than in the preceding text, but it might in fact be essentially the same representation and the final recommendation to worship the stars and the world (or the sky) joins up with the original Platonism completely. Like Celsus, Numenius should therefore be counted among the supporters of cosmic theology and religion which were still flourishing among the thinkers of the second century A.D.

On this same subject of Platonic theology in its hierarchical aspect, we read in another part of Porphyry's work a page that strikes a totally different note. Plato said that divinity proceeded in three hypostases in all: the supreme God is the Good; after him in second place comes the Demiurge; and, third, there is the soul of the world, "for divinity has proceeded as far as the soul" (*History of Philosophy* 4, fr. 16 Nauck [2nd ed.] p. 14, 3–7).[21] The principal idea of this text, which is formulated at the beginning and at the end, is that the divine goes no lower than the soul of the world. Porphyry's intention becomes even more evident if (unlike the editor A. Nauck, but like other scholars) we recognize in him the author of the following phrase quoted by Cyril of Alexandria: "the absence of the divine (*to atheon*) begins at the level of the body."[22] This Platonism is no longer that of Numenius but could be that of Plotinus, as is proved by comparing it with *Ennead* V 1 [10], whose thesis is that divine things end with the soul.[23] It would not be possible to believe, from this perspective, that the world or any of its parts had a share in divinity. The "sensible god" of the *Timaeus* is excluded in this Plotinian presentation of Platonism.

At least it ought to be so. But in the same treatise Plotinus expressly accepts cosmic theology—by the soul which makes it a living being, the world which we see is god, and similarly for the same reason the sun and the other stars (V 1 [10], 2, 40–41; cf. 2, 4 [divine stars]). There is no contradiction here to the concept of the soul as a lower limit of the divine, since it is the soul itself that confers divinity on the world. Nevertheless, we have seen more than once, especially in the Stoic context, this particular thesis integrated with the most authentic cosmic religion. On the other hand, Plotinus takes the idea of the world as "blessed god" (IV 8 [6], 1, 41–43 [with reference to the *Timaeus* 34B]) from the *Timaeus,* and it is as a Platonist that he joins those who address their prayers to the sun (whereas he attributes praying to "the stars" only to "certain others" (IV 4 [28], 30, 3–4; also 26, 1).

31. Votive Relief to Apollo (?) and Artemis. Attica. Ca. 325 B.C.

From this it is clear that cosmic piety is not alien to Plotinus, probably in reaction to Gnostic anticosmism. The same reference in the *Timaeus* to the world as blessed god reappears in a late treatise entitled *On Love* (III 5 [50], 5, 7–9). It is followed, one page further on, by a passage of great consequence for the new light shed by imperial Platonism on the religion of the world. It loses none of its validity but is established at a subordinate hierarchical level.

Plotinus asks whether divinity is limited to the intelligible world,

> or if "there are gods here also" and if the world is god, the "third god," as it is usual to call it, and if the beings above the moon and the moon itself are each of them a god. . . . The gods in the universe of sense down to and including the moon, the visible ones, are secondary gods which come after and correspond to those higher intelligible gods and depend on them, like the radiance around every star. (III 5 [50], 6, 17–24; trans. A. H. Armstrong)

It is clear that, at the beginning of this text, the philosopher opts for the second hypothesis. The first quotation, which colors everything that follows, is from Heraclitus; the world as a "third god" is a salute to Numenius without naming him. The divinity of the world, especially of the fixed stars and the planets, is affirmed unequivocally and the formula that designates them as "visible gods" echoing *Timaeus* 40D stamps it as of Platonic inspiration. The gods of the sensible sky yield ultimately only to the intelligible gods with whom they live symbiotically and of whom they are the manifestation. Far from being excluded from the sensible world, divinity impregnates it and sheds on it the brilliance of the intelligible gods. This is a very different tone from the thesis of *Ennead* V 1, according to which divine things descend no lower than the soul (V 1, 7, 49).[24] With these two contrasting opinions, one of them encountered in one of the oldest treatises (V 1), the other in one of the latest, we can imagine that, in the evening of his life, Plotinus was more aware of the divine character of the cosmos, in a similar development to that of Plato, whose cosmic piety blossomed particularly in the last dialogues, the *Timaeus* and the *Laws*.

We have seen Porphyry presenting Plato's theology as having no place for the religion of the world. It would be interesting, so as to complete our too brief survey, to know how he himself was personally situated in respect to this belief. We lack the evidence to answer such a question and can only mention two points. In his *Letter to Anebo,* Porphyry attributes the following to the Egyptian priest Chaeremon:

> [that he] acknowledges nothing above the visible worlds . . . nor other gods than the stars called planets, together with those which composed the zodiac and all those which rise in their vicinity. (2.12b; ed. Sodano p. 23, 7–24, 3)

Porphyry reproaches this profession of faith in a cosmic theology that is essentially that of the stars, reducing all things to physical phenomena and attributing nothing to incorporeal and living substances (*Letter to Anebo* 2.12c; ed. Sodano p. 25, 1-2). But in another work, very probably earlier, the *Cult of Images*, the same author praises beliefs and sentiments which, in their way, come close to the religion of the world, and so he quotes with approval a wonderful Orphic hymn, the main idea of which is to identify the details of Zeus's person with the reality of the universe. The head and the face of the god are the sky surrounded by the stars as hair. His eyes are the sun and the moon and his intellect is the aether, etc.—in short, everything here below is contained in the great body of Zeus. He concludes his quotation thus:

> Zeus is then the whole cosmos, a living being among the living beings and a god among the gods. (*De imaginibus* fr. 3, Bidez p. 3*, 12-6, 1)[25]

Elsewhere in the same treatise, he reviews the principal Greek and Egyptian divinities, noting the appearance and attributes given them in their figurative representations. Using these data, and in a style stamped with Stoic theology, Porphyry sees different cosmic forces designated in the various gods and goddesses. Thus, Hera is the force of the air, Ceres the seminal force, Themis the divinatory force, Hestia the terrestrial force, Ocean the force that produces water, etc. (fr. 4ff., Bidez p. 7*, 5ff.). The traditional Greek and Egyptian pantheon in this perspective becomes an allegorical doublet of the system of powerful movements which give life to the material universe; and where the constituted religion loses by this interpretation, the religion of the world certainly gains. This is undoubtedly to reduce the object of theology to physical phenomena—in other words, to lean toward the fault that Porphyry would criticize later on in Chaeremon, an inconsistency that did not escape the perspicacity of Eusebius, the Christian apologist to whom we owe the knowledge of these two groups of Porphyrian texts (*Praeparatio evangelica* 3.13.9).

The World and the Temple

The Temple, the Image of the World

The Etruscans and then the Romans used, among other places of worship, a pit covered by a vault, supposed to bring the world of the living into contact with that of the dead. This subterranean cell was called a *mundus*, because as Cato the Elder said, it was vaulted like the sky (quoted by Festus *De significatu verborum*; ed. Lindsay p. 144, 17-21).[26] This detail illustrates the tendency that is present in many religions to arrange buildings for worship and liturgical objects and vestments so that they might reflect the cosmos. It could be said that from a certain perspective the perfect temple would be a little cosmos, although this notion in ancient thought was generally applied to the human person. It is easy to understand how this ambition to make sacred buildings and instruments into true copies of the world draws strength from the cosmic religion and pays homage to it indirectly. In Rome too the cupola of the Pantheon was supposed to owe its rounded form to the desire to make it resemble the sky (Dio Cassius *Roman History* 53.27.2).[27] Finally, inspired as much by his classical as by his Christian culture, Isidore of Seville testified that:

> The Ancients used to make the roofs of their temples in the form of a tortoise shell; so as to represent the sky, which they could see was curved. (*Etymologies* 15.8.8)[28]

In Rome and throughout the Roman Empire there were many other vaulted temples, of the Persian god Mithra. Half buried, often arranged in grottos, these *mithraea* contained a ceiling that was either naturally or artificially curved, painted with constellations like those of the firmament. The intention was to make this place of worship a "replica of the cosmos."[29] Substantial archaeological documentation leaves no doubt on this point. We also have at our disposal a literary testimony from Porphyry in the same sense as follows:

> In the same way, the Persians consecrated a priest by initiating him into the mystery of the descent of souls into the underworld and their return from there, giving the place the name of "grotto"; as Eubulus affirms, Zoroaster was the first to consecrate in the mountains near Persis a natural grotto with flowers and springs in honor of Mithra, the creator and father of all things; he considered that the grotto offered an image of the world of which Mithra was the demiurge and the objects inside, through the proportion of their spacing, presented the symbol of the elements and the zones of the world: afterwards, Zoroaster imposed on other people also the custom of conducting initiations in caverns and grottos, whether natural, as the above mentioned, or artificial. (*De antro nympharum* 6)[30]

This passage from Porphyry poses various problems that we shall not touch upon here; in any case he attests clearly that to honor Mithra, the Demiurge of the universe, the mysteries of this god were unfolded in the beginning in a grotto, chosen for its significance as a whole as an image of the world and also because it contained objects symbolizing the stars (elements) and the circles of the sky. When later they came to construct temples for the mithraic initiation, these retained the appearance of a primitive grotto and even the name "grotto." To what can this conservative preference be attributed, if not to the desire to preserve in the *mithraea* made by humans the link with the cosmos which was apparent in the original grotto? (Was it original, or at least thought to be so by a sort of etiological justification of a sacred architecture?)

A comparable ideology was current in Hellenistic Judaism around the beginning of the Christian era, concerning the temple of Jerusalem. It is most often expressed in relation to Exodus 25–31, in which in great detail the divine will concerning the place of worship, its inner furnishings, its liturgical vestments, etc. is recorded. Philo admires the fact that the temple thus conceived should actually be consubstantial with the world:

> When furnishing a temple made by man for the Father and Guide of the universe, it was necessary to take the same substances with which the universe had been made. (*On the Life of Moses* 2.18.88; cf. *Questions and Answers on Exodus* 2.85)

This comprehensive observation is confirmed by a number of details: for instance, "the sacred chandelier with its seven lamps is an imitation (*mimēma*) of the celestial choir with its seven planets" (*Who Is the Heir* 45.221); the materials used to weave the hangings are a symbol of the four elements (*On the Preliminary Studies* 21.117); the altar of incense is the earth from which the exhalations rise (*On the Life of Moses* 2.21.101–22, 105; cf. *Questions and Answers on Exodus* 2.56, 73, 79, etc.). But the correspondence with the cosmos is nowhere more emphatic than in the case of the sacred garment of the high priest:

> The whole is a reproduction and an imitation (*apeikonisma kai mimēma*) of the world, as the parts are of each of the parts of the world. (*On the Life of Moses* 2.24.117; see also *On Dreams* 1.37.214)

It would take too long to go into the ingenious details of this parallelism, but we must understand the intention, which is to associate the universality of the cosmos with the cult of the temple:

> The high priest is bidden to put on the said tunic, a replica (*antimimon*) of the world in its totality, so that the world may celebrate together with man and man with the universe. (*On Dreams* 1.37.215)

The idea, striking and grandiose, is evidently to evoke, by means of this device, the immensity of the world within the walls of the temple, to expand the local worship to the dimensions of cosmic worship. Philo, moreover, was not the only one to have reflected fully on this point; decades later the historian Flavius Josephus expressed himself fully in the same vein, writing, for example, in a still more radical fashion, that "each of the objects of the Temple is intended to recall and to represent the universe" (*Antiquities* 3.180).[31]

There is no better way to conclude this development than to quote a page from the celebrated Renaissance architect Palladio, in which we can verify that the same outlook persisted through the centuries:

> When we consider this fine machine of the world and all the marvellous ornaments with which it is filled, the perpetual movement of the heavens making the seasons change in accordance with natural necessity and the way in which they maintain their delightful harmony and the balance of their course, we can be in no doubt that the little temples which we create must resemble this great temple created in its perfection by a single word issuing from the immense goodness of God.[32]

The World is a Temple:
The Permanence of a Theme

The text of Palladio introduces a second idea, which we have not yet considered, different from the one we have just seen but bound up with it. Given the fact that the temples have to reflect the cosmos, the cosmos becomes the temple *par excellence*. This new theme, which is often wrongly confused with the preceding one, appears throughout religion and literature. The beginning of Baudelaire's sonnet *Correspondance* is well known:

> Nature is a temple whose living pillars
> Sometimes let out confused words;
> Man passes through its forests of symbols. . . .

E. G. Leonard, for his part, quotes this Protestant hymn:

> O God, your temple
> Is the universe.
> When I contemplate
> The sky, the oceans,
> And its beauty,
> I am worshiping you
> O Father in your majesty.[33]

More important, along the same lines, is a page of Montaigne:

> For this world is a very holy temple into which man is introduced to contemplate it in the statues, not formed by mortal hands, but made perceptible by divine thought: the Sun, the Stars, the Waters and the Earth, which represent intelligible things to us. "The invisible things of God" says Saint Paul, "appear through the creation of the world, his eternal wisdom and his divinity being visible in his works."[34]

This text brings together two quotations. The end is composed of an almost word-for-word translation of Rom 1:20, in which one of the most famous formulations of the cosmological argument is to be found. The preceding lines, in which this argument does not appear at all, come from a completely different source. They summarize and adapt a development in Plutarch, which we shall look at below. It is from Plutarch that Montaigne takes the theme of the world as a very holy temple, but this image of pagan origin, in itself indifferent to all theological demonstration, is used by him to support the manifestation of God in creation. The same observation would also apply to the hymn quoted above.

How far back can we trace this theme? Cicero evokes a similar one in the case of Thales. According to this sage, it is said, humans must realize that whatever they see is full of gods, "for they would all be more holy if they were to find themselves in the most holy of temples" (Cicero *De legibus* 2.11.26). The idea is undoubtedly that that temple is the visible world, but we could not swear that this is not a conclusion drawn by Cicero from the saying, actually attributed to Thales, according to which "everything is full of gods" (Thales test. 22, Diels–Kranz). On the other hand, it has been thought that the assimilation of the cosmos to the supreme temple is featured in the *De philosophia* of Aristotle,[35] but a more careful reading of the two pieces of evidence has shown that the first is not concerned with the theme in question and that the second, which is in fact concerned with the theme, does not mention Aristotle.[36]

It seems that the first instance of a comparison of the world to a temple was actually attributed to the Stoic Cleanthes (in the middle of the third century B.C.), and even then the evidence from the doxographer is unclear.

> Cleanthes . . . used to say that the gods are priestly figures and sacred invocations, he added that the sun is a torch-bearer, he called the world a place of initiation and the keepers of divine truth the initiators. (*SVF* 1:538, p. 123, 7–10)[37]

This text makes sense if by "gods" we understand the stars, to which the Stoics actually did assign divinity. We are presented, then, with a parallel established between a temple of initiation like that of Eleusis and the cosmos itself. In the temple of Eleusis, there were constellations corresponding to statues and inscriptions on walls;[38] the sun was substituted for a *dadouchos,* and the natural philosophers conducted the initiation. Comparing stars to divine effigies, Cleanthes recalls the Platonic conception that we saw in the *Epinomis* 984A.[39] In still another instance this little dialogue had preceded him—the assimilation suggested by Cleanthes of the contemplation of the firmament with a religious initiation. We read in the *Epinomis* 986CD that the initiated man has a burning desire to know all about the marvelous order of the stars, [thinking] that after his death he would come to the place conducive to virtue, having thus received true and real initiation (*memyēmenos*) [. . .] he spends the rest of his time as a spectator among the most beautiful things which can be seen.[40]

This unequaled spectacle of the heavens certainly corresponds to the one that was revealed to the candidate in the liturgy of initiation; moreover, it surpasses it.

We cannot be sure that all authors who subsequently take up one or more of the themes contained in this rich document were inspired directly by it. But it was as though a school of Cleanthes had appeared—not immediately, but at least from the first century B.C. on. Some seem to attribute to him what he himself takes from the *Epinomis*—that is to say, the idea that the stars are divine images. This is what Philo does in taking up the theme of the cosmic temple as Cleanthes did:

[On the fourth day of creation, God] made the sensible stars, divine and supremely beautiful effigies (*agalmata*) which he placed in the sky as in the purest temple which exists in corporeal substance. (*On the Creation* 18.55)[41]

Another, more indirect way of formulating the same idea states: between the sky, the first to be created, and the human, the last to be created, there is an analogy and a reduction of scale; the human is a "miniature sky,"

[in that] he possesses within himself, like effigies, (*agalmatophorounta*) a number of natures which correspond to stars.

He does so through the arts, the sciences, and the theorems of virtue (*On the Creation* 27.82).[42]

Many other authors are content, in different contexts, to vouch for the conception of the universe as a temple. This is the case with Cicero in his famous Dream of Scipio, which concludes his *De republica*. Transported in a dream into interstellar space, the place of astral immortality, Scipio is heard to ask:

Can you not see into what temple you have come? (6.17; also 15)

Porphyry includes the theme in an *a fortiori* argument against the eating of animals offered in sacrifice, whose flesh, according to him, is a vehicle of demonic effluents. If, in the temples of human construction, even footwear must be pure, how could the contamination of our bodily garments be tolerated "in the temple of the Father, which is the world" (*On Abstinence* 2.46.1)? According to Proclus, finally, the recording of the ancient practices in the temples of Egypt presents the image of the stability of principles in "the holiest of temples, which is the world" (*In Tim.*, Diehl 1:124, 16–19).[43]

The most striking aspect of the evidence related to Cleanthes is still, however, the comparison he makes between the temple of initiation, its interior decoration, and its ministers, on the one hand, and, on the other hand, the world, the stars, and the theoreticians of cosmic religion. This point also commanded attention later on, beginning with Seneca, who also was a Stoic. In a eulogy of wisdom to which he refuses, unlike Posidonius, to assign technical inventions, Seneca shows it at work in the way it teaches us about the gods, the infernal powers, the Lares, the Genii, the divided souls. He continues:

> These are the initiations which it confers, as a result of which it is not a provincial sanctuary, but the immense temple of all the gods, the world itself which is revealed and which presents its true effigies, and true images to the intellect. For the physical eye is dulled by such great visions. (*Epistulae Morales* 90.28)

This important text is somewhat disconcerting. It is like that of Cleanthes in that here too the cosmic temple is magnified as the sacred place where the most real initiation is accomplished. We would expect that, as in Cleanthes, it would reveal the astral cult. In fact, it only treats the established religion of the Lares and the Genii. This first difference carries another with it, namely, that the effigies and images (*simulacra et facies*) of the cosmic temple, which it is tempting to identify as celestial constellations—as some historians have not hesitated to do—do not admit of this identification because it is stipulated that they are invisible and only perceivable by the intellect.

Any obscurity disappears if we proceed to a justly celebrated page of Dio Chrysostom, an orator at the end of the first and the beginning of the second century. It consists of two successive and parallel descriptions, one of the liturgy of initiation, as it was carried out in a temple like that of Eleusis, the other of the kind that we might suppose to be carried out on a cosmic scale.

> It is as though a Greek or a Barbarian underwent the initiation (*myeisthai paradoiē*) in the depths of a temple of mysteries (*mystikon tina mychon*) of unequalled beauty and grandeur; he would see many initiatory spectacles (*mystika theamata*), he would likewise hear many voices, darkness and light would alternate before his eyes, numerous other events would occur, and even as is customary in the ceremony called "enthronement" (*thronismōi*) the initiators (*hoi telountes*) would seat those to be initiated (*tous mnuoumenous*) and would dance around them. Is it conceivable that (such) a man would have no emotions in his soul and would not understand that what was happening was being achieved according to a design and an arrangement full of wisdom, even if he were one of those nameless Barbarians from the ends of the world,

even if there were no exegete or interpreter present, so long as he had a
human soul? (34) If that is impossible then, how could the community of
men, the whole human race, on receiving the complete and truly perfect
initiation (*tēn holoklēron kai tōi onti teleian teletēn mnuoumenon*), not in a
tiny chapel prepared by the Athenians to receive a limited congregation, but
in the world we see, a work full of variety and wisdom, in which each glance
alights on numberless marvels and where moreover it is not men like the
initiates (*tois teloumenois*), but immortal gods who initiate mortals (*telountōn*)
and who night and day in the light of the sun or of the stars, dance naturally,
so to speak, an eternal dance, how could humanity, I ask, remain insensible
to all these gods and completely unaware of the leader of the dance who
presides over the universe and directs the sky and the world like a good pilot
steering a perfectly prepared ship in which nothing is missing? (*Orationes* 12
[Olympian] 33–34)

   This sketch of religious initiation is one of the richest in existence, just
because Dio is led, in the interests of demonstration, to bring together
heterogeneous data. For instance, whereas the general style and the mention of the Athenians make one think of the rites of Eleusis, the reference
to "enthronement" belongs to the initiation conferred by the Corybantes,
priests of Cybele.[44] What Dio says brings out a certain number of elements
common to both the traditional initiation and cosmic religion and shows
that the latter is superior in every respect: by the immensity of the temple,
which is nothing less than the cosmos (we saw the same argument in
Seneca); by the initiatory spectacles, which are the stars in the sky; by the
alternating light and shade, which are night and day; by the *thronismos*
where the stars dance in a circle around the initiate; and finally by the dignity of the initiators, who are not simple humans but the sidereal gods
themselves. This practice of exalting the supremacy of the firmament by
making it the place of total and perfect initiation is extremely evident in
cosmic piety. It would be still more so here if Dio had stopped there, but
the religious celebration of the sky and the hymn to the visible gods which
inhabit it provide a final argument in favor of one invisible God governing
the universe. This theological practice, which was traditional in antiquity
and persists today, should not be integrated into the religion of the world,
but obviously we cannot exclude it from the brilliant and skillful description of cosmic initiation that serves as a premise to the demonstration.
   The intention of Seneca and Dio Chrysostom in the texts we have just
read seems to have been to magnify cosmic—that is to say, philosophical—
initiation at the expense of established worship. Plato was already tending
in the same direction when he modeled his philosophy on the pattern of
initiation. In other words, he showed the true initiation in his philosophy.
How are we to know if the ceremonies of Eleusis and other cults suffered

from this attitude of the philosophers? It is not possible. We must at least point out here a strange passage from Porphyry:[45]

> In the mysteries of Eleusis, the hierophant is dressed as demiurge, the torch-bearer as the sun; the priest of the altar is dressed as the moon and the herald of the sacrifice as Hermes. (*De imaginibus* fr., Bidez p. 22!, 4–7 = Eusebius *Praeparatio evangelica* 3.12.4)

The parallel becomes evident from the evidence concerning Cleanthes, who compared the sun to the torchbearer, but now the connection is inverted. It is the sacred ministers of Eleusis whose ornaments represent the planets. Whereas Cleanthes presented the cosmos as the model of a temple of initiation, Porphyry made the image of the cosmos enter the walls of the temple. It is as though, by a sort of return shock, the mysteries of Eleusis, when they had allowed the cosmic religion to be sumptuously formulated at their expense, came to open themselves to its influence.[46]

The Temple and the Temples

To say that the universe is a temple leads us almost inevitably to think of it as *the* temple, and it leaves all temples of stone and wood far behind it. This tendency is apparent in several of the documents that have been cited. To discredit temples made by the human hand is an old philosophical theme that goes back to Zeno, the founder of the Stoic movement,[47] and reappears in the speech of Paul on the Areopagus (Acts 17:24). The motives of Paul, like those of Zeno, were foreign to the notion of the cosmic temple; but elsewhere, on the contrary, it is this conviction that gives rise to hostility to the temples of human construction. Cicero imagines a journey of theological information through the air:

> [After Egypt,] we would see the splendid temples of Greece and of our country serving as sanctuaries for human representations of the gods which are considered sacriligious by the Persians; it is said that Xerxes set fire to the temples of Athens, solely because he considered it a crime against religion to keep the gods enclosed within walls, when the whole world is their abode (*quod deos, quorum domus esset omnis hic mundus, inclusos parietibus contineri nefas esse duceret*). (*De republica* 3.19.14; trans. Bréguet p. 58)

As a result of the existence of the temple of Jerusalem and its place in Jewish worship, Philo would necessarily be less radical than Xerxes. Nevertheless, he could maintain the distinction between the "very holy" cosmic temple, the first to be created, and the tabernacle of Exodus. The latter anticipated the temple of Jerusalem, which deserves only the term "holy" (*mundus factus est sanctissimum templum qui ante templum sanctum exstit*)

(*Questions and Answers on Exodus* 2.85; trans. Aucher). One page in particular establishes the necessary balance between the two temples. Here we detect an echo of Cleanthes, with the exception that the transmutation of the sacred ministers of Eleusis now allows the appearance of angels:

> We must believe the supreme temple, the real temple of God to be the world in its totality, which has as a sanctuary the most sacred part of subsistent reality, the sky, which has the stars for votive offerings and for priests the angels serving under its powers [. . .] . The other temple is made by the hand of man. (*On the Special Laws* 1.12.66–67)[48]

Philo goes a step further in the same direction when he says, for example, that not even the world in its totality would be an adequate temple to honor God (*On Noah's Work as a Planter* 30.126). In his eyes there exists a sanctuary even superior to the sensible cosmos, which is none other than the soul of the wise person (*On the Cherubim* 29.100–130; *Who Is the Heir?* 17.88; *On Dreams* 1.37.215).

We saw in some of the evidence above that Christian theology generally appears hostile to cosmic piety, but it does not always reject the idea that the universe is a temple. Origen, for example, affirms that this belief is shared by the simplest of Christians. Although he naturally does not suggest emptying the basilicas on this basis, he does at least find that it supports the Pauline injunction to "pray everywhere"(1 Tim 2:8; Origen *Against Celsus* 7.44).

Every Day Is a Feast Day

It is clear that in giving the cosmic temple precedence over defined places of worship, or in simply placing it on a par with them, we come to extend religious practice to the dimensions of the universe and to recognize, for example, the practice of praying everywhere. We must add at all times, since the temple of the world evidently ignores all restrictions to set liturgical times. It is a well-known opinion of Philo that, for the wise person, "each day is a feast-day," "the time between birth and death is an uninterrupted feast," "the whole of life is a feast," "no season fails to make life joyous, and the year's cycle is one long feast" (*On the Special Laws* 2.12.42–13.48).

We have known for a long time that this idea of Philo, strangely enough, may have originated with the Cynics.[49] Plutarch claims that the Cynic Crates, master of Diogenes, went through life joking and laughing "as if living were a feast" (*De tranquillitate animi* 4.466E). Less attention has perhaps been paid to the kinship that this representation has—above all, in the form that Philo gives it —with the belief that the universe is a temple.

This emerges from another page of Plutarch, in which Diogenes the Cynic is seen to observe to someone who was making great preparations for attending a feast: "But is not every day a feast for a good man?" On which Plutarch continues immediately:

> Certainly, and even a brilliant feast, if we are properly informed. For the world is a very holy temple and most worthy of God; man is introduced into it by his birth and there he does not contemplate statues (*agalmatōn*) made by the hand of man (*cheirokmētōn*) and deprived of movement, but the sensible realities which the divine Intellect has brought into being in imitation of the intelligible realities, as Plato says, and which have within them by nature a principle of life and of movement: the sun, the moon, the stars and the rivers constantly renewing their water, the earth from which comes food for plants and animals. Our life which is an absolutely perfect admission and initiation into these mysteries (*myēsin onta kai teletēn teleiotatēn*) must be full of confidence and joy.

After recalling that gaiety, whether vulgar or more refined, is characteristic of ritual feasts, Plutarch deplores that this is not also true of cosmic religion:

> But these feasts which God offers to us and in which he is the mystagogue (*mystagōgei*) are profaned if we spend the best part of our lives in lamentation, recriminations and exhausting anxieties. (*De tranquillitate animi* 20.477CE)

This text would need a long commentary. The most obvious part of it perhaps is the theme of the universe as temple, with its specific *agalmata*, which in this case are not only the stars but also certain sublunar realities. The introduction of the duality of the sensible and intelligible, absent from the parallel texts we have seen thus far, causes some confusion of ideas. In any case, the assimilation of cosmic religion to initiation is stressed, with the help of technical vocabulary. These are the elements that interested Montaigne, since it was this page of Plutarch that we saw him quote earlier on, in shortened form. But the originality of the text lies elsewhere—in the desire that cosmic initiation should engender the cheerfulness and hope that was sought in initiation through the cult. Once we understand this truth, says Plutarch, the religion of the world will be experienced with uninterrupted joy; the consequence is (and the causal relationship is clearly marked in the text) that, unlike in established religions, every day will be a feast day. This is why Plutarch approves of the saying of Diogenes. We cannot be certain that Diogenes himself would have arrived there by the same route! But it must be the case with Philo, whose attachment to the plan of the cosmic temple we have seen. At any rate, this hypothesis is more likely than that of his dependence on the Cynics, with whom there is no proof that he had any affinity.

Translated by Jane Curran

Notes

1. It is clear that, despite the insistence on its *totality*, the cosmos designates here the earth and its riches. See H. Sasse, "kosmeō, etc.," in *Theological Dictionary of the New Testament*, ed. G. Kittel (Grand Rapids, MI: Eerdmans, 1964) 3:888.

2. Information of the same type, but historical, is provided in 2 Kings 21:3-5; 23:4-5, 11-12: The abominable king of Judah, Manasseh, prostrated himself before the whole army of the heavens and built altars to the stars in the Temple itself, but the good king Josiah, his grandson, suppressed this worship of the stars and destroyed the altars and the liturgical materials.

3. See, for example, *De diversis quaest. ad Simplicianum* 2.1-5 (*PL* 40, col. 133), in which we learn that, in "the spirit of God carried on the waters" (Gen 1:2) some saw the animating principle of the mass of the universe—that is to say, the soul of the world; for his part, Augustine saw in it the Holy Spirit (see *De octo Dulcitii quaest.* 8.1 [*PL* 40, col. 166]; *Letter 118* 4.24-26 [ed. Goldbacher, pp. 687-90]).

4. Until the Christian era, Epicureans had been almost the only adversaries of cosmic religion, to which they opposed their own conception of divine nature. The principal evidence is this essay by Velleius in Cicero, which is clearly inspired by his contemporary, the Epicurean Philodemus (see the edition by A. S. Pease of *De natura deorum* [Cambridge, MA: Harvard University Press, 1955] 1:39-42). There are already signs of this hostility in Epicurus himself: "The strongest confusion arises in human souls when they think about the heavenly things being at the same time blessed and incorruptible and, completely opposed to this, having wills, activities and motivations" (*Letter to Herodotus* 81.2-5; ed. Arrighetti, p. 71). Lucretius took up the attack: "Perhaps, intimidated by religion, you still believe that the earth and the sun and the sky, the sea, the stars, the moon, in virtue of their divine essence, ought to be eternal. . . . And yet the things I am speaking of are so far removed from divinity, so unworthy of being counted among the gods that one might believe them instead to be destined to make us recognise a body deprived of the movement and feeling which belong to life" (*De rerum natura* 5.114-25; trans. Ernout; see also 144-45). But the Epicurean pages of Cicero on the same subject remain the richest in doctrine and history.

5. This is exactly what Epicurus wrote himself; see n. 4.

6. These are by far the most rich with regard to this aspect of Plato's theology. This does not mean that the others do not contain anything on the subject, but their contribution needs to be used with care.

7. Information on this pioneering role played by the Syrians and the Egyptians in astral religion can be found in later authors. According to Theophrastus, the Syrians (the Jews?), "during the night, devoted themselves to the contemplation of the stars, looking up at them and invoking them in prayer" (*De pietate* fr. 13, 7-10 Pötscher p. 172; quoted by Porphyry *On Abstinence* 2.26.3; ed. Bouffartigue-Patillon [there is a mention of it on pp. 58-67] p. 93). According to Chaeremon, the Egyptian priests "divided their time in two, devoting the night to the observation of celestial phenomena, combined sometimes with devotion, and the day to the worship of the gods to whom, four times a day—at dawn, in the evening, when the sun was at its zenith and when it went down to rest—they addressed their hymns" (again quoted by Porphyry *On Abstinence* 4.8; ed. Nauck, p. 240, 7-12=Chaeremon fr. 10, Van den Horst p. 22).

8. A.-J. Festugière "L'Epinomis et l'introduction des cultes étrangers à Athènes," in *Mélanges A. Fridrichsen* (Coniectanea neotestamentica 11; Lund-Köpenham: Neotestamenticum, 1948) 73.

9. We should at least mention the pioneering work of W. Jaeger, *Aristotle: Funda-mentals of the History of His Development* (2nd ed.; Oxford: Clarendon, 1948) 124–66; and, in recent literature, B. Effe, *Studien zur Kosmologie und Theologie der aristotelischen Schrift "Über die Philosophie"* ("Zetemata" 50; Munich: Beck, 1970); A.-H. Chroust, *Aristotle:* vol. 2, *New Light on His Life and on Some of His Lost Works* (Notre Dame, IN: University of Notre Dame Press, 1973) 145–15; B. Dumoulin, *Recherches sur le premier Aristote (Eudème, De la Philosophie, Protreptique)* (Paris: J. Vrin, 1981) 41–112. On the religion of the world, see T. G. Sinnige, "Cosmic Religion in Aristotle," *Greek, Roman and Byzantine Studies* 14 (1973) 15–34, esp. 24–26.

10. Velleius's tirade in Cicero *On the Nature of the Gods* 1.8.20.

11. The premise is that the aether, of all the elements, is the most subtle, always mobile and active.

12. The premise is that the only kinds of movement are natural, forced, or voluntary and that the movement of the stars is neither natural nor forced. These words make clear the distinction between doctrine and piety. We should add to these texts the famous and difficult fr. 26, Ross p. 94 = Cicero *On the Nature of the Gods* 1.13.33, in which we see that Aristotle, in *De philosophia* (book 3), in a precise outline, conferred divinity on the universal intellect and on the world (*menti tribuit omnem divinitatem, modo mundum ipsum deum dicit esse*).

13. Even though historians are not in agreement about their identity (Posidonius? Panaetius? etc.); see the edition of *On the Nature of the Gods* by A. S. Pease (above n. 4) 1:45–48.

14. *SVF* 2.1015, p. 303, 23–34, of which I have translated the last three lines.

15. *SVF* 2.92, p. 30, 17–20; this doxography actually serves as an example of the Stoic theory of *katalēpsis,* but this does not diminish its effect.

16. *SVF* 2.1027, p. 306. 23–24. In all these texts, "intellect" translates the Greek word *nous* (=*mens* in Latin).

17. *SVF* 2.1022, p. 305, 26–28; the word for "matter," as often among the Stoics, is *ousia.*

18. The main points of which I have given in *Théologie Cosmique. . . ,* 131–35.

19. Very badly cut up in *SVF* 2.634, p. 192, 7–9, and 644, p. 194, 14–15.

20. These points of doctrine are attributed to Plato, mentioned just above. "The world as second god" (*deuteros theos ho kosmos*) is also a Hermetic representation (Hermetic Corpus 8.1; ed. Nock, p. 87, 9–10; 8.5, p. 89, 5).

21. See the translation and excellent annotation by A. Segonds in the appendix to the edition by E. des Places: Porphyry, *Vie de Pythagore, Lettre à Marcella* (Budé; Paris: Les Belles Lettres, 1982) 190–91.

22. Quoted by A. Segonds, appendix to Porphyry, *Vie de Pythagore,* ed. E. des Places, 190 n. 5.

23. Well elucidated by A. Segonds, appendix to Porphyry, *Vie de Pythagore,* ed. E. des Places, 191 n. 1.

24. It should be observed that the Greek phrase translated in this way is, in reality, much more vague—literally: "And until these beings (*mechri toutōn*) [are] divine things." There is nothing against thinking that "these beings" designate not the soul but the beings engendered by it and inferior to it—that is to say, the sensible world. And "until" is inclusive, which would give a meaning compatible with treatise III 5.

25. The hymn is in no. 168 of the *Orphicorum fragmenta* of O. Kern, pp. 201–2. I have borrowed some words of the translation by E. des Places of Eusebius *Praeparatio evangenlica* 3 (in which the two pieces cited here from *De imaginibus* are to be found) 191, 193.

26. See R. Bloch, in *Symbolisme cosmique et monuments religieux* (Paris: Musée Nationaux, 1953) 1:20.

27. Cited by M. H. Quet, *La mosaïque cosmologique de Merida* (Paris: E. de Broccard, 1981) 18 n. 26. R. Bloch expresses doubts about this explanation in *Symbolisme* 1:23). See particularly M. Zepf, "Der Mensch in der Höhle und das Pantheon," *Gymnasium* 65 (1958) 355–82.

28. Cited by P. Boyancé, *Études sur le Songe de Scipion* (Biblioth. des univ. du midi 20; Bordeaux: Feret & Fils; Paris: E. de Broccard, 1936) 118–19.

29. See L. A. Campbell, *Mithraic Iconography and Ideology* (EPRO 11; Leiden: Brill, 1968) 49–50: "Mithraeum, a replica of the cosmos." See also R. Turcan, *Mithra et le mithraicisme* ("Que sais-je?" 1929; Paris: Presses Universitaires de France, 1981) 72–74.

30. Ed. "Arethusa Monographs," I, p. 8, 13–23; cf. 20, p. 20, 23–25. A good commentary is R. Turcan, *Mithras platonicus* (EPRO 47; Leiden: Brill, 1975) 23–27, 65–67.

31. See J. Daniélou, "La symbolique cosmique du temple de Jerusalem," in *Symbolisme cosmique et monuments religieux*, 1:61–64; A. Jaubert, *La notion d'alliance dans le judaisme aux abords de l'ere chrétienne* (Patristica Sorbonensia 6; Paris: Seuil, 1963) Appendix III: "Note complementaire sur le culte dans Philon; culte cosmique, culte aaronique, culte spirituel," pp. 483–89.

32. Palladio, *Quattro Libri dell'Architettura* (Venice, 1570) preface to book 4, trans. Chastel in *Symbolisme cosmique et monuments religieux*, 1:89. Among the ancient examples that Palladio uses for support are the Pantheon of Rome and the temple of Vesta.

33. E. G. Leonard, in *Symbolisme cosmique et monuments religieux*, 1:93.

34. Montaigne, *Apologie de Raimond Sebond* (*Essais* II 12), ed. Plattard p. 164.

35. So the most recent editors of the fragments of Aristotle (fr. 14a and b, Ross pp. 83–84); A.-J. Festugière, *La révélation d'Hermès Trismégiste* 2: *Le dieu cosmique* (Paris: Lecoffre, J. Gabalda, 1949) 235–36. I thought so as well in my *Théologie Cosmique*, 289 and n. 1; I am more skeptical nowadays.

36. See H. Cherniss, review of A.-J. Festugière, *La révélation d'Hermès Trismégiste*, *Gnomon* 22 (1950) 212 n. 2.

37. The Greek text has been subjected to several corrections; see von Arnim's apparatus and A.-J. Festugière, *Le dieu cosmique*, 235.

38. On the statues of the temples and their functions, see (along with P. Boyancé, "Sur les mystères d'Eleusis," *Revue des études grecques* 75 [1962] 471) Varro *Antiquitatum* 16 fr. 225, 1–3 Cardauns p. 96 = Augustine *City of God* 7.5: "The Ancients made statues, distinctive images as effigies of the gods, ornaments of such a kind that by perceiving them with the eyes, those who had come to receive the initiation of knowledge could see through the spirit the soul of the world and its parts, that is to say "true gods.""

39. Compare *Timaeus* 37C, where it is the world that is said to be an "image created by the eternal gods," with F. Cornford's commentary ad loc., pp. 99–102.

40. A text opportunely produced by A. Wlosok, *Laktanz und die philosophische Gnosis* (Abhandlungen der Heidelberger Akademie der Wiss. Philos.-histor. Kl.; Heidelberg: C. Winter, 1960) 39; see also p. 40. Compare *Phaedo* 69C, for philosophical initiation as a condition of beatific immortality.

41. The word *agalmata* is from *Epinomis* 984A. Philo uses it sometimes to refer in the same way to the "divine effigies" that adorn the sky (*On Abraham* 30.159). With a remarkable phrase, which doubtless reflects a Hebraism, he expresses there (and also in *On Rewards and Punishments* 7.41) the preeminence of the sky in calling it "true world in the world."

42. The idea is connected with the theme of the human being as microcosm. On the sensible world as temple of God, see *On Dreams* 1.37.215, and U. Früchtel, *Die kosmologischen Vorstellungen bei Philo von Alexandrien* (Arbeiten zur Literatur und Geschichte des hellenistischen Judentums; Leiden: Brill, 1968) 69ff., 81ff.

43. Perhaps we should compare a note in Hermetic *Asclepius* 24, ed. Nock p. 326, 16–20, where the ground of Egypt is called *imago caedi* and *mundi totius templum.*

44. See Plato *Euthydemus* 277D; for "holoclear" initiation, see *Phaedrus* 250C.

45. With P. Boyancé, "Sur les mystères, 466–67.

46. Explicated by M. P. Nilsson, *Geschichte der griechischen Religion* (2 vols.; 2nd ed.; Munich: Beck, 1961) 2:352. As indicated by P. Boyancé, "Sur les mystères."

47. See *SVF* 1:264–67, pp. 61–62; and E. des Places, *La Religion grecque* (Paris: Picard, 1969) 337–40.

48. See the commentary in I. Heinemann, *Philons griechische und jüdische Bildung: Kulturvergleichende Untersuchungen zu Philons Darstellung der jüdischen Gesetze* (Breslau: M. & H. Marcus, 1932) 48–50. It is interesting that in order to designate the temple "made by the hand of man," Philo uses the same word (*cheirokmētos*), borrowed from Aristotle, for denying any assimilation of the cosmic god to a manufactured work.

49. See I. Heinemann, *Philons griechische und jüdische Bildung,* 106–10.

18

The Spiritual Guide

I. HADOT

IN GRECO-ROMAN ANTIQUITY the spiritual guide appears to us principally in the following forms: as educator, musician, and poet; as legislator, sage, statesman, or king; and as philosopher. According to ancient thought his work is considerably aided by two factors: authority and friendship.

The Educator, Musician, and Poet as Spiritual Guide

As the beginnings of spiritual guidance in Greco-Roman antiquity coincide with the beginnings of general education, so too the function of the spiritual guide coincides with that of the educator, insofar as we understand education (*paideia*) to include the whole of the endeavor to make a person fit for life and, consequently, the formation of a person's moral attitudes as well. The earliest sketch of the ideal educator that has come down to us appears in a myth: it is the sage of semidivine nature embodied in Chiron the Centaur, half-brother of Zeus, educator of heroes and of the children of gods, who, on the basis of this his nature, unifies every form of wisdom and knowledge in himself. He first comes to our notice as Achilles' instructor in the art of healing in the Homeric poetry of the eighth century B.C. (*Iliad* 9.831ff.), while the plastic arts depict him as Achilles' teacher on the lyre, which was at that time inseparable from instruction in singing.[1] Chiron is subsequently mentioned as the educator of Medeios, son of Jason and Medea, in Hesiod's *Theogony* (1001), in a passage whose authenticity is admittedly subject to dispute. Most of the details concerning this mythical figure are transmitted to us by Pindar in the first half of the fifth century: Chiron is the educator of the heroes Jason (*Pythian* 4.102ff.; *Nemean* 3.53f.) and Achilles (*Nemean* 3.43ff.) and of the god Asclepius, whom he instructs in the art of healing (*Pythian* 3.5f.; 45f.; *Nemean* 2.53).[2] Other authors mention him as the educator of Aristeios (Apollonius Rhodius *Argonautica* 2.509f.), of Theseus (Xenophon *Cynegeticus* 1.2),[3] of the Dioscuri (Xenophon *Cynegeticus* 1.2), and of Actaeon (Apollodorus *Bibliotheca* 3.4.4). Pindar celebrates Chiron as a sage (*Pythian* 3.63, *sōphrōn*); he lauds the depths of his wisdom (*Nemean* 3.53, *bathymēta*), his intelligent advice, and his prophetic gifts (*Pythian* 9.38f., 51ff.). Pindar attests Chiron's capacities as a spiritual guide through Jason, who refers to the education he enjoyed under Chiron and can claim that in the twenty years that he spent in Chiron's cave under the care of Chiron's daughters, he never spoke a word or committed a deed for which he needed to feel ashamed before the "pure" daughters of Chiron (*Pythian* 4.103ff.). Chiron, however, proves himself as a spiritual guide not only in the moral realm but also in the religious sphere. An author of the first century A.D., Ptolemaios Chennos, reports that Chiron taught the god Dionysus as a boy the bacchic rites and mystic solemnities (*in Photius Biblioteca* 190).[4] It is probably as a symbol of divine religious instruction that the wise centaur was given a place in the stucco relief of the Roman Neopythagorean basilica at the *Porta maiora*, which also dates from the first century.[5] Plato, too, speaks of the "wisest" Chiron as Achilles' teacher (*Hippias minor* 371D), and for Euripides Chiron becomes a symbol of piety (*Iphigenia in Aulis* 927).

Chiron unites all the traits of an ideal educator in himself insofar as, on the basis of his semidivine nature—he is the son of Kronos and a mortal— he possesses all the means of favorably influencing both body and soul of his pupils. He is sports instructor, doctor, and spiritual guide in one. He knows how to direct his charges to suitable athletic activities (the plastic arts show him as instructor in hunting and boxing,[6] and to nourish them in accordance with their physical disposition (the centaur feeds Achilles with the marrow and guts of lions, boars, and bears) (Euripides *Iphigenia in Aulis* 703f; Apollodorus *Bibliotheca* 3.13.6; Statius *Achilleis* 2.382ff.),[7] and thus to help them attain health and top physical form. But he also knows how to heal sick bodies, on account of his knowledge of the art of healing. He influences the soul by means of instruction in singing and in playing the lyre or cithara—that is, through the union of poetry and music—for in the consciousness of antiquity, as we shall see, music and poetry were especially suited to affecting the emotions. By means of intelligent advice and moral guidance, and finally by initiation in religious rites and mysteries,[8] Chiron knows how to provide the soul with all the spiritual nourishment it needs.

In contrast to the later mythical tradition, Homer knows Chiron only as Achilles' instructor in the art of healing and introduces the aged Phoenix as the educator of Achilles.[9] The speech of advice that Phoenix gives in the ninth book of the *Iliad* to still the wrath of Achilles was considered throughout the whole of Greco-Roman antiquity to be a model of this genus and was memorized and quoted again and again until the end of the epoch.[10] The means of spiritual guidance that are employed in this speech—the use of allegory (9.502ff.), of mythical or historical examples of exemplary behavior in similar situations (9.527ff.), and the counsel of moderation, based on the correct assessment of human nature in comparison to the far superior nature of the gods (9.496–514)—remain central pieces of popular ethical and philosophical exhortation even in later centuries.

While Chiron's authority rests on his divine nature and wisdom, Phoenix's authority is derived on the one hand from his age, and on the other hand from the fact that Peleus, the father of Achilles, transfers his paternal authority to Phoenix—that is, chooses him to be the educator of his son on the basis of his human qualities and later even gives Phoenix to his grown son as an advisor and companion in the Trojan War. What particularly strengthened the authority of Phoenix's admonition, however, was its composition by a poet and the formal and religious aspect associated with this: formal, because its verse form raises it above the level of everyday speech and makes it more impressive; religious, because it comes from the mouth of a poet inspired by the Muses who, according to the view of the time—which was of influence for centuries to come—is able with their help to speak the truth (*alētheia*) and to proclaim the will of the gods.[11] Thus Hesiod as well in his admonitions to his brother Perseus refers to the inspiration of the Muses which enables him to proclaim to his brother the commands of Zeus (*Works and Days* 661–62). In this work the ethical instructions are not yet separated from professional information, and thus we find a colorful mixture of agricultural rules and ethical maxims.

This literary form of spiritual guidance, consisting of ethical and practical instructions presented in a succinct form and directed from a brother to his brother or from a father to his son, was already widespread in the Near East long before Hesiod.[12] The use of animal fables in this connection, too, which first appears in the Greek realm with Hesiod, had become a common property of the literary genus of admonition in the Near East.[13] A special literary form of this paraenetic literature is the "mirror for princes," which also has a long tradition in the Near East and to which I shall return briefly below.

Let us return once more to the realm of the myth, which we had already left behind with Hesiod, and let us turn now to a personality who in a certain way embodies the mythical guide of souls most purely: Orpheus.[14] The earliest surviving pictorial representations of the citharist Orpheus are probably a small Boeotian bowl and the metope of the treasure house of the Syracusans in Delphi (sixth century) where he can be seen on board the Argo as a participant in the voyage of the Argonauts. The earliest literary evidence is a fragment of the poet Simonides (fr. 27). From this earliest evidence onward Orpheus is attested continuously in the plastic arts and literature until the end of antiquity. The mythical significance of the Thracian Orpheus, son of the Muse Calliope, lies on the one hand in the power of his music to give spiritual guidance—that is, in the magical effect of his singing accompanied by the playing of the lyre. Orpheus is poet and musician at the same time. A bronze hand mirror of the fifth century B.C. depicts Orpheus playing while wild animals listen attentively, and beside him is a basket of scrolls. Just as great, on the other hand, is his significance as initiator of religious movements and mysteries. Our earliest evidence for him in this capacity is to be found in the writings of the comedian Aristophanes (*Ranae* 1032; cf. Euripides *Rhesus* 943)[15] and of Plato (*Protagoras* 316D). We can trace the existence of a religious literature (poems in hexameters) current under Orpheus's name from the end of the fifth century (Euripides *Hippolytus* 952; Plato *Republic* 2.364E; Aristophanes *Ranae* 1032), although it almost certainly goes back further than this. Like Chiron, but in an even more pronounced way, Orpheus is a spiritual guide in the ethical and religious sphere, and, like Chiron, he is credited with medicinal knowledge (Euripides *Alcestis* 962; *Cyclops* 646). The magical effect of his soul-guiding singing works wonders not only on human beings and animals, trees, cliffs, and entire mountain ranges but also on the powers of death and the underworld, as is demonstrated by his journey to Hades on the occasion of the death of his wife Eurydice. In addition to the commonly known myth of Orpheus's journey to Hades, I would like to add only one more example: the *Argonautica* of Apollonius of Rhodes portray Orpheus settling a dispute among the Argonauts by means of a performance of his Orphic theogony (1.494–511). Completely pacified, the men remain silent and motionless for a while after the end of the song before finally bringing a libation to Zeus and going to sleep. Somewhat later (1.916ff.), in keeping with his role as a religious spiritual guide, he persuades the Argonauts to land in Samothrace and there to have themselves initiated in the local mysteries of the Cabiri, as the founder of which he is mentioned elsewhere (Diodorus Siculus *Bibliotheca* 5.64.4 = Ephorus fragment of *Greek History* 70 fr. 104).

The myth of the magical power of the music of Orpheus can be understood only against the background of the ancient Greek doctrine of the moral effect of music, which sets out the ethical effects of music in all its aspects—word (verse), rhythm, melody, mode, sound of the instruments, and gesture (dance)—on the spiritual behavior of human beings. It is not possible in this context to go further into this important doctrine, elements of which can also be traced in the Orient (in China in the teaching of Confucius and in Egypt). I can here only refer to pertinent articles in text-books on the history of music.[16] In any case, it should be borne in mind that, in keeping with this doctrine, music in all the forms mentioned above constitutes an important means of spiritual guidance, that the rhythmic word order (poetry, later also rhetorically structured prose), the melodies and modes, and the characteristics of the various instruments are capable of evoking deep effects in the human soul, and that accordingly rhythms and modes selected according to particular aspects have significant educational value. There is a direct and mutual correspondence between music (in the early Greek comprehensive sense) and ethical life, indeed between music and wisdom. As music can evoke certain moral dispositions, so inversely the ethical personality of the musician, of both the composing and the performing musician, has the greatest influence on the manner of writing and representation. Only the wise person is capable of creating works that have ethical value. This essential connection between wisdom and music is expressed as late as the first century A.D. by Quintilian in the following way:

> For myself I should be ready to accept the verdict of antiquity. Who is ignorant of the fact that music . . . was in ancient times the object not merely of intense study but of veneration: in fact Orpheus and Linus, to mention no others, were regarded as uniting the roles of musician, inspired poet and sage (*musicus, vates, sapiens*). Both were of divine origin, while the former, because by the marvel of his music he soothed the savage breast, is recorded to have drawn after him not merely beasts of the wild, but rocks and trees. So too Tilagenes asserts that music is the oldest of the arts related to litera-ture, a statement which is confirmed by the testimony of the greatest of poets in whose songs we read that the praise of heroes and of gods were sung to the music of the lyre at the feasts of kings. Does not Iopas, the Vergilian bard, sing "The wandering moon and labours of the Sun"(*Aeneid*1.742) and the like? whereby the supreme poet manifests most clearly that music is united with the knowledge even of things divine. (*Institutio Oratoria* 1.10.9–11; trans. H. E. Butler)[17]

This doctrine of the ethical effect of music and poetry accounts for the prominent place that, as we shall see, verses, maxims, and admonitory speeches or spiritual exercises structured according to rhetorical rules occu-pied in spiritual guidance until the end of antiquity. Beside Hesiod, in archaic Greece early lyrical poetry provides examples of exhortations of a moral and political nature,[18] and we find the expression of a centuries-old aristocratic ethic at the center of Theognis's collection of elegies (sixth cen-tury B.C.), a handbook of practical morality: "Because I mean well to you,

Kyrnos, I will pass on to you such advice as I myself learned as a child from good (*agathoi*)[19] men (*Elegies* 27–28, Carrière [Budé]). Thus Theognis justifies his undertaking, which, in the midst of the confusions of political and social upheavals, had as its aim to keep alive and strengthen the consciousness of noble birth in Kyrnos and with it the quality of the innate disposition. This disposition, according to the archaic outlook, was the only guarantee of heroic courage in war as well as of the steadfast and noble endurance of all misfortune, whereas the man of lower birth breaks down under the blows of fate (*Elegies* 319–22, Carrière). It should be mentioned briefly here that the first beginnings of the ideal of the Stoic sage who is able to maintain his spiritual calm in all the storms of fate are to be found in the archaic aristocratic ethos, which even underwent an intensification of its values in Theognis's time, on account of the disappearance of the external power and wealth of the Megarian nobility.[20]

The Spiritual Guide of a Collective

Archaic Greek lyric poetry leads up to our second section, on the legislator and wise statesman as spiritual guide. The Athenian statesman Solon, who lived at the turn of the seventh and sixth centuries, author of exemplary laws aimed at social balance, gave his political ideas extremely effective expression in his elegies. They are urgent exhortations to his fellow citizens in the sense of paraeneses or admonitions to return to moderation and the just mean in all actions and demands and to hold to these henceforth. A clear, if simple, ethic is therefore what he considered to be the necessary basis of his politics, and politics is essentially the moral education of the citizens. In his elegy *Eunomia* ("good order") Solon emphasizes the importance of good laws for the ethical and economic well-being of the citizens:

> Obedience to the law (*eunomia*) shows forth all things in order and harmony and at the same time sets shackles on the unjust. It smooths what is rough, checks greed, dims arrogance, withers the opening blooms of ruinous folly, makes straight the crooked judgement, tames the deeds of insolence, puts a stop to the works of civil dissension, and ends the wrath of bitter strife. Under its rule all things among mankind are sane and wise. (fr. 3, 32–39, Diehl p. 29)[21]

This conviction of the importance of laws for the moral education of the citizens remained valid throughout the whole of Greco-Roman antiquity. With the founding of the Greek schools of philosophy in Athens, philosophy took up the relevant questions, always with the expressed goal of spiritual guidance. The philosophical discussion of these themes found expression in countless tractates about the state and the laws, which have for the most part been lost. Politics remained part of philosophical ethics until the end of antiquity.

Solon had his laws carved on wooden steles and set up in public. Similarly, in archaic Rome the first laws codified in writing—which were, incidentally, regarded by later tradition as an adaptation of Solon's laws to Roman conditions (Augustine *City of God* 2.16)—were engraved on twelve bronze tablets (hence the name "the Twelve Tables") and were set up in front of the curia so that they were visible to all citizens as a constant admonition. Into the time of Cicero's youth, Roman boys were required to memorize these laws *ut carmen necessarium,* "like a necessary poem" (Cicero *De legibus* 2.23.59). (The translation of *carmen* as "poem" reflects only part of the meaning of the Latin word; it omits the sacral, magical-incantatory aspect.)

Solon was one of the seven sages whose maxims were used for centuries in the moral education of the Greeks. The seven sages were not warlike heroes, as the Homeric epic portrays them, nor, with the exception of Thales, were they philosophers. Rather, literary tradition depicts them as statesmen and legislators, judges and counselors.[22] With the exception of Solon, historical testimony for the individual representatives is very sparse, not to say nonexistent. The seven sages—Plato mentions Thales of Miletus, Pittakos of Mytilene, Bias of Priene, Solon, Kreobulos of Lindos, Myson of Chen, and the Lacedaemonian Chilon (*Protagoras* 343A)[23]—are regarded as contemporaries and as authors of archaic rules of life that are still closely associated with the wisdom of the gods and are consequently valid for all times. Set in relation to the cult of Apollo in Delphi at an early stage, the pronouncements of the seven sages profit from the cultural and political radiation of this cult.[24] As we know with certainty only since recent times, two series of pronouncements of the seven sages were set up in the temple at Delphi: a short series of five sayings, which Plato mentions in the *Protagoras* (343B1ff.),[25] and a long series of some 140 maxims, which latter were carved into a stone column or stele before the beginning of the third century B.C. and displayed either in front of the temple or in the porch.[26] It was there that Clearchus of Soli, a student of Aristotle, subsequently "carefully copied"[27] them and, at the outermost reaches of the Greek East, in a Greek city situated on the Oxus in Bactria (in modern Afghanistan), had them carved on a stele and set up in a central place visible to all inhabitants.[28] Other archaeological finds indicate that the long series of maxims of the seven sages was likewise carved on a stele in Miletopolis in Mysia at about the same time.[29] The short series had already found a place in the gymnasium of Thera in the fourth century B.C.[30] These are only individual examples that have come down to us of a practice, which was widespread in antiquity, of using inscriptions as a means of collective spiritual guidance. And the fact that cities or individual patrons found it worthwhile to establish such monuments at great cost attests to the belief in the efficacy of such an enterprise. Thus, too, according to the pseudo-Platonic dialogue *Hipparchus*, the son of the Athenian tyrant Peisistratus (sixth century) is supposed to have had short verse inscriptions of his own creation carved into the herms that were set up along the streets leading from Athens to the various demes, so as to educate morally the rural population as well. In this way, he believed, his fellow citizens would no longer simply have to admire the wise inscriptions of the temple at Delphi, such as "Know thyself" and "Nothing too much." By reading these precepts at every coming and going they would find pleasure in them and allow themselves to be stimulated to further self-education. The place name is supposed to have stood on the one side of each herm, and on the other side, for example: "This is a monument of Hipparchus: Follow the paths of righteousness" or "This is a monument of Hipparchus: Thou shalt not deceive thy friend" (Pseudo-Plato *Hipparchus* 228D–229B). Yet even the public decrees of honor which were set up in the form of inscriptions served as a means of civic spiritual guidance: they served as examples of good civic behavior and as an incentive and exhortation to imitation.

A further initiative of civic governments that was similarly aimed at the moral good behavior of its citizens consisted in collecting oracles on important subjects—for example, the nature of God—as well as the consequences of the oracular response for the relation of both the individual and the whole populace to the divinity and for the cultic rites. These oracles were then carved in stone and set up in appropriate places, such as the city wall or the market.[31] As in the Middle Ages the frescoes and paintings in the churches could be regarded as a kind of Bible for the people, so the public inscriptions in the cities of Greco-Roman antiquity represented an important means of ethical, religious, and civic education.

Like the cities, so too the kings made use of inscriptions as a means of spiritual guidance—for example, the inscriptions that the Indian king Asoka erected in the third century B.C., in what is now Afghanistan, for his Greek subjects. Part is carved in stone,[32] and part engraved in stone blocks belonging to buildings.[33] In these texts, translated into a Greek of a philosophical stamp, the king speaks personally. He preaches a moral code of tolerance and of brotherly love and expresses his conviction that compliance with this moral code will lead humanity to happiness.

Finally, the theory of kingship that was developed on a philosophical basis primarily in the Hellenistic age defined the ideal king as the spiritual guide of his subjects. The numerous "mirrors of princes" never tire of asserting that the shortest and surest way to the ethical regeneration of the populace is to ensure that a single individual, the king, achieves virtue. The ideal king embodies virtue in himself and by his behavior as a living model makes it visible and desirable to all.[34] For this reason the admonitory genre of the "mirror of princes" is of particular importance in the ancient view: it is a question of educating the educator of the people.

The Philosopher as Spiritual Guide

With the emergence of the philosophical schools in Athens in the fourth and third centuries B.C., a new type of spiritual guidance developed, that of the philosopher. However, the types of individual or collective spiritual guidance that were discussed above continued to exist. Philosophical spiritual guidance also made considerable use, at least in its initial stages, of maxims of all kinds, whether in the form of aphorisms or in verses.

It must be pointed out here that philosophy meant something entirely different in Greco-Roman antiquity from what it means today. It was not a systematic thought structure à la Hegel intended to serve as the theoretical explanation of the world and the events of the world; philosophy was, above all, an education toward a happy life—happy life here and not only in some hypothetical life after death, even if the latter was not always left entirely out of consideration.

All Hellenistic and Imperial schools of philosophy, including the Cynics and Skeptics, regarded guidance toward a happy life as the most important goal of their philosophy. What was understood by happy life could vary considerably in theory,[35] but in all cases it had the practical end of strengthening the individual inwardly against all the vicissitudes of fate and, as far as possible, of making the person self-sufficient. Ancient philosophy was, above all, help with life's problems and spiritual guidance, and the ancient philosopher was, above all, a spiritual guide.[36] Only secondarily—namely, insofar as this was considered essential to spiritual guidance—was ancient philosophy a theoretical explanation of the world.[37] Cynics and Skeptics refrained completely from this theoretical aspect, regarding themselves as true followers of Socrates in this. For as Socrates, without expounding a definite philosophical doctrine, thrust his interlocutors into great confusion by means of skillful questioning alone—so that they became conscious of their ignorance and were eventually brought to the point of reflecting on themselves and of questioning their entire previous life[38]—so the Cynics confined themselves to exercising a salutary moral shock on their fellow human beings through their sermons and their way of life. The Skeptics, on the other hand, carried Socrates' aporetic approach to extremes.[39]

This subordination of the theoretical side of philosophy, as far as this side existed, to the ethical-practical side finds perhaps its purest expression in the Epicurean school. Epistemology and the explanation of the world (physics) are, according to Epicurus, only the necessary intellectual conditions for a happy life because they free one from superstition and fear of the beyond. They can never become ends in themselves. A life free of want, lived in retirement in the narrowest circle of friends, under the direction of a common teacher and spiritual guide, constitutes the external prerequisite. In the Stoic school as well, however, which was not fundamentally opposed to political activity, the daily living together of the students with the teacher-spiritual guide was the ideal situation. The same had been the case formerly for the Pythagoreans, for the Platonic Academy, and for the school of Aristotle and would also be the case later for the Neoplatonists.

The Greek term for the philosopher-spiritual guide was *kathēgemōn* or *hēgemōn*, that is, "the one who leads, who shows the way," which corresponds almost exactly to our modern term "spiritual guide." The Neoplatonist Proclus, for example, says of his teacher Syrianus that, after the gods, Syrianus had been for him "the guide to all goodness and beauty" (*Platonic Theology* 1.1, Saffrey–Westerink). By the time of Philodemus at the very latest,[40] that is, in the first century B.C., the Epicurean philosophical teachers and leaders were also called *kathēgemones,* and this term was still common among the Epicureans in the time of Hadrian.[41] In the Neoplatonic tradition it was used from the school of Plotinus up to the last heathen Neoplatonists of Athens and Alexandria known to us.[42] We have no information about the usual term for the philosopher-spiritual guide, but we can assume that it was identical to the term current among the Epicureans and Neoplatonists.

The Qualities Necessary in the Spiritual Guide

Understood as spiritual guidance, philosophical instruction was necessarily most effective when it was based on personal and friendly intercourse between student and teacher. After Plato and the founding of the Academy in the fourth century B.C., all philosophical schools had regarded the written word, the book, only as a temporary measure in place of personal instruction.[43] For Plato the only valid form of philosophical instruction was a dialogue, which consists of questions and answers—dialectic (*Phaedrus* 276A–277A). This form of instruction actually presupposes the active participation of the student, because the dialectical dialogue can only proceed when the respondent gives critical approval at every stage of the dialogue—that is, when questioner and respondent, teacher and student, reach agreement at every stage of thought. For the student as well, it is therefore a case of actively thinking and not simply of pure memory work. Even this lively instruction, however, can achieve success only when mutual affection unites teacher and student. Plato expresses this clearly in the *Symposium* (209BD), where he makes the affectionate attachment of the teacher to the student a prerequisite for the philosophical activity of the teacher as well. With justification, L. Robin has related this passage to the Platonic Academy:

> It [the Academy] represents for him [Plato] that "correct understanding of the love of youths" of which he later speaks (211B), an organized work of love. It was born of that ardent feeling of educator and legislator which had always animated him. . . . It lived from the attachment of the students to the initial pact and from the loving fidelity of their voluntary devotion to the Master's thought.[44]

Robin furthermore relates this passage in the *Symposium* to a text from the *Phaedrus* on which he comments as follows:

> The image which this passage of the *Phaedrus* evokes seems to me to be that of an association between the master and his students for the common pursuit of the truth, in which the master is only a guide. How should such a community not be founded on love, love of that truth which is its principle and object, love of the master for the souls he has chosen to improve, love of the chosen souls for him who guides and oversees their blossoming, and love of all together for that which is the imperishable fruit of their mutual love?[45]

Plato's albeit sublimated pederastic tendency is replaced by Aristotle with a more neutral theory of friendship, which was taken up and developed with minimal changes by all the schools of philosophy and which was to play a great role in ancient spiritual guidance. The view, supported by all the Hellenistic schools of philosophy, that moral and ontological self-knowledge must precede all moral progress and all other philosophical knowledge soon led to the question whether self-knowledge, even in the limited degree to which we are capable of it, can be realized only with the help of a friend, in whom we can contemplate, as in a mirror, our alter ego.[46] It is therefore revealing that for the purposes of spiritual guidance the combination of spiritual doctor and friend in a single individual was regarded as almost ideal. But the philosophical discovery of the truth as well, proceeding from the ontological recognition of one's own human existence requires a friend or, even better, friends. As long as it is a case not of sages but of those still in need of progress—and this is the usual situation—ideal conditions exist whenever one of the friends has advanced further along the path of progress than the others and can serve as leader—when he can give the others a hand and draw them upward.[47] In general, the instructors of

32. Stone Relief of Daedalus and Icarus. Greek. 4th century B.C.

all the Hellenistic schools of philosophy would have liked to regard themselves as being in the position of the advanced friend as against those friends
desirous of advance. It is in this position that the Stoic philosopher and
statesman Seneca saw himself in relation to Lucilius, the recipient of a
course of spiritual guidance in epistolary form. Seneca regretted, however,
that he could only correspond with Lucilius by means of letters: community of life would have been more advantageous to both (*Epistulae Morales*
6.5–6).[48] The Stoic philosopher Cornutus also regarded himself in this position of teacher-friend in relation to his pupil, the poet Persius,[49] and the
same holds true for the Christian Augustine in relation to his pupils during
his stay in Cassiciacum, and to his fellow brothers in the monastery that
he founded in Thagaste.[50] During this period the teachings of the Neoplatonists still played an important role for Augustine, and the organization
of the monastery in Thagaste, of life in Cassiciacum, and, somewhat earlier,
of the project conceived in Milan with nine of his acquaintances of a friendly
common life based on community of goods and devoted exclusively to
study (*Confessions* 6.14.24) rests entirely on heathen philosophical—more
precisely, Neoplatonic—conceptions.[51]

The Neoplatonists had actually caught up, as if in a reservoir, all the
different streams that justified this ideal: Plato's skepticism with regard to
the ability of the written word to transmit philosophical teachings and the
importance that he attached to a dialectic that makes demands on the
partner; Aristotle's doctrine of friendship; the more or less mythical tradition of the Pythagorean communities; the general conviction of the dogmatic schools of philosophy that only he can study philosophy who has the
necessary leisure to occupy himself with it his whole life long and that the
necessary means thereto could best be found through the frugal way of life
peculiar to philosophers and through community of goods among friends;
that hardly anyone is able to achieve virtue or become godlike by himself,
but that for this he needs the help of friends striving toward the same goal
and the guidance of the teacher-friend. A résumé of these theses is to be
found some one hundred years after Augustine in the writings of the Neoplatonist Simplicius.[52] An example of this, in addition to the school of
Epicurus in Athens, is the Neoplatonic school of Athens, which after being
closed by Justinian at the beginning of the sixth century was to find its
continuation in Harran (Carrhae), not far from the Persian border.[53]

Not just anyone can be a friend in the ancient philosophical sense, but
only he who devotes himself to a virtuous life. Even being a philosopher,
however, means above all striving for a morally exemplary life: teaching
and life must not diverge from each other. He who does not live his
teaching is not only no philosopher, but neither does he possess the

necessary authority to make his philosophical teachings credible. It is a mark of genuine authority that it can find credibility and obedience of its own power without proofs. It is the function of proof by living example that the authority of the spiritual guide has to fulfill, proof for the soundness of doctrines whose validity the student in the first phase of spiritual guidance—that is, of philosophical instruction—is not yet capable of understanding and judging. Even if the demand for authority must have fallen on particularly favorable ground among the Romans,[54] this aspect is nevertheless by no means lacking among the Greeks. The very thought of such an authoritative personality can do much. The Stoic Seneca cites Epicurus when he advises Lucilius to choose some virtuous man and keep him always in view, in order that he may live and act as if that man were watching (*Epistulae Morales* 11.8–9=Epicurus fr. 210, Usener). That Seneca is conscious of representing such an authority for Lucilius follows from his words in the thirty-second letter: "Live," he addresses Lucilius, as if everything that you did came to my ears, no far more, as if I saw it" (*Epistulae Morales* 32.1). Epicurus writes to one of his students: "Carry out all your actions as if Epicurus were watching" (Seneca *Epistulae Morales* 25.5=Epicurus fr. 211, Usener). Augustine, too, in the second book of his dialogue *De ordine*, under Neoplatonic influence,[55] emphasizes the role of authority:

> Because no one has yet come to knowledge without previously being ignorant, and because one who is ignorant knows neither what condition he must be in if he wishes to go to teachers to study nor what form of life can make him capable of learning, it follows, that it is authority alone which can open the door for those who wish to master the Good in its greatness and in its mysteries. (2.9.26)

Only after the student, Augustine continues, has, so to speak, blindly obeyed the rules set up by the authority for the attainment of a perfect life, does he subsequently learn their justification.

Selection of the Students

The role of friendship in philosophical spiritual guidance and the fact that the ancient philosophical theories of friendship consider the latter to be realizable only among morally worthy people have the necessary result that the philosopher and spiritual guide does not in general admit anyone and everyone as his student—at any rate, not into the narrower circle of students. Plato and Aristotle repeatedly express themselves very clearly on this point.[56] The close community in Epicurus's Garden likewise had to be careful to exclude any elements that could not be assimilated on account of character. The Stoic Seneca also expressly emphasizes that the philosopher must not waste his efforts on unsuitable students, which in no way contradicts the Stoic theory that all persons are by nature equally capable of realizing virtue. The individual effort—that is, the personal will of every person to develop the innate disposition to virtue—remains decisive. Where this will is absent and where the readiness to recognize one's own faults is lacking, every pastoral effort is condemned to failure from the outset. Seneca explicitly refuses—and in this he agrees with the Epicureans, Peripatetics, and Academicians or Platonists—to speak publicly, in the manner of the Cynics, in the marketplace to the masses, to all, whether they wish to hear or not (*Epistulae Morales* 29.1). Seneca writes:

> This very thing, my dear Lucilius, is, I believe, exactly what a great-souled man ought not to do; his influence is weakened; it has too little effect upon those whom it might have set right if it had not grown so stale. The archer ought not to hit the mark only sometimes; he ought to miss it only sometimes. That which takes effect by chance is not an art. Now wisdom is an art; it should have a definite aim, choosing only those who will make progress, but withdrawing from those whom it has come to regard as hopeless. (*Epistulae Morales* 29.3)

Exercises

The content to which the spiritual guidance of the Hellenistic schools of philosophy refers, which I have already described briefly above, can be characterized by two formulas: "learning to live" and "learning to die," where the latter formula can be regarded as the logical presupposition of the former.[57] To accustom oneself to not regarding death—one's own as well as that of relatives and friends—as an evil is the necessary precondition for the attainment of that inner freedom that allows one to follow only one's own conscience in all circumstances and to maintain peace of mind in every situation. Every philosophical tradition of antiquity wishes to teach its adherents how to die and how to overcome the fear of dying. The Stoic Seneca cites two statements of Epicurus in this connection: "Think on death" and "it is a wonderful thing to learn thoroughly how to die," on which he comments as follows:

> In saying this, he bids us think on freedom. He who has learned to die has unlearned slavery; he is above any external power, or at any rate, he is beyond it. What terrors have prisons and bonds and bars for him? His way out is clear. There is only one chain which binds us to life, and that is the love of life. The chain may not be cast off, but it may be rubbed away, so that, when necessity shall demand, nothing may retard or hinder us from

being ready to do at once that which at some time we are bound to do.
(*Epistulae Morales* 26.8–9)

"Learning how to live," on the other hand, means freeing oneself from one's usual irrational fears and passions without whose elimination a happy life is not possible. The greatest fear, and that which is the greatest obstacle to a happy life, is, in the ancient view, the fear of death, but all other strong irrational emotions and ambitions are also to be eliminated—such as, for example, wrath, striving for wealth and power, and fear for their loss.

The dogmatic foundations for overcoming the fear of death as well as other fears and passions may vary greatly, but the methods employed by the spiritual guide to achieve this end are almost always the same. The spiritual guide prescribes a frugal way of life—some philosophical tendencies prescribe vegetarianism[58]—in order to harden the body and, to a certain extent, remove its susceptibility to suffering, but also to maintain the body's health so that it will not represent an obstacle to spiritual activity. In fighting the fear of death and the various other fears and passions, dogmas no doubt play an important role in the Epicurean, Stoic, and Neoplatonic schools, but the spiritual guide not only expounds his philosophical dogmas in lectures but also applies himself to their practice, using the power of suggestion in its various forms. Above all, he does not immediately confront the beginner with all of the philosophical problems, but presents the beginner with a résumé (*epitomē*) in the form of individual maxims—for example, the *Fourfold Medicine* (*Tetrapharmakos*) and the *Principal Propositions* (*kyriai doxai*) among the Epicureans, and the *Little Handbook* of Epictetus among the Stoics, which was even used, along with the Pythagorean *Golden Poem*, by the Neoplatonists in elementary education.[59] The *Little Handbook* of Epictetus also found favor among the Christians.[60] In the field of ethics one also begins with traditional worldly wisdom, preferably in the form of maxims or verses. Collections of maxims and verses were very popular in antiquity, because they were regarded as particularly effective in the first stages of spiritual guidance, since they are particularly able to move the listener on account of their terse form (Seneca *Epistulae Morales* 108.9ff). When the fundamental doctrines have been memorized, it is a question of gradually extending the student's knowledge. Epicurus, for example, begins specific instruction in physics with the Small Epitome, that is, the *Letter to Herodotus,* which he then augments with the Great Epitome, in order finally to conclude the course of instruction with his thirty-seven-book *Physics.* As I have argued elsewhere regarding the Epicurean *Letter to Herodotus* in comparison with Seneca's method, the widening of knowledge occurs very gradually, and the fundamental dogmas have to be memorized again and again after, or simultaneously with, every advance in knowledge.[61] For what is desired is not knowledge, but rather knowledge as *habitus,* the transformation of the individual through knowledge. The heterodox Stoic Ariston, who, in the statement cited here, agrees with all ancient philosophers except the Skeptics, states:

> Philosophy is divided into knowledge and state of mind. For one who has learned and understood what he should do and avoid is not a wise man until his mind is metamorphosed into the shape of that which he has learned. (Ariston in Seneca *Epistulae Morales* 94.48)

First of all, the elements of knowledge must be appropriated, which is a purely intellectual process. Then, knowledge must be impressed upon the mind in such a way that it is always at hand and that it cannot be limited or lost on account of any external circumstances—in other words, in such a way that it becomes one with the individual and a constituent part of the person's being. This second stage can be attained only through practice and habituation with the incorporation of one's emotional components. Let us take as an example the dogma "Death is not an evil," which was professed by all the ancient schools of philosophy. The philosopher-spiritual guide knows that it is not sufficient to know this and to be familiar with and to have grasped intellectually the philosophical proofs that are the foundation for this statement; one must be convinced to such a degree that one's whole inner nature is penetrated by it. In order to achieve this transformation, the spiritual guide employs various pedagogical methods that are supposed to appeal to the emotional part of the soul. If he is a Stoic or Platonist, he will, for example, use historical examples of people who have sacrificed their lives either for the fatherland or for some other great cause, who in other words value their own lives less than the good that they defend with the sacrifice of their lives. He will, moreover, strive to develop these examples according to all the rules of rhetoric, so as to produce the greatest possible emotional effect through beauty of delivery as well as through beauty of subject matter. In the Imperial age rhetoric becomes the necessary aid of almost every philosopher, including the Epicureans.[62] Furthermore, the spiritual guide uses instruction in one of the three main branches of philosophy—namely, physics—again and again to bring the organization of the universe before the student's eyes (depending on the doctrine either as a product of chance or as a product of rationality) and to make clear to the student in relation to this the insignificance of the individual human fate. The vision of the universal leads to the experience of the smallness of human affairs. Thus, Marcus Aurelius writes with reference to a passage in Plato's *Republic:*

"Do you really imagine that an intelligence endowed with greatness of heart and a vision of all time and all reality thinks this mortal life to be a great thing?" "Impossible," was his answer. "Then such a man as that will consider even death not a thing to be dreaded, will he not?" "Most assuredly." (*Meditations* 7.35)

Theoretical instruction is thus always—the *Quaestiones naturales* of Seneca are a good example of this—interspersed with implementations that have an emotional basis themselves as well as exercise an emotional effect on the listener or reader, and whose frequent occurrence, finally, was intended to produce a very specific and permanent spiritual condition, which was called "greatness of soul." These and similar exercises in meditation, such as the Stoic practice of looking ahead to or intellectually anticipating all possible evils with their own peculiar method or "analysis,"[63] the spiritual guide himself undertakes together with his student, as well as urging the latter to undertake them himself, orally or in writing, several times a day. The *Meditations* of Marcus Aurelius are a good example of the practice of such intensive exercises in meditation.

Next to the transmission of knowledge and above all the realization of this knowledge with the help of the power of suggestion, the other great task of the spiritual guide consists in leading the student to the recognition of his faults, that is, to critical self-analysis, and to teach him to keep an exact diary of his spiritual illnesses. "Therefore, as far as possible, prove yourself guilty," Seneca advises Lucilius (*Epistulae Morales* 28.10), "hunt up charges against yourself; play the part, first of accuser, then of judge, last of intercessor. At times be harsh with yourself." And Epictetus advises his students to ask themselves the following questions:

How do I conduct myself? Do I behave like a wise man, like a man who can control himself? Can I really say of myself that I have learned to be prepared for everything? Am I, as one who knows nothing, also really conscious of my ignorance? Do I go to my teacher prepared to obey him like an oracle? Or am I not also one of those, who in their folly only go to school in order to learn the history of philosophy, to understand books which they did not understand before and to explain them to others should the occasion arise? (*Discourses* 2.21.9–10)

This self-examination, common to almost all of the philosophical schools of antiquity and in general derived from Pythagorean practice, is usually undertaken in the evening and in the morning. Thus, Porphyry writes of Pythagoras, that he especially recommended two times of day for self-examination, the time of going to bed and the time of getting up (*Life of Pythagoras* 40, des Places p. 54). At both times one was supposed to examine what one had done and what was to be done now, to account to oneself for what had been done and to reflect with care on one's future actions. For this reason everyone was supposed to sing the following verses to himself (here given in prose) before going to bed: "Sleep shall not descend upon your soft lids until you have considered your every activity of the day in threefold manner: Wherein did I err? What did I do? What duty did I neglect?" (Pythagorean *Carmen aureum* 40–42). And before rising the following: "First of all, when you awake from sweet sleep, consider carefully the coming work of the day" (*Carmen aureum* 43–44). We have many witnesses in ancient philosophical literature for the use of morning and evening self-examinations,[64] of which I would like to mention only a few lines of Seneca:

> Can anything be more excellent than this practice of thoroughly sifting the whole day? And how delightful the sleep that follows this self-examination— how tranquil it is, how deep and untroubled, when the soul has either praised or admonished itself, and when this secret examiner and critic of self has given report of its own character! I avail myself of this privilege, and every day I plead my cause before the bar of self. When the light has been removed from sight, and my wife, long aware of my habit, has become silent, I scan the whole of my day and retrace all my deeds and words. I conceal nothing from myself, I omit nothing. (*De ira* 3.36.1–3)[65]

The goal of such a twofold practice is obvious: extreme attentiveness and consciousness were desired. Not a single moment of daily life was to pass by without rational control, and, beyond this, the comparison between what had been planned and what had been achieved was supposed to enable the examination of ethical progress. For the examination of progress written notes are also necessary. With regard to this or that emotion which has been recognized as a particular individual fault through self-examination, the student is encouraged to keep a sort of diary, in which he records the frequency of his lapses:

> If you wish to stop being irascible, then do not give your habit any further nourishment, do not give it any opportunity of growing. Suppress the first outburst and count the days in which you did not lose your temper: "I used to lose my temper every day, now only every second day, and so forth: every three days, every four days." If you have been able to control yourself for thirty days, bring a thank offering to God. At first the habit of losing your temper will be weakened; in the end it will be completely overcome. "Today I did not give in to melancholy, nor the following day, nor after that for two or three months, but I kept a close watch on myself whenever an inclination that way arose." (Epictetus *Discourses* 2.18.12–14)

We even possess a work by the middle Platonist Plutarch with the title "How one can ascertain that one is progressing in virtue," which represents a catalogue of the various signs of progress.[66]

The result of self-examination naturally had to be communicated to the spiritual guide, a practice that we know from the Christian sphere under the name of "confession." From the school of Epicurus we possess extracts from a course in which detailed instructions are given to the Epicurean spiritual guide as to how he is to bring the student to confession and how he can formulate the discussion in an individual and considerate way: The spiritual guide must never speak in a tone despairing of the sinner. Even if the sinner is himself without hope or lets his dissatisfaction be very noticeable, the spiritual guide must never forget what is kind and beneficial. The spiritual guide must not make himself disagreeable to the student. The spiritual guide may choose the way of indirect reprimand by censuring the same fault in another or even by transferring it to himself and saying that he committed it in unbridled youth. The spiritual guide must not let himself be carried away to abuse, mockery, and humiliation. He must not hurt the student; neither must he employ flattery. He should determine whether the student is sensitive or somewhat sturdier or so recalcitrant that he will hardly mend his ways even if shouted at. The spiritual guide must note what sort of family the student comes from and what education he has had the benefit of, and so forth.[67] A further task of the spiritual guide was to encourage the student to analyze his dreams: the last flaring up of sensual desire manifests itself in dreams.[68]

This highly developed practice of spiritual guidance was completely adopted by the Christians, albeit with different premises. Paul Rabbow has demonstrated this with regard to the *Exercitia spiritualia* of Ignatius Loyola,[69] and Pierre Hadot with regard to monasticism from the fourth century on.[70] The figure of the philosopher as spiritual guide with the philosophical schools as the center of his activity is now replaced by the person of the clerical spiritual guide in the Christian orders. An albeit weaker, yet no less effective, reflection of this practice is to be found in the secular priest's practice of confession.

In conclusion I would be so bold as to ask, Has modern spiritual guidance or contemporary psychology, which is so proud of its scientific researches, brought the slightest advance over the millennia-old practice of spiritual guidance?

Translated by Margaret Kirby

Notes

1. See the collected examples in the Lexicon Iconographicum Mythologiae Classicae (*LIMC*): Figures *Achilleus* nos. 50–62 in volume 1/2 (1981); commentaries with literary references volume I1/1(1981), pp. 40–42, 48, 198.

2. See also Apollodorus, *Bibliotheca* 3.10.3. According to Pseudo-Justinian (*De monarch.* 6), besides Asclepius Apollo took part in Chiron's medical instruction.

3. Xenophon mentions twenty-one students of Chiron.

4. Vol. 3, p. 61 Henry (Budé; Paris: Les Belles Lettres). See also R. Turcan, "Chiron le mystagogue," in *Mélanges offerts à J. Carcopino* (Paris: Hatchette, 1966) 927–939.

5. See figure *Achilleus* no. 79 in the *LIMC,* vol. 1/2. Cf. J. Carcopino, *La basilique pythagoricienne de la Porte Majeure* (Paris: L'artisan du livre, 1926) 126ff. The attribution "Neopythagorean" is uncertain.

6. See, for example, figures *Achilleus* nos. 64–72 and 77–79 in the *LIMC,* vol. 1/2 as well as Catalogue, vol. 1/1, pp. 50–51.

7. See figures *Achilleus* nos. 21 and 81 in *LIMC* vol. 1/2 as well as Catalogue, vol. 1/1, pp. 45, 51f.

8. We have only late evidence for this tendency, from the first and second centuries A.D.; see nn. 4 and 5.

9. It is not possible to assume, with Friedrich Pfister (*Götter und Heldensagen der Griechen* [Heidelberg: C. Winter, 1956] 127), that in Homer's view Chiron was responsible for the education of Achilles until he was six years old and that only his later education in Phthia fell to Phoenix. The admonition makes it clear that Phoenix already had Achilles with him as a small child (*Iliad* 9.485–91). On the various mythical traditions relating to Achilles' childhood, see *LIMC,* vol. 1/1, pp. 40–42.

10. Last of all probably by Simplicius, *In Enchiridion Epicteti,* p. 70, 47–48 Dübner.

11. See M. Detienne, *Crise agraire et attitude religieuse chez Hésiode* (Coll. Latomus 68; Brussels: Latomus, 1963) 43.

12. See P. Walcot, "Hesiod and the Didactic Literature of the Near East," in *Revue des études grecques* 75 (1962) 13–36.

13. Ibid., 17–20.

14. On this question, see K. Ziegler, "Orpheus und Orphische Dichtung," *Realencyclopdie der classischen Altertumswissenschaft* vol. 18, cols. 1200–1320, 1341–1417.

15. See F. Graf, *Eleusis und die orphische Dichtung* (Berlin and New York: de Gruyter, 1974) chap. 1: "Die orphische Dichtung und Eleusis."

16. E.g., the article "Ethos" by W. Vetter in *Musik in Geschichte und Gegenwart,* vol. 3, cols. 1581–91.

17. This is the Loeb Classical Library edition, with minimal changes.

18. E.g., Kallinos fr. 1, Diehl; Tyrtaios fr. 7, Diehl, beginning; Solon *Eunomia* and fr. 10, Diehl; Phocylides frs. 57–60.

19. There is an untranslatable union of social and ethical superiority in this concept.

20. See F. Wehrli, who has convincingly demonstrated "the organic growth of philosophical ethics among the Greeks from their original estimation of things" (*LATHE BIOSAS* [Leipzig: Teubner, 1931] introduction).

21. Quoted in the translation by Kathleen Freeman, *The Work and Life of Solon: With a Translation of His Poems* (Cardiff and London: University of Wales Press, 1926; reprint New York: Arno Press, 1976) 208.

22. Aristotle *De philosophia* fr. 8, Rose (=Philopon *In Nicomachi Isagoge Commentaria* 1.1; Cicero *De republica* 1.12; *De oratore* 3.137).

23. There are various catalogues of the seven sages; see Barkowski, "Sieben Weise" in the *Realencyclopädie der classischen Altertumswissenschaft,* vol. 3, cols. 2243–47.

24. See Barkowski, "Sieben Weise," cols. 2251–52; Plato relates that the seven wise men met in Delphi and set up their gnomic maxims "Know thyself," "Nothing too much," etc. as a consecration gift for Apollo in his temple (*Protagoras* 343A8–B7).

25. See L. Robert, "De Delphes à l'Oxus: Inscriptions grecques nouvelles de la Bactriane." *Comptes rendus de l'Académie des inscriptions et belles-lettres* (1968), 438.

26. Robert, "De Delphos," 421–57, esp. 438ff.

27. See the epigram of Clearchus of Soli to be found on the base of the stele (Robert, "De Delphos," 422–24).

28. Robert, "De Delphos," 438–54.

29. See W. Dittenberger, *Sylloge Inscriptionum Graecarum* (3rd ed.; Leipzig: S. Hirzelium, 1920) 3:392–97); and Robert, "De Delphos," 440f. See also O. Hense, "Die Kyzikener Spruchsammlung," *Berliner Philologische Wochenschrift*, June 15, 1907, cols. 765–768. This series is also known to us through Stobaeus *Anthologium* 3.1783, Hense p. 125 (under the title "Sosiades' maxims of the seven sages").

30. *Inscriptiones Graecae* XII 3, 1020.

31. See L. Robert, "Un oracle gravé à Oinanda," *Comptes-rendus de l'Académie des inscriptions et belles-lettres* (1971) 597–619.

32. D. Schlumberger, L. Robert, A. Dupont-Sommer, and E. Benveniste, "Une bilingue gréco-araméene d'Asoka," *Journal Asiatique* 246 (1958) 1–48.

33. D. Schlumberger, "Une nouvelle inscription grecque d'Açoka," *Comptes rendus de l'Académie des inscriptions et belles lettres* (1964) 1–14.

34. See P. Hadot, "Fürstenspiegel" in *Reallexikon für Antike und Christentum* (Stuttgart: Hiersemann, 1950) 8:555–632.

35. In spite of their different theoretical foundations, happy life and virtuous life were identical or almost identical for most schools of philosophy. Even the so-called ethics of pleasure of the Epicureans boils down, in practical terms, to a virtuous life.

36. See Seneca *Epistulae Morales* 16.3: "Philosophy is no trick to catch the public: it is not devised for show. It is a matter, not of words, but of facts. It is not pursued in order that the day may yield some amusement before it is spent, or that our leisure may be relieved of a tedium that irks us. It moulds and constructs the soul: it orders our life, guides our conduct, shows us what we should do and what we should leave undone; it sits at the helm and directs our course as we waver amid uncertainties. Without it, no one can live fearlessly or in peace of mind (Seneca *Ad Lucilium Epistulae Morales,* trans. Richard M. Gummere [Loeb Classical Library; Cambridge, MA: Harvard University Press, 1970–71) 1:105).

37. The Peripatetics are an exception here. For them scientific research constituted an essential element of the happy life. See Aristotle *Nicomachean Ethics* 10.7.1177a121ff.; see also I. Hadot, *Arts libéraux et philosophie dans la pensée antique* (Paris: Etudes augustiniennes, 1984) 18–23, 34–36.

38. See P. Hadot, *Exercices spirituels et philosophie antique* (Paris: Etudes augustiniennes, 1981) the chapter "La figure de Socrate."

39. Because for the Skeptics nothing can be perceived or known, the development of dogmatics is not applicable to them.

40. Philodemus *De libertate dicendi* (*Peri parrēsias*) fr. 41.5, Olivieri. The term *kathēgētēs* is also common; see fr. 45.5, Olivieri.

41. *Corpus inscriptionum latinarum* 3, 12283 and 14203: Letter from Plotina to Hadrian with Hadrian's reply.

42. See Porphyry *Life of Plotinus* 17.42; Julian *Orationes* 9 [6] 202d (the cynic Crates referred to as *hēgemōn* of the Stoic Zenon); Damaskios *Vita Isadori* Zintzen p. 10, 5 (Damaskios refers to Isidor as his *hēgemōn*); Simplicius *In Aristotelis Physica Commentaria* 642.17, Diels, and 774.28, Diels: (Simplicius mentions Damaskios as his *hēgemōn*); Simplicius *In Aristotelis De Caelo Commentaria* 271.19, Heiberg. If the teacher's

activity as commentator on Plato or Aristotle is rather to be emphasized, then the term *exēgētēs* is used.

43. See Plato *Phaedrus* 276CD and the disputed Seventh Letter.

44. L. Robin, *Platon, Le Banquet* (Budé; Paris: Les Belles Lettres, 1929) XCI.

45. L. Robin, *Platon, Phèdre* (Budé; Paris: Les Belles Lettres, 1933) LIV.

46. See, e.g., Aristotle *Magna Moralia* 2.1213a13ff.; *Eudemian Ethics* 7.12.1245a35.

47. *Manus (dextram) porrigere (dare)*: it is a matter of a *terminus technicus* of spiritual guidance; see Seneca *Epistulae Morales* 55.2; 29.4; see also Augustine *De beata vita* 1.5; *Epist.*, 26 (Corpus scriptorum ecclesiasticorum latinorum 34:89, 4).

48. On the significance of friendship for Seneca's spiritual guidance, see I. Hadot, *Seneca und die griechisch-römisch Tradition der Seelenleitung* (Berlin: de Gruyter, 1969) 164ff.

49. See the *Vita Auli Persi Flacci* from the Probus commentary, which reveals the close friendship of Persius and his teacher, the Stoic Cornutus: "When he (Persius) was sixteen years old, he entered into a relation of friendship with Annaeus Cornutus, such that he never left his side" (§4).

50. See I. Hadot, *"amicitia"* in *Augustinus Lexikon* (Basel and Stuttgart, 1985) vol. 1.

51. I. Hadot, *"amicitia."*

52. *In Enchiridion Epicteti* p. 87, 51–88,8; p. 88, 20–21; p. 89, 11–14, Dübner.

53. See Michel Tardieu, "Témoins orientaux du *Premier Alcibiade* à Harran et à Nag Hammadi," *Journal Asiatique* (1985).

54. In this connection, see I. Hadot, *Seneca*, 173–76.

55. See my interpretation of the second book of the dialogue *De ordine* in *Arts libéraux*, 101–31.

56. See the theory of education that Plato develops in the *Republic:* only an elite, in the moral and intellectual sense, is capable of concerning itself with philosophy. For Aristotle, see the theory of friendship he develops in the *Nicomachean Ethics* and, above all, the last chapter, where the pedagogical possibilities of the philosopher are discussed (10.9.1179b7–15; see also Aristotle *Politics* 7.13.1332a40–42).

57. On exercises, see P. Rabbow's fundamental book *Seelenführung: Methodik der Exerzitien in der Antike* (Munich: Kösel, 1954); and P. Hadot *Exercices.*

58. E.g., the Pythagoreans, the Neoplatonists, Sextius (on the latter, see Seneca *Epistulae Morales* 108.17).

59. On this, see I. Hadot, *Le problème du néoplatonisme alexandrin: Hiéroclès et Simplicius* (Paris: Etudes augustiniennes, 1978) 160–64.

60. We possess several Christian adaptations of the *Little Handbook* (*Enchiridion*).

61. See I. Hadot, "Epicure et l'enseignement philosophique hellénistique et romain," in *Actes du VIIIe Congrès de l'Association Guillaume Budé (Paris 1968)* (Paris: Les Belles Lettres, 1969) 347–54.

62. *Inscriptiones Graecae ad res Romanas Pertinens* IV, 99: Inscription from Samos in honor of the Epicurean Gaius Iulius Sosigenes with the nickname "Isokrates," which can only refer to his rhetorical accomplishments. On the important role of rhetoric in the Academy from Philon of Larissa (first century B.C.) on, see I. Hadot, *Arts libéraux*, passim.

63. For more on this method, see P. Rabbow, *Seelenführung,* 42ff.

64. E.g., Seneca *Epistulae Morales* 28.10; Epictetus *Discourses* 4.6.33; 3.13.8; 2.21.9; 2.18.13–17; Hierocles *In Carmen aureum* 9, Köhler p. 80–84.

65. Seneca, *Moral Essays,* trans. John W. Basore (Loeb Classical Library; Cambridge, MA: Harvard University Press, 1928) 3:341).

66. See also Plutarch *De ira cohibenda* 464BC.

67. Philodemus *De libertate dicendi* = a summary of lectures by the Epicurean Zenon. See Rabbow, *Seelenführung*, 269. On the Epicurean practice of confession, see W. Schmid, "Epikur" in *Reallexikon für Antike und Christentum*, vol. 5, cols. 741ff.

68. Zenon the Stoic in Plutarch *Quomodo quis sent. prof. virt.* 12.82f. = (*SVF* 1:234, von Armim p. 56).

69. Rabbow, *Seelenführung*, 151–59, 189–214.

70. P. Hadot, *Exercices,* chapter "Exercices spirituels antiques et 'philosophie chrétienne.'"

19

The Spiritual Importance
of Not Knowing

R. T. Wallis

IN HIS INTRODUCTION TO THIS VOLUME, Professor Armstrong has stressed the close link in the ancient Mediterranean world between philosophy and spirituality, and the present article will be confined to philosophers and authors using philosophical terminology. It is not that philosophy provided the only form of non- or super-rational experience of the divine or even, for the average person, the most accessible one. But our knowledge both of such nonphilosophical experiences and of the external preparations for them is generally limited, and what we do know, for instance, of Dionysiac ecstasy, has been fully treated elsewhere, especially in E. R. Dodds's monumental *The Greeks and the Irrational*.[1] We shall therefore not attempt to repeat it here.

With the important exception of Pyrrho of Elis, our concern will be the various sources' accounts of the inadequacy of human knowledge and language in discussing God or a supersensible reality such as the Platonic Forms and the means they propose for overcoming this. Here we may recall Dodds's valuable distinction of six senses in which a god may be "unknown."[2] These are (1) unknown because foreign or nameless, (2) unknown to humanity in general owing to the necessary limitations of human knowledge, (3) unknown to all who have not enjoyed a special revelation or initiation, (4) unknowable in his essence but knowable by inference from his works or analogy from other causes, (5) unknowable in his positive character but definable by negations, and (6) unknowable but accessible in a supralogical mystical union, which is not, properly speaking, "knowledge." It is the last four of these that will concern us here; in other words, we shall deal not with simple ignorance or agnosticism but with the view of God as too perfect to be grasped by human thought and its consequences for religious belief and practice.

Even where abundant evidence exists, however, as it does for most of the sources to be considered here, its spiritual significance is not always easy to grasp. Publication of the Nag Hammadi Coptic Gnostic library, discovered in Egypt after World War II, for instance, has freed our knowledge of Gnosticism from dependence on the hostile accounts of the church fathers and the texts they chose to quote.[3] Yet we shall find that the significance of Gnostic negative theology remains as controversial as ever. Similar controversy surrounds virtually all we shall say about Plato. Plotinus we may take as the archetype of the mystic in classical antiquity—that is, of one who believes himself to have experienced or realized a superrational union with God or Ultimate Reality. But with other authors the case is less clear. We may pose three main questions. Least important is whether an author is describing his own experience or another's—whether, in Dodds's terminology, he is a "mystic" or only a "mystical theorist."[4] More important is the *kind* of experience that is reported. What, for instance, is the relation between mysticism and theurgy in later Neoplatonism? Finally, there is the problem of the *depth* or *level* of experience in question. And here a key problem is posed by the term *Nous*. Originally and in Homer the term conveyed the notion of "seeing," especially in the sense of insight into the meaning of a situation. In Plato and Aristotle *Nous* sometimes means "reason" in general, and elsewhere it connotes the highest of human intellectual powers, direct insight into truth.[5] By the time of the Roman Empire, in the Middle Platonists and *Hermetica,* it appears also to be used of a mystical union of a Plotinian type. The difficulty of deciding which sense is meant in a particular passage is obvious, and not until Plotinus is a clear distinction drawn between the three levels. For all these reasons we must often rest content with A.-J. Festugière's observation that "the historian knows only what he is told; he cannot penetrate the secrets of the heart."[6] I shall therefore, as far as space permits, extend my account to cover all levels of experience transcending discursive thought and ordinary language found in our sources and, further, to show how in many of them unknowability is present in varying degrees on several, sometimes on all, levels of reality. *Nous* I shall often leave untranslated; elsewhere I shall use "intelligence," "intellect," and their cognates or, where appropriate, such terms as "direct insight" or "intuitive vision," while giving my own views, wherever possible, on the type of experience described in the passage in question.

Plato

The greatest stress on the inadequacy of language in Plato's dialogues comes in the *Cratylus,* a work emphasizing the doctrine that the sensible world is in perpetual flux. It follows from this that we can have no knowledge (*epistēmē*) of that world, but only opinion (*doxa*) and that our account of it, in the words of *Timaeus* 29D, can be only a "likely story" (*eikōs mythos*). Knowledge is possible only of the changeless world of Ideal Forms, of which the sense world constitutes an imitation produced by the *Timaeus*'s divine craftsman (or "Demiurge") on the basis of the unstable "Receptacle of Becoming," itself graspable only by a "bastard form of reasoning" (*Timaeus* 52B). But verbal knowledge, in Plato's view, is an imperfect way of grasping even the Forms, or, to quote *Phaedo* 94D, a "second-best course" (*deuteros plous*). Words and names are only images (*eikones*) of the Forms, drawn from the sense world, and no image can ever exactly reproduce its original. Hence, the *Cratylus* declares, we need a kind of knowledge that grasps reality directly, "without names."[7] The deficiency of language is further stressed in the *Phaedrus*'s criticism of the written word, and in the *Seventh Letter*.

The vexed questions of Plato's philosophical development and the *Letter*'s authenticity need not be pursued here, since we shall find substantially the same attitude to our subject in all the relevant dialogues and in the *Letter*, whether it is Plato's own work or that of a close disciple. Here names (*onomata*), definitions (*logoi*), images (*eidōla*), and knowledge based on them (grouped together as "the four") are expressly stated to be inadequate to express the nature of the "Fifth" (the "thing-in-itself" or Form). All four attain only a thing's quality (*to poion ti*), not its essence (*to ti*). Intellectual insight (*nous*) is, however, declared to be closer to the Forms than discursive thought (*dianoia*) or opinion (*doxa*). But only by passing through the "four" can insight into the Fifth be attained. After a long communion between two souls in a common search for truth (the philosophical discipline which the *Republic* calls "dialectic"), a light suddenly springs up in the soul of suitable pupils.

That the supreme vision comes "suddenly" is likewise affirmed in the *Symposium*, which describes the philosopher's ascent through successive levels of beauty to the vision of the Form of the Beautiful. But it is in the central books of the *Republic* that the ascent is most clearly fleshed out. Here *dianoia* (discursive thought, exemplified by mathematics) is stated to be inferior to *noēsis* (intuitive insight) on two grounds. First, it starts from hypotheses that seem self-evident but of which it can give no account, though its objects are "intelligible in conjunction with a First Principle." *Noēsis*, in contrast, the faculty involved in dialectic, ascends from hypotheses to the unhypothetical First Principle, the Form of the Good, the source of the being of the Forms and therefore located by Plato "beyond Being" (*Republic* 509B). Second, although *dianoia* necessarily employs sensible images of the Forms, the philosopher's ascent to the Good and subsequent descent therefrom dispense with them. A full account of dialectic Plato declines to give, on the grounds that his audience has been concerned with "images" and would not be able to follow an account of Truth itself. In other words, the nature of dialectic is intelligible only to those who have passed through it. We can thus see that the accounts of the *Republic*, *Cratylus*, and *Seventh Letter* complement one another and explain why knowledge based on words or images is inadequate. In particular, the *Republic* does not confine to the Good an ineffability extended by the *Letter* to all the Forms. Similarly, the *Symposium*'s intuitive vision of the Form of Beauty extends to all the Forms in the *Phaedrus* myth. It is doubtful, however, whether Plato anywhere envisages a mystical experience like Plotinus's union with the One. P. Merlan is probably right in seeing his vision as closer to Zen Buddhist *Satori*.[8] Still more emphatically should Plato's *noēsis*—for him (as for the Neoplatonists) the crown of human intellectual life—be distinguished from prophetic or poetic inspiration, states he regards as lacking a basis of intellectual discipline and therefore as unreliable, if not positively dangerous. Finally, for both Plato and the Neoplatonists philosophical insight involves moral as well as intellectual purification, "turning the whole soul towards the light," and aiming at "likeness to God as far as possible" (*Theaetetus* 176B).

It is less certain how far we should press the declaration in *Timaeus* 28C that "it is hard to find the maker and father of this universe and . . . impossible to declare him to all." What is clear is that, since neither sensible nor Intelligible world is expressible in words, the shortcomings of language and conceptual thought will be clearest in attempting to describe the relation between them. Hence Plato's use of metaphors like "imitation" and "participation," whose inadequacy is exposed in the *Parmenides*. It is likewise the failure of language drawn from the sense world to express Intelligible Reality that best explains the antinomies of the second part of that dialogue. If we use such predicates in their everyday sense, a Form cannot be subject to them. Alternatively, if we apply such terms to the Forms, we end with the opposite absurdity, ascribing to them all the limitations of the spatio-temporal world. The Neoplatonists were therefore wrong in seeing in the *Parmenides*'s first two hypotheses a higher and a lower One. Yet they were not wholly in error; for, though Parmenides names Unity only as one of the concepts to which the antinomies could be applied, Plato is said by Aristotle to have come to regard the One (which we have reason to identify with the Good) as the Supreme Principle. It follows that the Supreme One is indeed strictly describable only in negative terms and, hence, like the Good in the *Republic*, lies beyond Being—and, *a fortiori*, beyond conceptual knowledge. In fact, Plato's nephew and successor Speusippus postulated as his first principle the One, which he placed beyond Being and the Good, and also beyond *Nous*. He apparently regarded the One as the seed whence all evolves, a comparison accepted by Plotinus, provided other entities are not regarded as a more perfect actualization of the One (a criticism that Aristotle, using his own criteria of perfection, levels at Speusippus). In contrast, Xenocrates, Speusippus's successor as head of the Academy, identified *Nous* with the Monad, his supreme principle,[9] and we shall find in pre-Plotinian Platonism a not-very-satisfactory oscillation between these positions.

Aristotle

Such a tension appears already in Aristotle, for, although his *Metaphysics* identifies God with a self-contemplating Intellect, his *Eudemian Ethics*, like his lost work *On Prayer*, hesitates whether God may really transcend Intellect.[10] Elsewhere, according to Plutarch, he followed Plato in describing the highest part of philosophy as a vision comparable to that enjoyed by initiates in the mysteries. That *nous* is needed to grasp the first principles of reasoning is stated in the *Posterior Analytics* and *Nicomachean Ethics*, whereas the *Eudemian Ethics* ascribes the practical person's common sense to divine inspiration, and the work *On the Soul* conceives of knowledge as the result of an eternally active, immortal Intellect operating within the human soul. Most remarkable is the reluctance of Aristotle's followers to discard this side of his thought.[11] Thus, his successor Theophrastus regarded the First Principles of Being as apprehensible only by an "intuitive contact," while even the materialist Dicaearchus attributed prophecy to a divine element within the soul. Finally, we may note the transcendentalist interpretation of the Active Intellect (identified with God) by the second century A.D. Aristotelian, Alexander of Aphrodisias, a major influence on Plotinus's view of *Nous*.

Pyrrho

The fascinating parallels between Greek and Indian thought cannot be considered here; still less the possible influence of one on the other. An exception is the unique development of "not knowing" by Pyrrho of Elis, founder of the Greek Skeptical school, whose philosophy blends traditional Greek agnosticism with the developing ideas of Buddhism, which he encountered on accompanying Alexander's expedition to India.[12] Its fundamental principle is "suspension of judgment" (*epochē*), on which tranquillity (*ataraxia*) naturally follows. Any assertion about the nature of things is no more true than its opposite. Phenomena we indeed experience, but the reality, if any, underlying them remains unknowable. Skeptics, therefore, feel pleasure and pain like others, but, since they do not regard them as good or evil, their tranquillity remains undisturbed. Hence the formulas "determining nothing" and "asserting nothing." These formulas, it is stressed, are not dogmatic assertions, for Skepticism has no positive tenets. Thus, in asserting nothing, we refrain from asserting even that we assert nothing. Similarly, the declaration that one alternative is no more true than another is, in turn, no truer than its opposite; it merely expresses the Skeptic's refusal to assert one alternative rather than another. The Skeptical method is thus to propound opposing arguments for contrary positions and thereby to show the equal unprovability of either. This achieved, his method destroys itself like a purge which, after purifying the body, expels itself. How far Pyrrhonism influenced Neoplatonic views on divine unknowability (as later Skepticism certainly influenced Plotinus on other points) remains uncertain. But at least two of its principles are echoed by the Neoplatonists. First, statements about Ultimate Reality are mere expressions of our own attitude thereto; second, negations used of the Supreme must in turn be negated.

New Transcendentalisms

A transcendentalist version of not-knowing, prefiguring Neoplatonism, apparently reappears in the first century B.C. with the rise of Neopythagoreanism, a revival of the religious side of Pythagoreanism, with the vital difference that the school's original dualism is often replaced by a monism in which the highest principle is a One which, as in Speusippus, transcends Being and *Nous*. Such a system occurs in various pseudepigrapha (writings falsely ascribed to early Pythagorean sages) of the time and in the Pythagoreanizing Platonist Eudorus of Alexandria.[13] It may be these circles that first gave a theological interpretation to the *Parmenides* and expounded the doctrine of divine ineffability, read into *Timaeus* 28C by Cicero (*On the Nature of the Gods* 1.30) and first expounded in detail, among extant authors, by the hellenizing Jewish commentator Philo of Alexandria. Between Philo and Plotinus we find at least five "transcendentalist" movements: (1) the Middle Platonists, (2) the Neopythagorean systematizers, especially Numenius of Apamea, (3) the *Chaldaean Oracles* and *Hermetica*, texts from what Dillon calls the "Platonic underworld,"[14] (4) Gnosticism, and (5) the Alexandrian Christian Platonists Clement and Origen. Alexandrian Christianity falls outside the scope of this volume, and Philo also is discussed in detail elsewhere. His omission here is less serious, since it seems only with the Christians, and perhaps Numenius, that we encounter Philo's own influence. His importance is in fusing the Jewish insistence on God's utter transcendence with the Platonic-Pythagorean doctrines just noted.[15] This shows that negative theology is neither a Hebraic incursion into classical Greek thought nor an unfortunate accretion to the Judeo-Christian tradition. The influence of Neoplatonic negative theology on Christian and Muslim thought and mysticism must also be left for other volumes.[16] It is the Middle Platonists who must now claim our attention.[17]

Among the Middle Platonists it is chiefly the Aristotelian group, led by Albinus, the second-century A.D. author of an *Epitome* of Platonic doctrine, and the anti-Christian polemicist Celsus, attacked by Origen, who offer the most relevant material for our purposes. (It is noteworthy that Plutarch of Chaeronea, the best preserved of all Middle Platonists, shows virtually no interest in negative theology.) Albinus himself is a good example of the equivocal attitude of contemporary Platonists. On the one hand, his supreme God is a self-contemplating Aristotelian *Nous*, containing the Platonic Forms; on the other hand, Albinus hints, he may be rather the transcendent cause of *Nous*. Hence Albinus's description of him as ineffable (qualified elsewhere to "almost ineffable") and apprehensible only by *Nous* (which is elsewhere said to grasp the Forms by a "non-discursive apprehension"). God's ineffability is upheld on the grounds that he transcends logical classification and has no quality; nor, indeed, Albinus adds, is he without quality. He likewise transcends the predicates "good" and "evil"; for "good," for a Platonist, involves participation in the Primal Good, which is the supreme God himself. Yet Albinus describes God as beautiful—indeed, as "most beautiful of all things." Albinus also teaches the "three ways" of knowing God found in contemporary Middle Platonists, Plotinus, and Medieval Scholasticism, those of Analogy (*kat'analogian*, illustrated by the *Republic*'s comparison of the Good to the Sun), Negation (*kat'aphairesin*, as a geometrical point is reached by abstraction), and Eminence (*kath'hyperochēn*, represented by the *Symposium*'s ascent through successive levels of beauty). Such mystical trends are qualified, however, by Albinus's interpretation of Plato's "imitation of God." Since this is achieved through virtue, he argues, we cannot imitate the Supreme God, who transcends virtue; our imitation must rather be of the World soul (a view indignantly repudiated by Plotinus).

Of other Aristotelianizing Middle Platonists, the rhetorician Maximus of Tyre likewise identifies God with Aristotle's Active Intellect, yet describes him as ineffable. He also prescribes what is evidently "an established tradition of exercises in introvertive contemplation"[18] leading to the divine vision. A similar system emerges from Celsus's extant remains, largely based on the *Republic*. Hence his stress on the way of Analogy (though he mentions the other two ways, using different terminology from Albinus). Celsus, however, places God beyond *Nous*, and hence describes him as intelligible only by "a certain ineffable power."

Of the Neopythagorean systematizers, most important is Numenius of Apamea. At the summit of his universe is a first God, identified with the Monad and the Good, though our extant fragments do not explicitly call him the One. On other points Numenius's statements appear contradictory. Thus, his supreme God is, on the one hand, termed the primary *Nous* and "Being itself." Yet, though identified with the *Timaeus's* Ideal Animal (the sensible world's Intelligible model) and described as "concerned with the Intelligibles," he is elsewhere said to be prior to Being and Form. It is Numenius's second God, whom, like Albinus, he terms "good," not "*the* Good," who constitutes the Platonic Demiurge proper. We may also note that the first God is said to exercise intelligence "by using the second God"; his essential activity would thus be something higher than *Nous*.

The first God Numenius regards as unknown to most humans. He is, however, attainable in contemplation, for, as in Plotinian, though not Iamblichean, Neoplatonism, the individual soul for Numenius contains the whole Intelligible world and in its pure state is identical with the principles whence it derives. Like contemporary Platonists, Numenius stresses withdrawal from the senses, to consort with the Good in an unspeakable and tranquil solitude, apprehending it "with a single glance." The echoes of Numenius's account of contemplation in Plotinus's descriptions of mystical union (including the phrase, in itself a commonplace of contemporary religious writing, "alone with the alone") suggest that Plotinus regarded Numenius as envisaging a similar experience. This is not disproved by Numenius's prescription of mathematics as a preliminary to contemplation, since Plotinus does the same.[19]

Significant resemblances also exist between Numenius and the *Chaldaean Oracles*, a collection of verses made in the second century A.D., which greatly influenced later Neoplatonism. For instance, both systems proclaim an Intellect above the one generally known. Elsewhere, however, the *Oracles* describe the highest principle as the supreme Intelligible, the "Father," who has "rapt himself away" beyond the reach of Intellect (whereas on a lower level Father, Power, and Intellect form a triad). Following another line of thought, the Father is described as "all things, in Intelligible mode." To know him the soul must practice self-concentration and avoid conceiving of the Supreme as an object of intellect, or trying forcibly to grasp him. Instead, the soul must "stretch out an intellect void of content"; the final vision is performed by a faculty termed the "flower (i e., finest part) of intel-lect" (*nous anthos*). The *Oracles* thus seem to describe mystical union, for which traditional vocabulary has once again proved inadequate. A problem arises, however, over the relation of this experience to theurgy, the system of purification by ritual magic expounded in the *Oracles* and accepted by most later Neoplatonists. Whether at some point ritual is left behind, or even whether the "mystical" passages are a mere literary device, are vexed questions, to which we shall return.

The profusion of experiences and spiritual exercises in the writings ascribed to the Egyptian Hermes Trismegistus cannot be discussed here. We must confine ourselves to a single text, the tenth of the Greek *Hermetic Corpus*,[20] which contains the clearest anticipation I have found in our Greek sources of Plotinus's mystical union. We shall see, we are told, when we can say nothing about the vision; for the knowledge of God is divine silence, bringing inhibition of all the senses and cessation and forgetfulness of all bodily movements. The divine Beauty illumines the contemplative's soul and *nous*, pervades his body, and transmutes his whole being into the divine essence (though full divinization is declared to be impossible while one is still in the body).

But it is in Gnosticism, with its ambivalent attitude of scorning phil-osophy vis-à-vis revelation while making full use of traditional philosophical concepts, that we find the strongest pre-Neoplatonic affirmations of divine unknowability. Negative theology is most prominent, among the Nag Hammadi texts, in the *Apocryphon of John* and *Allogenes* (a text used by Plotinus's Gnostic opponents), and elsewhere in the heresiologist Hippoly-tus's account of the second century Gnostic Basilides. The following points are fundamental to these systems. (1) The Supreme God utterly transcends knowledge, language, and indeed existence (being termed "nonexistent" or "preexistent"). (2) What partial knowledge humans can have of him is conveyed through an intermediary or intermediaries; (3) yet even the latter are very imperfectly knowable; hence (4) humans must rest content with knowing the Supreme by "ignorance" and "silence." Among the more interesting negative terms used of God in the *Apocryphon* are "ineffable," "innumerable," "immeasurable light," "pure light which no eye can behold," "neither corporeal nor incorporeal," "illimitable" (or, in one version, "neither limited nor unlimited"), "not an existent, but superior," and transcending even the term "God."[21] As in Plotinus, the reason for these negations is that such predicates apply only to beings who *need* them and receive them from another, whereas God, as their source, transcends them. Hence, as in Neo-platonism, he is called "Good" and so forth, not as possessing such qualities but as bestowing them on others.

33. Archaic Grave Relief. Attic. Ca. 520 B.C.

The *Apocryphon* is a work of Christian mythological gnosis, whereas *Allogenes* is a non-Christian text with strong philosophical tendencies, which we shall find echoed in the Porphyrian version of Neoplatonism.[22] Most important are that there and in Basilides we find the first explicit Western spiritual references to "unknowing" or "ignorance," and that in *Allogenes* the intermediary between the supreme God and lower realities is his manifestation or "reification," the Triple Power Being-Life-Intellect. But this "reification" is, in turn, incomprehensible, and the same negations are often used of it as of its source. The latter is described by a negative theology based on and expanding that of the *Apocryphon*, culminating in the paradoxical phrase, "nonbeing existence." We reach God by turning our energies within and ascending by stages from self-knowledge to the One who is known only by ignorance. We must cease seeking the incomprehensible and receive the supreme revelation in silence and without effort. Basilides goes further, describing God as "nonexistent," or simply as "nothing." He "wished" (a term used only for the sake of saying something) "without intelligence, sense, will, choice, or passion" to create the archetypal cosmos (also termed "nonexistent"). Finally, we hear, God will send the "great ignorance" upon the universe: beings will then cease to strive beyond their natural limits and, resting content with ignorance of all that lies beyond them, will cease from suffering.[23]

Is the point of the Gnostic negations simply to emphasize that we must be content to accept a revelation of what we cannot know? Such a view gains support from the second-century system of Valentinus.[24] Here not merely is the supreme God unknowable and ineffable, but even the Son (or *Nous*), who manifests his glory to lower beings, for long keeps his knowledge hidden from them. Evil originates in the desire of Sophia (Wisdom) to comprehend the Father. Hence, Sophia is nearly swallowed up and dissolved in his boundless sweetness, until she is saved by receiving limit. Yet the more philosophical Gnostic texts, including *Allogenes*, appear to describe a quasi-mystical ascent of a Platonic type, guided by an external revealer but dependent on the soul's own efforts. And perhaps Basilides and the Valentinians are simply warning humans, first, to recognize their limitations or, in Plotinus's words, that "to set oneself above *Nous* is to fall below it" (II 9 [33], 9, 51–52), and, second, that the final stage requires total passivity and abandonment of intellectual effort or, as *Allogenes* puts it, in terms recalling the *Chaldaean Oracles*, is attained "not firmly but calmly."

Plotinus

At all events, with Plotinus, the founder of Neoplatonism, we certainly encounter mystical union proper. His pupil and biographer, Porphyry, describes Plotinus as having attained it four times during the six years of their acquaintance, although Plotinus, by his own testimony, had often attained it before then (Porphyry *Life of Plotinus* 23.12–18; Plotinus IV 8 [6], 1, 1–11). With him too we once more encounter the inadequacy of language on every level. Hence Plotinus's constant use, progressively more frequent the higher we ascend, of such Greek words as *hoion* and *hōsper* ("so to speak") and his insistence that words can never express problems resolvable only by direct experience. Yet, unlike Plato, he continually exhausts the resources of language in pointing the soul toward the Transcendent. Equally fundamental is his continual reversal of commonsense views of Reality that start from the apparent solidity of the spatio-temporal universe and the type of consciousness dependent on the senses. This is clear from Plotinus's analysis of the material world, which consists of the reflections cast by the Ideal Forms on the unsubstantial basis of Prime Matter, termed by Plotinus "non-being," the point where the outflow of Reality from the One fades away into darkness.[25] In contrast to the One, which, we shall find, is the Good as being too perfect to *need* Form, Matter is Absolute Evil in its utter *lack* of form. It is apprehended by a kind of "non-seeing," as the eye "perceives" darkness from the absence of light.

Everyday human consciousness, based on discursive thought, memory, and sense perception, is indeed useful, Plotinus concedes, in dealing with the sense world and the memories and desires associated therewith. For not merely are many of the latter unconscious; it is precisely the unconscious ones that are most dangerous in binding the soul to this world. But such consciousness, involving separation between subject and object, and being based on words or images derived from the senses, is a weakening of the pure consciousness of *Nous*. Hence the paradox that the philosopher's well-being is most intense when he is unconscious of it (in the sense of our everyday awareness). For we know most when (again by our everyday standards) we seem to know least, just as sickness makes its presence more forcibly known than does health. On a more familiar level, actions such as reading are more intense when we are less conscious of them.[26] Finally, since plurality equals fragmentation and weakness, the greatest energy is produced by beings who keep their energy concentrated within. Action is therefore a weakened form of contemplation and an inferior substitute for those unable to pursue the latter directly. Contemplation need not, however, be conscious; even Nature (*physis*), the lowest level of Soul, which directly molds the sense world, has a "sleeping contemplation," while the divine Hypostases produce "without inclination, will, or movement" toward or knowledge of their products.[27]

For Plotinus *Nous* is eternally active within us, though we are normally unaware of it. In contrast to most other Platonists, he regards the highest level of our soul as enjoying perpetual contemplation of *Nous;* hence, to realize this we need only turn our awareness within. That the resulting union with *Nous* is an actual experience seems clear both from such vivid accounts as those of V 8 [31], 4 and VI 7 [38], 12, 22–30, and from Plotinus's exhortations to attain the experience for ourselves and his insistence that only so can our difficulties regarding *Nous* be resolved.[28] It is likewise *Nous* that best reveals the tension between the traditional Hellenic equation of perfection with Form and Limit and Plotinus's mystical sense of its inadequacy.[29] The Forms are finite in number, and *Nous,* although infinite in power, is still a self-limited, self-contained system comprising the Totality of Being. Yet on Plotinus's principles it is defective in *needing* Form, Limit, and Intelligence, all of which the One transcends. And Plotinus's view of *Nous* as "boiling with life" shows the inadequacy of traditional views even on that level. The revolutionary implications are best seen in his account of Beauty, which he regards as consisting not in Form (as in traditional Greek thought) but in Life, the radiance cast on *Nous* by the One, without which the Forms themselves would fail to stir us. That Beauty is inferior to the Good Plotinus declares on the grounds that the love of Beauty is violent and "only for those in some degree awakened," whereas the Good is the object of a more ultimate love, which is present in all beings even in sleep.[30] It is this that inspires the mystic's quest.

The One, Plotinus declares, as the source of Being, Form, and Limit, must be Unmeasured, Formless, and Infinite (Infinitude consisting for him on all levels in power, not in size or number). The One thus gives its products what it does not possess. Nor does it exercise Intelligence, though it is not ignorant or unconscious. It is too perfect to *need* Intelligence, which is only an "eye for the blind," whereas the One transcends all duality, including that of subject and object. For the same reason it transcends all predicates, including Being, since significant predication connotes duality and limitation. Hence, denial of one predicate to the One does not entail affirmation of its opposite, but sets the One on a level where opposites no longer apply. Still less should we regard the One as nonexistent or confuse the negations applied to it with those applied to Matter, at the opposite end of the metaphysical scale. The One is the Good as the supreme object of desire, in virtue of its utter freedom from want. Hence, neither "Good" nor "One" applies to the Supreme as a predicate. The term "One" connotes mere absence of plurality or signifies that we attain it by unifying our own minds. Similarly, in calling the One "cause," we are merely describing lower beings' relation to the One, without ascribing relation to the One itself. The

One, like other Hypostases, is unaffected and undiminished by what it produces and would not care if it had no products at all. We must therefore not demean our notion of the One by "exalting" it with a plurality of epithets; we must rather beware lest we have not *removed* enough from our conception of it.[31]

Another traditional view of the One emerges, however, from Plotinus's equation of plurality with fragmentation, which implies that the One contains its products in "unfragmented" form. Hence Plotinus's description of the One as "all things and none of them" or the "productive power of all" (*dynamis pantōn*). According to this line of thought, we can conceive of the One as exercising, or rather being, an act of consciousness prior to the emergence of subject and object, a "hyper-intellection," or a "simple self-apprehension." Similarly, transcending all limits, the One is supremely free. This term, however, like others used in the treatise VI 8 [39], such as "will" and "love of itself," is useful only to refute erroneous views of the One; their literal absurdity is clear from the One's absolute simplicity and freedom from want.[32]

Plotinus's account of mystical union follows from his view of the One. Just as the summit of our soul remains in eternal union with *Nous*, so the highest level of *Nous*, termed "*Nous* in love" or "that in *Nous* that is not *Nous*," remains in eternal union with the One. Hence, the One does not need to turn toward us; it is always present at the core of our being. To realize this we must "take off everything" or "put away otherness" and "confound the distinctions of *Nous*." We thereby "make ourselves formless" and wait for the sudden appearance of the One, resisting the fear that we may be left with nothing and the temptation to return to the reassuring familiarity of the sense world. As in Philo, the content of the vision is identical with the light by which it is seen. But, since the union transcends the subject–object duality, it is indescribable in words, and to convey it Plotinus prefers imagery drawn from the sense of touch to that from sight, as conveying closer intimacy. Elsewhere he refers to "presence transcending knowledge." While the union lasts, all distinction between the soul and the One is abolished. But though mystical union is gained through our own efforts, the One is not our highest self, but our transcendent source, with which we are united by love. The comparison Plotinus suggests is that of the centers of two circles, which are indistinguishable while they coincide and whose difference becomes clear only when they move apart. Hence, while Plotinus's denial that the One loves its products separates him from theistic, especially Christian, mysticism, he is equally removed from the monism of Advaita Vedanta.[33]

Porphyry

Porphyry claims that he too attained mystical union late in life. The surviving works that are certainly his, however, make little reference to the One. Especially important is his introduction into Neoplatonism of the concept, already found in the Gnostics, of "learned ignorance." Thus, he terms the One "Non-being above Being," apprehended by a "pre-intellection" or a "non-intellection superior to Intelligence." Similar references occur in Arabic texts probably derived from Porphyry's lost commentary on Plotinus. Porphyry further describes the One as containing all "non-intellectively and hyperessentially."[34] More surprising is his alleged identification of the One with the Father, the supreme member of the Chaldaean triad, which later Neoplatonists set on a lower level. A similar ambivalence occurs in the fragments of an anonymous commentary on the *Parmenides*, which P. Hadot regards as Porphyry's work, and which echo both his doctrine and that of *Allogenes*, especially in their twofold view of the One as exhibiting on the one hand an extreme transcendence, and on a lower level manifesting itself as the triad Being-Life-Intelligence. Here, however, we can deal only with the commentator's negative theology.[35]

We should not, the commentator argues, conceive of the One's absolute simplicity as a deficiency, since the term connotes merely denial of all multiplicity. The One, through its infinite power, is the cause of all other things and, hence, is identical with none of them, so that even the term "One" falls short of its nature. Remembering this, we can avoid attributing anything to the One without falling into the opposite pitfall of nihilism. We thus abide in a "non-comprehensive comprehension" and an "intellection that intuits nothing," and we can attain an "ineffable preconception that represents the One in silence, without even awareness of that silence, or consciousness that it is the One's image, or knowledge of anything whatever" and which constitutes "an image of the Ineffable that is ineffably identical with the Ineffable."

Nor should the fact that the One is not identical with *Nous* lead us to describe it as "other than *Nous*"; for otherness, like all relations, implies limitation, and thus has meaning only in the realm of derived reality, whereas the One remains unaffected by its products. Similarly, references to the sun as rising and setting erroneously attribute our own relation to the sun to that body itself. Since any comparison between God and his products would falsely situate them on the same ontological level, we cannot know the One. But, while negative theology terms the One "non-being," in fact the One is the only true Existent, in the face of which other things are nothing. The One further exercises a mode of knowledge transcending the subject–object duality and the opposition of knowledge and ignorance. But, the commentator concludes, it is better to renounce such speculations than to risk "fragmenting" our notion of the One with words deriving from our own incapacity. Negative theology is thus superior even to the affirmative theology of the *Chaldaean Oracles.*

Such affirmations, we read, may be true, but, since we lack the faculty of apprehending God, they pass all human comprehension and are as valueless to us as statements about color to one born blind. Moreover, the Chaldeans subsequently perform a complete *volte-face,* declaring that their affirmations must be abandoned; so what is the point of learning them, only to abandon them so soon afterward? Since God transcends both quality and essence, neither reasoning nor intelligence can apprehend him. The soul must therefore rest content with its innate ignorance both of God himself and of the manner in which beings proceed from him.

Later Neoplatonism

Following his tendency to multiply ontological levels within Neoplatonism and motivated by the same extreme negative theology as the commentator and Damascius after him, Iamblichus, the "second founder" of Neoplatonism, postulated a further supreme principle above the One, which he termed simply the "Ineffable."[36] Ineffability, however, in Iamblichus's view extended much further down the metaphysical scale; for he regarded the highest level of the Intelligible world as unknowable even for the *Oracles'* "flower of intellect." Yet more important was his view of the *means* of attaining the higher Hypostases; for, like most later Neoplatonists, he denied that the human soul has either an unfallen element or a transcendent individual *Nous.* The operation of a divine force is therefore needed for salvation, and this is provided by theurgy, which now assumes a higher value than philosophy. Otherwise, Iamblichus's *De mysteriis* argues, the theoretical philosopher could attain divine union. The vital element in theurgy is the ineffable symbols (*synthēmata*) sown by the gods in the material world as images of their own ineffability, and, though operative on more than one level, its final goal is union with the supreme God "beyond being and thought." The foundation for the ineffable mystical union is the knowledge of God innate in every soul, prior to thought and reasoning and therefore leaving no room for doubt. Its very simplicity makes the term "knowledge" inadequate and Iamblichus therefore follows Plotinus in preferring the term "contact." It is this principle that motivates every soul's aspiration to the Good.[37]

For Proclus, the great systematizer of Athenian Neoplatonism, the One is once more the Supreme Principle. Firmly rejecting any notion of the One as containing the causes of all, he regards a transcendent Ineffable principle as unnecessary, arguing that neither the term "One" nor that of "Good" detracts from the One's ineffability, since both merely describe its effect on lower beings (as the cause of Unity, or of Goodness and as the Supreme object of aspiration) without characterizing the One itself. Moreover, the negations used of the One must finally themselves be negated, and the soul must rest content with the silence of the mystical union.[38] The way of Analogy, which Proclus retains along with that of Negation, itself ends in the negative description of the Good as "beyond Being," while the transcendent source of plurality is now found in the divine Henads, or subordinate "unities."[39] Hence, the One is completely unknowable; but, though the Henads are unknowable in themselves, some conception of their nature can be formed from the beings that participate in them. The notion of degrees of unknowability is explained by the Athenian school's doctrine of Relative Infinitude. Since each level below the One constitutes an appropriate combination of Limit and Infinity, the higher levels are infinite (and therefore unknowable) to lower beings, but finite (and therefore knowable) to themselves and their superiors.[40]

Like Iamblichus, Proclus ranks theurgy higher than philosophy. It is, however, uncertain whether either of them regards ritual as leading directly to union with the One. We can be more confident about the psychological prerequisites involved. For our soul, like everything else, contains an image of the divine unity. Hence, it is by the "one" in us that we make contact with the One. Normally Proclus uses the Chaldaean term "flower of intellect" for this faculty, but elsewhere he argues that, since we are not only *nous* but a complex of mental faculties, we need a more central principle, on which all those faculties converge, termed by Proclus the "flower of the whole soul." The virtue by which divine union is achieved is faith (*pistis*), a term derived from the *Chaldaean Oracles.* Superrational faith, to be distinguished from its subrational counterpart, is the faculty whereby we leave reason behind and attain "the unified silence superior to all knowledge," the attitude of trusting dependence on what we cannot know conceptually, which links both us and the gods to the One.[41]

How frequently mystical union was attained in post-Porphyrian Neoplatonism is doubtful. Proclus's biographer and successor as head of the Athenian school, Marinus, nowhere describes his master as having attained it, though he does ascribe to Proclus a direct intuitive vision of the Forms.[42] Marinus's successor, Isidorus, on the other hand, is described by his pupil Damascius, the last head of the Athenian school, as having approached the gods within, "in the hidden depths of unknowing," which reads like a description of mystical union.[43] Damascius himself, more than any other Platonist, carries to its logical conclusion the principle of the inadequacy of language and conceptual thought, increasing as we approach the Supreme but present to some extent on every level, a defect that can be remedied only by pitting opposing concepts against one another and thereby transcending them.[44] Returning to the position of Iamblichus, he postulated an Ineffable principle above the One, on the grounds that Unity entails relation to plurality and hence cannot be the Ultimate, which must be free from relations. Similarly, since "cause" has meaning only in relation to its effects, in postulating the One as cause we deny its claim to the title of First Principle. Furthermore, on the view of reality as a hierarchy of degrees of unity, the One contains all its products in perfectly unified form; hence, once again, it needs those products and cannot be the Ultimate we seek. The solution is thus to postulate a principle that is simply Ineffable, neither coordinated nor uncoordinated with lower realities, neither immanent nor transcendent. We have an intuition of such a principle, but in seeking to characterize it, even in negative terms, we project onto it the divisions of our own thought and demonstrate only our own ignorance of it. The Ineffable thus appears as "nothing," but we must not confuse it with the opposite extreme of simple nonexistence. The One envelopes all in its absolute simplicity, but we must proceed further, to a principle that is "neither unique nor enveloping nor even ineffable." Since the Supreme transcends even our negations, our only recourse is to negate those negations *ad infinitum.*

A similar reversal of thought, though to a lesser extent, takes place with regard to the One and on yet lower levels (with which we cannot deal here). The One is not absolutely unknowable, but indescribable in words, while the negations used of it merely exclude positive notions without telling us anything about the One itself. The One mediates between the absolutely Ineffable and lower realities and thus retains much of the former's ineffability. Hence, we have no "knowledge" of the One, only a mere "suspicion" (*hyponoia*) thereof. Analogies derived from the "fragmented" world of sense experience become less useful the higher we proceed and, in the case of the One, provide a very imperfect pointer toward its transcendent simplicity. Since each level of Reality contains all in more or less unified mode we may proceed upward, simplifying our thought, until we reach the One. Here the term "One" symbolizes that principle's absolute simplicity, the term "All" its all-embracing nature; but since neither is adequate, we negate the former term by the latter, and vice versa. The One, thus, is known only imperfectly and from afar, and the closer we approach it the less we know it.

With Damascius pagan Greek metaphysics, especially the trends we have surveyed, reaches its conclusion. Its influence must be treated in other volumes; here I simply record my conviction that neither its influence nor its value is yet at an end.

Notes

Passages in quotation marks are generally my own translations or paraphrases (sometimes adapted from existing translations) of the original texts.

1. Berkeley and Los Angeles: University of California Press, 1951; see especially chap. 3 (pp. 64–101), "The Blessings of Madness," and appendix 1 (pp. 270–82), "Maenadism."

2. E. R. Dodds, *Proclus: Elements of Theology* (2nd ed.; Oxford: Clarendon Press, 1963) appendix 1, pp. 311–12.

3. The translation of the Nag Hammadi documents can be found in *The Nag Hammadi Library in English,* ed. James M. Robinson.

4. Dodds, *Pagan and Christian in an Age of Anxiety,* 69–70.

5. For more details, see R. T. Wallis, "*Nous* as Experience," in *The Significance of Neoplatonism,* ed. R. Baine Harris, 121–53, and the further literature cited there.

6. Festugière, *La Révélation d'Hermès Trismégiste:* vol. 4, *Le Dieu Inconnu et la Gnose,* 267.

7. For full references to Plato's distinction between *noēsis* and *dianoia* and his views on the inadequacy of language, see R. T. Wallis, "*Nous,*" 128–31.

8. P. Merlan, "Greek Philosophy from Plato to Plotinus," in *The Cambridge History of Later Greek and Early Medieval Philosophy,* ed. A. H. Armstrong (Cambridge: University Press, 1967) 30.

9. On the above, see Merlan, "Plato to Plotinus," 15–19, 30–32; and J. M. Dillon, *The Middle Platonists,* 1–18, 24–26.

10. See Merlan, "Plato to Plotinus," 42–47, 59, 86, and Wallis, "*Nous,*" 131–33.

11. Merlan, "Plato to Plotinus," 108, 112, 117–122.

12. See E. Conze, *Buddhism* (London: New York: Harper, 1951) 140–43; idem, *Buddhist Thought in India* (London: Allen & Unwin, 1962) 212–13; idem, *Thirty Years of Buddhist Studies* (San Francisco: Wheelwright Press, 1967) 217–20.

13. Merlan, "Plato to Plotinus," 84–86; Dillon, *Middle Platonists,* 117–21, 126–29.

14. Dillon, *Middle Platonists,* 384–96.

15. On Philo's negative theology, see Dillon, *Middle Platonists,* 155–58. On his mysticism, see David Winston, *Philo of Alexandria: Selections* (New York: Paulist Press, 1981) 21–35; for relevant texts, see 124–43, 164–74.

16. For a brief study, see the final chapter of Wallis, *Neoplatonism,* 160–70.

17. On the Middle Platonists, Neopythagorean systematizers, and *Chaldaean Oracles,* see Festugière, *Révélation,* 4:92–140; Merlan, "Plato to Plotinus," esp. 64–73, 80, 90–106; Dillon, *Middle Platonists,* esp. 280–85, 299–300, 312–13, 341–61, 366–74, 392–96.

18. Dodds, *Pagan and Christian,* 92–93.

19. See Dodds, *Pagan and Christian,* 86–87, 93–94.

20. For a summary of other Hermetic writings see Frances A. Yates, *Giordano Bruno and the Hermetic Tradition* (London: Routledge & Kegan Paul, 1964) 20–43; see also Dodds, *Pagan and Christian,* 76–77, 82–83.

21. *Nag Hammadi Library* II.1, esp. pp. 100–101.

22. Ibid., XI.3, pp. 443–52.

23. See W. Foerster, *Gnosis: A Selection of Gnostic Texts*, 1:64–74.

24. See Foerster, *Gnosis*, 1:127–45; for an analysis of Valentinus's system, see Hans Jonas, *The Gnostic Religion* 174–99; and, more briefly, Dillon, *Middle Platonists*, 384–89.

25. See Wallis, *Neoplatonism*, 48–50; for our "knowledge" of Matter, see Plotinus II 4 [12], 10.

26. Wallis, *Neoplatonism*, 81.

27. Ibid., 61–64, 84–85.

28. See Wallis, "*Nous*," esp. 123–125; A. H. Armstrong, "Plotinus," in *Cambridge History*, 245–46.

29. See Wallis, *Neoplatonism*, 53–57.

30. On Plotinus's view of beauty, see Wallis, *Neoplatonism*, 86–88; Armstrong, "Plotinus," 232–34.

31. For Plotinus's negative theology, see Wallis, *Neoplatonism*, 57–59; for the One as *dynamis pantōn*, see *Neoplatonism*, 60–61.

32. Ibid., 63–64.

33. On Plotinus's mysticism, see further Wallis, *Neoplatonism*, 88–90 (and the discussions cited there), 189.

34. See Wallis, *Neoplatonism*, 114.

35. On the fragments, see P. Hadot, *Porphyre et Victorinus*, 1:102–43; and, more briefly, Wallis, *Neoplatonism*, 114–18.

36. See J. M. Dillon, *Iamblichi Chalcidensis in Platonis Dialogos Commentariorum Fragmenta*, 29–35.

37. On theurgy in Iamblichus, see Wallis, *Neoplatonism*, 120–23; and Andrew Smith, *Porphyry's Place in the Neoplatonic Tradition*, 83–110.

38. See especially *Proclus: Théologie Platonicienne*, ed. H. D. Saffrey and L. G. Westerink, vol. 2 (Budé; Paris: Les Belles Lettres, 1972) chaps. 4–7, 10–12 (pp. 31–51, 61–73).

39. On the Henads see Proclus *Elements* props. 113–67, with Dodds's commentary; also *Théologie Platonicienne*, ed. Saffrey and Westerink, vol. 3 (Paris: Les Belles Lettres, 1978) IX–LXXVII; and Wallis, *Neoplatonism*, 146–51.

40. See Proclus *Elements* prop. 93, with Dodds's commentary; and Wallis, *Neoplatonism*, 149.

41. See Wallis, *Neoplatonism*, 153–55; Smith, *Porphyry's Place*, 111–21; on faith, see also the discussions cited in *Neoplatonism*, 154 n. 1.

42. Cited in Wallis, "*Nous*," 150 n. 73.

43. Quoted by A. C. Lloyd, "The Later Neoplatonists," in *Cambridge History*, 313.

44. I am indebted to Professor L. G. Westerink for permission to use the typescript of the edition with French translation that he and J. Combès are preparing of Damascius's *De principiis*.

Bibliography

Editions and translations of Plato and Aristotle are numerous and therefore not included here. Representative translations can be found in the General Bibliography.

Editions

Anonymous *Parmenides* commentator. Edited with French translation and notes by P. Hadot, *Porphyre et Victorinus* (Paris: Études Augustiniennes, 1968) 2:64–113.

The Budé series (text, with French translation and notes) includes the *Chaldean Oracles, Hermetica*, Iamblichus's *De mysteriis*, Numemius, Plotinus, and Proclus's *Platonic Theology* (4 vols. published out of 6). Collection des Universités de France. Paris: Les Belles Lettres.

Dillon, J. M. *Iamblichi Chalcidensis in Platonis Dialogos Commentariorum Fragmenta.* Leiden: Brill, 1973.

Diogenes Laertius. *Life of Pyrrho.* In *Lives of the Philosophers*, vol. 2. Edited with English translation by R. D. Hicks. Loeb Classical Library. Cambridge, MA: Harvard University Press, 1925.

Iamblichus. *Platonic Commentaries.* See Dillon.

Plotinus. *Enneads.* Edited with English translation by A. H. Armstrong. 7 vols. Loeb Classical Library. Cambridge, MA: Harvard University Press, 1966–.

Porphyry. *Life of Plotinus.* See Plotinus.

Proclus. *Elements of Theology.* Edited with introduction, English translation, and commentary by E. R. Dodds. 2nd ed. Oxford: University Press, 1963.

Translations

Translations of many important texts from pre-Plotinian Platonists and Neopythagoreans otherwise inaccessible in English can be found in Dillon, *Middle Platonists.*

Foerster, W. *Gnosis: A Selection of Gnostic Texts.* Translated by R. McL. Wilson. 2 vols. Oxford: University Press, 1874.

Hallie, P., ed., and S. G. Etheridge, trans. *Skepticism, Man and God.* Middletown, CT: Wesleyan University Press, 1964. Select passages from Sextus Empiricus, including book 1 of his *Outlines of Pyrrhonism.*

Origen. *Contra Celsum.* Translated by H. Chadwick. 2nd ed. Cambridge and New York: Cambridge University Press, 1967.

Plotinus. *Enneads.* Translated by S. MacKenna. Revised by B. S. Page, with an introduction by P. Henry. 4th ed. London: Faber & Faber, 1969.

———. *Plotinus: A Volume of Selections.* Translated by A. H. Armstrong. New York: Collier Books, 1962.

Porphyry. *Life of Plotinus.* See Plotinus.

Robinson, James M., ed. *The Nag Hammadi Library in English.* New York: Harper & Row, 1977.

Modern Studies

Armstrong, A. H., ed. *The Cambridge History of Later Greek and Early Medieval Philosophy.* Cambridge: University Press, 1967. Corrected edition, 1970.

Dillon, J. M. *The Middle Platonists.* Ithaca, NY: Cornell University Press, 1977.

Dodds, E. R. *Pagan and Christian in an Age of Anxiety.* Cambridge: University Press, 1965.

Festugière, A.-J. *La Révélation d'Hermès Trismégiste.* Vol. 4, *Le Dieu Inconnu et la Gnose.* Paris: Librairie Lecoffre, 1954.

Hadot, P. *Porphyre et Victorinus.* 2 vols. Paris: Études Augustiniennes, 1968.

Jonas, H. *The Gnostic Religion.* 2nd ed. Boston: Beacon Press, 1963.

Rist, J. M. *Plotinus: The Road to Reality.* Cambridge: University Press, 1967.

Smith, A. *Porphyry's Place in the Neoplatonic Tradition.* The Hague: Nijhoff, 1974.

Wallis, R. T. *Neoplatonism.* New York: Scribner, 1972.

———. "*Nous* as Experience." In *The Significance of Neoplatonism*, 121–53. Edited by R. Baine Harris. Proceedings of the International Society for Neoplatonic Studies 1. Norfolk, VA: I.S.N.S., 1976. Distributed by SUNY Press.

20

In Praise of Nonsense

Patricia Cox Miller

IN A COLLECTION OF RELIGIOUS TEXTS from late antiquity now known as the Nag Hammadi Library, there is a long poem entitled *Thunder, Perfect Mind*.[1] The poem is the self-revelation of a powerful goddess: she is "perfect mind," and she "thunders." Even a brief glance at this text suggests why the revelations of perfect mind might be connected with the awesome but incomprehensible rumblings of thunder, for Perfect Mind speaks in riddle and paradox, thus subverting the reader's ability to comprehend her in any straightforward or univocal way. Like the elemental "speech" of thunder, her speech cannot be reduced to logical propositions. Indeed, from a rational analytical perspective, the structure of her language is nonsense; it offends the ear with its noisy incongruities.

To understand Perfect Mind, one must leave the world of discursive language behind and enter the structure of paradox, where a potentially endless play of opposites is entertained:

> For I am the first and the last.
> I am the honored one and the scorned one.
> I am the whore and the holy one.
> (*Thunder, Perfect Mind;*
> *Nag Hammadi Library*, p. 271)

How can the first be last? How can Perfect Mind be both whore and holy one? Part of the genius of her language is precisely to force the hearer to ask such questions and thereby to lead that hearer more deeply into her mystery.

Her mystery is, of course, a thunderous silence. As Plotinus once remarked, all visions of divinity "baffle telling" (VI 9 [9], 10–11), and they frustrate the understandable human desire to tell the story plainly, to capture truth in words at last (VI 9 [9], 11).[2] At the end of words, the mystery still remains, majestically silent:

481

> I am the hearing which is attainable to everyone
> and the speech which cannot be grasped.
> I am a mute who does not speak,
> and great is my multitude of words.
>> (*Thunder, Perfect Mind;*
>> *Nag Hammadi Library,* p. 276)

Words cannot capture truth, but they can carry its resonant echoes. Plotinus goes so far as to say that visions of primal reality "break into speech," whose "sounds labor to express the essential nature of the universe produced by the travail of the utterer and so to represent, as far as sounds may, the origin of reality" (V 5 [32], 5).

Like Plotinus, Perfect Mind knows that her thundering riddles are the echoes of her reality in words, and it is those words that give her mystery a place in which to dwell in human consciousness. Toward the end of her self-revelatory poem, she says:

> I am the name of the sound
> and the sound of the name.
> I am the sign of the letter
> and the designation of the division.
>> (*Thunder, Perfect Mind;*
>> *Nag Hammadi Library,* p. 277)

She identifies herself not only with the paradoxical *images* of language but with *language itself.* Perhaps the ultimate revelation is that this goddess is the very process of speaking that she uses to characterize herself. The structure of her language carries her nature in it: she *is* what she *speaks,* as well as teaching how to speak. In the beginning was the word.

Such is the nature of divinity. There are, of course, many ways of responding to this poetic statement of the linguistic qualities of fundamental reality. In this essay, our interest lies in exploring a particularly (and peculiarly) appropriate linguistic response to linguistic reality in certain religious texts from late antiquity. Designated by scholarly convention as "magical" texts, they embody in a most strident form the *Thunder, Perfect Mind*'s perspective on the intimate relationship between being and speaking.[3]

The Sounds of the Spirit

Perfect Mind calls herself "the sign of the letter" and exhorts her followers:

> Hear me, you hearers,
> and learn of my words, you who know me.

> I am the hearing that is attainable to everything;
> I am the speech that cannot be grasped.
> (*Thunder, Perfect Mind;*
> *Nag Hammadi Library,* p. 277)

If one accepts such a conception of deity as the framework for one's own reality, how is it possible to show that one has learned the words of the speech that cannot be grasped? The Coptic *Gospel of the Egyptians,* also called "The Holy Book of the Great Invisible Spirit," offers the following reply to our question:

> And the throne of his (glory) was established (in it, this one) on which his unrevealable name (is inscribed), on the tablet (. . .) one is the word, the (Father of the light) of everything, he (who came) forth from the silence, while he rests in the silence, he whose name (is) in an (invisible) symbol. (A) hidden, (invisible) mystery came forth iiiiiiiiiiiiiiiiiii(iii) ēēēēēēēēēēēēēēēēēē-ē(ēē o) ooooooooooooooooooooo uu(uuu) uuuuuuuuuuuuuuuuu eeeeeeeee-eeeeeeeeeeeee aaaaaaa (aaaa) aaaaaaaaaa ōōōōōōōōō(ōō)ōōōōōōōō ōōō. And (in this) way the three powers gave praise to the (great), invisible, unnameable, virginal, uncallable Spirit. . . . (*Nag Hammadi Library,* p. 197)

Here is the "sign of the letter" with a vengeance! It would seem that the author of this prayer to the God of silent mystery knew that when language is revealed for what it truly is—a speaking of the unspeakable—it is incomprehensible, not to be resolved in a final word or in words at all. When the God who is "an invisible symbol" breaks into human speech, his sounds are the echoes of the alphabet, the vowels.

Elsewhere in this gospel, in an ecstatic invocation of the God that comes near the end of the text, the same kind of "language" appears:

> O glorious name, really truly, aiōn o ōn, iiii ēēēē eeee oooo uuuu ōōōō aaaa(a), really truly ēi aaaa ōōōō, O existing one who sees the aeons! Really truly, aee ēēē iiii uuuuuu ōōōōōōōō, who is eternally eternal, really truly, iēa aiō, in the heart, who exists, u aei eis aei, ei o ei, ei os ei! (*Gospel of the Egyptians; Nag Hammadi Library,* p. 204)

A text from the magical papyri, entitled *Monas or the Eighth Book of Moses,* makes the same point more directly:

> Lord, I represent you faithfully by the seven vowels; come and listen to me; a ee ēēē iiii ooooo uuuuuu ōōōōōōō. (*PGM* 13.206–9)

This alphabetical language, which attempts to sound the secret name of God, also gives voice to human reality. In one of the passages from the *Gospel of the Egyptians* quoted above, God's name is "really truly" "in the heart." As the narrative continues, one learns that "this great name of thine is upon me, O self-begotten Perfect one, who art not outside me. . . . Now that I have known thee, I have mixed myself with the immutable" (*Nag Hammadi Library*, pp. 204–5). To say the name is to become mixed with God.

Another Coptic document, *The Discourse on the Eighth and the Ninth*, also links the substance of God with the substance of humans through the vowels:

> O grace! After these things I give thanks by singing a hymn to thee. For I have received life from thee when thou madest me wise. I praise thee. I call thy name that is hidden within me: a ō ee ō ēēē ōōō iii ōōōō ooooo ōōōōō uuuuuu ōōōōōōōōōōōōōōōōōōōōōōō. Thou art the one who exists with the spirit. I sing a hymn to thee reverently. (*Nag Hammadi Library*, p. 296)

Clearly the vowels of the alphabet designate that point at which the human and divine worlds intersect, at least from the perspective of this text. To speak this language is not only to invoke the God; it is also to sound the depths of one's own primal reality. These strings of vowels are hymnic recitations of praise to the God and to human Godlikeness.

Ecstatic though it may be, there is something ominous about this language of the spirit. In the words of a modern poet, we confront

> . . . the murderous alphabet:
> The swarm of thoughts, the swarm of dreams
> Of inaccessible Utopia.
> (Wallace Stevens,
> "The Man With the Blue Guitar")[4]

Paul of Tarsus agreed. Writing to his unruly congregation in Corinth, some of whom felt that their utopia was not only *not* inaccessible but fully present, Paul felt compelled to warn them about the dangers of the spiritual language that they were speaking. The kingdom was showing itself in Corinthian worship in the form of glossolalia, that speaking "in the tongues of angels" which the "swarms" of alphabetical combinations we have just seen attempt to represent in writing.[5] Christian tradition sometimes attributed such language to Jesus himself, as in the following passage from the Coptic *Pistis Sophia:*

> Then Jesus stood with his disciples beside the water of the ocean and pronounced this prayer, saying: "Hear me, my Father, thou father of all fatherhoods, thou infinite Light: aeēiouō. iaō. aōi. ōia. . . ." (136)[6]

So also Paul, in another mood and writing to a different congregation, could say that "the Spirit helps us in our weakness; for we do not know how to pray as we ought, but the Spirit himself intercedes for us with sighs too deep for words" (Rom 8:26). Such "sighs" or "groans" were, as one scholar has pointed out, the "characteristic form of magical utterance"; in writing, they appear as alphabetical combinations by which the devotee "calls the spirit in the spirit's own language."[7] This, for Paul, is how we "ought" to pray. But, if this kind of praying is truly evidence of the spirit speaking through the prayer, why did Paul castigate the Corinthians for their angelic speech, comparing it with "noisy gong and clanging cymbal" (1 Cor 13:1)?

The problem, says Paul, lies with the impact of such speaking on "outsiders and unbelievers" (1 Cor 14:16, 23). For them, the "tongues of angels" are not supremely inarticulate, but merely unintelligible, buzzing swarms of letters:

> If even lifeless instruments, such as the flute or the harp, do not give distinct notes, how will anyone know what is played? . . .So with yourselves; if you in a tongue utter speech that is not intelligible, how will anyone know what is said? (1 Cor 14:7, 9)

Paul concludes by saying that the ecstatic praying can continue only if it is interpreted; for the benefit of the understanding of the uninitiate, spirit must be yoked with mind (1 Cor 14:13–15). This concern that spiritual language might be heard and so dismissed as mere gibberish occurs in the magical traditions as well. The *Pistis Sophia,* for example, does what Paul was advising the Corinthians to do:

> And Jesus cried out as he turned to the four corners of the world with his disciples, and . . . he said: "iaō. iaō. iaō. This is its interpretation: iota, because the All came forth; alpha, because it will return again; omega, because the completion of all completions will happen. (136; see also 10, 62)

Whatever we as modern readers may think about the seeming unintelligibility of even the interpretation given here, it is clear that for the ancient writer the inspired language of the alphabet did carry meaning and could be interpreted.

Fully initiate in this language, Paul everywhere shows his respect for it, even in the midst of protests against it: "If the whole church assembles and all speak in tongues, and outsiders or unbelievers enter, will they not say that you are mad?" (1 Cor 14:23). The verb used in this passage for madness (*mainomai*) is the one used to characterize the oracular utterances of the Delphic priestess and the Sibyls, as well as the rapturous language of the followers of the god Dionysus, all of whom were also said to speak in a tongue.[8] By his use of this verb, Paul has, perhaps in spite of himself, placed glossolalia squarely in a context of sacred utterance.

What are the dimensions of that context? As Professor Armstrong has remarked in the introduction to this volume, the spirituality of the hellenized Mediterranean world had an "archaic base"; it was indebted to "the immemorial observances, always there and underlying all the changes right down to the establishment of Christianity in the Roman Empire, and after." Paul, who *talks about* what the magical papyri *do*, has in his first letter to the Corinthians described basic aspects of alphabetical language. They are aspects that carry the archaic sensibility of that language, especially as it shows itself in the magical papyri where spiritual language is best and most fully preserved. The information from Paul concerns the form and qualities of this language: it is ecstatic prayer that does not sound like normal language but rather like music (as Paul's repeated musical metaphors suggest—gong, cymbal, flute, harp, bugle); it is not intelligible, but it is rhythmic; and it is also powerful, for it brings manifestations of the Spirit. Further, those manifestations take the verbal form not of reasonable words ("For if I pray in a tongue, my spirit prays but my mind is unfruitful") but, as we know from other sources, of strings of letters, particularly of vowels, and these somehow give expression to "mysteries in the Spirit" (1 Cor 14:2).

In the next sections of this essay, the piety of the alphabet will be discussed as a late antique phase of two much older ways of thinking, one of which connected language with the charm or spell, the other of which identified the letters of the alphabet with the elements of the cosmos.

The Spell of Language and
the Language of the Spell

It is curious that modern scholars, if they have studied alphabetical language at all, have tended largely to take precisely the view that Paul had predicted of outsiders and unbelievers: in various ways, it is nonsense. The range of scholarly reaction to such language has run from outright disapproval to a kind of amused fascination. On the negative side, such language has been viewed as compulsive and egotistic, presuming as it does to summon divine presence into the human realm. Establishing a "lien on God" rather than a "means of approach to him," the users of such language mock the true spiritual life with their mutterings of meaningless sounds.[9] On the positive side, such mutterings are transformed into "mystical gibberish," fit to be compared with Rimbaud's "Sonnet to the Vowels"![10] They are, in other words, symbolic, attempting to reflect in human writing and speaking the "heavenly writing" of the stars. And they are playful, carrying into adult life the alphabetical games of the child learning the letters, reciting them backward, forward, from the ends to the middle, and so on.[11] The child is initiated into the reality of humans, the speaking animals, by playing with the elemental parts of that speech.

A final characterization will serve to locate the perspective of the present essay, which is that alphabetical language is neither mere fancy nor selfish manipulation. It is rather, as Morton Smith has said, "jabberwocky."[12] Anyone who has read Lewis Carroll's famous poem knows that it speaks the language of the Looking-Glass House. It is an enchanted language that reflects a dimension of reality that is normally hidden. The "inside," "other side," or even "underside" of ordinary reality is best spoken in a poetic language that scrambles ordinary words and shows their imaginal potential. When Alice encounters the whiffling and burbling Jabberwock, she remarks, "It seems very pretty, but it's *rather* hard to understand!"[13] Alice's comment is insightful: such linguistic play *is* difficult to understand, and that is precisely the point. The idea that words create a meaningful universe is, as a poet said, the "supreme fiction"; language is phantasmal, not transparent to whatever "reality" might be.[14] Travailing and laboring, Plotinus said, we speak, and it is jabberwocky, a creation of the world in metaphor: "We must be patient with language," everywhere reading "so to speak" (VI 8 [39], 13).

It is this recognition of the creative and destructive functions of language, which weaves and unweaves meaning with every word, that is so well captured by the alphabetical language under consideration here. Using language against itself by breaking it down into its elemental parts and then reconfiguring those parts in endless permutations and combinations, the magical prayers constitute an iconoclastic piety. Consider, for example, the following passage from *Monas or the Eighth Book of Moses:*

> I invoke you iueuo ōaeē Iaō aeē ai eē aē iouō euē Ieou aēō ēi ōēi iaē iōouē auē uēa iō iōai iōai ōē ee ou iō Iaō, the great name; be to me (as) lynx, eagle, snake, phoenix, life, strength, necessity, phantoms of gods, aiō iōu Iaō ēiō aa oui aaaa eiu iō ōē Iaō ai (etc.). (*PGM* 13.876–87)

Such an invocation clearly breaks the normal forms of language, but the non-sense that then appears bears the "phantoms" (*eidōla*) of the gods! Ultimate meaning dwells in the breaking of form. The "nonsense" prayers are violently reverent.

When ordinary language is scrambled, the "insides" of the great name of God are revealed. It is not surprising, then, that for the texts under consideration here language casts a spell, and its aura is divine. One of the ways in which this conviction appears is in the alphabetical play with a name of God composed only of vowels: *Iaō*, the Greek name of the Hebrew *YHWH*, the holiest name of God. This is the most frequently petitioned God in the magical papyri, and it seems fitting that invocations to *Iaō* should so often consist of staccato-like combinations of the letters of his name (as in *Pistis Sophia* 136, quoted above: "Thou infinite Light, aeēiouō iaō aōi ōia . . ."), since this is the God who confused human language, reducing it to babble, as well as the God who gave speech to humanity in the first place, granting the power to name.[15]

God seems to dwell in the making and unmaking of language. This is suggested further by the frequent invocations to Hermes in our texts. The presence of Hermes, second only to *Iaō* in popularity among devotees of alphabetical language, points to one of the dimensions of archaic sensibility that lived on in the magical papyri. It is that the origin of language is divine. Among numerous theories of the origin of language in its written form, the one that captured the imagination of Greek antiquity named the god Hermes as the inventor of the alphabet.[16] Hermes carried into Greek tradition the linguistic genius of the Egyptian god Thoth, with whom he was identified.[17] The *locus classicus* for discussions of these two figures lies in the writings of Plato, whose ideas about writing are fundamental for understanding the alphabetical fantasies of late antiquity.

In the dialogue by Plato entitled *Phaedrus,* Socrates tells the story of the god Thoth presenting various arts (number, astronomy, and so on) to the king of Egypt as useful gifts for the people. Last of all, Thoth gives the king writing: "Here, O king, is a branch of learning that will make the people of Egypt wiser and improve their memories; my discovery provides a recipe for memory and wisdom." The king, however, disagrees: "If men learn this, it will implant forgetfulness in their souls; they will cease to exercise memory because they rely on that which is written, calling things to remembrance no longer from within themselves, but by means of external marks." Writing, from the king's perspective, is a mere semblance of wisdom (274D–275B).

Socrates goes on to explore the "strangeness" of writing by using an analogy to painting:

> The painter's products stand before us as though they were alive, but if you question them, they maintain a most majestic silence. It is the same with written words: they seem to talk to you as though they were intelligent, but if you ask them anything about what they say . . . they go on telling you just the same thing forever. And once a thing is put in writing, the composition . . . drifts all over the place. . . . (*Phaedrus* 275DE)

There is something uncanny about writing. It is God-given and, from the perspective of the God, offers a "recipe for wisdom." From the human perspective, however, the written word is a most frustrating crutch: it merely imitates the truth, and when questioned concerning its meaning it "drifts all over the place." Yet, like a painting, its silence is at the same time iconic, bursting with possibility. It is in such a context that the alphabetical words of the magical prayers belong. Attempting to write the ultimate wisdom, the name of God, they imitate that wisdom with explosions of drifting letters, icons of a divine silence. As one of the Coptic documents that speaks the language of the alphabet says, "the one who is saved" is "in the word in the way in which he exists" (*Zostrianos; Nag Hammadi Library*, p. 380). As with the Goddess in *Thunder, Perfect Mind*, so with the human being. Expression and existence form an inseparable pair.

Plato, however, was not comfortable with the kind of writing that is only an "external mark." The discussion in the *Phaedrus* continues as Socrates asks: "But now tell me, is there another sort of discourse, that is brother to the written speech, but of unquestioned legitimacy?" When Phaedrus, his conversation partner, asks what kind of discourse he has in mind, Socrates replies: "The sort that goes together with knowledge and is written in the soul of the learner. . . ." Phaedrus then says, "Do you mean the discourse of a man who really knows, which is living and animate? Would it be fair to call the written discourse only a kind of ghost of it?" "Precisely," says Socrates (276A–B). Wisdom is "written" on the soul, and writing in the letters of human language is the "ghost" (*eidōlon*) of that living writing.

The idea that tangible writing is ghostly compared with the invisible writing on the soul is indeed uncanny, but we have seen these ghosts before in an invocation from *Monas or the Eighth Book of Moses*, where strings of vowels are called *eidōla tōn theōn*, ghosts of the Gods who haunt human language. The persistence of the linguistic metaphor for wisdom is striking, yet it is a metaphor from which we cannot escape. As one scholar has argued in a careful and provocative study, "While presenting writing as a false brother—traitor, infidel, simulacrum—Socrates is for the first time led to envision the brother of this brother, the legitimate one, as *another sort of writing*: not merely as a knowing, living, animate discourse, but as an *inscription* of truth in the soul." Further, the living discourse "is described by a 'metaphor' borrowed from the order of the very thing one is trying to exclude from it, the order of its simulacrum."[18] The "written" character of wisdom is inescapable, even when it is an invisible inscription on the soul.

This conundrum lived on in the texts under consideration here. Recall, for example, *The Discourse on the Eighth and the Ninth*, in which the devotee praises the God who has made him wise by calling the God's name that is hidden within him. In the text, that calling takes the form of writing, and it is alphabetical nonsense. An interesting variant on the same phenomenon is offered in the "Mithras Liturgy," a particularly famous portion of the great Paris magical codex. At the end of this text, there are instructions concerning what the devotee is to do to consecrate himself so that the prayers and requests to which most of the text is devoted will be effective. Part of the ritual describes the devotee's "presentation before the great god": he must write "the eight-letter name" on a leaf and lick off the leaf while showing it to the God; then the God will listen to him. The name is "i ee oo iai," and the text says, "Lick this up, so that you may be protected" (*PGM* 4.785–90).[19] The written form of the god's name must be "licked up," eaten, and ingested; to be consecrated is to internalize the written word.

But that written word is an alphabetical fantasia, and it is precisely here that magical language preserves the Platonic conundrum that living language, which cannot be captured by writing, is itself a kind of writing! By writing the name of God, the ultimate form of living discourse, in jumbles of letters that do not make sense, these texts show that it is really ordinary writing that is scrambled and confused, a mere imitation of another kind of inscription. Magical writing takes the form of ordinary writing by using its letters and so is faithful to it, but it betrays that writing by its nonsensical use of those letters and is thus faithful to the writing that is an invisible inscription on the soul. Yet it betrays the invisible inscription as well by writing it in actual letters!

Magical language is thus thoroughly paradoxical, betraying and safeguarding with every vowel. It carries forward the Platonic sensibility in a radical way.

Of course Plato also spoke about language under the aegis of Hermes, who is often invoked in the magical papyri as the inventor of letters and as the God with whom the devotee asks to be united. The "inventor of articulate speech" whose name had a hundred letters and who could be approached through "the barbaric names," Hermes was a much-sought-after figure, accompanied in the magical prayers and spells by a great many nonsensical alphabetical formulations.[20] Ancestor to the magical Hermes, the Platonic Hermes is presented in the dialogue entitled *Cratylus*, which is, fittingly, one of the most playful of Plato's writings.

One of the main topics of conversation between Socrates and his companions in the *Cratylus* is the meaning of the names of the gods. What can names tell us about the nature of the gods, and how can the meaning of names be investigated? Socrates proceeds by breaking down the name of each god he considers, finding in the supposed "parts" of each name allusions to two or even several other words. What he offers are highly fanciful etymologies, yet for each name the allusive meanings carried by the etymologies actually reflect the nature of the god. Name after name, Socrates takes the words apart, grouping the syllables now one way, now another, and finds in each case "a hive of wisdom" (401E).

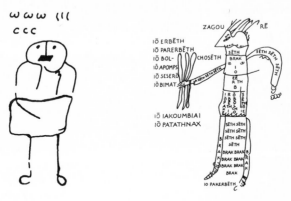

34. Charm to Inflict Illness.　　35. Charm to Restrain.

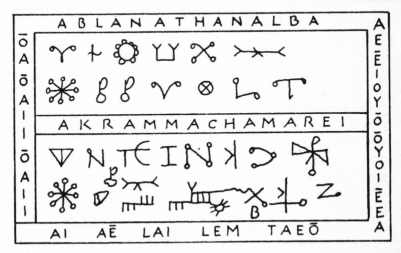

36. Charm to Restrain Anger.

Finally his companion Hermogenes asks about the name "Hermes."
Socrates says:

> I should imagine that the name Hermes has to do with speech, and signifies
> that he is the interpreter (*hermēneus*), or messenger, or thief, or liar, or
> bargainer; all that sort of thing has a great deal to do with language. As I was
> telling you, the word *eirein* is expressive of the use of speech, and there is
> an often-recurring Homeric word *emēsato,* which means "he contrived." Out
> of these two words, *eirein* and *mēsasthai,* the legislator formed the name of
> the god who invented language and speech. (*Cratylus* 408AB)

The name of the inventor of language and speech tells quite a story about
his inventions: they interpret and give messages, but they also thieve, lie,
and bargain. There is something contrived about language, yet it is divine.
As though this were not enough, Socrates goes on to speak about Pan, "the
double-formed son of Hermes": "You are aware that speech signifies all
things (*pan* = all) and is always turning them round and round, and has two
forms, true and false?" (408C). The progeny of the divine inventor of
language is double-formed; turning things round and round, words are
double-edged and, like Pan, perpetually in motion (408D). Hence, Socrates
shows again and again that if one wants to understand words, one must
enter the perpetual motion of their letters.

"Names rightly given," says Socrates, are "the likenesses and images of the
things which they name." Further, "imitation of the essence is made by
syllables and letters." Thus, the analyst's task is first to distinguish the letters
and then to distinguish *among* the letters, dividing them into vowels,
consonants, and so on. Entering the flow of words entails, as Socrates says,
"taking them to pieces" (439A; 424B–425A).

When juxtaposed with the magical papyri, the *Cratylus* reads like the
manual of instructions out of which the authors of those texts worked,
patiently dividing language into letters, letters into vowels, and so on, often
invoking the authority of Hermes as they worked. Yet, for the authors of
the papyri, Hermes as inventor of the alphabet was not only trickster but
also spellbinder. Along with the alphabet, he invented the philter, a charm
or spell.[21] This close association of language and the charm through Hermes
takes us back to the *Phaedrus,* where Thoth (Hermes in Egyptian disguise)
called his invention, the alphabet, a "recipe for wisdom." The word for
"recipe" here is *pharmakon,* also a philter, but one which truly captures the
double-edged quality of language, for it is a drug that can *both* poison *and*
heal.[22] Writing, then, is a *pharmakon,* and the wisdom it offers is a dangerous potion.

The connection between the word and the charm, stated by Plato and put
into action by the magical papyri, is a very old one. When, in a prayer for

protection against malevolent spirits, *Monas or the Eighth Book of Moses* says, "I invoke you, Lord, with a musical ode I chant your holy power; aeēiou-ōōō" (*PGM* 13.630–31), it has petitioned an ancient tradition that one scholar has named the "therapy of the word."[23] Legends about such shamanistic figures as Pythagoras and Orpheus characterize well the therapeutic dimensions of language. Pythagoras, for example, was said to chant his disciples to sleep with soothing and melodic rhythms; his musical words healed sufferings of both soul and body. Orpheus, who accompanied his poems with the music of the lyre, was a master of the *epode*, the incantation; he not only healed the *pathos* of human beings but could also charm beasts and stones and even the hostile spirits of the underworld.[24] When the magical papyri of late antiquity speak their alphabetical words in the context of music, invocation, protection, and healing, they are carrying forward the linguistic sensibility of this shamanistic tradition, for which the musical word or the sung charm was truly enchanting.

Given the transformative powers of such metrical speech, as well as the idea that the rhythmic word can heal, it is not surprising to find in the magical papyri an emphasis on the touching of the *tongue* in spells for healing.[25] Nor is it surprising that there is an insistence on the importance of correct pronunciation of the alphabetical words of power as well as careful reminders of exactly how many letters each string of letters contains.[26] And there is the further conviction that the one who says such words must be divinized—initiated into the nature of the God—because such words of power cannot be spoken with a merely human mouth.[27] Finally, the authors of the magical papyri have also carried on the rhythmic qualities of the spellbinding word. Indeed, so musical is the magical piety of the alphabet that one scholar was led to suggest that "each aeēiouō ēiouō . . . must have been a study of scales in a mystical voice-training academy," and another likened it to "hymnenpoesie"![28] We have already seen *Monas or the Eighth Book of Moses* name its magical language explicitly a "musical ode," yet much more frequent in our texts are graphic depictions of the rhythmic character of their alphabetical chants. Typical examples are *PGM* 13.905ff., 17, and 42, which are presented on p. 494. As an eminent student of these papyri once noted, such configurations were not "jeux d'esprit." "The letter and the word kept their full potency."[29]

From the archaic shamanistic tradition, the association of word and charm moved into philosophical, rhetorical, and poetic thinking. Xenophon, a contemporary of Plato and a fellow-admirer of Socrates, wrote that Socrates had characterized his own teachings as *philtra* and *epodai*—spells and odes! (*Memorabilia* 3.2.16).[30] Plato himself described Socrates' words as "tunes" with a "magic power" that left listeners "absolutely staggered and bewitched,"

```
        a   a
       ba   ak
      lba   akr
     alba   akra
    nalba   akram
   analba   akramm
  hanalba   akramma
 thanalba   akrammac
athanalba   akrammach
nathanalba   akrammacha
anathanalba   akrammacham
lanathanalba   akrammachama
blanathanalba   akrammachamar
ablanathanalba   akrammachamari
blanathanalba   akrammachamar
lanathanalba   akrammachama
anathanalba   akrammacham
nathanalba   akrammacha
athanalba   akrammach
thanalba   akrammac
hanalba   akramma
analba   akramm
nalba   akram
alba   akra
lba   akr
ba   ak
a   a
```

(PGM 17)

```
        a a a a a a
         e e e e e
        ē ē ē ē ē ē
     i i i i i i o o o o
         u u u u u
         ō ō ō ō ō
```

(PGM 42)

```
aeēiouo        aeēiouōō       aeēiouōouō
eēiouōa        eēiouōōa       eēiouōouōa
ēiouōae        ēiouōōae       ēiouōouōae
iouōaeē        iouōōaeē       iouōouōaeē
ouōaeēi        ouōōaeēi       ouōouōaeēi
uōaeēio        uōōaeēio       uōouōaeēio
ōaeēiou        ōōaeēiou       ōouōaeēiou
```

(PGM 13.905ff.)

with the "whole soul turned upside down" (*Symposium* 215CE).[31] Further, in his dialogue *Charmides*, Plato connects the *epode*, incantation, with the *pharmakon* and goes on to speak about the curative effect that noble words have on the soul (157A).[32] So also in the poetic tradition: Pindar, for example, said that the words of a poet could persuade "as with a *philtron*," a spell.[33] And in rhetorical circles as well, Gorgias, "the theoretician of the magic spell of words," used whole catalogues of magic-related words to describe the power of language to change reality.[34]

Running through all of these traditions that connect the word with the charm is an emphasis on the power or forcefulness of words. Compulsion, from their perspective, was built into the nature of language.[35] The authors of the magical papyri seem also to have been working out of such a realization. The nonsense words, for example, are often accompanied by imperative commands to the Gods being invoked to "come!" "guard!" "save!" and the spells themselves are frequently closed with the words "now! now! quick! quick!" This compulsive nature of the magical papyri has been repeatedly highlighted by the scholars who have studied them. But scholarly assessment of this compulsion has been negative. Magicians and their spellbinding commands have been seen as arrogant intruders on divine prerogatives.

Yet, from the perspective of the therapeutic, soul-transforming word that we have just discussed, the compulsive nature of magical nonsense words is not arrogant but pious. Such language is both the medium and the message of stark reality. It recognizes precisely the divine power of words, and it uses language in accordance with language's own qualities. Speaking to the gods in the gods' own language, the alphabetical words of the magical papyri expose the inner forcefulness of human language, and they expose that power in a most appropriate way, by placing those words in spells. It has been said that the magic of Socrates' words rested on their "obstinate destruction of all illusions."[36] Such can also be said of the authors of the magical texts: their alphabetical nonsense—rhythmic, incantatory, persuasive—destroys the illusions of language. It is truly a therapy of the word.

The Alphabet and the Cosmos

From the perspective of our fanciers of the alphabet, invoking God shatters human words, breaking them up into their elemental parts. Indeed, language is sometimes so shattered that only its most basic elements, the vowels, remain. Yet these phonetic components of language carry a world: if the vowels offer direct insight into language, they also offer access to the structural components of the cosmos itself. As we will see, the vowels sound a cosmic fullness through the one who speaks—and writes—them.

A striking example of the cosmic dimensions of the letters of the alphabet is given by Zosimus of Panopolis, an alchemist of the fourth century A.D. In a section of one of his treatises in which he is speculating about the proper names of generic man, he comes to the name "Adam," "a name from the speech of the angels." This is a name "with respect to the body," and it is "symbolic, composed of the four elements (stoicheiōn) from the whole sphere." Next Zosimus reveals the symbolic meanings of Adam's name by breaking it up into its letters (stoicheia):

> For the letter (stoicheion) A of his name signifies the ascendant east, and air; the letter D of his name signifies the descendant west, and earth, which sinks down because of its weight; and the letter M of his name signifies the meridian south, and the ripening fire in the midst of these bodies, the fire belonging to the middle, fourth planetary zone. On the Letter Omega 9)[37]

A, D, M; east, west, south; air, earth, fire: the letters of the name of man
(his "body") signify the elements that compose the cosmos. From this perspective, the alphabet is a kind of elemental grammar within which the
entire cosmos presents itself in human, earthy terms, as the symbolic body
of essential human being. By making these associations, Zosimus has not
reduced the cosmos to the merely human but has rather divinized the
human, since for him as for Greek antiquity generally the cosmos was
divine, the visible body of the Gods. Again the alphabet carries a piety, as
in one of the briefest of the magical papyri in which the devotee conjures
the presence of a God "with the twelve elements (*stoicheiōn*) of heaven and
the twenty-four elements (*stoicheiōn*) of the cosmos" (*PGM* 39.17–18). The
twenty-four letters of the Greek alphabet are cosmic, and they form the
exact "double" of the heavenly elements.

These connections between letters and elements can be made because of
the multiple meanings of the Greek word *stoicheion*, a word with an
interesting history. The basic meaning of the word is "something that
belongs to a series." In ancient linguistics, where the enduring meaning of
stoicheion was first developed, it was used to refer to a sound in a series with
other sounds in a word, and so was distinguished from *gramma*, the proper
name for the letters of the alphabet which make up a word.[38] Eventually,
however, the series of sounds that weave in and out of the letters were identified with the letters themselves, so that *stoicheion* came to be used more
or less synonymously with *gramma* and carried into the alphabet a vocal
quality like the *Thunder, Perfect Mind*'s "name of the sound and sound of
the name." Plato attributed this process to Thoth:

> The unlimited variety of sound was once discerned by some god, or perhaps
> some godlike man; you know the story that there was some such person in
> Egypt called Theuth. He it was who originally discerned the existence, in
> that unlimited variety, of the vowels—not "vowel" in the singular but
> "vowels" in the plural—and then of other things which though they could
> not be called articulate sounds, yet were noises of a kind. . . . In the end he
> found a number of the things, and affixed to the whole collection, as to each
> single member of it, the name "letters" (*stoicheia*). (*Philebus* 18BC)

As Plato goes on to say, after dividing all of these *stoicheia* into various
groups according to their sounds, the God "realized that none of us could
get to know one of the collection all by itself, in isolation from all the rest."
Thus "he conceived the 'letter' (*stoicheion*) as a kind of bond of unity uniting
as it were all these sounds into one, and so he gave utterance to the expression 'art of letters,' implying that there was one art that dealt with the
sounds" (*Philebus* 18CD). Plato has done some "weaving" himself here: to
the original meaning of "order" or "series" carried by *stoicheion*, he has

added "letter" and "sound" and has suggested that understanding this collection is an art given by a god.

To hear the sound of the letter is to be placed in a divine order, according to Plato, and it is particularly noteworthy that he emphasizes the vowels in this context. Later authors not only emphasized the vowels but saw them as first among the *stoicheia*. Thus, Philo of Alexandria, writing in the first century, could call the vowels the best and most powerful of the *stoicheia*, and Plutarch and Zosimus could write, respectively, on why alpha is the first letter, and omega the last letter, of the alphabet (Philo *Allegorical Interpretation* 1.14; Plutarch *Quaestiones convivales* 9.2.2).[39] The magical papyri, with their strings of vowels in constantly shifting order, also attest to the power of such *stoicheia;* yet, as we have seen, that power is often extended to include the entire cosmos. That extension is witness to yet another meaning which the word *stoicheion* came to hold.

As one scholar has suggested, "from sound as the original part of a word *stoicheion* probably came to be transferred to the cosmos," and it was used to designate the fundamental principles or constituent elements of the universe.[40] Thus, Philo could write about the heavenly word that places itself between the cosmic elements, thereby preventing them from destroying each other, just as the vocal elements in human words are placed between the silent elements and so perform the same protective function (*On Noah's Work as a Planter* 10).[41] What is here in Philo an analogy between cosmic elements (*stoicheia*) and alphabetic elements was in the hands of Stoic philosophers an identification. *Stoicheion* came to mean *both* letter *and* element.[42] Thus, the cosmic elements (earth, air, fire, water) and the letters of the alphabet could in some sense be said to mirror each other and, since the human being was thought to be composed of the same elements as the cosmos,[43] a further set of relationships could be added to an already complex phenomenon. It was to such an intricate net of associations that Zosimus was indebted as he took apart the name of Adam and discovered the whole cosmos there.

By the time of late antiquity, *stoicheion* had come to designate not only the constituent components of language and the cosmos but also, with the help of astrologers, the seven planets and even the stars. Astrologers, indeed, found more and more correspondences between human writing and heavenly phenomena; when they contemplated the skies, they saw what one modern scholar has called "Himmelschrift,"[44] a celestial text whose lights formed the moving script of divine order.[45] The "Mithras Liturgy" offers one example of how that divine script is mirrored in human writing. During one of this text's ceremonies of invocation, the initiate must invoke "the living, immortal names" that cannot be spoken with mortal sound or speech: ēeō oēeō iōō oē ēeō ēeō oē eō iōō (and so on, for several lines). The initiate is instructed to "say all these things with fire and spirit, until completing the first utterance; then, similarly, begin the second, until you complete the seven immortal gods of the world." When this is accomplished, the "cosmos of the gods" opens (*PGM* 4,605–25).[45] The immortal sounds of the seven vowels of the human alphabet, when they are spoken with "elemental" force ("with fire and spirit") reveal the seven planetary Gods and their realms. It is striking, of course, that such a divine script can be not only spoken but also written in human "language," yet it is here that the overflow of meaning carried by *stoicheion* can best be seen.

The idea that the seven vowels, most potent of the alphabetic *stoicheia*, and the seven planets, divine *stoicheia*, are related is an implicit assumption of the "Mithras Liturgy." This connection was made explicit by Nicomachus of Gerasa, a Neopythagorean thinker of the second century A.D. who carried into late antiquity the old Pythagorean doctrine of the music of the spheres. Pythagoras, who in the sixth century B.C. discovered the orderly arrangement of the musical scale, had elevated that order to the heavens. Like the seven notes of the octave, the seven planets moved in a harmonic progression and so made a "music" which, as tradition had it, Pythagoras claimed to have heard on several occasions. For Nichomachus, the vowels sound this mystical music. They are "sounding elements" (*phonēenta stoicheia*) and each vowel rings out the tone appropriate to each planetary sphere.[47] The heavens sing, and the sound is that of the vowels.

In the magical papyri, it is often the case that this Pythagorean music of the spheres is made audible as a human song. One of the most striking of the texts that utter the celestial harmony in earthy tones is the following:

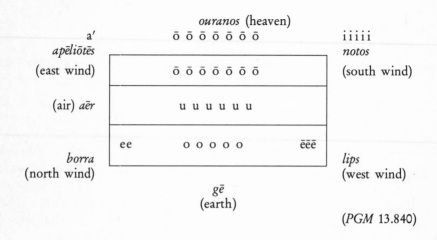

(*PGM* 13.840)

This diagram, which coordinates seven cosmic elements (heaven, earth, and air plus the east, west, south, and north winds) with the seven vowels of the Greek alphabet, is accompanied by instructions. It is a "picture" of what the initiate is to recite. Samples of the recitations are: "looking to the north wind, with one fist stretched out to the right, say 'e'"; "looking to the heavens, with both hands lying on the head, say 'ō'" and so on through all the elements and vowels in the diagram. Ultimately the initiate says to each of the cosmic elements the whole string of the vowels, and ends by invoking the God "as the cosmos: o uu ōōō aaa eeeee ēēēēē iiiiiii" (*PGM* 13.824–40). The initiate here is called upon to enact with his body and with his voice the entire cosmic scheme, all of which is effected by chanting alphabetical nonsense. It is a song both human and divine and displays fully the multidimensional power that the *stoicheia* had gathered by late antiquity. Archaic speculation lived on in the "elemental" piety of the magical texts.

The Allure of Language

The alphabetical nonsense that we have been discussing in this essay is informed, I would suggest, by a radical philosophy of language best expressed by the Neoplatonist Plotinus, who advised that we must be "in collusion with" language, reading all words as metaphors (VI 8 [39], 13).[48] That he followed his own advice will be clear from the following passage, in which he is speaking about Being itself, the ultimate reality that underlies everything:

> We cannot think of it as a chance existence; it is not what it chanced to be but what it must be—and yet without a 'must'. . . . Neither thus nor in any mode did it happen to be; There is no happening; There is only a 'Thus and no otherwise than Thus.' And even 'Thus' is false. (VI 8 [39], 9)

We must read metaphorically, letting language do its work of evocation. Strictly speaking, "we should put neither a This nor a That" to reality: "we hover, as it were, about it, seeking the statement of an experience of our own, sometimes nearing this Reality, sometimes baffled by the enigma in which it dwells" (VI 9 [9], 3). Nonetheless, the word for Plotinus is an "outshining" of soul, and discussion, while it cannot capture Being, does call to vision (III 2 [47], 16; VI 9 [9], 4).

Yet the vision baffles telling, perhaps because of the spellbinding character of reality itself. Plotinus had quite a lot to say about magic, most of it negative. "Everything that looks to another is under spell to that. . . . We move to that only which has wrought a fascination upon us" (IV 4 [28], 43).

In this latter statement, Plotinus has used the verb *thelgein* (to "enchant," "bewitch," "charm"), one of the words used by Gorgias long before him to describe the magical charm of words. Yet Plotinus has used it negatively. He is speaking here about the man who is captured by the charm of the external world and so neglects the inner, deeper world of the soul. There is, however, a positive magic: if nature is an allurer, administering as he says a "deceptive philter," Being itself is also beguiling, but beneficently so. In Plotinus's words, "So great is it in power and beauty that it remains the *allurer*, all things of the universe depending from it and rejoicing to hold their trace of it and through that to seek their good" (VI 6 [34], 18 [italics added]). Again the verb *thelgein* appears, but this time it refers to the bewitching allure of reality!

As we saw earlier in this essay, Plotinus thought that attempts to speak and write about this alluring reality were agonistic. Hence, he commends the "wise men of Egypt," who "left aside the writing forms that take in the detail of words and sentences and drew pictures instead." The language most appropriate to reality is hieroglyphic; that is "the mode in which the Supreme goes forth" (V 8 [31], 6).

Plotinus was not, of course, recommending that we abandon words and draw pictures instead; he wanted to see the "hieroglyphic" quality of all language. So also the authors of the alphabetical nonsense words. They did not abandon language either but formed their hieroglyphs with the letters of the alphabet. That this was not, for them, mere play or a deceptive philter is nowhere more poignantly voiced than in the alphabetical philosophy of Marcus, a Christian teacher of the second century. It is with his thoughts that we will close.

Marcus had taken the first verse of the Gospel of John seriously: "In the beginning was the word." God's creation was linguistic, and the letters of the first potent word that he uttered contained all of the forms of creation, each form presided over by the name of a letter of the alphabet, which is in turn composed of letters, each of which has a name, and so on to infinity. Thus, alpha, the name of the letter *a*, is composed of the letters *a*, *l*, and so on, and these letters have names in their turn, so that, for example, *l*'s name, lambda, contains yet more letters, and more names. Creation, in other words, is eternal and ongoing: "the multitude of letters swells out into infinitude," and "letters are continually generating other letters." The alphabet speaks a divine language, and it does so in a radically generative, metaphoric way, each letter calling up, but never pinning down, the enigmatic nature of reality, the word of God.[49]

Marcus, and his fellow magicians as well, was under spell to the bewitchment of language itself, which had the power to evoke the very heart of being—but it had that power only when broken apart. Shattered in this way, the alphabet was "the body of truth," "the figure of the element," "the character of the letter," and it was emblazoned on the body of the human being as well as in the cosmic spheres.[50] Indeed, Marcus describes the human being, who *is* the element that the alphabet figures, as "the mouth" of the silent God, and the song the human sings echoes the elemental sounding of the heavens, each one of which pronounces its own vowel (Irenaeus *Against Heretics* 1.14.3, 7). Marcus's illustration of the sound of this song, which brings letter, element, God, and human being together in one long wail, is the sorrowing cry of a newborn baby. Composed only of vowels, the baby's cry is a hymn of praise, sounding the elemental glory of the heavens and their linguistic creator (Irenaeus *Against Heresies* 1.14.6).

A figure for all attempts to express in language what is ultimately meaningful, Marcus's baby speaks, sorrowing and rejoicing at once. Here is "the murderous alphabet" indeed, and it shows what Plotinus described as the "agony" of speaking in a most wrenching way. As we suggested at the beginning of this essay, the piety of the alphabet is a violent one; its praise is nonsense.

Appendix

Two of the important categories used in this essay are "gnosticism" and "magic." They are typically used by scholars as normative categories that designate philosophical and theological positions. Such usage has recently been questioned, however, and I offer the following remarks both to alert the reader to these issues and to clarify my own use of the two terms.

Most of the texts in the collection called *The Nag Hammadi Library* have been considered by modern scholars to be expressions of "gnosticism," which is generally defined as a dualistic, antihistorical religious system with philosophical and mythological elements taken from Platonism and Judaism. The use of the term "gnostic" to describe these texts is, however, highly problematic. The term "gnostic" was used by the second-century Christian heresiologist Irenaeus to describe certain thinkers in the Christianity of his day as heretics whose theology was unsound. Hence the term "gnostic" carried, and tends still to carry, polemical overtones of a decidedly negative sort.

Further, as Morton Smith has pointed out in a ground-breaking essay, most of the thinkers whom Irenaeus branded with the name "gnostic" did not consider themselves to be part of such a "movement" and did not even use the word! In the present essay, use of this term is avoided where possible. Its usefulness is limited to convenient designation of texts and does not extend to descriptions of the contents of such texts. For a pointed discussion of these issues, see Morton Smith, "The History of the Term Gnostikos," in *The Rediscovery of Gnosticism,* ed. Bentley Layton, 2:796–807.

Like the term "gnostic," the term "magical" is problematic because of a negative theological bias that the word still carries from antiquity. What was called "magical" was considered by an earlier generation of scholars to be a debased form of religion in which conjuration replaced contemplation and arrogance toward the Gods replaced humble submission to them, but texts designated as "magical" have more recently been shown to be much more sophisticated and complex. Indeed, the term "magic" itself had in antiquity a very wide range of applicability from true piety to quackery; hence, the reductive use of the term in modern scholarship is not an accurate reflection of the ancient usage or phenomenon. In this essay, "magic" has been used only as a convenient designation of a collection of texts edited by Karl Preisendanz (see bibliography) and as a designation of those portions of texts from the Nag Hammadi Library that share the "alphabetical piety" so common in the magical papyri. For recent discussions of magic in late antiquity, see the excellent studies by Alan F. Segal and Morton Smith listed in the bibliography.

Notes

1. The collection of texts to which *Thunder, Perfect Mind* belongs was discovered in 1945 in the Naj' Ḥammādī region of Egypt and has now been translated into English from the Coptic and published as *The Nag Hammadi Library,* ed. James M. Robinson.

2. See also V 5 [32], 6, where Plotinus describes the attempt to speak about profound reality as an "agony."

3. Most of the magical texts discussed here are located in Karl Preisendanz, *Papyri Graecae Magicae.* Texts from this collection will be cited *PGM,* with papyrus and line numbers following. All translations are my own unless otherwise noted.

4. *The Collected Poems of Wallace Stevens* (New York: Alfred A. Knopf, 1977) 179.

5. For the connection between speaking in tongues and alphabetical writing, see Morton Smith, *Clement of Alexandria,* 232–33; and J. Behm, "glōssa," in *Theological Dictionary of the New Testament,* 1:722–23.

6. *Pistis Sophia,* ed. Carl Schmidt; trans. Violet MacDermot (Nag Hammadi Studies 9; Leiden: Brill, 1978) 707.

7. Smith, *Clement of Alexandria,* 232.

8. For sources pertaining to mantic speaking in tongues, see Behm, "glōssa," 722; and E. R. Dodds, *The Greeks and the Irrational* (Berkeley and Los Angeles: University of California Press, 1951) chap. 3: "The Blessings of Madness," pp. 64–101.

9. See A. D. Nock, "Greek Magical Papyri," in *Arthur Darby Nock: Essays on Religion and the Ancient World,* ed. Zeph Stewart, 1:176–94; A.-J. Festugière, *La Révélation d'Hermès Trismégiste:* vol. 1, *L'Astrologie et les Sciences Occultes,* 283–309; and Behm, "glōssa," 722.

10. See Franz Dornseiff, *Das Alphabet in Mystik und Magie*, 52 ("mystische Kauder-welsch") and 25 (Rimbaud).

11. See Dornseiff, *Das Alphabet*, 18–19; and Albrecht Dieterich, "ABC-Denkmaeler," *Rheinisches Museum für Philologie* 56 (1901) 77–105.

12. Smith, *Clement of Alexandria*, 232.

13. Lewis Carroll, *Through the Looking Glass*, in *The Annotated Alice*, ed. Martin Gardner (New York: Clarkson N. Potter, 1960) 197.

14. Wallace Stevens, "Notes Toward a Supreme Fiction," *The Collected Poems*, 380–407.

15. For uses of *Iaō*, see Smith, *Clement of Alexandria*, 233 n. 10. For the Hebrew *YHWH* who both makes and unmakes language, see Gen 2:19; 11:1–9.

16. Dornseiff, *Das Alphabet*, 3–8.

17. Ibid., 7 n. 4; Festugière, *L'Astrologie*, 287–93.

18. Jacques Derrida, *Dissemination*, trans. Barbara Johnson (Chicago: University of Chicago Press, 1981) Part I: "Plato's Pharmacy," p. 149 (italics in original).

19. I have used the English translation of this text by Marvin W. Meyer, ed. and trans., *The "Mithras Liturgy*," 25.

20. See, e.g., *PGM* 8.1–22, 50–53; *PGM* 5.400–423; French translations of many Hermetic magical texts can be found in Festugière, *L'Astrologie*, 287–96.

21. Festugière, *L'Astrologie*, 287–88.

22. See Derrida, *Dissemination*, 95–117; Pedro Lain Entralgo, *The Therapy of the Word in Classical Antiquity*, 95; and Jacqueline de Romilly, *Magic and Rhetoric in Ancient Greece*, 34–35.

23. Lain Entralgo, *Therapy of the Word*.

24. Porphyry *Life of Pythagoras* 30, in *Porphyrii philosophi platonici opuscula selecta*, ed. A. Nauck (Leipzig: Teubner, 1886); Iamblichus *De vita Pythagorica*, ed. Ludovicus Deubner (Leipzig: Teubner, 1937). For discussion of these figures, see Lain Entralgo, *Therapy of the Word*, 44–52, 75–86; Romilly, *Magic and Rhetoric*, 14–15; and Walter Burkert, "*Goēs*: Zum Griechischen 'Schamanismus,'" *Rheinisches Museum für Philologie* 105 (1962) 36–55.

25. Smith, *Clement of Alexandria*, 223.

26. Hans Dieter Betz, "The Formation of Authoritative Tradition in the Greek Magical Papyri," in *Jewish and Christian Self-Definition*: vol. 3, *Self-Definition in the Greco-Roman World*, ed. Ben F. Meyer and E. P. Sanders, 167; Dodds, *The Greeks and the Irrational*, 292–93.

27. Betz, "Formation of Tradition," 167; see Smith, *Clement of Alexandria*, 218 for a translation of *PGM* 13.783ff., in which a magician identifies himself with a spirit.

28. Albrecht Dieterich, *Abraxas*, 43; M. P. Nilsson, *Geschichte der griechischen Religion*, vol. 2, *Die hellenistische und römische Zeit* (Munich: Beck, 1950) 668.

29. A. D. Nock, "The Vocabulary of the New Testament," in *Arthur Darby Nock: Essays on Religion and the Ancient World*, ed. Zeph Stewart, 1:346.

30. Translated and discussed in Lain Entralgo, *Therapy of the Word*, 122 n. 21.

31. See also *Meno* 80AB.

32. Romilly, *Magic and Rhetoric*, 34–37; Lain Entralgo, *Therapy of the Word*, 121–26.

33. Romilly, *Magic and Rhetoric*, 4, 7–9.

34. Ibid., 3–22; Lain Entralgo, *Therapy of the Word*, 88.

35. For discussions of *bia* (force) and *anankē* (necessity), see Lain Entralgo, *Therapy of the Word*, 89–91.

36. Romilly, *Magic and Rhetoric*, 36.

37. In *Zosimus of Panopolis: On the Letter Omega,* ed. and trans. by Howard M. Jackson, 29.

38. Gerhard Delling, "stoicheion," in *Theological Dictionary of the New Testament,* 7:670–71.

39. Cited in Delling, "stoicheion," 671.

40. Ibid., 672.

41. Ibid., 671.

42. Ibid., 672–75; Dornseiff, *Das Alphabet,* 14–17.

43. See, e.g., the theories of the Greek physician Galen, discussed in Delling, "stoicheion," 673.

44. Dornseiff, *Das Alphabet,* 89.

45. Ibid., 81–90; see also Delling, "stoicheion," 679–83 for astrology and the elements.

46. Meyer, *Mithras Liturgy,"* 13.

47. See Albrecht Dieterich, *Eine Mithrasliturgie,* 32–35; Dornseiff, *Das Alphabet,* 82–91.

48. The verb *synchōreō* has a range of meanings including to "defer," "concede," "be in collusion with," "connive at."

49. The teachings of Marcus are most fully reported by the Christian heresiologist Irenaeus in *Against Heresies,* book 1. On the reliability of Irenaeus's accounts, see Rowan A. Greer, "The Dog and the Mushrooms: Irenaeus's View of the Valentinians Assessed," in *The Rediscovery of Gnosticism,* ed. B. Layton (2 vols.; Leiden, Brill, 1980) 1:146–75. I have used the English translation in *Ante-Nicene Fathers:* vol. 1, *The Apostolic Fathers,* ed. by A. Roberts and J. Donaldson, 336–37. The passages cited here are from Irenaeus *Against Heresies* 1.14.1–2.

50. See Irenaeus *Against Heresies* 1.14.3: Truth, who is also human, is described as follows: "Behold, then, her head on high, *Alpha* and *Omega;* her neck, *Beta* and *Psi;* her shoulders with her hands, *Gamma* and *Chi,*" and so on through the whole body.

Bibliography

Editions

Preisendanz, Karl, ed. *Papyri Graecae magicae.* 2 vols. 2nd ed. Revised by Albert Hinrichs. Stuttgart: Teubner, 1973–1974.

Translations

The Anti-Nicene Fathers. Translations of the Writings of the Fathers down to A.D. 325. Edited by A. Roberts and J. Donaldson. 10 vols. Edinburgh, 1866–72. Reprint Grand Rapids, MI: Eerdmans, 1979. Vol 1, *The Apostolic Fathers with Justin Martyr and Irenaeus.*

Meyer, Marvin W., trans. and ed. *The "Mithras Liturgy."* Missoula, MT: Scholars Press, 1976.

Pistis Sophia. Translated by Violet MacDermot. Leiden: Brill, 1978.

Plato. *The Collected Dialogues.* Edited by E. Hamilton and H. Cairns. Princeton, NJ: Princeton University Press, 1961.

Plotinus. *The Enneads.* Translated by S. MacKenna. 4th edition revised by B. S. Page. London: Faber & Faber, 1962.

Robinson, James M., ed. *The Nag Hammadi Library.* San Francisco: Harper & Row, 1977.

Zosimus of Panopolis: On the Letter Omega. Edited and translated by Howard M. Jackson. Missoula, MT: Scholars Press, 1978.

Modern Works

Behm, Johannes. "glōssa." In *Theological Dictionary of the New Testament*, 1:719–27. Edited by Gerhard Kittel. Translated by Geoffrey M. Bromiley. Grand Rapids, MI: Eerdmans, 1964–.

Betz, Hans Dieter. "The Formation of Authoritative Tradition in the Greek Magical Papyri." In *Jewish and Christian Self-Definition.* Vol. 3, *Self-Definition in the Greco-Roman World*, 161–70. Edited by Ben F. Meyer and E. P. Sanders. Philadelphia: Fortress, 1982.

Delling, Gerhard. "stoicheion." In *Theological Dictionary of the New Testament*, 3:670–87. Edited by Gerhard Kittel. Translated by Geoffrey W. Bromiley. Grand Rapids, MI: Eerdmans, 1964–.

Dieterich, Albrecht. *Abraxas.* Leipzig: Teubner, 1891.

———. *Eine Mithrasliturgie.* 3rd ed. 1923. Reprint Stuttgart: Teubner, 1966.

Dornseiff, Franz. *Das Alphabet in Mystik und Magie.* Leipzig: Teubner, 1922.

Festugière, André-Jean. *La Révélation d'Hermès Trismégiste.* 4 vols. Vol. 1, *L'Astrologie et les Sciences Occultes.* Paris: Librairie Lecoffre, 1944.

Lain Entralgo, Pedro. *The Therapy of the Word in Classical Antiquity.* Translated by L. J. Rather and John M. Sharp. New Haven, CT, and London: Yale University Press, 1970.

Nock, Arthur Darby. "Greek Magical Papyri." In *Arthur Darby Nock: Essays on Religion and the Ancient World*, 1:176–94. Edited by Zeph Stewart. 2 vols. Cambridge, MA: Harvard University Press, 1972.

Romilly, Jacqueline de. *Magic and Rhetoric in Ancient Greece.* Cambridge, MA: Harvard University Press, 1975.

Segal, Alan F. "Hellenistic Magic: Some Questions of Definition." In *Studies in Gnosticism and Hellenistic Religions*, 349–75. Edited by R. Van Den Broek and M. J. Vermaseren. Leiden: Brill, 1981.

Smith, Morton. *Clement of Alexandria and a Secret Gospel of Mark.* Cambridge, MA: Harvard University Press, 1973.

Contributors

A. H. ARMSTRONG, editor of this volume, is Emeritus Professor of Greek at the University of Liverpool, England, and Adjunct Professor of Classics at Dalhousie University, Halifax, Nova Scotia. He has translated Plotinus for the Loeb Classical Library series (5 volumes published to 1984) and is the editor of the *Cambridge History of Later Greek and Early Medieval Philosophy* (1970). He is the author of *The Architecture of the Intelligible Universe in the Philosophy of Plotinus* (1940, reprinted 1967; French translation with new preface by author, 1984) and *Plotinian and Christian Studies* (1979).

P. ATHERTON is Professor of Classics at Dalhousie University, Halifax, Nova Scotia. He is a well-known Canadian Aristotelian scholar and editorial secretary of the Dalhousie journal *Dionysius*.

W. BEIERWALTES is Professor of Philosophy at the University of Munich, Germany. He is the leading scholar on Platonism and its place in European thought from ancient times to our own. On this he has published a series of studies, *Platonismus und Idealismus* (1972), *Identität und Differenz* (1980), and *Denken des Einen* (1985).

K. CORRIGAN is Professor of Classics at Athol Murray College of Notre Dame, Saskatchewan, Canada. A classical scholar specializing in Aristotle and Plotinus, he is the author of "The Internal Dimensions of the Sensible Object in the Thought of Plato and Aristotle" (1980) and "The Irreducible Opposition Between the Platonic and Aristotelian Concepts of Soul and Body in Some Ancient and Medieval Thinkers" (1985).

P. COX MILLER is Professor of Religion at the University of Syracuse, New York. A specialist in the Gnostics, Origen, and Plotinus, she is the author of *Biography in Late Antiquity: A Quest for the Holy Man* (1985) and a number of articles on the more strangely interesting aspects of late antique thought.

J. M. DILLON is Professor of Greek at Trinity College, Dublin, Ireland. He is the editor of the fragments of Iamblichus's commentaries on Plato (1973) and the author of *The Middle Platonists* (1977).

J. GWYN GRIFFITHS is Emeritus Professor of Egyptology at University College of Swansea in the University of Wales. He has produced two major commentaries on ancient works illustrating devotion to Isis in the Roman Empire—*Plutarch's De Iside et Osiride* (1970) and *The Isis-Book of Apuleius* (1975)—and other works on Egyptian religion.

I. Hadot is Maître de recherche at the Centre National de Recherche Scientifique, Paris, France. She is the author of *Le Problème du néoplatonisme alexandrin: Hiéroclès et Simplicius* (1978).

P. Hadot is Professor of Hellenistic and Roman Thought at College de France, Paris, France. He is the editor (with Paul Henry) of the theological treatises of Marius Victorinus (1960) and the author of *Plotin* (1963), *Porphyre et Victorinus* (1968), *Exercises Spirituels et Philosophie Antique* (1981).

J. P. Kenney is Professor of Religion at Reed College, Portland, Oregon. He has a book forthcoming on the history and philosophy of theism.

A. A. Long is Professor of Greek at the University of California at Berkeley. He is the author of *Hellenistic Philosophy* (1974) and a number of articles on Hellenistic thought.

P. Manchester is Professor of Religious Studies and Philosophy at the State University of New York at Stony Brook. A student of philosophical theology with particular interest in the problem of time and eternity, he is the author of a number of studies on this theme in Greek philosophy, including a forthcoming book *The Syntax of Time*.

J. Pépin is Professor at the École Pratique des Hautes Études, Paris, France. He is the author of *Théologie Cosmique et Théologie Chrétienne* (1964), *Idées Grecques sur l'Homme et sur Dieu* (1971).

J. Pinsent is Senior Lecturer in Greek at the University of Liverpool, England. A historian of the Roman Republic, he has written also on Greek myths (*Greek Mythology*, 1979).

H. D. Saffrey is Maître de recherche at the Centre National de Recherche Scientifique, Paris, France. He carries on the tradition of French Dominican scholarship inaugurated by A.-J. Festugière in the field of the thought and piety of late antiquity. He is the editor (with L. G. Westerink) of the new edition (the first since the seventeenth century) of the great *Platonic Theology* of Proclus (4 volumes published to 1981).

F. M. Schroeder is Professor of Classics at Queens University, Kingston, Canada. A scholar in the field of ancient philosophy, specializing in Plotinus, he is the author of "The Platonic Parmenides and Imitation in Plotinus" (1978) and "Representation and Reflection in Plotinus" (1980).

J. B. Skemp is Emeritus Professor of Greek at the University of Durkam, England. A leading English Platonic scholar, he is the author of *The Theory of Motion in Plato's Later Dialogues* (1942, 2nd enlarged edition 1967) and a number of articles on Plato.

†R. T. Wallis was Professor of Classics at the University of Oklahoma and the author of *Neoplatonism* (1972).

Photographic Credits

The editors and publisher wish to thank the custodians of the works of art for supplying photographs and granting permission to use them.

1. The Metropolitan Museum of Art, Museum Excavations, 1928–1929, and Rogers Fund, 1930.
2. The Cleveland Museum of Art. Purchased by The John Huntington Art and Polytechnic Trust.
3. The Metropolitan Museum of Art, Rogers Fund, 1915.
4. The Louvre, Paris.
5. The Metropolitan Museum of Art, Museum Excavations, 1911–1912.
6. Cincinnati Art Museum. Gift of Mr. and Mrs. Fletcher E. Nyce.
7. The Metropolitan Museum of Art, Rogers Fund, 1914.
8. Courtesy of the Trustees of The British Museum.
9. Courtesy, Museum of Fine Arts, Boston. Classical Department Exchange Fund.
10. The J. Paul Getty Museum.
11. The Metropolitan Museum of Art, Purchase, 1955, Joseph Pulitzer Bequest.
12. Courtesy, Museum of Fine Arts, Boston. Catherine Page Perkins Fund.
13. The J. Paul Getty Museum.
14. The Metropolitan Museum of Art, Bequest of Walter C. Baker, 1971.
15. ©1986, Dumbarton Oaks, Trustees for Harvard University, Washington, D.C.
16. The J. Paul Getty Museum.
17. Courtesy of the Trustees of The British Museum.
18. The Cleveland Museum of Art. Purchased by Income J. H. Wade Fund.
19. Courtesy, Museum of Fine Arts, Boston. Classical Department Exchange Fund.
20. Courtesy, Museum of Fine Arts, Boston. H. L. Pierce Fund.
21. Courtesy of the Trustees of The British Museum.
22. Wellesley College Museum. Gift of Miss Hannah P. Kimball.
23. The Metropolitan Museum of Art, Harris Brisbane Dick Fund, 1950.
24. From Homer A. Thompson, "Excavations in the Athenian Agora: 1959," *Hesperia* 29 (1960) fig. 4.
25. From G. Lugli, *Roma antica. Il centro monumentale*, Rome, 1946, pl. 5.
26. The Victoria and Albert Museum, London.
27. Courtesy, Museum of Fine Arts, Boston. Francis Bartlett Fund.
28. ©1986 Dumbarton Oaks, Trustees for Harvard University, Washington, D.C.
29. The J. Paul Getty Museum.
30. Walters Art Gallery, Baltimore.
31. Courtesy, Museum of Fine Arts, Boston. Gift of Mr. and Mrs. Cornelius C. Vermeule, III.
32. The Metropolitan Museum of Art, Bequest of Walter C. Baker, 1972.
33. The J. Paul Getty Museum.
34. From *The Greek Magical Papyri, Including the Demotic Spells*, edited by Hans Dieter Betz, p. 321. ©1986 by The University of Chicago Press. By permission of The University of Chicago Press.
35. From *The Greek Magical Papyri, Including the Demotic Spells*, edited by Hans Dieter Betz, p. 269. ©1986 by The University of Chicago Press. By permission of The University of Chicago Press.
36. From *The Greek Magical Papyri, Including the Demotic Spells*, edited by Hans Dieter Betz, p. 149. ©1986 by The University of Chicago Press. By permission of The University of Chicago Press.

Indexes

Subjects

Akhenaten, in Amarna experience, 30–32
Albinus, 224; transcendentalism of, 466
alphabet, spiritual importance of, 495–99
Amarna experience, and aftermath, 30–32
animals, kinship with, 11
anthropomorphism, in Olympian polytheism, 272–73
Aphrodite, piety toward, 85–87
Apollo, piety toward, 84
apotheosis, and joyful adoration, 56–59
Aristotle: conception of gods, 123–29; divine *archē*, 123–26; Eleatic challenge, 123–24; god and human beings, 121–22, 131–33; god as *nous* (intellect), 129–31; spiritual importance of unknown, 464; spirituality of, 121–34; vision of nature, 123–29
Artemis, worship of, 196–99
Athena, piety toward, 83–84
Athenian tragedy, and Greek pieties, 96–98

baptism, rite of, 52–56
beauty, love of, 293–313; Dionysian concepts, 309–10; *nous* characteristic, 299–303; Platonic concepts, 294–99; Plotinian concepts, 299–306; Proclus's concepts, 306–9
body: "independent" living, 370; soul and sky, 366–73
body and soul: in ancient religious experience, 360–83; Aristotle's views, 376–77; celestial immortality, 379; cosmic god and Presocratic philosophy, 369–72; Heraclitus's view, 368–69; Homeric concepts, 361–63; hypercosmic dimension, 379–80; internal/external distinction, 368–69; Orphic views, 364–66; Platonic concepts, 374–76; Plotinian view, 379–80; poetic, prophetic, telestic, and erotic inspiration, 363–64; Pythagorean views, 364–66; self concepts, 347–48; sky and, 366–73; Socrates' views, 373–74; Stoic concepts, 378; suffering and illumination, 372–73

cannibalism, 12–14
Catullus, and Roman spirituality, 167–70
celestial immortality, of soul, 379
Chaldaean Oracles, 227, 253; transcendentalism and, 467
children, prayers and offerings of, 204
Chiron, as spiritual guide, 436–38
Cicero: and Greek philosophy, 161–67; on superstition, 162–65
city: Achilles legend, 322–24; in ancient religious experience, 314–36; archaic and classical, 325–31; bureaucratic priesthood, 326–27; civic attributes, 314–15; as commonwealth, 315; demonstrations in, 195–96; early development, 315–20; Ephesus, 195–99; gods and piety, 319–20; Hellenic contributions, 315–20; Hellenistic and Roman, 331–35; Homeric foundation, 321–25; in late antiquity, 195–99; military organization, 327; Olympian aspects, 321–24; Olympic games, 327–28; philosophy as wisdom, 330–31; social arrangements and primitive science, 326–27; Sophistic aspects, 330; sovereignty aspects, 317; wealth and instability, 326–27
confession, as initiation rite, 52–56
contemplation and prayer, Neoplatonist views, 255–56
cosmic dualism, of Plutarch, 217–19
cosmic god, and Presocratic philosophy, 369–72
cosmic piety, 408–35; Aristotelean tradition, 413–14; condemnations of, 408–9; feast days and, 430–31; Judaic and Christian views, 408–9; Platonism and, 410–12,

509

cosmic piety (*continued*)
    416–21; Plotinian tradition, 418–20; Stoicism and, 414–16; tradition of, 410–21; world and temple in, 421–30
cosmos, alphabet and, 495–99
countryside, in late antiquity, 199–202
creation doctrines, of Pharaonic period, 8–10
cultic polytheism, 270, 288
cults: Egyptian, 39–65; foreign, 171–78; mystery, 72

daemons, Plutarch's views on, 220
Damascius, Neoplatonist spirituality of, 250–64
Delphic divinity, 215–17
depth psychology, in religious study, 338
devotion, Neoplatonist views, 260–62
Dionysius (Pseudo-): love of beauty and god, 309–10
Dionysus: piety toward, 87–91
divine intellect, two kinds of life of, 242–44

educator, as spiritual guide, 436–41
Egyptian cults: apotheosis and joyful adoration, 56–59; encounter with divine, 56–59; initiation rites, 52–56; national religion, 40–46; nature of appeal, 42–46; oecumenical spiritual significance, 39–65; universal goddess of love offers salvation, 46–51
Epicureanism, 138–45; as alternative community, 138–39; nature of gods, 140–144
Erōs: Pseudo-Dionysian concept, 310; piety toward, 85–87; Platonic concepts, 294–95; Plotinian concepts, 304–5; Proclus's concept of, 306–9
erotic concept, of soul, 363–64
eternity: and intelligibility, 402. *See also* time and eternity
ethics, and Platonism, 219
evil, origin of, 381

feast days, and cosmic piety, 430–31
female divinities, in mystery cults, 72
foreign cults, influence on Roman spirituality, 171–78
forgiveness doctrine, in Egyptian cults, 52–56
friendship, Aristotle's doctrine of, 448–49

Gnosticism: and nonsense, 501–2; spiritual importance of unknown, 468–70

God, love of, 293–313; Dionysian concepts, 309–10; Platonic concepts, 294–99; Plotinian concepts, 299–306; Proclus's concepts, 306–9
gods: humanity and self, 352–54; personification of, 343; and self, 341–46
Greco-Roman antiquity, spiritual guides in, 436–59
Greco-Roman spirituality: divinity concepts, 269–70. *See also* Mediterranean spirituality
Greek pieties: ancient and continuing, 66–101; Athenian tragedy and, 96–98; earth powers and dead, 91–93; epic and lyric poets, 94–96; holy places and temples, 69–70; individual gods, 81–94; influence of externals, 67–72; influence of poets, 94–98; and morality, 79–81; mystery cults, 71–72; Orphism movement, 98–99; spirituality of ancient worships, 73–81

happiness, self and, 350–52
Hellenic monotheism, 280–89; Aristotle's role in, 282–84; cosmogonic aspects, 282; forms of being, 281; Middle Platonism and, 284–88; Platonic concepts, 280–82; Plotinian concepts, 286–89
Hellenistic city: in ancient religious experience, 331–35; philosophical sects, 332–33; political condition, 332
Helios, piety toward, 93–94
Heraclitus, and Olympian polytheism, 277–78
Hermopolite doctrine, 8–9
Homer, *psychē* and body, 362–63
Homeric polytheism, 271–74
Horus, in Pharaonic system, 40–46
humanity: and gods, 352–54; Plotinian view, 353–54; post-Aristotelian definition, 381
hymns, Neoplatonist views, 256–60

Iamblichus, Neoplatonist spirituality of, 250–64
illumination, suffering and, 372–73
Isis, as universal goddess of love, 46–51

judgment doctrine, in Egyptian cults, 52–56

language: allure of, 499–501; spell of, 486–95; spiritual importance of, 482–95
Lucretius, and Greek philosophy, 161–67

Mâat, importance of, 22–23

magic: and nonsense, 490–95, 501–2; and sensuality, 54–55; and technology, 15

magical language, 490–95

Mars, in Roman spirituality, 182–83

Maximus, transcendentalism of, 466

Mediterranean spirituality: monotheistic and polytheistic elements, 262–92

Memphite theology, 9

monks, fanatical activities of, 200–201

monotheism: biblical traditions, 289–90; in classical Mediterranean spirituality, 269–92; defined, 270; Hellenic, 280–89; heritage of, 289–90; "scholastic" model, 270–71

music, as wisdom, 440

musician, as spiritual guide, 436–41

mystery cults: goddesses in, 72; in Greek piety, 71–72

mystical experience: definitions, 236–39; in Neoplatonist spirituality, 245–46

national religion, Egyptian cults as, 40–46

Neferti, prophecies of, 20–21

negative theology, mystical union and, 247–48

Neoplatonism, spiritual importance of unknown, 475–77

Neoplatonist spirituality, 230–65; from Iamblichus to Proclus and Damascius, 250–65; and pagan piety, 262; Plotinus and Porphyry, 230–49

nonsense: allure of language, 499–501; alphabet and, 495–99; gnosticism and magic, 501–2; "jabberwocky," 487; language and, 486–95; sounds of spirit, 482–86; speech and, 482–86; spiritual importance of, 481–505

Numenius, transcendentalism of, 467

Olympian polytheism, 272–78; anthropomorphic aspect, 272–73

Olympic games, 327–28

oracles, and theurgy, 252–54

ordinary men and women: in cities, 195–99; in countryside, 199–202; piety and prayers of, 195–213; pilgrimages of, 205–7

Orpheus, as spiritual guide, 438–40

Orphism: and Greek pieties, 98–99; hymns, 259; view of soul, 364–66

Osiris: identification with, 24–26; judgment before, 33–34; in Pharaonic system, 40–46

pagan piety, survival of, 262

paradox. See nonsense

perfect mind, self-revelation of, 481–82

Pharaonic period, 3–37; Amarna experience and aftermath, 30–32; basic cults reconciled, 5–6; confident faith and some doubts, 21–29; doctrines of creation, 8–10; early phases, 3–20; judgment before Osiris, 33–34; life after death belief, 23–29; new horizons, 20–34; people and priest, 15–20; pluralism of, 6–8; primitive echoes, 10–15

philosophers, as spiritual guides, 444–45

Phoenix, as spiritual guide, 438

piety and prayers: of ordinary men and women, 195–213. See also cosmic piety

pilgrimages, in late antiquity, 205–7

Plato: and cosmic piety, 410–412; intellect and passion, 113–14; love of beauty and god, 294–99; metaphysical doctrines of, 110; Pythagorean influence on, 114–16; Socratic influence on, 112–13; spiritual importance of unknown, 461–64; spirituality of, 110–19

Platonic love, 294–99

Platonism: and cosmic piety, 416–21; Delphic divinity in, 215–17; ethics and, 219; and Hellenic monotheism, 284

Platonists, second century, 214–29

Plotinus: experience of union, 233; and Hellenic monotheism, 286–89; journey of soul to god, 234–36; life of divine intellect, 242–44; love of beauty and god, 299–306; mystical experience, 236–39, 245–46; Neoplatonist spirituality of, 230–49; soul united with intellect, 239–41; spiritual importance of unknown, 470–73

pluralism, of Pharaonic period, 6–8

Plutarch: cosmic dualism of, 217–19; Delphic divinity, 215–17; ethics of, 219; and second century Platonism, 214–29; soul and intellect, 220–23; views on daemons, 220

poet, as spiritual guide, 436–41

poetic concept, of soul, 363–64

polytheism: ancient aspects, 271–80; in classical Mediterranean spirituality, 262–92; defined, 270; Homeric conception, 271, 273; Olympian, 271–78; in Pharaonic period, 7

Porphyry: Neoplatonist spirituality of, 230–49; self and intellect, 232–33; spiritual importance of unknown, 474–75 prayers and offerings, of ordinary men and women, 202–4

priesthood, in Pharaonic period, 15–20

Proclus: "book of hymns," 256–60; contemplation and prayer, 255–56; devotion to divinities, 260–62; love of beauty and god, 306–9; Neoplatonist spirituality of, 250–64; oracles and theurgy, 252–54; scientific theology, 250–52

prophetic concept, of soul, 363–64

psychē: Homeric concept, 362; from sixth to fourth century, 367–68. See also soul

Ptolemaic tradition, 41–42

Pyrrho, spiritual importance of unknown, 464–65

Pythagorean view, of soul, 364–66

Rê, 4–6; identification with, 27–28

riddles. See nonsense

Roman city: in ancient religious experience, 331–35; private interest and public concern, 333–34

Roman spirituality, 154–94; degeneration theme, 154–55; early religion, 154–57; Greek influence, 155–56; historical periods, 191–93; influence of foreign cults, 171–78; later phases, 187–91; patriotic element, 157, 189; specific gods, 178–86; universalist cults, 188; Virgil and secular games, 158–61

scientific theology, Neoplatonist views, 250–52

self: in ancient religious experience, 337–59; body and soul concepts, 347–48; care of, 346–48; defined, 337–38; gods and, 341–46; Greek concepts, 338–39; and happiness, 350–52; Homeric view, 340; humanity and gods, 352–54; Jungian concept, 337; personification and, 343; and unity of virtue, 348–50

Seneca, as spiritual guide, 450

shrines, in late antiquity, 206–7

Sibylline books, and Roman spirituality, 160–61

sky: Greek view, 367; soul, body and, 366–73; in time and eternity images, 403

Socrates: agnosticism of, 109; criticisms of, 104–5; on individual conscience, 106; science vs. ethics, 102–3; spirituality of, 102–10

Solon, as spiritual guide, 442–43

soul: body and sky, 366–73; early notions, 360; "extended," 370; Heraclitus's view, 369; Orphic views, 364–366; Platonic concepts, 374–376; Presocratic philosophy, 369–72; Pythagorean views, 364–66; from sixth to fourth century, 367–68. See also body and soul

speech, spiritual importance of, 492–95

spell, of language, 486–95

sphinx, significance of, 4

spiritual guides, 436–59; Chiron and Phoenix, 436–38; collective form, 441–44; Cynics and Skeptics, 444–45; educator, musician and poet, 436–41; exercises and instruction, 450–55; friendship theme, 448–49; legislators and statesmen, 441–43; music as wisdom, 440; oracles and kings, 443–44; Orpheus, 438–40; philosophers as, 444–45; Plato and Aristotle, 445–48; qualities necessary in, 445–49; selection of students, 449–455; self-examination theme, 453–55; Solon, 442–43

stars, veneration of, 412

Stoicism, 145–51; body and soul in, 378; and cosmic piety, 414–16; rationality and spiritualism, 146–49; religion and intellect, 149–50

Stoic theology, 48

suffering, and illumination, 372–73

telestic concept, of soul, 363–64

temple: cult of, 423–24; image of, 421–24; and temples, 69–70, 429–30. See also world and temple

theurgy, oracles and, 252–54

time and eternity: afterlife concepts, 391–92; apocalyptic image, 404–5; astronomical image, 403; cosmological image, 397–401; Freud's infantile amnesia, 388; future image of, 404–6; Greek views, 387; historical beginnings, 388–93; image of, 393–404; memory concepts, 388–89; mythological origins, 385–87; in philosophical religions, 386; Plotinian image, 393–97; religious experience of, 384–407; ritual and myth, 390–91

transcendentalism: Albinus, Maximus and Numenius, 466–67; movement, 465; spiritual importance of unknown, 465–70 unknown: Aristotle and Pyrrho, 464–65; Gnostic views, 468–70; Iamblichus and Proclus, 475–76; Neoplatonist views, 475–77; Platonic concepts, 461–64; Plotinian concepts, 470–73; Porphyry's affirmation of, 474–75; spiritual importence of, 460–80; transcendental view, 465–70

Venus, in Roman spirituality, 184–86
Virgil, and secular games, 158–61
virtue, self and, 348–50

words, magic of, 492–95

worship: ancient spirituality, 73–81; gods and human beings, 76–79; meaning of gods, 74–76; piety and morality, 79–81; places and practices in late antiquity, 207–10; poetry and, 80
world and temple: in cosmic piety, 421–30; early comparisons, 425–26; image of, 421–24; permanence of theme, 424–29
writing, "strangeness" of, 488–90

Xenophanes, and Olympian polytheism, 277

Zeus: in Olympian polytheism, 274–76; piety toward, 81–82

Names

Achilles, 322, 323, 324, 339–43, 346, 348–49, 362, 436–38
Achilleus, 82, 342
Achoris, 23
Adonis, 75, 172
Aelius Aristides, 55, 205, 207
Aeneas, 157–59, 168, 171, 180, 183–84, 189–90, 333
Aeschylus, 92, 96, 97, 181, 276, 331, 366
Aetius, 413, 415, 417
Agamemnon, 92, 322, 324, 342–43
Akhenaten (Amenhotep, Amenophis), 30–32, 47
Albinus, 214, 219, 224–25, 227, 379–80, 466–67
Alcibiades, 105, 112, 375
Alexander the Great, xvii, 39, 43, 188, 331, 464
Amaunet, 9
Ambrose, 248
Amenhotep. See Akhenaten
Amenophis. See Akhenaten
Amûn, 9, 11, 30, 33
Anaxagoras, 102–3, 278, 370
Anaximander, 369, 399–402
Anaximenes, 367
Antiphon the Sophist, 366, 368
Antoninus, 196
Antony, 158
Anubis, 19, 24, 42, 44
Aphrodite, 81, 85–87, 97, 181, 183, 186, 256, 258, 323
Apollo, 43, 48, 68–69, 71, 76, 79, 82, 84–85, 87, 90–91, 96, 107–8, 158–59, 171, 205–6,

214–15, 217–18, 253, 260, 273, 322, 326, 344, 346, 442
Apollonius of Tyana, 226
Apopis, 8
Apuleius, 46–48, 52–54, 56, 59, 107, 177–78, 187–88, 207–8, 214, 224–25
Archilochus, 368
Ares, 186, 256, 342–43
Aristophanes, 102–3, 367, 439
Aristotle, 71, 102, 105, 110, 118–19, 121–34, 136, 140, 145, 208, 219, 224, 232, 238, 242, 247, 282–84, 331, 341, 352, 366, 376–78, 403, 410, 413–14, 425, 442, 448–49, 461, 463–64
Artemis, 43, 79, 159, 195–99, 202, 204, 259
Asclepius, 55, 74, 207–8, 261, 363, 436
Asoka, 443
Aten, 30–32, 47
Athena, 78, 82–84, 92, 97, 181, 256, 258, 261, 320, 323, 328, 342–43, 360, 362–63
Attalus, 192
Atticus, 214, 219, 224, 226, 228, 381
Attis, 50, 75, 172, 174–75
Atum, 6, 8, 11–12
Augustine of Hippo, 178–79, 181–82, 188, 231, 248, 386, 389, 397, 409, 415–16, 442, 448, 449
Augustus, 154, 156, 158–60, 167, 179, 182–83, 187–89, 192
Aulus Gellius, 179, 223
Aurelian, 192

Balbus, Quintus Lucilius, 414
Basilides, 468–69

Bes, 42, 44
Boethius, 397
Buddha, 30

Caesar, Julius, 154, 161, 182–83, 189, 192
Caligula, 192
Calliope, 439
Caracalla, 190
Cato the Elder, 155, 421
Catullus, 5, 167–71, 174–75, 179, 187
Celsus, 416–18, 466–67
Ceres, 147, 178, 421
Charon, 28
Cheiron, 363
Cheops (Khufu), 15
Chiron, 436–39
Chrysippus, 146, 149, 353, 415, 417
Cicero, 105, 140–42, 144, 146–47, 161–62, 164–67, 350, 352–53, 372, 378, 380, 410–11, 413–15, 425–26, 429, 442, 465
Claudius, 192
Cleanthes, 47, 146–48, 150, 425–27, 429–30
Clement of Alexandria, 135, 465
Commodus, 192
Confucius, 440
Constantine, 193
Crates, 430
Critias, 370
Croesus, 78, 275, 339, 341, 344, 346
Cupid, 53, 146
Cybele, 172, 175, 204, 428
Cyril of Alexandria, 418
Cyrus, 339

Damascius, 250–64, 475–78
Dat, 24
Demaratus, xvi
Demeter, 44, 72, 91, 96, 166, 363, 372, 391–92
Demetrius Poliorcetes, 332
Democritus, 366, 370, 413
Diana, 159, 171, 181
Dio Cassius, 422
Dio Chrysostom, 427–28
Diocletian, 192
Diodorus Siculus, 439
Diogenes Laertius, 149, 232, 344, 366, 415, 417
Diogenes of Apollonia, 367, 369–70, 410
Diogenes the Cynic, 109, 430–31
Diogenes the Dog. See Diogenes the Cynic
Dionysius of Halicarnassus, 160

Dionysus, 44, 48, 81, 85, 87–88, 90–91, 97, 175, 205–6, 208, 259–60, 364–65, 391–92, 437, 485
Diotima, 112, 294, 299
Djedi, 15
Domitian, 156, 187, 192, 198

Empedocles, 99, 278, 343–44, 352, 362, 365, 369–70
Eös, 75
Epictetus, 146, 149, 151, 378, 451, 453–54
Epicurus, 138–42, 144, 164–66, 186, 410, 413, 445, 448–49, 451, 455
Eris, 342
Eros, 85–86, 146, 341–42
Eunapius, 254
Euripides, xv, 96–97, 105, 136, 175–76, 202, 218, 341, 364, 367–68, 437, 439
Eusebius of Caesarea, 187, 208, 226, 421, 429

Fabius Pictor, 178
Firmicus Maternus, 50
Flavius Josephus. See Josephus

Gaius Velleius, 165
Galen, 352
Geb, 6, 8
Gregory of Nyssa, 248

Hadrian, 161, 177, 188, 192, 198, 206, 445
Hannibal, 157, 171, 192
Hardedef, 15
Harkhuf, 19, 20
Harpocrates, 46
Hathor, 11
Hecataeus, 39
Hecate, 254, 256, 368
Hector, 82, 324, 339–40, 350
Helios (Sol), 81, 93–94, 192–93, 210, 215, 256, 258
Hera, 82, 147, 177, 274, 354, 421
Heracles, 74, 259, 341, 344, 346, 354
Heraclitus, 125, 136, 218, 277–78, 315, 344, 367–69, 399, 402, 420
Hercules, 166, 171, 190
Hermes, 44, 87, 96, 204, 368, 488, 490, 492
Hermes Trismegistus, 169, 468
Herodotus, xvi, 26, 39, 78, 275, 321, 339–40, 347

Hesiod, 7–8, 79, 85, 95–96, 136, 159, 206, 271, 273, 276, 321, 361, 368, 370, 390, 436, 438, 440

Hestia, 260

Hippolytus, 409, 468

Homer, 7, 73, 79, 95–96, 136, 147, 181, 186, 271, 273, 315, 321, 324, 326, 328, 339–42, 349–50, 353, 360–63, 366, 372, 377, 381, 437, 461

Horace, 155, 167, 186–87

Horus, 4–8, 10–11, 24, 26, 40, 42, 44, 46

Iamblichus, 205, 217, 223, 250–64, 288, 475–76

Intef, 29

Irenaeus, 208, 501

Isidore of Seville, 422

Isidorus, 50, 259–60, 476

Isis, xx, 5–6, 34, 41–44, 46–50, 52–55, 59, 72, 177, 187, 218, 224, 392

Janus, 181, 256

Jesus Christ, 30, 94, 208, 392, 405, 408

Josephus, 423

Julian, 199, 253, 335

Julius Caesar. See Caesar, Julius

Juno, 159, 179, 181, 183

Jupiter, 179–83, 189, 193

Justinian, 34, 448

Juvenal, 177

Kauket, 9

Khefren, Pharaoh, 4

Khufu. See Cheops

Kuk, 9

L. Calpurnius Piso Frugi. See Piso Frugi Lucius Calpurnius

L. Calvanus Taurus. See Taurus, L. Calvanus

L. Manlius Torquatus. See Torquatus, L. Manlius

L. Septemius Severus. See Severus, L. Septemius

L. Tarquinius Priscus. See Tarquinius Priscus, L.

Leto, 84, 195, 215

Libanius, 200–202

Livy, 171–72, 175–76, 182

Lucian, 174, 205

Lucilius, 448

Lucilius Balbus, see Balbus, Quintus Lucilius

Lucretius, 141, 161, 164, 165–67, 172, 174–75, 184, 186, 189

Lysias, 366

Mâat, 8, 22, 23, 33

Marcus, 500–501

Marcus Aurelius, 146, 149, 151, 154, 192, 227–28, 335, 378, 452–53

Marinus, 254–55, 259, 261–62, 264, 476

Mars, 179, 182–83, 186

Maximus of Ephesus, 199, 253

Maximus of Tyre, 214, 224–25, 253, 466

Mèn, 201, 209

Menes, 6

Mercury, 172

Minerva, 181, 183

Minos, 82

Mithras, 55, 58, 71, 188, 392, 422, 489, 497–98

Muhammad, 30

Naunet, 9

Neferhotep, 29

Nefer-seshem-re (Sheshi), 18, 20

Nefertiti, 32

Nephthys, 6, 44

Neptune, 147, 172, 179

Nero, 192, 195

Nerva, 191–92

Numa, 178, 215

Numa Pompilius, 154, 180

Numenius, 214, 218, 226–28, 380–81, 417–18, 420, 465–67

Nun, 8

Nut, 6, 8

Octavian (Augustus), 158, 183

Odysseus, 80, 83, 87, 273–74, 321, 323, 339, 349, 354, 362–63, 368

Oedipus, 341, 343–44, 346, 348, 373

Orestes, 92, 97

Origen, 135, 227, 288, 416–18, 430, 465–66

Orpheus, 98, 393, 438–40, 493

Osiris, 4–8, 10, 19–20, 22, 24, 26–27, 33–34, 40–42, 44, 46, 48, 50, 56, 58, 59, 218

Ovid, 105, 179–80

Pan, 204, 259, 262, 492

Paris, 323

Parmenides, 250, 278, 463

Patroclus, 340

Paul of Tarsus, 105, 195–96, 208, 310, 408–9, 429, 484–86
Pausanias, 205
Pericles, 215, 332, 343, 347
Persephone, 72, 91–92, 372
Petosiris, 34
Petronius, 159
Pheidias, 332
Philip of Macedon, 331
Philo of Alexandria, 209, 217, 227, 288, 413–14, 423, 426, 429–31, 465–66, 473, 497
Philolaus, 366, 370
Philostratus, 207, 226
Phlegon of Tralles, 161
Phoenix, 437–38
Pindar, 83, 96, 136, 343, 352, 361, 364–66, 368–69, 372, 436–37, 494
Piso Frugi, Lucius Calpurnius, 172
Plato, xv, 68, 78–79, 86, 93, 99, 102–10, 112–19, 122–24, 136, 140, 145–46, 167, 206, 208, 217–19, 222–24, 226–27, 230–31, 233, 235, 238, 246–47, 250–54, 256, 264, 280–84, 286, 294–99, 303, 305–7, 320, 330, 340, 344, 346–50, 353, 365–66, 373–77, 379–80, 387, 394, 402–3, 410–14, 416, 418, 420, 428, 437, 439, 442, 445–46, 448–49, 452, 461–64, 471, 488–90, 492–94, 496–97
Plotinus, xiv, 59, 70, 95, 217, 223, 227, 230–49, 285–88, 294, 299–306, 308, 346, 353–54, 379–81, 393–94, 396, 398–400, 403–4, 418, 420, 445, 461, 464–68, 470–75, 481–82, 487, 499–501
Plutarch, 43–44, 46, 48, 107, 119, 146, 214–23, 225, 227–28, 262, 352, 372, 380–81, 425, 430–31, 454, 466, 497
Polybius, 157
Polycrates, 105
Pompey, 161
Porphyry, 138, 217, 230–49, 403, 418, 420–22, 426, 429, 453, 470–71, 474–75
Poseidon, 78, 315
Posidonius, 415, 427
Priam, 324
Proclus, xiv, 83–84, 217, 238, 250–64, 288, 294, 306–10, 426, 445, 475–76
Prometheus, 360, 363
Protagoras, 298, 372
Pseudo-Dionysius, 238–39, 248, 294, 309–10
Pseudo-Plutarch, 225
Psyche, 53, 54

Ptah, 9, 42
Ptahhotep, 22
Ptolemy I Soter, 39, 41–42
Pyrrho of Elis, 460, 464–65
Pyrrhus, 192
Pythagoras, 85, 99, 112, 208, 216, 226–27, 391, 453, 493, 498

Quintilian, 440
Quintus Lucilius Balbus. See Balbus, Quintus Lucilius
Quirinus, 179, 189

Rê, 3–5, 8, 20, 22–24, 26–28, 30, 32, 56, 58
Remus, 189
Romulus, 189, 193
Rutilius Claudius Namatianus, 190–91

Sakhmet, 42
Sallust, 154
Sappho, 86–87, 168–70, 364, 368
Sarapis, 41–42, 44
Sarpedon, 82
Saturn, 159, 179
Selket, 11
Seneca, 146, 353, 378, 427–28, 448–54
Servius, 178
Seth, 6–8, 11
Severus, L. Septemius, 160
Sextus Empiricus, 415
Sheshi, 18. See also Nefer-seshem-re
Shu, 6, 8, 42
Socrates, xv, 68, 93, 102–7, 109–10, 112–17, 136, 220, 222, 252, 299, 330, 340, 344, 346–49, 352, 373–75, 411, 444, 488–90, 492–93, 495
Sol. See Helios
Solon, 78, 328, 338, 339, 344, 441–42
Sophocles, 70, 96–98, 210, 328, 343, 367–68, 373
Speusippus, 284, 464–65
Statius, 11
Syrianus, 250, 252, 262, 264

T. Lucretius Carus. See Lucretius
Tacitus, 191
Tarquinius Priscus, L., 160
Taurus, L. Calvanus, 214, 219, 223
Tefênet, 6, 8
Tellus, 178

Tertullian, 135
Thales, 410, 425, 442
Theodosius I, 200
Theognis, 368, 440–41
Theophrastus, 133, 350, 464
Theseus, 318, 437
Thoth, 6, 8, 11, 33, 42, 44, 488, 492, 496
Thrasymachus, 104
Thucydides, 347
Tiberius, 192, 208
Timaeus, 387, 394
Torquatus, L. Manlius, 170
Trajan, 177, 191–92
Typhon, 44, 46

Valentinus, 470
Varro, 156, 158, 179, 181, 415–16
Venus, 183–84, 186, 189
Vespasian, 192, 198

Virgil, 158–60, 167–68, 171, 178, 180, 182–83, 187, 189–91, 379

Wadjet of Buto, 11

Xanthippe, 105
Xenocrates, 284, 412, 464
Xenophanes, 68, 79, 95, 167, 277, 369
Xenophon, 102, 104–5, 107–8, 115, 346–47, 366, 415, 437, 493
Xerxes, xvi, 429

Zeno, 352, 410, 415, 429
Zeno of Citium, xvi, 146
Zeus, 47–48, 75, 81–84, 92, 96, 136–37, 145, 147–50, 159, 181, 195, 201, 208–9, 215, 253, 258–59, 273–76, 278, 318, 322–25, 328, 330, 335, 342, 354, 361, 365–67, 375, 421, 436, 438–39
Zoroaster, 30, 422
Zosimus of Panopolis, 495–97

Colophon

Classical Mediterranean Spirituality: Egyptian, Greek, Roman,
Volume 15 of World Spirituality: An Encyclopedic History of the
Religious Quest, was designed by Maurya P. Horgan and Paul J. Kobelski.
The type is 11-point Garamond Antiqua and was set by
The Scriptorium, Denver, Colorado.